Creativity in the Classroom

Creativity in the Classroom, sixth edition, helps teachers link creativity research and theory to the everyday activities of classroom teaching. This foundational textbook is relevant for any course dealing wholly or partially with creativity and teaching. The sixth edition has been revised and updated throughout, informed by cutting-edge research on neurobiology, curiosity and imaginative play, questioning, and motivation, particularly the relationships among creativity, intrinsic motivation, and motivation to learn.

Alane Jordan Starko is Professor in the Department of Teacher Education at Eastern Michigan University, USA, and author of the blog creativiteach.me. A former elementary school teacher, teacher of the gifted, and head of the Teacher Education Department at Eastern Michigan University, she also served on the board of directors of the National Association for Gifted Children.

Creativity in the Classroom

Schools of Curious Delight

Sixth Edition

Alane Jordan Starko

Routledge
Taylor & Francis Group

NEW YORK AND LONDON

Sixth edition published 2018
by Routledge
711 Third Avenue, New York, NY 10017

and by Routledge
2 Park Square, Milton Park, Abingdon, Oxon, OX14 4RN

Routledge is an imprint of the Taylor & Francis Group, an informa business

First edition published by Longman Publishers, USA 1995
Fifth edition published by Routledge 2014

Library of Congress Cataloging-in-Publication Data
Names: Starko, Alane J., author.
Title: Creativity in the classroom : schools of curious delight /
    Alane Jordan Starko.
Description: Sixth Edition. | New York : Routledge, 2018. | "Fifth edition published by
    Routledge 2014"—T.p. verso. | Includes bibliographical references and indexes.
Identifiers: LCCN 2017008011 (print) | LCCN 2017021253 (ebook) |
    ISBN 9781315391625 (ebk) | ISBN 9781138228818 (hbk) | ISBN 9781138228825 (pbk)
Subjects: LCSH: Creative thinking.
Classification: LCC LB1062 (ebook) | LCC LB1062 .S77 2018 (print) |
    DDC 153.4/2—dc23
LC record available at https://lccn.loc.gov/2017008011

ISBN: 978-1-138-22881-8 (hbk)
ISBN: 978-1-138-22882-5 (pbk)
ISBN: 978-1-315-39162-5 (ebk)

Typeset in Minion
by Apex CoVantage, LLC

Printed and bound in Great Britain by
TJ International Ltd, Padstow, Cornwall

Dedicated to Tom and Gloria Jordan, on whose creative shoulders I'm grateful to stand.

And always, to my husband, Bob Starko, Pied Piper of all things feline. For more than 40 years his creativity has inspired and amazed me. I'll happily sign on for 40 more.

To me, a picture has delight in it, or it isn't a picture. . . . The theme may be ugly, there may be a terrifying, distressing, quality. . . . Yet it is all, in some strange way, swept up in the delight of a picture. No artist, even the gloomiest, ever painted a picture without the curious delight in image-making.

—D. H. Lawrence (1930)

Contents

Preface

Why Creativity in the Classroom?

At many points in the writing process, an author asks her- or himself, "Why am I doing this? Why write this book?" For me, the answer has two components: belief in the importance of creativity in the constant reshaping of the world in which we live and, more specifically, belief in the importance of creativity in the schools. It is easy to consider the essential role of creativity in bringing joy and meaning to the human condition—without creativity, we have no art, no literature, no science, no innovation, no problem solving, no progress. It is, perhaps, less obvious that creativity has an equally essential role in schools. The processes of creativity are inextricably tied to those of learning and motivation. The skills students need for the 21st century will require them to learn deeply and to solve problems, raise questions, and venture into ideas we can only imagine today. These processes will take them there. Classrooms organized to develop creativity become places of both learning and wonder, the "curious delight" of the book's title.

Why This Book?

Creativity in the Classroom: Schools of Curious Delight is a book about creativity written specifically for teachers. It was designed for a graduate course that helps teachers incorporate important aspects of creativity in the daily activities of classroom life. Teachers who understand the creative process can choose content, plan lessons, organize materials, and even create assessments in ways that help students develop essential skills and attitudes for creativity. To do this well, teachers need both a firm grounding in research and theory regarding creativity and a variety of strategies for teaching and management that tie research to practice. This book is designed to do both.

This is not another book on research regarding creativity, although research and theory are important components of the book. It is not a book of creative activities or "What do I do on Monday?" lessons, although it contains numerous examples and strategies for teaching and classroom organization. It does build bridges between research and practice, providing the reflective teacher with appropriate strategies for today and enough background to develop effective strategies for tomorrow.

What's Here?

The book has two parts. The first part, Understanding Creative People and Processes, provides the theoretical framework for the book. It has five chapters. Chapter 1 is an introduction that considers the nature of creativity and how it might be recognized in students. Chapter 2 begins consideration of how culture and creativity interact and then examines models of the creative process. Chapters 3 and 4 review theories and models of creativity, including theories focusing on the individual (Chapter 3) and theories involving systems of individuals within environments (Chapter 4). Chapter 5 reviews the characteristics of creative individuals. Although the purpose of the first part is to build understanding of research and theory, it considers each from the viewpoint of teachers and schools, examining how theories may be applied to young people and considering the implications for classroom practice.

The second part of the book, Creativity and Classroom Life, deals directly with strategies for teaching and learning. Chapter 6 describes techniques developed specifically to teach creative thinking and examines how they may be applied to the classroom. Chapters 7 and 8 examine approaches to teaching that support and encourage creativity in the major content areas—language arts, and social studies in Chapter 7 and mathematics and science in Chapter 8. Rather than approaching creativity as a supplement to classroom content, these chapters concentrate on creativity as an organizing strand that shapes the core curriculum. Chapters 6 through 8 include lesson ideas developed by teachers with whom I have been privileged to work. Their contributions immensely improve the work. Chapter 9 addresses classroom management and organization, showing how they might hinder or support the intrinsic motivation underlying creativity. Chapter 10 discusses two types of assessment: classroom assessment that is supportive of creativity and assessment of creativity itself.

Each chapter includes periodic "Thinking About the Classroom" activities that help the reader tie material to a particular teaching situation. Also included at the end of each chapter are three types of activities. "Think About It" suggestions apply the content and can be used for individual reflection or class activities for those using this as a textbook. New "Try It Tomorrow" suggestions are designed to do exactly what the name suggests—apply chapter ideas immediately in real-world contexts, most often in classrooms. Through both types of activities, I hope readers might not only develop creativity in their classrooms and plan creative opportunities for students but find creativity in their own lives as well. Perhaps they may find, there, a source of curious delight. Each chapter ends with "Tech Tips," providing resources to help apply content using apps and websites. This kind of feature always carries risks, particularly for the many suggestions on the Web. I know full well that by the time you read this book, some of the links I suggest will be gone. But the alternative is to make no specific suggestions, so I believe the risk is worth it. If the particular link is gone, search for something similar. I feel confident you'll be able to find it.

And while it is not technically part of the book, my blog Creativiteach (creativteach.me) focuses on the intersection of creativity and teaching and allows me to address issues, present new resources, and share new thinking on an up-to-the-minute basis. It also gives me a chance to talk to you. I really hope you'll come. Sharing ideas is a fine exercise in collaborative creativity—and talking only to myself is way less fun.

What's New in This Edition?

Beyond the usual updating, the most obvious change in this edition is the addition of the new "Try it Tomorrow" activities in each chapter to help you get off to a quick start applying principles for supporting creativity. There are also several sections that have been substantially expanded and updated. Perhaps the two most important are the more extensive section on current research on neurobiology and creativity and the section on curriculum planning. The research in neurobiology is expanding rapidly and clarifying the links between creativity and learning. It is complicated (one researcher repeatedly uses the term "messy") but fascinating. I've also added a section on general principles for developing curriculum supportive of creativity—thinking about creativity in the "What?" "Why?" and "How?" of curriculum planning. Using these as guidelines, regardless of the subject or standards you are using, will help you support students' creativity in the day-to-day planning of lessons and assessments. Information on characteristics of creative people has been reorganized and updated to reflect neurological and other contemporary research. Other areas with substantially expanded content are on curiosity and imaginative play, design thinking in schools, and the research on creative business environments. There are also new suggestions for helping students become effective questioners, and new apps for you to try, as the world—and the field—keep changing.

Acknowledgments

It is always impossible to acknowledge fully the many individuals whose contributions, critiques, support, and friendship allow a publication to evolve from dream to reality. Certainly that is true for this work. I do, however, express my gratitude publicly to a few individuals whose assistance was particularly essential.

First, I acknowledge the contributions of Jared Chrislip and David Jernigan, two talented young men who, as high school students, created the illustrations for the first edition of this book (with one assist from David's brother Nathan). For the second and third editions, we retained half the original illustrations and created new ones for the other half. As will be obvious, Jared and David have grown into extraordinary talented young adults. Jared has gone on to law school and beyond, so I worked with David to update the illustrations for the fourth edition, which are retained here. Still, both young men are essential parts of the fabric of the book. After all, a boring-looking book about creativity would seem the ultimate oxymoron! David and Jared's imagination, energy, and professionalism have been a joy to watch and an enormous asset to this endeavor. They are fine human beings as well as fine artists, and I am grateful to work with them.

Second, I thank the students in my creativity and assessment courses for their assistance in the development of my ideas, their practical insights, and their ever-present imagination. Perhaps most of all, I appreciate their patience as we struggle together to understand the complexities of this topic. Thanks also to Susan Wright, who convinced me that new forms of creativity were not beyond my reach. Venturing into the visual arts for the first time at this stage of my life has helped me reflect on my process and understand risk taking in a whole new way—and it has been loads of fun. Special thanks also are due to Elizabeth Gray, who helped double-check the many links included here, find relevant apps, and shape the "Try It Tomorrow" activities. Without her assistance, the ends of chapters would be much less interesting.

I owe much to the many professionals at Routledge who helped this book reemerge in a sixth edition. In particular, thanks to Alex Masulis and all the others whose behind-the-scenes work has made the process practically painless.

I express gratitude for and a warning about the houseful of black cats who have been my companions at the keyboard during almost all the hours of my writing. Any strange sets of letters appearing in the manuscript can be attributed to their wandering paws. Their purrs remind me it will all work out.

Finally, as always, I must acknowledge that my work would be impossible and my life a lot less fun without the constant love, support, and confidence of my husband, Bob. When I'm looking for an example of creativity, I never have to look very far. For more than 40 years, his creativity has been a wonder to me, a joy to watch, and a privilege to share. What could be better?

Part I
Understanding Creative People and Processes

This book has two parts. The first section provides the theoretical framework for the book. It is intended to help you think through the basic questions: What is creativity? What does it look like? How will I recognize it? Where does it come from? You will be introduced to the controversies and mysteries faced by researchers and theorists alike. This theoretical background will allow you to look at your classroom practice and make professional decisions based on the ideas that make the most sense to you. Along the way, we will consider other important questions: How might this operate in young people? How might it vary in different subjects or in different cultures? What might that mean for the students in my charge? Can I teach for creativity while also teaching my essential content? I believe the answer to the last question is "Yes, absolutely, and they'll learn more than ever." So let's begin!

1
What Is Creativity?

In 1905 an unknown clerk in the Swiss patent office published a paper in which he advocated abandoning the idea of absolute time. This fundamental postulate of the theory of relativity suggested that the laws of science should be the same for all observers, regardless of speed. The clerk's name was Albert Einstein.

Vincent van Gogh began painting in 1880. His adaptations of the impressionist style were considered strange and eccentric, and his personal life was complicated by illness and poverty. He sold only one painting before his death in 1890.

In 2003 Mark Zuckerberg hacked into Harvard's website and downloaded student ID photos into a website designed to compare student photos as "hot or not." The website lasted just a few days. Four months later he launched a new social networking website called "Thefacebook." The rest is history.

In a quiet space under an ancient tree, the storyteller recounts a familiar tale. The audience listens carefully to each nuance, appreciating both the well-known story line and the new turns of language and elaboration that make the characters come to life.

Harvard student David Sengeh, originally from Sierra Leone, was part of a group challenged to use biology to light the London Olympics in 2012. Three members of the team were from Africa and thought, "Why light London when we can light Africa, where hundreds of millions are off the electric grid?" The resulting project uses buckets of dirt and water to power LED lights and led to a $200,000 prize from the World Bank's Lighting Africa competition.

(Wagner, 2012)

In first grade, Michelle was given an outline of a giant shark's mouth on a worksheet that asked, "What will our fishy friend eat next?" She dutifully colored several fish and boats, and then wrote the following explanation: "Once there was a shark named Peppy. One day he ate three fish, one jellyfish, and two boats. Before he ate the jellyfish, he made a peanut butter and jellyfish sandwich."

At 19, Juan was homeless and a senior in high school. One cold evening he thought that a warm space inside the school would be a more appealing sleeping place than any he could see.

Getting into the building was no problem, but once he was inside a motion detector would make him immediately detectable to the guard on the floor below. Juan entered a storage room and carefully dislodged a pile of baseball bats. In the ensuing commotion, he located a comfortable sleeping place. The guard attributed the motion detector's outburst to the falling bats, and Juan slept until morning.

Who is creative? What does creativity look like? Where does it come from? What role do our classrooms play in the development—or limiting—of creativity? The word "creativity" suggests many powerful associations. In some contexts it seems almost beyond the scope of mere mortals—few of us can imagine treading in the footsteps of Einstein or Curie, Picasso or O'Keeffe, Mozart or Charlie Parker. Their accomplishments are stunning in originality and power, not just contributing to their disciplines but transforming them.

However, many of us have created a new casserole from ingredients in the refrigerator, jury-rigged a muffler to last to the next service station, or written a poem or song for the enjoyment of a loved one. What about Michelle and her peanut butter and jellyfish sandwich or Juan and his decoy bats? Were they creative? Can there be creativity in recounting a familiar story? Are we all creative? And what does any of this have to do with education?

The word "creative" is used frequently in schools. Virtually all of us, as teachers or students, have had experiences with creative writing. Teacher stores abound with collections of "creative activities" or books on "creative teaching" of various subjects. Such sources frequently provide interesting and enjoyable classroom experiences without tackling the fundamental questions: What is creativity? Where does it originate? What experiences or circumstances allow individuals to become more creative? Although collections of activities can be useful, without information on these more basic issues, it is difficult for any teacher to make good decisions on classroom practices that might encourage or discourage creativity in students.

This book examines the basic questions, theories, and research about creativity with an eye to classroom practice. It brings together basic principles underlying creativity, learning, and motivation to form a "Creativity in the Classroom" model that allows teachers to establish a classroom supportive of all three. Although the investigation of a phenomenon as complex and elusive as creativity will, of necessity, raise more questions than it answers, it provides a place to begin. I hope that thoughtful teachers who raise these questions will go far beyond the strategies suggested in this book to experiment, try new ideas, and observe what happens. Only through such efforts can we expand the body of knowledge on the development of creativity, its impact in classrooms, and its manifestations in young people.

Really, Why Bother?

It is interesting and sad to think that 20 years ago, when I wrote the first edition of this book, it wasn't necessary to ask why developing creativity in young people would be a good idea. Teachers might have wondered about taking time away from the curriculum or the role of creativity when addressing state standards (both of which I'll discuss later in the chapter), but rarely did they ask whether creativity itself had value. Today, I occasionally meet teachers who do. They wonder why they should do anything they aren't "accountable" for. If it isn't going to count, what's the point? This seems a bit like a captive rowing in the belly of a ship, concerned only about the number of strokes the overseer is counting and not really thinking about where the ship is headed.

I don't think the trend toward school accountability is equivalent to an uncaring, whip-bearing overseer (at least not on my good days). I teach courses in assessment, and I believe that it is an important thing. But the overemphasis on high-stakes tests has caused some teachers to lower their sights to the oar in ways that are not healthy for our students or our world. There are more important tests than the ones with fill-in bubbles. One of them is our stewardship for the young people we serve and the places in which we live.

We need creativity for our economy—and more. A few years ago, I had a wonderful opportunity to visit schools in China and speak to Chinese educators. Everywhere I went, teachers and administrators asked me the same questions: How can we help our students to be more flexible thinkers? How can we help them be better at creative and imaginative thinking? I was struck by the contrast between the conversations we had there and the ones I most often hear in schools in the United States. In recent years (and for logical reasons), conversations in U.S. schools have focused largely on improving standardized test scores. In China, where test scores—at least for the schools I was visiting—were already high, they recognized those scores as an insufficient goal. They were interested in learning more about the kind of education that has fueled the United States' traditional strengths in innovation and creativity.

Of course, conversations about the need for creativity are not unique to China. Dr. Kyung-Hee Kim's research was the subject of *Newsweek's* widely publicized "Creativity Crisis" feature (Bronson & Merryman, 2010), sparking water-cooler conversations about creativity across the United States. Is creativity really declining? Perhaps. For example, Weinstein and colleagues found that when examining adolescents' creative art and writing, it depended on the genre. Some aspects were better over time, some worse (Weinstein, Clark, DiBartolomeo, & Davis, 2014). Either way, there is a level of ambivalence regarding the role of both critical and creative thinking in American education. Conversations about a "Creativity Crisis" often advocate infusing more creative thinking into students' experiences—as long as it doesn't depress test scores.

Focusing on test scores first or, as it sometimes seems, exclusively is a shortsighted goal. As Zhao (2012) so forcefully points out, time is a limited resource. Every choice we make about the allocation of our time and energy limits another choice we could make. For centuries, the path to advancement in Chinese society has been through scores on various tests. As a result, they have had what Zhao calls a "laser focus" on the types of activities that raise test scores. Not surprisingly, they are very good at taking tests. However, the kind of test-taking focus that has created those scores has come at the expense of students' ability to question, problem solve, and innovate. The Chinese recognize that this is a serious problem and are working diligently to learn about the kinds of education that have supported the United States' traditional strength in innovation. Meanwhile, the United States is running toward the cliff of total test focus at breakneck speed, tossing aside nonmandated curriculum as we go. It is a giant step backward.

One of Zhao's most compelling points comes from a study in which he looked at the relationship between math scores on the Programme for International Student Assessment (PISA) and the annual Global Entrepreneurship Survey (GEM), which tracks various aspects of entrepreneurship across 50 countries. He found a significant negative correlation between the two; that is, countries with the highest PISA scores scored lower on measures of entrepreneurship than countries with more modest scores. Of course this does not mean that high test scores cause a less innovative economy, but it does suggest that the practices that produce exceptionally high test scores may not support innovative thinking. This possibility becomes all the more disturbing when considering that the United States' "creativity crisis" has emerged exactly at the point when education has become more and more test driven.

Meanwhile, writers considering the business world are clear that innovation and entrepreneurship are precisely what the United States needs to remain competitive in a global economy. Bookstores are full of titles such as *Creating Innovators: The Making of Young People Who Will Change the World* (Wagner, 2012), *Imagination First* (Liu & Noppe-Brandon, 2009), *Where Good Ideas Come From* (Johnson, 2010), *The Creativity Challenge: How We Can Recapture American*

Innovation (Kim, 2016) and Zhao's (2012) *World Class Learners: Educating Creative and Entrepreneurial Students.* The themes across such writings are consistent: (1) If the United States (or any highly developed nation) is to succeed in a global economy, it will require increased entrepreneurial, flexible, and imaginative thinking, and (2) success in those areas will only be possible if our education system supports the type of thinking required—entrepreneurial, flexible, and imaginative. The contrast between what the economy will require and the demands being made of U.S. schools could not be more dramatic.

Sir Ken Robinson, senior advisor to the Getty Foundation (and YouTube sensation), talks about two great crises in our world (2001, 2005, 2015). The first crisis is global warming, which threatens our environmental resources. The second he describes as a cultural crisis that impacts our human resources, the climate of fear and risk aversion in our educational system, spurred by overemphasis on single standardized measures. He says,

> The educational reforms really needed now are actually being held back by the attitudes to education that many policy makers learned when they went to school—20, 30, or 40 years ago. Many seem to believe the way to the future is simply to do better what we did in the past. The truth is we need to do something completely different for today's students.
>
> (2005, p. 2)

Robinson believes that only with experiences in creativity will our students be able to prepare for the shape-shifting world they must embrace.

Of course, not all tests are bad, and we want to ensure that students are learning valuable content, but (and this is a really big BUT) if schools focus all their efforts on preparing students for tests, they will not be successful in preparing students for life. The 21st-century pace of change, as well as the global economy, demands young people who can learn on their own, solve problems, and respond to situations unlike any their parents or teachers dream of. How do we prepare them for that? We help them to be independent learners and creative thinkers.

Interestingly, Ambrose and Sternberg (2012) tied the need for creativity to national and international issues beyond the economic. In a series of essays written by authors across domains, they argue that dogmatism—the absolute adherence to a prescribed set of beliefs, regardless of circumstances or additional information—is at odds with creative and critical thinking. When contemplating the partisan logjams that seem to characterize much of U.S. politics in the 21st century, it seems more creative thinking is definitely in order.

We Need Creativity for Learning

Fortunately, the voices calling for increased attention to creativity are spreading to the education arena. Sir Ken Robinson's (2015) *Creative Schools* is only one of a number of recent books aiming to help students be more curious, creative, or entrepreneurial (see, for example, Boss, 2012; Drapeau, 2014; Ostroff, 2016). This makes sense, because creativity and learning are inextricably linked.

I want to encourage creativity in schools because I want schools to be places in which students learn. Few critics would argue with the idea that schools should teach students to think critically and understand deeply. Abundant evidence suggests that the strategies that support creativity—solving problems, exploring multiple options, and learning inquiry—also support depth of understanding.

Sadly, all of us have had experiences in which we "learned" something in school without ever understanding it. Think about the tests for which you memorized facts you could not explain or the assignments for which you quoted relevant passages of the textbook without a clue what they meant or why they mattered. You aren't alone. Gardner (1993b) stated:

> The findings of cognitive research over the past 20–30 years are really quite compelling: students do not understand, in the most basic sense of that term. That is, they lack the capacity to take knowledge learned in one setting and apply it appropriately in a different setting. Study after study has found that, by and large, even the best students in the best schools can't do that.
>
> (p. 4)

Gardner was part of a Harvard research team, Project Zero, aimed at determining the types of curriculum and activities that allow students to build understanding. We'll talk more about curriculum development in Chapter 7, but for now the important key is: Students develop understanding by applying content in diverse ways and multiple settings, acting flexibly with what they know. When we ask students to use the content in diverse ways—to think and create with what they know—we not only have a glimpse into their level of understanding, but we develop it as well. Creative applications of core content are among teachers' most powerful tools in building students' understanding. When we consider some basics of learning theory, it makes sense.

Early theories of learning were often based on a behaviorist perspective. In this tradition, researchers observed, in carefully controlled conditions, the behaviors of various learners in response to certain stimuli. The learner was perceived as a passive receptor of stimuli—as outside forces directed, so the learner learned. The basic processes of learning were considered to be uniform across species. "It does not make much difference what species we study. . . . The laws of learning are much the same in rats, dogs, pigeons, monkeys, and humans" (Hill, 1977, p. 9). I actually studied from that book, many years ago!

This view of the learner as a passive absorber of stimuli appears to have little in common with the processes or purposes of creativity. However, contemporary learning theory acknowledges human learning to be a more complex, constructive process than previously thought. Increasing consensus among researchers suggests that learning is a goal-oriented process (see, for example, Bransford, Brown, Cocking, Donovan, & Pellegrino, 2000). Activities undertaken in pursuit of a meaningful goal offer more fertile ground for learning than activities undertaken without an obvious cause.

Learning as a constructive process implies that learners build their own knowledge as an engineer builds a new type of computer, not as a sponge absorbs water or a billiard ball bounces off the table. Psychological processes associated with this vision of learning are organizing information, linking new information to prior knowledge, and using metacognitive (thinking-about-thinking) strategies to plan the accomplishment of goals. Neurobiologists are also finding that in-depth thinking and learning requires an emotional connection, some tie to students' lives and interests. In order to build in-depth understanding, students must be engaged in activities they perceive as interesting and relevant (Bransford, Sherwood, Vye, & Rieser, 1986; Bransford et al., 2000; Immordino-Yang, 2016).

The processes of building cognitive structures underlie all learning. The development of expertise in an area might be seen as developing spaces or ties in the cognitive structure into which new information can fit. An expert's framework parallels the structure of his or her subject, allowing the expert to fit new information easily in the appropriate place, just as a chip might fit readily into a computer's already-prepared slot. Helping students become more expert entails assisting them in readying a framework—creating the slots.

To me, it is fascinating that multiple paths seemingly lead to very similar recommendations. Our understanding of neuropsychology is in its infancy, yet it appears to lead us to conclusions very similar to those derived from learning theory. Studies in this area begin with the brain and its functions. Many of our neural pathways are already established at birth (e.g., those that control breathing and heartbeat), but many more are created through our interactions with our environment. Each interaction uses and strengthens neural connections. The more we use particular connections, the stronger they become. As we create new connections, we build the capacity for more flexible thought. Psychiatrist John Ratey (2001) stated:

> We always have the ability to remodel our brains. To change the wiring in one skill, you must engage in some activity that is unfamiliar, novel to you but related to that skill, because simply repeating the same activity only maintains already established connections. To bolster his creative circuitry, Albert Einstein played the violin. Winston Churchill painted landscapes.
>
> (p. 36)

> Every time we choose to solve a problem creatively, or think about something in a new way, we reshape the physical connection in our brains. The brain has to be challenged in order to stay fit, just as the muscles, heart, and lungs must be deliberately exercised to become more resilient.
>
> (p. 364)

It is precisely such stretching of patterns that we hope to achieve when we teach in ways that enhance creativity. Students think about content from different points of view, use it in new ways, or connect it to new or unusual ideas. These associations strengthen the connections to the content as well as the habits of mind associated with more flexible thinking—and thus build understanding. In recent years, researchers have been able to identify some of the areas of the brain active in creative thinking. We'll look more at that in Chapter 3.

When researchers attempt to delineate teaching strategies that are most effective in supporting student learning, such lists typically include the activities required for finding and solving problems. For example, Mansilla and Gardner (2008), when discussing optimum strategies to develop understanding of disciplines, include the inquiry strategies that are at the root of creative endeavors. When Wiggins and McTighe (2005) discuss strategies to develop in-depth understanding, they state, "If we don't give students sufficient ongoing opportunities to puzzle over genuine problems, make meaning of their learning, and apply content in various contexts, then long-term retention and effective performance are unlikely" (pp. 37–38). Current books on "brain compatible learning" are full of suggestions for helping students solve problems, look at content from multiple perspectives, and express ideas in varied ways (see, for example, Armstrong, 2016; Gregory & Kaufeldt, 2015). All of these strategies are discussed in Chapters 7 and 8.

How, in the end, do these recommendations tie to creativity? Simply stated, if we want to help students build understanding, the strategies that support creativity will help us do so. Giving students opportunities to be creative requires allowing them to apply content in flexible ways to find and solve problems and communicate ideas. Learning takes place best when learners are involved in setting and meeting goals and tying information to their experiences in unique and personal ways. Creativity aside, we know that raising questions, solving problems, tying information to personal and original ideas, and communicating results all help students learn for understanding. How much better it is, then, to find and solve problems in ways that facilitate original ideas and to give students tools for communicating novel thinking. Structuring education around the goals of creativity is a wonderful two-for-one sale—pay the right price for the learning and you may get creativity free. But it doesn't stop there.

We Need Creativity for Motivation

There is one more variable in the Creativity in the Classroom triangle. When you were in school, did a teacher ever try to "motivate" you like this?

"You'd better study this because it is going to be on the TEST!"
"If you don't do well in this class, you will never get into a good college."
"This grade is going into your PERMANENT FOLDER!"

I don't know about you, but these kinds of threats may have convinced me that my test grades could pose some threats to my future, but they (and this is crucial) never motivated me to actually understand anything—at least not about the content. If anything, I learned to be test-smart and to engage in the type of study that would enhance my short-term memory of specific facts rather than long-term understanding of key ideas.

These experiences point out the difference between two key types of goals students (and others) may set for themselves: performance goals and mastery goals. Performance goals are goals that are undertaken to meet the approval of others or to gain external indicators of success—such as grades or a winning score in a ball game. With such goals, the individual is, in a sense, "performing" for others and awaiting the applause. When I was studying for some of my worst-memory school tests, I was setting a performance goal—a good grade on the test.

Mastery goals, in contrast, are undertaken because individuals want to master something—to best their own time, to understand a complex idea, to play a piece of music with their own interpretation and flair. Can you guess which type of goal is more likely to lead to learning for understanding (Ames, 1992; Ames & Archer, 1988; Elliott & Dweck, 1988; Grant & Dweck, 2003; Wolters, 2004)?

The concepts of performance goals and mastery goals are tied directly to extrinsic and intrinsic motivation. Performance goals are tied to intrinsic motivation—motivation that stems from within and is focused on the task, as opposed to extrinsic motivation, which is focused on a reward. Intrinsic motivation is strongly tied to creativity.

Amabile (1989) found that intrinsic motivation was fundamental to the creative process. She compared it to the feelings of a rat in a maze. If the rat is motivated by an extrinsic reward (cheese, for example), it takes the straightest line to the reward and gets out of the maze as quickly as possible. If the rat is intrinsically motivated, it enjoys being in the maze. It wants to explore it, take time in it, and find all the interesting nooks and crannies there. Of course, the intrinsically motivated rat is more likely to find an interesting or creative way through the maze—more on that in Chapter 4. Intrinsic motivation is—not surprisingly—also strongly tied to learning.

In schools, we tend to think of intrinsic motivation as finding joy in learning, but motivation in schools is a bit more complex than that. If we define intrinsic motivation as enjoying each task and seek it every minute of the school day, that's probably not realistic. To promote creativity in the classroom, we need to think about motivation in more complex ways. Consider a time when you learned something because you wanted to. Maybe you were learning to drive, to speak another language, or to play an instrument. Not all the tasks on the way to your goal may have been enjoyable—learning how to engage a clutch, speaking awkwardly, or practicing scales. But for many of us, we were motivated to continue to do these things because we valued the knowledge and skills we were gaining.

This is what Brophy (2010; Wentzel & Brophy, 2014) termed "motivation to learn," and it combines with intrinsic motivation in the Creativity in the Classroom model. In this case, classroom motivation doesn't necessarily mean that students will always feel, "this is fun," but they may also feel, "I'm learning" or "I'm really getting better at this" or even "This is worth doing." (Can you hear mastery goals here?) This kind of motivation helps students press forward when the activity isn't their favorite because they value the learning. Both aspects of motivation, the affect (This is so much fun I want to do more!) and the cognitive (Look at how much I've improved!) are important for creativity and learning.

So we need intrinsic motivation and motivation to learn, for learning. We need intrinsic motivation for creativity. We need creativity for learning—and learning for creativity. When we add them together, they create a Creativity in the Classroom model, which we could call the Learning in the Classroom model or Intrinsic Motivation in the Classroom model just as well. We'll examine the various aspects of the model in more detail throughout the book, but Figure 1.1 shows the overall relationships. Creativity, and the flexible thinking that is associated with it, is not "fluff." It is fundamental to the processes that lead to motivation and deep learning. It is essential for progress in our economy. But that isn't all.

We Need Creativity for Joy

Joy matters. I don't believe that any good teacher can limit his or her responsibility to the transmission of content. We want our students to have zest for life and hope in their capacity—and we want them to have those things in school. It is no coincidence that in an article titled "Joy in School," Steven Wolk (2008) cited "Let students create things" and "Take time to tinker" among the key elements of a joyful school life. In schools, we aren't punching out widgets; we are nurturing young people. In my view, an essential part of preparing students for life is helping them

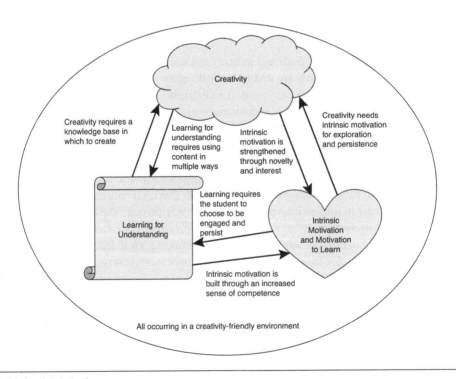

Figure 1.1 Creativity in the classroom

see that life is interesting and filled with the potential for joy. One way we do that is to help them experience creativity.

Thinking About the Classroom

If you teach young children, watch your students on the playground. Look for behaviors that use novel or original ideas for play activities. If you teach older students, observe their interactions during extracurricular or other social activities. Look for evidence of originality. Do you also see evidence of learning?

In Case There's Any Doubt: We Need Creativity for Everybody

I'm ashamed to say that this conclusion required three "aha!" moments regarding students with special needs and creativity. A few years ago, I was teaching a basic research class that is taken by students in a number of master's degree programs. Several of the students, knowing I had written this book, asked if I could take some time at the end of the term to talk about creativity in schools. Of course they didn't have to ask twice! When the time came, and I was about to introduce the "Three Keys to Creativity in the Classroom" (see Chapter 6), I made an offhand comment to the special educators in the room, apologizing if the material was not appropriate for their students.

Well, those teachers let me know in no uncertain terms that I was wrong. Not only, they insisted, was developing creativity appropriate for students with disabilities, it was possibly more important for them than for anyone else. As I thought about it, I realized that of course the special educators were right. Everyone needs to think flexibly. And students who struggle in school may need the chance to feel the excitement of generating and following their own ideas more than anyone else. Properly chastened, I promised them that the next time I was planning to revise the book, I would make sure to include examples appropriate for students with disabilities.

When the time came to begin the revisions, I bribed a special educator friend with Thai food and had a fascinating conversation about creativity for students with special needs. This was my second "aha!" moment. The more she talked, the more I realized that all the ideas she was sharing were things we taught in our basic curriculum classes as universal design principles: Students need to learn content in multiple ways, students need to express themselves and represent content in multiple ways, and students need to find content relevant to their lives. The key is, students with special needs must do all those things with appropriate supports. They need to learn creative thinking the same way. I can just see all of you out there saying, "Uh, didn't you know that?" Yes, but for some reason, that day it struck me more powerfully.

The truth is, some of the brightest people I know have disabilities. I have a gifted uncle who is blind. I have friends—young and old—with exceptional intelligence and attention disorders. A professor friend, a national leader at the top of his field, has trouble reading quickly. I could go on.

Sadly, as anyone in the field of special education can tell you, too often a focus on identifying and addressing disabilities can shift attention away from the many gifts that are present. A friend's young son was placed in a class for students with serious cognitive deficits. He spent his time in daily repetition of basic skills. When I met him a year later (when, fortunately, they had moved from that district), I was dumbfounded. I could not believe that anyone, let alone a teacher, could have had a 5-minute conversation with that young man and not recognize his bright, creative mind. Yes, he had attention issues. Yes, he had trouble with reading. But he had curiosity, and ideas aplenty. Later, thanks to persistent parents and some fine educators, he found his voice and vocation through film. But perhaps, if he'd had more opportunities for flexible thinking within his original school program, his path could have been smoother.

If we intend to provide classrooms that are supportive of creative and flexible thinking, it is essential that we consider, "How do we structure classrooms with opportunities for creative thinking available for *all* students?" Certainly there are students with severe cognitive limitations who will have trouble with abstract thinking, including some creative thinking activities. But *most of the students in our classes who have disabilities are also capable of flexible and original thinking, given the proper supports.* We just have to think about what supports are needed.

Those of us in general education can sometimes look to special educators to have the "magic stuff," the secrets to helping students with special needs learn. If we perceive ourselves as not having "the stuff," we can take our responsibilities to special needs students less seriously, and that would be a terrible mistake. I didn't need new strategies for students with special needs—I just needed to think more carefully about how to support those students with the strategies we already have. And, of course, you do, too. For one place to start, see the CAST website listed in the Tech Tips at the end of this chapter.

Interestingly, our conversation seemed to lead my friend to her own "aha!" moment. "You know," she said, "In special education we often teach students to think flexibly about practical content. For example, we teach students with cognitive impairments to think of multiple ways to approach the problem if their bus doesn't come when expected. But we rarely think about multiple options or flexible thinking for academic content. There we tend toward rote learning and memory. Those aren't the best ways to learn, and they certainly aren't the best ways to learn to think creatively." Wise woman, my friend. We all have a part of this work.

Getting Started: Defining Creativity

Definitions of Creativity

There are many definitions of creativity (e.g., Kaufman & Sternberg, 2006, 2010; Runco, 2014; Sternberg, 1999). Some definitions focus on characteristics of individuals whose work is determined to be creative (What is a creative person like?), whereas others consider the work itself (What makes this creative?). Since the mid-20th century, most definitions have two major criteria for judging creativity: novelty and appropriateness (Barron, 1955; Runco & Jaeger, 2012; Stein, 1953). Sometimes definitions take aim at the processes involved. For example, Kounios and Beeman (2015) define creativity as "the ability to reinterpret something by breaking it down into its elements and recombining these elements in a surprising way to achieve some goal" (p. 9). Still, the elements of surprise and goal directedness echo the two traditional elements of creativity. At its most basic, creativity involves the generation of a new product (idea, artwork, invention, etc.) that is appropriate in some context. Each aspect of this simple definition poses questions.

Novelty and originality may be the characteristics most immediately associated with creativity. Works of literature that imitate those before them or scientific discoveries that are merely a rehash of earlier work are seldom considered creative. To be creative, an idea or product must be new.

The key dilemma is, new to whom? If a researcher at the University of Michigan works for years to engineer a gene transfer to cure a particular disease only to discover that a researcher at Stanford published the same techniques only 2 weeks before, is the Michigan researcher's work no longer creative? Must elementary school children devise ideas that are unique in the world before their efforts can be considered creative? Either of these questions becomes, in the end, a semantic or a value issue. Some researchers—including some of the most active today—are focused on high-level creativity, creativity that changes some aspect of our world in dramatic ways. For them, only ideas new to a particular discipline or culture are designated creative. It is the purpose of this book to describe the development of creativity in the classroom. Therefore, the following definition seems most reasonable for our purposes: To be considered creative, a product or idea must be original or novel to the individual creator. By this standard, Michelle's peanut butter and jellyfish sandwich can be considered original, as can the unhappy researcher's discoveries, because both efforts were new to their creators if not to the world.

Thinking About the Classroom

With a friend, examine the same set of student papers or products. Do you both agree on which are the most original? Why or why not?

The second aspect of creativity is appropriateness. If I am asked the time and I reply, "The cow jumped over the computer yesterday," my response would certainly be novel—but would it be considered creative or simply inappropriate? Again, the definition can be fuzzy. Was Juan's late-night entrance to the school appropriate? Because van Gogh's works were not accepted by the public of his time, were they inappropriate? If they had never been accepted, would they have been creative?

One important factor in determining appropriateness is the cultural context in which the creativity is based. Just as intelligence is viewed differently in various cultures (Sternberg, 2000b, 2004), so the vehicles and focus of creativity vary from culture to culture and across time. Works by van Gogh or Manet that 19th-century audiences rejected are considered masterpieces today. The expressive individualism of some African American young men can take the form of creative stances, walks, and gestures that can go unnoticed or misunderstood by those outside their culture. Contemporary artists see beauty and power in graffiti that escape much of the general public.

Cultures, in fact, differ in their conceptions of the nature of creativity itself (Kaufman & Sternberg, 2006; Liep, 2001; Lubart, 1999, 2010; Niu & Zhou, 2017; Weiner, 2000). The product-oriented, originality-based phenomenon emphasized in this book is a Western orientation, whereas some Eastern or traditional cultures conceptualize creativity as a process of individual growth, spiritual journey, or evolution (rather than revolution) in shared community culture.

It is interesting to think about which areas in our culture are most tied to our cultural values and how that may affect our openness to creativity. It seems likely that the types of problems and modes of expression will vary in any multicultural society such as the United States. Certainly, the dulcimer music of Appalachia differs from New Orleans jazz. In a similar fashion, the styles of art and language as well as the modes and themes of expression show great diversity. In facilitating creativity in schools, it is important for the teacher to consider the cultural contexts of students' lives. It is necessary to provide multiple vehicles or strategies to appeal not just to students' varied abilities or learning styles but also to their diverse social and cultural values. This varied sense of appropriateness perhaps makes defining creativity more complicated, but it also allows richness and diversity in the types of creative efforts that are attempted and appreciated.

I consider a definition of appropriateness here that is nearly as broad as the term itself: An idea or product is appropriate if it meets some goal or criterion. Creativity is purposeful and involves effort to make something work, to make something better, more meaningful, or more beautiful.

In much adult creativity, criteria are set by the culture and the discipline. Most paintings, for example, must have some balance and composition. The question becomes much trickier as the norms change in a discipline. Although styles of painting vary and evolve, works of art are seldom considered creative unless they are eventually appreciated by some audience. Van Gogh was originally considered dysfunctional. Our revised standards consider him creative.

Each culture and discipline sets standards for creative activities. In many Western cultures, a story has a beginning, a middle, and an end, as well as an identifiable conflict and climax. In other cultures with elaborate oral traditions, the shape of a story may be very different, embracing multiple side roads and circles. Criteria for judging African ceremonial masks are very different from those for evaluating Italian commedia dell'arte masks. Nonetheless, the creative efforts in each case are eventually considered to meet some standard and be accepted by some audience.

Adult standards of appropriateness, however, are generally not suitable for children. Few expect elementary school students' paintings or stories to match those of Cassatt or Fitzgerald. We can consider children's efforts appropriate if they are meaningful, purposeful, or communicative in some way. If students successfully communicate an idea or endeavor to solve a problem, their efforts can be considered appropriate. If they do so in a way that is original, at least to them, we can consider the efforts creative.

Even such broad parameters can be difficult to translate into reality. Consider the following cases. Which behaviors would you consider creative or not creative?

1. In the middle of a discussion on plants, 6-year-old Toshio raises his hand. "Do you think the plants would grow taller and stronger if, instead of watering them, we milked them?"
2. Jane dressed for the first day of eighth grade in long underwear bottoms, a purple satin blouse, and grapes hanging as earrings.
3. Maria wrote the best essay on federalism her teacher had ever seen. It was clear, well documented, and thorough, including implications of federalism seldom considered by high school students.

Creativity takes many forms around the world

4. Eduardo's first-grade class has been taught to subtract by taking away the designated number. Numerous manipulatives are available for students' use. Eduardo refuses to use the method he has been taught. Instead, he uses his fingers to count up from the smaller to the larger number.
5. Sam is wearing a baseball cap on hat day. Unbeknown to his teacher, he has installed a mirror under the brim. When the hat is cocked at the correct angle, he can see the desk next to his. This will be handy during the sixth-period quiz.
6. Karin has recently become captivated by the early TV series *Leave It to Beaver*. She frequently uses her journal to write new adventures of Wally, Eddie, and the Beaver.
7. Susan is asked to illustrate a scene from the biography of Frederick Douglass her second-grade teacher is reading. Having heard that he traveled through England and Wales, she draws Frederick Douglass walking across a row of smiling whales.
8. Max's music class has been given the assignment of composing a short piece in the style of one of the classical composers they have studied to date. Max creates a rap about Beethoven's hair (and its lack of style) using the rhythms of Beethoven's Fifth Symphony.
9. Tzeena is known for her caricatures. During English class, she has at times passed around sketches in which she has drawn her teacher's head attached to the body of an ostrich.

Whose behavior did you consider creative? When Toshio wonders about the possibility of milking rather than watering plants, it is almost certainly an original idea. It is unlikely he has seen or heard of anyone putting milk on plants. Because the idea of plants' growing stronger with milk is perfectly consistent with what Toshio has been taught about children needing milk to grow strong, it is also appropriate and can be considered a creative response.

Jane's case is a little trickier. Attire is not necessarily novel simply because it is unusual. Did Jane originate the grape earrings? Is she the first to wear long underwear as middle-school fashion? If so (and because it certainly meets the adolescent criterion of being different from her parents' fashions), her dress can be considered creative. In many cases, however, clothing that may appear innovative to an outsider may be the latest craze in some groups. Jane may not be creative in her dress at all but may be conforming completely to unwritten standards.

Maria's report on federalism, although appropriate, is probably not creative. Although it is thorough, well written, and unusual for her grade level, we have no clear indication that she has developed any new ideas on the subject. If her assessment of the implications of federalism represents an unusually careful analysis or logical extensions of her sources, she should be commended for her efforts, but her work probably is not original. However, if she is able to approach the idea in a new way (perhaps using parallels to classrooms in a school) or to derive new and unusual implications from her reading, it is possible that her efforts can be considered creative. It is important to note, however, that even unusually well-written and -documented analyses and summaries generally are not considered creative when they are representations of someone else's ideas.

Eduardo's subtraction method may be creative if he has devised the method for himself. It is certainly appropriate because he is able to derive the correct answers by using it. If, however, Eduardo was taught the method elsewhere (e.g., at home, on the school bus), it cannot be considered creative.

What about Sam? If his mirrored cap is original, we must (perhaps grudgingly) consider it creative. It may not be considered appropriate by his sixth-period teacher, but it is purposeful to its creator. The same standard can be applied to Juan, the young man described at the beginning of the chapter, whose tumbling-bat distraction allowed him into the school after hours. Although breaking and entering are not appropriate as measured by legality, the strategy is purposeful. Juan was able to stay warm for most of the night because of his creative action. Although allowing the creator to be the primary judge of appropriateness poses some difficulties (e.g., should people with mental illnesses determine whether their responses are appropriate?), it still seems the most reasonable standard for children, whose ideas of purposeful behavior may be meaningful to them but not to adults.

Karin's *Leave It to Beaver* stories probably are creative if they are original stories consistent with the characters she chooses. If, however, they are a reprise of televised adventures, they cannot be considered original. The same criterion can be applied to student artists who while away the hours sketching countless Batman or Harry Potter characters. Elaborate drawings of well-known characters, however technically impressive, are not creative unless the content of the drawings is original. A standard pose of a familiar character cannot be considered creative, no matter how well it is drawn. If, however, the drawings represent characters in new and unusual settings, tell a story, or portray an original message, they may be creative.

Susan's illustration of Frederick Douglass walking across whales probably is novel. It is unlikely that she has seen a similar drawing! However, if the originality resulted from a misunderstanding or lack of prior knowledge of the difference between Wales and whales, the drawing is not a clever visual pun; it is a mistake. Although mistakes often can provide stimulus or inspiration for creative endeavors, they usually are not considered creative. In creative endeavors, the originality must be purposeful. In very young children, it is possible to confuse originality with immature understanding. When, as a toddler, I begged for a new jumper so I could jump higher, it was not a purposeful, novel thought. I thought that was what jumpers did. I was not being creative but made a logical connection the word "jump," just as an adult might accidentally misuse new vocabulary. (I was also sadly disappointed in my new jumper!)

Max's response to the composition assignment is certainly original. However, is it appropriate? If we gauge appropriateness as meeting the criterion for the assignment, probably not. Max, after all, created a piece about the style of Beethoven rather than in his style. However, if appropriateness is judged from Max's point of view—"How can I use music I value to do this assignment?"—the effort falls closer to the mark. Perhaps we can view Max's composition as falling short of the criterion for the assignment while still demonstrating considerable creative thought. It might also be relevant to ask whether it is good rap. That is, does it meet criteria in its own domain?

Tzeena's caricatures can probably be considered creative, if not kind. The idea of teacher-as-ostrich is probably original, and the drawings certainly portray a meaningful message. As with Max's music, it is important to remember that creativity is not necessarily channeled into school-appropriate behaviors. Although we can certainly endeavor to change students' vehicles for creativity, it is important to recognize creativity in a variety of forms.

Thinking About the Classroom

Creativity is not always expressed in school-appropriate ways. For 1 week, pay careful attention to students causing disturbances in your room. Do you see evidence of creativity in their behavior? Perhaps that originality can be channeled in other ways.

Levels and Domains of Creativity

Before going further, it is important to acknowledge that the term "creativity" can be used to describe acts at several different levels. The everyday creativity described earlier is certainly different in scope, if not necessarily in process, from the world-changing efforts of da Vinci or Einstein. Writers sometimes distinguish between "Creativity with a big C" that changes disciplines and "creativity with a little c," the more commonplace innovations of everyday life. Yet considering the creative pathways taken in everyday life may help us understand creative processes on the "big C" scale (Tanggaard, 2015). In an effort to represent the broad range of creative possibilities, Beghetto and Kaufman expanded the notion of big C and little C creativity to include four levels (2017; Kaufman & Beghetto, 2009). The first, Mini-C, represents the kinds of novel interpretations of personal experiences that occur in learning, specific to an individual. The other added level, Pro-C, fits between the "Little" and "Big" levels and represents substantial creative accomplishments that require a professional level of expertise but don't change disciplines in the way "big C" creativity would. Similarly, Sternberg (2003) proposed eight types of creative contributions, varied by their impact on a discipline. These ranged from replication to the integration of two formerly diverse ways of viewing a phenomenon. In this text, we will include in our discussions all types of creativity, from the everyday to the once-a-generation varieties. It will become clear that some theorists deal primarily with one, some primarily with the other. Certainly the kind of creativity we hope to enhance in our students is likely to be, at least for the moment, of the "little c" variety, but we hope that understanding the bigger picture and wider goals can make us better stewards of the talents in our midst.

As we consider the many unanswered questions about creativity, one of the most often mentioned is whether creativity is a general or discipline-specific phenomenon. A substantial body of research suggests that at least some parts of creativity are domain specific (see Baer, 2010, for example). Real-world creativity takes place in a domain—we recognize creative scientists, artists, writers, and the like. Although some individuals may demonstrate creativity across domains, except for some creativity measures, we have no way to recognize creativity that is domain free. Yet even when creativity measures do identify domain differences, there remains enough overlap between, say, creativity in language arts and creativity in science to suggest that there are some general creativity processes at work (Kaufman, Cole, & Baer, 2009; Lubart & Guignard, 2004; Plucker, 1998).

The question then becomes, is it all the same? Are the processes used by a creative physicist the same as those used by a creative artist? Are the characteristics associated with a creative entrepreneur similar to or different from those of a creative mathematician? Are individuals more productive in a particular discipline because their abilities are domain specific or simply because of human limitations of time and energy? As you read about creative people and processes, be alert to areas in which there appear to be similarities and differences across domains. These differences may be a function of the disciplines themselves or of the type of training essential to make creative contributions in a particular field. Although there is much yet to be investigated, there is evidence that both positions are true—some aspects of creativity (e.g., flexibility in thinking or persistence) are important across domains, whereas there may well be characteristics that systematically differ between creative physicists and creative rock musicians.

Why Do People Create?

Why did Emily Dickinson write? What prompted Scott Joplin to compose or Edison to invent or Pacific Island people to tell stories with dance? Examining the forces that motivate individual creativity may be crucial to encouraging those behaviors in school settings. Consider the statements of these creative individuals.

I think I teach people how to find meaning. I write about the most chaotic, tragic, hard-to-deal-with events, and these events are sometimes so violent and so horrible that they burst through bounds of form and preconceptions. I'm hoping that readers will find how to get the meaning out of these events. How do you find beauty and order when we've had this bloody horrible past?

(Maxine Hong Kingston, in Moyers, 1990, p. 11)

When we fantasize in our daily lives, that's easy, because fantasy by definition is sufficient and compensating. But, the writer's fantasy is not complete until he can transmit it to somebody else. . . . Where it flows, where you find yourself going on and the writing generates more writing—there's your book.

(E. L. Doctorow, in Ruas, 1984, p. 203)

I drew them several times and there was no feeling in them. Then afterwards—after I had done the ones that were so stiff—came the others . . . HOW IT HAPPENS THAT I CAN EXPRESS SOMETHING OF THAT KIND? Because the thing has already taken form in my mind before I start on it. The first attempts are absolutely unbearable. I say this because I want you to know that if you see something worthwhile in what I am doing, it is not by accident but because of real intention and purpose.

(Vincent van Gogh, in Ghiselin, 1985, p. 47)

In each case, individuals created works of art or literature because they had something to communicate. The message was not always easy to express. The ideas were sometimes difficult or the forms hard to manage. Despite the difficulties, the creators persisted. They wished to allow the audience to make meaning in new ways or to share a vision of the world. The process of making meaning and shared vision can be seen in the efforts of visual artists, storytellers, musicians, dancers, myth makers, playwrights, and other creators throughout history. It is expressed in contemporary terms by neuroscientist Mary Helen Immordino Yang as reflecting the imperative toward social connectedness.

By virtue of its evolutionary connection to bodily feeling and survival, our social mind motivates us to create things that represent the meaning we have made by processes of noticing, feeling, and understanding, so that others can notice, feel, and understand what we have.

(2016, p. 109)

Such an observation almost seems so obvious as to be meaningless: Of course writers and artists strive to communicate. Yet this most basic process of creativity, the effort to communicate, is missing in many so-called creative school activities. How often does a student in school write or paint or use another form of expression not because it has been assigned but because he or she has something to say? Others use creative processes in slightly different ways. Consider the forces that motivated these creators.

In 1873, Chester Greenwood received a pair of ice skates for his 15th birthday. Unfortunately, Chester was unable to enjoy the skates, because each time he ventured on the ice, the chill Farmington, Maine, air made his sensitive ears uncomfortable enough that he was forced indoors. The earmuffs Chester designed to solve this problem were sold across New England by the time Chester was 19.

(Caney, 1985)

In Chicopee, Massachusetts, a group of middle-school students read about the city's sludge problem. The state had ordered Chicopee to stop burning sludge because doing so violated air quality regulations. In the winter, the sludge froze before it could be hauled away to a landfill. (Another difficult New England winter!) Officials suggested constructing a brick building around the sludge to keep it from freezing, but the city did not have the necessary $120,000. Students at the Bellamy Middle School brainstormed numerous solutions and sent them to the chief operator of the sludge plant. Their suggested solar greenhouse successfully kept the sludge warm and was constructed for $500.

(Lewis, 1998)

In 1924 Kimberly-Clark began to market Cellucotton sheets as disposable cloths for removing makeup. In 1929 they patented the pop-up box and renamed the product Kleenex. Sales were still only moderate. A marketing survey revealed that over half the people purchasing Kleenex were using them, not to remove makeup, but as disposable handkerchiefs. A new marketing strategy and slogan, "Don't put a cold in your pocket," led to a 400% sales increase in 2 years.

(Caney, 1985)

In these cases, individuals exercised creative thinking not only to communicate but also to solve problems. The inventors of modern lighting, heating, and cooling devices used creative thinking to address the problems of comfort in their homes. Mail-order catalogues are full of devices designed to address less dramatic problems. Products that locate the end of the masking tape, clean the blinds, or protect the shoe that works the gas pedal from scuffing all resulted from someone's creative thinking about a particular problem or annoyance. And, of course, working to solve the problem "How can we learn more about Mars?" led to the NASA rover *Curiosity*.

Many times, the most important part of this process is realizing that a problem exists. Until their marketing survey, sales personnel at Kimberly-Clark had no knowledge of a need for a disposable handkerchief. It is hard to imagine now that a few years ago, no one thought offices needed the now-indispensable stick-on, pull-off notes. In a similar fashion, someone realized that there was a need (or at least a market) for bottled-water flavoring, tablet computers, and online social networks before those creations existed. In scientific research, it may be at least as important to select a potent research question as it is to solve it. The researcher who first wondered whether it was possible to alter the structure of genes opened up new worlds of medical research and treatment. Imagine the impact of the first human being to realize that the inability to record language was a problem. Identifying a problem to solve rather than solving a preset problem is called problem finding.

Problem finding, in its broadest sense, underlies all types of creativity. Some of the most basic research in problem finding was done with visual artists (Getzels & Csikszentmihalyi, 1976). In those studies, artists were considered to be problem finding as they manipulated materials to find ideas for their paintings. Finding the idea or theme to communicate, as well as finding a societal problem or need, can be considered problem finding. I consider both of these themes as the underlying (and overlapping) purposes of creativity in Western cultures. Within the primary culture in which I work and teach, individuals are often creative in their efforts to communicate an idea or to find and solve problems. Extending these processes into classroom situations can allow creative activities to occur there naturally. Introducing these procedures also holds implications for classroom learning because the purposes of creativity have much in common with key attributes of learning theory.

Thinking About the Classroom

Try giving two assignments on the same general topic, one demanding accuracy and one requiring originality. For example, if the class is studying the Civil War, one assignment may ask students to develop a time line of key events or to describe the causes of the war, and the other may ask students to describe our lives today if the South had won the war. Do the same students give the most accurate and the most original responses? Are the original responses also appropriate?

Teaching for Creativity Versus Creative Teaching

Structuring teaching for creativity can be a slippery goal. I once attended a class in which graduate students demonstrated lessons designed to enhance creative thinking. One activity in particular stands out in my memory. The teacher of the lesson took the class outside, a welcome break from the stuffy college classroom. She then brought out a parachute and proceeded to show us how the chute could be used to create various forms—a flower, an ocean wave, and other shapes. We were taught a specific, tightly choreographed series of moves to tie one form to the next in a story line. As the teacher narrated, we marched and ducked and raised our arms so that the parachute was transformed into various shapes to accompany the story. We acquired an audience of passersby, and the striking visual effect we created earned us hearty applause. We enjoyed the exercise and activity, especially the break from the usual routine and the enthusiastic acceptance by our audience. When we finished, however, I was struck by a clear question. Who was being creative? The living sculpture of the parachute activity certainly seemed original, and it communicated in novel and effective ways. Yet as a participant, my thoughts were not on communication or originality but on counting my steps and remembering when to duck—hardly the chief ingredients of creative thought. A teaching activity that produces an enjoyable or even creative outcome does not necessarily enhance creativity unless the students have the opportunity for creative thinking. The parachute activity might be considered creative teaching because the teacher exercised considerable creativity in developing and presenting the exercise. However, creative teaching (the teacher is creative) is not the same as teaching to develop creativity.

This distinction becomes clearer when books of so-called creative activities are examined. In some cases, the illustrations are adorable and the activities unusual, but the input from students is fairly routine. For example, a color-by-number dragon filled with addition problems may have been an original creation for the illustrator, but completing the addition problems and coloring as directed provide no opportunities for originality among the students. A crossword puzzle in the shape of a spiral was an original idea for its creator, but it still requires students only to give accurate responses to the clues and fill in the correct spaces. In these cases, those who created the materials had the opportunity to be creative. The students do not. In other cases, classroom teachers may use enormous personal creativity in developing activities that allow few opportunities for students to be original.

Teaching to enhance creativity has a different focus. The essential creativity is on the part of the students. If the students develop parachute choreography or a new form of crossword puzzle, they have the opportunity to exercise creative thinking. Creativity also can be developed as students devise their own science experiments, discuss Elizabethan England from the point of view of a woman at court or a farm woman, or rewrite "Snow White" as it might be told by the stepmother. When teaching to enhance creativity, we may well be creative as teachers, but we also provide students the knowledge, skills, and surroundings necessary for their own creativity to emerge. The results may not be as flashy as those in the parachute story, but they include real problem finding, problem solving, and communication by students.

Thinking About the Classroom

Examine a book on creative activities or creative teaching. For each activity, identify the person who has the opportunity for original or innovative thought. Is it primarily the author, teacher, or student?

Authentic Problems and Processes

Structuring education around the goals of creativity involves shifting our visions of teachers and learners. Robinson (2015) suggests teachers fulfill three essential purposes for students:

Inspiration—inspiring students with passion for their disciplines,
Confidence—helping students acquire the knowledge and skills to become independent learners, and
Creativity—enabling students to inquire, experiment, question, and develop both the skills and dispositions of original thinking.

Learning activities designed to foster creativity cast students in the roles of problem solvers and communicators rather than passive acquirers of information. Teachers, in turn, are transformed from founts of all wisdom to problem setters, problem seekers, coaches, audiences, and sometimes publicity agents. If students are to solve real problems, teachers have the responsibility not only to teach them the necessary knowledge and skills but also to set problems for which the teachers have no answers and to work together with students to find the solutions. If students are to communicate, teachers must help them find ideas worth sharing and audiences with whom to share them. These are fundamentally different processes from those most of us experienced as learners in school. This type of restructuring also has major implications for the content in curriculum areas to be addressed.

It is essential to be clear that restructuring curriculum does not mean eliminating it. Students can and should learn required content while also enhancing their creative thinking—the two should be inextricably entwined. One cannot solve problems involving plants without knowledge of botany, and teachers have the responsibility to help students gain that knowledge. Contrary to some quickly turned phrases, sometimes the sage *should* be on the stage. In fact, the processes of identifying and solving problems form an effective context in which to gain content knowledge. But students who are to be taught strategies for finding and solving problems and for communicating information must be taught not just the what but also the how of the disciplines in the curriculum. For example, students who are to be problem solvers in history must know not only facts, concepts, and generalizations about history but also how history works and what historians do. How does a historian decide on an area for study? What types of problems do historians find and solve? How do they gather information? Learning as much as possible about the authentic methodology of the disciplines allows students to become seekers and solvers of real or authentic problems while learning content about history in more complex ways.

The investigation of authentic problems was espoused by educators such as Dewey (1938) and Renzulli (1977, 2012) throughout much of the 20th century. Such problems were emphasized in literature on authentic learning (Brandt, 1993), situated learning (Brown, Collins, & Duguid,

1989), and problem solving ranging from opportunities for astronomical data gathering to solving dilemmas of real-world businesses (Bollman, Rodgers, & Mauller, 2001; Holt & Willard-Holt, 2000). Although more complete discussions on the nature of problem types and authentic learning are included in Chapters 7 and 8, for now, a simple definition will suffice. An authentic problem (a) does not have a predetermined answer, (b) is personally relevant to the investigator, and (c) can be explored through the methods of one or more disciplines. Students who are to address authentic problems must be provided with the knowledge and tools that allow them to be successful. In a parallel fashion, students who are to be effective communicators not only must have an idea worth communicating but also must be taught the skills of communication in a variety of formats.

As you can see, this book does not view teaching for creativity as something to be pulled out on Friday at 2:00 P.M. or when students are restless after an indoor recess. Teaching for creativity entails creating a community of inquiry in the classroom, a place in which asking a good question is at least as important as answering one. Building this climate includes organizing curriculum around the processes of creativity, providing students with content and processes that allow them to investigate and communicate within disciplines, teaching general techniques that facilitate creative thinking across disciplines, and providing a classroom atmosphere that supports creativity.

Teaching for Creativity in a Time of Standards

One of the most important educational trends of the early 21st century is the increased emphasis on teaching to specific state and national standards (Hollingsworth & Gallego, 2007; National Governors Association Center for Best Practices, Council of Chief State School Officers, 2010). This has been associated with increases in high-stakes testing. As I have met with teachers and discussed barriers to teaching for creativity, the most common response is some variation of "there are no standards for creative thinking" or "it isn't on the test." In a powerful and troubling piece, Berliner (2012) described our narrowing curriculum to the frame of high-stakes assessment as "Creaticide by Design." Creaticide was defined as "the national design to kill literary, scientific, and mathematical creativity in the school-age population of the United States of America, particularly among impoverished youth" (p. 79). For at least some prospective teachers, imaginative thinking seems to be outside what they perceive as essential in schools. In one study, the largest number of prospective teachers cited first grade as the time when students should start to focus on memorization rather than imaginative thinking (Beghetto, 2008). As a former first grade teacher, it makes me want to weep.

It is true that no responsible teacher should devote significant amounts of time to activities that will not enhance students' opportunities for success, both on high-stakes tests and on the more complex challenges of life and continued intellectual growth. If teaching for creativity is simply an add-on of cute activities, teachers should question its value. However, teaching for creativity is not additional curriculum. It is a set of strategies for designing curriculum so that both content learning and creative thinking are enhanced. Used in conjunction with careful curriculum alignment, teaching to enhance creativity can help students identify and solve problems, see from multiple points of view, analyze data, and express themselves clearly in multiple genres. These are the very activities that will enhance students' learning and (assuming reasonably designed assessments) are highly likely to enhance their test scores as well.

In the current education climate, this point cannot be made too often: Activities that engage students in problem solving, meaningful communication, questioning, and original representations of ideas enhance learning and motivation. In fact, some of the newest findings in neurobiology suggest that learning occurs best when in the context of personally meaningful activities (see Chapter 3). When such activities are planned around core curriculum goals, they constitute effective curriculum alignment. Good teaching is not dull, rote, or constantly repetitious. Good teaching finds multiple ways to help students think about important content. If we use content standards wisely, the biggest change in teaching is that we will more clearly delineate the content about which we want students to think—more on standards in Chapter 7.

Is Creativity Really Good for Us?

Given the fact that I have invested time and energy in writing a book on developing creativity, it would be reasonable to assume that if someone were to ask me if creativity is a good idea, I would answer, "Yes." And I believe it is, for reasons already described. But if I think carefully, I can also answer, "It depends." It depends on the definition of creativity and on how the power of creativity is used.

Ariely (2012) suggests that creative people are more skilled at lying. History has taught us that creativity can be used for good or evil, in ways both large and small. We celebrate beautiful art and discoveries that allow us to live healthier and more productive lives. Yet it is possible to use creative thought to devise new and original ways to do terrible things. As with all kinds of education, teaching for creativity demands a context of shared human values. Teaching about and for creativity brings with it the responsibility to discuss the ways new ideas bring joy and benefit to others in our collective community.

In the foreword to John-Steiner's (2000) book on creative collaboration, David Feldman described the 21st century as the "Era of Community" (p. xiii), in which the dominant challenge will be striking a balance between individuality and social connectedness. John-Steiner (2000) begins her work:

> We have come to a new understanding of the life of the mind. The notion of the solitary thinker still appeals to those molded by the Western belief in individualism. However, a careful scrutiny of how knowledge is constructed and artistic forms are shaped reveals a different reality. Generative ideas emerge from joint thinking, from significant conversation, and from sustained, shared struggles to achieve new insights by partners in thought.
>
> (p. 3)

Helping students find their way to creativity that lives in the balance between self and others, individuality, and community will require experiences both new and familiar.

And Do We Really Want It?

A 1995 article by Westby and Dawson has been widely cited in the blog world as evidence that teachers "don't like" creative students. Such claims seem wildly overstated based on data from 13 elementary school teachers, particularly because the descriptors for creative children were more negative in tone than those deemed "less typical" of creative students. But regardless of the research flaws, it must be admitted that opening our classrooms to creative responses, by definition, means opening them to the unpredictable and the unplanned. It means we won't always know the direction a discussion may take or the solution that may emerge. It means we must leave the comfortable position of knowing the correct answer. It will not always be easy. And it is true that creative students' behaviors are not often a welcome part of classroom routines (Aljughaiman & Mowrer-Reynolds, 2005). Sometimes what we think we want is, upon arrival, more difficult than we hoped.

This is complicated by a phenomenon uncovered by Mueller, Melwani, and Goncalo (2012), who found that individuals react negatively to creativity when faced with uncertainty. Individuals faced with uncertainty were also less likely to find or accept creative solutions to problems. Their findings point out a great irony—when we are uncertain and most need creative solutions, we are less likely to recognize them. I suspect this phenomenon operates in classrooms as well. The very conditions that support creativity lead to uncertainty—which may make us less inclined to choose the creative path or see the creative ideas before us. If we are to create the classrooms we need—and the classrooms our students deserve—we must recognize this danger and work against it. Classrooms that support creativity will require determination along with flexibility and persistence in the face of ambiguity. Additionally, Ozkal (2014) found that teachers' support for creativity was associated with their self-efficacy beliefs (confidence) about teaching, particularly their confidence in their ability to engage students and use effective instructional practices. Along with determination, we will need skills! I will do my best to provide many of them here.

Wagner (2012) asked a provocative question:

> In the past, our country has produced innovators more by accident than by design. Rarely do entrepreneurs or innovators talk about how their schooling or their places of work—or even their parents—developed their talents or encouraged their aspirations. Three of the most innovative entrepreneurs of the last half century. . . . had to drop out of Harvard to pursue their ideas. . . .
>
> So what would it mean if we were to intentionally develop the entrepreneurial and innovative talents of all young people—to nurture their initiative, curiosity, imagination, creativity, and collaborative skills, as well as their analytical abilities—along with essential qualities of character such as persistence, empathy, and a strong moral foundation?
>
> (pp. 22–23)

I hope this book is a place to begin answering Wagner's challenge.

Structure of the Book

Each of the dimensions of teaching for creativity is addressed in this book. The text is divided into two parts: Part I, "Understanding Creative People and Processes," and Part II, "Creativity and Classroom Life." Part I concentrates on research and theory about creativity in an effort to tie research to classroom practice, whereas the second part deals directly with classroom activities, organization, and practice. As you read, you will find several types of activities that can be used to explore the ideas presented. Throughout the book, Thinking About the Classroom activities will help you apply material to your particular teaching situation.

There are three features at the end of each chapter to help you extend your learning. At the end of each chapter, "Think About It" suggestions provide questions and activities to assist your reflections on each aspect of the creative process. For those using this book as a class text, Think About It activities may sometimes prove interesting class activities. You also may find it helpful to keep a journal as you read, recording your thoughts, questions, and ideas. Do not feel limited to the suggestions at the end of each chapter. You could use your journal to explore your own experiences with creativity, ideas that puzzle you, classroom observations, dilemmas, and solutions.

The second feature at the end of each chapter is titled "Try It Tomorrow." These are suggestions specifically for educators (or parents) who want to apply chapter ideas with young people in quick and easy ways. Of course, the Thinking About the Classroom activities also can be used for that purpose, so you might want to review them when looking for a place to start.

The final end-of-chapter feature is "Tech Tips." Our modern world is so full of technology that I, for one, struggle to keep up with the many ways I can incorporate new technologies into my teaching. I've started a blog on creativity and teaching (http://creativiteach.me), in an effort to join the technological conversation. Also, I've added a list of technology tips, usually but not always tied to chapter content, at the end of each chapter. I do this with some hesitation, knowing that some links that are functioning as I write will likely be outdated by the time you read them. And the newest and latest will pass my list by as soon as it is published. But because the alternative is to ignore this essential part of our educational context, we do our best. And, of course, I'll continue to update the creativiteach.me blog as I learn of new options. I really hope you will join me there. Blogging is much more fun when there is a conversation.

Finally, this book has two goals. First, I hope you will leave the book with an understanding of theories of creativity, the characteristics of creative individuals, and aspects of the creative process that reflect the status of contemporary research. The second (admittedly lofty) goal is that you will use these ideas to transform the ways you think about and act toward education. Teaching to develop creativity touches the very heart of the educational process, the ways that we, as teachers, interact with our students. I hope you may find here some ways to interact that are both power- ful and empowering, ideas that help your students find the curious delight of creativity. I cannot imagine a more valuable investment than time spent helping students learn in ways that allow them to solve problems, create, and share.

Think About It

1. One of the most interesting and effective ways to explore creativity is to undertake a creative project of your own. In my course, Developing Creativity in the Classroom, graduate students must identify a problem and invent something to address it. Their inventions have ranged from an enormous version of a dentist's mirror that allows the user to check leaves in building gutters without climbing a ladder to a device that signals forgetful teenagers to retrieve their wet laundry. You may want to try a similar activity. Look around you for everyday annoyances or dilemmas that you might solve. What things around you might be improved, simplified, or elaborated? Alternatively, you might want to undertake a creative writing project, artistic endeavor, or other creative task. Whatever you choose, record your thoughts, feelings, and activities in your journal. As you read, compare the research, theories, and techniques to your own experiences. How do you feel as you contemplate such a project?

2. Examine today's newspaper or news website. What evidence of creative thought do you see in the stories or advertisements? Look for original ideas appropriate to the situation. Are all creative ideas socially appropriate? You might make a chart of evidence of creativity in one day and see what proportion of the ideas you consider appropriate or ethical. It would be interesting to discuss how often ethical versus nonethical creativity makes the news.

3. Think about the influence of culture on your conception of creativity. Do you consider some forms of expression or activity more creative than others? Talk to others about what they consider creative. Think about how the responses might differ if you asked your colleagues, your neighbors, or your students. You might undertake a mini-research study to find out.

Try It Tomorrow

1. Talk to your students about creativity, particularly the many ways creativity can be dem- onstrated. Start a bulletin board (in the classroom or online) with examples of creativity in many disciplines and from many cultures. Encourage students to add examples. Help them distinguish the difference between creativity and celebrity.

2. Make a chart of the ways creativity can be displayed by people in different fields. For example, could a basketball player be creative? How? You might start the chart with a list of occupations and work with students to imagine how each might be creative. Then challenge students to add to the list.

Tech Tips

The world of technology is a marvel of creativity. Every day, new websites, new apps, and new devices bring us the possibility of innovative ways to teach. So at the end of each chapter, you'll find "Tech Tips," suggestions for technology resources that can help you support creativity, both for yourself and for your students. In most cases, there will be links between chapter content and the tips, but you'll also find occasional random tips that are just too good to omit. This chapter will focus on "tech basics" that will be helpful to any professional.

1. If you'd like to see examples of creativity in action, you need to visit TED. TED (www.TED.com) houses an extraordinary collection of talks by individuals across a variety of disciplines. TED is a nonprofit devoted to "Ideas Worth Spreading." It started out (in 1984) as a conference bringing together people from three worlds: technology, entertainment, and design. Since then, its scope has become ever broader. It includes two annual conferences, the award-winning TED Talks video site, and a variety of other programs. Fair warning: TED can be addictive. Once you start exploring the talks, you may not want to stop!

    An exciting branch of TED, TED-Ed, is subtitled "Lessons Worth Sharing." TED-Ed helps teachers link to outstanding lessons by capturing lessons on video and amplifying them via added animation. And all this is managed in 10-minute intervals designed to fit neatly into school schedules. TED-Ed is hoping to recruit outstanding teachers (you??), as well as interested animators, to help create the lessons. Here is a chance to start using interesting videos or to get in on the ground floor creating them (ed.ted.com).

2. One of the interesting questions debated in creativity literature today is whether creativity is individual or collaborative (or both). If you want to engage in collaborative creativity, you'll need ways to work together with colleagues and share information. Two basic ways to do that are through Google Docs/Drive and Dropbox. Google Docs (docs.google.com) is a free suite of editing tools that allows collaborative writing in real time. You can work on a document that is shared with a friend, and he or she will see the edits immediately—or whenever your friend next views it. Google Docs documents (or anything else) can be stored "in the cloud" through Google Drive, which is like an invisible extra drive you can access through any of your devices. If you share something with a friend, your friend can access it, too. No more sending missing attachments to your curriculum committee!

3. Another option for sharing files online is Dropbox (www.dropbox.com). In Dropbox, you create folders of information that can be shared with various groups. Any time you make a change, the change is instantly available. Think about how many times you send a colleague or friend something you want to refer to or update. Shared creativity has become much easier since the advent of "the cloud"!

4. The final basic website is CAST (www.cast.org). If we are to support creativity in all students, including those with disabilities, we need support. Originally known as the Center for Applied Special Technology, CAST is a nonprofit organization that works to expand learning opportunities for all individuals, especially those with disabilities. They do this through

principles of universal design for learning (UDL) and creative uses of technology. Here are a few examples—explore the site and find many more.

- Explore the UDL editions of several classic works, found under "Learning Tools." With online supports in mastering the stories, students can then participate in analytical and creative discussions of the ideas in the texts without being hampered by reading difficulties.
- Once you've seen how exciting the UDL books can be, use the UDL Book Builder to create your own custom-built books. You are guided every step of the way to preparing supportive texts for students ages 3 and up.
- Manipulate three-dimensional solids online using Interactives.
- See how CAST Science Writer supports middle and high schools students in writing science reports.

These are just a tiny sampling of the scores of supports provided at the CAST website and linked National Center on Universal Design for Learning. Most are free and available online. Take some time to explore and see which options are most appropriate for your students. I found it helpful to start at any point of the Checklist for UDL Guidelines and then click the various checkpoints to explore different resource options.

2
Models of the Creative Process

When I am, as it were, completely myself, entirely alone, and of good cheer—say, traveling in a carriage, or walking after a good meal, or during the night when I cannot sleep; it is on such occasions that my ideas flow best and most abundantly. Whence and how they come, I know not; nor can I force them. . . . Nor do I hear in my imagination the parts successively, but I hear them, as it were, all at once. What a delight this is I cannot tell! All this inventing, this producing, takes place in a pleasing lively dream. . . . This is perhaps the best gift I have my Divine Maker to thank for.

(Wolfgang Amadeus Mozart, in Ghiselin, 1985, pp. 34–35)

Generally speaking, the germ of a future composition comes suddenly and unexpectedly. If the soil is ready—that is to say if the disposition to work is there—it takes root with extraordinary force and rapidity. . . . In the midst of this magic process it frequently happens that some external interruption wakes me from my somnambulistic state: a ring at the bell, the entrance of my servant, the striking of a clock. . . . Dreadful, indeed, are such interruptions. Sometimes they break the thread of inspiration for a considerable time. . . . In such cases cool headwork and technical knowledge have to come to my aid. Even in the works of the greatest master we find such moments, when the organic sequence fails and a skillful join has to be made. . . . But it cannot be avoided. If that condition of mind and soul, which we call inspiration, lasted long without intermission, no artist could survive it.

(Peter Illich Tchaikovsky, in Vernon, 1975, pp. 57–58)

Molly wanted to write a song for an upcoming church musical. She had never written a song before, but she played several instruments and was convinced that if she could manage the task, the musical would be much improved. For several days she was frustrated with her efforts. Her ideas seemed either stiff and mechanical or very similar to popular songs she enjoyed. One evening, in the shower, she found herself singing a new, interesting chorus to her song. Hair still dripping, she ran to write it down. With this new beginning, the rest of the song followed easily.

Individuals who have created music, told stories, solved problems, and dreamed dreams have probably been the objects of curiosity and wonder from the earliest times. From the beginnings of recorded history, scholars have speculated about the source of creativity, how it works, and how individuals identified as creative differ from others. Studies, theories, and models of creativity have traditionally focused on four areas, all starting with P. Some examine characteristics of the creative *person*. They investigate personal characteristics, family dynamics, or essential abilities of individuals who have been identified as creative. Other theories and models are organized around the creative *process*. They examine the processes by which individuals generate creative ideas. Still others study and theorize about the creative *product* itself. They answer such questions as what makes something creative or how creative ideas are different from other ideas. As the role of context has become more important in creativity research, theories have also focused on a fourth P, *press*, or environment (Rhodes, 1961). Many theories of creativity, especially contemporary theories, examine all four areas.

Just as theorists have emphasized different aspects of creativity, they also have examined it through different lenses (e.g., Sternberg, 1988a, 1999). Each individual views the creative process from the perspective of a specific culture. Psychologists espousing particular theories of human learning and development have viewed creativity in those frameworks. The next three chapters examine models and theories of creativity from several vantage points. In this chapter, I will discuss models of the creative process and then examine cultural perspectives on the concept of creativity. Chapters 3 and 4 will focus on theories about the origin, nature, and systems of creativity—theories focusing on the individual in Chapter 3 and systems theories in Chapter 4. As you read, you may find it helpful to consider how each theory fits with others of a similar orientation, which aspects (person, product, process, or press) it emphasizes and how the theory fits with your experience. Finally, it is helpful to consider how each theory might influence classroom practice. Ask yourself, "If this theory is valid, how might it affect the way I teach—or perhaps the way I live?"

The Creative Process

Probably the most common source for models of the creative process can be found in the experiences of individuals who have developed creative ideas or products. Much of the early information on these experiences came from writings or interviews of individuals whose creativity is generally accepted, such as the letters of Mozart and Tchaikovsky excerpted at the beginning of this chapter. It also is likely that most scholars have been influenced by their own experiences in generating new and appropriate ideas. Certainly, if Molly, whose composing in the shower was cited earlier, were to describe the creative process, she would want to develop a model that rang true not just with outside sources but with her own experiences. Thus, traditional models of creativity tend to be based on descriptions of experienced creativity, as seen through the lens of the creator.

Think for a moment about a time you had a new idea, solved a problem, or created a piece of art or literature that was particularly meaningful to you. It might have been the time you planned a new interdisciplinary unit, fixed an appliance with a paper clip, or finally painted the picture that expressed your frustration with the pain some children bring to school. How did your idea happen? Did it come all at once, as Mozart described his inspiration, or did it demand the "cool headwork" of Tchaikovsky? As you read the descriptions of the creative process, consider how they fit with your experienced creativity.

Dewey and Wallas: To Incubate or Not to Incubate

One of the earliest contemporary models of creativity can be found in Dewey's (1920) model of problem solving. Dewey described the process of problem solving in five logical steps: (a) a difficulty is felt, (b) the difficulty is located and defined, (c) possible solutions are considered, (d) consequences of these solutions are weighed, and (e) one of the solutions is accepted.

Wallas (1926), Dewey's contemporary, studied the writings of creative people and generated a series of four steps that probably is the classic description of the creative process. In it, Wallas went beyond Dewey's logical sequencing to include unconscious processing and the experienced "aha!" described by many creators. The first step in the process is *preparation*. During this stage, the creator is gathering information, thinking about the problem, and coming up with the best possible ideas. Molly, whose experience is described at the beginning of the chapter, must have gathered ideas and experimented with melodies and lyrics as part of her preparation. The second stage, *incubation*, is the heart of the Wallas model. During incubation, the individual does not consciously think about the problem. He or she goes about other activities while, at some level, the mind continues to consider the problem or question. Molly may have been incubating while in the shower. How incubation functions (and whether it exists) has been one of the key debates among theorists in creativity. Whatever the means, the third stage in Wallas's model is *illumination*, the "aha!" experience. It is the point at which ideas suddenly fit together and the solution becomes clear. In Molly's case, the melody for the finale ran through her mind. This is followed by *verification*, in which the solution is checked for practicality, effectiveness, and appropriateness. During this stage, the solution may be elaborated and fine-tuned as necessary. Molly may have needed to rework lyrics and write a melody for the verse before the song was complete. If the solution is found to be unsatisfactory, the cycle may begin again.

One of the examples frequently used to illustrate the Wallas model is Kekulé's description of his discovery of the benzene ring, a basic structure in organic chemistry. Kekulé had been working on the problem of how the carbon atoms fit together when his oft-quoted experience occurred.

> I turned my chair to the fire and dozed. Again, the atoms were gamboling before my eyes. This time, the smaller groups kept modestly to the background. My mental eye, rendered more acute by repeated vision of this kind, could now distinguish larger structures, of manifold conformation, long rows, sometimes more closely fitted together, all twining and twisting in snakelike motion. But look! What was that? One of the snakes had seized hold of its own tail, and the form whirled mockingly before my eyes. As if by a flash of lightning I awoke.
>
> (Weisberg, 1986, p. 32)

Sometimes creative ideas need to be incubated

Kekulé's early work provided preparation. His incubation occurred during his doze (also translated "reverie") and ended on his awaking with illumination. Subsequent thought and experimentation provided verification.

The most examined stage of Wallas's model is incubation—the idea that taking time away from a creative problem can lead to a productive "aha!" moment of illumination. Research on incubation has had mixed results, perhaps not surprising as the definitions of incubation differ so widely across the studies. But Sio and Ormerod's (2009) meta-analysis, combining the results of 117 studies, found taking a break increases likelihood of problem solving, particularly with divergent-thinking tasks. Interestingly, incubation didn't necessarily require complete rest. In fact, for some types of insight problems, a "low cognitive demand" (easy) task seemed a more effective environment for incubation than no stimulation at all.

A number of researchers have tried to identify effective incubation strategies. Baird et al. (2012) found that participants who were encouraged to let their minds wander while completing a low-demand activity were better able to complete creative tasks than when they were given plain rest or a difficult task to complete. Gilhooly, Georgiou, and Devery (2013) found that not only did a break with an alternative task enhance completion of creative tasks, the type of task made a difference. When participants took a break by working on mental exercises very different from those in creative tasks at hand, the incubation was more effective than when they used similar tasks. The title of their article included the phrase "Do something different," which may be one of the keys. It may be that simply shifting your thoughts to something else may be the best way to give your conscious thoughts an incubation break. In subsequent research, Gilhooly and colleagues found that a break in which individuals were specifically directed not to think about the task but were not given an alternative task was also effective (Gilhooly, Georgiou, Sirota, & Paphiti-Galeano, 2015).

Some accounts of creativity across cultures seem to parallel Wallas's stages—likely with the same neurological underpinnings. Cajete (2000) described the creation of ceremonial art in indigenous societies as a process that begins with personal preparation (purification) and attention to materials, suitable time and place, and the like. This stage also includes a self-effacing "letting go and becoming" (p. 50) that is necessary for the artist and the artifact to become one. Only when both physical and spiritual preparation are complete can the work be brought into physical existence. Similarly, the Indian mathematical genius Ramanujan said that after he had worked hard without success, the goddess Namagiri revealed the answers to him in his sleep. His process of study, rest, and illumination follows the path of the Wallas model (Rao, 2005). Interestingly, contemporary medical researchers studying sleep have demonstrated that sleep is associated with increased inferential judgments, bringing together ideas not associated in initial learning (Ellenbogen, Hu, Payne, Titone, & Walker, 2007), and novel solutions to math problems (Stickgold & Walker, 2004). The thought that a period away from work may enhance creative production has caused companies such as Google, Cisco Systems, and Procter & Gamble to install EnergyPods, leather recliners with egglike hoods to shield noise and light and enhance napping possibilities (Berlin, 2008). I can only hope this trend eventually reaches higher education!

The four steps of the Wallas model, particularly the incubation and illumination stages, provide a key to understanding the differences among many theories of creativity. They also provide food for thought for those of us who are teachers. If a break from focused work is helpful in generating creative ideas, how might that be implemented in schools? Think about how "low-demand" cognitive tasks might be interspersed with more challenging ones to allow for incubation. For example, perhaps students might spend time brainstorming variables for an original science experiment, then take a break to work on organizing their research notebook pages. It would be interesting to see if such strategies allowed students to better solve creative challenges. More information on neurobiological research regarding incubation and insight is found in Chapter 3.

Torrance (1988) put forth a definition or process model of creativity that included "sensing" creative problems—identifying a creative problem to begin with. Similar to Dewey's model, it is made up of logical stages: (a) sensing problems or difficulties; (b) making guesses or hypotheses about the problems; (c) evaluating the hypotheses and possibly revising them; and (d) communicating the results. The final stage, which implies actually doing something with the idea, is missing from both the Dewey and Wallas models. It raises an interesting question: Is an idea less creative if it is never used or shared? If Emily Dickinson's poems had never been discovered or valued, would that have affected their creativity? Such concerns are part of some theories of creativity.

More recently, Cropley and Cropley (2012) suggested dividing several of Wallas's stages into an expanded model that meshes with business models of the innovation process. In this version, Wallas's preparation is divided into preparation (familiarity with the field), activation (dissatisfaction with current situation, problem finding), and generation (of ideas). The Cropley model continues with illumination and verification but then adds communication (to potential users) and validation (acceptance or rejection from users). One of the most interesting things about the Cropley model is that it is designed to address some of the paradoxes of creativity, in which creative people need to be flexible but logical, driven but patient, and so on (see Chapter 5). If different characteristics are essential at different stages of the process, paradoxes become a necessary part of the picture.

Sawyer (2012) has made the most ambitious attempt to synthesize multiple process models and has proposed eight stages of the creative process in a model that looks a bit like Creative Problem Solving (see below), with clear roles for knowledge and incubation. The stages are: Find the Problem, Acquire the Knowledge, Gather Related Information, Incubation, Generate Ideas, Combine Ideas, Select the Best Ideas, and Externalize the Ideas. The model makes it clear that creativity requires generation of new ideas, evaluation of ideas, and sharing of ideas in order to be complete.

Thinking About the Classroom

Consider how incubation may (or may not) operate in your classroom. Try giving two assignments: one that must be completed immediately and one for which there is incubation time between the assignment and the activity. Do you notice any differences? You may want to experiment with different amounts of incubation time or different activities during incubation.

The Osborn-Parnes Model

The Osborn-Parnes model of Creative Problem Solving (CPS) was developed over more than 50 years by several theorists. It differs from the models of creativity previously described in that it was designed not so much to explain the creative process as to allow individuals to use it more effectively. CPS is a model designed for action, but it can also bring us insight.

The CPS model was developed originally by Osborn (1963), who originated brainstorming and was highly successful in advertising. He was interested not just in theorizing about creativity but also in finding ways to use it well. The process was developed and elaborated by Parnes (1981) and later by Isaksen and Treffinger (1985). Each version of the process includes a number of steps that involve both divergent (finding many ideas) and convergent (drawing conclusions and narrowing the field) stages of problem solving. Early versions were represented in a linear form with alternating periods of convergent and divergent thought. The processes were designated as finding the ideas needed at each stage: (a) Mess-Finding, (b) Data-Finding, (c) Problem-Finding,

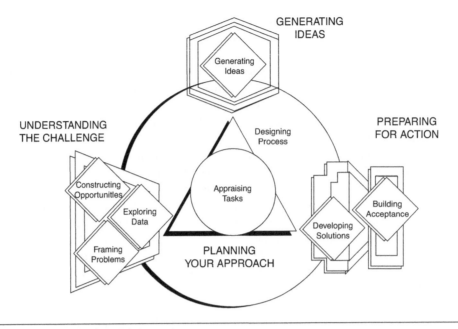

Figure 2.1 Creative Problem Solving (CPS) Framework

Source: CPS Version 6.1, © 2003 Center for Creative Learning, Inc. and Creative Problem Solving Group, Inc. Reproduced by permission of the authors.

(d) Idea-Finding, (e) Solution-Finding, and (f) Acceptance-Finding. In the early 1990s, a more fluid model was suggested, dividing the stages into three general components: Understanding the Problem, Generating Ideas, and Planning for Action (Treffinger & Isaksen, 1992; Treffinger, Isaksen, & Dorval, 1994). This view presented the stages not as a prescribed sequence but as a set of tools that can be used in the order and to the degree necessary for any problem.

The most recent version of CPS (6.1) continues this evolution (Isaksen, Dorval, & Treffinger, 2000; Treffinger, Isaksen, & Dorval, 2000, 2003; Treffinger & Isaksen, 2005). It reframes the components (specifying four) and renames stages and components to clarify functions (Figure 2.1). In addition, the newest model makes the fluidity of the process explicit by incorporating the decisions about the ways CPS should be used into the model itself.

For the purposes of illustration, I will assume that I am concerned about a situation still near and dear to the heart of those who frequent university campuses: the lack of available parking. Given the complexity of the situation and my inability to generate any immediate solutions, I decide to consider each stage. In reality, I would select and use only the components I need, but because I want the opportunity to describe each possible stage, I assume here that I need them all.

The first component I describe, Understanding the Challenge, involves investigating a broad goal, opportunity, or challenge and clarifying thinking to set the principal direction for work. Notice how the more inclusive language shifts the focus from the traditional view of understanding a problem. Within that component, I am likely to begin with the stage Constructing Opportunities. In that stage, I state a broad, brief, and beneficial goal. In this case, I might start with the goal "I want to improve the parking situation on campus."

The second stage in Understanding the Challenge, Exploring Data, entails examining many sources of information from different points of view and focusing on the most important elements. In my parking problem, I might gather data about the number of spaces available, the number of classes held at various times of the day, and so on. I also might interview students and staff to find out whether the frustration with parking differs for different groups of people, at different times, or in different situations. The most important data can be used at the third stage in this component, Framing Problems. In this stage, alternative problem statements are generated, usually starting with "In what ways might we . . . " (IWWMW). The intent is to identify ways to state the problem that will open the door to creative ideas. If the challenge to be considered is lack of adequate campus parking, the problem statements might include the following:

IWWMW build more parking lots?
IWWMW create more parking spaces on campus?
IWWMW limit the number of students parking on campus?
IWWMW limit the number of vehicles on campus?
IWWMW match the number of vehicles to the number of spaces available?
IWWMW provide students who live outside walking distance easy access to campus?

Clearly, the problem statement selected will affect the types of solutions considered. The broader the problem statement, the broader the range of possible solutions. The first problem statement, which is limited to creating traditional parking lots, offers limited options. The second might lead us to consider parking underground, in elevated structures, or on top of buildings. The last problem statement could lead to a range of possibilities—from traditional lots to bus routes, online classes, or helicopter pads!

The second general component of CPS, Generating Ideas, has only one stage. In it, ideas are generated for the selected problem statement(s) using a variety of tools. These may include brainstorming or any of the other tools for divergent thinking described in Chapter 6.

The third component is Preparing for Action. This involves exploring ways to make the promising options into workable solutions—translating ideas into action. It has two stages. The first, Developing Solutions, applies deliberate strategies and tools to analyze, refine, and select among ideas. Often, Developing Solutions entails using criteria to evaluate each of the proposed ideas systematically. In the case of the parking dilemma, possible criteria might include these:

How much would it cost?
Is it legal?
Is the technology available?
Would it be convenient for students?
Would it be convenient for staff?
Would it be acceptable to the university administration?

Criteria often are presented in a grid (Figure 2.2) that allows each idea to be evaluated by each criterion.

The final stage in this component is Building Acceptance. In this stage, plans are made for the implementation of the chosen solution. Possible difficulties are anticipated and resources are identified. This stage usually results in an action plan, with steps, resources, and individual responsibilities outlined.

The fourth component of CPS Version 6.1 is Planning Your Approach. This component reflects the need to monitor your thinking throughout the problem-solving process to make sure that you are moving in the desired direction and using an appropriate selection of CPS stages. One aspect of this component, Appraising Tasks, involves determining whether CPS is a promising choice for this situation. If a situation is open ended and would benefit from thinking about a number of possible options, CPS is an appropriate method. However, if the problem at hand truly has only one

	How much would it cost?	Is it legal?	Is the technology available?	Would it be convenient for students?	Would it be convenient for staff?	Is it acceptable to the administration?
Build a new parking structure						
Build a lot at the edge of campus with a shuttle						
Run a shuttle from parking lot near the highway						
Create car pool lot for cars with three or more passengers						

Figure 2.2 Solution-finding grid

correct answer and the task is to identify that answer, CPS may not be the best option. A second aspect, Designing Processes, involves selecting from among the CPS options the components and stages most likely to be helpful. Planning Your Approach can be considered the metacognitive facet of the CPS process that operates throughout the entire process.

While other models describe "naturally occurring" creativity, the CPS model is designed to be used, and programs and possibilities for teaching with it are presented in Chapter 6. At this point, however, we consider how well it and other process models fit with various theories of creativity. One of the important principles illustrated in the CPS model is the importance of both divergent and convergent—flexible and critical—thinking in solving complex creative problems. It, too, has ties to neurobiology, as researchers are discovering important links between brain networks that engage in different types of thinking, all required for the creative process (see Chapter 3).

Problem Finding

Whether or not it appears as a formal part of a particular model, problem finding, or the identification and framing of problems, is fundamental to creative processes. In Chapter 1, I noted that individuals undertake creative activities to communicate ideas or solve problems. Problem finding is the process by which individuals select those ideas or problems. Because this most basic of creative processes underlies all others, we will examine it in some detail. The most quoted passage in the problem-finding literature is probably from Einstein and Infeld:

> The formulation of a problem is often more important than its solution, which may be merely a matter of mathematical or experimental skill. To raise new questions, new possibilities, to regard old problems from a new angle, requires imagination and marks real advance in science.
>
> (Dillon, 1982, p. 98)

A parallel argument could be made in virtually any discipline. A painter who merely duplicates work created by others or an author who replicates others' writing probably will not be called creative or make an important contribution to his or her field. Seeking the piece worth painting or the story worth telling is at the crux of the creative process and key to the progress of the disciplines. If we are to encourage students to be creative, we must learn how to help them find problems.

Creative people find problems worth exploring

The Nature of Problems

To help students become successful problem finders, we must understand problems. Problems come in various shapes, sizes, and forms, some with more potential than others. A "problem" is not necessarily a difficulty; it may be a shift in perspective or a perceived opportunity. Blues musician Moby said,

> I think that creativity can create a lot of problems. I think that creativity can solve a lot of problems. . . . I don't see the world as a big mess of problems that need to be solved; I see the world as a really interesting miasma of things going on. And something that looks like a problem to us right now might end up looking like a wonderful thing from a future perspective.
>
> (Vaske, 2002, p. 122)

Problems can be categorized in several ways. Getzels (1964) distinguished between presented and discovered problem situations. These differ according to the degree to which the problem, method, and solution are already known. Later, Getzels (1987) identified three problem types. In a type 1 problem, there is a known formulation, a known method of solution, and a solution known to others but not to the problem solver. Students who have been taught the formula for computing the area of a square use this formula to calculate the area of a particular square. Most classroom problems are of this type. The teacher presents students with a problem and expects that they will arrive at a specific answer through a particular means.

Type 2 problems also take the form of a presented problem, but the method of solution is not known to the problem solver. In this case, students might be asked to calculate the area of a rectangle before they have been introduced to that particular formula. They must discover a satisfactory method before they can solve the problem.

With type 3 problems, there is no presented problem. The problem itself must be discovered, and neither the problem nor its solution may be known to anyone. In the Getzels series of examples, a type 3 problem might entail drawing a rectangle on the board and asking, "How many questions might be posed about this rectangle?" or "Pose an important question about this rectangle and solve it." Type 1 problems primarily involve memory and retrieval processes. Type 2 problems demand analysis and reasoning. Only type 3 problems, in which the problem itself becomes a goal, necessitate problem finding. I wonder what Getzels would think of a classroom task that asked students to invent a holiday story problem to reflect a particular formula or relationship.

Thinking About the Classroom

Examine your lesson plans for the week. Tally how many opportunities you have planned for presenting Getzels's type 1, type 2, and type 3 problems. Try to plan at least one problem of each type.

Another model for categorizing problems comes from Dillon (1982), who distinguished the levels of problems as existent, emergent, or potential. An existent problem is evident. A problematic situation exists, and the appropriate activity is to recognize it and solve it. An emergent problem is implicit rather than evident. It must be discovered before it can be solved. Emergent problems are important to people in management dealing with complex situations and data sets. A good manager is able to discover what the problem is before setting out to solve it.

Students also may have the opportunity to discover emergent problems in school content. This is probably most common in math, in which students may be asked to find the errors in a problem or solution, but such discoveries could also be appropriate in other disciplines. For example, students could identify problems with purported historical artifacts using their knowledge of appropriate attributes as clues (like the experts on PBS's *Antiques Roadshow*) or seek to identify and address civic problems in their community.

Like Getzels's type 3 problems, a potential problem does not yet exist as a problem. Perhaps potential problems are most clearly seen in the invention process. No one was assigned the problem of inventing stick-on, pull-off notes. However, some astute observer was able to combine the elements of temporary glue with office logistics and identify a problem that had previously gone unrecognized. In a parallel manner, an author finds a story that must be told where none existed before. If students devise original story lines or plan scientific investigations to test a question of interest, they have discovered their own problems.

Csikszentmihalyi and Sawyer (1993) proposed that the creative process varies in presented and discovered problems. On the basis of interviews with eminent contemporary creators in a variety of fields, they noted a common structure in descriptions of creative insight. Their subjects described four stages closely paralleling those of Wallas: (a) hard work and research preceding the moment of insight, (b) a period of idle time alone, (c) a moment of insight, and (d) elaboration needed to bring the idea to fruition. However, although the stages remained relatively constant, subjects described them as occurring in time frames from a few hours to several years. Csikszentmihalyi and Sawyer suggested that these widely varying time frames may represent the ends of a continuum of creative insights ranging from short-term presented problems to long-term discovered problems. Presented problems may be thought of as part of the normal work in a particular field, whereas discovered problems require the creator to think outside the usual boundaries, question existing paradigms, and ask questions no one else is asking.

In examining the means teachers may use to enhance creativity in students, one of the issues we must address is how we may vary the types of problems students solve in schools. Certainly, the vast majority of problems assigned to students would be categorized by Getzels as type 1 problems. The problem is clearly defined by the teacher or text, and the students are expected to derive the correct answer using the correct methods. Only rarely are students required to identify emergent problems or even to identify multiple ways to solve a problem. Still more rarely are students asked to create problems to solve. Yet if we consider the processes necessary for problem solving in real life, it is clear that real-world challenges do not come in neat packages with an answer key in the back. The kinds of problems that matter must be discovered and focused before they are solved. Although there is little research on problem finding by young people, it seems logical that practice in the processes of problem finding may be an important component in our quest for creativity.

Research Describing Problem Finding

The processes that creators use to discover or create problems have been studied in a variety of disciplines. Key to the development of this body of research is Getzels and Csikszentmihalyi's (1976) study of problem finding in art. College art students were presented with two tables, a drawing board, paper, and a variety of dry media. On one table were placed 27 objects used to create still-life problems. The students were asked to use one or more of the objects to create a still life on the empty table and to produce a drawing based on the still life.

Researchers observed the strategies used in creating the problem: the number of objects examined, the amount of exploration of each object, and the uniqueness of the objects used. These variables were used to rank students according to the breadth, depth, and uniqueness of their problem finding. The drawings were evaluated by artist-critics on graphic skill or craftsmanship, originality, and overall aesthetic value. These scores were correlated with the problem-finding rankings.

The correlation between craftsmanship and problem finding was positive—that is, more elaborate problem finding was associated with better technique—but not statistically significant. However, correlations between problem finding and both originality and overall aesthetic value were statistically significant and, in the case of originality, highly significant. Seven years later, the original problem-finding rankings were compared with the success of the former students as artists. Although the relationship was not as strong, it was nevertheless statistically significant. In a later follow-up evaluation, 20 years after the original study, the correlation between problem finding in art school and success of artists at midlife still was positive and significant (Getzels, 1982). The identification of problem finding not just as a significant predictor of creative achievement but as one that endures for decades provided the foundation for a variety of other research.

A review of the research on problem finding (Starko, 1999) suggested several hypotheses that may have implications for education. Firsthand accounts of the process vary from the mystical to the methodical, but at least some creators are able to describe the conscious manipulation of ideas that underlies their processes. Studies investigating these behaviors have made tentative ties between exploratory behavior and the successful finding of problems and solutions in a variety of fields. Problem finders were not assigned a problem, nor did they wait for an idea to appear from the blue. They explored, manipulated, and combined ideas until they found a problem worth solving.

A key variable in several studies is time: Subjects who are more successful in problem finding spent more time than others in deliberate exploration. In some cases, they explored more stimuli or more unique stimuli. Possibly we may be able to enhance students' problem-finding abilities by providing experiences that help them practice spending time in exploratory behavior before attempting to find or solve a problem. We also may be able to provide exercises that help them identify situations in which they will want to examine many unique ideas or variables before proceeding and also to find those in which it is most important to focus on a few key ideas. Much about problem finding remains to be uncovered. Although some researchers (Porath & Arlin, 1992; Rostan, 1992) have found correlations among various areas of problem finding, the relationships among the many processes and tasks currently designated as problem finding remain largely unknown. Interesting potential variables for investigation include the type of problem and the role of content knowledge.

Lee and Cho (2007) found that the variables associated with problem finding differed with the type of problem. When fifth-grade students were provided with a very open-ended, realistic situation, students with greater scientific knowledge were better able to find problems. Divergent thinking—the ability to come up with many different ideas—was actually negatively related to problem finding in that situation. When the problems were more structured, providing more scientific information, divergent thinking was positively associated with problem finding. This is only one of many areas in which the role of content knowledge in creativity appears to be important. Logically, this makes sense. I would be very bad at developing research questions regarding childhood cancer. I simply don't know enough about the topic to do a reasonable job. Similarly, my pediatric oncologist friend is likely to struggle at generating questions for educational research. If we want to teach young people to generate good questions, it seems logical that we must make sure they have a sufficient knowledge base to reasonably do so. Wildly "flexible" ideas may be less likely to generate interesting investigations than those based on some level of expertise.

Also unclear is how problem finding differs in children and adults. A key question in such investigations must be the relationship of problem finding to the development of other cognitive processes. Arlin (1975, 1990) postulated that problem finding can develop only after a person is capable of formal operational reasoning, which typically emerges in early adolescence. If problem finding emerges as postoperational thought and not before, efforts to identify it as a variable in young children may be futile. However, we still do not know whether problem finding is a single variable or whether it is multidimensional or domain specific. It is possible that various types of problem finding may develop along different time lines or that individuals may have profiles of problem finding, perhaps paralleling Gardner's (1983) multiple intelligences. Certainly, a number of studies have identified problem-finding behavior in elementary and secondary school students (Hoover, 1994; Lee & Cho, 2007; Londner, 1991; Moore, 1985; Starko, 1993, 1995; Wakefield, 1985, 1992).

One of the most interesting questions regarding the development of problem finding in young people is whether it can be influenced through intervention. Delcourt (1993) noted problem-finding activity in adolescents identified as creative producers in secondary school. These students were described as "continuously explor[ing] their many interests as they actively sought project ideas through a variety of techniques including reading, sharing information with others, and taking courses both in and out of school" (p. 28). In this study, the opportunities and encouragement for students to identify and pursue individual problems occurred during specialized services for gifted students. Information on the problem-finding processes of students not participating in such services is not available. Without a comparison group, it is impossible to tell whether Delcourt's students' problem-finding processes were affected by their participation in a program designed to facilitate individual investigations. Burns (1990) examined a similar program for elementary students. Although not writing specifically about problem finding, she investigated the effects of training activities on students' initiation of creative investigations. Students who engaged in a series of lessons on identifying interests and problem focusing initiated significantly more investigations than students not receiving such training.

In essence, it is clear that problem finding is an important component in adult creativity. We can identify some of the variables that make it more effective, but we have a great deal yet to learn. Even less is known about problem finding in children. From the middle grades up, evidence seems to point to the same processes seen in adults. In young children, we are not sure (Starko, 1993, 1995). It is possible that activities designed to teach students strategies for identifying interesting problems may enhance the possibility that they will choose to investigate some. But the evidence is not clear-cut.

In the meantime, however, children are going to school and facing an array of rigidly constructed, presented problems. We are left to choose whether we will continue business as usual until the research base is firmer or attempt to incorporate problem finding into our educational endeavors today. I opt for the latter. It seems only logical that encouraging the types of behaviors that make children explorers and questioners rather than passive accepters cannot help but enhance creativity, thinking, and learning. To help you begin, I discuss in Chapters 7 and 8 some examples of how you can teach problem-finding strategies and incorporate problem finding in the major curriculum areas. It remains for you to experiment, innovate, and observe how these principles translate into classroom activities in a variety of disciplines. This kind of innovation may not only enhance creativity and learning but also add to our knowledge of problem finding in young people. I am very eager to hear about your efforts!

Thinking About the Classroom

Try a mini-research project on problem finding. Gather a collection of objects that students may use as inspiration for an art or writing project. Observe whether some students spend more time than average examining the objects before beginning their projects. Do you notice any difference in their products?

Creativity Across Cultures

The definition of creativity holds that one of the keys to defining creativity is appropriateness. Creative responses are appropriate to the context in which they appear. Without understanding the context, our view of creativity can be limited. Sofaer (2015) explored how creativity was expressed in clay during the Bronze Age. Without her in-depth cultural knowledge, differences in vessels and figures would be invisible. With it, it is possible to analyze how cultural combinations, acceptance, and even failures influenced the creative development of clay forms.

Cultures across the world today vary in the types of creativity that are valued and the means used to display them. Some cultures have powerful oral traditions that are difficult to translate into written form. For example, much African poetry is only spoken or sung. Its rhythms are closely related to those of music and dance, and it often uses tone and pitch as well as words to express meaning (Hughes, 1968). Such art could hardly be evaluated by counting the iambs or looking for Western-style imagery. Cultures vary enormously in the style and materials of their visual arts. Chinese paper cutting and calligraphy, Navajo sand painting, and Ashanti wood carvings all express creativity in visual arts that demand measures of appropriateness different from those used for Impressionist paintings.

Cultures, however, do not differ only in their standards of appropriateness but also in the ways they conceptualize novelty and the processes of creativity itself. The notion of creativity as an original contribution has deep roots in the Western tradition of individualism. Since the Renaissance, Western thought has upheld the ability of individual artists, writers, and inventors both to imitate and to improve nature. By the late 19th century, the word *creative*, which had been used primarily to reference art and poetry, began to be applied to the wonders of a dawning technical age as well. The word *creativity* first entered the English language at the same time, although it was not in common usage until well into the 20th century (Weiner, 2000). Particularly in the United States, the image of a creative individual changing the face of the nation with a new invention became part of a national culture of individual enterprise and constant seeking for expansion and change. Other languages reflect differences in the development of this concept. The French word *créativité* appeared in the language only after World War II. Before that, commonly used terms would be translated as invention, discovery, and imagination (Mouchiroud & Lubart, 2006). Mpofu, Myambo, Mogaji, Mashego, and Khaleefa (2006) examined 28 languages of Africa and found that only the Arabic language had a word corresponding directly to creativity. Other languages had words that could be translated as creativity but also as a number of other descriptors, such as resourceful, intelligent, wise, talented, or artistic. Mpofu and colleagues expressed concern that the Westernized concepts being used in current creativity research may limit understanding of indigenous concepts of creativity within Africa. This issue surely may be a problem in other parts of the world as well.

In the United States, the notion of originality and inventiveness as both good and necessary for progress is deeply embedded in the culture. Our history of individual rights as part of a natural inheritance supports the image of rugged individuals struggling against cultural norms to bring forth progress. This can lead to implicit definitions of creativity suggesting that something new or original is intended to change society, move forward, and be significantly different from that which has gone before. Is that not what "original" means?

In contrast, many non-Western and traditional cultures have very different basic assumptions about the role of individuals in society, as well as the nature and purposes of creativity. In the Western perspective, "modern" society is considered dynamic and progressing, whereas "traditional" cultures are viewed as static. In fact "creative" and "traditional" can be used as opposites. Tradition, after all, does not change, whereas creativity is inherently novel.

The reality is not that simple. Each society determines the domains in which creativity will be more restricted and those in which it will be allowed more flexibility. These constitute, for each society, the parameters of appropriateness. Many of these parameters are shaped by religion. For example, the religious traditions of Orthodox Jews limit sculpture of religious images while encouraging thoughtful and creative interpretations of religious texts. Religion also shapes creativity in traditional societies across the globe, wherein many works considered art by outsiders are sacred objects with invariable forms. Their anonymous makers seek worship above artistry yet create beauty. Are they to be considered creative?

For many Hindu and Buddhist cultures, the notion of an individual striving to create something new to the world runs counter to the central goal of suppressing ego. Lubart (1999) described creativity within Hinduism as spiritual expression rather than innovation. Time and history are seen as cyclical. To make traditional truths come alive by finding a new interpretation—rather than by seeking to break with tradition—is the focus of such creative activity. Lubart (1999) stated, "If Eastern creation (and human creativity) can be characterized as a circular movement in the sense of successful reconfiguration of an initial totality, then the Western view of both creation and human creativity seems to involve a linear movement toward a new point" (p. 341). In contrast, Rao (2005) believes that Lubart's conclusions are based on too limited a view of both Asian creativity and Asian mythology. Rao believes creative processes to be transcultural, even if varied in their expression.

The question of whether, indeed, it is possible to generalize about Eastern and Western concepts of creativity is the subject of ongoing research. Niu and Sternberg (2002) summarized *implicit theories* of creativity in Eastern and Western cultures—theories used by everyday persons rather than researchers. They found that although implicit theories were similar in both groups, Asian people were more likely to view creativity as including social and moral values and to value the connection between new and old more than Westerners. In contrast, Westerners tended to focus more on specific individual characteristics. This seems consistent with a survey done by Yue and Rudowicz (2002). They surveyed 489 undergraduates in four Chinese cities, asking them to name the most creative Chinese people, historically and in modern times. More than 90% of the individuals named were politicians. The social influence of the individuals appeared to carry more weight than the originality of their thinking. It is interesting to consider how these conceptions may be changing over time, particularly as global communication increases. In contrast to Niu and Sternberg, Ramos and Puccio (2014) found that conceptions of creativity among laypersons in the United States and Singapore had a similar innovation focus. Tang et al. (2015) found that German and Chinese judges rated creative problem-solving tasks similarly—and both groups of judges rated the German efforts more original.

Kim (2005, 2007) compared Eastern and Western educational systems in regard to creativity. She found that the Confucian principles undergirding much of Asian society may make creativity more difficult by emphasizing rote learning, hierarchical relationships, and conformity. Individual differences are to be subsumed in the needs of the group: "Students seek to avoid appearing different from others, individuals learn to restrain themselves to maintain group harmony, and the fear of making a mistake or feeling embarrassed keeps many students silent" (p. 341). She also argued that gender roles based on Confucianism make it more difficult for women to have the independence necessary for creativity (2015). Still, when Seo, Lee, and Kim (2005) examined Korean science teachers' understanding of creativity, the teachers strongly associated the concept of originality with creativity.

The concept of "face," a strong cultural imperative to maintain a public image, can run counter to the risk taking associated with creativity. In one study, researchers found that individuals with a strong concern for face were less successful in creative tasks than those who were not as concerned with face. Interestingly, that relationship could be modified if participants' social image was affirmed before completing the task, so it may be that some cultural influences are modified by context (Miron-Spektor, Paletz, & Lin, 2015). Niu and Kaufman (2005) found that projects with a strong social impact were most valued by Chinese participants. Such a result is not surprising in a culture with strong collective values. While there are many international similarities in conceptions of creativity, it is clear, too, that there are important variations in views, often tied to long-standing ideals and traditions (Lan & Kaufman, 2013; Niu & Kaufman, 2013).

Understanding the intersection of creativity and collective values may be essential to those working to develop creativity in collective cultures. Because Western concepts of creativity and most creativity research have centered on individualistic concepts, recognizing and developing creativity in cultures with different values may take shifts in thinking. In general, cultures with more collectivist cultures, hierarchal structures, and less comfort with uncertainty are associated with lower levels of innovation (Hofstede, 2001). This is consistent with Zhao's (2012) analysis in which nations with intense focus on educational testing are less successful in measures of entrepreneurship.

And yet the answer cannot be as simple as "individualistic cultures are more creative." A quick look at the history of Chinese inventions or Egyptian art is enough to make it clear that those cultures have a rich creative history, and Paletz and Peng (2008) found that Chinese students were even more influenced by novelty (over appropriateness) than students in the United States or Japan. But for those of us who want to help develop creativity across cultures, the challenges are both interesting and perplexing. In the business world, researchers are investigating whether different organizational climates or different leadership styles are more effective in generating creative results in different cultures (Cabra, Talbot, & Joniak, 2005; Mostafa & El-Masry, 2008). It also seems likely that optimum classroom climate and activities for developing creativity are likely to have some commonalities as well as aspects that are culture specific (Cheng, 2010a, 2010b; Hennessey, 2015; Ng, 2004).

Thinking About the Classroom

What is your implicit theory of creativity? Is it the same as your friends' and colleagues'? Ask five of your friends to describe their ideas of creativity and creative people. Try to include as diverse a group as possible. Compare your results to those of your classmates. What did you find? Did the people you questioned represent the same cultural norms as the students you teach?

If we are to begin to understand cultural differences in conceiving creativity, it seems likely we will have to go beyond thinking of simply "Eastern" and "Western" views. Another lens through which to examine these differences is relatively traditional versus modernized cultures. One fundamental goal of many traditional societies is to preserve core cultural traditions. This goal shapes but does not eliminate opportunities for creativity within those cultures.

Cultural values affect whose creative efforts will be accepted and the areas in which creativity is and is not encouraged. Ludwig (1992) suggested that cultures are least likely to encourage creativity in areas affecting deep cultural patterns and described creativity in Bali:

> The more serious the art form, like sculptures of gods or ritual dances, the less the permitted change, and the less serious the art form, like carvings of kitchen gods, the theatrical performances of clowns, the playing of instruments or the weaving of containers, the greater the originality can be.
>
> (p. 456)

This is but one example of the ways that the basic concepts in the definition of creativity can vary across cultures. The concept of newness or novelty, particularly dramatic changes from previous ideas or practices, flies in the face of traditional cultures, in which the dominant social need may not be change but conservation. Without care, the traditions of many generations can be swallowed up in Westernization. In such circumstances, creativity may take a different form.

Many traditional cultures have types that are used for sacred religious symbols. These images not only represent the creativity of the maker but also provide impetus for diverse interpretations and insights on the part of those who view them. In cultures with rich oral traditions, the retelling of a familiar story may provide continually changing opportunities to elaborate and expand the tale. Although the story itself is not new or original, important richness is added to the cultural tradition with each new interpretation.

Of course, creativity within repetition is not limited to traditional cultures. In the Western performing arts, repeated interpretations of the same script, piece of music, or choreography offer new opportunities for creativity within often-classic forms. All creativity recognized by any society falls within some social rules, patterns, or definitions. Otherwise, it would not be recognized. However, definitions of creativity requiring that it be focused on transforming the society in which it operates limit our ability to appreciate creativity that enriches and preserves existing social systems.

Cultural transition itself offers plentiful venues for creativity. Mpofu et al. (2006) offer a model of creative expression in traditionalist, transitionalist, and modern cultures in Africa. Traditional societies value creativity within the values of the existing community. Transitional cultures require substantial innovation as they negotiate the space between traditional practices and modern economies. Creativity in these circumstances is represented not just in changing artifacts or performances but in increased flexibility in considering personal and cultural possibilities. Greenfield, Maynard, and Childs (2003) describe how the creative activities of the Zinacantec Maya people changed as their main source of income changed from farming to commerce. With the change came more abstract, innovative forms of weaving. This evolved, at least in part, because as the mothers were more involved in commerce, the younger girls learned to weave more independently than in previous times. As one aspect of the culture shifted, new opportunities for creativity emerged.

All of us are limited in our ability to recognize and appreciate creativity that is outside our cultural norms. In some cases, we fail to recognize innovation that represents a significant cultural shift; in others, we may perceive originality in unfamiliar forms that are, in fact, quite commonplace in context. One example can occur when impoverished people, of necessity, produce artifacts for Western audiences. Nottage (2005) describes Ugandan children engaged in a

> theatre of necessity . . . a ritualized performance event designed for audiences seeking authenticity and purity in indigenous cultures. . . . The reality of the situation is that certain indigenous rituals are exoticized and packaged for consumption and drained of their original meaning.
>
> (pp. 66–67)

The children described in Nottage's article are demonstrating creativity but perhaps not in the ways their audience perceives. The theatrical event itself may be composed of songs and dances that are familiar—perhaps even "old hat"—in their community. But realizing that outsiders would find such things exotic, finding ways to entice an audience to remote locations, and using innovative strategies to generate new sources of income for a traditional community represent original and creative problem solving.

Although most of the students in our schools will not come from areas as distant and unfamiliar as the interior forests of Uganda, our students do represent a mix of traditions whose variety must be considered if we are to help them develop their creative potential. In a multicultural society such as that in the United States, creativity situated in individual cultures can present collections of elements that hold fast to specific traditions and elements that draw from the outside. For example, the tradition of stepping, a contemporary dance form rooted in African American culture, draws from African dance forms, slave dance, Motown, and contemporary music and dance forms. Stepping both preserves and energizes African American culture. If it strayed too far from its roots, it would lose its power (Fine, 2003). And certainly, students whose family heritage promotes strong collective or "face" traditions will bring those nuanced conceptions of creativity to school. If we do not understand them, we will be less effective in supporting the students' creativity.

Cultural appropriateness also can be constrained by politics. For example, in the 1980s, the Soviet-style art instruction imported to China demanded that all students be able to render the same object or scene in exactly the same way (Xu Bing, 2001). It is interesting to contemplate whether artistic creativity could function under such circumstances or whether it could be held in abeyance until more flexible opportunities emerged.

Thinking About the Classroom

Visit a place or event in which a culture that influences your students is expressed. This might be a local cultural center, festival, performance, or museum. Observe the multiple ways that creativity is expressed and the values that are represented. Consider how they could be integrated into your curriculum.

Differing conceptions of the nature of creativity make the study of creativity across cultures both a challenge and a joy (Kaufman & Sternberg, 2006; Lubart, 1990, 1999). Most of the processes and theories described in this book are based on the individually focused Western orientation that emphasizes originality and problem solving. It is important to consider whether the processes and theories encompass the myriad ways creativity can be conceptualized, experienced, and expressed.

If concepts of creativity differ, what about the creative processes? Are they the same? Campbell (1996) described the concept of unique individual creativity as antithetical to the artistic and spiritual goals in much of Asia, particularly in traditional Indian art. Instead of seeking their own goals, traditional Indian artists have sought to open their minds through study and meditation in hope that the god they hope to portray will reveal itself in vision—a very different concept of problem finding. Campbell described much great Indian art as literal renditions of visions. The artist would not conceive of the image as his or her idea but as a much-appreciated gift.

Understanding creativity as literal visions from the gods is not limited to Eastern or ancient peoples. Norval Morrisseau (1997) was a shaman and one of Canada's most famous contemporary Native artists. He described his creativity as emanating not from his own mind, but from the House of Invention:

> Now what we're going to talk about is where and when did I get my creativity. Maybe twenty-five years ago, on one of my many visits to the astral plane [in dream], I came upon a group of beings who talked to me. . . . One of the spiritual helpers, who was called the Inner Master, said, "What's up above is down below. So while you're up here, we want you to go into the House of Invention and look over your artistic record and the picture you're going to bring down to your waking state, to bring down an art form for the people, for society in general."
>
> (p. 17)

Morrisseau continued to describe the pictures and colors experienced in the House of Invention and how they are to be brought to earth. He said, "Now, when I paint a picture I just allow myself to be used. I pick up the pencil and the canvas. I allow the interaction with soul to reflect in the mind" (p. 19).

Contemporary Native American cultures can reflect conceptions of creativity in both art and science that are more communal than individualistic. Cajete (2000) described the "primacy of a lived and creative relationship with the natural world" (p. 20) as essential to Native science, which is rooted in the understanding that creativity is the universe's ordering principle and process. From this perspective, human creativity, whether it be in art or science, is part of the greater flow of the creativity in nature. This type of thinking is particularly vital as knowledge comes in literal journeys or vision quests. Journeys and stories provide alternative ways to understand both the world and the creative process.

To outsiders, the idea of metaphoric journeys or seeking for oneness with the studied may seem strange or perhaps quaint. Yet Barbara McClintock, the Nobel Prize–winning biologist, credited her success to investigating and understanding key processes from the corn's perspective. A fundamental mystery of quantum mechanics is the apparent truth that at subatomic levels measurement affects reality. Objectivity appears to vanish, and the observer helps to determine the outcome. It may be that the key to creative discoveries in the next stages of physics is, after all, understanding our imperceptible connections to the natural world.

One of the great questions in studying traditional or non-Western conceptions of creativity is whether just the descriptions or the processes themselves differ. Think about how Cajete's components of Native science might map on stages of the creative processes in other models. If individuals set out to investigate a scientific principle using analytic investigative strategies, will they use the same mental processes to generate new ideas as individuals who have a similar knowledge base but whose concept of creativity leads them to seek heightened awareness and receive gifts from the natural world? Are those who claim their ideas come from the gods experiencing the same phenomena as those who believe their ideas to be their own? As yet, we have no certain answers to such questions, but I have to wonder what neurobiology might tell us.

It is interesting to contemplate the degree to which culture-specific concepts of creativity will continue or to consider whether our global communication will render the concept of creativity so Westernized that, like McDonald's, it has similar meaning but widely varied levels of appreciation around the world. Rudowicz and Yue (2000) questioned undergraduates across four different Chinese populations regarding characteristics associated with creative people and characteristics important for a Chinese person. They found some differences across the samples, but most of the characteristics associated with creative individuals were similar to those identified in Western conceptions. Interestingly, two characteristics consistently rated low by Chinese students were sense of humor and aesthetic appreciation. The most striking finding of the study, however, was that most of the characteristics associated with a creative person were considered as having a relatively low value for a Chinese person. A number of "specifically Chinese personality traits" (p. 187), such as following tradition or concern with face, were perceived as the least indicative of creativity. Does this mean that creativity is not valued by these audiences or that the characteristics associated with Western creativity are not valued? If the same students had been questioned about the characteristics of great Chinese writers or artists, what might they have said? Only further study will tell us.

Yet, there is evidence that understanding the differences in creativity across cultures can help students learn. Boykin (1994) identified ten cultural styles manifested in the learning preferences of African American children: spirituality, harmony, movement, verse, oral tradition, expressiveness, individualism, affect, communalism, and social time perspective. In school activities that build on these strengths, students are more successful (Boykin & Bailey, 2000; Boykin & Cunningham, 2001). Harmon (2002) analyzed the creative strengths associated with each preference. For example, expressive individualism may be manifested in personal style, independence, risk taking, or "cool pose." It can provide evidence of bodily kinesthetic intelligence and opportunities for flexibility and originality. Oral tradition can provide strength in metaphoric language, embellishment in phrasing, and facile code switching. It may be manifested in storytelling, freestyling, or in the rhythmic creative insults called dozens, snaps, or capping. In classrooms that build on these cultural strengths, students not only have more opportunities to be creative, but they may also be more academically successful.

Studying creativity across cultures poses numerous challenges. Current measures of creativity have been developed by and for contemporary Western populations. When such assessments are used to compare creativity in Western and non-Western or traditional and "contemporary" samples, it is difficult to determine whether identified differences reflect actual differences in creative thinking, differences in cultural responses to the instrument, or a missed opportunity to measure a different form of creativity. For example, Khaleefa, Erdos, and Ashria (1997) found differences on three creativity measures between Sudanese students educated in traditional schools and those trained in "modern" schools. Measures on two tests of divergent thinking favored the modern education, whereas a listing of creative activities actually practiced by the students favored the traditional education. Because the latter measure was developed in Egypt and emphasized verbal creativity, it is impossible to know whether the differences reflected real variations in the types of creativity displayed, greater familiarity with the cultures in which the instruments were developed, or both.

Despite the challenge involved, as we attempt to model creativity, it is important to recognize and examine differences in the ways human beings conceptualize and experience it. There is danger in assuming that the ways that seem most "logical" or contemporary are the only views we must understand. The linear path may not be the one we need. Understanding multiple perspectives may allow us insight into our students' lives and thoughts and perhaps into the nature of creativity itself.

Think About It

1. Interview a person you consider creative about his or her creative processes. Which model(s) do they most resemble? Share your findings with classmates.

2. Take a trip to explore a different culture. Think about areas near your home that represent a different culture than your own. In the Detroit area we have areas representing Latino, Greek, Arab, Polish, and many other cultures in easy reach. Area museums showcase art and inventions from around the world. You can also view creativity virtually, using some of the websites in the Tech Tips that follow or museums listed at the end of Chapter 7. (But I will say that telling your family that your homework requires a family outing would be much more fun!)

   Whatever you choose to explore, think about how creativity is expressed. Consider these questions.
   - In what areas (disciplines) is creativity expressed?
   - How did you identify these things as creative? How did your own culture affect your interpretations?
   - In what ways are characteristics of the culture expressed in the creativity? How are they different from those in your culture of origin?
   - What evidence do you see of creativity being similar or different across cultures?

3. Think about how problem finding operates in your own life. What kinds of problems do you address in your daily life? Are your problems presented? Emergent? Are there opportunities in your life for you to seek and examine original problems? This week, make notes of opportunities for problems you run across in your daily life. Try experiencing your day through the eyes of a writer, an inventor, or an artist and see what you find.

Try It Tomorrow

1. Teach students the "Do something different" strategy for inserting a brief incubation break in a creative project. Experiment with it together. For example, have students begin a creative writing project, then take a break for an unrelated low-stress activity, for example lunch or sorting papers. Return to the project. Discuss whether the break was helpful in generating new ideas.

2. Visit the 101 Questions website (www.101qs.com/) to help your students practice generating questions. Note there is a search option to help you select stimuli appropriate for your grade level.

3. Perhaps your class would like to try some group problem finding. Divide your class into groups representing creative problems to be found. Explore your class's surroundings for 30 minutes and come back to report what you found. Here are some possibilities for groups:
   - Inventors: Find situations where a new invention could solve a problem or inconvenience.
   - Visual artists: Find inspiration for a new work of art.
   - Musicians: Find sounds that might be combined to either create or inspire a new piece (yes, you are allowed to bang on things to find them!).
   - Playwrights: Look around for potential characters or situations to inspire a new play.
   - Naturalists: If your classroom provides access to the natural world, explore the plants and animals nearby. Think about the questions you might ask about them.

Tech Tips

1. Since we're talking about creativity around the world, this first Tech Tip will help you do some wandering. Have you ever wished to wander among the stones at Stonehenge, walk through the ruins of Pompeii, visit the shrines of ancient Kyoto, or even explore Yellowstone National Park? Now you can, through Google's World Wonders Project (www.google.com/culturalinstitute/beta/?hl=en).

   The ever-amazing folks at Google have collaborated with a host of partners, including UNESCO and the World Monuments Fund, to put World Heritage Sites online through pictures, video, and interactive three-dimensional models. You can sit at your computer and "walk" through Stonehenge in ways that would never be possible in real life. You can search the Wonders by theme or continent. If your class were studying Louis XIV, wouldn't it be more fun with a virtual field trip to Versailles? And if you are planning a family trip to Independence Hall, you could have a virtual preview.

   The World Wonders website has an Education link full of ideas and resources. Overview guides with suggested activities are available for primary (elementary) and secondary grades. There also are activities specific to some of the Wonders. I particularly like the activities suggested around the Pompeii website, because they provide a fine example of teaching students the investigative methodologies of the disciplines—in this case archeology. Students have the chance to explore an important archeological site and make inferences about how people lived based on the artifacts presented. It includes links to an eyewitness account of the eruption, allowing students to synthesize information from multiple sources. In addition to being fine curriculum, it is fascinating!

2. For more wandering, visit the International Children's Digital Library (http://en.childrenslibrary.org). It is a free online library of books for children from preschool into early adolescence, but I could easily browse there all day. Certainly it is wonderful for children, but don't underestimate its value to older students.

   The library truly is international, with books from scores of countries and in dozens of languages. The collection can be searched by language, age of reader, type of character, genre, topic, length—even color of cover! It will take a bit of exploring to get full benefit from this amazing resource, but it is well worth it. Here are just a few thoughts to get you started:
   - Explore the wonderful varieties of folk and fairy tales from around the world. Have students compare, contrast, and perhaps write a tale situated in their own unique time and place.
   - Use international children's books to provide multileveled resources around a given theme, allowing older students who struggle with reading to contribute something genuinely unique to the discussion. Be sure to preview the text, however, because some children's books contain complex language.

- Choose a book in a language you and your students do not speak. Create new stories to accompany the pictures. For example, *Dima*, written in Arabic, has wonderful fantasy illustrations of a young boy exploring the heavens.
- Have students who are studying world languages read children's books in those languages. When after many (many many!) years away from language study I had the chance to go to France, I found the most successful language practice for my rusty French was with children's television. Children's books can provide similar opportunities for success. Many of the books on the website are available in multiple languages, allowing interesting comparisons and study.

3

Theories of Creativity

The Individual

In rural India, 10th-grade student Remya Jose tried to balance the demands of continuing her high school education with responsibilities at home. She developed a pedal-powered washing machine that saves time, energy, and water.

As the carver holds the unworked ivory lightly in his hand, turning it this way and that, he whispers, "What are you? Who hides there?" And then, "Ah, Seal!"
(Carpenter, Varley, & Flaherty, 1968, n.p.)

There were things I knew right away. I knew how it was going to begin, I knew how it was going to end, I knew who Elphaba was, and I knew why—on some strange level—this was autobiographical even though it was about a green girl in Oz.
(Stephen Schwartz, composer of Wicked; *de Giere, 2008, p. 273)*

A recent holiday catalog claimed, "Anyone can be an artist! No matter what your background, easy-to-follow instruction making painting a pleasure, from the simple matching of paint to numbers, to advanced color mixing . . ."

In this chapter, we will examine theories of creativity that focus on the individual—the creative person. What is it that creative individuals do, and what allows them to do it? You'll note that theories in the next two chapters differ in the types of creativity they address and the scale of explanation they provide. Some researchers and theories target "big C" creativity, whereas others take a broader view. Some theories try to encompass all the key variables that influence creativity, whereas others look deeply into a single dimension. Be alert to these distinctions as you read. Sometimes contrasts between theories are genuine differences in perspective; other times it is simply that the theorists are addressing different questions.

You'll also see differences in emphases across time. The earliest theories, and more contemporary research in the 1950s and 1960s, focused on creative people. They aimed to figure out how creative people were different from others, often focusing on personality and affective variables. We'll discuss some of that work in Chapter 5. Next came theories with a more cognitive focus, examining the psychological processes that come into play when individuals are engaged in creative behavior. Most recently have come a group of researchers and theorists who examine creativity more broadly, across social and cultural contexts. Although early theories may have judged a person as creative or not-so-creative, a social cultural perspective would say that actions are only creative as they are judged in some context. These theories appear in Chapter 4. Notice how these theories interact—or at least, how they should. Because, of course, we don't need to consider the cognitive processes by which creativity operates *or* the ways cultures affect creativity *or* understanding of personality characteristics more common in people undertaking creative tasks. We need to think about all of these and about the ways they interact. If we look at only one aspect, we risk the blind-men-and-elephant dilemma that seems to come up so often when studying creativity. Studying and theorizing about each piece is important—as long as we know we're only studying one leg and have the rest of the elephant yet to examine!

We'll begin with some of the earliest examinations of the mysteries of the creative process, whose echoes continue into creativity research today.

Early Views

Both Plato and Aristotle described the creative process, but in very different ways. In *The Ion*, Plato writes about Socrates' responses to questions concerning the creative process in poetry. He describes the poet as under the influence of a divine madness that carries him out of his senses:

> The lyric poets are not in their senses when they make these lovely lyric poems. No, when once they launch into harmony and rhythm, they are seized with the Bacchic transport, and are possessed. . . . It is not they who utter these precious revelations while their mind is not within them, but . . . it is god himself who speaks, and through them becomes articulate to us.
> (Rothenberg & Hausman, 1976, p. 32)

Plato's emphasis on a mystic and external source of inspiration might ring true for Mozart. Both men saw the inspiration for creative activities as coming from outside, beyond the control of the creative individual, perhaps in the same way that Morrisseau (1997) saw his ideas as originating in the House of Invention. Creativity was considered unexplainable and outside normal human abilities. In fact, many of us listening to the music of Mozart may find it easier to attribute such beauty to divine intervention than to the powers of a fallible, vain, and possibly crass human being.

In contrast, Aristotle argued that creative processes must obey understandable natural laws:

> All makings proceed either from art or from a faculty or from thought. Some of them happen also spontaneously or by luck just as natural products sometimes do. . . . Anything which is produced is produced by something . . . and from something . . . The artist makes, or the father begets, a "such" out of a "this"; and when it has been begotten, it is "this such."
> (Rothenberg & Hausman, 1976, pp. 35–36)

Aristotle did not believe that creative products came through mystical intervention or unique creative processes. He believed that just as plants and animals produced young in a rational, predictable fashion, so art, ideas, and other human products derived from logical steps of natural law. His approach may have appealed to Tchaikovsky, for whom much of the creative process was the result of "cool headwork and technical knowledge" (Vernon, 1975, p. 58).

Although their arguments are complex, the basic contrast between Plato's and Aristotle's positions continues into modern psychology. Some theorists emphasize incubation, insight, or other processes unique to creativity that may occur in ways not discernible to the conscious mind. Others emphasize the similarities between creativity and other cognitive processes and postulate, as did Aristotle, that there is nothing unique or mysterious in the creative process. From that perspective, with enough understanding, we should be able to dissect creativity and understand how it works. Of course, modern neuroscience offers a third possibility—there may be unique processes (or combinations of processes) associated with creativity, but we may be able to analyze them, even when they are not available to our conscious minds.

Beginning in the 19th century, psychologists have presented a variety of theories to explain creativity. Each author brings to the task a specific theoretical perspective, the lens through which he or she views a range of human behaviors. A theorist who believes that human behavior is largely the result of subconscious forces will view creativity differently from one who believes that behavior can better be explained by conscious learning through experience. For the clusters of theorists presented in this chapter, think about how each theory of creativity fits into a broader perspective of thinking about human thought and behavior.

Psychoanalytic Theories

Psychoanalytic theories explain human behavior, development, and personality traits as shaped by powerful unconscious processes. Such theories attempt to uncover the unseen needs that motivate individuals' actions, often looking to childhood events to comprehend adult behavior.

Early Psychoanalysts

Of course, the granddaddy of psychoanalytic theory is Sigmund Freud. Freud believed that human behavior could be explained by examining conflicts between unconscious desires and acceptable outward behavior. He postulated three aspects of human personality: the ego (logical conscious mind), the id (primitive unconscious drives), and the superego (a conscience-like force that acts as mediator between the other two). Freud tied creativity and much other behavior to the sublimation of drives deriving from the id. If an individual cannot freely express his or her desires, those desires must find release in other ways or be sublimated. Freud believed that beginning in childhood, humans must repress their sexual desires in order to fit into conventional society. Thus he saw these sexual urges as particularly powerful forces that must be countered by psychic defenses. Many of the defense mechanisms, he postulated, resulted in unhealthy behaviors and various neuroses. Creativity, however, represented a healthy form of sublimation, using unfulfilled unconscious drives for productive purposes. In discussing creative writers, he stated,

> We may lay it down that a happy person never phantasies, only an unsatisfied one. The motive forces of phantasies are unsatisfied wishes, and every single phantasy is the fulfillment of a wish, a correction of unsatisfying reality. These motivating wishes vary according to the sex, character and circumstances of the person who is having the phantasy; but they fall naturally into two main groups. They are either ambitious wishes, which serve to elevate the subject's personality, or they are erotic ones. In young women the erotic wishes predominate almost exclusively, for their ambition is as a rule absorbed by erotic trends. In young men egoistic and ambitious wishes come to the fore clearly enough alongside of erotic ones.
>
> (Rothenberg & Hausman, 1976, p. 50)

Although we may speculate about the effects of Victorian society on Freud's assessment of the differing genders' needs, it is clear that he viewed fantasy and creative writing as the results of unfulfilled wishes, a continuation of childhood play. Heroic characters may express the need for conquest, and romantic heroines may express the need for love in a representation of the writers' daydreams. Personal desires for sex or power are cloaked in story, allowing writer and reader to experience pleasure without unacceptable guilt.

Other psychoanalysts such as Kris (1952/1976) and Kubie (1958) developed variations on Freud's theories, each emphasizing unconscious or preconscious processes as the driving forces in creativity. Carl Jung (1972), an associate of Freud, also believed in the importance of the unconscious mind in framing creative production, but went even further into the mysteries of the unconscious. He believed that important creative ideas come from influences greater than those in the mind of a single individual. Jung examined the patterns in human behavior, story, and myth that transcend time or culture. He believed that such patterns can be explained by postulating a human collective unconscious, "a sphere of unconscious mythology . . . [that is] the common heritage of humankind" (p. 80). The collective unconscious was seen as a series of inherited patterns that evolved through human history, predisposing individuals to think in particular forms. According to Jung, these archetypal images explain the similarities of earth-mother figures, creation myths, and resurrection and flood stories found in widely separated cultures. Jung believed that the individuals most adept at tapping into the collective unconscious are those most capable of high-quality creative activity.

Contemporary Psychoanalysts

Although views of creativity as a wholly unconscious or preconscious process are not widely held today, psychoanalysts continue to study the topic. For example, Rothenberg (1990) and Miller (1990) were particularly interested in the relationships among trauma, neuroses, and creativity. Miller studied the childhood of creative individuals and sought information on repressed childhood traumas that might give clues to their creative development. For example, in Picasso's painting *Guernica*, she identified images she believed are linked to an earthquake in Málaga during which Picasso, a terrified 3-year-old boy, escaped with his family through the crumbling city.

Rothenberg (1990) examined the creative process through extensive psychiatric interviews and experiments with artists and scientists, including Nobel and Pulitzer Prize winners, poets laureate of the United States, and recipients of numerous other honors. He identified specific thought processes that he believed are used by creative people across disciplines. These processes, he said, "distinguish creative people from the rest of us" (p. 11). The first of these he called the Janusian Process, after Janus, the Roman god of doorways and beginnings, whose two faces look in opposite directions. Contrary to much psychoanalytic thought, he viewed the Janusian Process as a conscious, rational procedure. In the Janusian Process, opposites are conceived simultaneously, a leap that transcends ordinary logic. Although not necessarily represented in the finished product, the idea of opposites being equally true represents an important stage in the creative process. For example, playwright Arthur Miller described coming up with the idea for his play *Incident at Vichy* while traveling in Germany. As he was driving on the Autobahn, he was struck with how beautiful Germany had become and the contrast between that beauty and Hitler's destruction. Rothenberg believed that Miller's ability to conceptualize the beauty and the horror simultaneously was central to his writing.

The second of Rothenberg's creative processes is the homospatial process, conceiving of two or more entities occupying the same space at the same time. This, he believed, is the process leading to the development of metaphors. A poet interested in the similar sound of the words "handle" and "branch" was able to bring these ideas together in a mental image leading to the phrase "the branches were handles of stars."

In an interesting series of experiments, Rothenberg created a set of slides in which subjects could be presented with images either side by side or superimposed (the superimposed pictures representing the homospatial process). Some writers and artists were shown a picture of soldiers next to a picture of a bed. Others were shown the two pictures superimposed, as if in a double-exposed photograph. A third group saw the photos with one on top, blocking part of the other. He found that in all three groups, significantly more creative products came from the subjects who had seen the superimposed photographs, suggesting that the homospatial process may, in part at least, be learned.

Thinking About the Classroom

Those of you who like to play with digital photography may want to experiment with Rothenberg's homospatial process. In one exercise, place two photographs side by side and use them to stimulate a writing or art activity. In the next class, try using two photographs that have been merged into a single image. See if you notice any differences in the originality of responses.

Finally, Rothenberg examined the relationship between mental illness and the processes he identified as underlying creativity. He determined that although creative processes differ from logical everyday thinking, as do those in mental illness, there are vast differences between the two. Whereas people engaged in the creative process may use ideas outside logic to facilitate their thinking, people affected by psychosis are more likely to believe contradicting or illogical ideas, to have no control over them, and to be unable to use them for creative purposes.

Behaviorist Theories

Psychoanalytic theorists consider human behavior to be determined primarily through the interaction of conscious and unconscious drives. Behaviorist psychologists, in contrast, view human activities as resulting from a series of stimuli and responses. The most famous advocate of this position was B. F. Skinner. The "Father of Behaviorism," Skinner believed that individuals' actions were determined solely by their history of reinforcement. If actions were followed by pleasant consequences, they were likely to be repeated. If the consequences were unpleasant, it was less likely the individual would try a similar action again. Theorists from this perspective focus on observable behaviors rather than internal drives or desires.

In a famous paper entitled "A Lecture on 'Having' a Poem," Skinner (1972) stated that a poet is no more responsible for the content or structure of a poem than a chicken is responsible for laying an egg. Each action is seen as a result of the creator's history, the stimuli and responses each creator has experienced. In this view, there can be no truly original behaviors or ideas except as they are an inevitable product of a unique individual's experiences. Presumably, another person who experienced every aspect of Shakespeare's life would have had no choice but to write the same plays. According to this theory, those who would influence creativity can do so through reinforcement. The more creativity or activities approaching creativity are reinforced, the more they should occur.

From this perspective, a teacher who wants students to generate more elaborate or original ideas should reward students for that behavior. Eisenberger and Cameron (1996), Eisenberger and Rhoades (2001), and Eisenberger, Armeli, and Pretz (1998) used a behaviorist perspective to argue for the positive influence of reward on creativity, at least in divergent-thinking tasks. This contradicts the current prevailing view regarding the often-negative impact of reward on intrinsic

Skinner believed that a poet is no more responsible for the content of a poem than a chicken is for laying an egg

motivation and creativity (see Chapter 9). More generally, a contemporary behaviorist theory of creativity would seek to analyze the contexts in which a combination of genetic characteristics and environmental events would cause creative acts to emerge, with an eye to natural selection (Cautilli, 2004). What circumstances "rewarded" our creative predecessors such that we viewed their diverging from the norm as a good thing? And what contexts continue to support such divergence today? Behaviorists want to know!

In a related theory, Mednick (1962) also viewed the production of ideas as the result of stimuli and responses, but he theorized that creative ideas result from a particular type of response, the bringing together of remote, unrelated ideas. Individuals who frequently bring remote ideas together should be more likely than others to produce creative ideas. This process may be influenced by several factors. First, individuals must have the needed elements in their repertoires. The person who invented the beanbag chair must have had some experience with beanbags or similar objects. This is of particular importance, because Mednick is one of the first modern theorists to theorize about the importance of a knowledge base in creativity. Second, individuals must have a complex network of associations with the stimulus. Those who are able to make multiple associations with a given idea are more likely to make unusual associations than those who give only a few stereotyped responses. This hypothesis was supported in Mednick's research using word-association tests with creative and less-creative research scientists.

According to Mednick, individuals who have had many experiences with a given stimulus in a familiar setting are less likely to make remote associations with that stimulus; their patterns of responses are too well defined. The greater the number of diverse associations with a given stimulus, the greater is the probability that remote ideas may be connected. An individual who has used a hair dryer to inflate a hot-air balloon, warm a bottle, dry a shirt, and play balloon catch will probably generate more ideas for its use or improvement than one who has used it simply to dry hair. Mednick developed the *Remote Associates Test*, still used in contemporary creativity research (see Chapter 10).

Humanist Theories

Developed at least in part as a reaction to behaviorism, humanist theorists do not emphasize either neuroses or reinforcement as predominant forces in human psychology. Instead, they focus on normal growth and the development of mental health. Humanist theorists view creativity as the culmination of well-adjusted mental development. Maslow (1954), founder of the humanist psychology movement, postulated a hierarchy of human needs that can be met in a generally ascending order, beginning with physical needs and progressing to needs for safety and security, love and belonging, self-esteem, and self-fulfillment. At the top of the hierarchy, one has the opportunity for self-actualization as a fully functioning human being. In examining the relationship between this development and creativity, Maslow found he had to reexamine his hypothesis that mental health, talent, and creative productivity went hand in hand. He could not match his ideas about creativity and healthy mental development with the apparently unhealthy behaviors of such great creators as Wagner or van Gogh.

To deal with this conflict, Maslow (1968) postulated two types of creativity. The first, *special talent creativity*, is "independent of goodness or health of character" (p. 35) and functions in creative geniuses. He concluded that we know very little about this type of ability except that we sometimes can recognize it when we see it. As described in Chapter 1, this is Creativity with a "big C."

The second type of creativity, *self-actualizing creativity*, is the basis for most of Maslow's writings on this topic. He believed that creativity of this type is a manifestation of mental health and movement toward self-actualization. It may be applied not just to the traditional creative arts but to any aspect of human behavior. Perhaps his most famous statement on the topic concerned a subject from whom he learned that "a first-rate soup is more creative than a second-rate painting . . . cooking or parenthood or making a home could be creative while poetry need not be; it could be uncreative" (Maslow, 1968, p. 136). Unless it changes the culinary world, a first-rate soup would be the product of creativity with a "little c."

According to Maslow, people with a high level of self-actualizing creativity tend to do everything creatively. They are characterized as more spontaneous and expressive than average, more natural, and less controlled or inhibited. He believed that the ability to express ideas freely without self-criticism is essential to this type of creativity and that this ability paralleled the innocent, happy creativity of secure children. Creativity was described as "a fundamental characteristic, inherent in human nature, a potentiality given to all or most human beings at birth, which most often is lost or buried or inhibited as the person gets enculturated" (Maslow, 1968, p. 143).

Maslow described the personality characteristics of subjects he identified as displaying self-actualized creativity. He considered them to be relatively unfrightened of the unknown, more self-accepting, and less concerned with others' opinions. These personality characteristics provide the essence of self-actualizing (SA) creativity.

Rogers (1961), another humanistic psychologist, also viewed creativity as the product of healthy human growth. Rogers viewed creativity as the emergence of novel products through the interaction of an individual and the environment. The characteristics associated with creativity allow this interaction to take place.

The first characteristic identified by Rogers is openness to experience. He believed that creative individuals are free of psychological defenses that would keep them from experiencing their environment. (Notice how this contrasted with Freud's idea that creativity is a psychological defense.) Openness to experience implies that an individual is willing to view experiences outside traditional categories, to consider new ideas, and to tolerate ambiguity if ambiguity exists. Of all the characteristics associated with creativity in various theories, openness—whatever the cause—is one of the most consistent.

The second characteristic is an internal locus of evaluation—that is, reliance on one's own judgment, particularly in gauging creative products. My actor-husband demonstrates this characteristic in his attitude toward his performances. After a performance, he does not judge his success by the volume of applause, the standing ovations, or the enthusiastic comments of audience members. Only when he judges his performance to be satisfactory is he happy. Unfavorable reviews for a performance with which he was pleased have little impact. With the exception of a few knowledgeable friends, other people's opinions have little to do with how he evaluates his achievements. His own (admittedly critical) judgment is the one he cares about.

Rogers's third characteristic is the ability to toy with elements and concepts. He believed creative individuals must be able to play with ideas, to imagine impossible combinations, and to generate wild hypotheses. This characteristic is associated with the same type of openness and lack of rigidity found in the first characteristic and appears to be fundamental to problem finding (see Chapter 7). When these three characteristics are present, according to Rogers, the natural human trait of creativity can develop.

One of the most important contemporary psychologists influenced by the early humanist approaches is Mihaly Csikszentmihalyi, whose concept of flow examines peak experiences. He is part of a recent branch of psychology called positive psychology because of its emphasis in studying and supporting positive life experiences. Csikszentmihalyi's work on flow will be addressed in Chapter 9. His theory of creativity will be discussed with systems theories in the next chapter.

Development of Creativity and Social Interactions

Surprisingly few theories examine the longitudinal development of creativity across time. One of the most interesting writers in this area was Soviet psychologist Lev Vygotsky. For years, Vygotsky's work was unavailable to Western readers. In 1992, Smolucha reconstructed Vygotsky's theory of creativity from three translated papers. Originally written in the 1930s, the papers are part of Vygotsky's sociocultural analysis of human thought, emphasizing the social and cultural interactions that underlie human thought and understanding. As such, they foreshadow the complex interactions among individuals and society that characterize the systems theories of creativity discussed in the next chapter. However, Vygotsky also characterized creative thought and activity in three major stages, so I consider his work first as a developmental approach.

Vygotsky believed that creative imagination originates in child's play. In particular, he saw the use of objects in symbolic play as key to the development of imagination. An often-cited example is a child using a stick as a play horse. The child at play is able to imagine a horse, creating an animal where none exists. Vygotsky distinguished between *reproductive imagination*, in which the individual imagines things from memory, and *combinatory imagination*, in which he or she combines elements of previous experience into new situations or behavior that characterizes creativity. The little child on the stick horse reproduces much of the experience from his or her prior understanding of horses, but the child may use and combine parts of this in new ways. Symbolic play experiences are influenced (and perhaps directed) by social interactions, such as an adult's suggesting that the stick might be a horse. (Additional discussion of contemporary research on pretend play can be found in Chapter 5.)

Despite the importance of early childhood experiences, Vygotsky saw them only as a beginning stage, not as the pinnacle of creativity. Because children have fewer interests, less complex understandings, and fewer diverse thoughts than adults, they are considered to be capable of less mature creativity: "The child's imagination is not richer, but poorer than the imagination of an adult; in the process of child development imagination also develops, reaching maturity only in the adult" (Vygotsky, 1930/1967, cited in Smolucha, 1992, p. 54). Vygotsky saw adult creativity as a consciously directed thought process in which individuals change and combine ideas in specific social conditions to create works of art, inventions, or scientific conclusions.

According to Vygotsky, the transition between the child's imagination and the adult's mature, thoughtful creativity occurs in the middle stage, adolescence. Before adolescence, imagination and thought are portrayed as separate strands of development. During adolescence, the strands come together. As adolescents develop the ability to manipulate abstract concepts, they begin to develop a more active and intentional creativity than that of childhood. Whereas children's actions in symbolic play may be mainly imitative or suggested by others, mature creativity is purposefully used and controlled. Vygotsky believed that the development of this type of creativity is influenced by inner speech, formal schooling, and thinking in concepts. Speech allows individuals to think about, represent, and communicate things that are not present. School also requires considerable thought about ideas and objects not in the immediate environment. Thinking in concepts allows individuals to process and combine experiences in new, more complex ways. In a parallel fashion, imagination is viewed as "a necessary, integral feature of realistic thought" (Smolucha, 1992, p. 65). We can think about things not present or ideas not yet achieved only if we can imagine them. This idea might give a few teachers pause. How can we teach about ancient Rome, negative numbers, or atomic theories if students do not have the capacity to envision them? It puts the importance of creativity in school in a whole new light!

Thus, Vygotsky proposed a developmental theory in which creative imagination begins in children's symbolic play and develops into a consciously regulated mental function influencing and influenced by inner speech and concept development. According to this theory, the linking of imagination and thought begins in adolescence but does not reach maturity until adulthood.

Vygotsky also foreshadowed contemporary systems theories by situating creativity in a particular time and place. "Any inventor, even a genius, is always a plant growing in a certain time and environment. His creativity issues from needs, which are given to him. He operates on the possibilities that exist around him" (Vygotsky, 1930/1967, cited in Smolucha, 1992, p. 54). Vygotsky continued to explain that the availability of resources explains the disproportionate distribution of innovators and artists in privileged classes. Such individuals have much greater access to the problems and processes of the disciplines.

Vygotsky emphasized that creativity, like other learning, emerges through interactions with other individuals. This occurs both at a micro level, as when an adult interacts with a child in imaginative play, and at a macro level, in which societies grow through the collective efforts of countless individuals. This view of creativity as both individual and cultural development provides a dialectic model in which creative processes are used in internal and external ways. Individuals use creative processes internally as they transform incoming social and cultural messages into a mind and personality. They also use creative processes externally to communicate new ideas and symbols, building and changing the culture around them.

A contemporary theorist influenced by Vygotsky is Vera John-Steiner. Her (2000) study of creative collaborations presented the idea that creative processes or ideas do not develop within individuals but in interactions among individuals within a sociocultural context. Feldman, in the foreword to John-Steiner's book, pointed out that the notion of creativity as a collaborative activity and Vygotsky's commitment to relationship as the "central ingredient in human development" (p. xi) are in marked contrast to the focus on individual responsibility for cognitive development and activity described by Piaget. Feldman viewed the shift in thinking as representative of society's shift from the "Age of the Individual" to the "Era of Community" (p. xiii). Additional information on collaborations is considered in Chapter 4.

Thinking About the Classroom

Vygotsky suggested that symbolic play is crucial in the development of creative imagination. Symbolic play may be influenced by social interaction—for example, an adult commenting that a box could be used as a boat. Observe a parent or teacher with young children. Note any comments that encourage symbolic play.

Creativity, Intelligence, and Cognition

The relationship between creativity and intelligence might best be described as "it depends." It depends on the definition and measures used to assess both creativity and intelligence. Perhaps the most common relationship postulated is the threshold theory. According to this theory, below a certain threshold (approximately 120 IQ), there is a strong, positive relationship between creativity and intelligence; the more intelligent the person, the more likely he or she is to be creative. Above the threshold level, however, the relationship is seen as weaker; a highly intelligent person may be highly or only moderately creative. At that point, theoretically, intelligence no longer predicts creativity. The threshold theory continues to be investigated and is discussed further in Chapter 5. In this section, we examine theories that treat creativity as part of intelligence or as comprising many of the same components as intelligence.

Guilford's Structure of the Intellect

Guilford's (1959, 1986, 1988) Structure of the Intellect (SOI) model is a complex model of intelligence including, in its later form, 180 components. The components are formed through combinations of types of content, operations, and products (Figure 3.1). Each type of content can be matched with each operation or product to form a separate cell of the cube associated with a particular intellectual ability. For example, intellectual abilities include the cognition of semantic relationships and the transformation of figural units.

Unlike previous models of intelligence, the SOI model includes *divergent thinking*, or thinking of many possible responses to a given question, as one of the basic processes of intelligence. Guilford identified components of divergent production that have formed the backbone of much research and assessment of creativity. They include fluency (generating many ideas), flexibility (generating different types of ideas or ideas from different perspectives), originality (generating unusual ideas), and elaboration (adding to ideas to improve them). Guilford identified two categories of abilities associated with creativity. The first is the divergent-thinking "slab." You might picture this as a slice cut out of the cube containing all the cells involving divergent production. The second is associated with transformations, the ability to revise what one experiences or knows to produce a new form. Transformations are part of the product dimension of the SOI model. Guilford also recognized the importance of sensitivity to problems and evaluation in generating and assessing creative ideas.

Whichever cells are identified as critical, the key to this perspective on creativity is that it is an intellectual function. Guilford did not portray creativity as rooted in conflict and childhood trauma or as a manifestation of mental health. Like any other aspect of intelligence, it represented to him a pattern of cognitive strengths that include but are not limited to the abilities to produce

CONTENT

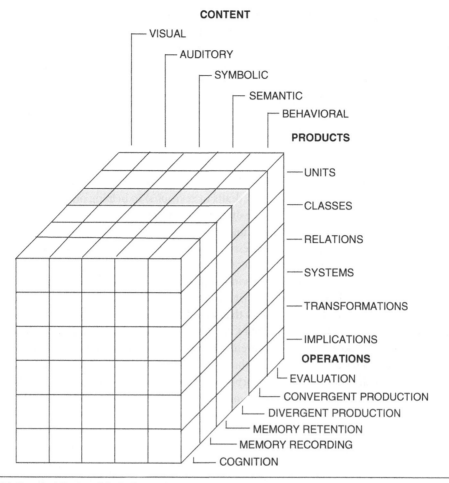

Figure 3.1 The revised Structure of the Intellect model

Source: From Guilford, J. P. (1988). "Some Changes in the Structure-of-Intellect Model," *Educational and Psychological Measurement,* 48, p. 3. Copyright © 1988 by Educational and Psychological Measurement. Reprinted with permission.

diverse responses to varied tasks. Similarly, several contemporary psychologists have attempted to identify cognitive processes underlying creativity. Although they may also identify personality or motivational characteristics associated with creativity, they do not view creativity itself as a mysterious force unlike other human experiences but rather as a manifestation of the same sorts of processes found in other types of thought.

Perkins, Weisberg, and Myth Busting

A number of contemporary researchers have questioned the concept of creativity as an extraordinary mental function, instead envisioning it as the result of normal cognitive processes. For example, Perkins (1981, 1988, 1994) examined ties between ordinary cognitive processes and the extraordinary processes sometimes postulated for creativity. He noted that many theories and ideas about creativity have their roots in the self-reports of creative individuals, such as the statements by Mozart and Tchaikovsky at the beginning of Chapter 2. Such reports are likely to be unreliable. Criminologists attest that eyewitness accounts of any event are likely to be contradictory, incomplete, and inaccurate. If the self-reports of creative individuals are to be believed, we must be convinced that the individuals remember the experience in sufficient detail at the time the report is made, understand the experience themselves, and are honest about the experience. It is not unreasonable to think that some individuals may be tempted to report their creative efforts in a manner that adds to their mystique or enhances their reputation. For example, Perkins (1981) noted that Coleridge, who reported an opium dream in which the poem "Kubla Khan" appeared to him, also wrote several earlier versions of the work. Even if no deliberate misrepresentation took place (a possibility that must be considered given other examples of Coleridge's inaccuracies in reporting his own work), his opium dream statement was made 16 years after the poem was written, leaving ample opportunity for selective or incomplete memory.

Perkins (1981, 1988, 1994) also examined the effectiveness of physical evidence documenting the history of a creative effort (such as early drafts or revisions) in helping one to understand the creative process. Based on those records, he did not find evidence to support the traditional view of incubation (creative leaps after extended unconscious activity) or unique creative thought processes. Rather, he viewed the creative process as made up of ordinary mental processes used in extraordinary ways. The key to creativity, according to Perkins, is not the process but the purpose. People involved in creative activities are trying to be creative. Perkins (2001) described "breakthrough thinking" as the kind of thinking that leads to discovery or progress by bringing together ideas not previously associated. In a model that sounds very similar to an elaboration of Wallas (without unconscious incubation, of course), he describes the need for a long search (thinking about the problem), followed by little apparent progress. Next, a precipitating event of some kind allows the thinker to reframe the problem that leads to a "cognitive snap," the "aha!" moment of understanding. Finally, the new idea is incorporated into thinking as a transformation. From this perspective, extraordinary breakthroughs can be explained by ordinary thought processes combined with persistence.

Weisberg (1986, 1988, 1993, 1999, 2006, 2010) attempted to demystify the creative process by debunking familiar myths about creative genius and examining research that ties creativity to familiar cognitive processes. As did Perkins, he questioned the validity of self-reports of creativity and used several classic examples to illustrate their fallibility. Mozart's letter about his creative process, quoted at the beginning of Chapter 2, is one of the most commonly cited reports of an individual widely acknowledged to be creative. Weisberg noted that there is, among musicologists, doubt as to whether Mozart wrote the letter at all. It may be a forgery. If it is authentic, there remains the question of whether it is (intentionally or unintentionally) accurate. Mozart's notebooks contain compositions never completed and compositions started and revised, indicating that his report of music emerging fully formed was, at best, only sometimes true.

Kekulé's dream of snakes forming a benzene ring is also subject to scrutiny. The word translated as "doze" can also be translated as "reverie," so Weisberg (1986) suggested that Kekulé was not dreaming but was lost in thought. Because the images Kekulé considered were described as "snakelike" and not as "snakes," Weisberg rejected the idea that an unconscious analogy allowed Kekulé's discovery. Rather, he believed that Kekulé thought about the problem, considered images in his visual imagination, and used the description of snakes to clarify the image.

In addition to his rejection of the unconscious as a source of complete creative products, Weisberg (1986, 2006, 2010) examined other prominent theories about creativity. He questioned the idea of creative leaps or flashes of insight by citing research showing that solutions to problems come not in a sudden change of direction but in gradual increments based on experience. For example, in the candle problem, a person given a candle, a book of matches, and a box of tacks is instructed to attach the candle to the wall. (You might want to stop and think a moment about how you might approach this task.) Most subjects either tried to tack the candle to the wall or tried to glue it with melted wax. The simplest solution is to use the box as a candle holder and tack it to the wall. Because this method involves using the box in a novel way, it is sometimes viewed as requiring creative insight. Weisberg examined verbal protocols (blow-by-blow descriptions of subjects' thought processes as they worked) and noted that all of the subjects who came up with the box solution started out by trying more common methods. Only when those failed did they experiment with other options, each building on the previous idea. One subject went from trying to put a tack through the candle to putting tacks next to the candle to using the box. Weisberg believed that this type of progression indicated that the solution came not as a creative leap but as an extension of past experiences.

Weisberg examined records of both artistic and scientific efforts ranging from *Guernica* to Beethoven's Ninth Symphony to the discovery of deoxyribonucleic acid (DNA). In each case, incremental steps (preliminary drawings, experimental themes, or unsuccessful models) can be identified leading from one idea (or theme or image) to the succeeding one. Ideas that appeared to be new and original emerged not fully formed from the depths of genius but bit by bit as part of a long, constantly evolving effort. More recently, Weisberg has worked toward a theory of problem solving that integrates both analytical analysis and the restructuring of thought that brings forth insightful (creative) solutions (Fleck & Weisberg, 2013; Weisberg, 2015). While he continues to believe many creative problems are solved through analytic means, the model opens the possibility that some examples of insight may occur another way. The options in Weisberg's model resemble the analytic and insightful problem-solving strategies described in Kounios and Beeman's (2015) neurobiological research discussed later in this chapter.

In one sense, Weisberg's view of creativity is that it does not exist, at least not as a unique process. Even "aha!" moments are based on analysis that comes before. But believing that creativity is not a unique process doesn't mean that genuinely creative products and insights do not exist. In many ways, Weisberg's view is an optimistic one, giving encouragement to those who might view creativity as outside their abilities. It would suggest all of us have creative capacity. We just need deep knowledge, persistence through many steps and detours, and determination to find a new way. It is also a good example of the general category of contemporary creativity theories based on cognition.

Creative Cognition

Other cognitive psychologists have investigated how fundamental cognitive structures and processes result in creative thinking. From this perspective, creativity occurs along a wide range of activities, beginning with the very ordinary processes of language use and concept development and extending to ideas representing fundamental shifts in various domains. Although few of us will exhibit earthshaking creativity, each time we express ourselves in a new sentence, we have created a new example within our linguistic framework. Each time we come to understand another idea, we have created a new cognitive structure. In this view, the ability to produce new ideas in everyday thought uses cognitive processes similar to those used in thinking recognized as creative (Ward, Smith, & Finke, 1999).

Ward (2001) stated, "The creative cognition approach concentrates primarily on the cognitive processes and conceptual structures that produce creative ideas" (p. 350). An important characteristic of this approach is its focus on basic conceptual processes rather than global thinking strategies. For example, instead of considering divergent thinking or the use of metaphors (two commonly cited examples of creative thinking), the creative-cognition approach would ask, "How does divergent thinking work? What basic component processes, such as retrieval, combination, or mapping, are used in divergent thinking?" This is the creative-processes-under-the-microscope view. In general, these processes are seen as similar to those used in other cognitive processes and across levels and types of creativity. Ward and Kolomyts (2010) explain, "Creative cognition explicitly rejects the notion that extraordinary forms of creativity are the products of minds that operate according to principles that are fundamentally different than those associated with normative cognition" (pp. 96–97).

Sowden, Pringle, and Gabora (2015) reviewed a number of dual-process models of cognition and found potential ties to creative thought. Dual-process models of cognition include two types of thinking. Type 1 processes occur outside our consciousness and allow us to make rapid associations and judgments. Type 2 processes are the kinds of analytical thinking we do consciously. The authors posit that the ability to switch between such processes may be key to creative thinking, like the back-and-forth movement between divergent and convergent thinking in Creative Problem Solving. Often, studies of creative cognition attempt to determine if cognitive processes that can be stimulated in a lab mirror creativity in real-world contexts. For example, when we develop new ideas, humans typically build those on very basic concepts already in place in the cognitive structure. If asked to imagine an alien creature on another planet, we are more likely to create something with two legs and symmetrical anatomy—not because that was part of the task but because those attributes are familiar to us and fit neatly into our experiences and cognition. Researchers investigating creative cognition explore circumstances that make it more likely an idea will be produced outside these familiar patterns (e.g., asking participants to think about abstract qualities such as need for nutrition; Ward, Patterson, & Sifonis, 2004). Understanding that moving up a level of abstraction can help move individuals out of familiar cognitive paths can help us understand why some creative thinking strategies (e.g., metaphors, or random input) can be helpful. Other studies include exploration of the processes of conceptual combination (what kinds of combinations of ideas yield more original results) and investigations of how culture and experience change the ways we process information.

This perspective does not claim that cognition alone can explain creative productivity. Motivation, culture, and timing are among the factors that can be used to explain why some individuals make creative contributions to the world around us. But creative cognition theories suggest that if, indeed, an intrinsically motivated person is more likely to persist long enough to find a new and interesting idea, he or she still uses the same cognitive processes used to generate more mundane ideas. This hypothesis is particularly important in two current veins of investigation: creativity and computers and the neurobiology of creativity.

The Ultimate Mechanics: Creativity and Computers

To most of us, the idea of a creative computer may seem at best absurd and at worst something out of science fiction. It summons forth images of mechanical poems or machinery gone awry, using intelligence in new and dangerous ways. Separating creativity from the uniquely human personality characteristics or cognitive styles postulated by most cognitive theorists is difficult. However, researchers in artificial intelligence are taking the next step beyond the creative-cognition approach and looking for algorithms that at least simulate creativity mechanically. If such a model can be found, it may provide insight into the microprocesses of human creativity.

Boden (1991, 1992, 1994, 1999, 2004), for example, described a computational model of psychology in which the semantic nets and systems of artificial intelligence can be used to represent possible models of human thought. Semantic nets are computer systems constructed to parallel the connections that cognitive psychologists hypothesize exist in the human brain. Connections among the nets offer possible explanations for apparent leaps of creative insight, much like the chance permutations in Simonton's (1988, 2004) associative networks (see Chapter 4). Boden

(2004) described three types of creative thinking that can be modeled through artificial intelligence networks: combinational creativity, which makes novel combinations of ideas already present in the network; exploratory creativity, which explores and experiments within a domain; and transformational creativity, which changes the "rules" of the discipline. She described computers using similar processes to create jokes, write poems, paint pictures, design buildings, and discover mathematical rules. Although none of these operates at the level of Langston Hughes, Georgia O'Keeffe, or Ada Lovelace, "this does not destroy the main point: that poetic [and other] creativity

Computers can help us model the creative process

requires a rich variety of mental processes, intelligible in . . . computational terms" (Boden, 2004, p. 146). Boden does not claim that computers duplicate the processes of human thought; in fact, after decades of study, she's blunt about their limitations (see Boden, 2015). But she suggests that if artificial intelligence can produce results that resemble human creativity, it may provide clues to how creativity operates within a human cognitive structure.

Some of the most interesting models of creativity have simulated collaborative creative processes. In 2003 in Sony's Computer Science Lab in Paris, a virtual orchestra of 10 computerized performers was assembled, each programmed to generate a simple sequence of notes. More important, the "performers" were programmed to "listen" to one another and improvise variations on other sequences. After several days of "rehearsals," the orchestra had produced new and original music (Sawyer, 2012). This model calls to mind the creative efforts of groups working in improvisational music and theater but also in teams of scientists.

And yet, as Boden (2015) points out, computer-driven art is typically bland. Without depth of cultural relevance and human emotion, it does not come close to the best human efforts. As Boden (2015) declares, "We need humans for that." Computers can't model the emotional and motivational components of creativity. They can solve problems but not find them. They have limited abilities to evaluate the value of their proposed solutions. A virtual orchestra can generate multiple pieces of music without the ability to assess which are beautiful and which mediocre.

Still, just as artificial intelligence can simulate many aspects of human thought, perhaps one day artificial creativity will simulate human ingenuity. In the meantime, computers offer one way to learn about the intricacies of the creative process.

Creativity and Neuroscience

There is no area in which our understanding of creativity has changed more in recent years than in the study of neurobiology. Such studies ask the question, "How do our brains work to allow creative ideas to emerge?" Now, armed with technology that can scan the brain in operation, neuroscientists are investigating brain activity during various creative activities. Creating such tasks is challenging. For example, Howard-Jones, Samuel, Summers, and Claxton (2005) asked participants, given varied conditions, to generate a story in 22 seconds while in an fMRI scanner. (Can you imagine?) The technologies that allow such explorations are still in their relative infancy, and conclusions must be tentative (see, for example, Sawyer, 2011), but already one thing is clear: It's complicated.

First, let's dispense with one of the most popular "neuromyths" (Goswami, 2006): Creativity does not occur on the right side of the brain. Creativity, like any complex activity, requires the whole brain. It is true that in some creative tasks, highly creative people use the right hemisphere of the brain more than less creative individuals. But everyone who has a whole intact brain uses all of it when attacking creative problems, from musical improvisation to story generation, designing book covers, and traditional creativity measures (Aghababyan, Grigoryan, Stepanyan, Arutyunyan, & Stepanyan, 2007; Bechtereva et al., 2004; Bengtsson, Csikszentmihalyi, & Ullén, 2007; Carlsson, Wendt, & Risberg, 2000; Ellamil, Dobson, Beeman, & Christoff, 2012; Howard-Jones, Blakemore, Samuel, Summers, & Claxton, 2005; Kounios et al., 2008; Kounios & Beeman, 2015). While there are patterns in the way our brains appear to operate across creative tasks, there are also differences. For example, Abraham, Thybusch, Pieritz, and Hermann (2014) found that in their sample, men and women were equally successful in divergent-thinking tasks, but the areas of their brains used were different. Another study found differences between the brain regions utilized in adults and adolescents (Kleibeuker, Koolschijn, Jolles, De Dreu, & Crone, 2013). As I said, complicated.

Kaufman and Gregoire (2015) describe highly creative people as having "messy minds" (p. xvii). Messy minds do not work in a linear step-by-step creative process. Rather, they switch back and forth among thought processes, seeming to engage in multiple, sometimes contradictory processes at the same time. Creative thinking can require jumping from generating ideas to expanding and elaborating the ideas to critically examining the ideas to shifting perspective and considering them from another's point of view. And, of course, the types of thinking required vary from discipline to discipline and even genre to genre. It is not surprising, then, that the biology behind this type of thinking is, indeed, messy—or at least tricky to understand. The wonder of it all is that in creative thinking, seemingly conflicting processes come together harmoniously to bring forth something new.

In order to think about the neurobiology behind creativity, we must first consider the brain. Contrary to the diagrams I viewed as a child, the brain's functions cannot be mapped out in neat geographical segments. There is no "reading" part of the brain, no "music" parcel, and certainly no "creativity" section. Rather, the brain is an amazing and complicated (there's that word again) collection of networks, each consisting of millions of connections across different parts of the brain. These networks work together to allow complex functions to occur. In order to think about how creativity functions, we need to consider at least three distinct networks.

If you have been to any kind of teacher development in recent years, you are likely to have heard about "executive processes" or executive control. In children, these terms typically refer to students' abilities to maintain focus and control distracting impulses. One neural network controlling executive processes can be called the *executive attention network*. While terminology varies, sometimes depending on the level of specificity being used, executive networks are involved in the regulation of attention, emotions, and memories. Because executive networks help us focus, they are essential in setting and carrying out goals. The executive attention network focuses on stimuli and goals outside ourselves. We need it to make sense of and shift among the many demands of the external world (Kaufman, 2013; Rueda, Checa, & Cómbita, 2012).

For years, neurobiologists focused their studies on executive processes, considering how we think about the tasks before us. Then, in one of those moments we can characterize as accident or insight, someone thought to examine what the brain was doing *between* thinking about tasks and goals (Buckner, 2012). Whereas early studies had looked at brain activity between tasks as "noise," researchers now recognize this as the activity of a different and essential network, dubbed the *default network*. It is the network that is typically activated when we are awake but at rest—those moments when we stop the whirring and attention to our to-do lists and let our minds roam freely. As far as the brain is concerned, it turns out, Immordino-Yang (2016) puts it succinctly, "Rest is not idleness" (p. 43). A drifting mind is an active mind!

Whereas the executive networks deal with external goals and tasks, the default network is active in considering our inner experiences. It is essential for understanding ourselves, making personal meaning, understanding another's feelings, and developing empathy. The default network helps us remember the past, think about the future, imagine other perspectives or options, understand stories, make personal connections, and think about mental or emotional states—ours or others' (Baird et al., 2012; Baird, Smallwood, & Schooler, 2011; Buckner, Andrews-Hanna, & Schacter, 2008; Kaufman, 2013). Time taken to let the mind wander, reflect, and consider in unstructured ways is valuable. In fact, without the meanderings of the default network, we are unlikely to fully consider the moral and ethical meanings of ideas or situations at hand (Immordino-Yang, 2016). Kühn et al. (2014) even found that there was an association between a measure of creativity and the actual amount of gray matter in areas of the brain used by the default network. Gotlieb, Jahner, Immordino-Yang, and Kaufman (2017) call the default network "[T]he Neural Engine of Imagination" (p. 310).

The third neural network with a key role in creativity is the *salience network*. The salience network has an important sorting function, It determines which of the many incoming stimuli are important and worthy of attention or action. It helps us recognize that the dog walking toward us is not unusual, but the bear on the sidewalk is—and requires immediate attention! It can also help us recognize when our feelings are important. Because the salience network is tied to emotions, it is important in motivation. It also may facilitate shifting between the executive and default networks (Koustaal & Binks, 2015; Menon & Uddin, 2010).

The dance among these networks—and sometimes a *pas de deux* of two networks at once—is necessary for the creativity. Not surprisingly, different networks take the lead at different parts of the process. Understanding them helps us understand creativity more fully and also its links to learning. It seems likely that the processes may vary with different types of creative tasks and even with the part of the process addressed. For example, Limb and Braun (2008) found that the areas of the brain activated during jazz improvisation are more associated with the default network than areas of the brain dedicated to focused goal-directed behavior (can you imagine improvising in a fMRI scanner?). Damage to some of those areas is associated with serious impairments on several measures of creativity (Shamay-Tsoory, Adler, Aharon-Peretz, Perry, & Mayseless, 2011). But other types of divergent-thinking tasks can pull from the same areas of the brain as other language-based tasks (see Yoruk & Runco's 2014 review for more detail).

Creative tasks sometimes bring multiple networks together simultaneously, effectively using at the same time functions that more typically conflict. Just as creative people have been found to be both playful and disciplined simultaneously (Csikszentmihalyi, 1996), so creative thinking can engage seemingly conflicting thought processes at once (Koustaal & Binks, 2015). In particular, creativity seems to be associated with greater connection between the default network and areas associated with cognitive control—the executive attention network. Typically, as one of these networks is actively engaged, the other is less active. We don't usually let our minds wander at the same time we are working toward a needed goal. But in creative thinking, the networks are utilized together. In fact, individuals identified as highly creative showed more connectivity between the networks even while at rest (Beaty et al., 2014; Ellamil et al., 2012; Immordino-Yang, 2016). In more creative people, the networks talk to each other more.

Logically, it makes sense that creativity would require diverse neurological connections—it is a complex process and requires both unfettered generation of new ideas and the ability to sort and evaluate the ideas to determine which are worth pursuing. Just how and why these processes coordinate is still a matter of study. One possibility is that creative people don't fully "deactivate" the default network when addressing a task that requires external attention—they let some part of their mind wander while considering a goal or task. It could be that creative thinking utilizes facile shifting from one network to the other as needed, using different areas for different parts of the process. It is also possible that the simultaneous use of both networks at once allows the executive attention network to monitor the "wanderings" of the default network to seek out original ideas and shift perspective when necessary. Or, of course, all these possibilities could operate together, or the coordination may happen in ways not yet envisioned (Beaty, Benedek, Kaufman, & Silvia, 2015; Beaty et al., 2014; Ellamil et al., 2012; Nusbaum & Silvia, 2011; Takeuchi et al., 2011; Zabelina & Robinson, 2010).

Some research focuses on the neurobiological underpinnings of the "aha!" moment in creativity, what Kounios and Beeman refer to as insight (2015; Bowden & Jung-Beeman, 2003; Jung-Beeman et al., 2004; Kounios et al., 2008). Insight, in their terminology, is when a new recombination of ideas occurs instantly, the kind of moment that might make you exclaim, "Hey! I just had an idea!" It parallels, in many ways, the "Illumination" phase in Wallas's (1926) model of creativity. Insight comes as part of a problem solving sequence in which an individual is immersed in a problem, comes to an impasse, and then suddenly (Aha!) is aware of a solution. Kouios and Beeman distinguish this from analytic problem solving, in which new ideas come forward slowly, in a step-by-step process. Most of us have probably had the experience of solving problems both ways.

Kounios and Beeman (2015) and colleagues have investigated the differences between analytic and insightful problem solving using a variety of methods. One type of study used EEG readings to pinpoint the precise timing of neural activity. Another type used fMRI machines to identify areas of the brain that were more active during particular types of thought. To check for insight, they used a particular type of word problem called remote associates. Creativity tests using remote associations are based in the theory that original ideas occur when existing ideas are combined (associated) in new ways—remember Mednick? (see information on the *Remote Associates Test* in Chapter 10). In such measures, three seemingly unrelated words can all be linked to a fourth word. For example, think about these three words.

Tree   Cone   Apple

What word can be linked to each of them to make a meaningful word or phrase? Think for a minute.

Now try "pine." Pine tree, pine cone, pineapple. Some of you probably solved this problem analytically. You picked one of the words, perhaps "cone," and tried to think of all the associations you could, testing each with the other words. Others of you just looked at the three words, and somehow, "pine" just popped into your head. When given such tasks, all people do both types of problem solving, but most people are more inclined to one type than the other, typically more analytic or more insightful.

Using such problems, Kounios and Beeman were able to pinpoint the moment an insightful solution occurred by observing a burst of high-frequency gamma waves just above the right ear. At the same time, the fMRI showed increase blood flow in part of the right temporal lobe. This pattern wasn't seen when people solved the problems analytically. As Kounios and Beeman point out, this meant they'd almost literally found a "spark of insight" (2015, p. 71). But that was not all. Just before the tell tale gamma burst, before the insight has (at least consciously) occurred, there was a burst of alpha waves in the right back side of the head. The authors describe this as mentally downshifting, momentarily cutting back on the information being taken in, the way many of us look at the floor or close our eyes when thinking hard. Think about when your insightful ideas appear. In the shower (very common)? Just before falling asleep? We often process insightful solutions better when other stimuli are minimized, and it seems our brains help that process along. Interestingly, individuals who tend toward insightful problem solving may do this a bit less—that is, they may take in more information (and also have more active right hemispheres)—while at "rest" than those who tend more toward analytical problem solving. And, in fact, an individual's brain state—the parts of the brain that are activated—is different before a problem is eventually solved through insight. As compared to "preparing" to solve a problem analytically, a brain prepared for insight has more activity in the temporal lobes of both hemispheres—ready for any type of idea that might emerge (Kounios et al., 2008). Aren't our brains amazing and wonderful?

Of course, this research is not without its limitations and critics. As Yoruk and Runco (2014) point out, originality is an essential element of creativity, making any kind of measurement a challenge. In particular, remote associates items have a single correct answer, making the processes of association potentially quite different from those of divergent or original thinking. When examining neurobiological research (like all research) on creativity, it is important to note how creativity was defined. Weisberg (2013) raises both methodological and theoretical critiques of neurological insight studies and questions how problem solving perceived as insight actually differs from more incremental processes.

Right about now, you are probably thinking, "Well, this is all very interesting, but what does this mean in practical terms? We don't have the option to teach to one area of the brain or another." There is some evidence that electrically stimulating particular areas of the brain can enhance originality, but again, school-based brain stimulation is unlikely to be popular, at least for now (Wei et al., 2014; Zmigrod, Colzato, & Hommel, 2015). True, but there's more.

Many of the things neurobiology is teaching us about creativity are linked to new understandings of learning as well. Immordino-Yang (2016) describes the essential links between feeling and learning. We cannot truly understand and use information unless we think about it deeply. We only think deeply about things we care about. She explains:

> Meaningful learning is actually about helping students to connect their isolated algorithmic skills to abstract, intrinsically emotional, subjective and meaningful experiences. . . . it appears to be essential for the development of truly useful, transferable, intrinsically motivated learning.
>
> (p. 20)

In fact, separating teaching and learning from the emotions and activities that help students care about them can be self defeating if our goal is learning for understanding. Immordino-Yang continues:

> [I]n teaching students to minimize the emotional aspects of their academic curriculum and function as much as possible in the rational domain, educators may be encouraging students to develop the sorts of knowledge that inherently do not transfer well to real-world situations. . . . Simply having the knowledge does not imply that a student will be able to use it advantageously outside of school.
>
> (p. 39)

That is, if students see no purpose or meaning in their learning—if they can not use it or tie it to their lives in some way—the rote learning that may occur might get them through an exam, but it will not last or prove useful. And where do those essential ties to personal meaning occur? The default network.

Think about what the default network helps us do. It is associated with self-awareness, personal memories, imagining the future, reflecting on the meaning of events, imagining the perspective of another person, improvisation, and moral reasoning. It is also deeply tied to emotion. Through it, we make social evaluations, experience empathy, and make sense of emotional reactions—ours and others'. If we are to bring personal meaning to learning, we must engage the default network by finding time and space for students to reflect on their learning without being in a race to complete the next task. As students have the chance to ponder content more broadly, they are better able to make personal connections and build ties that create learning. And when they do, they engage parts of the brain necessary for creativity as well. For example, if we pose a question or problem that links content to students' lives or interests and allow time and space for reflection, we both make learning more meaningful and allow incubation to occur. It is interesting to think about how that might occur in school. Teachers have typically seen wandering minds as impediments to learning, but we may have been wrong.

Immordino-Yang and colleagues found that the more participants reflectively paused, the greater the activity in the default network while feeling moral emotions. She argues reflection is necessary for learning, for making personal connections to content, and for helping students understand the moral and ethical implications of the content addressed (2016; Gotlieb et al., 2017). Baird et al. (2012) found that conditions that encouraged mind wandering during incubation were more beneficial to divergent thinking than plain rest. Tan, Zou, Chen, and Luo (2015) found that students who reported their minds wandering more during an incubation period were more successful in solving a mathematical pattern problem. So one practical implication of the research to date is that students need time to reflect, both for effective learning and for solving problems in creative ways. A classroom that requires constant engagement and focused activity is not necessarily the classroom in which either learning or creativity will develop best.

Gotlieb et al. (2017) make a number of recommendations for practice based on what they call "social emotional imagination." Here is a selection. Consider how they fit with neuroscience to date.

1. Schedule time for reflection or capitalize on moments that occur naturally. Consider the types of questions and activities that prompt students to ponder rather than recall the information. Rushing on to one more task can get us nowhere—but in a big hurry! Sometimes this can be just a brief pause. In a history class, take 30 seconds to have students imagine the scene they are studying and then describe their thoughts. Pause and imagine how a literary character is feeling. Envision a chemical bond taking place. Begin to build habits of taking in information, then pausing to consider what it means. Building in time for reflection seems likely to increase both learning and creativity.

2. Scaffold and model mindfully moving between task-oriented focus and meaning making. Talk to students about the usefulness of many types of thinking. Teach students about the functions of different brain networks. They don't need all the details about the brain's subsections, but it is valuable for them to know that there are different ways to use their brains. Explain your processes as you shift between energetic task focus and taking a few moments to think (you do that, right?) Help them develop meta-awareness of their thinking and strategies to help them take moments for reflection without losing focus entirely.

3. Encourage students to imagine pathways to goals, short and long term. Helping students envision both the future goals and the steps that can help them get there—and tying those things together—can help them in myriad ways, from long-term life planning to minimizing procrastination in assignments.

4. Use stories to help students build personal narratives. Help students know the people and the stories behind the content, whether they concern authors of literature, scientists who discovered key principles, or figures in history. As information is personalized and tied to story, students experience it from different perspectives—and with different networks. Let reflection on content be personal as well. Take a minute to allow students to think about what they would do in a historical situation, what feeling a painting gives them, or perhaps even what personal situation would feel like a particular algebraic equation!

5. Give students meaningful opportunities to make meaningful choices about curricular content. Gotlieb et al. (2017) say, "The best way to develop creative citizens is to give them supported practice at conceiving, developing and following their interests, curiosity, and talents." Choice is so important, and it can be a rare thing in schools. What can better encourage in-depth learning than content that is personally meaningful? Choice also can support curiosity, engagement, and motivation. More on that in Chapter 9.

I would add, building on incubation research, consider scheduling simpler tasks between opportunities to think about more challenging ones, allowing the brain a chance to relax focus a bit. For example, young children might begin thinking about a story idea, then take a break to draw a picture, have a few minutes of recess, or even go to lunch. Return to the story and see what new ideas emerge. Older students might break to organize their notes or listen to a few minutes of quiet music between generating ideas for science experiments or planning history essays.

Interestingly, neurobiology also provides evidence for the impact of mood on creative thinking. Early neurobiological research found that positive affect (associated with increased dopamine levels) was tied to cognitive flexibility and improved creative problem solving (Ashby, Isen, & Turken, 1999). Subramanian, Kounios, Parrish, and Jung-Beeman (2009) found that individuals in a positive mood solved more problems, and solved more problems using insight, than those in a more negative mood. Positive mood broadens our attention and makes more things seem relevant and interesting. It also activates several areas of the brain, one of which (the anterior cingulate) helps deal with conflicting ideas. When it is activated, we are more likely to recognize less obvious solutions rather than assuming them to be irrelevant or impossible. We know that positive mood in the workplace leads to more creativity for up to two days afterward (Amabile, Barsade, Mueller, & Staw, 2005)—and that creative activity can boost mood! These ideas echo the research of Mueller, Melwani, and Goncalo (2012), who found that even small amounts of anxiety resulted in less effective problem solving. While the interactions between mood and creativity can be complex, overall, positive moods are more likely to support creativity than more neutral ones (Baas, De Dreu, & Nijstad, 2008). And so, for multiple reasons, our classroom climate matters. More on creative environments in Chapter 9.

Kounios and Beeman (2015) describe out modern life as "an environment on steroids," (p. 217) with little time for quiet introspection. Certainly as I compare my field-wandering childhood to the pace of children today, the comparison is stark—to say nothing of the atmosphere in many classrooms today. Kounios and Beeman continue, "The inner world of the default-state network hardly has a chance. As a society, we are trading creativity for a narrow type of efficiency" (p. 217). While we cannot change the society in which our students live, if we want them to learn and create most effectively, we are going to have to find classroom ways to stop, take a breath, and have a thought. Classrooms in which every child is totally content focused every minute of every day have always been an illusion, but now we understand that they aren't even a good idea (see Chapter 4). And it seems that the links between creativity and learning are much deeper than I ever imagined.

Think About It

1. Read or watch descriptions of creative activities by creative people. A classic place to start is *The Creative Process* (Ghiselin, 1985). You also could explore accounts of creative people at TED.com or blogs of creative scientists or writers. Or invite creative people to talk to you. I've sometimes invited exceptionally creative professors from other departments to participate in a panel discussion for my class. Fascinating! Do any of the creators describe processes similar to your own?

2. Consider what Maslow and Rogers would recommend for a classroom atmosphere that would enhance creativity. We will address that question more fully in Chapter 9, but for now, observe the atmosphere in your classroom on different days. Do you see any differences in the flexibility of thinking your students demonstrate?

3. Go on a creativity hunt and observe what you see. One way to do this is to go to a place in which a group of people is engaged in open-ended activities. This could be children on a

playground, teens in the mall, or adults at a party—or even a planning meeting. Observe and take notes of examples of creative thinking you notice. Think about the circumstances in which they occur and how ideas seem to emerge. You may want to save your notes—or go on another hunt—to consider other variables that we examine in the text.

Try It Tomorrow

1. Go on a creativity hunt with your class. Explore the school grounds and perhaps a different grade level in action. Have students document (write, draw, voice-record) how many creative tasks are occurring during this. Stop into administrative offices, the lunch room, and the playground to get a full scope of what's happening in other areas of the school while they are in the classroom. Older students might be assigned to do an individual creativity hunt in their neighborhood and return to report their findings.

2. Think about what you can do to create a positive mood in your classroom before the next activity requiring flexible thinking and problem solving. Share a quick video, play some music, wear a costume, or whatever else might lift the mood in your class and see if you notice a difference in their responses. If you teach multiple sections, you might experiment with different strategies for different classes.

3. Review the list of neuroscience-based suggestions at the end of the chapter and try one or more. For example, briefly pause for reflection in the middle of a lesson, allowing students to envision the events or phenomena being studied, or help them make a personal connection to events, perhaps by uncovering the story in your content.

Tech Tips

This chapter's tips are a miscellany of ways to express creativity, with interesting constraints (see Chapter 6).

1. Ernest Hemingway once wrote a short story using only six words.

   "For sale: baby shoes, never worn."

   It is said that the story was the result of a bet with friends—who paid up. Hemingway thought it was one of his best. The six-word story is a unique and powerful art form. *Wired* magazine has published a number of six-word stories from famous authors, from the profound to the silly (www.wired.com/wired/archive/14.11/sixwords.html). The Six Word Stories website (www.sixwordstories.net/#sidebar) brings together stories from famous authors and Web readers—you can even submit your own.

   The powerful thing about six-word stories is that they force the writer to choose carefully, focusing on the ideas that are most central. The same process can be used to create six-word challenges in different curriculum areas. What about a six-word summary of a historical event or scientific/mathematical principle?

2. Flickr Five Frames (www.flickr.com/groups/visualstory) is a strategy for visual storytelling using just five images. It is a fine way to help students grasp the underlying structure of many stories. The best five-frames follow a similar sequence: (1) introduce the character, (2) introduce a problem situation, (3) involve the character in the problem, (4) resolve the problem, (5) end with something unexpected. I love the Humpty Dumpty sequence. It is worth searching for!

3. Many students like to create their own comic strips. Two options for doing this without cost are Make Beliefs Comix and ToonDoo. Make Beliefs Comix (www.makebeliefscomix.com/)

allows the user to drag and drop characters, objects, and talk or thought balloons into simple cartoons. While it doesn't allow for much customization, it is easy to use and has enough options for many story possibilities.

ToonDoo (www.toondoo.com) has more flexibility, allowing original characters, uploaded images, and either cartoon strips or books. Take a look at both sites and see which you'd like best for your cartoons.

4. Try having students create stories through dialogue via Google Story Builder (docsstorybuilder.appspot.com/). For a more complicated Google storytelling option, see the options for linking stories, photos, and Google Earth with Google Tour Builder (tourbuilder.with-google.com/).

4
Theories of Creativity
Systems in Context

Pablo Picasso is one of the most famous artists of the 20th century. Renowned as one of the cofounders of the cubist movement, he worked in many styles. Beginning in the 1890s with academic realism, his style transformed multiple times and remained in flux until the end of his life. Many of his later works were unappreciated until after his death.

[Thomas] Edison is in reality a collective noun and means the work of many men.
(Francis Jehl, Edison's longtime assistant, quoted in Kelley, 2001, p. 70)

Tall Horse, a collaboration between the Handspring Puppet Company of South Africa and the Sogolon Puppet Troupe of Mali, retold the true story of a giraffe walking from Marseilles to Paris in 1827. The production melded multiple languages, styles of choreography, and traditions of puppetry.

I make them because I have to support my son. When my son is happy, I'm happy. So I try to carve all the time. I see it as a normal kind of work. If I clean, it's all right. If I carve, it's all right. Anything I like to do, I'll just do it. . . . I look at my work like a job, something I have to do to support my family.

(Eva Aliktiluk, Inuit carver)

Systems Approaches

All creativity occurs in a particular time and place. In Chapter 3, we discussed Vygotsky's theories proposing a dialectic relationship between internal and external processes of creativity: Creativity was required to build individual understandings and insights regarding the surrounding culture, and creativity allowed innovation and change in the culture itself. This embedding of creativity in culture rather than simply in the cognitive or emotional processes of individuals is the basis of systems, or confluence, theories, the most influential theories studied today.

Systems theories approach creativity as an interaction between the individual and the outside world. In these theories, the mechanisms of the mind are not sufficient to explain the creative process or the determination of what is creative. Each must be placed in the context of an external environment. Simonton (1988) stated, "Creativity cannot be properly understood in isolation from the social context, for creativity is a special form of personal influence: The effective creator profoundly alters the thinking habits of other human beings" (p. 421). Of course, just as creative individuals affect those around them, systems theories propose that creativity is influenced by the environment in which it takes place.

For example, what of Eva Aliktiluk, the Inuit carver cited earlier (Auger, 2005)? The stunningly beautiful Inuit carvings, originating largely in northern Canada, pose a puzzling case study of the impact of context on creativity. Until the 1940s, Canada's Inuit lived in small family groups scattered across the Arctic, with minimal contact with Canada's south. In the mid-20th century, their nomadic lifestyle became increasingly endangered and, under a variety of pressures, many moved to build communities. In those communities, most of the skills that were essential to survive as nomadic hunters had little financial value. However, skilled carvers soon found a market for their carvings in "southern" markets, and Inuit art became a mainstay of Canadian galleries. The ability to carve or paint could make the difference between self-sufficiency and subsistence living.

When asked about their art, Inuit carvers express varied views. Contrary to Western images of starving artists striving to be understood, Eva sees carving as a way to make a living, equivalent to cleaning houses. Carvers must make what will sell. If southern people want to buy carvings of seals, one must make seals. For many Inuit artists, making art is a financial necessity. Similar situations exist in many parts of the world where indigenous art and artifacts are created for distribution elsewhere. But still, there are options. One might carve scores of virtually identical seals. One might carve seals, each one different from those before. Or one might carve tigers or cows or abstract forms—but perhaps not feed one's family. Where does creativity fit, and how is creativity possible? Systems theories examine such questions.

In most cases, researchers writing about systems theories deal with "big C" Creativity, or creativity that substantially influences a discipline or culture. We are left to consider the ways in which the forces operating in systems models may influence creativity of more modest proportions.

Creativity, Culture, and Csikszentmihalyi

Possibly the most influential of the systems models was put forth by Mihaly Csikszentmihalyi (1988, 1990b, 1996, 1999). Csikszentmihalyi (pronounced, approximately, "chicks sent me high") presented a three-pronged systems model of creativity, including aspects of the person, the domain, and the field (Figure 4.1). The model has been embraced by other prominent theorists (e.g., Feldman, Csikszentmihalyi, & Gardner, 1994). The model changes one of the basic questions in the study of creativity from "What is creativity?" to "Where is creativity?" It examines creativity profound enough to be described as "the transformation of a cultural system (e.g., chemistry, medicine, poetry)—the incorporation of novelty into the culture" (Nakamura & Csikszentmihalyi, 2001, p. 337).

Csikszentmihalyi saw creativity not as a characteristic of particular people or products but as an interaction among person, product, and environment. The person produces some variation in the information gained from the culture in which he or she lives. This variation may result from cognitive flexibility, motivation, or an unusual and inspiring life experience. However, according to Csikszentmihalyi, examining the mechanisms of novelty in the individual is only part of the picture.

Individuals are not creative in a vacuum (except perhaps on creativity tests). They create in a domain. A playwright creates in a symbol system and tradition of a culture. Without knowledge concerning the conventions of theater and script writing, it would be impossible to be a successful

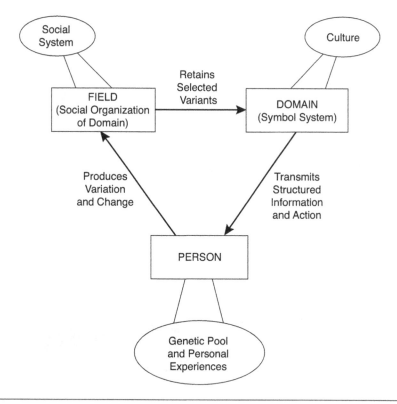

Figure 4.1 The locus of creativity

Source: From Sternberg, R. J. (Ed.) (1988). *The Nature of Creativity* (p. 329). New York: Cambridge University Press. Copyright © 1988 by Cambridge University Press. Reprinted with permission.

creative playwright. Creativity demands a domain-specific knowledge base. A creative mathematician must know mathematics. A biologist must know biology. A carver must be able to carve.

However, the domain is not the only entity that influences creative production. Variations also come into existence in the context of a field, or the social structure of a domain. The field comprises those people who can affect the structure of a domain. The field of theater, for example, is made up of theater teachers, drama critics, audience members (especially season ticket holders), producers, actors, directors, and any other individuals who help shape the definition of good theater at a particular time in a particular society. To be perceived as creative, the playwright must strike a balance with the order of the field. If the play is too similar to past standards, it will be considered mundane; if it is too different, it will not be considered art. If the variation is accepted, it becomes part of the domain to be transmitted by the field to novices. In some domains, notably the arts, it is possible for individuals to create works that are not accepted by the field at the time they are created. This rejection may mean poverty for the creator, but in time (possibly posthumously), acceptance may come. In the case of the Inuit carvers, multiple fields influence their creative efforts. First are the standards of the community of carvers. Once the art goes beyond the community, its success is influenced by its success in navigating the field at large. Shop owners who cater to souvenir seekers exert one kind of influence, prominent gallery owners another.

Even in seemingly objective domains such as the sciences, there is a structure to the field that influences the possibilities for high-level creative accomplishments. It is difficult to become influential without the ability to publish in the right journals or to be accepted by the right conferences.

Systems theories of creativity require an interaction of person and environment

A creative individual's work must be valued by some portion of the current field if it is to be given a professional hearing. In some cases, such as Mendel's work in genetics, the importance of creative ideas can be seen only later, as the field and domain change. It is interesting to speculate whether Einstein would have been viewed as a genius or a crackpot (and what his theories might have been) had he been born 100 years earlier when his field was very different.

Individuals are not only judged by the field; they are formed by it as well. In the course of preparation and in their environments of practice, individuals are shaped by those who practice around them, particularly those in mentoring relationships. The entire Inuit carving community was influenced by artist James Houston, who went north on a painting trip. His delight in their carvings and the impression his "souvenirs" made on the Canadian Handicrafts Guild marked the beginnings of commercial viability for the carvers (Auger, 2005). The potential interactions among individual, domain, and field are complex and may change considerably in different times, different environments, and different domains and fields. For example, the personal characteristics that might lead one to be a highly creative physicist in the 21st century in the United States might be very different from those that would have been necessary for one to be a 19th-century Parisian painter, because the personalities necessary to find acceptance in those domains and fields vary so enormously.

It is interesting to consider whether the linkages among individual, field, and domain described by Csikszentmihalyi are relevant in creativity on a smaller scale than the transformation of a cultural system. Although individuals may be creative in ways that do not influence a field or domain in significant ways (at least according to many definitions), all creativity does occur within a domain that exists within a context.

Consider, for example, the anonymous storyteller cited at the beginning of Chapter 1. A fine storyteller will bring to that effort a host of personal characteristics and processes. He or she works within the domain of storytelling, using the tools and conventions of that form. The storyteller also works within a context. The society provides the cultural context in which the storyteller's art is developed and practiced. It includes conventions within which the storyteller must work: traditional tales and frameworks within which variations are accepted, structures for learning to tell stories, and relationships with mentors, possibly even politics regarding who tells which tales under which circumstances.

Although they look somewhat different from the factors influencing innovation in Western science or theater, the interactions of individual, content discipline (domain), and context (field, surrounding culture) appear important in many types of creativity.

Thinking About the Classroom

Creative efforts are not always accepted by the field at the time they are initiated. Make a bulletin board of "Great Failures" to help students understand that new ideas are not always immediately appreciated (or successful!)

Building on Csikszentmihalyi's model, Gardner (1993a, 1993b) described an interactive perspective on creativity that recognized the importance of the interactions among individuals, domains, and fields. Drawing on his own theory of multiple intelligences, Gardner (1983) came to believe that individuals are creative in particular, domain-specific ways. Although an individual may certainly be creative in more than one domain (consider the poetry and artwork of William Blake), Gardner's definition of creativity reflects creative functioning not as a general personal characteristic ("He or she is a creative person") but in a particular area. He stated, "The creative individual is a person who regularly solves problems, fashions products, or defines new questions *in a domain* in a way that is initially considered novel but that ultimately becomes accepted in a particular cultural setting" (Gardner, 1993a, p. 35, italics added). The domain(s) in which a person becomes creative are affected by the individual's intelligences, personality, social support, and domain and field opportunities.

Gardner based his theories on in-depth studies of highly creative individuals. In his studies of eminent creators, Gardner found wide variations in the types of intellectual strengths demonstrated by creators in different domains. In addition, he found that the symbol systems to be mastered and the activities in which individuals must be engaged vary enormously across disciplines. He described five types of activities in which creative individuals may be involved:

1. *Solving a particular problem.* This includes primarily scientific or mathematical research questions but also covers tightly constrained artistic tasks, such as musical arrangements.
2. *Putting forth a general conceptual scheme.* This includes the development of artistic or scientific theories—for example, the theory of relativity or the characteristics of cubism.
3. *Creating a product.* Creative products include works of visual art, literature, or choreography.
4. *Giving a stylized performance.* Stylized performances are defined generally by a script or score but include opportunities for interpretation, improvisation, or innovation. Examples are dance, drama, or musical performances.
5. *Performing for high stakes.* Gardner described this as a type of creative endeavor in which one's words and actions are the substance of creativity and in which one may risk security, health, or life in the service of a mission. This type of creativity is exemplified by public

figures such as Gandhi. It is interesting to consider which of the activist strategies we view on the evening news could be considered performing for high stakes.

It is possible that the intelligences, personality traits, and cognitive processes necessary for creativity may vary depending on which type of creative product is necessary or desired. As additional components are considered—the language of the domain, the characteristics of the field at a particular time, or the type of product necessary for the desired contribution—the potential elements of the system defining or controlling creativity become increasingly complex. One fascinating potential twist on these ideas comes from Robert and Michele Root-Bernstein (2004). Their research suggests that many highly creative scientists also have creative avocations in the arts, whereas creative artists often have avocations exploring in the sciences. Perhaps the fact that few individuals make highly creative contributions in more than one domain is as much a matter of allocation of time and training as it is discipline-based creativity.

Thinking About the Classroom

One of the key questions in theories of creativity is whether there are general creative processes that span the disciplines or whether creativity is discipline specific. Baer (1993) found evidence of discipline-specific strengths in students in grades 2, 4, 5, 8, and college. Try giving your students creative tasks in several disciplines. Do the same students demonstrate exceptional creativity in every subject? You may want to ask a colleague to help assess the products to increase the reliability of your findings.

Feldman: Defender of Insight

Feldman (1994, 1999, 2003) can best be described as a systems theorist with a developmental perspective. As a systems theorist, he recognized the complex interactions that come into play to allow high-level creativity to function. He listed seven dimensions that may influence creative processes: (a) cognitive processes, (b) social and emotional processes, (c) family aspects—growing up and current processes, (d) education and preparation—formal and informal, (e) characteristics of the domain and field, (f) sociocultural contextual aspects, and (g) historical forces, events, and trends (Feldman, 1999, pp. 171–172). He believed that creativity occurs within specific domains and that there is no general trait of creativity.

As a developmentalist, Feldman (1994) believed that creativity develops along these multiple dimensions. In contrast to Rogers, who believed creativity was part of the natural developmental process for all human beings, Feldman's focus on extraordinary creativity led him to focus on extraordinary, or nonuniversal, development. Nonuniversal development encompasses developmental changes that are unique to highly creative individuals. All human beings, according to developmental theory, experience internal transformations as their cognitive systems respond to interactions with the world. Feldman (1994) stated, "Creativity is a particularly strong and powerful instance of development, in which a personal, internal reorganization also leads to a significant change in the external form of a domain" (p. 87).

This may be most easily understood by examining the relationship of Feldman's ideas to Piaget's theories. Piaget postulated two processes to account for all changes in thought structures: assimilation and accommodation. *Assimilation* is the tendency to fit information into past experiences, allowing for a constant reality. *Accommodation* is the process of adjusting one's perception of reality to fit new information (Boden, 1980). Neither process deals well with novelty, the really new restructurings of experience. Feldman postulated a third process: transformation. In the *transformation* process, the mind constructs ideas and images that are not based on experience. Transformation can lead to cognitive reorganization that is so profound it allows the individual to view the world in new and unique ways.

Feldman contradicted, to some degree, the basic premise of some contemporary theories that creativity represents the use of ordinary cognitive processes in unique ways rather than being an unusual or distinct process. He defended the importance of insight and the unconscious in the creative process. Feldman (2003) stated that creativity is involved in all developmental transitions—each time we reorganize our cognitive structures, as in Piaget's stage development, it requires creativity. He proposed a continuum of such transitions from the universal—the stages typical of human development—to discipline-based changes that stimulate a shift in thinking in a discipline. All these transitions occur within particular disciplines and in contexts that impact the degree to which creative transitions are recognized and appreciated.

As did Perkins (1981), Feldman believed that creativity is rooted in the desire for creative change. Feldman's third aspect would probably ring true for several other theorists: He believed that new creative efforts are inspired by the results of previous creative efforts. Although Perkins or Weisberg might attribute this influence to the effects of knowledge, Feldman emphasized that seeing the results of others' creativity illustrates that it is possible to make a difference. He believed that interaction with the creative efforts and products of others may allow the fruits of nonconscious transformations to enter one's consciousness. This emphasis on essential interaction with the crafted world is one of the key attributes that place Feldman among the systems theorists.

Thinking About the Classroom

Feldman believed that creative efforts are inspired by the creativity of others. Consider how this idea may affect your students. How might you share the creative efforts of other young people in a manner that encourages rather than overwhelms?

An Investment Model and Thoughts About Wisdom

Sternberg and Lubart (1991, 1993) and Sternberg and O'Hara (1999) proposed an investment theory of creativity: Individuals must buy low and sell high to achieve creativity. Instead of investing in stocks or diamonds, these individuals invest in ideas. Creative individuals pursue ideas that are novel or out of favor (buying low), then convince the field of the value of those ideas. Once the ideas gain favor, they allow others to pursue them (selling high) while they go on to other endeavors. Individuals who pursue already popular trends or solutions are less likely to achieve valuable original results. The investment theory suggests that six types of interacting resources contribute to creative performance: intellectual processes, knowledge, intellectual style, personality, motivation, and environmental context (Zhang & Sternberg, 2011).

As did Perkins and Weisberg, Sternberg and Lubart (1991, 1993; Sternberg, 2012) explained the intellectual processes of creativity with the same model they used to understand other intelligent activities. However, unlike these two theorists, Sternberg (1985b) devised a triarchic model of intelligence that includes components specifically tied to creative insight. For example, although selective encoding (sifting relevant from irrelevant information) is important to understanding any type of input, it may be particularly important in creative insights. Sternberg gave the example of Sir Alexander Fleming's discovery of penicillin. When Fleming's bacteria culture was spoiled by mold, he was able to recognize the important information at his fingertips and, rather than despair at his unsuccessful experiment, make an important discovery. Other components of intelligence seen as important to creativity are problem definition, strategic use of divergent thinking, selective combination, and selective comparison of information. Sternberg's (1988b) theory of creativity originates in this model of intelligence.

The investment theory also examines the role of knowledge in creative performance, hypothesizing that it is an upside-down U. A low amount of knowledge is associated with limited creativity. An extremely high amount of knowledge may limit creativity because the individual becomes so immersed in the current state of the art that he or she is unable to find a truly new perspective. It is possible that a moderate amount of knowledge may be the most supportive of creativity. What exactly constitutes a moderate amount of knowledge and how it might vary by age or discipline remain questions for further investigation.

In addition to linking creativity with knowledge and specific aspects of intelligence, Sternberg and Lubart (1991, 1993) believed that creativity is characterized by a mental style that prefers to create its own rules, to attack unstructured (rather than rigid or prefabricated) problems, and to be involved in tasks characterized as "legislative," such as writing, designing projects, and creating business or educational systems. They also noted ties to specific personality characteristics, such as tolerance of ambiguity, intrinsic motivation, and moderate risk taking. Finally, as did several other theorists, Sternberg and Lubart (1991, 1993) noted the importance of task-focused motivation and environmental variables in supporting creative activities. In this view, the complex interactions among the six types of resources necessary for high-level creativity account for the relative rarity of such accomplishments.

Sternberg (2000b, 2012) has been clear that just as he believes intelligence can be developed, so he believes creativity can be increased through specific choices (e.g., the choice to redefine problems or take sensible risks). He also has examined the relationships among creativity, intelligence, and wisdom (Sternberg, 2001, 2004b). He has described intelligent people as those who "somehow acquire the skills that lead to their fitting into existing environments" (2001, p. 360). Although what is considered intelligent behavior in one place may differ from behavior considered intelligent in another, behaviors considered intelligent generally are rewarded as appropriate to the society. The rewards are reaped as a result of adapting to an environment or environments.

In contrast, most definitions of creativity focus on ideas that are novel in a particular environment. Whereas intelligence may cause individuals to adapt to and succeed within cultural norms, creativity can cause them to reject such norms. The more novel the work, the more the individuals question existing paradigms, standards, and conventions—and the higher the level of personal and professional risk. Sternberg (2001, 2004b) described wisdom as a synthesis of intelligence and creativity, balancing the need for change with the need for stability and continuity in human affairs. Wise individuals, according to this theory, would be sought after as leaders because of their ability to seek both stability and progress. Surely, we can use more such individuals.

The role of wisdom in balancing continuity and change may be manifested differently within varied contexts. This could account, in part, for differences in the types of creativity considered appropriate across cultures. In societies threatened with the extinction of cultural traditions, wisdom may lead to an emphasis on creativity within those traditions. Rejection of cultural paradigms is less risky to society at large when practiced in dominant cultures.

Finally, as mentioned in Chapter 1, Sternberg (2003) proposed a propulsion model of types of creative contributions. In contrast to Gardner's types of creative products that vary more by type of activity, Sternberg's divisions categorize creative activities according to the ways they propel existing ideas forward. They vary in the degree to which the contribution accepts current paradigms and the direction in which it moves the field. He suggests that even children can be creative in different ways, ranging from minor replications to major redirections in their thinking. Sternberg's types include:

1. Replication: Demonstrates that the field is in the right place.
2. Redefinition: Leads back to the field's current state, but viewed in a new way.
3. Forward incrementation: Moves the field forward in its current direction.
4. Advance forward incrementation: Moves the field forward at an accelerated pace, further than others may be willing to go.
5. Redirection: Moves the field in a new direction.
6. Reconstruction/redirection: Moves the field back to an earlier state, then in a new direction.
7. Reinitiation: Moves the field to a different starting point, then in a new direction.
8. Integration: Integrates two formerly diverse ways of thinking.

Different people will prefer different types of creative activities, and different types of activities will be demanded (or accepted) in different contexts. For example, when economies are in turmoil, innovations in energy production may be more accepted than when things are more economically stable. When we believe we are doing well, there can be less motivation for—or tolerance of—innovations that send us in new directions.

Gruber's Evolving Systems

Gruber and his associates (Gruber & Davis, 1988; Gruber & Wallace, 1999, 2001; Wallace & Gruber, 1989) began with a basic assumption of the uniqueness of each highly creative individual. Believing that creative people develop along such idiosyncratic paths that generalizations about them are likely to be minimally useful, they used case studies to investigate in depth the distinctive processes of highly creative individuals. Gruber's (1981) most famous work, *Darwin on Man: A Psychological Study of Scientific Creativity*, examined the evolution of Darwin's ideas through a painstaking analysis of his notebooks and other writings.

The evolving-systems approach entails a set of complex attitudes and approaches for studying the efforts of creative people. First, the approach is developmental. It views creativity as developing over time and being affected by purpose, play, and chance. Second, it is complex, seeking to identify multiple insights, projects, metaphors, and so on in the work of a creative individual. An evolving-systems approach does not seek to identify a single "aha!" in the work of a creative individual but rather to track the many insights that occurred across time. The phrase "network of enterprise" (Gruber & Wallace, 2001, p. 347) is used to underscore the complex and branching nature of the creative endeavors studied. Third, it recognizes creative activity as interactive, affected by historical context, interpersonal relationships, and professional collaborations. The evolving-systems approach recognizes the creative individual both as a constructor of tasks and as a human being interacting with the world, with emotions, aesthetics, and needs. The degree of detail possible in individual case studies allows the researchers to consider multiple, complex factors interacting over time to influence a body of creative work.

Gruber and Davis (1988) noted major aspects of evolving systems that have been observed across case studies. First, and most clear-cut, is that creative activity takes a long time. As noted by Weisberg (1993), major creative insights do not come out of the blue but are the result of years of learning, thought, and preparation. Because of the length and potential frustration of this process, creative individuals must of necessity invent and pursue subgoals. Early sketches and metaphors also were seen as helpful in shaping and maintaining continuing efforts over time. Darwin's (1859) branching-tree image was part of his writing years before its use in *On the Origin of Species*.

The second aspect noted is a "loose coupling of knowledge, purpose, affect, and milieu" (Gruber & Davis, 1988, p. 266). The evolution of creative ideas is influenced by an individual's expertise, motivation, emotions, and environment. "Loose coupling" represents the limited effects of one on the other. As an illustration, although depression and discouragement may affect an individual's thought processes, they do not eliminate that person's knowledge and expertise.

The third aspect observed in the evolving-systems theory is nonhomeostatic processes, or processes designed to seek not closure but additional achievement and challenge. The creative individual seeks not just answers but additional questions. Despite these patterns, Gruber's focus remained on the idiosyncratic nature of creative processes: "Every creative person is unique in ways that are relevant to his or her creative achievements" (Gruber & Wallace, 2001, p. 348). Only by in-depth study of individuals, Gruber believed, can we recognize the multiple complexities of significant creative contributions.

Thinking About the Classroom

Consider having your students study in depth the life of a creative individual in your field, either through reading biographies or interviewing local citizens. Have them attempt to identify the experiences and incremental understandings that led to more substantial creative accomplishments.

Simonton and an Evolutionary Model

Simonton (1999, 2004) proposes a model of creativity that can be dubbed evolutionary because at its core is the "survival of the fittest" creative ideas. Simonton proposed that creative ideas are produced through random combinations of mental elements. Individuals vary both in the number of mental elements present in their unconscious and in the networks of combinations produced. The greater and more varied the number of combinations, the greater the likelihood of a creative idea. The best ideas, he proposed, will surface to the conscious mind for fuller consideration—thus "surviving." Simonton notes that many eminent creators have extended periods between major creative successes. He attributes this to the need to build a database of ideas and experiences that will form the basis of random combinations. The addition of chance encounters, experiences, and memories can provide just the ingredients necessary for a creative combination to emerge.

Simonton's model can be considered a systems model because, in addition to the mental evolutionary processes, it also takes into account the sociocultural "zeitgeist," or context. Some of Simonton's most interesting work has been in tracking creative accomplishments across historical time periods, examining patterns of high and low productivity for individuals and for disciplines as a whole. Art (or at least particular kinds of art) can flourish when wealthy patrons abound. Periods of war deeply constrain the types of scientific advances possible, as virtually all efforts are centered on areas necessary for national survival.

Finally, Simonton considers characteristics of creative individuals as essential components of a model of creativity. This has led him to a model of scientific creativity based on a confluence of logic, chance, genius, and zeitgeist.

Amabile, Motivation, and a Model of Creativity

Amabile's (1989, 1996, 2001) componential model of creativity has been particularly influential in its inclusion of noncognitive personal characteristics within a broader systems model. Amabile was interested not just in characteristics of creative individuals but in "creative situations"

(Amabile, 1996, p. 5)—what are the circumstances conducive to creativity? She found that the social environment can have a large effect on creativity, primarily through the mechanism of motivation. This insight led to the development of her componential model of creativity. The model brings together major components found in many models of creativity. It has three components: domain-relevant skills, creativity-related processes, and task motivation. While the model was later revised to detail the ways the three components map on different stages of the creative process (Amabile, 1996), for our purposes, the basic form will do (Figure 4.2).

Domain-relevant skills define the area in which the individual can be creative: factual knowledge about the domain, technical skills, or particular domain-related talents. If a person is to be creative in music, he or she must be knowledgeable about music, probably play an instrument, and, in most cases, be able to read musical notation. Particular talent in music would also be considered a domain-relevant skill. A scientist who is to make a creative contribution in astronomy or oceanography will need extensive education in that field before he or she is prepared to do original work. Creative contributions do not spring forth in a vacuum. They are built on the knowledge and efforts of those who have gone before. It is not enough for children to have fun with creative puzzles, activities, and games. They must know enough about something to change it, elaborate on it, derive implications from it, or use it in a new way. If we are to facilitate creative thinking, we must teach content in such a way that it supports rather than threatens the attitudes and habits of mind that allow creative ideas. Any of the content we teach can form the basis for creative activities if we provide students with the opportunity to learn information, techniques, and strategies and then encourage them to use these in new ways. Chapters 7 and 8 concentrate on teaching domain skills in a manner that is consistent with creative activity.

The second component in the model is creativity-relevant processes, originally called creative thinking and working skills. It includes cognitive style, implicit or explicit knowledge of means for generating novel ideas, and a conducive work style—generally including the orientation toward

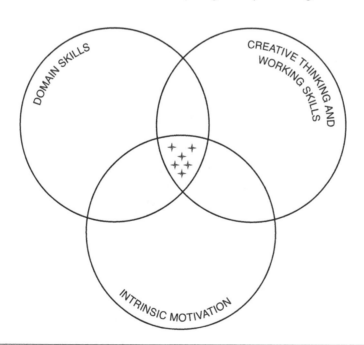

Figure 4.2 The creativity intersection

Source: From Amabile, T. M. (1989). *Growing Up Creative*. New York: Crown, p. 63. Reprinted by permission of the author.

hard work (Amabile, 1996, 2001). In this area are found the habits of mind as well as the specific strategies and abilities typically thought of as creative thinking. These might include looking at situations from many points of view, using metaphors, or exploring and problem finding. When we teach students brainstorming, use creative dramatics, or teach techniques for developing story ideas, we are developing creative thinking skills or general heuristics for approaching problem tasks. In the process, we also support habits of mind that are conducive to creative thinking, such as suspending judgment or looking for a novel response. This component also includes the creative-working skills that allow an individual to persevere at a task over time: concentration, focus, organization, and tolerance of ambiguity. The ability to maintain attention to a task over time has been identified as important in several aspects of creativity. It takes time in exploration to identify a problem. Gardner (1993a), Gruber and Davis (1988), and Weisberg (1999) all noted that high-level creativity activities demanded a commitment to task that spanned years. Creative thinking and working skills are the focus of Chapters 6 and 9.

The final component of Amabile's (1989, 1996, 2001) componential model is her most important contribution to the literature on creativity: task motivation, particularly intrinsic motivation, or motivation that comes from within a person and not from some outside source. A child who plays the piano for the joy of playing is intrinsically motivated. The child who plays to earn TV-watching privileges or to avoid a scolding is not. All the skills, habits, and abilities in the world will not ensure that an individual will persist with a task unless he or she wants to do so. In 1989, Amabile wrote, "People will be most creative when they feel motivated primarily by the interest, enjoyment, challenge, and satisfaction of the work itself . . . and not by external pressures" (p. 54). Her later work indicates that although intrinsic motivation is important, the interactions of motivation and creativity are complex.

Thinking About the Classroom

Have students make a list of things they like to do. Discuss why they like the activities. Try to determine whether they are intrinsically motivated or compelled by an outside reward.

No activity, by itself, is intrinsically motivating. It can be so only to a particular person at a particular time. Amabile (1989) identified three hallmarks of intrinsic motivation. The first and most obvious is interest. Anyone is more likely to be motivated by something that has captured his or her interest than something that is boring or of no perceived value. A second aspect of intrinsic motivation is competence. Individuals will seek out activities and persist in them longer if they feel they are mastering something on their own. I once took a community education class on playing the mountain dulcimer. It was an interesting and highly motivating experience. The instrument is uncomplicated enough that I was able to play simple melodies the first time I picked it up. This early success and feeling of competence made practicing enjoyable and left me eager to learn more. Later, as I struggled with more difficult techniques, I still enjoyed my growing feeling of accomplishment. Later, I decided to try to teach myself to play the folk harp. I found that my motivation to play has followed a similar pattern. As my efforts sound more and more like music, it is more and more fun. Although it is unlikely that I will ever become a professional-caliber musician, the satisfaction I receive from my gradual improvement is enough to keep me playing amid a schedule that allows very little free time. I am intrinsically motivated to do it. As I improve, I am able to explore new ideas and techniques and hope to become increasingly creative in my efforts.

An intrinsically motivated rat likes to explore the maze

This idea ties closely to Bandura's (1977) construct of self-efficacy. *Self-efficacy* is a person's assessment of confidence in his or her ability to perform a specific task. The more confident (efficacious) people feel, the more likely they are to begin the task and persist in the face of obstacles. As an illustration, I feel confident in my ability to bake bread. I have been successful in baking bread in the past and am willing to experiment with new techniques, ingredients, and recipes. Perhaps someday my exploration will lead to a wonderful new recipe or bread-making invention.

I feel much less sure of my mechanical abilities. I do not willingly take on mechanical projects. If I am forced to tackle a broken toilet, a flopping windshield wiper, or some other small disaster, I deal with it in the quickest, most efficient manner I can. I have no desire to explore, experiment, or be elegant; I just want to get through it. Recall from Chapter 1, Amabile (1989) compared these feelings with those of a rat in a maze. If the rat is motivated by an extrinsic reward (cheese, or a functioning windshield wiper), it takes the straightest line to the reward and gets out of the maze as quickly as possible. If the rat is intrinsically motivated, it enjoys being in the maze. It wants to explore it, take time in it, and see what can be discovered there. Of course, the intrinsically motivated rat is more likely to find an interesting or creative way through the maze. Until I feel more competent in tackling mechanical projects, I am unwilling to spend time in the maze and am unlikely to exhibit any creative activity in that area.

A third hallmark of intrinsic motivation is *self-determination*: the sense that we are working on something for our own reasons, not someone else's (Amabile, 1989). To be intrinsically motivated, I not only need to feel successful, but I also need to feel that I am pursuing the activity because I have chosen to do so. Amabile describes a research study in which college students worked on three-dimensional wooden block puzzles. All the students worked individually. Half the students were allowed to choose which of three puzzles they would do and how to use the allotted 30 minutes. The other half were told which of the puzzles to do and given time allocations. Clearly, the first group had much more self-determination.

After the 30-minute period was over, the subjects were left alone in the laboratory and told to do whatever they wished. The students in the self-determining group spent significantly more time playing with the puzzles during this period than the other group. They also were more likely to say "yes" when asked if they would be willing to return to the lab to work on additional puzzles. The group that had the opportunity to choose how they would pursue the activity was more intrinsically motivated to continue it than the group that had been given specific directions.

Two other important researchers in the area of intrinsic motivation (Ryan & Deci, 2000) write about intrinsic motivation and self-determination but also about goal-directed types of extrinsic direction that reflect the "motivation to learn" described in Chapter 1. Sometimes learners are motivated not by interest or joy in the immediate task (say, practicing an exercise on descriptive language) but because they believe it to be a step toward a goal they value (writing a really scary Halloween story). Both this type of "stick to it to reach the goal" motivation and the playfulness of intrinsic motivation are essential for creativity in schools—and, I would argue, creativity anywhere. It is a rare creative task that does not have moments when it is necessary to push forward through difficult times toward the creative goal. Ryan and Deci tie intrinsic motivation to autonomy and competence but also to *relatedness*—that sense of being part of a community in which one is respected.

These are challenging teaching goals. Help students find classroom activities interesting. Support them in independence and goal setting. Help them progress, and clearly communicate when they are doing so. And, along the way, make them all feel accepted and cared for. It can feel a bit overwhelming.

In traditional classrooms, students are assigned material in which they may or may not have any interest, given tasks at which they may or may not succeed (or which may or may not provide any challenge), and given specific instructions on how to proceed. A situation less conducive to intrinsic motivation can hardly be imagined! Chapter 9 focuses on motivation in the classroom and outlines strategies to maximize the possibility of intrinsic motivation for students.

Thinking About the Classroom

Try a mini-research project on self-determination. Try to identify two activities that should be equally interesting to your students (perhaps two art activities, if you teach elementary school). One week, do the activity with maximum control and direction. Put out extra materials and note how many students choose to use them. The next week, do the second activity. This time, give students more choice about how they pursue the activity (what to do first, which materials to use, and so on). Again put out extra materials and note who uses them. See if you find any differences.

The three components of Amabile's model parallel several of the creativity models discussed earlier. Where Amabile emphasizes domain-relevant skills, Sternberg focuses on aspects of intelligence that allow individuals to gain information and use it in novel ways, and Gruber and Weisberg discuss expertise in content areas. Amabile outlines creativity-relevant processes. Numerous theorists talk about the use of combinations, metaphors, divergent thinking, and problem finding as important strategies supporting creativity. Amabile's focus on task motivation ties to the persistence across time noted by Gruber, Weisberg, Csikszentmihalyi, and others. You can undoubtedly identify similarities to other models. Those familiar with literature on education of the gifted and talented will also see strong parallels with Renzulli's (1978) three-ring conception of giftedness. It is even possible to see ties to Bloom's (1985) phases of talent development. Individuals must develop a love of the discipline, skills in the discipline, and the ability to use them artistically.

Systems Continue and a Model for the Classroom

Of course, theories of creativity continue to evolve. For example, Baer and Kaufman (2005) proposed an Amusement Park Theoretical (APT) model in an attempt to address the dilemma of whether creativity is global or discipline specific. The APT model conceptualizes creativity as having initial requirements common to all creativity, such as intelligence and motivation (like the tickets common to all amusement parks), and then increasingly specific general thematic areas, domains, and microdomains, in which the characteristics and requirements for creativity will vary, like rides in an amusement park.

Glăveanu (2009, 2010) approaches creativity from the perspective of cultural psychology, concerned that systems models to date have not given adequate attention to the cultures in which creativity is embedded. A cultural psychology of creativity views the creative act as emerging from the interaction of an individual and a community, all building on existing cultural norms and artifacts (items or ideas). From this perspective, all creativity stands on what has come before—no creativity could exist without a context. Glăveanu builds on Csikszentmihalyi's model by broadening the concepts of domain and field to include more ordinary interactions than the major contributions on which the model was originally based. Even our smallest creative acts occur within a particular culture, so culture is relevant in creative acts from the latest Nobel Prize–winning research to my culinary inventions based on refrigerator necessity.

Glăveanu (2009) suggests principles on which a cultural psychology of creativity is based, often consistent with the definition of creativity used here. For example:

- Creativity is contextual. Novelty and appropriateness can only be defined in relation to a particular time and place.
- Creativity acts take place in a given culture and build on the resources and ideas there.
- Creativity should not be judged only by outsiders but in relationship to the creator and the society in which the creation takes place. It is socially defined within communities.

But what of the classroom? If, as current thinking proposes, creativity happens in systems within environments, what about the environments in school? Where do they fit? Building on her work with Amabile, Hennessey (2015) proposed a model that takes into account both the individual activities and characteristics essential for creativity and the multiple levels of culture that impact students in classrooms (Figure 4.3).

This model begins with the characteristics an individual brings to a task or problem: three circles representing the domain expertise, creative thinking skills, and motivation found in Amabile's model. But then it continues, adding additional "circles" to the system. First, Hennessey

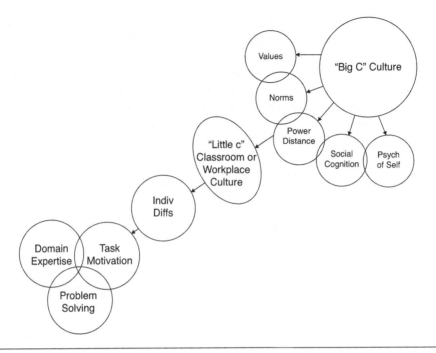

Figure 4.3 Hennessey Classroom System Model

Source: From Hennessey, B. A. (2015). Creative behavior, motivation, environment and culture: The building of a systems model. *The Journal of Creative Behavior,* 49 (3), 194-210. Reprinted with permission.

adds individual differences, particularly as they impact motivation. For example, as we'll discuss in Chapter 9, some people respond differently to rewards than others, based on their individual experiences and values. But considering individual variations isn't enough. In school, creativity occurs within a classroom environment and culture. Similarly, workplace creativity occurs in a culture reflecting a specific environment—a shop, a research team, a division, and so forth. Hennessey calls this the "little c" culture, reflecting the small scale of a classroom or possibly a school, not the level of creativity. Most of us, thinking about our own school experiences, can remember classrooms in which rules and expectations were so rigid that it was highly unlikely a divergent idea would be accepted—or, for that matter, expressed. On the other hand, if we are fortunate, we can recall teachers who welcomed our thinking and celebrated original ideas. Certainly our motivation was affected by both scenarios.

But that is not all. The classroom or workplace culture and the individuals who lead it are shaped by social psychological constructs—the values, norms, and so on that are part of the school or corporate environment. Those, in turn, are shaped by the "big C" Culture in which the setting is embedded, the national or regional culture. So if I am a student, with particular domain and creative thinking skills (which, of course, are also affected by my schooling), my intrinsic task motivation is affected first by my individual characteristics and experiences and next by the culture of the classroom in which I'm working. If, as I recall fondly, I was in Mrs. Fetter's second-grade class, I knew she loved my stories and took every opportunity to encourage them. Mrs. Fetter always seemed to want to hear what students had to say. In her room, it was safe to be curious. Mrs. Fetter's individual values about her classroom were affected by her personal experiences and the district in which she worked. These were shaped by the larger culture in the United States at that particular time. In those post-*Sputnik* days, there was a heavy value placed on developing bright children's thinking, particularly in math and science. How that translated into Mrs. Fetter's love of curiosity and stories, I'm not sure, but I'm glad it did.

Hennessey's (2015) model may be important in beginning to understand the development of creativity in schools globally. Her research demonstrated differences in the impact of extrinsic reward on students in Saudi Arabia and the United States—research results that seemed so clear and consistent in one context became different when the setting was changed. Such understandings will be critical as teachers around the globe work to foster students' creativity in widely varied contexts. Systems models can be complex to analyze but serve to help us view creativity as it occurs—in a particular place and time, with individual human beings.

Whichever theory or outline we study, at least three fronts must be addressed in the development of creativity. We must deal with the necessity that the creative person acquire knowledge and expertise in some content area. It also is important that we be familiar with strategies for manipulating content, finding problems, and looking at content in new ways. Finally, it is essential for us to foster the motivation and positive attitudes that keep individuals committed to a task long enough for exploration, problem finding, and creative thinking to take place. These are the challenges for the remainder of the book.

Creativity, Collaboration, and Organizations

Creative Collaborations

Systems theories invariably entail human interaction. Creative individuals exist within cultures and fields made up of other human beings. Vygotsky (1960) described the origins of creative thinking itself as occurring in social interactions. One of the more interesting questions raised by such theories is whether creativity is—or needs to be—an individual process. John-Steiner (2000), after studying creative collaborations wrote:

> The study of collaboration supports the following claim; productive interdependence is a critical resource for expanding the self throughout the life span. It calls for reconsidering theories that limit development to a progression of stages and to biologically preprogrammed capabilities. The study of partnered endeavors contributes to cultural-historical and feminist theories with their emphases upon the social sources of development.
>
> (p. 191)

John-Steiner proposed that the development and functioning of creative processes can be enhanced through collaborative thinking—thought communities—more powerful than that of a single individual. She cited mathematician Phil David, who described collaboration as "almost as though I have two brains" (p. 190). Playwright Tony Kushner (1997) wrote,

> The fiction that artistic labor happens in isolation, and that artistic accomplishment is exclusively the provenance of individual talents, is politically charged, and, in my case at least, repudiated by the facts. While the primary labor on *Angels* [*in America*] has been mine, more than two dozen people have contributed words, ideas and structure to these plays . . . Had I written these plays without the participation of my collaborators, they would be entirely different—would, in fact, never have come to be.
>
> (pp. 145–146)

The concept of creativity as a collaborative rather than an individual process flies in the face of stereotypical images of lone creators in garrets or laboratories. Yet history is full of creative collaborators, and the labs of the 21st century are inhabited by research teams.

Sawyer (2006) describes group performance, particularly improvisation, as "the creative process made visible" (p. 255). Many other types of creativity result in a visible product—a scientific paper, a song, a piece of art—but result from processes that occur behind closed doors. For actors (or jazz musicians), the doors are open. Much group creativity is necessary in the preparation for any theatrical production, and a vital part of the process happens before the audience. Sawyer suggests that studying the collaborative creativity that functions in improvisational theater or music can bring insights into collaboration in scientific teams or business collaborations. He and coauthor DeZutter (2009) coined the term "distributed creativity" (p. 82) to reflect times when a group of individuals collectively generate a creative product. In fact, Sawyer (2007) states, "Collaboration is the secret to breakthrough creativity" and "the lone genius is a myth; instead it's group genius that generates breakthrough innovation" (pp. ix, 7).

After many years of being married to an actor/director, I have come to a deep appreciation of the phenomenon Sawyer describes. Even in scripted works, creative actors and directors do not simply recite lines created by an author. Fine theatrical productions are the result of creative insights of multiple actors, sudden new moments, chance gestures, and unexpected interactions that suddenly "work"—not to mention the creativity of directors, designers, and costumers. None of this happens in a single individual but in a shared creative space that comprises a production. I've experienced similar creative energies in the professional meetings when ideas fly around the table and the group is able to move in new and creative directions. The creativity in those places is different from that which is feasible for a single human being.

Sawyer (2007) describes collaborations that exist in various configurations, from constrained problem-solving situations in business to the free-wheeling problem finding of improvisational theater. Even a creative endeavor as seemingly solitary as writing can have collaboration as a vital component. Sawyer describes the critical friendship between C. S. Lewis and J.R.R. Tolkien. The two men met at Oxford University. Both had a hobby they kept secret from most other colleagues: writing mythical fiction and poetry. They formed a group with other local scholars, the "Inklings," and met weekly to discuss Nordic myths and read aloud from their works in progress. Before the Inklings, Lewis had written a few poems and Tolkien had written fanciful stories as a private hobby. The Inklings became a sounding board and safe haven in which key themes for their later work emerged. The work developed there resulted in Tolkien's *The Lord of the Rings* and Lewis's *The Chronicles of Narnia*. It is hard to imagine that either of these works would have been created without the input, critiquing, and encouragement of the Inklings. Different types of collaboration require different structures, but each requires a balance of planning, structure, and improvisation in order for creativity to emerge.

John-Steiner (2000) described four different types of collaborative patterns that have characterized creative partnerships. In *distributive collaboration*, relationships are widespread and relatively informal. An individual draws on multiple relationships to enhance creative endeavors. Sometimes partnerships result. *Complementarity collaboration*, such as that of Marie and Pierre Curie, entails a division of labor based on complementary expertise. These relationships entail "mutual appropriation . . . the stretching of human possibilities through the collaborative partner's shared experience that sustains their endeavors" (p. 199). In *family collaborations*, relationships within the creative collaboration are more integrated across areas of expertise and may change significantly across time. They may involve collaborations of literal families or groups of individuals working together in intense relationships. The final type of collaboration, *integrative collaboration*, requires a long period of shared activity. John-Steiner hypothesized that the difficulty in transforming a discipline means that a new mode of thought or art form is more likely to be successful when it is the result of collaborations. It is particularly interesting to think about what factors contribute to the widespread creative relationships that characterize particularly fertile venues of artistic or scientific development such as the Harlem Renaissance. Similarly, as teachers, we must be challenged to think about ways to develop shared creativity in our classrooms in ways perceived as collaborative and not cheating.

A joy of writing books such as this one is that I sometimes hear from the people who read them. One of my most interesting correspondences has been with Welsh storyteller Michael Harvey. Michael sent me some extraordinary poetry created by elementary-age children (see Chapter 7). When I asked him to describe the strategies he used to help children write so beautifully, he explained that whereas older children might have individual responses, with children 7 to 11 years of age, he facilitates collaborative processes toward group products. It is interesting to consider that the collaborative creativity demonstrated by these elementary students may be similar to that used by some highly creative adults and increasingly emphasized in the business world. As we consider ways to structure school experiences to support creativity, it is important to remember that the approach need not always be targeted at individual responses. Facilitated group activities may be particularly appropriate for younger students, as well as for those whose cultural norms are more cooperative than competitive.

And, of course, technology is changing the opportunities for creative collaborations. It is easy to envision scientists sharing data from different parts of the world coming to insights that would not be possible with a single data source. But even in the arts, long-distance collaborations are evolving. One strangely fascinating effort was Rivers Cuomo's "Let's Write a Sawng" sequence on YouTube. Cuomo, a member of the alternative rock group Weezer, posted a series of videos, first asking for suggested song titles, then melodies, harmonies, and so on, resulting in a 15-step collaboration involving tracks recorded all over the country. And if you have never experienced Eric Whitacre's virtual choirs, go immediately to ericwhitacre.com/the-virtual-choir and listen to choirs whose members have never met.

Such opportunities greatly enrich options for student creativity on both local and global scales. Collaborative writing options such as Google Docs and online options for creating bulletin boards, mind maps, and shared projects are evolving each day. Students in your class can collaborate with one another, with students across town, or with students across the globe. Books such as Lindsay and Davis's (2012) *Flattening Classrooms, Engaging Minds* can help you begin.

Organizational Creativity

An interesting elaboration on the concept of collaborative creativity is organizational creativity (Puccio & Cabra, 2010). It is not unusual today to characterize whole organizations as creative or less creative based on both their organizational innovations and the institutional processes that facilitate them. Companies such as Google, Amazon, and Apple are known not just for their products but for their unique corporate cultures. With the rapid pace of global and technological change, companies that are flexible and innovative have a tremendous advantage. So it is not surprising that there is a growing body of research on the attributes of creative organizations.

For example, Puccio, Murdock, and Mance (2007) presented a creative change model, suggesting that innovations come about as a result of interactions among people, the processes they engage in, and the environment in which they work. Not surprisingly, individual creativity is central to organizational creativity. Amabile (1988a) stated, "It is individual creativity that provides the raw material for organizational innovation, and, therefore, individual creativity must be central to the organizational model" (p. 150). But unlike more general models of creativity, organizational creativity is particularly dependent on effective—or even transformational—leadership. The behaviors and policies of leaders in an organization can make the difference between a thriving dynamic business and a stagnant one. It is interesting to think about the parallels in classrooms.

Sternberg's (2015) "Mineralogical" framework for analyzing institutional creative change focuses on universities and describes institutions as ranging from "Rusted Iron" to "Diamonds in the Rough" based on three dimensions.

1. How much desire is there for actual creative change in the institutional culture as a whole?
2. How much desire is there for the appearance of creative change in the culture of the institution?
3. What is the perceived quality or potential creative quality of the institution?

(p. 255)

For me, the dimensions raised interesting questions about the cultures of many educational institutions. I have certainly experienced many schools in which the desire to appear to be changing is much greater than the desire to actually change!

The processes used to facilitate creative thinking in the workplace are very similar to those presented in Chapter 6, which include Creative Problem Solving, Synectics, analogies, and so forth. The characteristics of creative work environments can include both the corporate spaces and culture and the national/regional environments in which they operate. Just as individuals thinking creatively need to be flexible and open to new ideas, so, too, must corporate climates and cultures. Just as creative individuals must be willing to take risks, so, too, must creative organizations. Ekvall and Ryhammar (1999) identified 10 dimensions related to a creative organizational climate:

1. **Challenge** (How challenged and committed are employees to the work?)
2. **Freedom** (How much flexibility do employees have to decide how to do their job?)
3. **Idea time** (Do employees have time to think things through before having to act?)
4. **Dynamism** (Is there a sense of moving forward?)
5. **Idea support** (Are there resources available to support new ideas?)
6. **Trust and openness** (Would Rogers find this a psychologically safe place?)
7. **Playfulness and humor** (Is there room for fun?)
8. **Conflicts** (Is the workplace full of conflict? How are conflicts managed?)
9. **Debates** (Are there lively discussions about the work?)
10. **Risk taking** (Are risks and failures an expected part of innovation?)

Consider how these attributes, associated with successful innovation in business, might look in a classroom. In your classroom, how might conflicts impact students' creative options? Is there time for play? For risk taking? Kim and Hull (2012) investigated the impact of an anticreative environment, with troubling results. One of the interesting dilemmas for leaders of global corporations is determining whether the circumstances that support a creative organizational environment translate from one area of the world to another. Workers from highly individualistic cultures may need different kinds of leadership as compared to more collective societies (see, for example, Hon & Leung, 2011; Mostafa & El-Masry, 2008). And, as Hennessey (2015) points out, as we work to develop creativity in students around the globe, similar questions arise. For a multileveled review of the literature on organizational creativity and innovation, see Anderson, Potočnik, and Zhou (2014).

Patterns, Questions, and Issues

Having examined numerous complicated and conflicting theories, we are left to consider this: Are there any patterns here? Do the theories of creativity give us any firm ground on which to base classroom practice, or are they all so much ivory-tower speculation? Table 4.1 provides an

Table 4.1 Theories of Creativity—Some Possible Clusters

	Theorists	Explanation
Theories Focusing on Individuals		
Psychoanalytic theories	Freud Kubie and Kris Jung Rothenberg Miller	Creativity can be explained largely by unconscious or preconscious processes.
Humanist theories	Maslow Rogers	Creativity is a natural part of healthy development.
Behaviorist theories	Skinner Mednick	Creativity is the result of responses to specific stimuli.
Creativity as cognition	Guilford Perkins Weisberg Ward and associates Investigators in artificial intelligence Investigators in neurobiology	Creativity can be explained using the same processes as other aspects of cognition, possibly in unique combinations.
Theories Beyond Single Individuals		
Sociocultural theories	Vygotsky John-Steiner, Kaufman, and others studying creative collaborations	Creativity is developed in interactions among individuals.
Systems theories	Csikszentmihalyi, Feldman, Sternberg and Lubart, Gruber, Simonton, Gardner, Amabile, Hennessey	Creativity entails complex interactions of elements that may include cognitive processes, personality traits, and interactions with the environment, domain, and field.

overview of the available psychological theories. As I warned at the beginning, it is important to note the lens and scale used in each theory. The most current theories and research fall into the categories of Creativity as Cognition and also into Systems Theories. This is not a conflict but a matter of focus. A neuroscientist studying the brain processes involved in insight studies one individual human at a time—but each of those humans exists in a variety of systems. So we need it all.

As in most fields, I suspect, the more we understand about creativity, the more questions rather than answers we probably have. If nothing else, a review of these chapters should show that anyone who claims to have *the* theory of creativity or boasts that he or she can teach you all you need to know about creativity in four easy steps should be taken with a generous pinch of salt. However, it is easy to find commonalities among the theories that may provide a basis for both research and practice.

Several theories note that creativity demands time, persistence, and motivation. Classroom activities that always are completed in 15 minutes or are so simple that they offer no opportunities for struggle do little to develop commitment to task. Creativity also demands a knowledge base. Most theorists concur that individuals are creative in some subject area and need a base of knowledge and skills to succeed. Certainly, a student who is to be a creative physicist will need a solid background in physics. However, if we teach only the facts about classroom subjects, we have presented only half the picture. Students also will need to be taught the skills of questioning, investigation, and creativity in a variety of disciplines. Our budding physicist needs to learn how to frame a question, how to plan research, and how to represent ideas in a variety of forms. Students of creative writing need to learn about generating story ideas, using metaphors, and writing dialogue. Whether the processes and attributes of creativity are subject specific or cut across disciplines remains to be investigated. Either way, a knowledge base in a particular domain is necessary for high-level creativity in that area.

Some theorists postulate insight as a key element in the creative process. For some (such as Sternberg), insight represents a specific cluster of cognitive processes that can be enhanced through training. For others (such as Feldman), it is the result of nonconscious processes that are difficult to evaluate. Other theorists deny any role for insight—though neurobiological evidence may make that position harder to maintain. However, most theorists do postulate strategies, processes, or habits of mind that make creative ideas more likely. These may include generating analogies, defining problems, or looking for multiple solutions. It is possible that such strategies can be taught and improved. Several theorists stress the importance of purpose, attitude, and the desire to be creative as well as the effects of the outside environment.

Of course, there remains the question of whether any single theory, or even any conception of creativity, can encompass the multiple creative activities of human beings across many cultures.

In the succeeding chapters, I consider classroom ideas and techniques designed to provide the knowledge base, motivation, attitudes, and strategies conducive to creativity in a classroom environment. While the universally agreed-upon theory has not yet evolved, there are enough commonalities, especially among the most current theories, to provide a reasonable place to start.

Think About It

1. Sometimes it can be difficult to keep the various theories of creativity straight. Try making a picture or other graphic organizer to help yourself. You might make one picture for each set of theories (one for psychoanalytic theories, one for humanistic, and so on) or try to incorporate all of them into one complex graphic. Try not simply to list theorists in categories but use images and shapes that will help you remember them.

2. Write (or conduct) an imaginary debate between theorists. Think about which points they might argue about and which they might agree on. If you were to score the debate, who would win?

3. Carefully consider Hennessey's model of the systems influencing creativity in classrooms. Make a diagram indicating key factors and influences you see operating in your own school or home.

4. Think about a time you have been in a group successfully collaborating in a creative process—problem solving, performing, or improvising in any venue from jazz to cooking. What made the group "work"? Consider how that dynamic could be transferred to a classroom. Perhaps you can take a field trip to watch a theatrical rehearsal or a jazz session. Listen carefully for moments of innovation.

5. Examine Ekvall and Ryhammar's dimensions for creative organizational climate. Based on the dimensions, make recommendations for classroom practice. When you get to Chapter 9, compare your list to the recommendations there. If there are things I should change or add, write to me via creativiteach.me.

Try It Tomorrow

1. For 1 week, keep track of the things you say and do to try to motivate students. Think about the kind of motivation you are promoting. Save the list for consideration when you read Chapter 9.

2. Try adding choice to an activity that hasn't typically included choice. This could be something simple, like giving young students a choice of writing implements, or something a bit more complicated. For example, one teacher gave students five homework assignments for the week and told students they needed to choose three. Observe your students' responses to activities in which they feel more control.

3. Teach your students about how producer Brian Grazer's "curiosity conversations" have inspired his movies and brought him joy. You can find details with a quick web search—and even some videos. Challenge students to conduct a curiosity conversation of their own with someone who has done something they find interesting. You might even have them suggest a movie plot inspired by the conversation! Talk about all the factors that influenced the person they chose. Do you see evidence of systems? (Grazer & Fishman, 2015).

Tech Tips

1. Historypin (www.historypin.com) seems like a good Tech Tip for a chapter on systems, because it allows the user insight into the wonderfully complex systems in the history around us. Historypin is an online, user-generated archive of historical photos and personal recollections. Users are able to use the location and date of an image to "pin" it to Google Maps. Where Google Street View is available, users can overlay the historical photograph and compare it with the contemporary location. The site features collections of documents around particular topics, as well as "tours" that take the user through content to tell a story. But best of all, you (or your students) can become part of historypin by adding content about your own location.

2. No collection of Tech Tips focusing on creativity would be complete without some discussion of drawing. The options are always changing. Use your favorite search engine to explore "free drawing programs" or "free paint programs" and see what you find. This online sketchpad (https://sketch.io/sketchpad/) offers a wide range of tools; plus you can save, export, and share your drawing in a variety of formats. Of course, there also are many drawing apps for the iPod, iPad, and smartphones. The Brushes app has even been used to create covers for *The New Yorker*. I've enjoyed using the less-expensive ArtStudio, which can make even my amateur efforts look pretty impressive. And, of course, "There's an app for that!" Phone and tablet apps such as Draw 4 offer a variety of options for students' creativity.

3. If you'd like to try creating objects in three dimensions, try Google Sketchup (www.sketchup.com). Google presents it as a tool for creating images to be uploaded to Google Earth, and that certainly can be one function, but it also could be used to create fantasy buildings and to develop skill in three-dimensional thinking.

4. There's an app for that, too. Augmented reality (AR) apps allow students to create 3-D animated shapes from their colored pages. For example, the Quiver app (particularly Quiver Education) includes fanciful and curriculum-based coloring pages that can be brought to virtual life by holding a phone or tablet over them. While the students' part in this isn't particularly creative, the transformations from two to three dimensions are highly motivating, even to adults, and could serve as the basis for interesting writing assignments.

5. You can also explore 3-D in real life with 3-D design and printing options. One option is the Tinkercad app, which allows students to build designs online by combining shapes, then print them with a 3-D printer.

6. Since we're thinking about creative collaborations, explore some of the websites devoted to supporting international collaborations for schools. One place to begin is the Connect All Schools project; see www.connectallschools.org/node/132295.

5
Creative People

As a child, Angélica started her own business making and selling clay toothpick holders and crocheted glass covers in order to buy her own sewing machine. "I wanted to be a great person, a dress designer . . . What I have thought all my life, since I was a child, is that you only need a little interest and some gumption and you can get ahead" (Wasserspring, 2000, p. 67). Unfortunately, gumption was not a valued attribute for women in Atzompa, Mexico.

Elijah McCoy, son of former slaves who had escaped to Canada, studied mechanical engineering in Scotland. After the Civil War, he moved to the United States and worked for the Michigan Central Railroad. Because the railroad company could not imagine an African American engineer, he was hired to run the boiler and lubricate moving parts of the train. In 1872, Elijah patented his first invention, a self-regulating lubricator. His device was so successful that buyers of steam engines would ask if the lubrication systems were the "Real McCoy."

I hated school. From age 12 or 13 I knew I wanted to be a movie director, and I didn't think that science or math or foreign languages were going to help me turn out the little 8-mm sagas I was making to avoid homework. During class I'd draw a little image on the margin of each page of the history or lit book and flip the pages to make animated cartoons. I did just enough homework to get promoted every year with my friends and not fall to the wrath of my academically minded father. I give my dad credit for single-handedly keeping my math grades high enough so I wouldn't be held back. My other worst subject was phys ed; I failed that three years in a row in high school. I couldn't do a chin-up or a fraction. I can do a chin-up now, but I still can't do a fraction.

(Steven Spielberg, 1985)

Composer Stephen Schwartz said, "If someone says to you that a song isn't working, you wonder, well, maybe they're right. So when do you stand up and believe in yourself? When do you say, 'I don't care what you're saying, I know this is right'—when is it stubbornness or arrogance, and when is it [appropriate] conviction? It's a tricky thing."

(de Giere, 2008, p. 311)

Sarah's mother calls her Sarah Bernhardt for the dramatic emphases she puts on all her expressions. Sarah is never just happy; she is exuberant, dancing from one corner to the next, leaping over furniture, and singing. Sarah is never tired; she is exhausted, panting, and at risk of immediate collapse. When Sarah is angry, the family moves back. Sarah's teacher finds her a constant challenge. When Sarah is bored (which happens often), everyone knows it. And yet she can always be counted on to put a new spin on a class discussion or come up with a new amusement on a rainy day. Having Sarah in class makes life interesting.

José makes his teacher's life easy. She always knows where to find him—in the library or science room, usually buried in a book. Always interested in the latest discoveries, he reads several science magazines cover to cover each month. He doesn't say much in class; in fact, he doesn't say much at all. The rest of the students think José is a little odd, but they generally accept him. They joke about the "mad scientist" and speculate as to what he might be building in the basement. Occasionally his teachers wonder, too.

Words such as "artist," "inventor," and "musician" bring to mind images that often are larger than life. We may picture a starving painter shivering in rags in a windy garret, a wild-eyed Dr. Jekyll amid bubbling beakers, a rock star surrounded by screaming fans, or a violinist playing for coins on a street corner. It is difficult to tell which of these images are grounded in reality, which are products of Hollywood, and which may be helpful in identifying and nurturing students' creative potential. Are all highly creative people alike? Certainly creative individuals like Elijah McCoy, Angélica Vásquez, and Stephen Schwartz led vastly different lives. Students as diverse as Steven Spielberg, Sarah, and José can lead us to question what a creative student really looks like. In this chapter, I examine characteristics that have been associated with highly creative persons, imagine how they might be manifested in children, and discuss how they might be supported in classrooms.

Many kinds of personal characteristics may be important in the development of creative potential. Creative individuals may be distinguished by the ways they think; by their values, temperament, and motivation; and by the things that happen during their lives. It is important to note that these patterns and the relationships among them are enormously complex. Just as there is no simple theory of creativity, there is no generic creative person. The characteristics of creative individuals vary among people and across disciplines. A creative composer has strengths, needs, and values different from those of a creative physicist, and no two creative physicists are exactly alike. Despite these variations, there are enough patterns to suggest some commonalities worth exploring.

In examining these commonalities, one more caveat is in order. Identifying traits in highly creative adults does not guarantee that similar traits are present in creative children or children who may grow into creative adults. At the end of the chapter, I look at some research on young people who have been identified as creative and show how it dovetails with research on creative adults. It does present some promising beginnings. We must, however, admit that our knowledge of creativity as manifested in children is limited. Having done so, we use the research available as well as we can. Because we lack definitive answers, our most practical course of action is to consider identifying and supporting positive characteristics associated with creativity wherever we find them. Identifying them is our goal for this chapter.

Characteristics Associated With Creativity

Creativity and Intelligence

In Chapter 3, the most accurate description of the relationship between creativity and intelligence was designated "it depends." Even those who hypothesize that creativity is the product of the same basic cognitive processes as other thoughts recognize that the production of novel ideas is distinct from the production of accurate but unoriginal ideas. Yet experience and common sense seem to indicate a relationship between the two. We probably would be surprised to see an outstanding creative contribution coming from a person of severely limited intelligence. Notwithstanding the extraordinary accomplishments of some individuals with savant syndrome, the vast majority of inventions, scientific breakthroughs, great works of literature, and artistic innovations are made by intelligent people. How intelligence facilitates creativity has been the subject of study and debate for decades (Kim, Cramond, & VanTassel-Baska, 2010; Plucker & Esping, 2015).

In the 1950s, MacKinnon (1978) identified a minimal relationship between creativity and intelligence in creative architects, writers, and scientists. He found a low, positive relationship between intelligence and creativity in mathematicians. These findings do not mean that the architects and writers were not intelligent (they were) but that the most intelligent subjects were not necessarily the most creative. It was difficult or impossible to predict creativity on the basis of their IQ scores. Similar early research by Barron (1969) and Roe (1952) postulated a *threshold effect*, a minimum IQ necessary for major creative contributions. Beyond that level (perhaps IQ 120), other factors were seen as more important than intelligence in predicting creativity. If, as seems likely, the majority of MacKinnon's architects had IQs at or above the threshold level, little relationship would be expected.

The idea of a threshold relationship between creativity and intelligence is still common in the literature today. Although the majority of today's theorists tie intelligence to high-level creativity, it is not clear whether the threshold of intelligence is necessary or consistent. There are a number of both mathematical and definitional complications to the question. First, any studies attempting to compare the relationship between intelligence and creativity above and below the threshold level will face a statistical restriction-of-range problem. Because the range of IQs above 120 is much smaller than that below it, it will be more difficult to find a relationship there, even if one exists. Second, it is important to check definitions.

It is very difficult to draw conclusions from studies all purporting to examine creativity and intelligence but using completely different measures to do so. We know that the relationships between intelligence, as measured by any number of tests, and creativity, as measured by tests of divergent thinking or the number of remote word associations or the number of patents listed, are likely to differ. For example, Batey and Furnham (2006) suggest that the relationship between creativity and intelligence, when both are measured by paper-and-pencil tests, is likely to be stronger than when gauging creativity as real-world accomplishments. They suggest that divergent-thinking tests require neural efficiency for cognitive speed, retrieval from memory, and so forth, all of which are associated with intelligence. The skills and attitudes for authentic creative accomplishments are much more complex. And, of course, definitions of intelligence continue to expand (see Sternberg & Kaufman, 2011).

A number of researchers have found overall relationships between creativity and intelligence without evidence of a threshold effect (Cho, Nijenhuis, Vianen, Kim, & Lee, 2010; Preckel, Holling, & Wiese, 2006; Sligh, Conners, & Roskos-Ewoldsen, 2005). However, Jung et al. (2009) examined brain chemistry associated with cognitive ability and creative tasks and found patterns suggestive of a threshold effect. Jauk and colleagues found multiple threshold levels that varied depending on the definition of creativity used. A rigorous definition, using traditional creativity tests, was associated with a higher threshold. On the other hand, no threshold was found for real-life creative activities (Jauk, Benedek, Dunst, & Neubauer, 2013).

In 2005, Kim used meta-analysis to try to bring clarity to the matter. Meta-analysis is a technique that allows a researcher to gather a large number of studies on a particular question and then statistically "merge" all the data into one summary conclusion. Kim identified 21 studies that specified a relationship between creativity and intelligence, with a total sample of 45,880 people. Her analysis found little relationship between IQ scores and creativity test scores and no support for the threshold theory. Of course, all of the relationships described in Kim's analysis were, of necessity, based on creativity tests rather than measures of real-world creativity. It is possible that if the mathematics of meta-analysis allowed for other types of measures, different conclusions could emerge.

Park, Lubinski, and Benbow (2007) investigated just that—could they predict real-world accomplishments based on a test score? In a 25-year follow-up of highly able young people, they found that even when the entire sample was in the top 1% ability level, they still could predict real-world accomplishments based on SAT tests taken at age 12. Astonishing as that sounds, it still doesn't answer the creativity/intelligence question, as not all the accomplishments (for example, earning a law degree) necessarily required creativity. In another meta-analysis, Kim (2008) found that divergent thinking, particularly on the Torrance Tests of Creative thinking, was more likely to predict creative accomplishments than was IQ.

Other research investigates specific cognitive processes of intelligence and creativity, seeking to understand how they are related. Beaty and Silvia (2012), looking at how creative responses change over (short-term) time, found that they varied with intelligence. For years, I told my young students, "Your first idea is practically never your best idea." Overall, Beaty and Silvia found that to be true—as individuals progressed through a divergent-thinking task, their responses became more creative. But highly intelligent people progressed differently—they were more likely to generate creative ideas continuously through the task. Their study is an example of research suggesting that creativity is controlled, at least in part, by some of the same basic executive processes that constitute intelligence. That is, creativity and intelligence are related because they use many of the same cognitive "ingredients."

For example, both intelligence and creativity require monitoring and updating incoming information and inhibiting irrelevant responses, but in different combinations (Benedek, Jauk, Sommer, Arendasy, & Neubauer, 2014). Lee and Therriault (2013) suggested a model in which working memory predicts (is necessary for) intelligence, intelligence predicts associative fluency (naming many letters or animals quickly), which then predicts both divergent and convergent thinking. But, of course, saying one thing predicts another is not the same as establishing cause or saying they are the same.

Silvia and Beaty (2012) found people with higher intelligence generated more creative metaphors. But that was not the only difference. People who took a bit longer with the task came up with more creative metaphors than those who responded quickly. People whose personalities measured high in openness took more time and developed more clever metaphors. It feels in some ways like complex recipes using pantry staples. If I have flour in my kitchen, I can make a lot of different things. If I also have yeast, my options are greatly expanded. Similarly, it seems that our memory and cognitive processes can be used to do both analytic and creative things—with the addition of the right motivation and personality spices!

Because there are no universally agreed-on measures for either creativity or intelligence, the relationship between the two constructs cannot be cleanly defined, at least for now. There does seem to be a relationship, however, at least for adult-level creativity. A high level of adult creative accomplishment seems to be accompanied by at least high-average intelligence. It is possible that there is a minimum threshold of intelligence that makes this level of creativity possible. It is also possible that much creativity in our modern world requires study and/or formal education—and that an apparent IQ threshold may be more related to the need for education than to creativity itself. The relationship between IQ and creativity is less clear in children (Kim, 2005; Welter, Jaarsveld, van Leeuwen, & Lachmann, 2016), and it is important not to underestimate the creative potential of students with lower IQ scores. It appears that factors outside those measured by most IQ tests (e.g., divergent thinking and motivation) affect both school achievement and creativity.

Being alert to those factors may help us identify and nurture students whose abilities may not be fully assessed by traditional IQ testing.

The IPAR Studies: In Search of Human Effectiveness

The most extensive studies investigating the characteristics of creative individuals were conducted at the University of California at Berkeley from the 1950s to the 1970s. At the Institute of Personality Assessment and Research (IPAR), under the direction of Donald MacKinnon, psychologists examined effective functioning in a variety of fields, including architecture, creative writing, mathematics, industrial research, physical science, and engineering. Although MacKinnon's work with creative architects probably is the most well known, other investigations followed similar patterns.

The full results of the IPAR studies are much too complex to be summarized here. However, they have provided the basis for much of the writing on characteristics of creative people. Although groups varied by field (e.g., architects differed from writers or mathematicians), there were commonalities. MacKinnon (1978) listed seven of the "most salient characteristics of all the creative groups we have studied" (p. 123). Of course, the list reflects characteristics of highly successful creative professionals; how they relate to other kinds of creativity requires more investigation. According to MacKinnon, creative people are:

- Intelligent
- Original
- Independent
- Open to experience
- Intuitive
- Holders of theoretical and aesthetic interests
- Possessed of a sense of destiny and purpose

Thinking About the Classroom

Begin collecting books and stories about individuals who display the characteristics associated with creativity. Share them with your students. Consider the kinds of models presented in your literature, science, or social studies curricula. Would students be able to tell from them that you value flexibility, originality, or persistence? Will they see examples of collaborative creativity as well as independence?

Characteristics of Creativity and "Messy Minds"

In the years since the IPAR studies, characteristics associated with creative individuals have not changed dramatically, but our view of how those characteristics function has become more complex. Researchers have compiled a great many lists of characteristics associated with creative individuals, each slightly different (Feist, 2010; Runco, 2010b; Russ & Fiorelli, 2010; Tardif & Sternberg, 1988). But systems models point out that individual characteristics are not sufficient to explain creative activities. Individuals, however their personal characteristics and experiences might support creativity, still must function in a given domain in a particular time and place. As we puzzle as to whether creativity is general or domain specific, we must wonder if the characteristics of creative playwrights are likely to be identical to those of creative physicists. Abuhamdeh and Csikszentmihalyi (2004) take the next logical step, pointing out that the personal characteristics necessary for creativity may well vary across both time and discipline. In describing personal characteristics of artists, they state,

> [W]e propose that the notion of the "artistic personality" is more myth than fact. Although it describes some of the traits that distinguish aspiring artists at certain times under certain conditions, these traits are in no sense required to create valuable art at all time, in all places. . . . because the social and cultural constraints on the artistic process vary significantly across time and place, the nature of the artistic personality will vary accordingly.
>
> (p. 32)

For example, a painter who works in a time when the predominant style is realistic and precise may well need different characteristics than one who works in a time when success requires abstract improvisation and raw emotion. This may hold true in other disciplines as well. Characteristics of jazz musicians may differ from those of musicians in other genres (Benedek, Borovnjak, Neubauer, & Kruse-Weber, 2014). A specific characteristic traditionally associated with creativity may be found to greater and lesser degrees not just in different domains but also in time periods. Still, studying characteristics associated with creative individuals in a variety of situations gives us a place to begin when trying to identify and support creative behaviors in young people.

Recall that Kaufman and Gregoire (2015) described creative people as having "messy minds." Just as the neurobiology of creativity is complicated, so are the characteristics and behaviors associated with creative individuals. Rather than focusing on who creative people are, Kaufman and Gregoire examined what creative people do—differently, or perhaps more frequently than others. As you consider their list, look for evidence of paradox, what Kaufman has called the messiness of the creative minds.

Creative People Engage in Imaginative Play I have to admit, reading this made me smile, because for me, there are few things I enjoy more than letting my imagination roam free. But there is more to this activity than my joy in creating stories of fantastical islands. Many eminent creators engaged in imaginative play as children, but perhaps more importantly, creative artists, entrepreneurs, scientists, approach their work with a playfulness that allows creative connections to take play—the variation in constraints and flexibility described by Koustaal and Binks (2015). Playfulness with ideas is an essential part of both finding and solving problems (see Chapter 6).

Unfortunately, our culture tends to view play as frivolous. The phrase "child's play" is not considered a compliment. Children's free playtime has been in steady decline since 1955 (Gray, 2013). And this decline is reflected in schools. When I started teaching in 1972, my first grade classroom contained plenty of blocks, dress-up clothes, and other play materials (and, yes, they learned to read and add anyway!). Today, you'd be hard pressed to find such activities in many kindergartens. It is a significant—and damaging—loss. As Kaufman and Gregoire state, "Our widespread play deficit is an important reason to carve out spaces in which play is not only tolerated but *celebrated* [italics original]" (p. 11). A more complete discussion of the issues around play, creativity, and development is found later in this chapter, in the discussion of creative children.

Thinking About the Classroom

Teach your students the characteristics associated with creativity. Create a bulletin board on which you collect examples of these characteristics in the news, stories, or cartoons.

Creative People Have Passion for Their Activities Creative people have passion for their activities, often beginning early in life. Many creative people can remember the moment they realized "This is going to be my life. This is the thing I love." In Torrance's (1983) longitudinal studies, he found that students who fell in love with something early were more likely to be creative as adults—in fact, early dreams were a better predictor of adult creative achievement than academic achievement. Of course, creative people can have varied interests. Root-Bernstein and colleagues have studied eminent scientists and found that, in addition to their evident passion for science, they frequently had serious avocations in arts and/or crafts (Root-Bernstein, 2015; Root-Bernstein et al., 2008).

Of course, helping young people fall in love with a discipline is more complicated than simply saying, "Follow your passion." First, young people cannot fall in love with something to which they've never been exposed. So if we overemphasize students' pursuing today's interests without developing tomorrow's, students (especially students with fewer family resources) lose out. Students need a varied intellectual diet to find their tastes. And yet, in order to understand working with passion, they need some time to explore the things that bring them maximum joy today. It is also helpful to remember Vallerand et al.'s (2007) distinction between harmonious and obsessive passions. A harmonious passion is joyful and brings meaning to life. It helps people feel fully themselves. In contrast, obsessive passions bring stress and anxiety, with constant striving to improve because of external pressures, not inner motivation. Helping students find healthy passions is tied to intrinsic motivation (see Chapter 9) and involves focusing on learning and growth rather than impressing others.

Such motivation can be particularly valuable when the going gets tough. Every creative endeavor has times when ideas are fine, but what is needed is hard work. Passion—along with grit, tenacity, and optimism—can help pull us through. In fact, passion can drive persistence, which may account for *persistence or task commitment* often appearing on lists of characteristics associated with creativity. Willingness to continue in the face of obstacles, to maintain motivation without immediate reward, and to stay focused on a task for long periods are essential to successful creative efforts. José, described at the beginning of the chapter, showed enormous drive and commitment to his interest in science. And consider the enormous task commitment required of the mathematicians in the movie *Hidden Figures*. Without it, the problem solving required for space travel never could have been successful. If our students are to be creative in real-world situations, they must be able to maintain motivation and concentration long enough for it to happen.

We have a special obligation to dispel the common notion that really creative or really smart people do not have to work hard or that if you are good enough, ideas will come quickly and easily. In my own early research on problem finding in creative writing (Starko, 1989), I found that even among high school students, the most able writers consciously manipulated ideas and experiences to generate writing projects. Less able writers thought that if they just waited, ideas would "pop out"—if nothing popped, they had no ideas. They did not understand that they could improve their ideas through their own efforts.

It is important to provide models of struggle, failure, and continued efforts. If students equate a single failure with total failure, they are unlikely to continue creative or other efforts. Stories of creative individuals can be helpful models. If students learn about the number of filaments Edison tried before finding a successful material for the light bulb or the scorn heaped on Amelia Bloomer for wearing split skirts, or "bloomers," they may find courage for their own struggles. (In fact, it is likely you may be familiar with Ms. Bloomer only in conjunction with her infamous split skirts. She also was a journalist, whose paper *The Lily* was said to be the first owned and operated solely by women [Hanaford, 1882b].) Be alert to this need when exposing young children to biographies. Sometimes biographies written for children seem more concerned with modeling good behavior than portraying truth. They may omit realistic struggles and substitute simplistic stories of bright, kind children who grew up to be successful adults. Such stories not only are trivial, but they also can be damaging. If young children believe that achievement is supposed to come easily, the buffetings of real life will be an unwelcome surprise. And there may be added benefits. One study found that physics students who were exposed to the scientists' struggles (rather than solely stories of scientists' achievements) showed increased interest in science and more success learning physics content (Hong & Lin-Siegler, 2012).

Telling stories of your own efforts, struggles, and successes also can project a powerful model. One of my colleagues brought all the drafts of her master's thesis to school so her students could see how many times it was written and rewritten before it was completed. I have occasionally shared with young people my beginning efforts to learn a new instrument. I believe those struggling, flawed performances, although not providing a great model of musicianship, showed both the willingness to take risks and the necessary continuation of less-than-perfect efforts on the way to success.

Finally, it is important to recognize that creative individuals almost always persist and struggle over self-selected tasks, not over those assigned by others. When we look for evidence of passion, persistence, and drive in our students, we may not always find it in the areas we select. The fact that a student does not always complete math assignments or struggles to understand Chinese grammar is not necessarily an indication of potential creative failure. Although we certainly want to assist students in developing the self-discipline to complete less preferred tasks, we may look for evidence of their perseverance elsewhere. We may find it in the kindergarten student who does not want to stop building his imaginary village just because free time is over or in a high school student who wants to spend all her time in the robotics lab but frequently skips history. Recognizing such behaviors as inappropriate or inconvenient in school should not keep us from recognizing them as clues to positive, task-focused motivation.

Creative People Daydream They let their minds wander into the important spaces of the brain's default network. Daydreaming allows time and space for incubation and new connections, whether while staring into space, taking a walk, enjoying a hot shower, or even getting ready for a nap. This poses some interesting challenges in school. So much of our time is spent helping students learn to focus—must we also help them learn to unfocus on occasion? It seems so if we want them to learn all they should and open spaces for creative thinking.

Recall from Chapter 3, the recommendations for mind wandering and reflection suggested as pathways to the default network. If we want students to access those pathways in school, we need to schedule time for pausing, imagining, and thinking about the story in the content we are teaching. Students need to reflect on the content, not just absorb it.

It is also important to recognize that students who spend "unscheduled" time daydreaming are not necessarily wasting time, even if they are not engaged in the task at hand. The message we want to send such students is their minds can do many wonderful things. Sometimes they focus on a particular task or goal, and sometimes they wander in ways that help us think more deeply and imagine new things. Both kinds of brainwork are good. The key is to be mindful of which type of thinking we need at any given moment. Then, as the teacher, make sure you make space for both to occur.

Creative People Take Time for Solitude Here, too, we can tap into the functions of the brain's default network—what Kaufman and Gregoire (2015) call the creativity network.

[T]he pace of modern life leaves little time for seemingly unproductive activity as we face increasing distractions and demands for our attention. The mind must have the space to settle down if it is to come up with the insights that make for original creative work. When we're engaged in solitary reflection, the brain is able to process information, crystallize memories, make connections, reestablish a sense of identity and construct a sense of self, make meaning from our experiences and even guide moral judgment.

(p. 52)

Metaphorically, our brains need space to breathe, and solitude can bring that. It is interesting to think about how we might bring some quiet "alone" time in a group of 25 or more young people.

The idea that solitude is positive can be hard for parents and teachers who worry about children who prefer time alone. We worry about how they'll learn to get along with others or whether they might be secretly lonely. Of course it is important to be sensitive to young people's social needs and skills, but it is also true that creative endeavors often require quiet time away just to think. Just because technology gives us the ability to communicate 24–7 doesn't mean it is a good idea. While some creative children may have active social lives, others are more introverted and find socializing stressful. José may fit into that pattern. The pursuit of creative activities, for many, demands a great deal of alone time. It is important to distinguish between students who are alone because they are unhappy or rejected and students who are alone by choice. Although we certainly want all students to be able to communicate with others and get along socially, it truly is not necessary that every child or adult be a social butterfly. A quiet student who spends his or her time with one or two friends and a paintbrush (or a cello or a computer) may be perfectly happy and well adjusted. Well-meaning attempts to force students to participate in activities they do not enjoy so they will become one of the group may be counterproductive. At times, helping a student find another painter (or musician or web designer) with whom he or she can share the passion may be more appropriate. At other times, the best course of action may be to let the student paint.

Creative People Are Intuitive and Work Through Insight Since ancient times, creative people have described their ideas as mystical experiences, seeming to come from somewhere outside themselves. Now, of course, we know something of the brain mechanisms by which this occurs, but in some ways the creative unconscious is as mysterious as the Muses—even with the benefit of fMRI machines. Intuition is a form of thinking taking place largely out of conscious awareness. It is especially important in the generative part of the creative process, when divergent ideas and connections are explored. Once those ideas come into our consciousness, our more focused and analytical conscious thinking can be used to evaluate ideas and make plans to move forward. As described in Chapter 2, the "aha!" experience of insight can bring things together in new and unexpected ways.

The willingness to work through insight and (at least sometimes) go beyond careful analysis is tied to another characteristic linked to creativity, the ability to *escape entrenchment*. Individuals who can escape entrenched thinking are able to get out of the ruts of their everyday ideas and consider things in new ways. If creative individuals find themselves repeating predictable thought patterns, they look for a new angle, a new perspective, or a break in the pattern.

Children who are adept at this type of thinking may become bored or impatient with routines, repetitious assignments, or practice activities. Finding a balance between a secure and efficient classroom routine and the creative individual's preference for novelty can be difficult. Although practice can be important, as teachers, we certainly must be alert for assignments that are repetitious simply because we cannot think of anything else to do. A change from the daily journal entry or weekly vocabulary definitions not only will relieve boredom but also will allow students to understand that patterns can be broken. Students, too, can help to break the mold of entrenchment. If they are asked, "What is a new way we could practice French vocabulary, share information about Iowa, or line up for lunch?" they may just find one!

Creative People Are Open to Experience The notion that creative people are open to experience has been in the literature since the 1950s, but, like many aspects of creativity, our understanding of "openness" is becoming increasingly complex. Openness to experience (sometimes labeled Openness/Intellect) is one of the "Big Five," a model used to describe major aspects of personality. Individuals who are open to experience are said to be curious, imaginative, artistic, excitable, unconventional, and have wide interests. They consistently seek to understand the world around them and their own inner worlds of ideas. It is possible that such openness begins in early in life. In one study, "stimulation seeking" exploratory behavior at age 3 was associated with both greater intelligence and academic achievement at age 11 (Raine, Reynolds, Venables, & Mednick, 2002).

Kaufman and Gregoire (2015) describe Kaufman's dissertation research, in which he suggested there are at least three types of engagement that make up openness to experience: intellectual engagement, affective engagement, and aesthetic engagement. It is interesting to think about how different profiles of engagement could be associated with creativity in different domains. I think of a researcher friend who appreciates the aesthetics in the world around him but is primarily driven by intellectual curiosity. On the other hand, an artist friend's primary driving force is aesthetic, even while she is intensely curious. They are both open to experience, but different kinds of experience drive their passions. Whatever its type, openness to experience is very powerful. Kaufman and colleagues have found that openness to experience can be a better predictor of creative accomplishment than divergent thinking, IQ, or other personality traits.

Recently Kaufman et al. (2016) examined the two aspects of the Big Five characteristic of Openness/Intellect. Both aspects reflect openness to experience, but Openness is more associated with perception, emotion, and aesthetics, while Intellect reflects curiosity about abstract ideas. They found that creativity in the arts was more linked with Openness and creativity in the sciences with Intellect. Woo et al. (2014) also studied the structure of openness, developing a six-factor model. They found cross-cultural differences in the patterns of openness found between U.S. and Chinese samples, raising interesting questions about the breadth and variety in this important variable.

Openness to experience can provide creative individuals with constant sources of questions, ideas, and problems. This includes receptiveness to the complex input of all the senses. I once visited a beautiful formal garden on an island in Maine. As I walked amid the profusion of colored flowers, I noticed a woman painting at one end of the garden. Not wishing to disturb her, I avoided that area until I noticed her taking a break from her work. As I walked toward her, she exclaimed, "Can you believe all the greens here?" I looked at her canvas and realized that she was painting not the gardens but the woods surrounding them, all in various shades of green. Up to this point I had not noticed the greens at all. As I looked through her perspective, they were breathtaking. The subtle differences in tone and hue that had escaped me were the inspiration for her creative work. I have always been grateful to that woman. Greens have never been the same to me. However, without her observation of that diversity, neither I nor any of those who subsequently viewed her painting could have had that experience.

Openness to experience also is characterized by the willingness to try something new and different: octopus at an Italian restaurant, an exhibit of Japanese paper folding, a concert of Elizabethan (or contemporary) music, or lessons in tap dancing. Children who become entranced looking at the rocks in the driveway, middle school students who are willing to listen to opera with open ears and open minds, and high school students who, as one of my friends did, take their dates to a medical school film festival of exotic operations all are exhibiting a willingness to be open to the experiences around them.

Adults can help develop this capacity in young people. Pianist Jeannette Haien describes her father's influence on her openness and expectation in experiencing the world.

> One of my first memories is of my father calling excitedly to say, "Look." He was looking up at the sky. I couldn't see what I had to look at. Then he said, "Listen," and I heard this peculiar sort of sound, very distant. He kept saying, "Look higher, look higher," and I did. Then I saw my first skein of geese and heard their call. He took my hand and said to me, "Those are the whales of the sky." [Note the metaphoric language!] I have never forgotten it. And I never look up at a sky without the expectation of some extraordinary thing coming—airplane, owls at night. I'm a great looker up to the sky.
>
> (Moyers, 1990, p. 53)

I believe we must cultivate this openness to experience in ourselves before we can share it with young people. Unless we are able to experience the wonder, we cannot convey it. I know of no way to do this except by committing ourselves to look more closely and listen more deeply to the things that surround us. As I have learned to distinguish the songs of birds, the clamor in my yard is transformed from interesting noise to a series of conversations. As I have watched theatrical lighting more closely, I have come to appreciate and notice subtle changes I once ignored. If you are able to point out to students the marvels of the patterns on the snake's back, the subtle differences in descriptive language between authors, the elegance of an equation, or the fantastic patterns of crystals, these experiences may allow them to open their own eyes. If we do not see the beauty in the things we teach, how will our students see it? This type of openness is strongly related to curiosity, discussed later in the chapter.

Openness to experience also means openness to inner emotional experiences. Children who weep at the death of Charlotte the spider in *Charlotte's Web* or become irate at the treatment of homeless people are willing to experience emotions even when they are difficult. Dramatic Sarah, described earlier, experienced and expressed a wide range of emotions. It is possible that this type of openness ties to the emotional overexcitability described by Dabrowksi as a characteristic of highly creative individuals (Piechowski & Cunningham, 1985). Openness to experience can sometimes be painful and confusing. Opening one's mind to experiences also necessitates opening it to confusion and disorder. Especially in adolescence, creative individuals may be troubled by uncertainty as to life's goals or purpose, crises in religious beliefs, conflicts in personal or social roles, and so on. Although all young people experience such difficulties to some degree, the turmoil can be particularly painful to those who acknowledge and examine it rather than ignore it or wait for it to go away. Creative adolescents have enormous need for empathetic understanding that conveys confidence in their ability to overcome the anxiety while not belittling the intensity of its effects or the reality of its causes.

Of course, the need for such counsel and understanding is not limited to adolescents. Young children, too, can exhibit unusual openness to experience. A friend's daughter returned from a typical first-grade field trip to a farm determined to become a vegetarian. Whereas the other children had enjoyed seeing and feeding the animals, she was absorbed in thinking about why the animals were being raised. Her parents' respect for her values and assistance in planning her meals (she was permitted to omit meat as long as she consumed sufficient protein) allowed her to deal with the experience in a positive way. It should also be noted that she wrote a note of protest to one of the fast-food companies complaining that there were no children's meals for vegetarian children. She could order a salad, but she could never get a toy!

It is interesting to consider whether behavior that can sometimes be labeled "distractible" might also be labeled "open." In fact, decreased latent inhibition, that is, failing to screen out stimuli that had previously been irrelevant, can be associated with creative achievement, particularly in individuals with high IQs (Carson, Peterson, & Higgins, 2003). This makes sense to me. Something that was irrelevant in one situation can be exactly the idea needed in a new one, so a tendency to take in greater amounts of information—irrelevant or not—can be useful in problem solving. On the other hand, it can make focus more challenging. This may be one reason there can be issues distinguishing highly creative behaviors from ADHD, as described later in this chapter.

A related characteristic is *tolerance for ambiguity*, what Sternberg (1988b) once called a "sine qua non" of creativity. Clearly, one cannot be open to experience without being tolerant of ambiguity, for life is practically always confusing, contradictory, and ambiguous. If an individual cannot tolerate loose ends, unanswered questions, or gray areas where black and white would be easier, that person is left to a diet of TV situation comedies or rigid judgments.

The creative process itself also demands tolerance for ambiguity. Despite Mozart's claims, creative solutions rarely spring forth full blown. More often, they emerge over a period that includes moments of insight and times of struggle, persistence, and confusion. To survive this process, the creative individual must be able to live with half-formed ideas, possible solutions, and images that might be good but could be better.

Children who are able to tolerate ambiguity are willing to keep trying and experimenting although they are not sure if they are right. My experience in schools is that we do little to tolerate, much less encourage, ambiguity. Generally, school tasks deal with correct answers and incorrect answers, but nothing in between. Unfortunately, school probably is the only place on earth where answers are so clear-cut. I cannot think of any other aspect of my life that has an answer key!

If we are to help students tolerate ambiguity, there must be questions, assignments, and problems in school that do not have one best answer. There must be discussions in which there is room for genuine difference of opinion. Dillon (1988) said that the best discussion questions are the ones the teacher would like to discuss because he or she genuinely does not know the answer. Although sometimes such discussions may lead to consensus, it is important to understand that sometimes the real answer is "We don't know." Our best ideas today may not be good enough or may not be our best ideas next week. As teachers, we should not feel compelled to tie everything up in a neat package. Neat packages are easy to carry, but they do not make us think about the contents.

Creative people deal well with novelty

Creative People Are Mindful They observe. They pay attention. They are aware of the world around them, and of their own thought. This characteristic seems highly tied to openness. There is an interesting tension between mindful attention and mind wandering, and both are essential parts of the creative experience. Langer (2005) describes mindfulness as "an effortless, simple process that consists of drawing novel distinctions, that is, noticing new things" (p. 5). And yet, while Langer may view it as effortless, mindfulness requires giving up our fixed ways of looking at the world and being open to novelty and possibility. It requires recognizing when our thinking is on "automatic pilot" or when we are holding tight to assumptions or ideas. It means embracing uncertainty and ambiguity. Langer's version of mindfulness is not meditative but fully thoughtful. In particular, mindful learning requires questioning, examining possibilities, and considering alternatives to the content being learned. Only then can it be used flexibly. Langer's (2000) research suggests that content that is learned mindfully, as opposed to rote learning of absolutes, is more readily remembered and used—particularly in new circumstances.

Of course mindfulness can also have a more meditative meaning, and Kaufman and Gregoire (2015) recognize that as well. It would make sense that individuals who may be more prone to distraction might sometimes benefit from mindfulness meditation. But how they benefit may vary depending on the type of meditation involved. Traditional meditation is very focused, often on breathing. On the other hand, open-monitoring meditation asks participants to focus on their changing thoughts, moment to moment, remaining open to what may emerge. This form of structured mind wandering was more associated with improved divergent thinking, while traditional focused meditation was associated with more convergent thinking (Colzato, Ozturk, & Hommel, 2012).

Creative People Are Sensitive Creative individuals can be exceptionally affected by stimuli of all types—sights, sounds, and even emotions. This can be a paradox in itself. The same sensitivity that allows them to appreciate small beauties in the world around them can also make the chaos of everyday life extraordinarily difficult. Sensitive people see patterns, beauty, drama, and excitement where others might not. Sensitive children are more easily overstimulated and overwhelmed, particularly by others' moods and actions. This is not moodiness; it has a neurological basis. Highly sensitive people appear to process information differently, with more activation in areas of the brain relevant to the task at hand (Jagiellowicz et al., 2011). Again, creativity presents us with "messiness." The same openness that allows for creative flexibility and insight can pose particular challenges for individuals who are more easily overwhelmed by the sights and emotions that surround them.

Creative People Can Turn Adversity Into Advantage It is inevitable that major creative endeavors will be full of roadblocks, challenges, and discouragement. There is no question that creative people require persistence and often courage to overcome obstacles. But it is also the case that an exceptional number of highly creative people seem to have experienced exceptional trials and losses. Ritter et al. (2012) investigated the reasons this may be so. They found that, at least in virtual reality, an experience that is "diversifying," that is, outside expected reality, increased flexible thinking more than expected experiences.

Fortunately for all of us, creativity does not require trauma, but it can be a vehicle through which individuals can succeed against long odds. Perhaps losses—of people, health, home, jobs, and so on—force us to look at the world with new eyes—nothing is the same, so we look at everything differently. Clearly, no one would suggest supporting trauma as a way to strengthen students' creativity. But we can offer creative opportunities to all young people, and especially those dealing with challenging life events. While the opportunity to write or paint about life's challenges can be helpful to everyone, it can be a lifeline for some. Ritter et al.'s research also suggests that we can enhance students' creativity by providing them with new and unexpected experiences, without the need for added adversity.

Creative People Think Differently and Take Risks They can be nonconformists, unwilling to follow social conventions—or seemingly arbitrary school rules. It shouldn't be surprising that the same people who raise questions about biology or chemistry or art should question social norms as well. Having original ideas is, by definition, going against convention and opening oneself up to rejection or ridicule. Creative people must be willing to take risks, to accept the failures that almost inevitably precede successes. This is not necessarily the type of risk taking that spurs a person to bungee jumping or mountain climbing. Rather, it is a willingness to accept intellectual risks. It is the courage described by MacKinnon (1978) as necessary to think thoughts others are unwilling to think or express ideas that are off the beaten path. Creative risk taking opens an individual to criticism, ridicule, or feelings of foolishness. On any given night, a jazz musician standing up to improvise could perform poorly.

Actor Dustin Hoffman, speaking on the *Tonight Show* (Leno, 1992), compared his feelings about acting with Greg Louganis's 1990 Olympic diving. At the time, Louganis was the greatest diver in the world, yet on one dive he hit his head on the diving board. Hoffman noted that the goal of the dive is to come as close to the board as possible, so the difference between a score of 10 and a humiliating knock on the head was measured in a fraction of an inch. "I looked at that," said Hoffman, "and thought— there it is." Even an actor of Hoffman's quality recognized that in every creative endeavor, there is the risk of failure, sometimes by a fraction of an inch. Continuing to create means accepting that risk. There is a reason that in her 2012 book *inGenius*, Tina Seelig titles one chapter, "Move Fast, Break Things."

Students willing to take creative risks are not always at the top of the climbing bars or the bottom of the pile of football players. They may be the ones willing to express an opinion that differs from the teacher's, declare that they prefer classical to rock music, or submit an assignment in a form different from that of their friends. They may be willing to sing their original song, suggest a new due date for an assignment, or organize a schoolwide protest against cafeteria food or national politics. They are students willing to experiment to see what works in science, in art, or in fixing a broken automotive belt.

Lesson 5.1   *Perfection Is Not So Perfect*

One of the impediments to healthy levels of risk taking is perfectionism—students' sense that they must not make mistakes or they will be somehow inadequate. There are many ways to help students separate having high standards from perfectionism. One, of course, is to study the lives of creative people and note their circuitous paths to success. Another is through supportive stories. Some of my favorite stories of creativity trumping fear come from Peter Reynolds, whose *Ish* (Reynolds, 2004) and *The Dot* (Reynolds, 2003) delight and support readers from preschool to graduate school. *Ish* is about a young boy, Ramon, who loved to draw until his brother's criticism took the joy from his efforts. Younger sister Marisol wisely points out that his drawing may not look exactly like a vase, but it is vase-ish, and worthy of admiration. Reynolds's books can be used to spark discussions of when it is important to be as perfect as possible, and when "ish" is just fine. Information on Peter Reynolds's blog is available at the end of Chapter 7. Another fine story for similar but more abstract discussions is *Perfect Square* (Hall, 2011), a story of a square that is transformed in many ways and finds both adventure and beauty.

Supporting students in risk taking requires something of a balancing act because we must help them not only to take intellectual risks but also to assess which risks are worth taking and understand that with risk taking comes responsibility for consequences. Creating a classroom climate in which students are safe in expressing differences of opinion is an essential component in this type of support, as are ironclad rules against sarcasm and bullying. Even when students' efforts at originality are unacceptable (e.g., the new format they devised for an assignment omits critical elements of the task), it is important to help them see exactly what caused the problem. If a student's assignment was to give a persuasive speech and he instead did an imitation of the principal's morning announcements, the assignment was not fulfilled. Here you need to help the student understand that taking on a new character was not the problem and that an original element could have added interest to the speech. To be successful, however, he needed to portray the principal in a persuasive mode as the assignment required. (It also may have been appropriate to reiterate that class rules against sarcasm and unkindness toward other students also apply to adults. Young people sometimes need help finding the line between humor and cruelty.)

The truth is, for creative people, failures are part of the process. I once had the wonderful opportunity to hear Newbery Award–winning author Laura Amy Schlitz talk about her writing. Ms. Schlitz began her writing career with a successful romance novel. Buoyed by that accomplishment, she decided to write her first "real" novel—sure it would be the great Venetian novel. She went to Italy, studied, and worked for years to produce the 700-plus-page manuscript. She sent it off to publishers and waited for their excited responses. And waited. And waited. You can imagine the rest. No one wanted her novel. Saddened, she decided she wasn't an author after all and decided to focus on her career as a school librarian. As luck would have it, she later found herself in need of some car-repair cash (as any librarian can easily imagine) and eagerly volunteered for a curriculum-development task, writing some monologs that could be used in the social studies units on medieval life. Encouraged by the response to the monologs, she sent them off to publishers, they landed at Candlewick Press, and the rest is Newberry History. The story itself was fascinating, but my favorite part was when she brought out the enormous ribbon-bound manuscript of her failed novel and threw it on the ground with a thump. She stood up on it like a pedestal and said, "Stand on your failures. They are what push you forward."

Creative people take risks

Other Characteristics Associated With Creativity Treffinger, Young, Selby, and Shepardson (2002; see also Treffinger, Schoonover, & Selby, 2013) also reviewed characteristics associated with creativity—more than 300 of them—and clustered them in four general categories. They were Generating Ideas, Digging Deeper into Ideas, Openness and Courage to Explore Ideas, and Listening to One's Inner Voice. Generating ideas, naturally, reflected divergent thinking. Digging deeper into ideas reflected more convergent processes like evaluating and seeing relationships. At first glance, logical thinking skills as a creative characteristic may seem to present a paradox. We sometimes think about creativity as the opposite of logic or logic as a barrier to creativity. In fact, highly creative people have excellent logical thinking skills. If students are to be effective in gathering information about a situation, to focus on important issues, or to evaluate potential ideas, logical thinking is indispensable. Students who display logical thinking can use evidence to draw conclusions, give reasons for their responses, and make use of logical sequences such as if–then or cause–effect.

Logical thinking can even be a tool for dealing with novelty. In a new or different situation, starting with what is known or familiar often is an effective strategy. For example, if a student is challenged to create an animal that might live on Venus and a home for the creature to live in, that probably is a novel task. Yet one of the most powerful ways to begin is with the information he or she currently knows about Venus. What is the temperature? The atmosphere? The terrain? What types of adaptations would be most effective under these circumstances? Why? What resources are available for building? Such questions can lead to truly creative responses—those that are both novel and appropriate—rather than fanciful drawings of four-eyed green creatures. Also, this assignment provides the opportunity for students to synthesize information on the solar system with information on animal life, reinforcing and integrating two science units. Helping students to practice this type of assignment, in which logic is used to support originality, can impact both their creative thinking and content learning.

Treffinger et al.'s third category deals with the openness and playfulness already discussed. The fourth, Listening to One's Inner Voice, combines passion and reflective thinking with independence of thought. Individuals exhibiting independence in judgment are able to assess situations and products by their own standards. They do not feel compelled to seek approval from others or follow the latest trends. Stephen Schwartz, the composer cited at the beginning of the chapter, noted the tricky balance between independence and arrogance—in that case, standing up for the inclusion of the song "Popular" in the musical *Wicked*. Sarah, the young dramatic student at the beginning of the chapter, may be exhibiting similar independence. Her dramatic responses seem to be unaffected by others' judgments.

Independent students of any age may not always be easy to teach. They may be stubborn, argumentative, or resistant to authority. Sarah, when angry or frustrated, probably was not pleasant to have in the classroom. Students with independent judgment may resist correction or doubt the teacher's ability to assess their creative work. Our challenge is to help students develop independence in ways that support their creativity in school. To develop this type of independence in judgment, students of all ages must be encouraged to evaluate their ideas, writing, and other projects. Self-evaluation is discussed in more detail in Chapter 9. For now, it is important to note that independence in judgment demands some standards with which to judge. Such standards do not imply arrogance but rather knowledgeable assessment. Students must be taught about the criteria that might be used to assess various types of work. Kindergarten art students could be taught to be sure that they have used the whole paper. High school art students might examine their use of light and shadow. In creative writing, elementary students might look for a beginning, middle, and end to their stories, whereas older students might check the realism of their dialogue. Understanding that judgment is based on criteria, not whim, can help students move from "But do you like it?" to their own assessments. It is also possible that, as Gardner (1982) hypothesized, children who practice judging their work in childhood may not fall prey to the harsh self-judgments of many adolescents that squelch their creative endeavors in the teen years. Runco 1991b; Runco & Chand, 1994; Runco, Johnson, & Gaynor, 1999) noted the importance not only of independence in judgment but also of good judgment or evaluative skills in creativity. He stated that the creative process begins with identifying a problem or task and then requires generating multiple ideas. However, generating numerous ideas is not enough. Creative individuals must assess which of the many ideas produced are good ones. Runco noted differences in elementary students' ability to identify original ideas and suggested that the ability to evaluate creative ideas may be as essential as the ability to generate them. This theory would lend more support to activities that assist students in evaluating their own work, particularly in assessing which of their ideas are especially original.

Finally, independence in judgment does not mean that the judgment of creative individuals is self-centered or without concern for consequences. Helping students make independent judgments entails helping them develop means for evaluation along many dimensions, including the potential impact on self, community, and environment.

Thinking About the Classroom

Divide a large piece of paper into squares and list one characteristic associated with creativity in each square. Leave the paper on your desk for 2 weeks. Each time a student does something to demonstrate a characteristic, put his or her name in that square (after the first time, just use tally marks). Be sure to mark the characteristic even if it is displayed in a negative way. At the end of 2 weeks, see which students are listed most often. Are they the students you expected?

Creativity and Complexity

It is clear why both the minds and the characteristics of creative people can be described as messy. So many seem potentially contradictory: flexible yet logical, risk taking yet committed to task, daydreaming yet persistent. Csikszentmihalyi (1996) believed the complex personalities exemplified by these dichotomies are a hallmark of creativity. After interviewing nearly 100 extraordinary creators, he listed 10 dimensions of complexity on which creative individuals appear to develop both dimensions of a continuum simultaneously:

1. Creative individuals have a great deal of energy but also are often quiet and at rest. They may work long hours with great intensity yet value time for rest, reflection, and rejuvenation.
2. Creative individuals tend to be smart yet naïve and able to look with new eyes on the world around them.
3. Creative individuals are playful yet disciplined.
4. Creative individuals alternate between imagination and fantasy and a rooted sense of reality. It is this balance that allows their responses to be both original and appropriate.
5. Creative individuals seem able to express both introversion and extroversion as needed.
6. Highly creative individuals can be humble while simultaneously being proud of their accomplishments.
7. Creative individuals seem to be minimally affected by gender stereotyping, able to express both masculine and feminine dimensions of their personalities.

8. Creative individuals typically are seen as rebellious and independent, yet it is impossible to be an eminent creator without having internalized an existing domain. Therefore, creative people can be at once traditional and rebellious.
9. Creative individuals can be passionate about their work while maintaining objectivity in their judgments.
10. Creative individuals, because they are open, experience both suffering and enjoyment in connection with their creative activities.

It is clear from this list that any shallow, stereotyped, or simple characterization of a creative person does a disservice to complexity that appears to be associated with highly creative individuals—those whose creativity affects us on a daily basis. This complexity may provide one explanation for the sometimes-conflicting lists of characteristics and experiences attributed to creative individuals, particularly if researchers are not aware of all the dimensions of the person being studied.

It also is important to recognize that characteristics of creative individuals are not always positive. According to Csikszentmihalyi (1994), the characteristic that most consistently differentiated successful artists from those who give up an artistic career was a cold and aloof disposition. Flexible thinking may be used to create imaginative stories or to invent elaborate lies (see Ariely, 2012, for some interesting hypotheses). Although we may not wish to encourage aloofness, arrogance, or hostility in our students, it is important to recognize that the characteristics that allow individuals to be creative—independence, courage, and persistence—may not always be expressed in ways that are easy on classroom routines. Helping students channel their drive in ways that can be positive for both them and their community is one of our responsibilities as adults and mentors. Perhaps we can be facilitators of creativity that is confident without being arrogant and self-confident without being self-centered. In fact, Damian and Robins (2012) distinguished between authentic pride (in an accomplishment) and hubristic pride (pride in oneself as an exceptional human being) and found authentic pride more closely associated with both creativity and intrinsic motivation.

Creativity and Mental Illness

The image of "mad genius" has been part of Western culture for hundreds if not thousands of years. And yet healthy mental development is at the core of some models of creativity, and some research associates creative activities with increased mental health (Lepore & Smyth, 2002; Pennebaker, 1995; Richards, 2007). It seems unlikely that the sustained efforts required for major creative accomplishments would be possible in the face of major mental illness. Sawyer (2012) points out that much of the research linking creativity and mental illness is fraught with methodological difficulties, including far-reaching definitions of mental illness, the potential for preconceptions, and often-deceased subjects. And yet the questions continue.

The likelihood of creative success in the face of mental illness may vary considerably across disciplines. Ludwig's analysis of biographies (1995) found depression quite common in writers (particularly poets) and composers but much less common in other disciplines. Similarly, he found psychoses associated with schizophrenia evident in creative individuals in theater, architecture, and poetry, and not at all in creative explorers or sports figures. Kaufman (2001, 2005) found poets more likely to suffer from mental illness than other creative writers, and female poets in particular. It is interesting to consider how chicken/egg dilemmas and issues of image play into these differences. Might an individual who struggles with depression be more inclined to creative writing than physics because of the cultural stereotype of a sad, lonely poet? Might a depressed general keep that fact hidden at all costs? Might tales of illness make more interesting stories and thus result in more biographies? It seems likely that the educational requirements necessary to make creative contributions in some disciplines create barriers for those whose illness makes concentration a struggle. And, of course, the fact that some people with mental illness are able to create successfully in some disciplines does not mean either that most people with mental illness are creative or that most creative people have mental illness. Neither is true (Kaufman, 2014; Silvia & Kaufman, 2010).

An interesting question is the relationship between a genetic predisposition to mental illness (as opposed to the illness itself) and creativity. One measure of these is schizotypy, a personality continuum ranging from normal levels of imagination and openness to extremes of magical thinking and psychosis, particularly schizophrenia. Kinney et al. (2000–2001) investigated adoptees whose biological parents had schizophrenia and found that those with schizotypal signs (but not schizophrenia) had greater creative accomplishments than a control group. The researchers speculated that major psychological illnesses may have a positive component that accounts for their continuation in the population—in this case, the risk of illness may carry with it enhanced creativity. Abraham and Windmann (2008) investigated the relationship between schizotypy and problem solving. They found that individuals with schizotypy were better able to overcome the influence of examples when trying to generate original responses; that is, they were better able to escape entrenchment. However, later investigations have found that individuals with schizotypy have no advantage—or even a disadvantage—in divergent thinking, creative cognition, and creative problem-solving tasks (Armstrong, 2012; Rodrigue & Perkins, 2012). Other researchers have found that close relatives of individuals with schizophrenia, bipolar disorder, or serious depressive disorders are more likely to have creative occupations (Kyaga et al. 2011, 2013). It is possible that characteristics that in an extreme form can lead to mental illness in more "moderate doses" can support creativity.

A continuing avenue for investigation is the relationship between specific cognitive processes associated with creativity and those associated with mental illness. For example, latent inhibition is the process by which we mentally "screen out" stimuli we have previously identified as irrelevant. It is what allows you to be in the room with a ticking clock or a dripping faucet—or, as we did years ago, live near a passing train—and not be bothered by the sounds. Low levels of latent inhibition can be associated with psychosis (imagine being unable to screen out every drip and tick), but some reduction can also be found in young adults with major creative accomplishments (Carson et al., 2003). Kaufman (2009) found that adolescents with lower latent inhibition had more faith in their intuition, a characteristic associated with openness and creativity.

Research continues. Where there are relationships, they are complicated. Martín-Brufau and Corbalán (2016) found that in a group of Spanish college students (rather than eminent creators), the relationship between psychopathology and creativity appeared higher for men than women. Landgraf et al. (2015) found that both creativity and schizotypy varied across cultures (in this case, German and Russian) and that culture affected how the two were related. Damian and Simonton (2015) found the rate of mental illness was much lower among eminent African American creators than in Ludwig's (1995) majority culture sample. Among Iranian college students, there was a significant relationship between creativity and subjective emotional, psychological, and social well-being (Tamannaeifar & Motaghedifard, 2014). Other research found positive relationships between creative activities and feelings of well-being. Silvia et al. (2014) found that when sampling day-to-day activities, people who reported being happy and active were more likely to be doing something creative at the time. In a study of activity journals, Conner, DeYoung, and Silvia (2016) found people who were involved in everyday creative activities scored higher on measures of positive feeling and "flourishing" (minding purpose and meaning in life) the following day. So there is much to learn.

At this point, the most reasonable conclusions seem to be that (1) the notion of a mad creative genius is based in Romantic legends rather than reality, (2) where some individuals with mental illness are creative, the relationship between mental illness and creativity is complex, varying by degree of disability, discipline, and culture (see Kaufman, 2014), and (3) it is possible that engaging in everyday creative activities may lead to increasingly positive feelings. When considering how these affect our students, perhaps we are best served by remembering that the large majority of highly creative individuals have no major mental illnesses. We can feel confident that all efforts to facilitate our students' emotional and psychological well-being will pose no major threats to their creative potential—and creative activities may help us create a more positive classroom environment.

Biographical Traits: Learning From Life Stories

Biographies of Eminent Creators

Some studies of creative individuals have not examined their intellectual or personality characteristics but rather the kinds of things that have happened during their lives. Highly creative individuals in some disciplines are more likely to be firstborn and to have lost one or both parents early in life (of course, many of the individuals on which that research is based lived in a time when such losses were much more common than they are today). Despite this loss, they often have been reared in stimulating, diversified, and enriching home environments, exposed to a wide range of ideas. Some creative adults report that as children they liked school, enjoyed books, had many hobbies, and learned outside of school. Others either did not attend school or found it excruciating. Whereas some report warm, supportive peer groups, others were at the margins in social situations (Tardif & Sternberg, 1988). Other studies have reported that creative adolescents come from homes with clear expectations but few rules, that their parents have well-established interests, and that the adolescents have more childhood traumas than less creative students, more collections, and more unconventionally furnished homes (Dacey, 1989).

Of course, the difficulty with lists such as these is that they reflect particular bodies of research on specific populations during given times. You can, no doubt, think of a creative exception to virtually every item listed. Certainly, there are many creative individuals who have grown up with both parents, who had minimally stimulating childhood environments, and who did not collect anything. Moreover, the experiences in creators' lives, as do their other characteristics, vary by field. The family environments of creative scientists and mathematicians may be happier than those of artists and writers. They often have had more formal education and different hobbies (Piirto, 2004). Brazilian poets were more likely (almost unanimously) to name their mothers as their most important mentors than American poets were (Wechsler, 2000).

Examining biographies of eminent 19th-century creators across domains, Gardner (1993a, 1994) found some themes and characteristics that seemed to transcend disciplines, at least during that time period. Nineteenth-century creators lived somewhat removed from the center of society, came from families of moderate means who valued learning and hard work, and often were somewhat estranged from their immediate families. They were more likely to have warm relationships with a nanny or a more distant relative. Early in their careers, it was necessary for these creators to move to a larger city to develop their growing expertise. Gardner also noted two additional themes and a possible 10-year rule.

The first new theme that emerged from Gardner's (1993a) case studies was the matrix of support that surrounded the creators at the times of their creative activities. During periods of intense creative activity, these eminent creators needed both cognitive support in the form of someone with whom they could share newly formed ideas and affective support from someone whose friendship was unfailing. These roles could be met either by the same person or by different individuals. In either case, this type of support appeared necessary to major creative contributions. Albert (1990, 1993) also noted the importance of focal relationships in the developing careers of highly creative individuals.

Gardner (1993a) called his second emerging theme the "Faustian bargain." As did Faust, eminent creators made enormous sacrifices to their work. In many cases, they sacrificed interpersonal relationships. Some undertook lives of extreme asceticism. In making the preeminent force in their lives work, these highly creative individuals left little room for other pastimes, pleasures, or people.

Finally, Gardner (1993a) identified a pattern of achievements he called the 10-year rule. Individuals in a variety of domains tended to produce major ideas, breakthroughs, or other creative products at approximately 10-year intervals. It will be interesting to examine biographies of 21st-century creators to learn whether the 10-year rule continues to hold true during the contemporary knowledge explosion.

But the more we learn about the early experiences of highly creative people, the clearer it becomes that they vary across time and by discipline (Simonton, 1986, 2009, 2010). Authors are more likely to come from unhappy homes than scientists, and composers are more likely to be firstborn than creative writers. The more formal and logical the discipline, the more likely an eminent person is to be firstborn, educated, and from an intact family. And, of course, all of these things occur on average and at particular points in history.

We can get some sense of how experiences may transcend time by comparing Csikszentmihalyi's (1996) interviews, noted earlier, to Gardner's 19th-century examples. Csikszentmihalyi and his associates conducted interviews with 91 exceptionally creative individuals between 1991 and 1995. Individuals were selected according to three criteria: the person must have made a difference to a major domain of culture; he or she still had to be actively involved in that domain; and he or she had to be at least 60 years old. Csikszentmihalyi identified personality and biographical characteristics sometimes similar to and at other times divergent from those found by Gardner and other researchers. For example, whereas Gardner's creators struck Faustian bargains that often sacrificed personal relationships, most of Csikszentmihalyi's participants had stable and satisfying marital relationships. The most marked of Csikszentmihalyi's findings was the existence of contrast or paradox. Creative individuals experienced early years that were both nurturing and precarious, supportive and marginal. The patterns of the dualities varied from individual to individual, but the contrasts remained. For example, one individual may have grown up in a warm, supportive home but experienced racial discrimination. Another may have grown up in an economically struggling or dysfunctional family but experienced support from extended family or other mentors. This type of bimodal early experience, providing both support and challenge, appeared tied to later creativity (Gute, Gute, Nakamura, & Csikszentmihalyi, 2008). Perhaps it is not surprising that Csikszentmihalyi also found complexity and paradox in the personal characteristics of the people he studied. In fact, if the biographies of Csikszentmihalyi's (1996) subjects teach us one thing, it is that there is no one path to big C creativity. He says,

[W]hat is astonishing is the great variety of paths that led to eminence. Some of our respondents were precocious—almost prodigious—and others had a normal childhood. Some had difficult early years . . . others had happy family lives. . . . Some encountered supportive teachers; others were ignored and had bad experiences with mentors. . . . This kind of pattern—or rather, the lack of it—suggests an explanation of development that is different from the usual deterministic one. It seems that the men and women we studied were not shaped, once and for all, either by their genes or by the events of early life. Rather, as they moved along in time, being bombarded by external events, encountering good people and bad, good breaks and bad, they had to make do with whatever came to hand. Instead of being shaped by events, they shaped events to suit their purposes.

(p. 181)

Somehow, I find that profoundly encouraging!

Creativity and Multicultural Experiences

Creativity and culture intertwine in fascinating ways. Culture shapes the ways individuals conceive of creativity and the venues in which they create. It is part of the systems that both make creativity possible and judge its success. But there is also evidence that interacting with diverse cultures can be a factor in developing creativity and is a unique example of a biographical event that can be chosen.

In 2009, Maddux and Galinsky published a series of studies in which living abroad and, in particular, thinking about the kinds of adaptations that were necessary for living abroad were associated with higher scores on a number of problem-solving tasks (also Leung, Maddux, Galinsky, & Chiu, 2008; Maddux, Adam, & Galinsky, 2010). Lee, Therriault, and Linderholm (2012) found that college students who had studied abroad did better on measures of creativity than students who planned to study abroad but hadn't done so yet. There is some logic to these results. Living in another culture provides one experience after another in which you have the chance to look from another perspective, be open to new experiences, observe in new ways, and deal with confusion and ambiguity. Like traumatic events in early life, it can be a disruptive influence on thought patterns—but much more enjoyable!

Tadmor, Galinsky, and Maddux (2012) found that living in another country is not sufficient. Plenty of people live abroad but remain sheltered in a cocoon of familiar people and experiences, eating Kentucky Fried Chicken in Prague or Beijing and shaking their heads at the "strangeness" of whatever new experiences surround them. In order to have living abroad change your perception, you need to be able to envision more than one way of experiencing the world. The researchers call this "integrative complexity," but we can also call it "letting the new culture become a part of you." Individuals who identified with both cultures, "biculturals," scored higher on a creativity measure and produced more innovations at work than those who identified with a single culture—either their original culture or the one to which they had moved. Similarly, individuals of mixed race who had integrated two racial identities were more likely to show greater creativity, particularly when they had bicultural experiences at home (Viki & Williams, 2013). Those who continuously experience two cultures are less likely to think there is only one possible perspective.

It is possible that even more limited cross-cultural experiences may have an impact. Exposure to a presentation about a different culture before a creative-thinking task can enhance creative performance (Leung & Chiu, 2010; Leung et al., 2008). Tadmor, Satterstrom, Jang, and Polzer (2012) found that multicultural experiences had an additive effect in brainstorming teams—if both partners had multicultural experiences, teams did better than would have been predicted by the members' individual creativity. The multicultural experiences included living in another country but also exposure to other cultures through friends, food, music, and so forth.

Although most of us don't have the opportunity to move abroad for extended periods of time, thinking about how we can enhance our students' understanding and appreciation of diverse cultures may benefit both their cultural understanding and their creativity. For many of us, this is easier than you would think. Consider the cultures in your midst. Cultural community centers, museums, cultural fairs—even restaurants—can help students experience another way of looking at the world. And, of course, technology literally puts the world at our fingertips. Organizations change year to year, but a quick search for "global classroom connections" is likely to point you in the right direction. It is essential in structuring multicultural experiences that students are prepared to understand different perspectives rather than observing other traditions as oddities. None of this will change perspectives in the same way a long-term experience will. But if we approach each experience with the intent to understand, it can't hurt.

With this exception, perhaps the most relevant characteristic of biographical traits is that we cannot change most of them. We can support cultural exchanges, provide role models, encourage parents to provide a stimulating environment, and support hobbies and interests. We also can be part of the matrix of cognitive and affective support that may be necessary for creative activity. In that, we may take some hints from Gute et al.'s (2008) descriptions of the early home environments that supported eminent creators. The environments were characterized as complex because they included both integration and differentiation. Integration suggests an environment in which individuals feel valued and secure, and it was created through a combination of warmth and consistency. Differentiation was characterized as a place family members could "be themselves" by seeking out new challenges and opportunities. When I read Gute et al.'s descriptions of the themes that characterized these families, I couldn't help thinking how valuable these would be in a classroom. Imagine a classroom in which these are your goals.

Integration
- Supporting children's existing aptitudes and interests
- Spending time together
- Teaching core values and behavioral boundaries
- Learning to tolerate failure

Differentiation
- Learning to cope with difficult circumstances
- Stimulating new interests and challenges
- Modeling habits of creativity
- Building a demographically and psychologically diverse unit

It sounds like a classroom in which creativity could thrive (and note the parallels to creative work environments described in Chapter 4). When you read about classroom organization in Chapter 9, see how many of these attributes you notice. Finally, it may be productive for us to examine the characteristics and activities associated with creativity, hypothesize how they may appear in children, and consider how we may support some of them.

Thinking About the Classroom

Read two biographies of the same creative person—one written for adults and the other for children. Keep track of the emphases and information that are different. Do both books accurately describe the successes and failures in the person's life, the triumphs and setbacks? How might the differences affect your students?

Creativity and Talent Development: What Do Teachers Do?

The studies of talent development conducted by Bloom (1985) and his associates did not deal with creativity per se. The research was designed to examine "the processes by which individuals who have reached the highest levels of accomplishment in selected fields have been helped to develop their capabilities so fully" (Bloom, 1985, p. 1). It examined young adults of extraordinary accomplishment in a variety of areas, including athletic, aesthetic, and cognitive or intellectual fields. Although the talent development studies were not designed to center on creativity, it is clear that they chronicle the development of many creative individuals. We can question the degree of creativity necessary in swimming or tennis, but it would be hard to argue that the nation's most recognized young pianists, sculptors, research mathematicians, and research neurologists did not represent creativity of the highest level. As such, the generalizations on the development of talent hold promise as keys to the development of creativity as manifested in a variety of disciplines.

All the subjects, regardless of area, spent an enormous amount of time developing their talent. For example, the pianists had, on the average, spent 17 years studying, practicing, and performing before being identified for the talent development studies. This finding rings true with theorists such as Gruber (Gruber & Davis, 1988; Gruber & Wallace, 1999) and Perkins (1981), who emphasized the importance of time and persistence in developing creative ideas. However, time alone is not sufficient. I, too, have played the piano for more than 17 years, yet I am hardly a candidate for such a study. What the learner does with the time, how he or she does the activity, and how the activity changes over the years are critical to the development of talent and creativity (Sosniak, 1985).

The lengthy process of talent development was divided into three phases, first identified in interviews with concert pianists. Although the phases overlap, the timing varies, and the edges may be fuzzy, the three general areas were consistent across talent areas and may provide important clues to the processes underlying the development of creativity.

In the early years of talent development, learning was playful. Learners explored their fields: They ran their hands across keyboards, played with numbers, and experimented with paint, clay, and paper. Instruction was personal, informal, and enjoyable. Teachers were warm and affectionate, child centered, and nurturing. The emphasis was on exploring and curiosity, and early efforts were met with enthusiasm and approval. As the learners developed skills, they identified principles and patterns that made their learning more systematic. These discoveries helped them become aware that music, art, math, and science were not just areas for fun but that could be studied seriously.

The timing of the phases varied from discipline to discipline. The pianists, for example, began studying formally at around age 6. The mathematicians did not begin formal study of mathematics until high school. Thus the early years in one field may occur 10 years after they occur in another. The key is not chronological age but experience in the field studied. Whenever the first phase occurs, it provides the inviting atmosphere and early delight that sustain talented individuals through the intensity of the second phase.

At some point during the early period of exploration, it became clear that tinkering around was not enough. To develop effectively, the student needed to master the techniques, principles, and vocabulary of the chosen field. If the key word in the early years is exploration, the dominant theme in the middle years is precision. Pianists played the same thing over and over, consciously making slight variations. Mathematicians worked and reworked the same complex problems. The emphasis in all fields was technical mastery. Effective instructors in the middle years were knowledgeable, thorough, disciplined, and systematic. Eventually, middle-year teachers became instrumental in guiding students to new instructors for the third stage, in which learners make the transition from technical precision to art, regardless of discipline. During this time, students find their voice—their own interpretations, styles, problems, and research areas.

In one sense, it is at the third stage that creativity appears. After all, it is here that we find the truly new discoveries, proofs, and sculptures. Yet those accomplishments had their roots in each of the stages that went before. A teacher's role in developing creativity must vary according to the students' experience with the subject matter and stage of learning. Consider the development of creative writing. Primary-grade students will have little experience with writing and almost certainly will be in phase 1. They will need a playful approach to writing, exploring words in a warm, supportive atmosphere. A teacher will need to get them hooked on writing if they are to progress further.

Older students, some of whom may already be enthusiastic writers, may lack the technical skills to produce high-quality work. In that case, careful analysis of the work of expert writers, study of the techniques of plot and character development, and exercises to build vocabulary may be the most effective means to improve their work. The students may practice writing in the style of various authors, creating passages that convey a particular mood, or they may rewrite a particular piece numerous times until it is as tight and precise as possible. If students do not move from exploration and fun to mastery of technique, they can never improve. However, attempts to impose the precision of techniques before there has been sufficient exploration and enjoyment to foster commitment to the discipline are likely to fail.

For a teacher working with advanced students or professional writers, the dilemma is somewhat different. She needs to help her students go beyond her examples, to see multiple ways to approach a task and find their own unique voices. This can be a painful and difficult transition. Students who have always been successful imitating others may find it frightening to be themselves without a correct way of working. They will need to develop their own point of view and assessment of success. Their previous mastery of the standard techniques of the discipline can help them develop both the confidence and the judgment necessary to succeed at this level. At this point, students probably will spend little time in class and long hours writing. They may meet for individual critiques or peer editing groups. Emphasis will be on identifying the messages and techniques that characterize each individual and how that writer works most effectively.

Thinking About the Classroom

Think about the content area(s) you teach. Do you consider yourself primarily a phase 1, 2, or 3 teacher? Is your most important role introducing a subject area and developing interest, honing technical skill, or eliciting artistry? Do you teach in a manner that is effective for that stage? What would you do if one or more students were ready for the next stage? Compare your responses with those of someone who teaches the same level and subject you do.

Csikszentmihalyi's (1996) biographical studies provide examples not identical to but often supportive of Bloom's stages. Csikszentmihalyi's subjects reported childhoods that varied widely but were consistently characterized by a prodigious curiosity. As phase 1 individuals explored the world playfully, the individuals interviewed in Csikszentmihalyi's studies described a drive to explore the world in a variety of domains. Csikszentmihalyi (1996) cited a story told about Charles Darwin's youth:

One day as he was walking in the woods near his home he noticed a large beetle scurry to hide under the bark of a tree. Young Charles collected beetles, and this was one he didn't have in his collection. So he ran to the tree, peeled off the bark, and grabbed the insect. But as he did so he saw that there were two more specimens hiding there. The bugs were so large that he couldn't hold more than one in each hand, so he popped the third in his mouth and ran all the way home with the three beetles, one of which was trying to escape down his throat.

(pp. 156–157)

Certainly, not all early explorations Csikszentmihalyi described were quite as challenging to life and limb as young Darwin's, but most individuals did recall joy in early exploration. Future astronomers spent fascinated hours stargazing; writers and artists experimented with forms. In many cases, parents' efforts to provide intellectual stimulation and support were important factors in the discovery and development of talent. In other cases, parents were absent or unsupportive. School per se was rarely mentioned as a source of talent development, but individual teachers were credited. Two main factors were noted about the teachers singled out as important influences. First, the teachers noticed the students, believed in their abilities, and cared. Second, the teachers showed that care by providing greater challenges and opportunities to develop talent than those received by the rest of the class. For example, Rosalyn Yalow, a Nobel Prize winner in medicine (although trained as a physicist), recalled her interest in mathematics being awakened when she was 12 years old:

I was a good student, and they always gave me lots of extra work to do. I took geometry from Mr. Lippy. He soon brought me into his office. He'd give me math puzzles and math beyond what was formally given in the class, and the same thing happened in chemistry.

(Csikszentmihalyi, 1996, p. 174)

Some students found the recognition and support of their talents in extracurricular activities. Still others, particularly in the arts, found little or no support for their talent in their K–12 experiences. For many of Csikszentmihalyi's (1996) subjects, college or graduate school represented a high point of life. It was the place where they found their voice, identified their vocation, and were exposed to teachers who appreciated their unique strengths.

Although these biographical studies do not break down into neat phases, they do provide examples of a progression from playful exploration to the identification of adult voice and direction. Along the way, these individuals required exposure to advanced skills and challenges commensurate with their emerging talents.

Disciplinary, Gender, and Cultural Differences

At least when considering "big C" Creativity, it is unusual to see the same person contributing in more than one domain. There is evidence that some portion of creative ability is discipline specific (Baer, 2010; Kaufman, Cole, & Baer, 2005). So it is not surprising that biographical experiences and personal characteristics of creative individuals vary across disciplines. For example, whereas creative individuals in both art and science tend to be open to experience, artists may tend to be less emotionally stable and less conforming than scientists (Feist, 1999). Researchers have studied characteristics specific to scientific creativity, artistic creativity, creative writing, and a host of other disciplines (Innamorato, 1998; Neihart, 1998; Piirto, 2004; Simonton, 2009, 2010). It appears the patterns of intelligence and the personality characteristics necessary to be creative in the domain and field of mathematics are different from those necessary to make a contribution of equal stature in the domain and field of choreography. The more we come to understand the complexities underlying the creative process, the more difficult it is to give a one-size-fits-all description of a creative individual.

There also may be gender differences in the life patterns and characteristics of creative men and women. Although research using creativity tests and tasks to examine gender differences in creativity shows no clear differences (Baer & Kaufman, 2008), it is impossible to deny the differences in eminent creative accomplishments that appear to exist by gender. It is difficult to determine why this is so, both because there have been few studies of creative women and because studies of creative individuals seldom include enough women to allow valid comparisons. The types of differences that might be uncovered were illustrated in Helson's (1983) study of creative women mathematicians. As part of the IPAR project, the researcher examined female mathematicians who had completed their degrees between 1950 and 1960. Although differing in generally predictable ways from less creative women mathematicians (higher in flexible thinking, more independent, and less tolerant of rigid routines), they also differed from creative male mathematicians. Helson found that creative female mathematicians were more likely to describe themselves as nonadventurous and inner focused. Male mathematicians were more likely to emphasize ambition. Certainly, the fact that the women subjects had entered the workforce during a time when women's professional roles were more constrained than they are today must have had an impact on their perceptions of their careers and personal development. These issues continue to shift and change with changing cultures and times. Mpofu, Myambo, Mogaji, Mashego, and Khaleefa (2006) describe how many traditional African cultures expect men and women to be creative in different domains (healing vs. embroidery, for example) but that such dichotomies are much less influential in areas with transitional or modern African cultures.

It seems likely that many differences resulted not from innate differences in creative individuals but from the ways that creativity was met in homes, schools, and other environments. In some places, the differences are quite dramatic. Angélica Vásquez, the contemporary Oaxacan potter described in the beginning of the chapter, worked in circumstances in which well-behaved women are submissive and riding a bicycle is perceived as a challenge to cultural norms. Her struggles for creative independence were quite different from what a man in that society would face (Wasserspring, 2000). But differences can play out in more subtle ways. Fabricant, Svitak, and Kenschaft (1990) reviewed research showing that boys in math classes were allowed more freedom to deviate from rules and discover alternative solutions to problems, whereas girls were required to follow the rules more closely and were criticized more often. Such experiences, especially over a period of years, might certainly have had an impact on women's confidence, initiative, and ambition (Sadker, 2002; Sadker & Sadker, 1986, 1995). If we treat creative boys and girls differently, we should not be surprised if the end results are different.

Despite the changes of the last century, the differences in gender expectations make it likely that men and women may have different experiences exercising their creativity. bell hooks (1995) wrote,

> Long after the contemporary feminist movement stirred up questions about great art and female genius . . . we still must confront the issues of gender and work with respect to the politics of making space and finding time to do what we women artists do. Most artistic women I know feel utterly overextended. . . . We spend much time trying to figure out how to use our time wisely. We worry about not giving enough of our care and personhood to loved ones. Despite feminist thinking and practice, women continue to feel conflicted about the allocation of time, energy, engagement, and passion.
>
> (pp. 126–127)

The focus and devotion to task that can be viewed as necessary concentration in creative men may be viewed as selfishness when practiced by women—particularly women with families. Even if the individual "mechanics" of creativity are similar in men and women, it is possible that some women may need different characteristics and strategies to be successfully creative in their fields. For example, highly creative women may be freer to express that creativity within some disciplines during periods when they are not raising young children (Reis, 1987, 1998, 2002; Subotnik & Arnold, 1995). Of course, childrearing offers many opportunities for creativity, but not in most traditional disciplines.

Some have suggested that women's natural means of knowing and working are more collaborative than those of men (Belenky, Clinchy, Goldberger, & Tarule, 1997; Gilligan, Lyons, & Hammer, 1990). If so, women may have an advantage when developing creative collaborations. John-Steiner (2000) argued that interdependence is a human rather than a gender-linked characteristic but still believed that women's life experiences mean they "face fewer barriers than men when attempting collaboration" (p. 122). This may shape differences in the ways women pursue creative endeavors and the characteristics they bring to bear on the process. It also might impact the circumstances in which women are creative. Kemmelmeier and Walton (2016) found in their simulated creative challenges that women were more original if the task was designed to better others.

It is possible that, as Reis (1987, 1998, 2002) hypothesized, women and men often have different paths and time lines for creative accomplishment. They may bring different personal characteristics to their creative endeavors or encounter gender-defined responses from the fields in which they create. Until more research gives us a better understanding of these possibilities, we should recall that the vast majority of research underlying our understanding of creative individuals (and their processes) describes creative men. It simply is not clear whether the same characteristics are found with the same frequency in equally talented women. It also is important to monitor our own responses to characteristics associated with creativity in male and female students. Do we respond in the same way to males and females who are insistent in their questioning, persistent in their arguments, and independent in their manner? Do we encourage both individual creative efforts and the more collaborative processes for creative endeavors? Do we accept sensitivity and displays of emotion from female students while rejecting them in male students? If so, we may be at risk of encouraging creativity in some students while discouraging it in others. How do we respond to a powerful high school senior who wants to quit football to devote more time to theater? In at least one case I know, that decision resulted in an immediate conference between the senior and the horrified principal. The school's honor was at stake and clearly could not be upheld by outstanding theatrical productions! It is important that the full range of characteristics and processes associated with creativity be accepted and supported in all students, regardless of gender.

Just as our knowledge of possible gender differences in the characteristics or processes of creativity is limited by lack of research on creative women, little is known about how such characteristics or processes may vary across cultural groups. Virtually all research on characteristics of creative individuals reports the characteristics of European or European American men. It is possible that Samoans creating original dances, African Americans improvising gospel music, or Japanese manga designers may have different cognitive and personality traits from those thus far studied. We simply do not know. It seems likely that because the very nature and definition of creativity varies across cultures, the characteristics associated with creativity vary as well. In addition, the challenges presented by differing levels of support provided to individuals on the basis of gender or culture seem likely to affect the characteristics necessary for success. For example, if the time line for women's creativity is extended, it is possible that motivation or persistence may play particular roles in their creative development. Csikszentmihalyi (1994) described the political pressure on a talented African American painter in the 1960s that led to that individual leaving an artistic career. It is interesting to contemplate whether Spike Lee may have needed a different constellation of characteristics than John Sayles to be a creative director in the 1990s. How might Barack Obama's creativity be affected by the multicultural nature of his history? Perhaps your observations of the creative characteristics of children from varied cultures will add to our understanding of this important question.

Finally, we do not know the personal characteristics necessary for success in collaborative creative endeavors or how they may vary from those identified in the preceding discussion. Although it seems likely that some characteristics will be similar among individuals whose creativity is individually versus collaboratively focused, there may be important differences. Differences also may occur across different types of group efforts. It is interesting to consider whether the characteristics that might be necessary (or sufficient) for one type of collaboration (e.g., an informal distributed collaboration) may be different from those required for a more intense integrative partnership. Only more investigation into collaborative creative processes will provide the answers. In the meantime, it seems wise to be cautious about identifying only one type of individual as having the potential for creativity while all the while supporting characteristics that may help students develop creative strengths.

Thinking About the Classroom

Keep track of your responses to boys and girls who ask questions in class. See if you respond the same way to their calling out or probe to understand their thoughts equally. You may want to ask a colleague to observe you. When you look at student papers, notice how much emphasis you put on original content and how much on form or neatness. Do you weight them equally for boys and girls? You may want to make similar observations regarding your responses to students from different cultural, ethnic, or socioeconomic groups.

Play, Curiosity, and Creative Children

Perhaps even more difficult than the questions of whether the characteristics listed apply equally to men and women or to varying cultural groups is the question whether it is appropriate to try applying research on adults to young people. There are few studies on creative children, largely because such studies pose enormous logistical difficulties. Researchers who define creativity as adult creative accomplishment must either identify creative adults and work backward to determine what those individuals were like as children or identify a group of children, analyze their characteristics, wait for them to become adults, and hope some turn out to be creative! Neither course of action is simple. An alternative path is to identify students who seem to have creative potential, usually through a test of divergent thinking, and identify their characteristics. Of course, we then are left wondering whether the students who scored high on the tests are the same students who will be creatively productive as adults. The best answer to that question is "maybe" (see Chapter 10). Despite these challenges, some research suggests that the characteristics identified in creative adults also may be found in young people.

Play, Playfulness, and Creativity

One of the most interesting relationships in the creativity research is that between creativity and play. Play occurs throughout the world among humans and animals. Anyone who has ever watched kittens romp or otters perform seemingly endless variations of sliding understands that the urge to play seems an essential part of mammalian childhood (Kestly, 2014). The drive to play is strong. Brown (2009) describes a powerful interaction between sled dogs and a hungry polar bear, in which the bear's desire to play seemed to overcome its desire for a dog dinner. If you haven't seen one of the many videos, search YouTube. It is remarkable.

And yet play is dangerous. Certainly the dogs that played with the bear put their lives in danger. Young animals tussling can easily lose their footing and be hurt, just as children's tree-climbing adventures can come at a cost. And yet we all play. Why? Brown suggests that evolutionarily, play is an advantage because it helps young animals practice essential skills of adulthood, like hunting or even fighting. But what about us?

If childhood play helps us practice essential life skills, it seems one of the skills we practice is creative thinking. Playfulness, in dealing with ideas, is one of the hallmarks of the creative process. It allows creators to envision another way without being tied to the way things have always been. Not surprisingly, play is tied to a number of processes associated with creativity, including divergent thinking, insight, and problem solving (Fehr & Russ, 2016; Russ, 2014). In particular, imaginative play is tied to creativity across disciplines (Mottweiler & Taylor, 2014; Root-Bernstein, 2015; Russ, 2014). Play is important in other ways as well. It helps young people learn language development, impulse control, planning, problem solving, curiosity, emotional regulation, social negotiation, and a host of other skills (Barker et al., 2014; Bateson & Martine, 2013; Gray, 2011; Hoffman & Russ, 2012; Kestly, 2014; Weisberg, Zosh, Hirsh-Pasek, & Golinkoff, 2013; Panksepp, 2008). In school-aged girls, early pretend play predicted not only divergent thinking but also math achievement 4 years later (Wallace & Russ, 2016). There is some controversy over the links between childhood play and later creativity (Lillard et al., 2013; Russ, 2014; Silverman, 2016), but for me, the weight of evidence and logic suggest they are important.

Yet play is in short supply. Children's free time has been declining. Gray (2011) points out that the decline has occurred at the same time as a disturbing increase in psychopathology among young people—more anxiety, depression, feelings of helplessness, and narcissism. Of course, anyone who has taken basic statistics can tell you that just because two things are related does not mean one caused the other. There are many things about our complex world that could contribute to mental health problems. Yet Gray makes a strong case that play serves to help young people develop a repertoire of strategies that support their mental health. Serious play deprivation has been associated with a variety of emotional issues in young people, and even play-deprived rats are more aggressive and fearful (Bateson & Martine, 2013; Whitebread, 2012). Some research is even beginning to examine "play intervention" to help young people develop play skills and (the researchers hope) associated creativity (Hoffman & Russ, 2016).

Play is not just important for children. Magnuson and Barnett (2013) found that playful adults report feeling less stress and, when they do feel stress, cope with it in more positive ways. In one study, adults who imagined themselves as children with a day off from school were more successful in generating creative responses on a later test of divergent thinking. In that case, simply thinking about play increased the adults' divergent thinking (Zabelina & Robinson, 2010). The affective dimension of playfulness matters. Play includes elements of spontaneity, joy, and lack of stress. And it can lead to important innovations. Dale Dougherty, founder of *Make* magazine and Maker Faires across the country describes the origin of the maker movement as "experimental play." Dougherty recognized that makers played with technology to learn about it.

> Makers give it a try; they take things apart; and they try to do things that even the manufacturer did not think of doing. . . . makers are exploring what these things can do and they are learning as well. Out of that process emerge new ideas. . . . Making is a source of innovation.
> (Dougherty, 2014, p. 7)

Just as makers' play with technology can lead to technological breakthroughs, so play with ideas can lead to learning and insight in other content areas. Playfulness can range from Mozart's bawdy nonsense Latin to Alexander Fleming, who described his work saying, "I play with microbes. . . . it is very pleasant to break the rules and be able to find something that nobody had thought of" (Maurois, quoted in Bateson & Martine, 2013, p. 58). As we consider the role of playfulness in supporting creativity, it will be essential to consider both the ways we manipulate ideas and the mood with which we do it. Davis (2009), found that, in general, positive moods were associated with greater creativity, but like many good things, there comes a point when more is not necessarily better. Hyperexcitable moods are not helpful for creativity (or much else in classrooms!). And there are times in the creative process when grit and determination are more essential than playfulness. Still, mood matters. Particularly in the idea-generating phase of creativity, the positive affect associated with play is supportive (Bateson & Martine, 2013).

What makes something play? Gray (2013) says that play, first and foremost, is *self-chosen and self-directed*. If you have to do it, it isn't play. Play is a choice. Second, play is *intrinsically motivated*; that is, play is chosen for its own sake, without regard for external rewards or approval. Third, play is *guided by mental rules* but always leaves room for creativity. Play is never rigid. Fourth, play is *imaginative*; play is not bound by the constraints of reality. When playing, superpowers can be real. Finally, play is *conducted in a relatively unstressed frame of mind*. If it is not fun, it no longer functions as play. Even rats "laugh" while they are playing (Kestly, 2014). Fortunately, play is not "all or nothing." While in school, full-blown play is likely to occur only at recess, playfulness can be an important part of curricular activities across grade levels.

One option recommended for early education is guided play, a "middle ground" between free play and direct instruction. In guided play, adults guide the learning process through comments, questions, or coplaying, but the play is still child directed. The adult may initiate the play and work to focus the child's attention or take advantage of a play situation to comment on concepts from the curriculum. Guided play is associated with better academic and social outcomes than free play alone. Of course, guided play is only one way to engage students to play with ideas, physically or mentally. It helps them learn because "[I]t invites the learner in, implicitly asking for his or her engagement in a way that directly imparting the same information does not" (Weisberg, Hirsh-Pasek & Golinkoff, 2013, p. 109). In studying effective teaching strategies in middle grades, Conklin (2014) found numerous examples of playfulness that caused her to suggest "Play" as a dimension to be evaluated when observing teaching. In that case, play includes choice and self-direction, imaginative creations, and a nonstressed state of interest and joy. It was defined to include creating of imaginative products (for example, a *Monthly Mummy* magazine portraying life in ancient Egypt), role-play, lessons involving physical activity, choice, and self-direction, and the use of humor and unstressed conditions. There are challenges inherent in balancing play and imagination and curricular goals—for example, if the *Monthly Mummy* was not carefully structured, it might not address the needed content. And yet the joy and interest described in the "high play" classrooms make it a variable worth considering.

Fine (2014) suggests playfulness as an antidote to secondary classrooms in which rigor and joy are seen as mutually exclusive. She defines intellectual playfulness as grounded in tasks that are open ended, absorbing, and provide opportunities for intellectual risk taking appropriate (and necessary) for adolescent learners. She used an example of a poetry slam contest in which students were to identify an injustice and then draft, revise, and perform a poem using a variety of devices to communicate effectively. Throughout the revision process, consistent use of the words, "What would happen if?" shifted students' thinking from absolutes to possibilities. Another class created "physics jamz," songs created to review physics concepts. Neither of these tasks are free play, as one might find in a preschool classroom, but they are playful—interesting and engaging—while also pursuing academic rigor. As Fine laments, such moments are rare in current secondary schools but essential if students are going to learn in ways that carry them beyond the next standardized assessment.

Curiosity

It seems logical to assume creativity and curiosity are linked in important ways—especially when thinking about children. Almost any new idea or solution springs from a moment of, "I wonder if . . .?" or "I wonder how . . .?" One of the key characteristics associated with creativity is openness to experience—a tendency to embrace the wonder, puzzles, conflicts, and ambiguities of the world. And the perpetual "Why?" and "I wonder" that characterize many young people can be the beginning of such openness. If we want to help young people develop their creativity, it is important their curiosity be preserved.

Virtually any discussion of current curiosity research starts with Berlyne (1960), who viewed curiosity as a drive, like hunger or an itch that must be scratched. When faced with something novel or strange, he believed, humans (and other animals) are driven to explore. Since then, of course, there have been more theories and a variety of research (see Golman & Loewenstein, 2015; Jirout & Klar, 2012; Loewenstein, 1994; Silvia, 2006 for reviews). Loewenstein (1994) theorized that curiosity is sparked by negative feelings based in an information gap—"Something isn't clear or doesn't make sense, so I'll be unhappy until I understand." Litman (2005) expanded that idea to include both negative feelings and positive feelings of interest—"Something is unclear. That is interesting, and I want to know about it." Jirout and Klahr (2012) characterized curiosity as preference for complexity or the unknown—"This is unusual and puzzling. I love things like that!"

Curiosity can be conceptualized as a trait or a state (Silvia & Kashdan, 2009). Curiosity as a trait is a characteristic that varies among people. My friend Ellen is curious about everything. No matter where we are or what we are doing, she has questions. Other people seem content to let the world go by unexamined. Curiosity as a state is a more temporary phenomenon, sparked by something external. If you were to walk down the street and encounter what appeared to be a treasure chest, it is almost certain that you would be moved to a state of curiosity.

While the idea of curiosity is familiar, it can be tricky to define, particularly when thinking about children (Kashdan, Rose, & Fincham, 2004). My favorite practical definition comes from Engel (2011), who suggests "curiosity is simply *the urge to know more*" (p. 627, italics original). Not surprisingly, curiosity has been tied to learning and development. Piaget (1969) viewed curiosity as the urge to explain the unexpected, leading to new understandings. Kagan (1972) described curiosity the need to resolve uncertainly, leading to new understanding. While the areas of emphasis differ, both theories view curiosity as essential to children's development, sparking the explorations that promote learning. Curiosity is, in fact, associated with development in a variety of ways, sometimes in interactions we don't totally understand. For example, Bornstein, Hahn, and Suwalsky (2013) found that children who were more exploratory as infants had higher academic achievement in adolescence. Curiosity has been linked to the kinds of positive social interactions many of us hope for in our students. For example, curiosity is associated with tolerance of anxiety and uncertainty, positive emotional expressiveness, initiation of humor and playfulness, unconventional thinking, and a nondefensive attitude when faced with varied perspectives (Kashdan, Afram, Brown, Birnbeck, & Drvoshanov, 2011; Kashdan, McKnight, Fincham, & Rose, 2011; Kashdan, Sherman, Yarbro, & Funder, 2013). It is associated with longer life for older adults (Swan & Carmelli, 1996). Kashdan, DeWall et al. (2013) even found that curiosity was a protection against aggression, particularly relatively new romantic relationships. This makes sense to me. People who are curious enough to want to understand a partner are less likely to respond with aggression when something seems unexpected or "off."

Clearly, curiosity is valuable. Not surprisingly, students learn more from text when they find it interesting—when, in fact, they want to learn more. While the mechanisms for this aren't entirely clear, it appears that when readers are interested in the content, they process text more deeply rather than at a rote verbatim level (Schiefele, 1999, 2001; Silvia, 2006). VonStumm, Hell, and Chamorro-Premuzic (2011) found that, along with intelligence, consciousness (effort) and engagement (their marker for "intellectual curiosity") correlated with academic achievement in higher education more broadly. Adolescents who are generally interested in life experiences also score higher on a number of measures of psychological well-being than those who are more often bored (Hunter & Csikszentmihalyi, 2003). And there is some neurological evidence that curiosity, when satisfied, is associated with areas of the brain linked to memory (Jepma, Verdonschot, Steenbergen, Rombouts, & Nieuwenhuis, 2012). That is, if we have been curious about something and find the answer, we are more likely to remember it than something about which we had never wondered in the first place. That rings true with my experiences. I remember almost nothing of seventh-grade social studies, but I still remember the things we learned in a lesson on historical method that began with a simulated artifact we were to analyze. Decades later, I still recall my excitement as the puzzle began to make sense.

Curiosity can feel good. Kang et al. (2009) called curiosity the "wick in the candle of learning." They found that when people were curious, areas of the brain associated with anticipated reward were activated—as if the brain were (unconsciously) saying, "This is going to be interesting when I figure it out!" In fact, subsequent studies found that curiosity made it more likely that participants would remember novel information. Kang and colleagues stated,

> The fact that curiosity increases with uncertainty (up to a point) suggests that a small amount of knowledge can pique curiosity and prime the hunger for knowledge, much as an olfactory or visual stimulus can prime a hunger for food.
>
> (p. 972)

Think of it. Just as the crunching or sizzling images from your favorite restaurant can make you anxious to eat, so can a bit of information that spurs curiosity make students hungry to learn more.

With all the good things associated with curiosity, it would seem that schools would be full of opportunities to develop more curious students. Sadly, that is not true. Some of the most important—and disturbing—research about curiosity comes from Engel (2015) and her colleagues. Her studies are important enough I'd like to describe of few of them in some detail.

Engel (2011) describes a study in which she and her students set out to learn about how curiosity might be exhibited in fifth grade and in kindergarten. They visited classrooms over a period of 3 months, making five 2-hour visits to each classroom, at different times of day, observing different activities. The research team hoped to observe individual differences as well as differences across groups, but the project turned out to be impossible. There simply were too few expressions of curiosity—even among the kindergarten students—to make reasonable analyses. Any time a child asked a question in order to learn, any time he or she tinkered with an object, opened something up to look at it, or used other gestures to learn more about something, it was counted as a "curiosity episode." In the kindergarten classes, among 22 children, there were typically two to five curiosity episodes in a 2-hour observation. In fifth grade, the number dropped to zero to two. In other words, students in classes that were neither overcrowded nor underfunded, spent many hours each day without ever expressing curiosity or interest about anything.

Why would this be? Anyone who has spent time among toddlers knows that, given a supportive environment, young children are virtual curiosity machines. Every nook and corner of the world must be explored, and once they have language, children's early conversations can seem to be an unending stream of "What's this?" and "Why?" As children grow and become more familiar with their environment, curiosity can become more focused around particular interests. I can still remember driving my poor father crazy asking him to read me more about King Tut when I was too young to handle the text myself. Where does curiosity go? One clue comes from my memories of my King Tut period. While I was a very curious child, I also wanted to please my teacher and tried hard to "behave." I can still recall how the only times I got "in trouble" in first grade were when I forgot myself and started exploring. I touched the piano. I read books set aside for next year. I asked questions. I ended up standing in the corner. Yes, really. In the corner.

Curiosity in schools can feel like a distraction. It can pull us from carefully designed lesson plans or into discussions that don't reflect the core curriculum. But it is key to engaged effective learning. As von Stumm, Hell, and Chamorro-Premuzic eloquently state,

> Schools and universities must early on encourage intellectual hunger and not exclusively reward the acquiescent application of intelligence and effort . . . It is not only the diligent class winner who writes an excellent term paper but also the one who asks annoyingly challenging questions during the seminar (a habit that is, unfortunately, not appreciated by all teachers).
>
> (2011, p. 582)

Fortunately for me, my miserable first-grade year was followed by a much better one, with a teacher who delighted in my questioning ways. Adults' responses to children—and their curiosity—are profoundly important. In an early study, Moore and Bulbulian (1976) found that children in the presence of a friendly, supportive adult during one task were more likely to demonstrate curiosity or exploration in the next task than those with a more "critical" adult—even though the adult never criticized the children directly. Engel (2011) and her associates found a direct link between the number of times teachers smiled and talked encouragingly and the level of curiosity expressed in their classrooms. Another study (Engel, 2011, 2015) illustrated how tiny interactions affect students' choices to explore—or not. A teacher/researcher worked with individual students to complete a popular "bouncing raisins" activity that involved observing raisins rise and fall in a glass of water, vinegar, and baking soda, then answering questions on a worksheet. With some students, as the researcher began to pick up materials from the activity, she picked up a Skittle and dropped it in the glass saying, "I wonder what would happen if we dropped a Skittle in instead?" With other students, she just picked up materials and left them nearby. Then the researcher left the room, purportedly to get more materials, telling students they could do anything they chose while she was gone—use the materials, draw with crayons, or just wait. Students who had seen the teacher exhibit curiosity, even that briefly, were more likely to explore and experiment further with the materials. Other children tended to just sit and wait.

Teachers' goals and their students' beliefs about those goals appear to interact with curiosity in important ways. Why are we dropping raisins in water? Another study of the bouncing raisin activity (Engel & Randall, 2009) examined teachers' actions. This time the teachers were the research subjects and the students were assistant researchers. Before the activity, some teachers were told that the purpose of the activity is to help students "learn about science." Other teachers were told the purpose was to help students "complete the activity." This time it was the student who took a Skittle from the table and dropped it in the glass to see what would happen. Teachers who were told to focus on teaching science were more likely to respond with interest and encouragement. Teachers who were focused on completing the worksheet prompted students to return to the worksheet. It brings to mind my first experience in a rental car with a GPS system, many years ago when such things were less reliable. As I drove through the beautiful Tillamook Forest, the GPS showed me as off the road and the system repeatedly prompted me to "Return to the designated route," despite the fact that I was going exactly as I should. In this case, teachers did something similar, prompting students to stop observing and experimenting and return to a worksheet designed to help them learn to observe and experiment! Perhaps this study can help us understand Kashdan and Yuen's (2007) study in which adolescents with high curiosity thrived in challenging schools but had the lowest success rate in less challenging schools. The authors suggest that curious students may do best in environments in which they feel learning is valued. They are less interested in just going through the motions.

So, in these days of high-stakes assessments and stressful teaching situations, what do we do if we want to encourage curiosity (and its close associate, creativity) in classrooms? We will examine that dilemma throughout this book, but we can start with a few ideas.

1. Small interactions matter. We can encourage students' curiosity about the content or about the interactions that happen in the in-between moments. Whether it is a young child brandishing the enormous insect discovered at recess or the adolescent overheard describing a recent trip, a teacher's smile or expression of interest makes a difference in how our classroom spaces are perceived. If you are seen as a person who wants to know more, students will feel safer to wonder and question.

2. Consider how you can spur students to be curious about the curriculum. Students can be drawn in by novel, incomplete, puzzling, or ambiguous information. Don't make the mistake of thinking that the simplest presentation is always the most effective. Complexity can be interesting. Historical characters with all their quirks and incongruous experiments are more interesting than more bland presentations. Silvia (2006) points out that interest and enjoyment are not the same—and have different antecedents. Students may enjoy simple ideas and activities that make them feel confident, but they are more likely to be interested in—and learn more from—activities that are varied and complex. Helping students move from superficial, enjoyable interactions with content to deeper, more interesting ones is a challenge, but one worth tackling.

3. There is a difference between students who are engaged and those who are curious. As Engel (2015) states, "Friendly teachers, hands-on activities, engaged children do not automatically mean curiosity is alive and well" (p. 98). In the bouncing raisin activity, students whose teacher simply helped them complete the worksheet were engaged. They may well have enjoyed their participation. But when given the opportunity, they gave no indication of curiosity. Students can be engaged and even interested in a skilled presentation of content, but unless they have a chance to wonder about it, there are limited opportunities for curiosity and little to suggest it is valued. As you plan the activities through which the curriculum will be addressed, think about how you can integrate student questioning into the mix (see Chapter 6)—and how you can support it, even when not part of the plan.

Research on Creative Young People

While there is a fair amount of research on play and curiosity in young people, research on characteristics associated with creative young people is sparse. MacKinnon (1978) cited a 1968 study by Parloff, Datta, Kleman, and Handlon in which characteristics of creative adolescents paralleled those of adults. In that study, on a factor associated with disciplined effectiveness (e.g., self-control, socialization, tolerance, achievement through conformity), the creative adolescents scored higher than less creative adolescents, whereas creative adults scored lower than less creative peers. In this sample at least, although creative adults and adolescents seemed to have many personality similarities, creative adolescents had to learn to work the system in order to have opportunities to exercise their creativity. Well-established creative adults were more able to function as free, nonconforming spirits. It is possible that assisting students in maneuvering this balance may be valuable. Feist (1999) also found that personality characteristics associated with creativity tend to be stable, at least from adolescence on. The characteristics that distinguish creative from less creative adolescents parallel those that distinguish comparable groups of adults, and these characteristics appear to remain consistent across time.

In his research on creative adolescents, Walberg (1988) examined a national sample of 771 high school students from which he identified three groups: those winning competitive awards in science, those winning awards in the arts, and those not winning awards. The three groups were compared using a self-report biographical questionnaire. Members of both creative groups were more likely to describe themselves as friendly, outgoing, and self-confident, although they were also more likely than the third group to find books more interesting than people.

Creative young scientists were more likely to describe themselves as imaginative, curious, and expressive and to value creativity. They did not see themselves as more likely to generate wild ideas but did find satisfaction in expressing their ideas in new and original ways. They attached a greater importance to money than the less creative students, but when choosing the best characteristics to develop in life, they chose creativity more often and wealth and power less often. Their self-descriptions parallel in many ways the research suggesting that creative adults are curious, flexible, imaginative, persistent, and likely to value creativity.

Just as characteristics of eminent creators vary across disciplines, differences were noted in the characteristics of high school students who had received awards for creativity in the arts and in the sciences. The scientists, as compared with the artists, were less social and less involved in organized school activities. They had more detailed plans for the future and expressed more confidence in their own intelligence. Artists tended to have more diversified interests and confidence in their creativity.

Other patterns in young people echo trends found in adults. Runco (1991a) found a relationship between independence and divergent thinking in preadolescent boys. Keating (1983) reported that, as with adult creative mathematicians, junior high school boys who were highly able in math (and who thus, perhaps, had the potential for creative contribution in that field) had a high regard for theoretical values and a low interest in religious values. Unlike adult creative mathematicians, the junior high school students were low in aesthetic values. Zenasni, Besançon, and Lubart (2008) found a relationship between creativity and tolerance for ambiguity in adolescents—as well as a relationship between adolescents' creativity and that of their parents.

Piirto (2004) examined the writings of highly able and creative child writers. She defined 16 qualities that characterized their work, including playfulness with words, a sense of humor, an ear for the sounds of language, and the use of visual imagery and figures of speech. Many of these characteristics require cognitive or personality traits associated with creativity, such as metaphorical thought, visualization, openness to experience, and willingness to play with ideas. Watson and Schwartz (2000) found that the development of individual styles in children's drawings, some with higher aesthetic and creativity ratings, could begin as early as age 3.

Johnson and Hatch (1990) examined the behavior of four highly original young children. All four children were independent, persistent, fluent, and expressively elaborate. However, each had a specialty area that was the focus of his or her creativity, and thus each expressed that creativity in a different way. This study lends support to the idea that creativity may be specific to a given discipline or area beginning at a very early age. Similarly, Han and Marvin (2002) found that the 109 second-grade students in their study demonstrated a range of creative abilities across different domains of performance tasks rather than a single uniform strength or weakness, and Park, Lubinski, and Benbow (2007) found that the fields of adult creative accomplishments could be predicted with assessments at age 12. In contrast, Plucker (1999b) reported that a strong content-general ability could predict creative activities for high school students. Clearly, some of the key issues regarding both the nature and measurement of creativity in adults are puzzling for young people as well.

Finally, the complexities of life mean there are no guarantees that young people with exceptional creative abilities will maximize them in adulthood. A posthumously published study by Torrance (2004) revealed that students identified by peers as the most creative (admittedly not the most valid measure but an interesting one) were almost never among those who had the greatest creative accomplishments 30 years later. Among the factors that may have made a difference were divorce, childcare responsibilities (particularly for women), and problems finding creative focus. Torrance's "Beyonders," who had significant creative accomplishments, were more likely to be energetic, to love their work, and to have a sense of purpose.

Creative Activities and Misidentification

As noted in multiple examples cited, characteristics associated with creativity, when manifested by students in school, don't always lead to positive consequences. Students acting in creative ways don't make teachers' lives easy. It can be hard to reconcile teachers' images of an ideal student with characteristics associated with creativity. Students who are calm, compliant, follow the rules, and respond to content in predictable ways are much easier to deal with in large groups than those who have new ideas about how things should be done. Perhaps this is why one study found that teachers' self-efficacy (confidence) regarding their teaching skills was related to their nurturing of creativity (Ozkal, 2014). It takes skill and confidence as a teacher to flex with the new ideas creative students bring to the table. These issues are found across the globe. Günçer and Oral (1993) described Turkish teachers as perceiving creative students as nonconforming in matters of school discipline. It is not surprising that teachers' beliefs about the value of creativity can make it more likely that they foster it in their students (Chan & Yuen, 2014). Webb et al. (2005) tell the story of Steve Wozniak, founder of Apple Computers, who was suspended from school because he left his homemade electronic metronome running in his locker. He wanted to take it home to show his parents but neglected to turn off the "tick tick" sounds, resulting in a school visit by the bomb squad. Although the results aren't always quite that dramatic, highly creative behaviors can result in students being viewed as strange, eccentric, or troublesome by students and teachers alike.

In fact, sometimes students with high creative abilities can act in ways that lead them to be identified as having disabilities. Ironically, this can be a particular risk for highly able students for whom the traditional school assignments pose little challenge. After months—or years—of repetitive assignments and too-slow pacing, some such students use their imaginations to relieve the boredom. This can result in daydreaming or other off-task behavior. Such lack of attention to the school tasks at hand has led some highly creative children to be referred for evaluation of possible attention deficit disorder/attention deficit hyperactivity disorder (ADD/ADHD). Cramond (1994) compared "crossover traits" between creativity and ADHD. Webb et al. (2005) have created a similar chart noting similar behaviors associated with giftedness (including high creativity) and ADHD, while Baum and Owen (2004) have examined behaviors that can cause gifted and creative students to be misdiagnosed as learning disabled or as having ADHD. Their summary of Cramond's crossover traits is provided in Table 5.1. In each case, authors point out that the independence, flexible thinking, risk taking, and playfulness associated with creativity can be misinterpreted as disabilities when they are manifested in some classrooms. It certainly is possible for a child to be highly creative and also have ADHD or another learning disability. But, as Healey (2014) succinctly points out, "Most creative children probably do not have ADHD, and

Table 5.1 Comparison of Traits of Creativity and ADHD

Trait	Creativity	ADHD
Inattention	Broad range of interests, resulting in playing with ideas, visualizations, ease of making connections from what is said to other links; capable of multitasking	Not paying attention, unfinished projects
Hyperactivity	High energy for interesting tasks	Excessive movement, restlessness
Impulsivity	Risk taking and sensation seeking	Acting without thinking/thrill-seeking behavior
Difficult temperament	Unconventional behavior/daring to challenge the system	Deficient social skills
Underachievement	Focusing on own projects instead of those dictated by school	Difficulty with achieving school goals

most children with ADHD will not be notably more creative" (p. 246). It is important for teachers to find ways to discriminate between students who cannot attend in most situations and students who daydream when they are bored or simply engaged with their own imagination.

Despite potential confusion, there are helpful trends in the research. Although none of these studies assures that characteristics of creative children and creative adults are the same or that creative adults necessarily had the same traits when they were children, the patterns are consistent enough to suggest that the characteristics discussed in adults may well emerge in childhood. There certainly is no body of research suggesting that they do not. With that being the current state of the art, the most reasonable course of action is to support and encourage characteristics associated with creativity whenever possible. At the very least, our classrooms should be more flexible, responsive, and attuned to the wonders around us. At best, we may make a difference in the creativity of a young person who may one day bring greater knowledge or beauty into the world—sounds like a good risk.

What's Next?

1. Read a biography of a creative individual. Compare the individual's traits and experiences with those associated with creativity. You may want to compare an individual's autobiography with a biography written by someone else. Do the same characteristics emerge? Are some emphasized more in one work than in the other? Or examine descriptions of people in the news. Do you see evidence of characteristics associated with creativity?

2. This is another opportunity to invite a panel of creative people to visit your college or university class. (I have sometimes called university department chairs and asked them to nominate the most creative person in the department.) Ask them about their creative process and activities. Find out how they are alike and different and if you can identify traits listed in the chapter. How did you respond to the speakers? Were all the characteristics associated with creativity manifested in ways that were comfortable for you? Reflect on what these individuals might have been like as children.

3. Think about the dichotomies Csikszentmihalyi described as characteristics of creative individuals. Examine the characteristics of a media character who might be considered creative. Is the person portrayed simplistically or with depth of character? Consider what dimensions might make the character more interesting.

4. Pick one or two characteristics associated with creativity that you would like to increase in your own life. For example, you might want to become more open to experience or more persistent. For a month, try to exercise that characteristic whenever you can. Record your efforts and see if you find the characteristics can be changed.

5. This book considers the challenge of identifying and supporting characteristics associated with creativity in students. Reflect on how similar characteristics are supported—or not supported—in teachers. In your school, how are teachers who espouse novel ideas or persist in their own tasks received? Consider the types of professional experiences that would be most effective in supporting creativity in education professionals. Make a plan!

Think About It

1. If you wonder about the importance of play and playfulness, start by searching YouTube for videos involving huskies and polar bears. You should be able to locate footage of remarkable interactions between these two theoretical enemies, who seem to overcome the instinct for aggression, using the even more powerful instinct to play. Consider how other animals play. How could play be an evolutionary asset for animals, even with the potential dangers?

Try It Tomorrow

1. Share characteristics of creative people with your students. Together, collect examples from local people or people in the news. Have students think about a characteristic they'd like to develop in their own lives and have them write about it.
2. Devise an activity or even a brief interaction in which you can model your curiosity for students. Perhaps, as in Engel's experiment, you might model "what if?" curiosity about science activities. Or you might express your questions about something in history, in the news, or even in the life of a fictional character. Don't try to fake curiosity; ask questions about something that genuinely makes you wonder. Students can tell the difference!
3. Help students be curious about your curriculum. Consider how something you plan to teach can be tied to a puzzle or intriguing question. What about your content is likely to make them wonder? You might experiment with Ostroff's technique "Everything is Interesting" (2016, pp. 51). Challenge students to find something—anything—interesting that links to a topic that might initially appear dull. You could present the "dull" topics yourself or have students generate a list to challenge one another. Their task is to present the topic to the class in an interesting and thought-provoking way—thus proving "everything is interesting."

Tech Tips

1. One of the most interesting ways to expose students and ourselves to the thought processes of creators in various disciplines is to read their blogs.

Writer Blogs

Not surprisingly, writers are some of the people who have embraced blogging the most. The key, of course, is to sort through websites that are basically big advertisements and those that provide genuine insights into an author's process. Children's author Peter Reynolds has a website that includes both a blog and specific questions and answers about how he began thinking about some of his books. His blog sent me on a hunt for other helpful blog sources (www.peterhreynolds.com/).

Some writing blogs are specifically targeted at teachers and young writers. The Teaching Authors blog (www.teachingauthors.com) features six children's authors who teach writing. Utah Children's Writers (utahchildrenswriters.blogspot.com) is a similar blog (obviously) from Utah. Helena Pieli-chaty's Diary of a Children's Writer (www.helena-pielichaty.com/blog) is exactly what it sounds like—as is children's author David L. Harrison's blog (davidlharrison.wordpress.com). Take a few minutes to explore and find out if some of your favorite authors have blogs. I looked at random for a few authors on my bookshelf and found this splendid source from Amy Tan (amytanauthor.com) and this one from Laurie R. King (www.laurierking.com/).

Science Blogs

Because I don't offhand know the names of as many practicing scientists as I do authors, it seems much easier to seek out collections of blogs in the area of science. Fortunately, this is not hard to do. Science Blogs (scienceblogs.com) provides access to science blogs in different categories (life science, physical science, technology) and even some blogs in nonscience areas. Take a look and see what seems interesting. Another site claims to have located the 50 Best Female Science Bloggers (www.onlineuniversities.com/blog/2010/04/50-best-female-science-bloggers/).

Write a Blog

Another way to use blogs to enhance creativity is to create a blog yourself. You might use this as a place to express yourself or a place that allows your students to share their creativity. Some teachers create private blogs in which they post all the content, then (with permission, of course) post their students' work in a space to which only class students and parents have access. There are, of course, blogging sites that make this simple. Two of the most popular are Blogger and WordPress.

Of course I'd be delighted if you'd join the conversation—or even do a guest post—for my blog discussing creativity in the classroom (creativiteach.me). Who knows what kind of blogging may be in your future?

2. Perhaps instead of speaking through a blog, you'd like to speak through an avatar. Many technology tools use avatars in very sophisticated ways. Clearly, creating this type of avatar is beyond most of our technological skills. But there are options available that are accessible even for young students.

Voki (voki.com) is a website that allows you to create customized (if not totally original) avatars that can be made to speak through recordings or typed text. Although they cannot manage long speeches, they can deliver basic messages via websites or e-mail. Voki for Education provides suggestions and features specifically for teachers, some free at the most basic level and (naturally) more elaborate options with a paid subscription. Imagine having students create a Voki to express the three key points in a presentation, or the point of view of a historical character, which then could be elaborated on in written or verbal form.

In a similar way, the app Chatter Pix Kids allows students to take a photo, drawing, or doodle and give it a voice by drawing a "mouth" and recording their voice. A similar online option that can be used, with supervision, is Blabberize (blabberize.com). Blabberize does not (yet) have a section targeted at teachers, and not all the things you'll find browsing the site are student appropriate. Still, the site has potential for creative uses, so you might want to take a look.

If you'd prefer an app to an online option, Tellagami is a quick and easy way to create and share animated messages on phones or tablets. Even elementary-aged students can create customized animated characters in minutes, allowing for interesting and varied ways for them to share information or stories.

Part II
Creativity and Classroom Life

If we, as teachers, hope to help students increase their creativity, we need to determine which aspects of creativity can be influenced and what our role is in that process. As the preceding chapters make clear, there are diverse points of view as to the origin of creativity, how it is exhibited, and what types of activities might encourage it. Our role as teachers depends on the theories and models of creativity we apply. If, as did Plato, we believed that creativity stemmed from the intervention of the muses, there is not much we can do (unless we can determine what attracts the muses!). But as should be clear, as research evolves and our understanding of creativity becomes more complex, we understand that no single component is sufficient to either explain or promote creativity. Systems theories suggest we will have to attend to a combination of disciplinary knowledge, skills, and a classroom atmosphere supportive of creativity. Any attempts to enhance creativity must be grounded in our best understanding of how creativity operates. Part I of this book was devoted to building that understanding. Now we must get down to the business of teaching!

Part II discusses classroom activities, practices, and organizational strategies that are supportive of creativity. Chapter 6 reviews a variety of general strategies and techniques for developing creative thinking. Chapters 7 and 8 overview the major subject areas—language arts, social studies, science, and mathematics—as they might be taught through the goals and principles of creative thinking. They examine the question, "How might teaching look if we approached each area as an opportunity to find and solve problems and communicate ideas?" Chapter 9 examines the research on motivation and creativity and investigates the implications of this research for classroom management and organization. Finally, Chapter 10 discusses assessment and creativity—both assessments that can be used to evaluate creativity itself and classroom content assessments that are supportive of students' creativity.

6
Teaching Creative Thinking Skills and Habits

A group of workers were charged with solving the difficulties of potato-chip packaging. The standard bag packaging was inexpensive but fragile, allowing a large number of chips to be broken in transit. The workers tried using the Synectics approach, in which analogies are used to solve problems. They tried to imagine things in nature that are like potato chips, and one worker thought of dry leaves. These are brittle and break easily, as do chips. One worker recalled that after a rain, a large number of leaves are easily bagged without breaking, many more than can normally fit into a standard bag. The group convened outside, wet down some leaves, and noted that, indeed, wet leaves could be compressed easily into a compact space without breaking them. This analogy formed the basis of the Pringles potato-chip line, which features chips that are formed while wet into a shape that is easily and compactly packaged.

(Gordon & Poze, 1981)

In Sweden, a group of high school students received training in lateral thinking, a series of techniques for generating ideas by looking at situations from fresh perspectives. Corporate and industrial leaders provided problems for the young people to address. One of the problems involved the difficulty of motivating workers in a plant that needed to be kept running over the weekend. The students suggested that, rather than motivating the existing workers to take weekend hours, a fresh workforce be employed that only worked on weekends. The idea was tried, and applicants for the weekend jobs far exceeded the number needed.

(de Bono, 1992)

Ms. Cochran was concerned that her class's science project ideas were unoriginal and often represented displays or demonstrations rather than research. After teaching the differences among the three types of projects, she demonstrated how to use the SCAMPER acronym to generate ideas for improving projects. Beginning with the idea of a display on beekeeping, students suggested research projects that included assessing the effects of color on bees' attraction to flowers and comparing honey production in differently shaped hives. Ms. Cochran was pleased to see the variety of projects her students produced for that year's fair.

Mr. Brown was concerned about the lack of creativity his students displayed in both their art and creative writing. He purchased a book of creative activities and, using suggestions from the book, began engaging his students in activities for 30 minutes each Friday afternoon. One week the class brainstormed to name as many types of birds as possible. Another week they thought of ways to communicate with an alien, and another Friday they made all the pictures they could think of from a square. After several weeks Mr. Brown began to question whether these activities were a good use of class time. He had seen little evidence of improvement in students' art or writing.

Not surprisingly, if we are going to think about encouraging creativity in the classroom, we have to think about the factors that are supportive of both learning and creativity. Recall from Chapter 1 that the Creativity in the Classroom model illustrates the essential relationships among creativity, learning for understanding, and motivation to learn/intrinsic motivation. In this chapter, we'll begin thinking about the things we can do in school to support all three, individually and collectively. Figure 6.1 illustrates some of the key factors that influence the "Creativity" node of the model. Creativity requires knowledge bases in both the disciplines and creative thinking strategies, creative thinking habits, and an environment in which creativity can thrive.

Three Keys to Creativity in the Classroom

Imagine a classroom in which creativity is welcomed. If you are like many teachers, you may picture a wildly colorful room, busy students, and an enthusiastic—and perhaps eccentric—teacher. Our stereotypes of teaching for creativity sometimes lean toward Robin Williams's costumed character leaping across desks in the movie *Dead Poets Society* (or perhaps something out of Hogwarts). To be truthful, I probably would love to be a student in either place. Still, neither my talents nor my agility make it likely that I will be levitating feathers, dressing up, or clambering across the furniture in most of my classes. Does that mean my ability to create a classroom full of creativity is limited? I hope not. I believe there are at least three things we can do as teachers to help create a classroom in which creativity can flourish: teach the skills and attitudes of creativity, teach creativity-supportive curriculum, and develop a creativity-friendly classroom environment. We will address all three keys over the next five chapters.

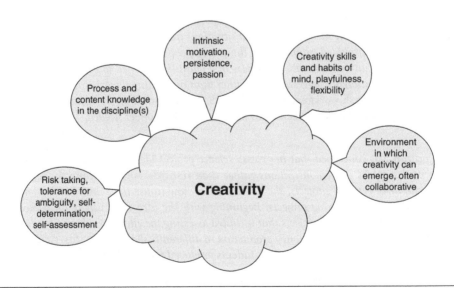

Figure 6.1 Creativity in the classroom model: Creativity

The first key, teaching the skills and attitudes of creativity, entails explicitly teaching students about creativity. It includes teaching about the lives of creative individuals, the nature of the creative process, and strategies that can be used to generate creative ideas. For example, the Story Collider website (storycollider.org) provides insight into the variety of things people find interesting about science, the range of careers they pursue, and the meandering paths they sometimes take to find them. If we want glimpses into the reality of scientific creativity, that is a fine place to begin. You'll want to consider all the places in your curriculum it may be appropriate to teach about the lives and characteristics of the individuals whose creativity framed the disciplines. In addition, this chapter will review a variety of strategies that can be used to directly teach creative thinking skills and develop related habits of mind.

The second key, teaching creativity-supportive curriculum, has changed a bit since the last edition of this book. I used to say that we must teach students how individuals are creative in the disciplines they study. In science, for example, this type of teaching entails learning the processes of scientific investigation in addition to the concepts and generalizations resulting from such investigations in the past. This is more complex than teaching the five steps of the scientific method, although that is a place to start. Real science rarely progresses in such neat and predictable steps. Learning how creative scientists operate entails learning the kinds of questions scientists ask and the methods they use to investigate them. It examines the obstacles that can impede progress, the circuitous paths that can lead to success, and the skills necessary to conduct investigations. Parallel kinds of knowledge can be examined for any field in which creativity emerges. I still believe disciplinary methods are important, but I also believe it is essential to teach the rest of the regular curriculum in ways that are supportive of creativity. To coin a silly phrase, we need to "creativize" the curriculum, considering both the content and the methods we use. Chapters 7 and 8 examine teaching content areas—building the needed knowledge base—in ways that are compatible with creativity.

The third key, developing a creativity-friendly classroom environment, entails creating a classroom atmosphere in which flexible thinking, questioning, and problem solving are welcomed. A creativity-friendly classroom provides a safe space for risk taking and organizational structures that support intrinsic motivation. In brief, a creativity-friendly classroom uses varied and flexible teaching methods, provides experiences with choice, offers informational feedback in assessment, encourages self-assessment, uses rewards thoughtfully, teaches both cooperation and independence, and promotes questioning and experimentation. Additional information on classroom procedures and structures that are supportive of creativity are addressed in Chapters 9 and 10. Chapter 10 also will address assessment of creative thinking.

Tools for Creative Thinking

Many techniques, sometimes called tools, for creative thinking have been designed to assist individuals in generating original ideas. A number of these strategies originated in business, where new ideas are essential for developing products and maintaining a competitive edge. Some techniques have been used in schools in an effort to help students become more creative. There is evidence that many of the strategies described can be effective in assisting both children and adults in producing novel appropriate ideas. Exactly why or under what circumstances they work is not always clear. Possibly some of the techniques mimic or stimulate the cognitive processes that underlie creativity. Some of the techniques may develop attitudes or habits of mind that facilitate creativity: independence in judgment, willingness to explore multiple options, and persistence beyond the first idea. In any case, familiarity with techniques designed to enhance creative thinking gives individuals a set of tools to use in their exploratory behavior. Instead of sitting and waiting for the muse to strike, students can use deliberate strategies to channel their thoughts in new directions.

Lesson 6.1   Artist to Artist: What Is It Like to Be Creative?

In *Artist to Artist* (Eric Carle Museum of Picture Book Art, 2007), 23 major illustrators talk to children about their art. It is a fine resource for teaching illustration (and a lovely example of flexibility in the varied ways pages are assembled), but it also can be used to talk about the lives and experiences of the illustrators themselves. Learning about the lives of creative individuals provides models for students, as well as examples of the not-always-straightforward path to creativity.

Having tools, however, is not always sufficient. As Mr. Brown discovered, practice with creative thinking skills does not automatically result in the transfer of such skills to other circumstances. Students must be taught how to use them, when to use them, and under what circumstances they might be useful. Using techniques in diverse circumstances and discussing their application elsewhere can enhance the possibility that they will be seen not as Friday-afternoon diversions but as valuable approaches to life's dilemmas. In addition, time spent in activities that specifically teach creative thinking skills and attitudes sends a valuable message to students: "Creativity is valued here. It is so important that we will spend precious time and energy to help you be more creative." Such messages are an important aspect of the creativity-friendly classroom. Students who have spent class time learning to question and explore seem much more likely to believe that these activities will be accepted and appreciated if they initiate them later.

Another, perhaps counterintuitive advantage to many of the strategies presented here is that they put constraints and conditions around creative tasks. Telling students to write, paint, or investigate whatever they want for as long as they like is not necessarily the optimum circumstance for creativity. Sometimes when constraints push our thinking into new paths or forms, such as haiku, Twitter recipes (follow Maureen Evans @cookbook), or the six-word story described in Chapter 3, our ideas become more original. Haught-Tromp (2017) called this the *Green Eggs and Ham* effect, after the famous Dr. Seuss book written after the author was challenged to create a children's book using no more than 50 words. Her research found college students wrote more creative couplets when constrained to use particular words than when given freedom to write anything.

This chapter examines a variety of techniques designed to help generate new ideas. It describes how they work and how they might be used with students. It also offers suggestions for helping children transfer the techniques from classroom exercises to real-life habits of mind. First, I consider Robert and Michélle Root-Bernstein's (1999) list of "thinking tools" for developing creative thinking. Next, I explore possible strategies for teaching the concept of problem finding and helping students ask questions. The rest of the chapter is divided into four major sections: divergent-thinking strategies, use of metaphors and analogies, imagery and creative dramatics, and commercial and competitive programs.

As you read, consider which strategies fit most smoothly with the content you teach and the developmental level of your students. Although many techniques, such as brainstorming, can be used at almost any level, others, such as some of the more sophisticated uses of metaphor, are best for students with more highly developed abstract thinking abilities. Only you can determine which ideas are best for your students, how they can be adapted, and which areas of the students' lives may provide the best opportunities for transfer.

The Root-Bernsteins (1999) suggested that to improve education, we need to redefine thinking. If we want to experience intellectual feasts, we must consider the tools used by the master chefs who have "learned to mix, blend and savor an entire range of mental ingredients" (p. 1). Of course, identifying the tools doesn't guarantee creative thinking any more than buying a whisk guarantees any of us a fluffy omelet. But as we're practicing, it helps to have a whisk! In an effort to identify creative thinking tools, the Root-Bernsteins examined the writings of a range of highly creative thinkers to find out how they experienced their processes. This effort doesn't claim to represent the whole range of forces that may be operating to influence creative activities. It does seek out commonalities in how highly creative people believe they work. Moreover, these commonalities entail both cognitive and affective aspects—in fact, one of the key findings is that highly creative activities cannot be described without both. Intuition and "gut feelings" are inseparable from the creative process. They quote Einstein, "Only intuition, resting on sympathetic understanding, can lead to [insight] . . . the daily effort comes from no deliberate intention or program, but straight from the heart."

Just as to understand characteristics of highly creative people required examining both cognitive and affective characteristics, so supporting creativity will require supporting both the more clearly defined creative thinking processes and the less-easy-to-identify attitudes and habits of mind that are supportive of creativity. The Root-Bernsteins (1999) identified 13 "thinking tools" of the highly creative people. The tools are intended to bring together imagination and experience—to help us understand the world in more creative ways. Notice the synthesis of convergent and divergent thinking they entail. As you read the remainder of the chapter, consider how the techniques described give students the opportunity to experience these tools. Next consider in what ways using these tools might support students in respecting their intuition and emotive connections with content.

1. **Observing.** Highly creative people pay attention to their senses. They are open to all the experiences of the body.
2. **Imaging.** The ability to recall or imagine feelings or sensations allows scientists or musicians both to recall past sensory experiences (e.g., a bird's song) but also to imagine sights, sounds, and feelings they've never experienced (the song of 1,000 birds, the feeling underneath a bird's wings).
3. **Abstracting.** Because sensory input and imagery are complex, creative people use abstracting to extract core principles from complicated data, ideas, or images.
4. **Recognizing patterns.** Recognizing patterns, as they occur in nature, in language, dance, or mathematics, is the first step to being able to create them.
5. **Pattern forming.** With this tool, creators combine elements in new and often unexpected ways.
6. **Analogizing.** The creation of analogies is a logical extension of recognizing and forming patterns. We recognize that two seemingly different things share important characteristics. This can lead to poetic images of life as a spider's web or the invention of a new pump based on the anatomy of a shellfish.
7. **Body thinking.** Many highly creative people describe awareness that comes through the body before it enters the conscious mind. A dancer may experience a dance physically before consciously describing it, or a scientist or mathematician might have a sensation of the patterns of electrons or nonrational numbers that only later can be explained through logic.
8. **Empathizing.** Empathizing is related to body thinking, as individuals lose themselves in the things they study. Actors can lose themselves in roles, historians may seek to enter the minds of those they study, and scientists "become one" with the subject of their research.

9. **Dimensional thinking.** In this tool, individuals are able to envision objects in three (or perhaps more) dimensions. Of course, this type of thinking is essential to architects, sculptors, and engineers.

10. **Modeling.** Although all of the earlier tools can be interrelated, the final four tools clearly require the integration of multiple tools. Modeling can range from modeling work on the accomplishments of others to using working models to understand and analogize situations.

11. **Playing.** Playing requires a "childlike joy in the endeavor at hand" (p. 26). It can entail approaching tasks with a level of irreverence that allows typical rules or procedures to be ignored momentarily.

12. **Transforming.** Transforming can move ideas from one form to another and/or move from one thinking tool to the next to further explore and understand ideas.

13. **Synthesizing.** Finally, synthesizing is used to bring together ideas, feelings, memories, images, and so on in a holistic way. Whereas transforming may change things one step at a time, synthesizing makes a more singular change to bring important elements together.

Problem Finding

I am frankly fascinated with problem finding. Thinking about the strategies used by creative individuals to identify the very challenges they address raises both my curiosity and my awe. Still, I have been a teacher long enough that my questions always come back to "Could we help people learn to do this—or learn to do it better? If I helped students think about their own problem finding, would they find better problems?" It seems a potentially important question. Carson and Runco (1999) found that problem finding and problem-solving skills were associated with more adaptive personal coping strategies in college students—and less linked with confrontation, avoidance, and the like as means of dealing with stress. Could we help students gain this advantage? As in many issues related to creativity, the answer is not clear. There is no established research base suggesting that training in problem finding will improve students' creativity. Likewise, there is no ready-made lesson manual to help us do it. However, I have found enough hints in the writings of creative individuals to help me get started, and my experiences sharing these ideas with children have been positive enough to encourage me. I believe that watching students find problems—in addition to watching them solve them—can be an important clue to understand their thinking (Starko, 2000).

Reading the writings of creative individuals about their search for new creative endeavors has led me to identify several themes related to problem finding: *exploring with interest, playing and wondering*, and *capturing questions*. Exploring with interest entails approaching the world with wonder. A strange new insect is an opportunity for curiosity, not disgust. Paint that drips in places we did not expect may be a discovery, not a mess. Ray Bradbury (1996) wrote, "[I]deas lie everywhere, like apples fallen and melting in the grass for lack of wayfaring strangers with an eye and a tongue for beauty, whether absurd, horrific, or genteel" (p. 8). Each new day, each new place brings something to think about. Naturalist Cathy Johnson (1997) exemplified exploring with interest when she described the value of wandering.

> Wandering is the best way I know to feed that flame [curiosity], to answer those questions. Wandering—but with a conscious step, an openness to experience. "Wandering" may *sound* aimless, . . . but it is as purposeful in its way as the migration of monarchs each fall. Like their erratic, drifting flight, it only looks aimless taken a step at a time. In the larger picture a good wander is a search for questions, for the answers that lead inevitably—and

happily—to more questions. . . . How will I know what lies over the next ridge, beyond the next trail's turning along a creek, in the corners of my mind, if I don't give myself permission to wander?

(pp. 59–60)

Students can be taught the value of wandering and wondering. Wanders may be physical or mental. Students can explore the paths of a nature trail or practice asking questions about a fish tank. In fact, Oppezzo and Schwartz (2014) found that walking, particularly walking outside, actually increased creativity for college students. Whether the wandering is mental or physical, creative people must observe, think, and wonder. Creative individuals are great observers. Composer Igor Stravinsky (1997) said,

The faculty of creating is never given to us all by itself. It always goes hand in hand with the gift of observation. And the true creator may be recognized by his ability always to find about him, in the commonest and humblest thing, items worthy of note.

(p. 192)

Lesson 6.2   Stories in Quilts: Problem Finding in the Visual Arts (5–12)

Share *Stitching Stars: The Story Quilts of Harriet Powers* (Lyons, 1997) or another book that explores the art forms of early story quilt makers. Harriet Powers's story is particularly important because she was both a slave and an artist. Her work can be compared with that of Faith Ringgold, whose quilts can be seen in the illustrations of her children's books. Talk about how the women found their ideas. Challenge students to find a story that could be expressed in either a quilt or a collage.

Science lessons that help students observe not just for accuracy but also for curiosity are part of wandering. So are writing lessons that help young people find interest in the characters they create or history lessons that inspire them to notice the words spoken by people long ago and wonder at their thoughts. Therefore, instead of always asking, "What do you see?" we might sometimes ask, "Is there something here that puzzles you? What questions might we ask about this character, this soap bubble, this math puzzle?" Part of teaching students to explore with interest is helping them understand school as a place where students ask questions rather than just answer them.

A second theme in the writings of creative individuals is playing and wondering. Creative individuals do not just explore; they play. They enjoy the chance to think about things just for the joy of it, the "Oh, wow!" of all human endeavors. My favorite description of this process is from Richard Feynman (1997), a Nobel Prize–winning physicist. He described a time when, after having success in his field, he found himself without ideas. After a period of considerable stress, he had an important insight.

I used to *enjoy* doing physics. Why did I enjoy it? I used to play with it . . . So I got this new attitude. Now that I am burned out and I'll never accomplish anything, . . . I'm going to play with physics, whenever I want to, without worrying about any importance whatsoever. Within a week I was in the cafeteria and some guy, fooling around, throws a plate in the air. As the plate went up in the air I saw it wobble and I noticed the red medallion of Cornell on the plate going around. It was pretty obvious to me that the medallion went around faster than the wobbling. I had nothing to do, so I started to figure out the motion of the rotating plate. . . . I went on to work out equations of wobbles. . . . The diagrams and the whole business that I got the Nobel Prize for came from that piddling around with the wobbling plate.

(p. 67)

Remember from Chapter 3: Play matters. It is not clear whether we can directly teach playfulness, but we can model and support it. Teachers who approach their subject with the attitude "This is so interesting. I just can't wait to show you" have the beginnings of playfulness. Playfulness entails thinking about things just for fun and sharing those thoughts with students. It is not the same as silliness. It is approaching a subject not as content to be covered but as a part of the world worthy of curiosity. Playing with ideas gives us the energy and impetus to ask new and interesting questions and provides a counterweight to the "way too sophisticated to care" attitude that seems to pervade some youth cultures. (Do you see ties to any of the Root-Bernsteins' [1999] tools here?)

Finally, creative individuals pay attention to their wonderings. They capture their ideas and build on them. This is the essence of the theme-capturing questions. In the example just discussed, Richard Feynman certainly explored his world with interest. He was open to curiosity about the plate wobbling above his head, whereas many of the rest of us would have concentrated on ducking. He was willing to play with his observations, thinking about the wobbling plate just for fun and curiosity. But he did not stop there. Although some individuals may have noticed the wobble, and still others may have been curious about the spinning, for most people, these would have been fleeting thoughts, immediately lost to the clamor of the demands of everyday life. Feynman continued to ponder and play with the ideas, to calculate and reexamine until his series of questions and answers led him to truly new territory. The persistence so often noted as a characteristic of exemplary creators is required not just for solving problems but also for sticking with an area of curiosity long enough to find the really interesting questions. Teaching students to nurture their ideas requires lessons that do not demand a problem be identified and solved in one 43-minute class period. Good problem finding is a serial drama, not a situation comedy.

It can be valuable to teach lessons the sole purpose of which is to ask questions or find problems. You may have students practice generating story topics, possibilities for plant experiments, or ways to get ideas for a painting. Later lessons may or may not actually entail writing the stories, conducting the experiments, or painting the paintings. At times, it may be useful to practice asking questions the way basketball players practice jump shots—understanding the way they fit into the game, even if we are not going to play four quarters today. For example, the book *A Rainbow at Night* (Hucko, 1996) contains paintings by Navajo children along with the artists' descriptions of how they chose their subjects. Many of the paintings can lead naturally to a discussion of how a similar strategy could help students find subjects for their own paintings. Figures 6.2 and 6.3 are taken from lessons designed to raise students' awareness of the ways people in various careers ask research questions (Schack & Starko, 1998; Starko & Schack, 1992). It may also be interesting to discuss the ways authors find the ideas to explore in a story. Sometimes this might be investigated through the authors' own explanations. Other times it can be interesting to hypothesize the kinds of experiences that may have led an author to a particular story. Tom Stoppard translated that type of speculation into an Oscar-winning movie, *Shakespeare in Love*. More information on helping students ask questions is found in the next section.

Who Does Research?

Who does research? Did you think of scientists wearing white coats boiling things in glass tubes?

There are many other people who do research. Think about the kinds of questions the people in the following table might investigate. What questions might they ask?

Person	Questions
Newspaper reporter who writes about schools	
Doctor	
Football coach	
Toy store owner	
Cancer researcher	
School principal	
Restaurant manager	
Author	
Think of someone you know. What questions might they ask as part of their job?	

Figure 6.2 Who does research?

Source: From Starko, A. J., & Schack, G. D. (1992). *Looking for Data in All the Right Places: A Guidebook for Conducting Original Research With Young Investigators.* Waco, TX: Prufrock Press, p. 9. Copyright 1992 by Prufrock Press. Reprinted with permission.

Lesson 6.3   More Problem Finding in the Visual Arts (5–12)

It is interesting to compare the problem finding of quilt makers (Lesson 6.2) with that of other artists. One interesting comparison is the life and art of Grant Wood, presented in the short book *Artist in Overalls* (Duggleby, 1994). The book explores the roots of Wood's art and also makes clear the many setbacks and disappointments that came before his success. This story could form the basis for lessons either on finding problems in one's surroundings or on the need for persistence and drive in creativity. Students might be challenged to find other examples of individuals who persisted in their creative endeavors despite hardship and rejection.

Our Ancestors (Rohmer, 1999) contains stories and pictures by a diverse group of artists who created art to honor their ancestors. It, too, provides glimpses into both the creative process and the influences that support it.

All Kinds of Questions

Just like newspaper reporters, researchers make use of key question words such as Who, What, When, Where, Why, and How. Using these keywords, it is possible to think of interesting questions on just about anything. For example, take a look at these questions about ordinary classroom pencils.

Who uses pencils?
What kind of pencil is easier for young children to use?
When did pencils become common household items?
Where are most pencils used?
Why do people choose to use a pencil instead of a pen?
How does the way you hold a pencil affect your handwriting?
How does a #2 pencil compare to a #3 pencil?
How could you gather samples that would demonstrate the differences?
How many pencils are sold by the school store?
What if they advertised the pencils? Would sales go up?
What if someone didn't have a #2 pencil? Would anything else work in marking a standardized test?

Pick a common item that seems interesting to you. Using the question systems, write the most interesting questions you can think of.

Who _____?
What _____?
When _____?
Where _____?
Why _____?
How _____?
How does _____ compared to _____?
How many _____?
What if _____?
What if someone didn't _____?

Figure 6.3 All kinds of questions

Source: From Schack, G. D., & Starko, A. J. (1998). *Research Comes Alive.* Mansfield Center, CT: Creative Learning Press, p. 25. Reproduced with permission.

We also may teach lessons focusing on the third aspect of problem finding: capturing questions. A great question or idea is unlikely to bear fruit if it flits across our mind and is gone. Lessons that practice problem finding can help students begin to attend to their own curiosity or flexible thinking. It also can be useful to teach students the value of recording ideas. Creative individuals in almost every domain keep notebooks in which they record sketches, snatches of dialogue, intriguing story ideas, or puzzling questions. Students can do the same.

Seelig (2012) describes an observation exercise taught by Stanford University professor Bob Siegel. Professor Siegel is accustomed to leading students on expeditions to far-off lands, but in this case he opens their eyes to their home environment in new ways. In the Stanford Safari, students are required to make a series of observations of the campus, recording them in a field notebook. In the process they learn a lot about their university but even more about the power of observation—and, I suspect, questioning. Seelig describes a similar focused observation in a shopping mall. She says, "It isn't enough to make acute observations. You need to find an effective way to capture them to make them stick" (p. 79). Whether in a notebook, through photographs, or in boxes full of paper scraps, creators must find ways to hold their ideas for future development.

The Appendix contains a series of lessons designed to teach problem finding in several domains. The lessons were designed originally for students in fourth grade, but they can easily be adapted for a variety of grade levels. They include lessons on problem finding in inventing, writing, and science, as well as discussions on creating an idea notebook and developing habits of mind that are conducive to problem finding.

Students as Questioners

Questions, it almost goes without saying, lie at the heart of all creative endeavors. Contented people do not make discoveries. Those who do not wonder do not invent, write, paint, or explore. They are contented with the world as is. Those who believe all the important questions have been answered miss the joy of asking new ones. And yet, when we consider the sad trajectory of students' questioning—from toddling question-generating machines to the often-unquestioning students inhabiting our classrooms, we must consider our roles in the process. How much energy do we spend teaching students to ask questions as compared to that teaching them to answer them? Do the questions we ask students cause them to ponder or simply to recall? Of course, the answers to such questions are complicated. More each year, teachers and schools are judged by their students' abilities to *answer* questions, at least the kind that appear on standardized tests. In the face of such pressures, it is too easy to leave students with the impression that answering questions is the important part when, in truth, it is only the beginning.

If we want students to use and benefit from their curiosity, we need to signal that we support it, well beyond asking, "Do you have any questions?" First and most basically, we need to teach students what a question is. Very young children, as all kindergarten teachers know, have trouble understanding the difference between a story and a question. Without guidance, a suggestion that young children ask questions of a visiting firefighter can result in long stories about vaguely fire-related events. Early childhood educators are accustomed to helping students discern the difference. But that is not the only area for potential confusion.

Less common is any effort to help students understand the difference between genuine questions and checks for understanding. Teachers ask a lot of "questions" to which they already know the answers. As teachers, we understand this as an important part of our formative assessment processes. We ask students to restate information, give examples, or solve problems as a way to determine how they understand content. The problem is, when we call these queries "questions" (and particularly if they are the only type of question students experience in school), we teach an unintended message. Students come to believe that, at least in school, questions have one correct answer and the teacher knows it. Their goal, under such circumstances, is to determine what the teacher is thinking and replicate that "answer." Such interactions bear little resemblance to the roles questioning plays in the real world, at least outside game shows.

Of course checks for understanding play an important role in school and, in fact, formative assessment is important in building a classroom atmosphere in which creativity can thrive. It simply is not the same as asking a genuine question. So why not teach students the difference? We can honestly say to young people, "You know, many times I ask questions in class and I already know the answers. When I do that, I'm trying to find out what you know and figure out how best to teach you. I need to check your understanding to make sure we are ready to go to the next idea. But that's not the same as a real question. When I ask a real question, I'm wondering about something and I don't know the answer. Sometimes there is no right answer at all!" Figures 6.4 and 6.5 represent activities that could be used to spark such a discussion, particularly if you want to teach students about research questions.

I Wonder . . .

Good researchers are always asking questions about the world around them. They notice things that are interesting and wonder about the things they do not know. This exercise will help you practice being a good questioner. For each topic, think of as many interesting questions as you can. Try to think of some unusual questions—questions no one else will think of.

For example, if the topic were baseball, you might wonder, How did the greatest baseball hitters learn to swing? What team won the most pennants? Why?

You could also wonder:

What type of food makes the most profit at the baseball stadium?
How has Little League changed since girls started playing?
Does the color or style of the uniform affect playing?

Now, you wonder about these topics:

Your school building
Cookies
Birds
Cars

What other topics (things) do you wonder about?

Figure 6.4 I wonder

Source: From Starko, A. J., & Schack, G. D. (1992). *Looking for Data in All the Right Places: A Guidebook for Conducting Original Research With Young Investigators.* Waco, TX: Prufrock Press, p. 8. Copyright 1992 by Prufrock Press. Reprinted with permission.

Question, Question, Who's Got the Question?

Albert Einstein once said that finding a good problem or asking a new question was the most important part of real advances in science. Good researchers are always asking questions about the world around them. They notice things that are interesting and wonder about the things they don't know. This exercise will help you practice being a good questioner. For each topic, think of as many interesting questions as you can. Try to think of some unusual questions, ones no one else will think of. For example, if the topic was athletic shoes, you might wonder:

Do athletic shoes really improve sports performance?
Do you really need different kinds of shoes for different sports?
When did athletic shoes become popular with people who weren't professional athletes? Why? How?

You could also wonder:

Which brands are most popular with athletes? Students at our school?
What is involved in celebrity endorsements of athletic shoes?
How many crimes involve the stealing of athletic shoes?

Now, what questions might you have about these topics?

Customs in your school:
Teenagers' eating habits:
Friendships:
Cars:

What other things do you wonder about?

Figure 6.5 Question, question, who's got the question?

Source: From Schack, G. D., & Starko, A. J. (1998). *Research Comes Alive.* Mansfield Center, CT: Creative Learning Press, p. 23. Reproduced with permission.

If we do this, we can (at least sometimes) frame our interactions so that students can identify the differences in purpose. A teacher might say, "OK, let me check to see if you understand," clearly signaling a particular goal. It is also possible to help students identify processes to check their own understanding. The teacher might suggest, "This is a good time for you to check to see if you understand. Is there something you'd like to clarify? You might want to ask a question about something that was unclear or try giving an example to see if it is correct. Sometimes, when I want to check my own understanding, I say to someone, 'Let me see if I understand. Did you mean. . . .?' Raphael, what might you say to me to check your understanding of this diagram?"

Other times, questioning might have a different goal. The teacher might say things like, "Lately, I've been reading a lot in the paper about the unusual algae growth in our lake this year. I have a lot of questions about that. Do you? For example, I've been wondering if this is a new kind of algae, or just more algae. I don't know, and I'd like to find out." This could lead to a discussion about what the students know about the local situation and what genuine questions it raises. The lesson here is quite different: questions can be used to express curiosity and guide us in seeking information. As students begin to understand that things phrased as questions can have very different purposes, they can begin to use questions strategically. Fortunately, there are a variety of questioning models that can help, each with particular purposes and strengths.

Question Formulation Technique (QFT)

Rothstein and Santana's (2011) journey into questioning began not with students but with parents. Working with parents in a dropout-prevention program in the 1980s, the authors repeatedly heard from parents that they did not want to attend school meetings because they "didn't even know what to ask." After initially thinking it would be a simple thing to provide parents with appropriate questions, Rothstein and Santana learned that what the parents really needed were the skills to generate and ask their own questions. Being able to ask questions turned out to be transformative, particularly for self-advocacy. When parents asked, "Why didn't we learn this in school?" Rothstein and Santana wondered, "Why, indeed?"

Thus began a 20-year journey exploring the role of questioning in a variety of venues. The key to their recommendations is a protocol for question generation called the Question Formulation Technique (QFT). Questions, of course, have many functions. In school, the QFT serves to support student engagement and learning by having them generate questions around a Question Focus provided by the teacher. This is not "What do you wonder about the world in general?" but "What do you wonder about this statement related to our core content?" This is the strategy's greatest strength and its biggest limitation. Having teachers provide the initial stimulus, if done well, means that the questions students generate should raise their curiosity and interest around areas planned for curriculum. This makes the process very school friendly while at the same time not being the optimum strategy for someone who wants students to generate individual questions about personal interests.

The process has three key stages for students:

- Produce Your Own Questions
- Improve Your Questions
- Prioritize Your Questions

Once the teacher presents a focus statement (or topic), groups of students generate questions using rules very similar to brainstorming. They categorize them as open or closed, understanding that both types can be useful, and practice changing questions from one type to the other to see which best reflect their key interests. Eventually students select the best three questions and use them for short- or long-term purposes, as determined by the teacher. You can find detailed guidance and resources at the Right Questions website (rightquestion.org).

A More Beautiful Question

One of the books that helped pushed questioning to the front and center of the education agenda is Berger's (2016) *A More Beautiful Question*. *A More Beautiful Question* is not a book about education specifically but a book about the way raising questions changes human learning, interaction, and invention. This is a book focused on innovation and the types of learning that will help move it forward. What makes a question beautiful? From the associated website, here's Berger's answer.

> A beautiful question is an ambitious yet actionable question that can begin to shift the way we perceive or think about something—and that might serve as a catalyst to bring about change.
>
> That definition makes clear that this book is not about grand philosophical or spiritual questions—Why are we here? How does one define "good"? Is there life after death?—all of those great questions that spark endless, impassioned debate. . . . The focus here is on questions that can be acted upon.
>
> (amorebeautifulquestion.com)

From that perspective, a beautiful question helps the questioner move forward—to learn more, solve a problem, imagine a better way. Berger suggests a three-stage progression in questioning: Why—What if—How. These categories envision the questioner looking at a situation and asking

1. Why does it have to be this way?
2. What if we could. . . . ?
3. How could we do it?

This is a powerful sequence to teach questioners of any age. If you teach about invention or innovation, work with maker activities, or just want students to envision the work differently, Berger's book (and the associated website) can be a fine resource.

Questioning Habits of Mind

One of my favorite tools for helping students move from being absorbers to questioners comes from Deborah Meier (2009). She cites five Habits of Mind underlying Boston's Mission Hill School, each of which can be framed as a question.

- **Evidence:** How do we know what we know, and what's the evidence?
- **Viewpoint:** Could there be another point of view?
- **Connections/Cause and Effect:** Do you see any patterns? Has this happened before? What are the possible consequences?
- **Conjecture:** Could it have been otherwise? If even just one thing had happened differently, what might have changed?
- **Relevance:** Does it matter? Who cares?

I would be hard pressed to think of a better set of questions for developing both critical and creative thinkers! These questions help students critique what they know but also ask that they consider other perspectives, examine possible changes, and look for new ways. Of course, the ways these questions would be implemented would differ across ages and subject matter. The kinds of evidence we'd look for in chemistry would be very different from those in literature, but they are all important. Changing one thing, or looking at relevance might be dramatically different in art versus history, but either requires flexibility of thought—the basis for creative thinking.

I do differ with Meier over one point. She believes the five mental habits are not to be taught or memorized but practiced together by both students and teachers. Clearly, using these perspectives in teaching subject matter would create a classroom atmosphere in which the Habits of Mind can grow. Still, I would teach the questions. I would post them in my classroom. I would point out times when I use them to consider the content before us, not in an attempt to have students memorize key questions but to explicitly model the types of thinking I'm hoping to support. Meier describes the schools she is helping to create as schools for democracy, schools that support an informed and intelligent citizenry. I believe these questions can do that. I also believe they can help develop classrooms in which students feel supported in thinking in new ways, trying different perspectives, and suggesting alternatives. So perhaps these Habits of Mind—along with the other questioning techniques—can help lead to schools for creativity, too.

Divergent-Thinking Strategies

Many techniques for enhancing creative thinking are designed to increase students' divergent thinking, or their ability to think of many different responses to a given situation. The most common definition of divergent thinking includes those types of thought discussed in Chapter 2 as part of Guilford's Structure of Intellect (SOI) model: fluency (thinking of many ideas), flexibility (thinking of different categories or points of view), originality (thinking of unusual ideas), and elaboration (adding detail to improve ideas). Fluency often is the basis of activities designed to improve divergent thinking. The more ideas you have, the logic goes, the more likely it is that at least one of them will be a good idea. There is some research to support this premise, beginning more than 40 years ago (MacKinnon, 1978; Parnes, 1963). However, the link between fluency and originality is not airtight. MacKinnon (1978) noted that some individuals have many ideas, including high-quality ones; some have many ideas with little originality; and others have only a few ideas but all of high quality. He suggested that no one approach will increase creative thinking for such diverse individuals. Individuals in the first group might be encouraged to develop their fluency, those in the second to consider criteria for evaluating their ideas, and those in the third to increase their output. He noted that people who produce only a few high-quality ideas often have many more ideas that they do not make public. Thus, fluency for its own sake may be questionable. And some activities designed to foster divergent thinking may not lead to the desired outcomes. For example, Rubenson and Runco (1995) found that the more people working in a brainstorming group, the less originality emerged.

And so, for years, researchers have been examining divergent thinking and seeking to understand and improve it. Some research has investigated links between training in divergent thinking and improved creativity. Baer (1993) examined the effects of training in divergent thinking on students' creative performance in a number of domains. Divergent-thinking activities were associated with higher-quality creative products in storytelling, collage making, and poetry writing for second-grade students. Basadur, Runco, and Vega (2000) worked with managers who learned a process similar to Creative Problem Solving and applied it to real-world problems. They identified the most important skill in generating high-quality solutions as the ability to generate a large number of solutions. Other studies have demonstrated that programs designed to enhance divergent thinking can improve creative thinking in school-aged and even preschool children (Alfonso-Ben-lliure, Meléndez, & García-Ballesteros, 2013; Doron, 2016), and learning about divergent thinking can improve divergent thinking (van de Kamp, Admiraal, van Drie, & Rijlaarsdam, 2015). Of course, in some cases, the measures used to assess creativity were very similar to the divergent-thinking skills taught, leaving open the question of relationship to real-world creativity.

Runco and Sakamoto (1999) cited a variety of research indicating that explicit directions asking for more fluent or more original ideas increase the likelihood of such ideas occurring. Yi, Plucker, and Guo (2015) found that providing creative models increased both verbal divergent thinking and artistic tasks. Such research continues, demonstrating that instructions to "be creative" are not as simple as they sound (Hong, O'Neil, & Peng, 2016). Directions to "be fluent" can result in more ideas, while "be creative" can lead to fewer but better ideas (Forthmann, Gerwig, et al., 2016; Nusbaum, Silvia, & Beaty, 2014). Forthmann et al. label this the "Be-creative effect." Not surprisingly, when students were both taught strategies to help them generate more ideas, and also instructed to be creative, their performance was significantly improved (Forthmann, Wilken, Doebler, & Holling, 2016, p. 25).

Still, it appears that although fluent thinking may not always lead to originality, at least some individuals increase their production of good ideas by considering many. And some measures of divergent thinking provide reasonable estimates of creativity or problem solving (Runco, 2010a). It is possible that the sheer number of ideas is important. Perhaps, too, the process of generating many ideas also encourages attitudes that are associated with creativity, experimenting with ideas in playful ways. It would seem that to be most effective, activities involving divergent thinking must make the purpose of the strategy clear. The goal is good ideas. Divergent thinking is one path to get there.

One approach, recommended in the Talents Unlimited model (Schlichter, 1986; Schlichter, Palmer, & Palmer, 1993), is direct teaching about divergent thinking. In the Talents Unlimited model, this type of thought, called productive thinking, is taught as one of several types that are important for success in a variety of tasks. Students are taught that when the task calls for productive thinking, they should do four things (Schlichter, 1986, p. 364):

1. Think of many ideas (fluency).
2. Think of varied ideas (flexibility).
3. Think of unusual ideas (originality).
4. Add to their ideas to make them better (elaboration).

In addition to teaching the model, instructors can encourage fluent, flexible, original, and elaborative thinking through their comments and questions. For example, asking, "How many ways can you think of to . . .?" encourages fluency. "What are some different kinds of ideas?" or "So far, all our ideas involve food. Try to think of ideas that solve the problem in a different way" encourages flexibility. Comments such as "Try to think of something no one else will think of" are designed to elicit originality, whereas "How can we build on this idea?" encourages elaboration.

I have taught students the four aspects of divergent thinking, along with the aphorism "Your first idea is practically never your best idea." I believe that teaching students this principle, along with a variety of strategies for increasing divergent thinking, can provide valuable tools as long as students understand the situations in which the tools are useful. There is no point in understanding how to use a lathe unless you are able to tell when you need it and when you might be better off with a saber saw, circular saw, or handsaw. Without such knowledge, you waste time, energy, and wood. In the same way, teaching students to think divergently without teaching them when such thinking is useful can lead to inefficiency and wasted time that our classes can ill afford.

Lesson 6.4 Flexible Thinking in Social Studies, Science, and/or Technology Education

Read a biography of George Washington Carver. Look for examples of fluency, flexibility, originality, and elaboration. Think about a substance that might be plentiful but not useful in your community—perhaps an invasive plant or plastic waste from a local business. Think flexibly about how the substance might be used productively. You might point out that the designers at Ikea have produced best-selling lighting and decorative features from what had formerly been industrial waste.

Consider the first three examples at the beginning of this chapter. In each case, individuals were trying to solve a problem or generate a new and better idea. These are the types of situations in which divergent thinking can be most useful. If we are trying to plan an original party menu, build an emergency shelter in the woods, or find a plastic that will suit a manufacturer's needs, it is unlikely that the first idea we consider will be the best possible idea. In such circumstances, there probably is value in considering multiple possibilities before choosing one.

In contrast, Mr. Brown's students, who are "brainstorming" as many types of birds as possible, are not trying to solve a problem or come up with a new type of bird. They are simply listing all the birds in their collective memory. They may even attack the task flexibly and generate responses such as a badminton birdie or a bird-of-paradise flower. Such tasks may provide a pleasant diversion for a Friday afternoon, but they do not provide clues into the nature or purpose of divergent thinking. Coming up with many ideas simply for the sake of making a long list does not teach students divergent thinking. It is essential for them to understand that divergent thinking is used when we need to solve problems or come up with new and better ideas.

The same caveat applies to the other strategies in this chapter. If students are to use strategies to increase their creative thinking, the strategies must be taught in meaningful ways. Students must understand how these techniques can be used—not just to talk to aliens but to communicate their ideas to friends and neighbors, come up with a better idea for their science project, or figure out how to get their baby brother out of the locked bathroom. The only possible value I can see in generating long lists of birds, things that are red, or uses for a brick is its value as a practice activity for students who already know about fluency and how it should be used. They could discuss how this task is different from the types of tasks in which they would really need to have many ideas or look to see whether their most unusual ideas were early or late in the list. Young children, in particular, may sometimes benefit from practice activities that are easier than most real-world problems.

Even so, the same goals could be better accomplished by using divergent thinking in a meaningful situation. When I was teaching in Connecticut, the state was hit with its first hurricane since 1938. Because the same trees that create the scenic tree-covered roads of New England also hang over the power lines, the hurricane caused millions of downed tree limbs and massive power losses. In the weeks after the storm, the branches were transformed into mountains of mulch along every roadside, far beyond the immediate demand for garden use. Rather than list the classic "uses for a red brick," which is fairly meaningless except to brick companies, my class used divergent thinking to come up with uses for the state's overabundance of mulch. This was a time when original ideas were needed and could be suggested to the proper authorities. Students could examine their list, realize that only after some effort had they come up with their best ideas, and begin to understand that this strategy might be useful in solving other problems. Similarly, the techniques described in this chapter can be used in the context of students' lives, community issues, and course content, allowing students to experience the strategies' usefulness.

Finally, it is important to help students see how divergent thinking fits into the whole of creative thinking. Divergent thinking alone is not creativity. Creativity entails finding a problem or issue worth addressing, generating ideas for addressing it, and evaluating the ideas generated— not to mention applying them. It may not be necessary for you to evaluate ideas in every activity involving divergent thinking, but it is important to do so often enough for students to understand that just having a lot of ideas is not sufficient. They must also be able to choose from the ideas those that are most original, most interesting, or most promising.

Brainstorming

Of all the strategies for generating ideas, brainstorming is probably the most familiar. It is based on Osborn's (1953) principle of deferred judgment: not evaluating any ideas until a number of them have been produced. Osborn compared the process to driving, noting that it is inefficient to drive while pushing on the gas and brake pedals simultaneously. In a parallel fashion, he believed that braking to evaluate ideas could hinder their production. According to this principle, generating many ideas and then applying evaluation criteria is more productive than judging each idea as it is produced. The intent is not to eliminate evaluation but simply to delay it.

The process of brainstorming strives for a nonjudgmental, supportive atmosphere in which idea production can flourish. One of the four cardinal rules of brainstorming even prohibits judgment. The four rules are:

1. Criticism is ruled out. No person is to evaluate any idea until all ideas have been produced. When you work with students, make sure they understand that this rule precludes both verbal and nonverbal criticism: no eye rolling, face making, or other signals.
2. Freewheeling is welcomed. In brainstorming, way-out notions are seen as stepping stones to creative ideas. Suggestions that appear to be far-fetched can open a new point of view that may lead to a workable idea. For example, while brainstorming ways to make a gloomy basement classroom more attractive, one student suggested replacing the glass block windows with stained glass. This suggestion was clearly not within the class's budget, but it led students to begin thinking about the windows and provided the inspiration for cellophane designs applied to the windows that were reminiscent of stained glass.
3. Quantity is wanted. Quantity is not desired for its own sake but because a large number of ideas seems more likely than a small number to yield a good idea.
4. Combination and improvement are sought. This rule is sometimes described as hitchhiking. It suggests that many good ideas can be found by building on or combining previous ideas. Such elaboration is to be encouraged. Sometimes extra effort is required to convey the notion of shared ideas to students accustomed to competition and individual ownership. One friend displayed a poster with the four rules of brainstorming. Underneath the fourth rule she wrote, "This is called teamwork, not 'stealing ideas!'" That phrase and the discussion about it helped her sports-minded students to understand that the successes of group processes are group successes, not individually owned triumphs or failures.

These four rules can be used in their original form or adapted for younger grade levels. One preschool teacher called brainstorming "popcorn thinking." Her students were taught that when they did popcorn thinking, they should try to have lots of ideas pop out, just like popcorn in the popper. They were also taught that no one is allowed to criticize ideas during popcorn thinking and that it is all right to use someone else's popcorn idea if you change it a little. The teacher did not find that her 3- and 4-year-olds needed any special encouragement to generate freewheeling ideas!

Whatever form the rules take, the focus during the first brainstorming sessions—as for the remaining strategies in this chapter—should be on learning the process rather than on analyzing complex content. If the first few experiences are fairly simple, such as planning a Halloween costume or selecting an animal as the class mascot, students will have the chance to learn the skill, see when it is useful, and be ready to apply it to many new situations.

Brainstorming can be an appropriate strategy any time you want a large number of ideas. This occurs most often when you need to solve a problem or come up with a new, original idea. Students could brainstorm new endings for a story, options for making a graph, strategies that might have aided a historical figure, variables for a possible science experiment, synonyms for an overused word, features for the school newspaper, or strategies for reducing cafeteria noise. They could brainstorm art materials for printing, resources in the school that could be recycled, or ways to encourage adults to use metric measurement. In each case, the strategy has a meaningful use. The list of ideas is generated so that one or more particularly good ideas can be selected, a much more purposeful reason than merely making a list.

In traditional brainstorming, participants work in groups with a leader or recorder to keep track of ideas and monitor the rules. Although some adults can manage groups of 10 or 12 individuals, such groups are probably too large for most students to manage independently. You may find group sizes of three to five more appropriate, except with highly motivated older students. Recall that Rubenson and Runco (1995) found that the larger the group, the less likely it would come up with a truly original idea. Bringing forth truly novel ideas is risky, and it may be more difficult in the face of a larger audience.

Usually in a heterogeneous class, the brainstorming groups should also be heterogeneous in knowledge, experience, race, and gender. There may be times when brainstorming is used with specifically targeted groups. A group of students with above-average interest, ability, or knowledge in a particular content area working together can provide an appropriate challenge that may not be possible in heterogeneous groups. Conversely, a group with less background or skill in a particular area may provide more opportunities for each student to contribute than might be found in a more diverse, fast-moving group. Flexible grouping patterns (whole-class groups, heterogeneous groups, or homogeneous groups) will allow you to use brainstorming in varied ways for different circumstances and content areas.

Whatever the group composition, groups typically brainstorm for a set period of time, perhaps 3 to 10 minutes, depending on the age of the participants, recording all suggestions without comment. At the end of that time, the group members review and evaluate the ideas using appropriate criteria. A group brainstorming alternative strategy that Lincoln might have used in dealing with Southern secession might consider the economic impact of the suggestions, their political viability given the climate of the time, and how the suggestions relate to Lincoln's expressed personal beliefs. Although the students themselves certainly could not implement any chosen suggestions, they may gain insight into the thought processes that go into such decisions. A discussion like this could be valuable in understanding the Civil War as well as the role of the presidency. A group brainstorming solutions to the cafeteria-noise problem might consider factors such as cost, whether the idea has the support of the principal or teachers, and the amount of noise likely to be affected.

There are numerous variations on brainstorming that can be effective under varied circumstances. Periods of brainstorming can be alternated with periods of evaluation. For example, groups can brainstorm for 5 minutes, select their best ideas, and then continue brainstorming, presumably in a productive direction. This process can be continued as long as necessary or desired. Students can brainstorm silently by writing ("brain writing") rather than verbalizing their ideas. Obviously, this technique is appropriate only for students who are old enough and sufficiently skilled that the writing itself does not get in the way of producing ideas. One way to organize this type of exercise is to group students as you would for a standard brainstorming session. Each person writes an idea on a piece of paper and passes it to the person on his or her right. That person may modify the idea or add a new idea before passing the paper on. Depending on the size of the group, the papers may circulate one or more times before the ideas are discussed. Brainstorming has been done all over the world. Preiser (2006) described variations on brainstorming used in Germany. These include having participants write ideas on cards before beginning a group activity and then "brainwalking" (p. 180), in which many versions of a topic are listed on papers posted around a room. Participants go from poster to poster, adding ideas and making notes on things that may relate to other posters. In electronic brainstorming, participants are not sitting in a group—in fact, they may not be in the same state. Using appropriate software, group members sit at computers and add ideas to a list, and the ideas are then immediately available to other group members. Just search for "online collaborative brainstorming" to find options. One advantage to electronic brainstorming is the opportunity to contribute ideas anonymously, so there may be less hesitation to add unique ideas.

In reverse brainstorming, the group proposes opposites of the desired ideas. Students might brainstorm ways to waste resources in school or increase arguments in the schoolyard. Reverse brainstorming is intended to open fresh perspectives and allow participants to attack the original problem from a new point of view. For this to be effective, students must be able to understand the purpose of the activity, which is to abstract principles from reversed data and to use them in a new situation. It is probably most effective with secondary students and adults, who are more likely to have the abstract reasoning skills to manage these transitions. Younger students may enjoy reverse brainstorming but are likely to become silly without making the transition back to the original issue; they might even want to implement some of the negative ideas suggested!

In other variations, individuals record their own ideas in an individual brainstorming session before joining a group. In one version, individuals list their suggestions and then read their ideas to the group in round-robin style, crossing out any duplicate ideas until all have been recorded. Ideas are then evaluated as usual.

A visual version of brainstorming, mind mapping, can be used by individuals or groups and is often the basis for online collaborations. In mind mapping, branching links and images are used to represent new ideas and their relationships to other ideas. This can be done on paper or a white board or through any of a number of mind-mapping apps. Seelig (2012) suggests brainstorming sessions in which individuals record ideas on individual sticky notes. These can be arranged and rearranged on a board as group ideas develop. They also allow individuals to record their ideas "on the fly" without worrying about whether someone else is talking, making it more difficult for one voice to dominate a group.

There is no one correct way to brainstorm, nor is there a single technique that guarantees positive results. Osborn himself did not propose brainstorming as a cure-all for any situation demanding creative ideas. Individuals vary in their approaches to and strengths in creative thinking, so no technique will work equally well for all. Some research suggests that the fluency associated with brainstorming increases the likelihood of participants' producing original ideas, but there is also research that calls into question the effectiveness of traditional brainstorming. As a strategy to teach students to think of multiple ideas before coming to closure, it may well have value. As a tool for generating quality ideas in real-world settings, it appears to have significant weaknesses.

Paulus and Nijstad (2003), among others, have reviewed the research on brainstorming and found it wanting. Individuals generating ideas alone are more effective and efficient than groups brainstorming similar topics. This doesn't mean that single individuals had more ideas than groups but that, for example, five individuals generating ideas separately are likely to come up with more good ideas than the same five individuals in a brainstorming group (Mullen, Johnson, & Salas, 1991). Sawyer (2007) synthesizes the critiques of brainstorming by describing three causes of productivity loss in traditional brainstorming. First, topic fixation occurs when groups get stuck in categories of related ideas and don't move from their rut. Some of the variations of brainstorming listed already (e.g., brain writing or brain walking) are less problematic in this regard. The second cause of lack of productivity is social inhibition. Despite the brainstorming rule regarding judging, brainstorming is more effective with noncontroversial topics and in groups of equals. Finally, brainstorming groups can fall victim to social loafing—some members of the group may relax and not feel as accountable for success in a group situation. Thus their individual efforts may produce better results than their efforts as part of a group. As we think about using brainstorming with students, it will be important to think about strategies to minimize these issues. We also may want to consider our ultimate goal. In a study comparing college students asked to generate many ideas versus those asked to come up with one good creative solution, researchers found that overall quality and originality favored the "one solution" group, even while the most original ideas came from the more fluent group (Reiter-Palmon & Arreola, 2015).

Finally, like adults, elementary school students faced with a divergent-thinking task are affected by the instructions given. Runco (1991a) reported a study in which students, some of whom had been identified as gifted and talented, were given five tests of divergent thinking. Some groups were given the standard directions asking for many responses, whereas others were instructed to give only original responses. Runco found that in all groups, those who were cued to be original were more likely to be original. They also were less fluent—a variation of the be-creative effect. An interesting observation in Runco's study is that the instruction to be original improved the scores of students not identified as gifted more than it improved the originality of students identified as gifted. In the end, brainstorming only results in creative ideas when participants understand that as a goal (Rietzschel, Nijstad, & Stroebe, 2014).

It appears that divergent thinking in general and brainstorming in particular may be helpful in generating new and appropriate ideas, but these strategies offer no guarantees. The quality of ideas is likely to improve when students understand the purpose of fluency—we are trying to be fluent not because the teacher likes long lists but because we are trying to come up with new and better ideas. Deferred judgment is an important component of brainstorming, but in some situations, considering the criteria for good ideas may not always hurt and may sometimes help. (It occurs to me that it requires tolerance for ambiguity simply to read creativity research!) It may be that, for teachers, the most important function of brainstorming and other divergent-thinking strategies is to practice the flexibility, risk taking, and other habits of mind associated with creativity. The classroom atmosphere associated with the activities may be more important than the strategies themselves. It is important for researchers and teachers to continue investigating the type and timing of evaluation that is best for varied circumstances, subject areas, and levels of expertise.

The remaining strategies in this section can be considered aids to divergent thinking. Divergent thinking suggests that it is good to think of many varied ideas, but it does not provide strategies for generating ideas when none are forthcoming. Although it is true that many brainstorming groups come up with original ideas after a period of dead time, it is also useful to know some cues for thinking of new ideas, changing direction, or getting started when you are feeling stuck.

Lesson 6.5   Flexible Thinking in Biology: DNA

Give each student a bag of 16 M&Ms™. The red candies represent thymine, white = adenine, yellow = cytosine, and blue = guanine. Have students line up the candies so that the white and yellow are on one side. Line the other candies up so that red is across from white and blue across from yellow. Have students rearrange the candies as many ways as possible. Think about the number of code combinations that would be available with millions of base pairs. What would happen if one color was missing? (Adapted from a lesson by Krista Adair.)

Thinking About the Classroom

If your students have not had previous experience with brainstorming, try some action research. Plan a lesson that requires them to generate many varied answers to a question or problem, such as planning new endings for a story or deciding how a character might solve a problem. Before the next lesson, teach students the rules and purpose of brainstorming. Then do a lesson that closely parallels the first lesson. With the students, examine the results. Under which conditions did students generate more ideas? Under which conditions were there more good ideas? If you want to avoid the effect of practice, randomly divide the class in half and give each half the same task, one with brainstorming instruction and one without. With older students, you might want to do (or repeat) the experiment with one of the variations of brainstorming.

SCAMPER

One of Osborn's original suggestions for improving divergent thinking was to use idea-spurring queries. His work included checklists of questions such as "How can we simplify? What combinations can be utilized? What adaptations can be made?" (Parnes, 1963, p. 35). When individuals or groups are generating ideas and suggestions begin to slow or become stuck in a single direction, such questions can point to a new perspective.

Eberle (1977, 1996) took some of Osborn's key questions and arranged them into an easy-to-remember acronym, SCAMPER. Eberle used the acronym to write a book using visual imagery and titled it, naturally enough, *SCAMPER*. It is described later in the chapter. The acronym SCAMPER can be a useful tool for many creative endeavors other than visual imagery. Because it is easy to remember, it can assist children as well as adults in using the idea-spurring questions that can help them generate diverse ideas. In this section, I examine the questions and strategies that underlie SCAMPER and how they may be used to facilitate divergent thinking.

The S in SCAMPER stands for *substitute*. It suggests asking questions such as "What could I use instead?" or "What other ingredients, materials, or components could I use?" Many new products and solutions to problems large and small are the result of substitution. The individual who first considered substituting artificial sweetener for sugar in soft drinks changed the country's habits forever. The person who realized napkins could be made of paper rather than fabric used substitution, as did the child who used a paper clip to repair a bicycle chain and the driver who held a car together with duct tape. In each case, a solution or innovation was found by substituting a new material or part for the original one.

The C stands for *combine*. It asks, "How can I combine parts or ideas? Are there two things I could blend rather than come up with something new?" Many common products are the result of combinations. Think of the things that have been combined with telephones: calculators, GPS systems, calendars, alarm clocks, music players, and so forth. Food products also frequently result from combinations. I once saw an innovation in a local grocery store that combined a serving of dry cereal with an individual-size carton of milk. This combination may be particularly useful for children who would like to serve themselves cereal but cannot manage a heavy milk jug without disaster.

Any of the SCAMPER verbs also can be used to stimulate works of art or literature. Lukman Glasgow's sculpture *Watergun* consists of a faucet at the end of the barrel of a pistol. Other combinations could be used to create interesting visual puns from compound words or figures of speech. Imagine how a carpool, a fan belt, or a handspring might be portrayed. Picasso used this technique to recombine elements of figures or objects that had been taken apart. A parallel process could be used to recombine parts of a familiar object in new ways to create a work of art. Similarly, characters from diverse literary forms could be combined for new story ideas. Imagine what kind of story might emerge if Curious George met the seven dwarfs or the personality of Lady Macbeth were one of the characters in *The Grapes of Wrath*.

Thinking About the Classroom

Look through magazines or gift catalogs. On your own or with students' help, collect pictures that illustrate the use of each of the SCAMPER verbs in developing new products. You may want to use the pictures to create a bulletin board. Younger students can use the examples to learn about inventing, whereas high school design students can use it to spur or improve their class projects. Alternatively, either group could pick a common household item and use the SCAMPER verbs to plan ways to improve it.

The A stands for *adapt*. It suggests questions such as "What else is like this?" or "Could we change or imitate something else?" In adapting, we change something known to solve the problem. Many communication apps for individuals without speech began as adaptations of boards that allowed the user to point (or blink) at the desired word. Countless fashion trends have started as adaptations of earlier styles. The first person to hook a trailer behind an automobile probably adapted the idea from wagons hooked behind horses.

Many times, creative solutions to problems come from adaptations of old ideas. In my graduate creativity class, the most daunting assignment probably is the requirement to identify a personal or social problem and invent something to solve it. Students are always relieved to realize that many inventions are adaptations of earlier ideas and products. Their adaptations have included a perforated pizza box that divides into individual plates, eliminating dishes and fitting more easily into the recycling bin, and a cutting board adapted for use by individuals with limited use of one arm. The board was equipped with prongs to hold food securely in place so that only one hand was needed for cutting. In these two cases, the adaptations must have been good ones, for we have since seen commercial versions of both.

The M can have several meanings. It can stand for *modify*. In modifying, we ask, "Could we change a current idea, practice, or product slightly and be successful?" Modifications might include changing the flavor or color of toothpaste to be more appealing to children or adding nuts and raisins to a popular cookie recipe. Slight changes in the styling of automobiles also could be characterized as modifications. The M can also stand for *magnify* or *minify*. Magnifying allows us to ask, "How could I make it bigger, stronger, more exaggerated, or more frequent?" It could lead to ever-larger television sets, giant Goldfish crackers and supersized meal portions, double-length garden hoses, or a weekly (rather than monthly) collection of recyclables. One of my students magnified the idea of a dentist's mirror by attaching an angled mirror to the end of a broomstick. He used it to check the gutters of his house without dragging out the ladder and climbing to the roof. Magnifying common objects to many times their size also can spur original works of art. Andre Peterson's *Staple Remover* is a 30-inch magnification of a familiar object. Viewed at that size, form becomes more important than function, allowing us to see the object in a new way. To minify is, of course, just the opposite. To go in this direction, we ask, "How can I make it smaller, more compact, lighter, or less frequent?" Minifying has led to Ritz bits (bite-size crackers), watch-sized computers, concentrated fabric softener, and 10-second commercials. (Actually, the shortened commercials combine both magnifying and minifying: They take less time, so we get more of them. I am not at all sure I am grateful for that innovation.)

The P stands for *put* to other uses. It suggests that we ask, "How can I use this in a new way?" The switch from advertising Kleenex as a makeup remover to billing it as a pocket handkerchief was a brilliant and profitable use of this strategy. Using resealable food storage bags to organize a

M stands for modify, magnify, or minify

suitcase, planting flowers in an old wheelbarrow, and recycling plastic milk jugs as part of a stage set all are examples of putting materials to uses other than those for which they were intended. A good friend used press-and-seal plastic wrap to keep her cast dry in the shower. When my elementary students considered alternate uses for the hurricane-generated mulch, they were using this part of the SCAMPER acronym.

The E is for *eliminate*. It leads us to ask, "What can be omitted or eliminated? Are all the parts necessary? Is it necessary to solve this problem at all?" Grocery stores are full of products from which fat or sugar have been eliminated. Poets constantly strive to eliminate unnecessary words. Concentrated laundry detergents are the result of omitting or reducing fillers. I occasionally think that fashion designers must delight in deciding which parts of women's clothing to eliminate next. Sometimes the problem itself can be eliminated if it is found to be unimportant or not worth the effort required to solve it. In some schools, efforts to reduce cafeteria noise were eliminated when would-be problem solvers determined that as long as students can hear emergency signals over the cafeteria noise, it may be good for students to talk in the cafeteria, or that the energy spent trying to keep them from doing so could more profitably be spent elsewhere.

Lesson 6.6   Put to Other Uses: Using Part of SCAMPER (K–12)

Joan Steiner's (1998) book *Look Alikes* is a fabulous example of putting objects to other uses, in this case, using common objects to create extraordinary landscapes. It can provide a challenge for anyone from child to adult to find new ways to use the things around us. *Note:* Many of the suggested activities in this text make use of picture books. Do not make the mistake of assuming picture books are appropriate only for young children. Many of the works of art and literature contained in such books speak powerfully to individuals of all ages. Moreover, they have the added advantage of being short enough to share easily in a brief period.

Finally, the R stands for *rearrange* or *reverse*. It suggests questions such as "Could I use a different sequence? Could I interchange parts? Could I do the opposite? What would happen if I turned it upside down, backward, or inside out?" Left-handed scissors, knives, and garden tools are examples of rearranging or reversing. I had a reversible winter coat that cut my dry-cleaning bills in half. One of my students used the principle of reversing to reduce the frustration she experienced in trying to get ketchup and salad dressings out of the bottles. She built a rack for her refrigerator door that holds all the bottles upside down. When she removes them from the refrigerator, they are ready to pour.

The questions generated by the SCAMPER acronym can be used to address many types of problems. Because the acronym itself is quite complex, teachers of young children may want to teach one or two letters at a time. Students of all ages can benefit by looking for examples of how others have used these strategies before using them independently. Students can look through magazines for examples of cartoons, advertisements, or products that illustrate the use of one or more SCAMPER verbs. These can be collected and displayed in the classroom. A commercial jingle may substitute new words in a popular song. A paper towel advertisement may use magnification as it portrays its product absorbing a small lake. Many new products can be identified as the result of idea-spurring questions.

You may find it easiest to have students begin to use the SCAMPER acronym in ways similar to those they see around them. They could use the questions to suggest ways to improve a familiar product or suggest new items for the school menu. Older students could try using idea-spurring questions to draw political or humorous cartoons or advertisements. However, the most important understanding is that all or parts of the SCAMPER acronym can be used any time students need to generate many ideas or solve a problem. They do not have to sit and wait for ideas to pop into their heads but can use the SCAMPER questions to help the ideas come.

Lesson 6.7   Reversible Poetry and More

Marilyn Singer's (2010) book *Mirror, Mirror* puts the "reverse" part of SCAMPER to use by creating poems that tell two different versions of fairy tales, one when read from the top down and another when lines are read from the bottom up. Challenge your students to create their own mirror poems or to try applying another SCAMPER verb to an original (or favorite) poem. What would happen to a poem if you substituted or eliminated words or perhaps magnified or minified aspects of the language?

In the example at the beginning of the chapter, Ms. Cochran used the SCAMPER questions to help students improve their science projects. Suppose second-grade students wanted to duplicate a demonstration in the science book that used colored water traveling up a celery stalk to illustrate the structure of the stem. The SCAMPER questions could be used to generate ideas for modifying the project. Students could ask a number of questions: "Could another plant be substituted for celery? Would it still work? Would other liquids work? Would they travel the same distance or at the same speed? Would big stems and little stems work the same way? What if you used a root instead of a stem? Would it work upside down? Do all colors travel the same way? At the same speed? If you cut a notch in the celery, what would happen?"

Older students could use a similar strategy for more sophisticated projects. If a seventh-grade student was interested in teaching mice to go through a maze, he or she might ask, "Does the shape or material of the maze affect the speed of learning? Could I combine this study with another variable, such as nutrition, noise level, or social interactions? Is there a famous experiment I could adapt? Does the height or width of the maze affect learning? If I reverse the maze in the room, will it matter? Could the idea of a maze be used in other types of experiments? How do human beings find their way through mazes? Are people who are good at paper-and-pencil mazes also good in three-dimensional mazes?" I can just imagine that last question resulting in a research study in a corn maze!

Lesson 6.8   Reversible Math (9–12)

To get a sense of whether students really understand a math principle, ask the question backward, giving the students the result and having them work through to where they must have started. For example, show students a graph of a line equation and talk them through how they could figure out what the equation is (without finding points). How can they determine whether the slope is positive or negative? Whether it's near zero or not? Whether the y-intercept is positive or negative? The same kind of process works with statistics (give them a mean and a median, asking them to come up with datasets that work), solving equations (give them an x and then ask them how many equations they can come up with that have that solution), story problems (give them the answer and ask them to come up with the scenario), and many other topics. (Adapted from a lesson by Sandy Becker.)

In either case, a variety of novel projects could be devised through responses to the SCAMPER questions. In a similar manner, SCAMPER can be used to modify and elaborate story plots, create ideas for three-dimensional art projects, or address school or community problems. It gives students a set of tools they can use when they are struggling to find an idea or to improve the ideas they have.

Thinking About the Classroom

Consider how SCAMPER could be used in more abstract ways. For example, in algebra, students could examine an equation for a line, then use the SCAMPER verbs to propose ways to change the equation. Play with that idea yourself. Try to graph each one and examine the changes that result. In this case, the acronym doesn't help to generate a new product per se, but it can help us think about mathematical relationships in many different ways.

Shape	Coating	Basic Filling	Additions	Size	Package	Tie-In
rectangle	milk chocolate	peanut butter	nuts	regular	singles	sports
circle	white chocolate	chocolate	caramel	double	buddy pack	sports figure
sphere	peanut creme	vanilla	cookie pieces	mini	family pack	cartoons
triangle	fruit coating	mint	coconut	varied	clear package	movie
prism	coconut	cashew butter	raisins	family	toys inside	TV show
animals	nuts	white chocolate	dates		package is a toy	news hero
rocket	cookie crumbs	orange	jelly		musical	story figure
truck	pretzel crumbs	cherry	sprinkles		personal	superhero
donut		other fruit	chopped candy			
			marshmallow			

Figure 6.6 Attribute listing for a new candy bar

Attribute Listing

Another strategy for generating creative ideas is attribute listing (Crawford, 1954). With this technique, the problem or product is divided into key attributes that are addressed separately. For example, an individual charged with creating a new candy bar might determine first what the key attributes of a candy bar are and then consider how each one might be altered or combined to form a new product. The attributes to be considered could include the shape, coating, basic filling, additions to the filling, size, packaging, and possible ties to famous characters. Instead of trying to plan a new product all at once, the candy designer might first think about variations in shape (What about a round candy bar or animal shapes?) and then consider each attribute in turn, using a list like the one in Figure 6.6. This process could result in a rocket-shaped bar filled with peanut butter and jelly or tiny orange-filled candies in a package tied to a Saturday-morning cartoon show.

A similar process might be followed by those designing cars, playgrounds, or any other complex product. By identifying the key attributes of the product, the design task can be broken into manageable components that can spur new combinations of ideas.

The same process can be used to address problems that do not result in a physical product. Imagine a town council trying to develop an advertising scheme to lure shoppers downtown. Attribute listing could be used to identify key features of the downtown area and how each could be used to attract consumers. A school library media specialist trying to ease congestion at the checkout desk might look at each step of the process separately. He or she might examine the path and direction of the line, the responsibilities of the student with the book, the position and responsibilities of the worker(s), and the physical arrangement of the desk. If he or she determines that young children cause delays because they have trouble placing their books on a high counter or cannot reach a scanner, perhaps a different area can be used when primary classes come to the center. If one person is responsible for supervising check-in while also giving directions for the next activity, perhaps those responsibilities could be separated. The strength of this process is that it forces the problem solver to examine the situation from several angles. If, for example, the problem solver had not used attribute listing but had simply viewed the desk traffic jam as a whole, he or she might not have noticed multiple causes for the difficulties.

Lesson 6.9 Attribute Listing in Spanish IV: "If" Clauses and the Mexican Revolution

This lesson should be taught simultaneously with lessons on contrary-to-fact "if" clauses—another example of Reversing. List key events of the Mexican Revolution on the board. For each event, use contrary-to-fact clauses to imagine what might have happened if each event had been altered in some way. For example, how would the revolution have been different if Carranza had not ordered the assassination of Emiliano Zapata? As an assignment, students can be asked to select an event not discussed in class and write a brief essay (in Spanish) describing what might have changed if the event had been altered. (Adapted from a lesson by Lynn Massucci.)

Students can be taught to use attribute listing in planning their school or personal projects. To be successful at it, most students will need assistance in learning to identify the important attributes of a product or situation. As they become adept at identifying key components, they can begin to consider the effects of changing each one, first by examining changes planned by others and later by instigating change themselves.

In an art class, students may use observation skills to identify attributes of a particular style of painting. They might then observe what changes resulted when one or more attributes were changed. After determining the key attributes of impressionist paintings (e.g., departure from realistic representation, a subject that is usually outdoors, varied colors to represent the effects of light and shadow), they might determine which attributes were altered by postimpressionists such as Seurat or Cezanne. Later, they might experiment with first mimicking a particular style then choosing some aspect of the style to change.

In science, students can identify the key attributes or variables in an experiment or demonstration and hypothesize what might happen if specific changes were made. One fifth-grade class examined the attributes of a tin-can solar cooker described in their textbook and speculated on what would happen if each were changed. The result was a "solar cook-off" that added considerably to students' understanding of solar energy. In a similar way, physics students may examine the attributes of a Ping-Pong ball launcher and hypothesize how changes in the length and angle of the mechanism change the velocity of the ball and the distance travelled.

A classic use of attribute listing is to represent story structure. After students learn about key attributes of stories (character, setting, conflict, and others), not only can they analyze the stories they read, but they also can use the knowledge to generate new stories. One possible exercise asks students to list 10 possible characters, 10 settings, 10 problems the character might have, and 10 sources of help. These can be combined to suggest many varied story lines. One variation is to require students to create a story based on the last four digits of their phone numbers. If my phone number ends in 0263, I would have to write a story using the tenth character, the second setting, the sixth problem, and the third source of help.

Davis (1998) described how Fran Striker used a similar technique to generate plots for the *Lone Ranger* series. Striker combined lists of characters, goals, obstacles, and outcomes to plan each episode. Older students may enjoy hypothesizing how such techniques may be used in planning contemporary television shows, perhaps using lists of attributes to develop a new episode for a favorite show.

Attribute listing also can be used to create fantasy characters, inventions, or products that can form the basis of creative writing. Very young children can combine lists of heads, bodies, and tails to invent new animals. Older students can use a similar process to invent new superheroes or other fantasy characters. They might list superpowers, animals, or other sources of unusual characteristics, secret identities, or weaknesses. These attributes may be combined to design new comic book characters. Older students might do a similar exercise but then compare superhero attributes to the attributes of heroes in Greek or Shakespearean literature. The idea of fantasy characters could be combined with science content to create characters that might live in a particular environment. Students might identify key attributes of the environment on Venus or deep ocean channels and then list possible features that could allow a living thing to exist in that situation. Characteristics could be used to develop characters for realistic science fiction writing. Students might also examine commercial science fiction and speculate on how the characters were developed, how attribute listing might have been used, or whether the characters could actually exist in the situations described. Attribute listing also can be used to modify existing products and to develop real or imagined inventions that could be the basis of persuasive speeches, advertisements, or stories. In social studies, attribute listing can be used to identify key issues or components in current events or historical stories and then predict the outcome if one attribute changed. In math, students can examine attributes of a polygon and hypothesize what will happen to the area as attributes are altered. Such exercises are particularly meaningful when put in a real-world context. What if that shape were used for packaging, and your company wanted a more innovative package without more materials cost?

Using attribute listing provides a fine opportunity to unite critical and creative thinking in the same activity. The types of critical analysis and evidence sharing emphasized by the current curriculum can be used to identify attributes. Hypothesizing about the possible results if one attribute were altered—and justifying the prediction—can allow students to process content in an interesting and flexible way while becoming aware of complex relationships across variables.

Lesson 6.10   Attribute Listing in Biology or Chemistry

Have students list the attributes of a particular animal and its habitat. Choose one attribute of the habitat and list all the ways it might change. For each, describe the impact on the animal studied, both short and long term. In a study of evolutionary biology, this could include predictions about the future of the species.

You could undertake the same activity with a particular molecule. What are its attributes? What could happen if one of them changed?

Morphological Synthesis

A variation of attribute listing, morphological synthesis, combines two attributes in the form of a grid. Young students wishing to invent a new animal could list animal heads on one axis and animal bodies on the other axis (Figure 6.7). Each square on the grid would represent a particular combination of head and body. Students could design an animal by choosing a particularly appealing combination or by random selection, such as pointing to the paper with their eyes shut or dropping a small object on the paper.

One of my favorite uses of morphological synthesis was created by a graduate student who lived in a house with several other international students. In addition to the usual stresses of graduate school, these students had to deal with language difficulties, limited budgets, and unfamiliar American food. One discovery that generated great enthusiasm in the group was prepared biscuit mix. It was inexpensive and flexible and could be mixed with a variety of foods to create new dishes. One student created a morphological synthesis grid to generate new recipes. Along one axis, she listed ways the biscuit mix could be cooked, such as baked, deep-fried, boiled for dumplings, steamed, or pan-fried. On the other axis, she listed things that could be combined

Animal Bodies

		Frog	Pig	Squirrel	Robin	Cat	Ant	Lion	Whale	Mouse
	Cow									
	Bear									
Animal Heads	Snake									
	Tiger									
	Elephant									
	Ostrich									
	Alligator									
	Goldfish									

Figure 6.7 Create an animal through morphological synthesis

with biscuit mix, with items ranging from chopped ham and onions to chocolate chips and raisins. Each square represented a possible dish. Although not all the combinations were delicious, the group was very pleased with some of the new dishes and planned to use the same technique to invent other new foods.

One advantage of using morphological synthesis with young students is that it teaches techniques that parallel those necessary to read and create graphs. When students identify the square that represents a giraffe head on a pig's body, they are reading x- and y-axes just as surely as they might in any math activity. Combining materials and strategies to invent a new game, mixing pop-up forms and unusual holidays to devise new cards, and adding seeds to growing media for a science experiment all provide opportunities for creative thinking that parallel those of many real-world creators while also giving students practice in several types of content and skills.

Random Input and Other Techniques of Lateral Thinking

In a book titled *Serious Creativity*, de Bono (1992) described strategies designed to promote lateral thinking and the creation of new ideas. De Bono, a prolific writer in the field of creativity for decades, has provided training in strategies designed to increase creative ideas for numerous companies and organizations around the world. The basis of de Bono's work is the systematic promotion of lateral thinking, defined as "seeking to solve problems by unorthodox or apparently illogical methods" (p. 52). He contrasted vertical thinking, in which the thinker delves more deeply into familiar or typical paths of thought—often compared with digging the same hole deeper—with lateral thinking, which tries a different perspective or vantage point—digging a new hole. De Bono believed that it is possible to increase lateral thinking through the systematic use of strategies that stimulate alternate paths of thought. His serious creativity does not rely on inspiration, intuition, or natural creative talent but teaches specific tools that anyone can use to increase the production of original ideas. Although the tools of lateral thinking are too numerous and complex to be fully explained here, we can examine a few examples.

Lesson 6.11   Morphological Synthesis in Kindergarten

After listening to *Color Zoo* (Ehlert, 1989), use morphological synthesis to choose three color–shape combinations to be used in creating a picture in the style of Lois Ehlert. Have students hold cards to create a human grid. Practice having designated students walk forward to create their combination. Read the book and discuss the shapes used by the illustrator. Have students use the morphological synthesis grid to create three shapes to be used in constructing an animal. (Adapted from a lesson by Melinda Spicer.)

The Creative Pause   One strategy an individual can learn for spurring creative effort is the creative pause. In using a creative pause, an individual stops midstream in a line of thinking not because there is a problem but because the thinker has chosen to stop. The pause allows the thinker to pay deliberate attention to some point, opening the possibility that there could be a new idea. A teacher might stop, purposefully, at a random point in lesson planning and consider whether there might be another way to approach the task about which he or she is thinking. Students could be taught to pause periodically in the midst of any potentially creative endeavor. Midway through a writing assignment, problem-solving task, social studies project, or art piece, they might pause and consider whether what they are doing might be approached in another way.

The creative pause is not used to focus on problems or force thinkers to wrack their brains for a novel response. It is an opportunity for focus and change. It is not the result of inspiration but a deliberate strategy that is undertaken purposefully, with the recognition that in any train of thought, there may be alternative, perhaps better ideas to be considered. If, after a brief period, no new ideas are forthcoming, the original line of thought can be continued. It is interesting to consider what ideas might result if every classroom held a sign reading, "PAUSE—and think." Students might occasionally look up, pause, consider their thinking, and perhaps move to new, more original ideas.

Provocations and the Use of Po One way to cue lateral thinking is to set up provocations. In using provocations, statements are put forward to provoke new patterns of thought rather than to describe realistic situations. De Bono (1970) suggested the word "po" to instigate provocations. When po precedes a statement, it indicates understanding by the writer or speaker that the statement is not true and may even be impossible, yet the speaker would like to consider it anyway in the hope that it might open new avenues of thought.

In many ways, po is parallel to children's use of "what if" or "just suppose." Young children often have little difficulty imagining what would happen if dogs could fly, if schools had no doors, or if pencils had to be kept in the refrigerator. Older students and adults sometimes have trouble maintaining focus on obviously ridiculous propositions long enough to see whether new, helpful ideas might be derived from them. The word "po" may be of particular value to middle-grade and older students who sometimes consider themselves much too mature to play silly games like Just Suppose. If they understand that po is a tool used by top business executives to spur creative ideas, they may be more willing to suspend judgment long enough to try it.

Four common provocations may be preceded by the word "po." The first is a reversal, similar to the R in SCAMPER. In a reversal provocation, you invert the situation being considered. Elements are not eliminated; they are reversed. For example, "po, the Native American Indians landed in Portugal in 1492." This provocation might form the basis of a class discussion on the impact of Columbus's voyage.

A second type of provocation is an exaggeration. This type of provocation takes one variable being considered and expands or diminishes it to unreasonable proportions. In developing a school recycling plan, the provocation might be po, each classroom produces 100 boxes of waste paper a week. This may suggest processes that might not otherwise be considered. An alternate provocation might be "po, each class may use only one piece of paper per year." Such an exaggeration might help students focus on how we might treat paper if it were a rare and valuable commodity.

The third provocation is distortion. Here, relationships between elements or time sequences are altered. An interesting provocation for a teacher education class might be "po, the students give tests to the teachers." A high school class studying the development of language might consider "po, written language developed before oral communication." Distortion provocations can be very challenging, yet powerful. The distortion "po, you die before you die" sounds bizarre, and yet it is the type of provocation that led to the development of living benefits life insurance, a successful form of insurance that brought profits to the insurance companies and financial relief to the terminally ill (de Bono, 1992). Of course, any of the provocations or other tools of lateral thinking also can be interpreted through visual or literary arts. Many art classes learn to enlarge or reduce images through the use of grids. When the grids are distorted, creating curves or angles not present in the original, students can find new perspectives.

As provocations become more unrealistic, the students will need increasing cognitive and emotional maturity to deal with them profitably. Young children can enjoy fantasy Just Suppose situations but may have trouble abstracting principles from the provocations to real life. You will need to use your professional judgment to gauge the types of provocations that are most powerful for your class. As students gain in sophistication and experience, they can recognize seemingly silly statements as serious invitations to new, innovative ideas.

Random Input Another way to cue lateral thinking is to use random input. With this strategy, the problem or subject for creative thought is juxtaposed with a randomly selected word, generally a noun. By attempting to make connections between the subject and the unrelated word, individuals may see the problem from a new vantage point or generate new ideas. If I were trying to think of a new approach to an upcoming social studies unit on westward expansion, I might try the random-input approach. In order to generate the word, I could either select one of several random word generators available online (just search for "random word generator") or as a phone/tablet app and use it to select a noun or use a hard-copy dictionary. If using the dictionary, I could open it to a randomly selected page (say, 68) and choose a random word position (perhaps the seventh word). If the seventh word is not a noun, I would continue down the page until I came to a noun. When I tried this exercise, the word I generated was bangalore torpedo. (You can tell this activity is authentic because I'd never make that up!) A bangalore torpedo is a metal tube that contains explosives and a firing mechanism and is used to cut barbed wire and detonate buried mines. One advantage to the online word generators is that you can choose to select from only common nouns, in which case I would not have ended up with such a challenging word, but let's go with it.

My task now is to make some kind of connection between a bangalore torpedo and westward expansion. Pioneers did not have to detonate buried mines, at least to my knowledge, so I have to consider other uses for explosives. Perhaps some students might be interested in the mechanics of the weapons used by pioneers. We might examine how explosives were used in creating pathways through the mountains or how settlers managed to get through the mountains without artificial pathways. Miners sometimes used explosives. Perhaps I could incorporate information on prospecting and mineral rights into my unit. We could examine the varying motives that led people westward. How were the solitary prospectors different from the mining companies or the homesteaders? The idea of focusing the unit on why people went west has potential for making ties to other aspects of the social studies curriculum.

I might take a totally different approach. How might the bangalore torpedo relate to my processes in planning the unit? Should I blow up all my previous plans and start over? Perhaps I need to review my ideas thus far for hidden mines or sources of difficulty. Whatever idea(s) I pursue, in approximately 5 minutes, an unusual and unrelated word has provided me with numerous avenues for potentially creative changes in my planning.

The same approach can be taught to students. High school students trying to develop a theme for a yearbook or dance, middle school students trying to develop a character for historical fiction, or elementary students brainstorming new ideas for the playground all may benefit from randomly selected input. Students can use random input when they have no ideas—for example, when they cannot think of a subject for an art project or cannot decide what area of independent study to pursue. Random input also can be useful when they have run out of ideas or when all their ideas are starting to sound the same. Perhaps they have already done three reports on various states and want to make the fourth project unique. A related option is to consider some of the toys designed to spur creativity and story writing, such as Story Cubes or Think-ets. Rolling a story cube can provide the next twist in a story or a random prompt for any kind of problem solving.

Practice activities with random input can work well during the last 5 minutes before lunch or at the end of the day. Pick a problem or issue from course content, school problems, or current events and match it with a random word. For example, "The problem is trash in front of the school. The word is lumberyard. What ideas does this bring us?"

Thinking About the Classroom

Try using random input in planning a lesson (or unit) when you are feeling stuck and looking for a new approach. Or, working with others who teach on your grade level, agree on a common topic. Try an online or tablet random word generator to select a different word for each group member, and spend 5 minutes individually using your words to generate ideas. Compare your results. See what varied directions the lesson might take from these random ideas. Try the same thing with a different type of problem— perhaps when you are trying to plan an interesting and novel party for your friends.

Six Thinking Hats and CoRT One of de Bono's best-known strategies is Six Thinking Hats. With this strategy, six different roles or ways of approaching a situation are defined as different-colored hats. A person taking on the white-hat role, for example, focuses on information. White-hat thinking asks questions such as "What information do we have? What information is missing? How are we going to get needed information?" The green hat requests creative effort, whereas the red hat looks for feelings, intuition, or emotion. Black-hat thinking requires critical judgment; yellow-hat thinking looks for benefits and possibilities; and blue-hat thinking monitors the kinds of thinking being used. By switching the type of thinking requested about a given problem, problem solvers can find new perspectives and avoid becoming trapped in familiar patterns of thought.

In using this strategy, teachers evaluating a textbook series might start with blue-hat thinking to define the goals of the group. Next, white-hat thinking might be used to gather information, and green-hat thinking could help in the development of possible selection criteria. Yellow-hat thinking could be used to look for good points about the list of criteria, followed by black-hat thinking to help in spotting weaknesses and flaws. Finally, red-hat thinking could be used to assess how the group feels about the criteria as they now stand (de Bono, 1991a, 1991b, 1999).

With young people or less complex tasks, a more limited sequence could be used. For example, students could use the thinking hats to respond to a poem. Students could begin with red-hat responses, explaining how they feel about the work: "I really like that poem" or "It gives me a feeling of loneliness." Next, the white hat could be used to identify interesting or missing information: "I can't tell why the writer went into the woods" or "I wonder what made him think the woods was like a cave." The yellow hat could be used to point out things students like about the poem: "I like the picture it makes in my mind of the bright stars near the dark woods" and "The last line has a lot of 's' sounds." If desired, this discussion could be continued using the black and green hats.

The key to each of these activities is that various hats, or frames of mind, are used and changed purposefully. The Six Thinking Hats strategy is designed to break apart different types of thinking, allowing the thinkers to concentrate more efficiently on each type of thought and ultimately provide a more rounded view of the task or situation. The effective use of Six

Thinking Hats demands more information than is possible in a brief overview. Information on resources supporting de Bono's teaching strategies is best obtained through his authorized website (edwdebono.com).

Another skills program that includes lateral thinking is CoRT (de Bono, 1986), an acronym for Cognitive Research Trust, the site of the program's origin. In using CoRT, students are taught strategies, each with an accompanying acronym, that provide cues for effective thinking. The first tool taught is called PMI (plus, minus, and interesting). The PMI tool is designed to overcome our natural tendency to continue thinking about a situation in the same direction as our original impression. Take a minute and think about what might happen if, starting tomorrow, all public schools were open 24 hours a day. Jot down a few of your ideas before continuing.

Chances are, if you look at your list, you will see that most of your ideas were generally positive or generally negative. If your first impression was that 24-hour schools were a good idea, you probably thought of several points to support that position. If your first impression was negative, it is likely that you listed several problems that might accompany 24-hour schools. Few people, unless cued, automatically look with equal care at multiple sides of an issue or situation. If you were to use PMI to think about 24-hour schools, you would list all the positive things and all the negative things you could. You would also list interesting things, those that are neither positive nor negative. Interesting things often are questions that might be raised, such as "What does 'open' mean? Would schools conduct traditional classes all day or would they take on different roles?" or "How would vacations be scheduled?" Other tools in the CoRT program provide similar cues for examining issues. Some but not all of the tools are designed to foster lateral thinking. The assumption underlying the program is that if students' perceptions of a situation can be broadened, their thinking about the situation can be more effective. Like Six Thinking Hats, CoRT demands more information and training than can be provided in a brief overview. Resource information is available through de Bono's website (edwdebono.com).

Using Divergent Thinking in Creative Problem Solving

As discussed in Chapter 2, Creative Problem Solving (CPS) is a model designed to facilitate as well as describe the creative process. Each of the components of CPS has both divergent and convergent aspects (called generative and focusing phases), so it is a natural context in which to use divergent thinking. Many of the tools described so far can be used effectively in the CPS process to enhance the number and diversity of ideas. Because CPS is complex, teachers of young children may wish to teach and use single parts of the process separately or to use them in a simplified fashion. Students of any age will need many varied experiences with CPS to master the stages and be able to apply them to varied situations. However, I believe the time and trouble required to teach CPS are worth the effort.

With CPS, students have a powerful process for attacking school, social, and personal problems from elementary grades into adulthood. Although early practice activities may focus on fantasy situations or fairy tales, CPS is most potent when used to interact with the real world. A book that will inspire you and your students to use your new problem-solving skills to benefit your community is *The Kid's Guide to Social Action* (Lewis, 1998). This book provides examples, skill instruction, and tips for problem solving that can be applied to a host of community issues. The basic components of CPS were discussed in Chapter 2. This section reviews each component and follows two classes through early problem-solving activities. As you review these two examples, it is important to remember that they are provided merely as examples of possible steps, not as an illustration of stages to be undertaken in every problem-solving activity. The effective use of CPS entails making good decisions about which components and stages to undertake in a given situation (Isaksen, Dorval, & Treffinger, 2000; Treffinger, 1995; Treffinger, Isaksen, & Dorval, 2000, 2003; Treffinger, Schoonover, & Selby, 2013).

Understanding the Challenge

Constructing Opportunities Recall from Chapter 2 that the first stage of Understanding the Challenge is Constructing Opportunities. Consider the way Barack Obama's first presidential campaign constructed opportunities to reach voters (and contributors) through the use of technology. Their identification of that opportunity has changed the face of political campaigning for the foreseeable future—but first they had to envision it as an area to address. It is necessary to identify a general sphere in which to focus problem-solving efforts. Sometimes opportunities are obvious or come up in day-to-day classroom conversation. In one class, a sixth-grade girl returned from a vacation outraged over the limitations in restaurant children's menus. Because the girl had a small appetite, her mother insisted that she order children's meals. Although her mother ate a variety of interesting food on her vacation, the sixth grader spent the entire week eating hamburgers, hot dogs, fried chicken, and spaghetti. For her, this was the beginning of a project that spanned nutrition, restaurant regulations, age discrimination, and many other issues. In another school, frequent injuries on the blacktop playground provided an obvious focus for concern.

If a challenge does not present itself immediately, students can be taught to look for problem areas. Newspapers or news websites can be used to generate lists of concerns. Local or school officials can be interviewed to identify issues affecting the community. For young children, teachers may wish to identify real or fictional challenges. I have selected two opportunities for following the CPS process through. The first is an imaginary primary teacher's fictional problem-solving exercise revolving around Horton and the Whoville situation (Seuss, 1954). In a second real-world example from my own teaching, the mess was not a trouble spot but an opportunity. Two middle school students became curious about the historical marker near the school and went out to read it after the school day ended. The marker described the town's beginnings, and, with a few calculations, the students realized that the town was approaching its 250th birthday. This was not a problem but an opportunity for creative problem solving.

In each case, students should be able to identify the general goal of the problem-solving activity and whether the goal was self-selected or presented by the teacher. Students who have some experience with Creative Problem Solving could begin by Appraising the Task to determine whether CPS is an appropriate tool for this opportunity. They might also Design the Process by selecting which stages of CPS are most appropriate for the situation at hand. In this case, I will describe each possible component as if the decision had been made to pursue each available stage.

Exploring Data In Exploring Data, students learn as much about the situation as possible. The young students investigating Whoville could write down everything they know about Horton's situation. The list should include facts, feelings, and impressions obtained by reading the book. Students could determine which ideas are facts, which are opinions, and which cannot be fully determined. They also could record information they would like to have if they could visit Horton at the site of his dilemma. This exercise would provide practice in Exploring Data and in supporting ideas with information from text.

For the 250th anniversary group, Exploring Data had a wider range. The curious students read town history, talked to local officials about planned celebrations (there were none), and spoke to community members about town activities during the 1976 national bicentennial. Several people believed that near the bicentennial (no one knew exactly when), some elementary school students had buried a time capsule in front of a local school. No one knew exactly where.

The first step in Creative Problem Solving is finding a challenge—or a mess

Framing Problems Framing Problems is a stage in which problem solvers identify potential sub-problems in their challenge. Problems usually start with IWWMW ("In what ways might we?"). In the *Horton Hears a Who* exercise, problem statements might start with "In what ways might Horton . . ." Students should list as many problem statements as possible before choosing the one (or a combination) that best expresses the dilemma they choose to address. The primary school group might ultimately settle for a problem statement such as "In what ways might Horton keep the people of Whoville safe without having to sit still all the time?" The anniversary group's problem was something like "In what ways might we celebrate the town's 250th anniversary so that it will be remembered?"

Generating Ideas In the Generating Ideas stage, problem solvers generate as many varied and unusual ideas as possible for solving the problem. At this stage of the CPS process, many other tools for divergent thinking can be useful. Attribute listing, SCAMPER, morphological synthesis, metaphorical thinking, and others all can be used to increase the number and diversity of solutions put forth. After the group has produced as many ideas as needed, a smaller number of ideas usually is selected to continue the CPS process. At this stage, no formal criteria are used for selecting the ideas. The group simply chooses the ideas that seem best. The Horton group might choose such ideas as building a stand to hold Whoville, getting someone else to hold it for a while, getting the people in Whoville to get off the dust ball for a vacation, and building a new Whoville. The 250th anniversary group suggested numerous ideas for a community celebration: a town festival, articles in the paper, commemorative souvenirs, a new time capsule, and a variety of school projects.

Preparing for Action

Developing Solutions In Developing Solutions, the short list of ideas is evaluated using criteria determined by the group. The number of criteria and the sophistication of the evaluation will vary with grade level. Young children should begin with a small number of criteria, simply evaluated. For example, in judging Horton's options, students might be asked how Horton could decide which was the best idea. They might ask, "Could he do it without dropping Whoville? Would the Who people be safe? Would the Who people be happy? Would Horton be happy?" These criteria might be evaluated with the simple grid shown in Figure 6.8. Each suggestion could be judged on each criterion and given a happy face, sad face, or neutral (can't tell or maybe) face. The solution with the greatest number of happy faces is likely to be the best solution. As students mature and gain experience with CPS, they can use more sophisticated focusing tools. Rather than smiling faces, students can use numerical rankings for each criterion, adding totals to determine the highest-ranked solution. If students use CPS in real-world contexts, they probably will soon determine that the point totals may not always identify the best idea. Sometimes an idea may rank high but be impossible to carry out. For example, if the 250th anniversary group had an idea that was ranked high on every criterion except "Will the principal let us do it?" the high rankings probably will not be sufficient to make it a viable idea.

	Could Horton do it?	Would the Who people be safe?	Would the Who people be happy?	Would Horton be happy?
Build a stand for Whoville	☺			
Get someone else to hold it	☺			
Get the people of Whoville off the dust ball	☺			
Build a new Whoville	☹			

Figure 6.8 Solution-finding for Horton

Lesson 6.12   Using CPS in American History

Understanding the Challenge

Review the immigrant groups who settled in the colonies and the varying types of technological knowledge they brought with them. Discuss why people moved to the frontier or backcountry. Brainstorm the types of challenges likely to be found on the frontier. Small groups of students choose a problem situation to study, researching facts relevant to the situation. For example, a group studying the problem "limited food" might study climate, soil conditions, vegetation, wildlife, and the like. They also would investigate the technology related to food production available in the 18th century. Frame a problem statement in the form "In what ways might we . . .?"

Generating Ideas

Using a period tool as a basis, groups use SCAMPER to modify the tool to improve it. Select criteria for evaluating the tool. (Evaluation criteria may be generated as a whole-class activity.)

Planning for Action

Plan the materials and steps necessary to create either the new tool or a model of the tool. (Adapted from a lesson by Linda Gayer.)

In other cases, students may realize that they omitted an important criterion (e.g., money or time available) or that some criteria simply are more important than others. In the actual 250th anniversary group, building a time capsule did not outrank all other ideas, especially those concerning community involvement, but the group really wanted to build a time capsule. The enthusiasm of many class members was much greater for that project idea than for any other. They determined that for this project, class interest was particularly important, so they gave it additional weight.

Students also need to understand that ideas do not have to be mutually exclusive, that sometimes they can be combined, or that many can be pursued simultaneously. The 250th anniversary group demonstrated this diversity. They divided in half, with one half planning to build and bury the time capsule while attempting to locate the previous mystery capsule on the school grounds. The other half, who had been investigating the stock market, decided to create a business to produce and market commemorative souvenirs. They planned to market company stock to finance their venture and, rather than plan a town celebration, to incorporate sale of their souvenirs into the town's annual spring festival. Other strategies for teaching focusing (the convergent pieces of CPS) can be found in Treffinger et al. (2013).

Building Acceptance The final stage of the CPS process asks problem solvers to create a plan of action. They are to determine what needs to be done, who will be responsible for each task, and what a reasonable time frame is. In addition, those involved in planning attempt to identify in advance what the major stumbling blocks might be. These barriers could be difficult parts of the plan, or they could be individuals or groups who oppose the plan. If planners can identify the problem in advance and develop strategies for avoiding or minimizing them, their chances of success are increased.

The primary school children trying to solve Horton's problem might decide on a simple three-stage plan for building a stand for Whoville: (a) gather materials, (b) build a sturdy stand with a soft top, and (c) gently put the dust ball on the stand. If Horton cannot put Whoville down to gather materials and build the stand, those responsibilities will need to be assigned to someone else. Maybe a friend would do it. Students also should identify any possible problems that might arise: What if the friend refuses to help? What if the Whos at the bottom of Whoville are crushed? Planning for these eventualities—Horton could call another friend, or he could ask the Whos to travel to the top of the dust ball while he puts it down—allows students to begin to envision how difficulties can be anticipated and avoided in other situations.

In real-world applications of CPS, Building Acceptance becomes particularly important. The 250th anniversary group needed detailed plans to realize their ideas. This stage of the process, in which they thought about the details of cost, timing, and responsibilities for each project, allowed them to plan ahead, thus avoiding many difficulties later on. From their difficulty in locating the bicentennial time capsule, they learned that if they wanted to be sure their capsule was eventually located, it would have to be clearly marked. In addition to leaving a map in the school office safe, the students topped the capsule with a large piece of scrap metal that could be located easily with a metal detector.

Even detailed planning will not eliminate all difficulties. At one point, the 250th anniversary souvenirs were not selling well, and the students' dreams of profits were rapidly evaporating. Divergent-thinking tools and strategies were never so welcome as when they were needed to salvage this important project. The group quickly devised new sales strategies and was able to sell the souvenirs. This example is perhaps CPS at its best. The skills the students had learned in one context were suddenly needed, used, and found successful in another. The wider the variety of contexts in which students practice these skills, the more likely they are to be able to transfer the skills to other situations. It is important for you to teach explicitly about transfer. As students learn the skills of CPS, you can ask them, "When else might we use this process? When have you had a problem that needed a creative solution?" It is also important that students understand that it is not necessary or desirable to use all the CPS components or stages in a given situation. The key (and a key purpose of the Planning Your Approach component) is to determine which processes are needed and to use them appropriately.

You also can use individual steps of the process as appropriate in many classroom contexts. Sometimes only one or two stages of the process are necessary or appropriate. Students may use Framing Problems to clarify conflicts in the classroom, Building Acceptance to plan class activities or projects, and Developing Solutions to select the site for a class field trip or to choose the class pet. High school students may find the process valuable in a variety of extracurricular venues, from prom or yearbook planning to designing stage sets within a budget. Any of the CPS stages can be used in various historical contexts, allowing students to envision the circumstances that could cause them to make particular decisions—or to change history. CPS could be combined with role-playing to consider how the Treaty of Versailles might have been negotiated differently while still maintaining the interests of various countries. Of course CPS is invaluable in technology, engineering, or robotics classes or maker clubs, where solving creative problems is the focus of activity.

The metacognitive skills required for deciding which steps to apply in a given situation provide powerful opportunities for analysis. If students think CPS must always be used in its entirety, they will miss valuable opportunities for transfer and critical thinking. In fact, at the beginning, you may choose to teach three broad components of CPS (Understanding the Challenge,

Generating Ideas, and Preparing for Action) rather than all the individual steps. Once students have seen the importance of understanding a problem before trying to address it, they will be better prepared to learn specific strategies for doing so. Whether students are dealing with fictional or actual problems, CPS can allow them to develop valuable problem-solving skills, foster habits of mind that are supportive of creativity, and process important content all at the same time. The depth and breadth of possible benefits make it clear that the time and effort expended in teaching this complex process can be well spent. A host of materials on using the Creative Problem Solving model with students is available at the Center for Creative Learning, Inc. website (creativelearning.com).

Thinking About the Classroom

Find a friend who teaches at the same grade level as you and list curriculum areas in which you might use CPS. Choose one example to try with your class. Remember that you could problem solve either real-world problems or problems from history or literature—either of which will provide lots of opportunities for finding evidence in texts.

Design Thinking

Want a better mousetrap? Want hotels that feel like home? How about a new way of thinking about literature? A new way to design curriculum? You might consider design thinking. While there are a number of varieties and definitions, design thinking is a process in which the strategies of designers are used to address all manner of needs and problems. Seelig (2012) points out that the scientific method of analytic thinking is useful when trying to investigate the world but that different types of thinking are needed when the goal is to *invent* rather than *discover*. The term "design thinking" has roots with David Kelley at Stanford's famous d[esign] school. It is the core of thinking at IDEO—source of innovations for businesses from HBO to the TSA. Design thinking is not all about high fashion, better curtains, or sleeker cars. It is a way of thinking that assumes change and innovation are possible. In an interview with *Fast Company*, Kelley said,

> [W]e moved from thinking of ourselves as designers to thinking of ourselves as design thinkers . . . What we, as design thinkers, have, is this creative confidence that, when given a difficult problem, we have a methodology that enables us to come up with a solution that nobody has before.
>
> (Tischler, 2009)

Design thinking assumes everyone can be creative given the tools and strategies to do it.

Design thinking can be used by teachers addressing problems in schools or curriculum (and we do have a few of those, yes?). It also can be taught to students. In fact, some schools are choosing design thinking as an organizing principle of their curriculum. For example, in my area, the Henry Ford Learning Institute structures middle and high school curriculum around quarterly design challenges. It is interesting to compare the stages of the Stanford model of design thinking to creative problem solving.

Empathize The first step in design thinking is unlike any other problem-solving strategy I've seen: Empathizing. In most cases, designers—and many others—are addressing problems that affect others. In order to offer the best possible solutions, it is essential to understand others. Design thinkers may observe, discuss, and listen to others in order to come to deeper understanding. Working with a team, design thinkers collect information about potential users or other people involved.

Define In this stage, you define the design challenge—or finding the problem. This stage is very similar to the Framing the Problem (or Problem-Finding) stage in CPS, except it is framed as a Point of View (POV) and may be more narrow than a typical problem statement in CPS. A good POV is grounded in insights about the users and focuses the problem, but it also captures the enthusiasm and imagination of the design team.

Ideate This stage parallels the Generating Ideas (or Idea-Finding) stage of CPS in generating many varied ideas for addressing the problem. Many other creative thinking strategies can be used here—mind mapping, sketching, SCAMPER, building, and so forth.

Prototype This is another stage that is, perhaps, idiosyncratic to the design thinking process. Prototyping asks the design team to produce an artifact of some type that can be shared with those whose problem is being addressed. It could be a model of a gadget, but it also could be a storyboard, a role-playing activity, or anything else that allows the ideas to be shared in an interactive way. A team may prototype several ideas to see which are most effective and appealing to the audience. The stage of CPS tries to anticipate problems that might be encountered in a prospective audience, but the design thinking process actually confronts them.

Test This is where that confrontation takes place—users are asked for feedback about the prototypes. Again, CPS addresses the need to build acceptance but doesn't specifically suggest trials by users, likely because CPS was created in order to address all manner of problems, and design thinking (not surprisingly) has its roots in designing "stuff," though its uses now are much wider.

Consider how the strategies of design thinking could be used for school problems and curriculum innovation. There are many resources to help you get started. Stanford's Taking Design to School project slightly adapts the design steps (dividing Empathize into Understand and Observe) for use with students. A quick search can help you locate their materials online. Edutopia's 5-Minute film festival has a list of short films featuring teachers and students using design thinking (www.edutopia.org/blog/film-festival-design-thinking-in-schools). The Design Thinking for Teachers website (designthinkingforeducators.com/) has many useful resources, including a Toolkit outlining strategies for using design thinking in your school or community. Gudipati and Sethi (2017) describe teaching children a four-step process of Feel-Imagine-Do-Share (FIDS). And Martinez and Stager (2013) present an even simpler design model for schools: TMI or Think, Make, Improve. Their model has strong ties to the Maker movement and aims to engage students in the messiness of real-world building and problem solving. They caution against projects pre-ordained by the teacher, but encourage open-ended prompts such as "Make something that will start here and end there in one minute" (p. 62).

Of course, as Goldman and Kabayadondo (2017) point out, the purpose of design thinking—particularly in schools—is not to learn the steps of a method but to change mindset: becoming more empathy driven in problem solving, committing to action, and understanding failures and persistence as necessary parts of success. It is the attitude more than the process that changes students' approaches to problems. Design thinking fosters an "I can" attitude. Whichever model of design thinking you investigate, it has the potential to engage your students in problem solving that mirrors that in real-world innovation and to help them become more confident and committed problem solvers as well.

Using Metaphors and Analogies

Several theories of creativity emphasize the importance of bringing together remote ideas to stimulate a new point of view or to forge a new synthesis. Among the most powerful tools in this process are metaphors and analogies. Their use can also be considered a mechanism for divergent thinking because it can produce many varied ideas, but it generally is focused more on the types of ideas produced than on the number. In analogical thinking, ideas from one context are transferred to another in a search for parallels, insights, fresh perspectives, or new syntheses.

Creative individuals have transformed, been inspired by, and occasionally plagiarized the ideas of others throughout history. Composers have based works on familiar folk melodies, other composers' themes, and their own earlier compositions. In the best cases, these original sources have been transfigured into unique wholes by being merged with new themes or set with interesting instrumentation. The new wholes may not only be valuable in themselves, but may also add to our understanding of the works from which they originated.

The same processes operate in art, literature, and other disciplines. Fashion designers pull key ideas from one era and merge them with the materials and sensibilities of another. Writers use imagery that evokes earlier stories, heroes, and times. We understand Frodo Baggins more fully when we place him in the context of mythic heroes such as Gilgamesh or Odysseus. We understand *West Side Story* because of *Romeo and Juliet*. Langston Hughes (1951) invited his readers to understand the consequences of a dream deferred by comparing it to a raisin in the sun, a festering sore, a sagging load, and an explosion. Each comparison brings a fresh perspective and raises new questions and understandings. Because we know raisins and sores, we may begin to know dreams. The power of metaphor and analogy to communicate and bring new insight is one reason for teaching children to use these techniques.

Metaphors also can play an important role in problem solving and scientific discovery. Numerous inventors and scholars have attributed their ideas to parallels with objects or events around them. Gutenberg developed the idea of movable type by looking at the way coins were stamped. Samuel Morse found the idea for the relays used to transmit telegraph signals over long distances while he was traveling by stagecoach and noticing the stations where horses were replaced as they began to tire. Eli Whitney said he developed the idea for the cotton gin while watching a cat trying to catch a chicken through a fence. (Others claim he usurped the idea from a Mrs. Greene, who could not obtain a patent in her own name because she was a woman! [Gordon & Poze, 1979; Hanaford, 1882].)

A variety of scientific insights originated in metaphor. Pasteur began to understand the mechanisms of infection by seeing similarities between infected wounds and fermenting grapes. Darwin's evolutionary tree was a powerful image that was unchallenged through years of research. Einstein used moving trains to gain insight into relationships in time and space. The process of seeing or imagining how one thing might be like something else can allow new parallels to unfold, spurring hypotheses, syntheses, and perspectives.

Lesson 6.13   Names for Snow

Beach's (2003) picture book *Names for Snow* can serve as a fine introduction to metaphor for young children or a charming inspiration for writers through adulthood. Imagining snow as a mother, a kitten, or a magician can open opportunities to view other natural beauties. What might be the names for rain, tree, or sky?

Synectics

Synectics is an original word coined to mean "the joining together of different and apparently irrelevant elements" (Gordon, 1981, p. 5). Synectic methods are metaphor- or analogy-based techniques for bringing elements together in a search for new ideas or solutions. They have been used by businesses, think tanks, and research organizations and have been the impetus behind the ideas for Pringles potato chips, magnesium-impregnated bandages, disposable diapers, dial-your-own-octane gas pumps, the space-saver Kleenex box, and a host of other innovations. Synectic ideas also have been adapted for teachers and students in a series of workbooks and curriculum development guides (Gordon & Poze, 1972, 1975, 1979, 1981, 1984).

Lesson 6.14   Use of Metaphor in Spanish IV or Social Studies: The Conquest of Mexico

In Spanish: Describe the process by which a germ enters the body and causes an infection. Discuss how this process is similar to the conquest of Mexico. As an assignment, students create their own analogy and create a visual image that illustrates the comparison between their analogy and the conquest of Mexico.

In social studies: Use a similar process to create analogies for other historical events. What natural processes could be considered analogous to the Mideast conflicts? To the era of space exploration? (Adapted from a lesson by Lynn Massucci.)

The basic processes of Synectics are "making the strange familiar" and "making the familiar strange" (Prince, 1968, p. 4). To make the strange familiar, you combine something familiar with a new problem or situation to solve the problem or come to an understanding. To make the familiar strange, you also combine something new or strange with something familiar, this time to gain new insights into or perspectives on the already familiar idea. These two processes are facilitated through the creation of various types of analogies.

Direct Analogies   Direct analogies are the simplest type of comparison. In a direct analogy, individuals look for parallels between one idea, object, or situation and another. Students first learning to make direct analogies start with simple comparisons between similar objects and progress to more abstract processes. Early comparisons might examine how a bird is like an airplane or how a kite is like a balloon. Beginning comparisons are most likely to be successful if they are based on clear similarities in either form or function. Even young students likely can see physical similarities between a tree and a hat rack or functional similarities between a campfire and a stove.

Students will be most successful if they first practice describing the connections in an analogy selected by someone else before they begin to create their own. They should have opportunities to identify the connections and similarities in such activities as how a comb and a rake are alike before being asked, "What things are like a comb?"

The power of the technique comes as students begin to generate their own analogies and see similarities between more remote objects. They might examine how a rock is like a tree or a dog or how a feather is like grass. As students mature and develop abstract thinking, direct analogies can encompass abstract ideas. Students might discuss how happiness is like fire, how freedom is like chains, or how erosion is like a thief. They can make these comparisons as exercises to practice metaphorical thinking or to process important curricular ideas. Students studying immigration might discuss how immigration is like banking, migrating, or cooking a meal. Students studying imperialism might be asked, "What animal is like imperialism?" By discussing student-generated analogies about content, students can process content at complex levels of thinking, and teachers can gain insight into students' understanding of key ideas. You might consider creating a graphic organizer to help students frame their understanding, with opportunities for them to note parallels.

Direct analogies also are powerful tools for creating visual images. Roukes's (1982) *Art Synectics*, although not directly paralleling all the Synectic processes, uses various types of analogies to stimulate art activities. Direct analogies can be made between emotions and a variety of objects: a twisted ribbon to signify laziness or a broken mirror glued over a photograph to signify anxiety. For one activity, Roukes (1982) suggested that such items be collected and displayed in a small box with many compartments to create an emotion box (p. 68). Other projects use strategies ranging from personal analogies to magnification, combination, and distortion to stimulate new points of view in the visual arts.

Personal Analogies For personal analogies, students are asked to be the thing. They do not physically act out the object or situation as they might in creative dramatics. In fact, many of the objects and situations that might be investigated through personal analogy do not easily lend themselves to dramatic interpretation. Doing a dramatic interpretation of a plant cell or a sedimentary rock would be difficult, but if students could imagine they were those things in specific situations (the cell splits or the rock is subjected to increasing heat and pressure), they could gain greater understanding and new perspectives.

The amount of experience students have had with personal analogies, as well as their developmental level, will affect their depth of connection and empathetic involvement in the analogies they create. The greater the conceptual distance between the person and the analogy, the more difficult it is for him or her to attain empathetic involvement but the greater the likelihood that the analogy will lead the person to new ideas.

Lesson 6.15 Metaphor in Religion: 1 Corinthians 13

Have students restate 1 Corinthians 13 in light of one of their roles. For example, "If I speak in the tones of men and of angels but have not love, I am only a resounding gong or a clanging cymbal" can be restated as it might be lived by someone who works at a fast food chain: "If I could take orders at the speed of light, but did not have love for each of my customers, I would be just as well sweeping the floor." (Adapted from a lesson by Tanya Hart.)

There are four levels of involvement for a personal analogy (Joyce, Weil, & Calhoun, 2009):

1. First-person description of facts. At this level, the person describes what is known about the object or animal but shows no empathetic involvement. In describing a porcupine, the student might say, "I feel prickly," or "I feel my tail bump on the ground."
2. First-person identification with emotion. At the second level, the person recites common emotions but does not present new insights. In describing the porcupine, the student might say, "I feel happy walking through the woods," or "I feel protected by my quills."
3. Empathetic identification with a living thing. At this level, the student shows more insight into the life, feelings, and dilemmas of a porcupine. For example, "It's confusing. Sometimes I like my quills; sometimes I don't. I feel safe with quills around me, but no one can come near. Even other porcupines don't come close because we might hurt each other. I wish I could take them off."
4. Empathetic identification with a nonliving object. At the highest level of personal analogy, students are able to make the same type of empathetic connection with nonliving things. They might express a plane's feeling of exhilaration on reaching the speed for takeoff or the sadness of skis being put away for the summer.

Personal analogies can provide the bases for class discussions, writing projects, or art activities. Primary school students might be asked to be a letter going through the postal service and to write in their journals about their adventures. Intermediate school students studying simple machines could be asked to discuss what it might be like to be a lever or a pulley. How would they feel as they were used? What might change their feelings? High school students might be asked to create a work of art or a written description of life from the perspective of an electron or a sound wave. Chemical bonds might take on a whole new meaning when viewed from the perspective of individual elements. What kinds of love songs might describe them?

Personal analogies can also form the basis for problem solving or design projects. If you were the kickball, what would you do about the fights on the playground? If you were the stop sign in front of the school, how would you get more people to come to a complete stop? If you were a seatbelt, how would you get people to wear you? If you were a school desk, how would you feel? How would you like to feel? How could the desk be redesigned so that it could feel that way? In each case, taking on the identity of the object may allow the designer or problem solver to view the situation in new ways.

Lesson 6.16 *Metaphor in Science*

Students studying elements, compounds, and mixtures can be challenged to create superheroes based on particular elements or perhaps compounds or mixtures. Each superhero must be based on the nature of the element chosen, with powers reflective of the element's characteristics. Students can be challenged to persuade others that their element is the most super of the group. (Adapted from a lesson by Chelsee Harris.)

Compressed Conflicts Compressed conflicts, or symbolic analogies, bring together words that express diametrically opposed ideas. In a technique reminiscent of Rothenberg's (1990) Janusian process, the user is forced to consider two opposite ideas at the same time. Sometimes these juxtapositions may be literal antonyms, such as happy sadness or cold heat. Other times they may express more complex or oblique yet conflicting relationships, such as shameful hero or independent follower. Compressed conflicts frequently have broad, abstract applications and can be applied to many varied situations. The level of abstraction they require makes compressed conflicts most appropriate for students in later elementary grades and above. They may form the basis of interesting and challenging writing projects or essays based on social studies or science content. Consider which historical figure could be considered a generous thief or which forces in physics might be considered powerfully weak.

Using Synectics Among the many ways Synectics can be used in classrooms, three applications are basic: stretching or practice activities, activities designed to help students investigate previously learned content from a new perspective (making the familiar strange), and activities designed to help students understand new content by tying it to something known (making the strange familiar). In stretching activities, students are taught the concepts of direct analogy or connections, personal analogy, and compressed conflict. These strategies are used in practice exercises, much as ball-handling exercises are used to practice the skills necessary for many sports. Practice exercises usually are not tied to new content but rather use familiar ideas or fantasy content to help students become comfortable with making connections. They may be tied to creative writing exercises or class discussions, or they may be used simply as a sponge for the 10 extra minutes left before lunch. Students might be asked questions such as the following:

Direct Analogies
How is snow like a merry-go-round?
What animal is like a clock?
How is fear like a grapefruit?
Which is harder, a rock or a scream?

Personal Analogies
Be a pencil. How do you feel during the school day? How do you feel at night?
Pretend you are your favorite animal. What are you? How do you feel? What do you want most?

Compressed Conflicts
What in nature is like a sad happiness?
What animal is like submissive independence?
How is a clock like a stopped stream?
What actions are like living death?

Stretches also can be used to process content in a manner that invites open-endedness, humor, and playfulness as well as critical analysis. If the topic is *Hamlet*, students might be asked, "What animal is most like Ophelia?" Students studying food chains might be asked, "Which is stronger, a food chain or an iron chain?" In a unit on the Revolutionary War, students might be asked to create a compressed conflict representing Benedict Arnold or to express the feelings of the bullets at Lexington and Concord. If the topic is the civil rights movement, what analogy would best characterize Rosa Parks's actions? These activities often are designed to help students think in new ways about previously presented content.

Joyce et al. (2009) presented two outlines (called syntax) for teaching with Synectics: one for creating something new and one for making the familiar strange. The outlines are adapted from *Teaching Is Listening* (Gordon & Poze, 1972), a self-instructional text on designing curriculum using Synectics. The first outline is designed to create something new by making the familiar strange. Although more complex than a simple stretching exercise, it can allow students to examine previously learned content from a new point of view. The steps of the outline are as follows:

1. Students describe the situation as they see it now.
2. Students suggest direct analogies, select one, and explore it.
3. Students become the analogy they selected, creating a personal analogy.
4. Students use descriptions from steps 2 and 3 to create a compressed conflict.
5. Students generate another analogy based on the compressed conflict.
6. Students use the last analogy (or the rest of the Synectics experience) to examine the original task or problem.

Imagine that Mr. Lopez's class has been studying Martin Luther King Jr.'s march in Selma, Alabama.

Mr. Lopez: Today we are going to talk again about Dr. King's march in Selma, but we are going to think about it in a new way. What do you remember about the march? [He records students' responses on the board.] Yes, those are the facts. Next, we are going to use Synectics to help us understand the facts in new and different ways. I'd like you to think for a moment about an animal that reminds you of the march on Selma.

Sam: It reminds me of mosquitoes. There are a lot of mosquitoes in Alabama—huge ones. I bet the marchers got bit a lot.

Mr. Lopez: That could be true, but we are not trying to think about animals that actually were on the march but animals that are like the march in some way. One way to do that is to think about one of the characteristics of the march and see if there is an animal that also has that characteristic.

Gina: Well, it could be like coral. Coral has lots of little parts, and the march had lots of people.

Jared: Yeah, but coral's dead. The marchers weren't!

Mr. Lopez: When we make analogies, there often are some characteristics that fit and some that don't. We'll think of several alternatives until we find one we can agree on.

Deb: It probably marched like a giant snake down the road.

Diane: I think it was more like an army of fire ants. Each ant alone isn't very strong, but an army of ants can be strong and dangerous. The march was strong because there were so many people.

Ben: Yes, but the people weren't violent like fire ants. They were more like a bunch of sheep, or . . .

Maria: Wolves! I read that wolves are really gentle animals; they only kill for food when they need it. They work together in packs to kill much bigger animals. [The class decides to work with the idea of wolves.]

Mr. Lopez: All right. Wolves. What does it feel like to be a wolf?

Bob: Furry!

Mr. Lopez: Bob, what kind of feeling might a wolf have? How does it feel to be a wolf?

Bob: Confident. I know I have my wolf brothers around me.

Katie: Nervous. I don't like killing, but sometimes I have to. I wish I could eat grass and be a peaceful animal.

Bruce: I'd rather be a lone wolf if I could.

Wendy: It's weird. There could be a lot of fear and bravery at once. A wolf would feel strong, but it still could be scary to try to kill a moose or some big thing. [The class continues to talk about the feelings a wolf might have. Mr. Lopez continues to record their responses.]

Mr. Lopez: Looking at the things you've said about wolves, do you see any words that conflict, words that are opposite or don't seem to go together? [The class makes several suggestions, including confident–nervous, peaceful–killing, lone–brothers, strong–scared. They choose strong–fear as the most interesting conflict.]

Mr. Lopez: Okay, can you think of another analogy for strong–fear? You may think of another animal or some type of machine.

Diane: A burglar alarm. It is strong, but you wouldn't have it if you didn't have fear.

Bob: A bird. Birds are really strong for their size, but they fly away at the slightest disturbance.

Wendy: A soldier. It's not exactly an animal, but a soldier is strong even though he might be afraid.

Deb: Salmon swimming upstream. They have to be really strong, but they don't know where they're going. They must be afraid.

Ben: How about a building being bombed? It's strong, but afraid it won't be strong enough.

At this point Mr. Lopez may either help the class select one of these analogies or let individual students select their own. They go back to the original topic, the march on Selma, and write about how the march is like the analogy selected. Deb might write about salmon willing to battle the stream for the sake of the next generation, and Bob might write about how flocks of birds stick together in times of danger. Each analogy has the potential to bring insight into the strength, motivation, and courage of the marchers.

In addition to processing content that has already been introduced, Synectics can be used to present new content. The second outline is designed to make the strange familiar by using familiar analogies for new material. The steps for this Synectics format are (Joyce et al., 2009):

1. The teacher provides information on a new topic.
2. The teacher suggests a direct analogy and asks students to describe the analogy.
3. The teacher has the students "become" the direct analogy.
4. Students identify and explain points of similarity between the new material and the direct analogy.
5. Students explain where the analogy does not fit.
6. Students reexplore the original topic on its own terms.
7. Students provide their own direct analogy and explore the similarities and differences.

Imagine that a teacher wanted to teach a lesson on animal habitats. She might provide the students with some basic information on food chains and how changes in one part of the chain affect all the other parts. Next, she could ask the students to look at a mobile hanging in the classroom and describe it: how it is made up of individual pieces, how they are connected by strings, how it is balanced, and so on. Next, students should be asked to become the mobile. (Gordon and Poze [1972] do not always include this step.) They should describe what it feels like to be the mobile. How do they feel blowing in the breeze? How do they feel if a string breaks?

Individually or as a class, they could identify elements of the mobile that are in some way like the animal habitats. For instance, each piece of the mobile is like a separate animal. The strings holding them together are like the connections between one animal and its food. If one piece is taken away, the whole mobile gets off balance. The students also may describe things about the mobile that are different from a habitat. For example, the mobile does not really demonstrate that there are many animals of the same type.

At this point, students may return to a discussion of the animal communities and try to develop their own analogies. The student-generated analogies allow students to process information in a creative way, and their explanations can provide valuable information for teachers on how well they understand the concept being taught.

As you can see, Synectics processes can have a wide variety of applications across curriculum areas and real-world problems. They may be used in simple, mind-stretching exercises or to provide a framework for presenting or processing key concepts.

Thinking About the Classroom

Plan a lesson using one of the Synectics outlines. Have a friend give you feedback on your plan. Teach the lesson and then discuss the results.

Other Uses for Metaphorical Thinking

The Synectics processes provide powerful tools for generating and using analogies, but there are certainly times when you may wish to help students use analogical thinking in other ways. In particular, experiences in metaphorical or analogical thinking can help students generate ideas and forms for creative expression. Interestingly, Garner (2007) suggests the use of metaphors as a strategy particularly appropriate for helping struggling students learn.

We probably associate metaphors and analogies most commonly with literature. Most students, at some point, must memorize the differences between the two. Less often, students actually may use such literary devices as tools for their own expression. To use metaphors and analogies in their own writing, students must become familiar with the use of analogies elsewhere, as in Langston Hughes's question about the dream deferred. Students might discuss why Hughes chose those particular images and what the images communicated. They may brainstorm other analogies Hughes might have used and another dream poem or a work about some other thought and its effects on an individual.

Analogical thinking can be used to create contemporary stories analogous to works of literature. The Lizzie Bennet Diaries, an online serial vlog (video blog) paralleling *Pride and Prejudice*, is an interesting and complex view of what can happen when a classic story is translated into contemporary dilemmas (see www.lizziebennet.com). Students could compare scenes between the book and the vlog or create their own scripts for contemporary scenes analogous to the literature being studied. Consider the textual analysis necessary to translate Huck Finn into a contemporary figure—a homeless adolescent with a passion for skateboards, perhaps.

When teaching a science lesson on alpha, beta, and gamma rays to eighth graders, one teacher used an analogy in the form of a story. Here's the beginning:

Once upon a time in a small town there lived Annie Alpha, Bobby Beta, and Gramma Gamma. Annie Alpha was a very positive yet rather large young lady. Everyone liked her because she was so positive about everything. However, Bobby Beta was much smaller, very fast, and created some negative attention. Gramma Gamma, on the other hand, just sat in her rocking chair and observed everything; she was rather neutral.

(adapted from a lesson by Sheri Noble)

The story goes on to describe the types of "houses" these particles lived in, such as a lead house for the gamma rays, how they would function in a magnetic field, and so on. Years later, students still remembered Annie Alpha! This creative (and effective) teaching example can then lead to teaching for creativity, as students learn to write their own analogies for different scientific principles.

The history of film is full of analogical thinking. Students studying mythic heroes might examine *Star Wars*, *Lord of the Rings*, or *Harry Potter* to find parallels that may have been inspired by ancient mythology. *The Matrix* and *The Lion, the Witch, and the Wardrobe* are potent sources of religious imagery. *The King of Hearts* examines war and peace, sanity and insanity. *A River Runs Through It* is, on the surface, a movie about fly-fishing, but it is also a movie about struggling, conquering, and growing up. One chief value of using films to explore analogical thinking, especially with secondary school students, is the insight that this type of thinking surrounds us and affects our understanding on a day-to-day basis.

Studying how these techniques are used commercially can provide the impetus for students to use them. The same strategies can be used to create a new mythic hero in a different time or place. What might a mythic hero have done during the American Revolution? (Do we have some?) What might a mythic hero in today's high school be like? Students might brainstorm other vehicles that could have been used to carry the message in *A River Runs Through It*. If the family had not gone fly-fishing, where might they have gone? Would the imagery work in the same way for a group of young women? What alternatives could be used? This type of exercise can move analogical thinking from an example on a multiple-choice test to a tool for personal expression.

Analogical thinking also can provide insights and creative stimuli in the arts. Students can examine paintings and sculpture for images that use one form to portray another idea before they try generating new images for the same idea. This type of exercise can be considered as part of the technical skills instruction necessary for talent development. Sometimes a more constrained activity, demanding the use of a specific technique to portray a given idea, can be more valuable in developing creative expression than unstructured projects. Certainly, there are times when students should express their own ideas in their own ways, but training in analogical expression or other specific techniques makes their own efforts richer.

Analogical thinking can provide exercises in fashion design or architecture. Contemporary design shows can provide inspiration here. Like designers on a popular TV show, students might be challenged to create clothing or buildings inspired by pieces of art, places in the environment, or even items in the grocery store. Analogies also can be used to create political or other cartoons. I have a cartoon in my office from the years I lived in New England. Entitled "Moses in Connecticut," it pictures Moses raising his arms to part the snow drifts in front of a New England home. Although Moses probably would not be an appropriate theme for public-school class activities, it is easy to imagine how a similar image could be used in a variety of settings. Picture Moses on the football field, Moses at rush hour, or Moses finding a parking place on campus! Other cartoon analogies could be expanded in a similar manner.

Political cartoons are frequently based on familiar literature, children's stories, or fables. Cartoons have portrayed George W. Bush and Saddam Hussein as cowboys in a faceoff at sundown and Donald Trump as claiming he can spin straw into gold. Crusaders attempting to go against established interests can be portrayed as tilting at windmills or "huffing and puffing and blowing the house down." Those with a new political view can be pictured as leading the country to Camelot or Never-Never Land, all depending on the cartoonist's point of view.

Students from upper elementary grades on can use these techniques with varying degrees of sophistication. Younger students can learn how to use familiar stories or images to create more original posters or advertisements. Certainly, many fire-prevention or substance-abuse posters I have seen would have benefited from original use of analogies. Middle school students can study the use of metaphors and analogies in political cartoons, perhaps graphing the number of times cartoons are based on children's stories, seasonal events, or other sources. As students learn to recognize metaphorical images, they can use them to create their own humorous and political statements.

Frequently, various techniques of creative thinking can be used together for even more power-ful results. Analogical thinking can be triggered through the use of morphological synthesis. For example, current events or issues could be listed on one side of the grid and children's stories or current movies on the other side. The grid could be used to generate ideas for political cartoons. Examine the grid in Figure 6.9. Consider how a cartoonist might create a drawing about pollution using "Cinderella" or "The Three Bears." Similarly, a grid could be created with important ideas about friendship or common teenage dilemmas on one side and possible settings on the other side. These could be used as the basis for short stories. In either case, students have a tool for gen-erating creative analogies while becoming aware that the same statement can be made in many different ways.

Thinking About the Classroom

Start collecting cartoons that use metaphors or analogies to make a point. Use them as the basis for a lesson or bulletin board.

A songwriter friend of mine makes frequent use of analogies in helping students learn to write songs. Young children can begin with activities as simple as changing the words to "Row, Row, Row Your Boat." If the beginning were changed to "Drive, drive, drive your car" or "Slide, slide, slide your skates" or even "Stretch, stretch, stretch your smile," the parallels could be continued through the song. The book *If You're Hoppy and You Know It* (Sayre, 2011) takes the children's song about happiness and transforms it into a ballad about animals that cries out for additions ("If you're sloppy and you know it, you're a hog"). Older children can learn how music portrays ideas and emotions without lyrics by listening to a variety of music. Students can draw the images the music brings to mind and discuss the feelings it elicits. This idea can be extended by writing lyrics that fit the mood of the music. The Beethoven's Wig CDs can inspire students to write words to classical music, just as "Weird Al" Yankovic can inspire older students to write parodies. Eventu-ally, students can begin writing original songs that express their own ideas.

As in all creative activities, we must recognize the stages in the processes of analogical think-ing. Students must recognize analogies before they can create them. They must be able to generate ideas in a structured situation before they can do so alone. I suspect that when students' creative efforts in school fall short, it often is because they have been given freedom but no tools. Simply saying, "Write a song about something that interests you" presents an overwhelming task for most students—and adults. Beginning gradually by recognizing the images in familiar songs and

Try creating a political cartoon by matching a political issue with a children's story and creating an analogy.	
Issues	**Stories**
Pollution	Cinderella
Homelessness	The Three Bears
Recycling	Snow White
Endangered species	Peter Pan
Drugs	Jack and the Beanstalk
Gun control	The Three Pigs
TV violence	Aladdin

Figure 6.9 Using analogies to create political cartoons

adapting them or by writing lyrics to familiar tunes is much less intimidating. Learning how other composers used and reused melodies can give students the freedom to do the same. Students also should have experience in understanding how others have used analogies in design or cartooning before attempting to use these devices in original ways. No real-world creative works come forth in a vacuum. It is unrealistic to expect such efforts from children.

Visualization and Creative Dramatics

Two additional strategies for enhancing the production of creative ideas are visualization and creative dramatics. Both techniques involve bringing ideas to life, one in the imagination and the other in physical activity.

Visualization

Visualization involves creating mental images of something that cannot be seen or that does not exist. If I were to say, "Picture your bedroom," you probably could easily conjure up an appropriate mental image, even if you are not in your bedroom right now. If I were to ask you to picture your bedroom in the home in which you grew up, it is likely that it, too, would be a clear image. In fact, for many of you, that image probably is laden with emotion. For the fortunate among us, picturing home brings feelings of love and security. For others, the emotions are much more painful. In either case, a mental image of home demonstrates one characteristic of visualization. Clear visual images are frequently accompanied by powerful corresponding emotions. This combination can make visualization a potent learning tool but one that must be used with caution and sensitivity. Perhaps it is the power of visualization to carry strong emotions that has made it a target of some political groups.

Parents concerned about mind control have attacked the use of visualization in schools as inappropriate and potentially dangerous. As mentioned in Chapter 5, it is important that you take local sensibilities and concerns into account when planning the content and format of visualization activities. Although some individuals may be uncomfortable with fantasy images involving witches, dragons, or water sprites, few parents object to picturing a journey through the digestive system, imagining a new invention, or visualizing spelling words if such activities are approached sensitively.

Visualization can be used to reinforce course content. Elementary school students may be asked to visualize the roaring seas, crowded conditions, and bad food aboard the *Mayflower*. Secondary school students may gain insight into Shakespeare's theater by visualizing the experiences of the groundlings in the Globe Theatre.

Inaccurate pictures (visualizing the Globe as a movie theater, for instance) can be counterproductive. Students will need prior knowledge and careful guidance if their images are to increase their content knowledge effectively. Visualization assisted in this way is sometimes called guided imagery.

To be most effective in stimulating this type of visualization, the teacher should have a script, written or mental, of the images to be portrayed. Students can be encouraged to sit in a comfortable position, usually with their eyes covered or closed, while the teacher guides them through the content. The descriptions and suggestions should be presented slowly and clearly, with time allowed for students' images to develop. For example, a teacher guiding students through the circulatory system could start with oxygen entering the system:

> Picture yourself in a tiny submarine, just big enough for you. Everything you need is there. You have a comfortable chair and plenty of air for the journey. You even have food in case

you get hungry. Picture yourself in your comfortable capsule. . . . Today you and your capsule are going on a wonderful journey all through your body. First you will have to shrink until you are very, very small—small enough to fit into the tiniest blood vessel. You are so small that you can see all the molecules in the air around you. In front of you is a person breathing. He looks so big you can't even see the whole person; all you can see is the giant nose. Oh! You are being inhaled. Into the nose you go, along with all the air molecules and dust around you. . . . Now you are in the nose. It is hard to maneuver around the hairs in there; dust particles are trapped on all sides of you. . . .

Clearly, students would need prior experience with guided imagery before they could be expected to focus on such an extended image. Early exercises can be as simple as picturing spelling words in the shape of the object (e.g., picture the C in "cat" turning into a cat) or visualizing the characters in math story problems. Students also can be encouraged to draw illustrations for books without pictures or books for which the illustrations have not been shown.

Guided imagery focused on content can enhance students' memory and stimulate their writing or other creative expression. Students who experience the difficulties on the *Mayflower* through imagery are more likely to begin to understand the emotions of the people there than students who merely read a section in the social studies text. If they write about the experiences of a child on the ship, their writing is likely to be more vivid. A high school student who has experienced life as a groundling is less likely to associate Shakespeare only with highbrow intellectual elitists.

I once did a guided imagery experience about traveling under the sea with a group of second graders. The images portrayed in their writing were far superior to those usually demonstrated by the group. In one of my favorite pieces, a student described what it felt like to "feel the sand under my stomach . . . see the sun shining down through the water and not feel the wind." I believe it is unlikely that this degree of insight would have occurred without the imagined experience of being under water.

Lesson 6.17   *Using Multiple Strategies:* Hansel and Gretel *or* King Lear

This series of lessons was designed to prepare students for a theatrical production of *Hansel and Gretel.* Consider which of them would be appropriate with a novel or play at your grade level.

- Read the story, preferably from a version without illustrations so students must visualize the story themselves.
- Brainstorm new endings for the story under a variety of circumstances:
  What if the witch was a fairy godmother?
  What if the father refused to leave them in the forest?
  What if the birds did not eat the bread crumbs?
  What if the candy house could talk?
  What if the children had a magic charm?
- Create a grid containing the characters, the settings, and the main events of the story. Scramble the attributes so different characters do different things in different settings. Create a new story. For example, what might happen if the father found the candy house?
- Play a selection from Humperdinck's opera *Hansel and Gretel.* Have the children close their eyes and describe an open-ended visualization. For example: "You are walking

in the woods. Listen to the sounds around you. What do you hear? Walk down the path until you see a very unusual house. Look at it carefully. . . ." Have the students open their eyes and describe what they visualized.

- Use creative dramatics to allow children to experience being Hansel, Gretel, and the talking Candy House. Imagine what they could say to each other. (Adapted from a lesson by Patricia Barnes.)

Imagine using similar strategies for *King Lear.*

- Choose animals or other symbols to serve as metaphors for the king and his daughters. Create a poster (paper or online) and explain why the images are appropriate.
- Imagine how the play might have been different if Lear had sons rather than daughters. What are the strengths and limitations of Shakespeare's choice?
- Choose characters from current television or movies who share characteristics with Lear's family. Explain the parallels and differences.
- Have students anticipate what might happen next. Outline the plot of a sequel. What if Lear had lived? How might the sequel be different?
- If Lear were to be converted to a graphic novel, which scenes would be most essential? Perhaps one of your students would like to create it.

Of course, guided imagery and visualization also can be used to imagine things that do not exist. Eberle (1977) provided a series of visual images that were created using the SCAMPER acronym. In one piece, students picture doughnuts filled with various substances stretching into different shapes and enlarging to the size of a house. A potent image has them jumping into a swimming pool filled with applesauce in the middle of a giant doughnut. That portion of the experience is invariably met with giggles and squirms. Students can be guided to picture an imaginary trip in a hot-air balloon, a tour through an enormous strawberry (echoing *James and the Giant Peach* [Dahl, 1961]), or a voyage to a distant planet. These types of images can spur artwork, creative writing, or discussions of literary forms such as science fiction.

Finke (1990) discussed the use of imagery in the invention process. Finke conducted numerous research studies in which individuals used selected images to generate new ideas for inventions. In such exercises, subjects might be asked to visualize combinations of a cone, half a sphere, and a hook. They could change the size and position of the images as desired until they found an image that gave them an idea for an invention. Finke was particularly interested in the function of preinventive forms in the creative process—that is, combinations of simple images that may be interpreted in various ways to solve diverse problems (Ward, Smith, & Finke, 1999).

One of the more interesting results of Finke's (1990) research was that subjects, generally college undergraduates, were more successful at devising creative inventions when the task was somewhat restricted. Subjects given a large range of shapes from which to devise any invention were less creative in their responses than those given a limited number of images from which to work and a particular category of object to create. Subjects also had more original ideas when they generated a preinventive form combining images into an interesting and potentially useful shape before identifying the category of object to be devised instead of trying to plan a form to suit a particular category.

Perhaps the common thread in these results is exploratory behavior. If an individual has a limited number of images to consider, it is possible for him or her to explore each one more fully. If it is necessary to select a form for an unknown purpose, multiple possibilities for that form must be considered. It would be interesting to experiment with variations on Finke's (1990) techniques with younger students. They could be given specific geometric forms to visualize, manipulate mentally, and use to create new ideas for inventions. It also may be worthwhile to consider whether the concept of restricted tasks could be valuable in teaching other creative thinking techniques.

Creative Dramatics

In creative dramatics, students are asked to explore ideas with their bodies as well as their minds. These exercises can be valuable for developing concentration, sensory awareness, self-control, empathetic understanding, and a sense of humor. In creative dramatics, students have the opportunity to be someone or something else in a safe and accepting context (Heinig, 1992; McCaslin, 1999).

It is important to distinguish creative dramatics and role-play from children's theater. As will be discussed in Chapter 8, students involved in role-play activities address problem situations by taking on a variety of roles and portraying their decisions. Children's theater is theater produced for children to watch, often by adults, and sometimes by talented student actors. It is derived from a script, rehearsed, and presented to an audience. Creative dramatics, like role-play, is not scripted and is seldom intended for an audience. Although creative dramatics or role-play activities may be repeated, they are not rehearsed for consistency but reexplored for new ideas and interpretations. Research suggests that improvisation—verbal or musical—is associated with increases in divergent thinking in both children and adults (Lewis & Lovatt, 2013; Sowden, Clements, Redlich, & Lewis, 2015).

Students involved in creative dramatics explore a situation physically in an effort to find and express creative ideas. At times, this may involve the types of problem-solving activities and exploration of issues described in the discussion of role-playing. Creative dramatics can be seen to encompass such activities. However, it also includes explorations of less realistic situations and investigations of animals or objects. In role-play, students typically take on fairly realistic roles to solve a problem. Creative dramatics often moves also into fantasy; students can become melting snow, stalking animals, or the walls of a building.

Like role-playing, creative dramatics activities can be divided into three stages: warm-up, dramatic activities, and debriefing. Warm-up exercises are used to warm up both brain and body. Physical and mental stretching activities provide a transition from other class activities and allow muscles to loosen. Warm-ups can sometimes be used to focus students on the issue or topic of the day. At other times they may be unrelated to the activities that follow. My experience has shown that older students need warm-up activities more than younger ones. Most young children readily throw themselves into any kind of dramatic activity. At the drop of a hat, they are ready to be a lion, a rubber band, or a lost child. Students from the middle grades on are much more self-conscious and need more warm-up and focus activities before proceeding. It is helpful to point out that many of these same activities are used by professional actors preparing for the stage or screen. Warm-ups can include the following:

Stretching. Students stretch all their muscles from the head down. Students should be cued to stretch as many muscles separately as possible.
Relaxing. Students lie on the floor and relax one group of muscles at a time.

Mirrors. Each student needs a partner. One person becomes a mirror, reflecting each movement the partner makes. Mirrors work most easily with slow, smooth movements. Occasionally students may be directed to switch roles without disrupting the flow of the movement.

Catch. Students play catch with a variety of imaginary balls. They should try switching from a softball to a beach ball to a bowling ball.

Walking. Students walk in place under a variety of circumstances: through the jungle, on hot sand, or going to school when their homework is not done.

Rubber bands, ice cubes, and other objects. Students become an object whose form changes. They might portray melting ice, frying bacon, or a stretching rubber band. Older students may imagine stretching rubber bands around various parts of their bodies.

Dramatic activities may include movement exercises, sensory-awareness exercises, pantomime, and other forms of storytelling. Movement exercises are designed primarily to help students gain control of their bodies and become aware of how their bodies move. Most of the warm-up activities described in this discussion could also be used as movement exercises. Other movement activities could include the following:

Puppets. Students pretend to be pulled by strings attached to various parts of their bodies.

Tug-of-war. Students are divided into teams pulling an imaginary rope over an imaginary line.

Animals. Students imitate animals' movements and mannerisms. Secondary students may develop human characters based on some aspect of the chosen animal.

Human machine. Students in small groups form machines, or they can create one giant machine as a whole-class build-on activity. There are many variations to this exercise. One of my favorites entails having each participant identify one sound and one movement. One student may choose to raise and lower one leg while whistling with each downward movement. The goal is to build the parts into a machine in which each piece is attached to the next in a logical fashion, with moving parts interacting. If your class can assemble the entire machine before dissolving in hysterics, they have demonstrated enormous self-control!

Sensory-awareness exercises are exactly what the name implies: exercises to increase students' awareness of their five senses. You may ask your students to eat imaginary food, listen to imaginary sounds, or feel imaginary textures. You may find that limiting one of the senses can enhance the others. The opportunity for students to feel a variety of textures while they are wearing blindfolds may sharpen their ability to imagine other textures.

Perhaps the most familiar dramatic activities involve pantomime and other forms of storymaking activities. Students are asked to use their bodies to portray situations with or without the use of dialogue. These may range from simple activities, such as pantomiming someone using a common household tool, to complex problem-solving scenarios. More complex dramatic activities may require a planning phase as well as an acting phase. Students who are asked to act as an interviewer with a panel of presidential candidates, portray Phillis Wheatley discussing her poetry, or present the story of *Peter and the Wolf* will need discussion time—and content knowledge—before the activities can be presented successfully. Also, most creative dramatics activities are enhanced by a debriefing discussion. Students may discuss what they did, how it felt, what worked, what did not, and what they might try another time. These discussions make it clear that creative dramatics activities, although enjoyable, are not part of recess. They are kinesthetic activities that can bring insight into a variety of situations.

Creative dramatics also can provide impetus for content discussions, art activities, and writing projects. Like visualization, they can bring an enhanced understanding, especially of the emotions underlying problems or events. If students are given sufficient background knowledge, a creative dramatics activity about a young woman wanting to go to battle during the Civil War can increase their understanding of women's roles during that period. A representation of key individuals in the French Revolution can help students focus on the characteristics that motivated important participants and more fully understand their interactions.

Fantasy activities such as creating the human machine can be used as the basis for discussion and journal writing. One second-grade class, after doing the human machine activity, talked about what things could be done by an amazing machine such as the one they had built. Students then wrote their ideas and created illustrations of their own amazing machines. The stories included machines that ate foods the owner did not like, one that turned bad people good, and one that made scrambled eggs. In the scrambled egg story, the author's mother became jealous of the machine because everyone preferred the machine's scrambled eggs to those she made for breakfast. However, this was not because Mom's cooking was inferior but because the machine served breakfast in bed. One day the machine made breakfast for Mom, too. After that, she loved it "like a pet."

Like the stories that students wrote after their underwater visualization activity, these efforts were much better than everyday journal entries. Similar results can be attained when older students write about their experiences surviving in a hostile environment, dealing with a cyberbully, or asking someone out on his or her first date after living these events through creative dramatics. Creative dramatics techniques, with the new perspectives, emotional insights, and enthusiasm they can generate, can be a valuable asset to any language arts or history program. With some creative teaching, they can enrich math and science as well.

Thinking About the Classroom

Invite some children and adults to participate in creative dramatics together. See if you notice any differences in the ways they approach the activities. Adults all should have the chance to participate! You also might try this activity with students of different ages. See what you observe about their approaches.

Commercial and Competitive Programs

A number of commercial programs and interscholastic competitions designed to enhance creative thinking are available. The CoRT program and Six Thinking Hats have already been described. Because the number of options is increasing so quickly, it is impossible to discuss all of them. This section samples the menu and describes some of the better-known offerings.

Future Problem Solving Program International

The Future Problem Solving Program International (FPSPI), originated by Torrance and Torrance (1978), involves students in using CPS to address problems of the future. It offers both competitive and noncompetitive programs. In the original Global Issues Problem Solving program, teams in four divisions (grades 4 to adult) work to complete problem booklets on assigned topics. Each year, FPSPI topics are selected from three strands: business and economics, science and technology, and social and political issues.

The topics for the problems are the same internationally for any given academic year. The first two topics are considered to be practice problems through which students learn and practice the steps of CPS. Practice problems typically are submitted to a state or national affiliate organization for evaluation and feedback. The third problem, which must be completed by the teams without assistance, is the basis for competition. Teams earning the highest number of points on the third problem may be invited to an affiliate and possibly the international FPSPI competition.

Several variations on the FPSPI process are offered. Action-based problem solving is a similar noncompetitive program designed to teach problem solving to students from grades K–3 and up. Scenario writing is a competition in which individual students write scenarios of life as they see it at least 20 years in the future, focused on one of the FPSPI topics for that year. Scenario performance gives students the opportunity to build on the ideas of the scenario-writing activities to create a storytelling performance. Community problem solving is an opportunity for students to use their problem-solving skills to address issues in their own community. For additional information and links to local affiliate organizations, visit the FPS website (www.fpspi.org).

Destination ImagiNation

Destination ImagiNation is a team-based program with an affiliate and international structure similar to that of FPS. However, the problems addressed and the types of products produced in the two programs are very different.

Students participate in Destination ImagiNation in teams of up to seven members who work to solve two different types of challenges: team challenges and instant challenges. The five possible team levels are primary, elementary, middle, secondary, and university. Teams have the opportunity to present their solutions in tournaments, and all but the primary level are evaluated by appraisers.

In a team challenge, teams work over a period of several months to solve a problem and prepare a presentation of their solution. Each year, Destination ImagiNation presents challenges in categories such as "Engineering Challenge," "Fine Arts" or "Scientific Challenge" (and one noncompetitive Early Learning Challenge), and teams select one to solve. In contrast to FPSPI, in which students generate and record ideas for solving problems, many Destination ImagiNation team challenges require students to create some type of vehicle, structure, machine, or other physical object that must function to solve the problem. Each challenge also includes a performance element. For example, in 2016–17, the Technical Challenge "Show and Tech" teams were challenged to build a stage and put on a show, with an opening act and a headlining act. The stage had to be capable of moving a performer from one area to another, and teams were encouraged to incorporate technical effects in their productions.

Although Destination ImagiNation and FPSPI both require divergent thinking and have similar competitive structures, the nature of the problems often makes the competitions appealing to different students. Students most successful in FPSPI are comfortable with library research and written and verbal communication. In some schools, FPSPI is incorporated into the social studies curriculum. Students who most enjoy Destination ImagiNation often are tinkerers or performers. They like to solve three-dimensional problems or use their creativity in artistic or dramatic ways. For additional information on Destination ImagiNation, visit its website (destinationimagination.org).

Odyssey of the Mind

Odyssey of the Mind (Micklus & Micklus, 1986) is a competitive program in which teams solve problems very similar to those in Destination ImagiNation. In fact, the two groups represent a split in the original Odyssey of the Mind (then abbreviated OM), in which Destination ImagiNation continued as a nonprofit organization and Odyssey of the Mind affiliated with Creative Competitions, a for-profit organization. Both groups address both short- and long-term problem solving. Both include problems with both building and performance elements. You will need to check your local schools to see which organization is most active in your area. See the Odyssey of the Mind website (www.odysseyofthemind.com) for additional information.

Inventing and Invention Conventions

One of the most interesting and enjoyable ways to learn about creativity is through the invention process. Learning about inventors' experiences and walking in their footsteps bring students unique insights into the generation and implementation of new ideas. Numerous companies, foundations, and organizations sponsor activities designed to teach students about inventing and provide audiences for young inventors. I have also found that identifying a problem and inventing something to solve the problem is a powerful assignment for adults. The task seems initially intimidating, but I have watched scores of graduate students find success, pride, and renewed faith in their own creativity by tackling this challenge (and never once has a student been unable to find something that needed inventing).

Regardless whether you and your students become involved in a formally organized invention program, the basic steps of inventing are essentially the same. At the beginning, it is important to become aware of inventors and stories of inventions. It is easy to go through life assuming that Scotch tape or facial tissues or drinking straws always existed. If questioned, most of us probably would realize that these ideas must have come from somewhere, but it is easy to forget that all the objects that fill our lives, from paper clips to computer chips, are the product of someone's new idea. Someone had to ask, "What is needed here?" "What is the problem here?" or "How could this be better?" There is an ever-growing collection of books and websites available to help students learn about inventors and inventing. A quick search will get you started.

While you are searching, it is very important to seek out invention stories of men and women from a variety of races and cultural groups. If you limit yourself to the stories that are easiest to find, you are likely to leave the impression that all major inventions were created by a very limited group—something that is far from the truth.

New inventors need to become sensitive to problems and opportunities around them. One way to do this is to brainstorm "things that bug me." In small groups, students generate lists of everyday annoyances. These vary enormously—from second-grade students, who may be bugged by too-small lunch boxes or demands to clean their room, to adults who hate walking to the mailbox on a rainy day, cleaning up after their children in restaurants, and finding unidentified fluids leaking from their cars.

It also is sometimes helpful to look through catalogs, especially the unusual gift catalogs that arrive in November and December. Many of the products in them are the result of someone's effort to alleviate one of life's annoyances. On several occasions, students have appeared in my office with catalogs offering solutions to problems that appeared on their bug lists the year before. Frequently, they accompany their discovery with wails of "Why didn't I think of that?" or "They're selling my invention!" Young students may enjoy seeing children's inventions in *The Kid's Invention Book* (Erlbach, 1999). My favorite is an edible pet food server designed by a first-grade student who was disgusted by the dirty spoons used to scoop pet food. Her server could be crumbled into the pet's dish, and the pet food never touched human hands! I also enjoy the periodic "Fallonventions" feature on *The Tonight Show*, where young inventors share their problems and solutions. You can find a collection of young inventors' videos and options for sending materials to the show by searching for "Fallonventions" on the web or YouTube. Becoming aware of inventions and the need for inventions can change the way individuals look at the world. During this process, it is not uncommon to hear people say, "This is driving me crazy. Everywhere I look, I see inventions. Everything I do, I think, 'How could this be easier or better?' Everywhere I go, I look for something to improve. It's driving my spouse (or parent) up the wall." With due sympathy to the beleaguered families, this sensitivity to opportunities is an essential part of problem finding and a valuable asset to any inventor.

Once the problem has been identified, the exploration begins. Many of the divergent-thinking strategies discussed earlier can be helpful in generating beginning solutions. In many cases, numerous designs and materials must be tried before a workable solution is found. Sometimes it is necessary to find technical assistance for engineering questions or physical assistance for molding new materials. All of these are difficulties encountered by real inventors as a normal part of the invention process. An invention log can help students record the process, keeping track of their successes, failures, and untested ideas. It is a place for them to draw and revise plans, jot down ideas, and record dreams. If carefully kept and dated, the log can also serve as a record in case the invention should be patented.

After the planning, the building can begin. In some cases, students construct their initial efforts using alternate materials or a miniature scale until they can fine-tune the idea. It is important, however, that they be encouraged to plan inventions they actually can create. It is enjoyable to imagine fantasy inventions beyond available levels of technology, but for a student to decorate a box and say, "This would be a machine you could touch to the fluids leaking out of your car and it would instantly analyze them" does not expose him to the same problem-solving processes that he could learn by creating a simpler but manageable invention. Even so, such far-fetched ideas sometimes lead to practical applications. The student with the leaking car but few technical skills created a large pad on which he sketched a full-scale drawing of the underside of his car. By driving the car in the tire prints drawn on the pad, he could position the vehicle so that its underside was exactly over the corresponding parts in his drawing. Then, when the car leaked, the drip fell from the real car part onto the analogous part of the drawing, allowing him to locate the origin of the leak. A color key to identify brake fluid, oil, or other liquids completed the product. It worked!

If you would like students to work on inventions but are not part of a formal invention program, you may want to organize an invention convention yourself. The steps for organizing such a conference parallel those for any science fair. There is one caution you may want to consider. Be sure participants understand that inventions must be self-contained. That is, they must not require running water, outside electricity, or other such externalities. Without the self-containment rule, you could easily find yourself with 30 projects needing electricity and 5 needing running water, all in a gym with two electric outlets and no faucets! Organizations sponsoring invention competitions for children seem to come and go, so it is probably best to search and see what is current. Related information on teaching innovation can be found at the Henry Ford Museum website. Go to www.thehenryford.org and then look for the "Teach Innovation" section. There are lesson plans and useful videos, all available without cost.

Science Olympiad

Science Olympiad is a national nonprofit organization devoted to improving the quality of science instruction, increasing interest in science, and providing recognition for outstanding accomplishments in science. Although it is not targeted specifically at increasing students' creative thinking skills, Science Olympiad does provide the opportunity for them to use creativity in a content area.

Science Olympiad provides a menu of activities at various levels. These represent a balance among life science, physical science, and earth science and also among events requiring knowledge of science facts, concepts, processes, skills, and applications. Some of the activities, particularly those that are fact based, have single correct answers and offer minimal opportunities for creative thinking. In other activities, the application of scientific principles leads to the possibility of many correct solutions. For example, in Division B (grades 6–9), one event asked students to identify various rock samples by using standard testing procedures. Although this is a fine activity for developing the domain skills that students will need eventually to be creative in earth science, it probably is not an activity for which original answers are appropriate. Another activity at the same level asked teams to construct, in advance, an insulated houselike structure, 20 to 40 cm on each side, that will retain the heat of 100 ml of water in a 250-ml beaker for 20 to 30 minutes. In this case, many varied solutions are possible. Using flexible thinking within the parameters of the discipline is likely to increase students' success (Science Olympiad, 1990). For additional information, visit the Science Olympiad website (www.soinc.org).

Science Fairs in Cyberspace

As I look at the science fair and related activities available today and compare them to the activities I remember from my childhood, I'm tempted to say, "This is not your mother's science fair!" For example, the Google Science Fair is a global online science and technology competition open to individuals and teams from ages 13 to 18. To see amazing projects from around the world, go to Googlesciencefair.com. For information on how your students can participate, look for the Teachers and Mentors section.

For an alternative science competition, you might want to explore the Breakthrough Junior Challenge, a competition in which students ages 13 to 18 submit short videos (no more than 5 minutes) that bring to life a principle in life sciences, physics, or mathematics. There are substantial scholarship opportunities for the winners, but they may be most exciting as models for scientific video production at a school or district level. For more information, see breakthroughjuniorchallenge.org. An even shorter video option was the now-discontinued Science Vines, which challenged users to create a video illustrating a scientific principle in 7 seconds or less. Sadly, the Vines option appears to be unavailable, but that shouldn't stop interested students and teachers from creating 7-second videos to share in other ways.

You can also be inspired by adult competitions. I was fascinated to discover the Vizzie Awards, sponsored by the National Science Foundation and *Popular Science*. The awards honor outstanding visualizations of scientific principles. The web address is too long to include here, but just search for "Vizzies" and be inspired. Imagine creating your own Vizzie-inspired event, challenging students to visually display the science they are learning.

Makers and More

In recent years, a new variety of groups encouraging young people to be "makers" have emerged. Organizations such as Maker Corps (makered.org), the DIY Maker program (diy.org), and Make magazine's Maker Faires (makerfaire.com/education), all encourage young people to solve problems by building, often with a technology focus. Such things may be organized in maker spaces, community-operated spaces in which people with common interests can meet, share equipment, and collaborate. The field still seems a bit in flux, so you might want to explore and see what kinds of maker opportunities are available in your area, or check makercamp.com for options for creating your own summer making adventure. The DIY maker anthem "Build, Make, Hack, Grow" could be the theme song for youthful creativity.

Numerous interscholastic programs are available that facilitate creativity in particular disciplines. Young Author's programs encourage and support young writers. History days, organized to parallel a science fair, provide outlets for creative research and presentations in history (www.nhd.org).

In all cases, teachers will need to assess the impact of such programs on several dimensions. Does the program help students use important content and processes? Do the products required allow flexible responses? What is the impact of the competitive aspect of the program? Chapter 9 offers evidence that competition in creative endeavors may inhibit students' intrinsic motivation and creativity. Others may argue that rewarding creative products parallels processes in the real world and may encourage students to greater progress. Only you can judge what is best for your students as you balance the benefits with the risks for any given group of students.

Thinking About the Classroom

Find out when the local Destination ImagiNation tournament is taking place and visit it. Or contact local coaches or participants in FPSPI, Science Olympiad, or other competitions. Perhaps there is a maker space or maker organization nearby. Find out what is going on in your area.

Commercial Products, Transfer, and the Real World

Many commercial products and programs designed to enhance creativity are available: books, kits, software, and more. Some are single activities or books focusing on a targeted idea or skill. Others are comprehensive programs. Most recently, there has been a proliferation of apps designed to spur divergent thinking and help record and organize ideas. Where there has been any evaluation, the assessed effectiveness of materials and programs varies from study to study, requiring careful analysis of the research. It is one thing to discover that students using a particular program become better at exercises very much like those used in the program. It is quite another to discover that students can develop skills in commercial or other activities and transfer them into new, real-world situations. The ways materials and strategies are introduced and taught can affect how or whether students use them outside a teacher-directed situation. If teachers cue students that the skills might transfer, the students are more likely to try using them in other situations (Bransford, Sherwood, Vye, & Rieser, 1986; Cramond, Martin, & Shaw, 1990).

As you select activities, whether commercially produced or teacher designed, consider first how they mesh with the research and theory available and also how they might be adapted to enhance the possibility of transfer. If any of these activities and the processes they teach are to be of long-term value, they must develop skills and attitudes in students that help them think creatively both inside and outside the classroom. They also must support students' increasing independence in their use. Although imaginative activities can be valuable and important in themselves (e.g., using CPS to solve Horton's dilemma or planning a new space creature), I believe their value is enhanced when students understand how they can use similar processes to improve their ideas at school, at home, or in other locations.

I have frequently used my experience with my first Thanksgiving turkey as an introduction to lessons on fluency or brainstorming. I learned all my cooking skills in a family of seven. This practice provided me with unique advantages and disadvantages. I learned to cut a pie into seven pieces equal enough to pass the most discriminating judgment. I also learned to cook turkeys averaging 20 to 25 pounds. The first Thanksgiving I was married, I prepared the turkey as I had done before, only to realize once it was placed on the table that there was no longer room even for our two plates. Needless to say, we ate turkey for some time after the holiday. I needed many ideas about what to do with leftover turkey.

This story and students' stories about times they needed many ideas have helped children make the transition from seeing brainstorming sessions as an enjoyable diversion to viewing them as useful exercises. Using brainstorming to solve class dilemmas is an even more powerful tool for transfer. Whatever creative thinking techniques you choose to teach, students eventually should be able to answer the questions "What are you doing?" "Why?" and "When might this be helpful?" Without such cueing, we may end up like Mr. Brown, described at the beginning of the chapter, whose students enjoy creative exercises on Friday afternoon but demonstrate little creativity in other aspects of their lives.

The transfer process might be viewed as paralleling any other tool we might give students. Few adults could imagine giving a young person a box full of saws, wrenches, and hammers and then hope that he or she would figure out when to use them. If we are to provide students with mental hammers and creative nails, we must also help them see how many things in the world could benefit from a little hammering and a few nails. In some places, we could use the whole box.

Think About It

1. Make a table listing the 13 strategies identified by the Root-Bernsteins. Examine the creative thinking strategies in the remainder of the chapter, and see which of the 13 skills are represented. Are there skills that don't appear? How and where might they fit into classroom routines?
2. Choose at least two strategies from the chapter and use them in an area of your life that would benefit from increased creativity. You may use them to work on your creative product or in any other aspect of your life. Record your feelings while using them and the results of your efforts.
3. Examine quotations from famous inventors or other creative people. Look for evidence of the use of metaphor or other strategies in their thought processes. Discuss the strategies that individuals seemed to use most successfully.

Try It Tomorrow

1. There are a number of commercial dice-like products that can help generate random input for storytelling or other problem solving. For example Story Cubes are available both as dice and as an app with virtual dice. But your students can make their own paper dice with a basic cube pattern and some imagination. They could create dice specifically for storytelling with characters, settings, and so forth or more truly random dice with generic nouns that can be tied to any problem-solving situation. You might try dice with verbs and adjectives as well and see which are more helpful.
2. Experiment with both perspective taking and personal analogies by imagining conversations by animals or inanimate objects. Choose (or have students choose) a photo or other illustration of an environment and have students add thought bubbles to clarify what might be occurring. The catch is, the thoughts can not be those of any humans in the picture. Pictures could be general or designed to illustrate science concepts, historical events, or any other aspect of the curriculum.
3. If you teach art, you might want to experiment with Scalin's (2011) Photo Mash-up technique as an example of the SCAMPER verb "combine." In a photo mash-up, two photos are cut into strips and woven together to create something new. Students can experiment with straight or wavy lines, different widths, etc. to see what emerges. Scalin's book *Unstuck* is full of strategies to help get creative juices flowing.

Tech Tips

1. In this age of iPods, iPads, and smartphones, there are apps for just about everything—including creative thinking. One of the most useful for those odd 5-minutes-before-lunch moments is Creative Genius on the Go for iPod, iPhone, or iPad. Creative Genius on the Go is a collection of divergent-thinking challenges that can be used anywhere you have a handy phone. Also good for road trips!

   A similar tool for adults and older students is called brainsparker. It offers random creativity prompts for generating divergent ideas. For example, the app might suggest you write down 10 ideas without stopping or take your problem to its most extreme conclusion (brainsparker.com/brainsparker_app).

   When doing divergent thinking, you might also enjoy using mind-mapping apps like Popplet or Ideament to display ideas in a visual format. Popplet has subscription options and suggestions specifically for schools, so that can be a user-friendly introduction for those who are new to virtual tools. Like all things app, things change rapidly, so be sure to look to see what is available.

2. Of course there are also plenty of other online options for mind mapping. SpiderScribe (www.spiderscribe.net) is a free online tool that allows you to create visual representations of ideas and their links. It isn't as flexible in creating shapes as a mind map that you draw, but it allows you to upload files, pictures, and maps, in addition to text. One nice thing about SpiderScribe is that it can be shared, so you could record your ideas and send them to a friend (or a lot of friends!) or use it for online brainstorming. The map is available from anywhere, because it is stored "in the cloud." The site has a print function, so you can also print out your map for later use.

3. If flexible thinking entails thinking from another perspective, it certainly would include taking on another person's point of view. Fakebook, from Classtools.net, allows users to create simulated Facebook pages for literary characters, historical figures, or new fantasy characters. Check out the sample pages for historical characters like Benjamin Franklin and imagine how this could be used for language arts or social studies projects.

4. For a real-world exercise in flexible thinking for older students, examine the Room for Debate feature of the *New York Times* online. In Room for Debate, four or five experts from various perspectives write a short response to a question in the news. The *Times* suggested that Room for Debate could be used to address the Common Core standard "Constructing Arguments," a skill requiring logic and critical thinking. But not only is that skill something that can also be brought to bear on creative tasks, it is also something that can be taught in a way that facilitates creativity at varied grade levels. Your students don't have to be able to read the *Times* to use the Room for Debate format. Imagine constructing Room for Debate entries like these:

   Should Jack be prosecuted for the theft of the Golden Goose? (From the perspective of Jack, the Giant, and the Goose)

   Why was the first Thanksgiving important? (From the perspective of a Pilgrim, a Native American from 1620, and a person today)

   Should a bike path be built along the creek next to the school? (From the perspective of a student, a parent, and a fish in the creek)

   Why did you choose your housing material? (From the perspective of the three pigs)

   Which simple machine is most useful? (From the perspective of a lever, a pulley, and a wedge)

Figure 6.10 Chapter 1 Wordle

5. Wordle (www.wordle.net) and Tagxedo (tagxedo.com) are two of several available options for creating word clouds from text, with words appearing larger depending on how frequently they appear in the text. Figure 6.10 is a Wordle for the first chapter of this book. Just glancing at it allows me to see which ideas are featured most prominently. Students can use word clouds to analyze text (theirs or texts they are studying) or to create graphics. Tagxedo allows a bit more flexibility, because the user can choose the shape of the word cloud. Look on the Tagxedo website for a presentation on "101 Ways to Use Tagxedo."

7
Creativity in the Content Areas
Language Arts, Social Studies, and the Arts

When Dave stopped by to greet his colleague, Nancy, Nancy looked glum.

"What's up?" asked Dave. "Bad day?"

"I just don't know how I'm going to do it all," replied Nancy.

"All what?"

"Everything. You know how much I care about the creative activities in my class. I love my students' energy and excitement when their imagination really gets going. But now that we have these new standards, I guess that's all over. There are no standards about creativity—and there's so much there. How will I fit in anything extra—especially something that isn't in the assessments? Maybe creativity has to go."

What would you say if you were Dave? Teaching content is at the heart of most school activities. We know that the continuing explosion in the amount of information available ensures that much of the knowledge our students will need in the future is not available today—and most of us acknowledge that many students may not remember the details of the Taft-Hartley Act or the importance of equivalent angles for the rest of their lives. Still, most teachers spend the school day teaching content in four basic areas: language arts, mathematics, social studies, and the sciences. Content can help students understand the world around them, gain an appreciation for cultures, live healthier lives, express themselves more clearly, and make more knowledgeable decisions in many areas of their lives. It also can be a vehicle for learning the types of problem solving and critical and creative thinking that may be considered the basic skills of the 21st century.

This chapter examines the teaching of content and how it relates to the basic goals and processes of creativity. Creative acts entail finding and solving problems and expressing individual ideas in unique ways. Neither the problems solved nor the ideas expressed exist in a vacuum. People are creative in one or more disciplines, functioning as creative scientists, creative musicians, and creative writers. Individuals need knowledge in order to be creative; finding problems of increasing sophistication demands increased understanding of the domains in which the problems are found. It is possible to become so entrenched in established knowledge that it is difficult to view a field with a fresh perspective (Sternberg & Lubart, 1991; Sternberg & O'Hara, 1999). However, too much knowledge is seldom a concern of teachers in elementary or secondary schools. A more immediate issue is determining how the major disciplines might be taught so that they are supportive of students' creativity while also teaching for understanding.

As noted in Chapter 1, recommendations for strategies that enhance understanding of content have, in fact, described activities that involve students in creative thinking. Sternberg (2003) describes a series of research studies in which students who are taught content using analytical, practical, and creative thinking skills were more successful across academic disciplines than those taught in traditional ways alone. He summarized, "In short, by encouraging students to think creatively—to create, imagine, suppose, discover, invent—teachers can help students improve their achievement" (p. 132). There is reason to believe that teaching content in ways that support creativity can develop skills that are essential for 21st-century citizens. Wagner (2008) interviewed several hundred leaders in business, education, and philanthropy, asking about skills that students will need as they move into adulthood. One of the first responses from a business leader was, "First and foremost, I look for someone who asks good questions. We can teach them the technical stuff, but we can't teach them how to ask good questions—how to think" (p. 20). Wagner summarized the skills he identified as follows (note the parallels to creative thinking):

1. Critical thinking and problem solving
2. Collaboration and leadership
3. Agility and adaptability (flexible thinking)
4. Initiative and entrepreneurialism
5. Oral and written communication skills
6. Accessing and analyzing information
7. Curiosity and imagination

Virtually every element listed echoes a key attribute of creativity: curiosity, finding interests and problems, flexible thinking, communicating personal ideas, and solving problems. Yet the list was not developed to focus on creativity but to describe activities that best assist students in 21st-century careers and citizenship.

Teaching to support creativity does not minimize the importance of factual information. An individual seldom finds a powerful and interesting problem without having substantial background knowledge. It does suggest that this content can be put to work. It also forces us to look on both the content and the students with new eyes. When we teach students to find and solve problems, we can never know exactly where the problems may lead. We must look at students not as empty vessels or blank slates but as fellow investigators who come to us with ideas, experiences, and thoughts worth pursuing.

Figure 7.1 represents the Learning for Understanding portion of the Creativity in the Classroom model.

Note that in order to learn for understanding, students need to focus on understanding goals, goals that lead them to the key concepts and generalizations we want them to learn. They must use the information they learn in meaningful ways and receive clear feedback. As you continue through the next three chapters, observe how the strategies designed to support creativity can lead in exactly those directions.

The next two chapters examine content teaching from several angles. First, I will describe general principles for developing curriculum supportive of creativity. Next, I'll address one of the most important and controversial curriculum developments in recent years, the Common Core

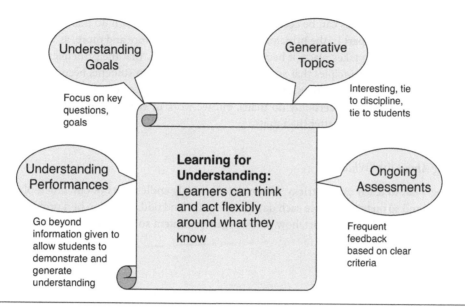

Figure 7.1 Creativity in the classroom model: Learning for understanding

State Standards being adopted in many of the United States. If Nancy is to find a way to incorporate creativity into her teaching, she—and thousands of teachers like her—must be able to do so while addressing required standards. And, in truth, it doesn't matter if your curriculum is defined by the Common Core or some other curriculum standards; in most cases, the same principles apply. Third, we'll survey four major areas of curriculum (language arts, social studies, science, and mathematics) and give examples of content teaching that may support creativity. Finally, Chapter 8 examines additional strategies that cut across disciplines, including inductive teaching, role-play, simulation strategies, and discussion techniques.

Curriculum for Creativity

Let's start with curriculum. We all have it. And if we can't figure out how to help students develop creativity within the regular curriculum—as opposed to the last half hour on Friday afternoon—it isn't going to happen. I sometimes say we need to "creativize" our curriculum. It's a silly word but appropriate. We need to consider how to structure our curriculum so that it supports students' creativity—and, as we now know, their understanding as well. There are at least four basic principles for creativizing curriculum. You can think of them as representing curriculum's key questions: What? How? Why? And how do you know?

- What? In curriculum supportive of creativity, content is organized around key ideas and questions that can be viewed from multiple perspectives. Where possible, it includes information about the creative methods of the discipline being taught.
- How? The methods of such curriculum include instructional techniques that require students to ask questions, generate varied options, and consider multiple perspectives.
- Why? The tasks students undertake to apply curriculum are tied to the real world in complex ways, asking genuine questions and solving real-world problems.
- How do you know (they understand)? Assessment includes multiple formative and summative assessments, including some that offer choices and use content in new ways.

Each of these principles can be considered in more depth, and we'll do that over the remaining chapters. The best part is, the principles serve double duty. More and more, as we understand how in-depth learning takes place, it becomes clear, once again, that the principles that support creativity are also the principles that support learning. As we help students become curious, ask questions, take on new perspectives, and tie content to their lives, we not only become more interesting teachers (though we certainly do that!), but we work in sync with our students' growing brains. And what could be better than that?

Thinking About the "What?"

Knowing what to teach can be tricky. Given the seemingly endless lists of outcomes, objectives, core ideas, and so on teachers face each day, that might sound odd. But it can be a problem. When the lists are long and time is short, how do we organize content so that learning happens?

Here are three thoughts:

Big Ideas
Big Questions
Real Processes

Like so many other things about teaching for creativity, these key features serve two purposes—creativity and learning. First, the basic content supportive of creativity is organized around key questions or ideas, ideas that are robust enough that they can be viewed from multiple perspectives. This can be harder than it seems, as most of us have spent many years in fact-driven education. I'll bet many of you could still tell me the dates World War I occurred but are fuzzy on exactly why. Or you can recite a formula from math or physics but have no idea when it might be useful. Curriculum that focuses on "facts first" does not help students learn in ways they can remember and apply later. Facts are important but only in the service of bigger ideas. They are the leaves on the tree, not the trunk.

How do we find the trunk? One way to do it is to stop and consider what is really important. What do we want students to take from this unit that they can apply elsewhere? Big ideas are most often expressed either as statements of relationship or as key questions. One of my favorite examples was from one of my students, years ago, who was teaching a unit on Japan to third graders. While there is much in Japanese culture that could be of interest to young people, she wanted to start with an idea that could go beyond the unit. In her case, she wanted students to understand that the geography of Japan shaped the culture. If students understood that, they would have learned a powerful idea that could apply to many times and cultures. But my favorite thing about that unit was the way she did it. She started with a question.

Why do students in Japan often have rice in their lunches instead of sandwiches?

That was a puzzle. But once students started learning about how rice grows and compared it to the way wheat grows (so essential for those jelly sandwiches), the differences in lunch choices made complete sense. It was an "aha" moment of understanding. And, of course, that understanding made possible other questions and inquiries about the ways geography was important across the two cultures.

Good curriculum moves students toward "aha" moments, particularly those that can apply to different situations and perspectives. They are the grist for flexible thinking in ways that facts alone seldom provide. When we choose ideas that can be applied to varied times, places, and perspectives, not only is curriculum richer, but it supports flexible and original thinking as well.

There is only so much one can think about a specific fact. "Many people in Japan eat rice." Tying it to a bigger idea brings it to life. "People in Japan eat rice because the geography of their land supports rice. The flat plains in the United States are good for growing wheat, which is needed to make bread. That is one reason bread is a staple food in the U.S." Even for young children, such an understanding can lead to questions like, "Do people on other islands also grow rice?" Or even, "If people lived on the moon, what would they eat if plants don't grow there?"

While a full discussion of curriculum organization is impossible here, McTighe and Wiggins's (2013) *Essential Questions* is a fine resource to help you organize curriculum around big ideas. My student's lunchbox question was a bit narrow, but it served as an essential (and very motivating) question for that unit. Similarly, other "meaty" questions planned to facilitate understanding can support creativity as well.

The other "what" of curriculum supportive of creativity is "real processes," teaching students how the creative individuals within each discipline ask and answer questions. From that perspective, teachers should teach each subject in such a way that students have the opportunity to use the creative methods of the fields we teach. Students might, at least at times, view language arts as would a creative writer, see science from the perspective of a creative scientist, and approach social studies as would a creative investigator in those domains. They must learn not just the content of the disciplines but also how the disciplines work. Content teaching should, at least at times, include strategies for finding problems, gathering information, focusing on important ideas, and expressing discoveries in the forms and language of the domain.

For example, consider artist George Szekely. He fell in love with children's art. He was captivated by the honesty and the excitement of their work. He also was struck by the ways in which the work of young artists paralleled the activities of adult artists. When absorbed in their paints, clay, or dances, they were engaged in authentic ways in the processes of art. Unfortunately, as an art teacher, he also was struck with the contrast between the ways student artists made art on their own and the ways they were expected to make art in schools. School art usually involved tasks selected and planned by the teacher. Any deviation from the plan was considered to be misbehavior or failure. He describes one young art teacher who burst into tears because one of her students refused to complete her carefully planned projects—all he wanted to do was paint!

Szekely's (1988) efforts to design school art activities that allowed students to act as artists required his interaction with students as fellow seekers. He realized that when teachers assume that students can make artworks simply by following instructions, they are forgetting how important thinking about art ideas and preparing for the artwork are in the art process. Artists prepare for art making by thinking about their ideas, visualizing the works they might make, recording ideas in notes and sketches, planning for the works, searching for materials, and playfully experimenting with various possibilities for carrying out the ideas. Lessons that place the major emphasis on following instructions and learning set techniques of art making do not come to terms with the basic problem of introducing students to the art process. Instead of preplanned art projects, Szekely's lessons involved students in the messy processes of finding ideas and making art—and were rarely completed in 45 minutes!

Parallel concerns, challenges, and potential solutions can be found in any discipline. Just as art instruction should exemplify the processes of art, instruction in other content areas, at least part of the time, should share the processes of creative individuals in those areas. Students learning science need to learn information about the world around them. If they are to develop as creative scientists, they also need to begin learning how scientists view the world—how they question and explore. Students learning mathematics need to begin seeing the wonder with which mathematicians view the patterns around them and the types of questions they ask.

Thinking About the Classroom

Think about the subject or subjects you teach. Consider the types of questions professionals in that field or those fields pursue. Jot down a list of skills necessary to identify and explore problems in at least one area you teach. How many of them are taught in your curriculum?

Although each discipline has investigative techniques to be learned and particular types of questions that may be explored, there also are ideas, values, and attitudes that support creativity across domains. I recall a summer conference at which, as a graduate student, I was serving in several capacities. In the morning, I was teaching investigative techniques in science to a group of elementary teachers. In the afternoon, I was serving as an assistant to a well-known expert on visual arts, a subject about which I knew very little. I hoped that by assisting, I might gain enough knowledge and confidence to do a better job teaching about that area. After a few days, I was startled to realize that my morning and afternoon activities were parallel. In each class we taught students to observe carefully, to look for patterns, to decide what was interesting, and to investigate further. In art, as in science, we encouraged students to value their observations and ideas and to approach the world as a source of inspiration and amazement.

Students can capture many types of ideas in a notebook

The tools we used to explore were different, but the processes of questioning were often the same. Looking back now, I can see that the shared experiences follow the patterns of problem finding described in Chapter 6.

Szekely viewed himself as an artist-teacher, making and living art while he shared it with students. Teachers can model the processes of exploration, finding and solving problems by sharing their own efforts in a variety of disciplines. Writer-teachers might describe the walk through the woods that inspired their latest poem or the interesting character they observed in the Laundromat. Mathematician-teachers might describe their search for natural spirals and their delight at finding a new, interesting shell. Historian-teachers could share their efforts to learn about the history of their house or their curiosity about the town's defunct trolley system: Where did those tracks once lead? Whatever the discipline, teachers will be better models if, in at least one area, they are involved themselves in the processes of exploration.

Initially, such involvement may prove a challenge. Teachers' lives are very busy, and the pursuit of outside interests may feel like a luxury we can ill afford. Or worse, we, ourselves, may have spent so many years pursuing teacher-designed, teacher-assigned projects that we may have difficulty imagining ourselves pursuing an academic task without an assignment. It may be easier to look for opportunities to be creative in cooking, woodworking, or making Halloween costumes than in language arts, history, science, or math. Yet although creativity is valuable in any area from costumes to casseroles, if we expect creative questioning in academic domains from our students, we must be willing to experience it ourselves. Think about how you might use at least one of the disciplines you teach to explore the world in ways that interest you, and then share your experiences with your students. A teacher who is also an artist or a mathematician or a scientist or a writer can better share the adventures of these domains with the people around him or her.

Thinking About the Classroom

Examine your curriculum materials. Are there any areas in which students are encouraged to ask and answer questions? Does your curriculum teach processes for investigation, problem solving, or creativity in your area of study?

Thinking About the "How?"

Of course, once we've determined the "what" of the curriculum, it is also important to consider the "how," the types of teaching methods that help students consider the content from varied perspectives. These include instructional techniques that require students to ask questions, generate varied options, and consider multiple points of view. In other words, our students need to think about the things they are learning. Examining the "how" of our teaching to enhance creativity doesn't mean changing everything we are doing—sometimes small changes make a big difference. In one study, simply changing the type of lesson introduction to a more creativity-supporting option enhanced both creativity and learning (Webb & Rule, 2014). It is a matter of being mindful of the variety and types of teaching methods we use.

There are many ways to do this. In Chapter 6, we examined strategies for helping students ask questions. There are also many ways to get students to think about things from multiple perspectives. For example, we could consider these planning basics.

- Is there a place in this lesson it would be helpful to generate many ideas?
- Could students take a different perspective or point of view about the content?
- How could I use a "what if" question to get students to look at content in a new way?

- Would asking students to add detail enhance their understanding? Could they fill in missing pieces?
- How could I incorporate metaphor into our discussion?

You can also use many of the strategies in Chapter 6, adapted to your content, to generate activities supportive of creative thought. But there is a caveat. Beware of what I've sometimes referred to as "Twinkie Curriculum," or Twinkie activities, named after snack cakes popular with young children. Those cream-filled wonders can make children's eyes sparkle with delight, but they don't actually help when children are hungry. They don't bring needed nutrients for a balanced meal. They are (at least for children) just fun. A few Twinkies in a healthy diet probably won't hurt, but they shouldn't be children's main food source. Similarly, activities in which students generate many ideas for naming nail polish colors might be useful for teaching students what fluency means, but they don't teach important principles, except perhaps in an art course studying color variation or perhaps a unit on advertising. Similarly, using flexible thinking within content, but not important content, can be a waste of its power.

Activities in which students ask questions and think flexibly take time and are potent learning experiences. It is important to focus their power on key ideas and not on the less important details of the curriculum. For example, in studying *Romeo and Juliet*, students might have fun devising a more effective escape plan for the young couple. They might even use considerable original thinking in doing so. But why? It would not help them focus on important ideas. It would be a Twinkie activity. What would be better? It depends what you are trying to teach. If you are teaching about Shakespeare's use of imagery, perhaps you want students to consider all the ways light and dark, day and night are used, not always in traditional ways. In that case, having students generate a list of contemporary songs or movies in which light and dark are used symbolically could enhance their understanding of imagery while helping build meaningful ties to their lives. They might be challenged to write a description of something in their world that reflects darkness or light in complex ways. Of course, if your teaching emphasis is on another aspect of the play, the places you would employ flexible thinking would change. The key is: Help students think in multiple ways about the ideas you care about most. Use flexible thinking, metaphor, and perspective taking as powerful teaching tools rather than a break from routine.

No Twinkies. Except maybe for dessert.

Thinking About the "Why?"

The third principle for developing curriculum supportive of creativity suggests that students should be able to understand why the content matters.

The tasks students undertake to apply curriculum are tied to the real world in complex ways, asking genuine questions and solving real-world problems. As with the first principle, this can be summarized in a few key phrases:

- Real world
- Real questions
- Real problems

All good lessons involve practice. Whatever the key ideas we are teaching, students must practice them to reinforce their learning. The question is, how? When we ask students to apply content in new ways, it requires them to think about the ideas more flexibly. When those applications are relevant to authentic questions, they make learning real. Studying the volume of solids as a geometrical formula and then completing a set of calculations is one thing. Considering how best to design a container to hold a particular volume of popcorn is another. Learning the difference between a simile and a metaphor is standard language arts content. But developing metaphors that could be used to justify a new school mascot makes the concept of metaphor meaningful beyond the textbook. Students in both cases have the opportunity to use flexible thinking and develop original ideas. They also begin to see how the things they are learning relate to their lives.

It makes sense that thinking about something in more than one way helps students learn, but it is more than that. Think back to the discussion of neurobiology in which Immordino-Yang (2016) said,

> [E]motion and cognition are supported by interdependent neural processes. It is literally neurobiologically impossible to build memories, engage complex thoughts, or make meaningful decisions without emotion. . . . Put succinctly, we only think about things we care about.
>
> (p. 18)

You probably should read that again, because this is vital. **We only think (deeply) about things we care about.** Unless students care about the things they are learning, they won't think about them. If they don't think about them, they won't learn them, not really. They may be able to repeat facts for a test, but they won't remember them, transfer them to another situation, or use them in useful ways. Hardly seems as if that should qualify as "learning" at all, regardless of the test score.

How do we help students care about content? Not by giving out stickers or snacks. Those are more likely to generate interest in the anticipated rewards. Rather, helping students see content as meaningful in their lives—not just interesting but also useful—is a start. Open-ended problems can be particularly powerful, because they allow students to wrestle with defining the task and find ways to tie to their own interests and creativity. Projects that might, at the surface, feel much less efficient than a traditional test or straightforward "report" may actually be the best route to the learning we all want—and creativity, too! More in-depth information on developing real-world problems is found later in this chapter.

Thinking About the "How Do You Know?"

The final general principle for developing curriculum supportive of creativity is:

> Assessment includes multiple formative and summative assessments, including some that offer choices and use content in new ways.

In all good curriculum, we start with big ideas. Then we decide what we want students to be able to do with those ideas. That process can lead us to develop both effective practice activities (which can serve as formative assessments) and appropriate major (summative) assessments. We know when we ask students to apply information, they will learn the most and showcase their ideas most effectively if they are engaged in projects that are meaningful to them. And while it is true that most public school teachers must prepare students to take traditional tests, if traditional tests are the primary type of major assessments, we may teach an unintended message—"Only test scores count." While, sadly, sometimes public schools feel like that, if we want learning for understanding and creativity to occur, we need to create assessments that both require students to use the information and send the message, "Your thinking about the content counts." Information on developing assessments supportive of creativity can be found in Chapter 10.

Creativity and the Common Core

Of course, for most teachers, all these strategies must be implemented within the curriculum standards required by our schools and districts. In the United States, the Common Core State Standards Initiative is one of the most powerful educational forces in decades. The Common Core State Standards Initiative is designed to develop shared curriculum standards across the affiliated states—at the point of this writing, more than 40 of the 50 states at various levels of implementation. The Common Core State Standards are not technically a national curriculum, because they were developed through collaboration across states rather than by any federal body, but they are exerting tremendous influence on schools across the country. The political future of the Common Core State Standards is unclear, but it seems likely that, at least in the United States, all of us will be teaching toward some kind of standards for the foreseeable future. The question then is: Can creativity and the Common Core (or any other set of required standards) coexist peacefully?

There are many good things about the Common Core. In particular, the emphases on critical thinking, logic, research, and mathematical thinking can be important supports for creative thinking and innovation. But here's my fear. Under pressure to raise the ever-looming test scores, schools and teachers may feel compelled to focus their efforts entirely on Common Core standards, with everything else lost in the chomp of giant accountability jaws.

But remember what the standards' authors say under "What is Not Covered by the Standards":

> While the Standards focus on what is most essential, they do not describe all that can or should be taught. A great deal is left to the discretion of teachers and curriculum developers. The aim of the Standards is to articulate the fundamentals, not to set out an exhaustive list or a set of restrictions that limits what can be taught beyond what is specified herein.

This leads us to the first of three key principles to consider regarding creativity and the Common Core, also applicable to most other standards documents.

Creativity and Common Core Principle 1: They Are Not the Whole Curriculum

These are the Common *Core* State Standards. They are not the whole apple. If we limit what we teach to exactly what is in the Core documents, students will miss out on important experiences and ideas—to say nothing of most of social studies, world languages, and the arts! The "What Is Not Covered by the Standards" list addresses this specifically:

> While the Standards make references to some particular forms of content . . . they do not—indeed, cannot—enumerate all or even most of the content that students should learn. The Standards must therefore be complemented by a well-developed, content-rich curriculum.
> (National Governors Association Center for Best Practices,
> Council of Chief State School Officers, 2010, p. 6)

Creativity and Common Core Principle 2: They Don't Tell You How to Teach

The Common Core State Standards Initiative outlines core math and language arts content to be addressed at each grade level (with science content outlined in the Next Generation Science Standards). That is, the Core Standards carefully delineate *what* is to be taught at each grade level, at least in those subject areas. But they don't address the ways that content is to be taught. In fact, when listing "What Is Not Covered by the Standards," the first sentence states, "The Standards define what all students are expected to know and be able to do, not how teachers should teach." It is important to understand what the Standards do and do not mandate and then look for ways to integrate both creative teaching and teaching for creativity into the mix.

For example, suppose that you are teaching fourth grade and you want to incorporate creative thinking strategies into your instruction. Imagine you are working on the following standard:

> Describe in depth a character, setting, or event in a story or drama, drawing on specific details in the text (e.g., a character's thoughts, words, or action).

Your goal for today is to help students describe a character. You could have students read a paragraph and pull out the descriptive words and phrases—I'm beginning to doze off just imagining it. What other options might allow for more creative thinking and more interested students? Start by asking yourself the basic curriculum planning questions described earlier:

- Is there a place it would be helpful to generate many ideas?
- Would it be helpful to take a different perspective or point of view?
- How could I use a "what if" question?
- Would asking students to add detail enhance their understanding?
- How could I incorporate metaphor into our discussion?
- How can I get students to ask questions and investigate?

These questions could trigger a number of ideas. Let's take Alice, because *Alice in Wonderland* is one of the suggested texts for fourth grade:

- I could pick a pivotal scene and ask students to generate many possible choices the character could make. Then they need to choose which choice the character is most likely to make, supporting their choice with evidence about the character's personality, beliefs, and so on. For example, early in the story, Alice is stuck in a room, too big to get through the door, and she sits down and begins to cry. What could she do next? Which choice is more likely based on what we know about Alice?
- I could ask students to describe a character, then ask them to describe the same character again but from the perspective of another character. For example, how might the Cheshire Cat describe Alice? Or the Duchess? They must provide evidence for why the second character is likely to hold those views.
- There are lots of possible "what if" questions in *Alice in Wonderland*, but it is a bit trickier to come up with a "what if" question that will help students better be able to describe Alice's characteristics. I might save "what if" for another day.
- Thinking about adding details made me remember another Common Core Standard: Make connections between the text of a story or drama and a visual or oral presentation of the text, identifying where each version reflects specific descriptions and directions in the text. It would be interesting to have students compare the details in the text with the original illustrations. Are there details they'd like to add to the illustrations to make them better match the text?
- Metaphors for Alice could be fun! If Alice were an animal, what animal would she be? What about Alice is like that animal?
- How could students investigate Alice? Perhaps at the beginning of the book, students could generate hypotheses about Alice's characteristics. Is she curious? Brave? Not very careful? As they continue to read, they could chart evidence to support or not support their hypotheses.

Any of these activities help students look at details and describe a character, but they also provide opportunities for flexible thinking and imagination.

Of course there are scores of other creative activities possible with Alice, but the basic questions listed here can help give direction to almost any subject and standard, and the strategies in the next two chapters provide additional options. Remember, the goal of the standard is set, but as Alice found out, even if you know where you are going, there are a lot of ways to get there, not to mention adventures along the way!

Creativity and Common Core Principle 3: They Don't Tell You What Students Should Do With the Content

The standards also do not address how students might use the content being taught. The Common Core Standards list the basic processes students are to use ("Describe," "Explain," "Write," "Compare") but do not, generally, say what students should do in order to demonstrate those processes. This is where performances of understanding fit in: What could students do to demonstrate they understand and can use the content?

For example, imagine high school students are to do the following.

> Analyze how an author's choices concerning how to structure a text, order events within it (e.g., parallel plots), and manipulate time (e.g., pacing, flashbacks) create such effects as mystery, tension, or surprise.

There are many possible ways that understanding could be expressed. They could write a traditional paper, perhaps focusing on the standards for writing informative text. Alternatively, they could analyze several texts—perhaps several mysteries—and then write their own mini-mystery using the mystery strategies identified. The mini-mysteries could take the form of a mystery e-mail story-starter, a traditional short story, or an oral story to be told at a "scary story" event—perhaps around Halloween. All of these activities support standards either in narrative writing or speech, as well as the initial analysis. The difference is, the teacher included an additional question: "How could students use this content in an original way?"

Students also could support the Common Core Standards on using technology in writing by contributing to an online bulletin board or poster defining "What Makes a Mystery?" or "Time Travel in Text," sharing their observations about authors' techniques across multiple texts. Such marvels are possible using websites such as Padlet, Corkboard Me, Popplet, or Glogster or related apps. The important thing is, *in any of those tasks, students are analyzing authors' choices concerning how to structure text and doing something meaningful with the information.* The activities also support one of the keys to developing creativity by helping students understand the tools and methods of professional writers.

Or say you were addressing the following standards:

> Summarize categorical data for two categories in two-way frequency tables. Interpret relative frequencies in the context of the data (including joint, marginal, and conditional relative frequencies). Recognize possible associations and trends in the data.
> Make inferences and justify conclusions from sample surveys, experiments and observational studies.

You could have students complete the handy problems undoubtedly available in your math textbook. Or you could, as one of my students did some years ago, turn statistics on its ear. He devised a project in which students had to conduct a brief survey, analyze the data, and then present the data, first accurately, then as deceptively as possible without lying, using common strategies of presenting incomplete data, truncating graphs, and so on. The project allowed him to assess students' understanding of statistics and their ability to interpret surveys while also providing a great cautionary lesson for the next time they read a "data-based" claim. In similar ways, having students identify and solve problems within disciplines can provide powerful experiences of both learning and creativity.

The Common Core State Standards set a high bar for student learning and critical thinking, but they are not a cure-all for education, nor will they, alone, support creativity. But if we are wise, it is possible to address Common Core (or other) Standards and creativity simultaneously—and with better understanding, as well. Doing so will require both creative teaching and teaching for creativity. We need teachers who can look at key content and say things like, "I don't need to have students demonstrate their understanding of the systems of the human body by writing a report. We did that for our last unit. This time, they could build Rube Goldberg–type models to demonstrate the systems and explain them—incorporating oral communication standards and creativity at once." By examining ways to use content in flexible ways, both content learning and creativity benefit.

Thinking About the Classroom

Examine the Common Core or other local standards for your grade level. Look for standards that could be taught while investigating real-world problems. Be sure to check the language arts standards that support content areas for possible options.

What Is a Problem?

When I say curriculum should focus on key concepts and questions of a discipline, most teachers feel they are in familiar territory. But if we are also to assist students in finding and solving problems in content areas, the terrain may be less familiar. It is important to consider, first, what is a problem? What characteristics define real or authentic problems, and how are they distinct from the kinds of problems typically addressed in schools? Theorists espousing authentic outcomes, real-world tasks, and multidimensional problem solving fill the pages of educational journals (Mansilla & Gardner, 2008; Newmann & Wehlage, 1993; Renzulli & Reis, 1997). However, in many cases, the meanings of such terms are unclear. The authors assume, perhaps, that we will know real tasks when we see them.

One helpful key to defining real problems is in the work of Renzulli (1977; Renzulli & Reis, 1997), whose Enrichment Triad Model centers on individual and small-group investigations of real problems. This model was originally developed for the education of gifted and talented students, but many of its components are appropriate for all students, and the strategies for the pursuit of real problems can hold the key to problem finding and solving in many arenas.

First, a real problem springs from the interest of a student or group of students. A real problem has personal interest and value to the student who pursues it. If everyone is assigned to do it, it is less likely to be a real problem. This characteristic poses challenges for teachers. Rarely, in general content teaching, do we have the option to have each student investigating unique interests. But we can approach the ideal by being alert to student interests and concerns and working with them to tie content to their worlds.

Second, a real problem does not have a predetermined correct response. It involves processes for which there cannot be an answer key. As I consider the real problems with which my students have become involved, they seem to fall into three general categories:

1. Some real problems are research questions. They involve gathering and analyzing data and drawing conclusions. True research questions entail collecting information from primary sources through observation, surveys, interviews, or document analysis. The students who surveyed food preferences in the school cafeteria, those who interviewed local citizens on life in the community during World War II, and the first graders who observed the effects of milk on plant growth all investigated research questions.
2. Other real problems fall into the category of activism. In these activities, students attempt to improve some aspect of the world around them. Students who set up school recycling programs, teach peers what to do if they suspect a friend is being abused, create community nature trails, or lobby for bike lanes on local roads are pursuing this type of real problem.
3. Finally, real problems in the arts entail the expression of some theme, aesthetic, or idea. Adult creators use words, movement, paint, or clay as tools for expression. Students whose artwork explores the changing light, whose stories reflect their ideas about friendship, or whose dance reflects their rage all address real problems in meaningful ways.

In pursuing real problems, students should use authentic methodology as much as possible. That is, they should address the problem the way a professional would address it. Students who are to survey cafeteria preferences must learn something about survey design. The first-grade students with the bean plants should make a hypothesis and have a control group. Although some types of authentic methodology are easier to implement than others, each aspect of a project provides opportunities to stretch students toward professionalism. It can be easier for students to use authentic historical research techniques in a local history project than in a project about a distant place. However, even when primary sources are limited, students can use professional techniques for sharing information in a manner that is appropriate to the discipline.

Finally, when they are pursuing real problems, students eventually share information with a real audience. What constitutes a real audience will vary enormously with the age of the students and the sophistication of their problems. The key is that the audience should have a genuine interest in the product instead of viewing it as a source for a grade or other evaluation. Some real audiences are part of the natural school environment. A group of first-grade students may write an original play and produce it for the class next door. Other audiences may be created by school events to provide a vehicle for student efforts: art exhibits, invention conventions, and science fairs (Schack & Starko, 1998; Starko & Schack, 1992). Still other audiences may be part of the local community. Our local chamber of commerce was pleased to display a student-produced brochure on the history of local buildings along with other pamphlets the chamber made available to the public. The radio station often aired student-generated public service announcements. Local-access cable television, historical societies, and other community organizations can provide enthusiastic audiences for appropriate student products. And, of course, Internet technologies provide the opportunity for students to share their world with interested audiences across the globe.

Certainly, the types of problems pursued, the methodology employed, and the audiences approached will vary enormously from a kindergartener's first puppet show or garden experiment to a high school senior's computer program for displaying the location of archeological artifacts. However, at each stage, students may be nudged just one notch closer to professionalism: the kindergarten student to plan a puppet before building it, the high school senior to present his or her work to the state archeological association. Each represents a legitimate step toward pursuing real problems.

The time required to pursue fully authentic problems means that not every unit will involve a full-blown investigation. Sometimes simulated problems, like the previous example of devising a new popcorn container in geometry class, are most appropriate. But the vision of students genuinely involved in bringing content to bear on real-world issues can guide us and push us toward more meaningful and memorable content experiences. The next four sections examine finding and solving problems, learning the methodologies of disciplines, and structuring teaching to enhance creativity in various disciplines. In no case are the suggestions intended to be a comprehensive program in the discipline discussed. Rather, they reflect activities, points of view, and organizational strategies that can form an important part of many programs.

Thinking About the Classroom

Examine a local newspaper, looking for real-world problems that might be investigated by students. You may want to look daily for a week or two. See if you discover any that might tie to your curriculum.

Finding and Solving Problems in the Language Arts

Helping students find and solve problems in the language arts requires a major shift in perspective. Students must—at least at times—shift from thinking "I write because I have an assignment" to "I write because I have an idea." Understanding that good writing and good language are based in the communication of ideas is at the heart of creativity in the language arts.

Finding Purpose and Technique for Communication

Authors write for a variety of purposes. Some writing is designed to convey factual information, some to persuade, some to share emotions or ideas, and some to raise questions. Other important communication uses oral language or other media or symbolic forms for similar purposes. If students are to use writing or other forms of language to share their own ideas, they must recognize the efforts at communication in the works they read or hear.

In considering the role of language and language arts in creativity, teachers must be aware of at least two perspectives. The first is that language, oral or written, is an essential vehicle for communicating creative ideas, strategies, and solutions across disciplines. Students may write about problems and ideas in math, science, social studies, or any other area. A second perspective is that schools may play a role in supporting the kind of creativity inherent in the language arts themselves: poetry, storytelling or story writing, play writing, creative nonfiction, and so on. In either case, the heart of the process is identifying an idea worthy of communication. This section deals primarily with the second perspective: creativity in the more traditional language arts. Keep in mind, however, that writing and language activities can and should be organized around the problem-identification and -solving experiences in the other disciplines discussed later.

The links among thought, speaking, and writing are at the heart of current literacy approaches. Students learn that if they can think it, they can say it. If they can say it, they can write it and read it. Writing is, above all, communication. In addition, the acts of reading and writing are seen as inquiry driven and purposeful. As students develop as readers and writers, they can approach the processes of finding and expressing ideas with increasing sophistication. Among other things, the

National Council of Teachers of English (NCTE) statement on Professional Knowledge for the Teaching of Writing (2016a) states that teachers need to understand:

- The wide range of purposes for which people write and the different kinds of texts and processes that arise from those purposes;
- Strategies and forms for writing for public participation in a democratic society;
- How people make creative and literary texts, aesthetic genres, for the purposes of entertainment, pleasure, or exploration;
- The ways digital environments have added new modalities while constantly creating new publics, audiences, purposes, and invitations to compose;
- Appropriate genres for varied academic disciplines and the purposes and relationships that create those forms.

Sound familiar? The writing process can support many of the attitudes and ideas associated with creativity, involving students in problem solving, communication, and flexible thinking. Done well, language arts instruction places communication squarely at the center of all writing, speaking, and other forms of communication. Although the terminology may vary, most advocates of the writing process identify at least five stages: prewriting, drafting, revising and editing, rewriting, and publishing (NCTE, 2016b).

A complete description of the writing process is beyond the scope of this chapter, but we consider here how some stages may tie to research and theory in creativity. In the prewriting stage, students can engage in problem finding and focusing if they are given the flexibility to choose an idea, topic, or question of personal concern. The prewriting stage may include at least three components: caring, observing, and focusing. Writers first must care about something; they must be moved to say something. Caring can spring from previous experiences and interests or from experiences structured by the teacher. This component also includes time to let ideas brew or incubate.

After caring comes observing. The author observes his or her experiences and attitudes regarding the idea or topic, past or present. (Do you recognize the parallels to problem finding here?) This can be followed by focusing: determining point of view, identifying audience, selecting relevant observations, and narrowing goals. In one class, sixth-grade students were challenged to think about an interesting character they had come across during summer recess. The prewriting process included thinking about people who were interesting, people who related to topics of interest, or people who made a difference in their summer. A student might consider the camp counselor with the purple hair, the coach of a well-loved sport, or the woman next door who hired him or her to do yard work.

One student chose to write about an older woman whose stories of days gone by had made summer evenings interesting. The student cared about the woman and wanted others to care about her as well. Next, the student considered all the sensory and emotional details she could recall about the woman. Webbing, or mind mapping, is often used to organize such ideas and information on a topic. Even emergent readers with limited writing skills can use mind maps by drawing in items, locations, or activities associated with an idea. Finally, it was necessary for the student to sort the information and decide what she wanted to convey about her friend. Her decision to use descriptive language to portray the dignity and grace with which the woman spoke gave focus to the project. The activities of caring, observing, and focusing allowed the student to find and focus on a specific problem in a general assignment.

Later stages of the writing process, particularly revision, in which students often work together to examine a draft from the reader's point of view, also support creativity by helping students develop the necessary internal locus of evaluation and standards for judgment (see Chapter 9). Skills instruction can include not just lessons on punctuation or grammatical form but also activities that help students focus on the techniques or strategies used by proficient writers in many disciplines—and use some flexible thinking along the way. Such lessons can make skills instruction come to life. Students of any age who have read *The Aunts Go Marching* (Manning, 2003) and seen how cleverly homonyms are used may have a completely different purpose for learning homonyms than students whose sole goal is to complete a worksheet. Imagine setting the task of creating a new set of children's stories based on homonyms. You'd have language study and creativity all in one! Middle school students learning about concrete poetry through Grandits's (2004) *Technically It's Not My Fault* can learn about voice and structure in poetry, with a goal toward poems that reflect their lives as vividly (and humorously) as do Grandits's. And while it is intended for students aged 8 to 14, almost anyone can benefit from Alison Wilcox's *Descriptosaurus* (2013). Wilcox describes *Descriptosaurus* as a "thematic expansion of a dictionary and thesaurus" (p. viii). It is a resource designed to help students expand their descriptive vocabulary and experiment with language based on settings, characters, and creatures.

The basic *Descriptosaurus* is thematically to allow young authors to find just the options they are seeking, For example, in the Settings section, there are subsections for Landscapes, Settlements, and Atmosphere. Each of those is further divided. If I wanted to describe a foggy day, I could easily turn to the page on "Rain, mist and fog" to find related words, phrases, and sentences. Do I want my fog to be icy, damp, or swirling? Is it brooding or a blanket of grey mist? Did it drift up from the soggy soil or perhaps descend from a mountain? There are also specialized *Descriptosaurus* options to vocabulary specific to ghost stories, adventures, or mythologies. Just browsing the pages makes me want to write something and provides countless examples of the differences key word choices can make.

Young beginning authors can examine the ideas and emotions underlying stories they hear. They might discuss the feelings the author tried to convey in *The Snowy Day* (Keats, 1962) or what ideas the author tried to share in *Ira Sleeps Over* (Waber, 1972). They can experiment with listing words that might make the reader feel happy or frightened or try to write a brief story that evokes a particular feeling. There are a variety of "feeling wheels" online to help develop more varied vocabulary. They could discuss why authors might write happy stories or sad stories. Later, students might write a piece designed to evoke a particular feeling, share the piece with peers, and discuss whether readers understood the intended mood. What kinds of emotions are crucial to *The Crucible?* How might they be experienced by John Proctor as opposed to Abigail Williams?

Students also can explore the language play fundamental to some works of literature. Children, young and old, reading *Ding Dong, Ding Dong* (Palatini, 1999) can enjoy the many plays on words in the story of the giant gorilla (Ding Dong) who climbs the Empire State Building attempting to sell Ape-On cosmetics. More sophisticated readers can examine the word play in the dialogue of *The Importance of Being Ernest* or Tom Stoppard's plays. Understanding the authors' enjoyment of the clever use of language can inspire students to new types of writing while reinforcing flexible thinking about the words they choose. If your school celebrates Valentine's Day, consider a lesson on point of view inspired by *I Love You More Than Moldy Ham* (Armstrong-Ellis, 2015), an account of a young monster's loving devotion framed in all things gruesome. How might other creatures express their loving thoughts? Elementary students could also examine the flip-flopped point of view of *How to Put Your Parents to Bed* (Larsen, 2016) and imagine how other activities might look from a different vantage point. Other writing tasks might encompass broad areas, allowing students to write about topics they identify as important: their favorite after-school activity, the thing about school they would most like to change, or a person they think is important. Although such tasks are still relatively constrained, they do begin to convey the idea that writing is designed to communicate ideas and feelings that matter to the author.

Go beyond haiku and experiment with some new forms of poetry. Perhaps you'll enjoy book spine poetry, in which you stack books in such a way that the titles form a poem. One of my friends and her young son started by stacking *Mary Poppins* on top of *The Girl Who Plays with*

Fire and went on from there. Or try found poetry, constructed by arranging text mined from existing documents. *The New York Times* has an annual contest for poems "found" in its pages. Think about finding poetry in a newspaper, a historical document, or even a science text. It could provide students with a new perspective on news or content.

Students in intermediate and higher grades can begin to discuss how authors get ideas for their writing. Reading biographies and blogs and interviewing local authors can give students clues to the writers' processes. Older students can analyze the writings of creative adults describing their work. They can begin to practice the careful observations and sense of wonder that characterize many authors. When students view the world through writers' eyes, every experience becomes a potential story source. Many authors look at the world and think, "Isn't that strange—or interesting—or sad—or confusing" and want others to notice as well. From those desires, perhaps, springs their drive to write.

One of my favorite examples of an author describing his process is Ray Bradbury's (1996) *Zen and the Art of Writing: Essays on Creativity*. In it, Bradbury describes the process of finding stories within oneself and nurturing the muse that stores them there. "Ideas," he writes, "lie everywhere, like apples fallen and melting in the grass for lack of wayfaring strangers with an eye and a tongue for beauty, whether absurd, horrific, or genteel" (p. 8). His suggestions for finding the ideas range from reading poetry every day and reading to improve color sense to long walks in the country to long walks through bookstores. "By living well, by observing as you live, by reading well and observing as you read, you have fed Your Most Original Self" (p. 43). Bradbury writes of masterful problem finding. His thoughts on finding ideas could be particularly meaningful to students studying Bradbury's science fiction—and perhaps writing their own. Or if you want to share the possibilities of random combinations as inspiration, try Sacher's (2012) *Random Story Generator*, a book in which pages are cut in thirds, representing opening phrases, characters, and conflicts that can be mixed and matched at will. It is, at its heart, an expanded version of Attribute Listing. You might want to create your own story generator, with students determining the characters and situations that most interest them.

Lesson 7.1   Mama, Do You Love Me? Using Flexible Thinking in Language Arts (K–12)

Read the picture book *Mama, Do You Love Me?* (Joosse, 1991). The book uses images and examples from Inuit culture to describe a mother's love for her child. Students could write a similar book using images from their own culture or a culture they research.

Students can begin to observe the world around them as writers through the vehicle of a writer's notebook. Separate pages might be set aside for jottings of a particular type. Students might create sections for "Things I wonder about," "Strange things people do," "Peaceful things," "Nice-sounding words or phrases," "Ideas about the future," "City things," or any other categories that suit their interests and needs. Some categories might be required as a basis of class discussions. For example, a class that read *Gilgamesh* or the *Autobiography of Malcolm X* (X, 1965) might spend several days looking for ideas or examples regarding heroics. These might be shared in a class discussion on how such ideas may form the basis for a new piece of literature. The pieces may or may not be actually written.

At other times, students may engage in activities that parallel those described by particular authors. Students who have read how Toni Morrison (1987) found the idea for the novel *Beloved* by reading a 19th-century newspaper might be assigned to examine a paper (past or present) for possible story ideas. Younger students might be challenged to imagine the story behind the story in familiar tales. Why did Goldilocks go into the woods that day? Why weren't the three pigs sharing a house? Books such as *The True Story of the Three Little Pigs* (Scieszka, 1989) can help students view familiar stories from another perspective and provide an example of an author finding ideas in seemingly common sources. Even older students can consider the use of perspective in fairy tales by considering the roles of traditional—and not-so-traditional—characters in the *Shrek* movies. In what other story might Shrek take a part or reveal a misunderstanding of the original?

Students who have heard of E. L. Doctorow's struggle with writer's block might follow his example. According to a television interview I heard years ago, after the success of *The Book of Daniel* (1971), Doctorow found himself struggling for a new idea. As an exercise in self-discipline, he forced himself to write for a portion of each day, hoping to find an idea among the unsatisfactory efforts. One day, lacking any inspiration, he sat staring at a spot on the wall. Because he had no immediate ideas, he began thinking about the wall. The wall made him think of the house, and he let his imagination wander to the time the house was built. He imagined the people who might have been walking by, what they might have been doing, and where they might have been going. The result, in the end, was the novel *Ragtime* (Doctorow, 1975). Students, too, might pick a familiar place or object and imagine connections that might lead to a story idea. Again, the stories may be written, or the ideas may be simply discussed and set aside for another day.

Lesson 7.2   Reading in the Dark: **Using Flexibility in Language Arts (Secondary)**

One way to encourage flexible thinking is to change form or genre. Students can write "autobiographies" of fictional characters, using excerpts from a favorite song to create a poem, or create a sound poem by sampling bits of music. The website ReadWriteThink, a joint venture of the National Council of Teachers of English (NCTE) and the International Reading Association (IRA), shares a lesson plan based on the book *Reading in the Dark* (Golden, 2001). The lesson plan asks students to create a soundtrack based on a book they have read (www.readwritethink.org/lessons/lesson_view.asp?id=861).

Apol (2002) described an exercise in which secondary students were challenged to write poetry about ordinary things. First, they read poetry that centered on common objects, discussing the way big ideas can be attached to small objects, Next, their instructor presented a table full of familiar objects that could suggest poetry. In this case, Apol modeled the way problem finding might have occurred in others before presenting the opportunity for students to have a similar experience. In addition to stories and poems, students should examine authors' purposes in a variety of fiction and nonfiction formats. Think about the diversity of purposes that may be represented in the following forms, each involving writing: poems, novels, short stories, essays, blogs, vlogs, plays, screenplays, documentaries, technical reports, pamphlets, grant applications, research reports, project proposals, legislative bills, advertising copy, and song lyrics.

Perry (1999) interviewed more than 75 best-selling authors about their experiences and strategies in writing. She was particularly interested in their accounts of writing in the flow state, described in Chapter 9. The resulting book, *Writing in Flow*, can be helpful in working with secondary school students who want to experiment with strategies that have been helpful to professional writers. Her five keys to writing in flow offer suggestions very similar to those discussed previously: (a) have a reason to write, (b) think like a writer (deferring judgment, taking risks, and being open to experience), (c) loosen up (play with ideas), (d) focus in, and (e) balance among opposites (work with both thought or craft and inspiration). You also may find her suggestions useful as you experiment with your own writing processes.

Don't forget the possibilities that technology gives us for supporting students with special needs in their creative expression. Students who may have trouble expressing themselves often have a lot to say. The CAST website listed in Chapter 1 can lead you to a wealth of options (www.cast.org). For example, the CAST Book Builder option (bookbuilder.cast.org) can assist students of all ages in creating their own online books.

You can also go to the Universal Design for Learning website (www.udlcenter.org), and click on "UDL Guidelines." Find the links for Three Primary Principles, then choose "Provide Multiple Means of Action and Expression: Expression and Communication." From there, select Guideline 5.1, "Use Multiple Media for Communication," where you should find an option for "Examples and Resources." There you will find suggestions that are supportive for all kinds of learners, with options for creating stories, comics, and even videos. In the best spirit of universal design, these really are appropriate (and delightful) for all students, from Animoto (videos) to ToonDoo (cartoons) and so on. Of course tablets can also provide support for speaking, writing, and all manner of communication. The Autism Speaks website provides a listing of iPad apps that have been successfully used with students with autism. Many of these can be used to support creative expression (www.autismspeaks.org/autism-apps).

Lesson 7.3   Sipping Spiders Through a Straw

Enjoy some flexible thinking while teaching about both literary analysis and parody by comparing parodies to their originals. At Halloween, examining *Cinderella Skeleton* (San Souci, 2000) and comparing the elements that parallel the original can provide an experience in story structure. Perhaps your students will write Snow Ghost and the Seven Cats, or a story of a witch named Rapunzel held captive by a princess! The purported collection of campfire songs for monsters in *Sipping Spiders Through a Straw* (DiPucchio, 2008) provides another example of parody and flexible thinking and is likely to inspire additions to the collection. Older students can be inspired by more sophisticated parodies of literature and film. Scout the Web for parodies of Shakespeare and poetry (there are plenty), or consider how song spoofs can illustrate meter and rhyme and what makes a good one so funny.

As we consider the possibility of creativity as a collaborative process, it is important to envision how we can support that collaboration in our classrooms. An extraordinary example of collaborative creativity was shared with me by Michael Harvey, a Welsh storyteller. Michael (personal communication, 2002) sent me some poetry written by groups of elementary and middle-level students based on his telling of Bible stories. I was so touched by the poems that I had to learn how they were created. How did primary-grade children come up with ideas like "I can feel a winged woman inside me with thunder and lightning in her heart"? Michael generously shared some of his process with me. As you read, think about the aspects of problem finding exemplified in this class.

[After telling the story] What I start on is their experience of listening to and being in the story . . . We talk about what it was like for them. I try [to] keep this part of the conversation based in the senses so as to avoid anxiety about how much they remember. . . . In the early establishing stage I try [to] maintain the group dynamic by avoiding competition between the kids and giving approval to whatever is said. . . . Before long they're giving me vivid sense impressions of the story. This age range (7–11's) have incredible group consciousness and this gives focus and momentum to this part of the process.

It really does feel like an archaeological dig to me. The thing, whatever it is, is out there and we need to use such skill as we have to find it. Sometimes I talk about metal detectors—when the thing goes "bleep" you know you've found something but you don't know what. It's like that going through a story. When we go through it after the proper telling—they're looking out for an internal imaginative prompting that says "there's something there." They all know what I mean . . .

In an older group you would expect a lot of individual responses but with the 7–11's they negotiate a group response. What is great is that they always choose—I never have to prompt them or hurry them along or play referee. [Once] we've decided which bit we're going to look at in more detail, usually I retell this bit of the story to take them back to the images and feelings and then I just ask what they experienced. . . . If, say, we're inside the Temple where Samuel is asleep and someone says they can see the walls in the lamplight, I'll ask what they're like. "Smooth."

"OK, what kind of smooth?"

"Very smooth."

"Uh, huh, can you think of anything that might be as smooth as the walls?" They get stuck.

"Is there anything in the temple that smooth—or outside the temple?"

"A sand dune!"

Great! I can see a high level of consensus behavior not to mention smiles of creation and no doubt relief, so I write it down . . .

When I run these sessions, although I am in charge and have done it before, I play the game of doing it with them. In that respect I am as delighted as they are when things go well and as frustrated when we get stuck. This means that it is easier to move onto a more demanding and subtle level by asking "Is that right, or nearly right?" If they say "Yep, that's exactly right," then I leave it even if I've got a brilliant idea just bursting to come out. I've seen so many teachers destroy rapport by saying something along the lines of "Don't you think it would be better if . . ." You can see the light going out in the kids' eyes when they do that!

Michael went on to describe identifying the form that fits the ideas emerging. Notice the opportunities for exploring the story, identifying something that speaks to the group, and shaping the words to fit their images. Think about the type of classroom atmosphere created in this type of collaborative effort. The poem about Samuel is as follows:

> *Samuel Asleep in the Temple*
> *The temple walls were as smooth as a sand dune's shadow*
> *The lamp's flame shone like a sword glistening in the sun*
> *On the battered ark's ancient patterns.*
> *They swirled like a sand storm in the desert—as wild as freedom.*
> *God's voice whispered like the wind on the waves*
> *rumbled like the deep Red Sea*
> *murmured like a baby in a cradle sighed*
> *like the Angel of Death . . . Samuel!*
> —Bryn Deri, CP School, Year 6 (age 10)

If you are interested in reading more from Michael and his students, visit his blog (yrawen.word-press.com/taliesin) or his website (www.michaelharvey.org). You can find poetry and text in both Welsh and English, as well as information about Michael's activities. One day I want to travel to Wales for a workshop!

Genre Studies

Sloan (1991) suggested that students can learn the strategies and conventions of literature not just as authors but as critics. She emphasized the importance of developing a sense of story and the centrality of narrative in students' lives. A sense of story is one of the key methodologies needed by any writer. Sloan suggested that students who understand the structure and function of stories may be able to identify and use literary conventions and to identify the stories of value in their own lives. Students develop a sense of story by examining the stories of others, often in guided reading experiences. They may discuss the type of story (What signs and signals indicate whether a story will have a realistic or fantasy setting?), setting and plot (Suppose you thought of a new ending—how would the rest of the story have to be changed to fit the new ending?), characters (Are there any characters that could be eliminated? How would that affect the rest of the story?), point of view, mood, tone, style, theme, or illustrations. Basic story types can be discussed with varying degrees of sophistication. Whereas older students may examine quest patterns in literature, young children can address similar issues by looking at circle stories in which the main character leaves home, has an adventure, and returns home again. When students are aware of these conventions, they become part of the methodology of the discipline for the students, as their own stories portray crafty foxes (or, defying convention, heroic foxes) or use seasonal imagery to support themes.

Taken more broadly, Sloan's approach was a precursor to the genre studies that can be pursued across grade level. Just as young children need to know the "rules" when writing their first haiku or fairy tale, so older students who study the conventions of science fiction, historical fiction, auto-biography, or creative nonfiction will be better prepared to write them. Multigenre studies, when multiple types of literature are studied (and written) around a single theme, have the added creative benefit of modeling multiple points of view around a single topic. Consider broadening the genres you study beyond the basics. Have your students studied the conventions of "spooky stories" to learn how to induce fear without gore. Hitchcock did it! Search online for "Two Sentence Horror Stories" for a short but challenging format. Some violate my "no gore" rule, but you can be selective in your examples. What about creative nonfiction? I was recently introduced to *Creative Nonfiction* magazine, full of interesting and inspiring memoirs and other essays to inspire you. How about six-word stories, inspired by Hemingway's famous challenge? If you don't know it, a quick web search will bring lots of examples. Remember, sometimes constraints can inspire the most creativity.

In this process, students should be exposed to the conventions and purposes of culturally specific forms. These could include anything from Irish Finn McCool stories to rap poetry, from Faith Ringgold's story quilts (Ringgold, 1991) to storytelling forms from diverse cultures. If the first part of problem finding is caring, at least some of the literature students read and the writing or oral expression they create must center on ideas and forms they care about. The communication usually fostered in language arts programs also may be expressed in nonlinguistic forms instead of or in addition to language assignments—as Ringgold's story quilts led to the written telling of her stories. Students can express ideas and values of importance through creating artworks from many traditions. These expressions can be explained orally or in writing, providing variety in problem finding and new opportunities for expression.

Lesson 7.4 Family Treasures: Historical Research and Creative Expression (K–12)

Read *The Lotus Seed* (Garland, 1993), the story of a Vietnamese family's immigration to the United States, and the way a lotus seed became an important symbol of their strength and heritage. Have students talk to family members about important stories from their past. These may form the basis for many types of creative expression: stories or essays, dance or theater, or a variety of visual arts.

Language Arts: Creative Strengths

Many aspects of creativity can be supported in any discipline, but each discipline has aspects of the traditional curriculum that lend themselves particularly well to creativity. In language arts, the most obvious vehicle is creative writing. Imaginative writing activities can provide natural opportunities for the use of creative thinking skills and strategies. Most of the strategies designed specifically to enhance creative thinking (see Chapter 6) lend themselves to language arts activities. Students can write stories based on metaphorical thinking, visual imagery, or creative dramatics experiences. They can use metaphors and Synectics techniques to enhance descriptions, plan advertisements, or improve poetry. However, it is important for teachers not to lose track of the possibilities for enhancing students' creative thinking through content writing.

Writing in content areas can give students the opportunity to express their questions, concerns, and interests in addition to their understanding of content. Worsley and Mayer (1989) described a variety of writing assignments as part of secondary school science instruction. Suggestions include not just giving the typical lab reports but also relating histories of specific places (a river bed or a phone booth), describing sensory experiences, rewriting textbooks, describing inventions of the future, recounting a history of one's personal ideas, and "positing wild theories" (p. 72). One of my favorite examples was a student essay about television written by a high school junior. Almost the entire essay is a series of questions, for example:

> What type of people watch exercise programs? Are they uncontrollably fat? Are they exercise fanatics? Do they watch Channel 7 exercise at 5:20 A.M. or Channel 4 where the girls always jump around in those tight-fitted leotards? Maybe it depends on if they are male or female, or maybe it depends on how hard they want to work out.... Why do people become addicted? How do people decide the amount of time they have to watch TV?
>
> (Worsley & Mayer, 1989, pp. 116–117)

That essay sounds like an exercise in problem finding! While it is more common for writing in content areas to be more formal and factual, if such writing explains the investigation of real problems, it represents authentic creativity at work.

Finally, language arts activities provide multiple opportunities for modeling creative behaviors. Students can examine the problem solving and flexible thinking of characters from Pippi Longstocking to Harry Potter to Sherlock Holmes or Oliver Twist. Selecting literature for young people that models the characteristics we seek is one more way to demonstrate that our classrooms are safe for creative thinking.

Lesson 7.5   Flexible Thinking in the Language Arts

Talk about stories in which the size of characters is an important aspect of the story, for example, *Jack and the Beanstalk*, *Tom Thumb*, *Alice in Wonderland*, or *Gulliver's Travels*. Young children could read *Inch Boy* by Junko Morimoto (1988). Discuss his creative adjustments to his size. You might create a morphological synthesis chart of characters and sizes. Use the grid to imagine how stories might have changed if the characters had been different sizes. Alternatively, think about the relationships between size and age in movies such as *Big* or *The Curious Tale of Benjamin Button*. Use them to envision a story in which a character does not age in typical fashion. (Adapted from a lesson by Cindy Pinter.)

Thinking About the Classroom

Plan a class activity in which you discuss writers' purposes and problem finding with students. Many authors' blogs or websites can provide important clues to their thinking. Send the students out in search of interesting problems to write about and see what happens.

Finding and Solving Problems in Social Studies

At the beginning of its guidelines for creating state social studies standards, the National Council for Social Studies (NCSS) (2013) states:

> Now more than ever, students need the intellectual power to recognize societal problems; ask good questions and develop robust investigations into them; consider possible solutions and consequences; separate evidence-based claims from parochial opinions; and communicate and act upon what they learn. And most importantly, they must possess the capability and commitment to repeat that process as long as is necessary.

It sounds a long way from my memorize-the-facts social studies experiences many years ago. Needless to say, with this focus, social studies offers many options for creative thinking. Although definitions may differ slightly, most discussions of social studies center on two general types of student goals: to gain important understandings from the social sciences and to prepare to be knowledgeable participants in a democratic society. If students are to find and solve problems in social studies, the problems would logically fall into a similar division. We will first briefly consider the general opportunities for flexible thinking offered by social studies instruction, then consider the types of content and teaching methods that may allow students to find and solve problems in the social science disciplines and to identify and address problems as citizens of a community, state, or nation.

Flexible Thinking Through Points of View

The "social" in "social studies" makes it clear that all the social science disciplines focus on human interactions. History and archeology are about humans past and sociology about humans present. Geography is not just about landforms (that's geology) but about the way humans interact with the land. Whatever we study in social studies, at the base, is about people, and all those people have points of view. Learning to look at the world through others' eyes is fundamental to the social science disciplines, and it provides grand opportunities for flexible thinking.

There are many ways to help students think about multiple perspectives. In history, some basic questions could include:

- Why would this person do that? What would he or she be thinking?
- What options did the person have? What else could he or she have done?
- What if the person (or group) had chosen [fill in another course of action] instead? What might have been the consequences?
- What if [fill in some way in which the circumstances could change]? How might that have changed what this person thought or did?

The intent of such questions is to help students understand historical figures as human beings who made decisions based on what they knew and believed—just like we do. Similarly, when studying other cultures, helping students understand that cultural practices that might seem odd to them make logical sense given the environment and history of a people is not just good for cultural understanding but for flexible thinking as well.

Thinking About the Classroom

Seek out history books with multiple viewpoints appropriate for your grade level. For example, young children studying the Revolutionary War could be introduced to *George vs. George* (Schanzer, 2004). Slightly older students could use *Everybody's Revolution* (Fleming, 2006) or the Civil War materials described in Lesson 7.8. Share what you find with colleagues, and encourage your librarians to add the books to their wish lists. Consider how you could use the materials to help students examine multiple perspectives.

This kind of understanding can begin in elementary grades. Recall my student's unit on Japan, described at the beginning of this chapter. It allowed American third graders to look, for that moment, through Japanese eyes and see rice as a very sensible and delicious lunch food. It just required a shift in perspective. One amazing opportunity to help older students (teens) understand varied cultural viewpoints is through the Voices of Youth blog. Built and maintained by UNICEF, Voices of Youth is a venue for sharing ideas for youth around the world (www.voicesofyouth.org).

Many teaching strategies can facilitate students taking on varied perspectives, some of which are described in Chapters 6 and 8. Consider role-play, simulations, point–counterpoint writings, or taking on the personas of historical figures through Fakebook (www.classtools.net/FB/home-page), blogs, or imagined Twitter accounts of historic events. Put your students in the shoes of Lin-Manuel Miranda and write the lyrics for a new hip-hop musical, giving voice to figures from another period in history. Such things both provide variety to your instruction and allow students to momentarily look at the world differently, certainly an essential skill in our global world.

Students as Historical Researchers

If students are to identify and investigate problems in the social science disciplines, they must have two types of knowledge. First, they must have knowledge of the discipline itself. Historians must know something about history, and geographers must know geography. Second, they must know how the discipline works. Historians must understand the sources of historical information, what kinds of questions it answers, and how to investigate them, and geographers must know what geographers do, what kinds of information they value, and how geographical information is gathered, assessed, and used.

Unlike language arts, in which both the content of literature and the strategies for creating it have traditionally been included in school curricula, many students go through school experiencing social studies only as a body—or perhaps more accurately, a disembodied mass—of content. Some of you probably recall reading social studies texts and answering countless Chapter Checkup questions, many of which entailed copying the appropriate sentence from the text onto your paper. In such cases, social studies facts can be emphasized in ways that limit students' understanding of more important concepts and exclude any consideration of the origin of the facts in question. How do we know what the Pilgrims ate or wore or played? How do we know which kings were loved or hated, how medieval communities were organized, or how the public viewed the United States' involvement in World War II as compared with the Vietnam War? How have public views on the war in Iraq compared to contemporary views about Vietnam? Without a consideration of the methods or the content of the disciplines, students are left with little choice but to believe it is true if it is in print, particularly in a textbook—hardly a healthy assumption for a discipline that purports to prepare students for citizenship!

If students are to be prepared for creative thinking in the social science disciplines, they need to understand not only the facts but also the broad trends and concepts that organize the disciplines. These include ideas such as interdependence and systems; cause, effect, and change; and conflict, power, rights, and justice. They also will need skills for gathering, organizing, and analyzing information, as well as a knowledge concerning social scientists' habits of mind. For example, Parker (1991) cited examples of "History's Habits of Mind," including "Appreciate the often tentative nature of judgments about the past, and thereby avoid the temptation to seize upon particular 'Lessons' of history as cures for present ills" (p. 74). How could one better learn the values and habits of history than by acting like a historian?

Although students certainly can be taught the methodologies of many social science disciplines, I discuss here only strategies for historical research. Space precludes a full discussion of all areas, and the emphasis on history in social studies curricula makes it a logical place to begin. Involving students in historical research allows them to identify and investigate problems in the same manner as creative historians.

Historical research answers the question, "How did things used to be?" Its purpose is to reconstruct the past as accurately as possible, taking into account multiple perspectives. A magazine interview with a former politician discussing key events of his or her term, a book on changes in 19th-century fashion, or a newspaper article on the memories of local residents older than 100 years are reporting historical research. Students who interview their parents about the parents' school experiences, investigate the past occupants of stores on Main Street, or learn about the Civil War by examining the lyrics of popular music of the period also are doing historical research.

Much historical research is interesting and appropriate for elementary school students. There is, however, one important caution: the younger the students, the closer to home the research must stay. Young children have a difficult time distinguishing history and fantasy. After all, George Washington and Snow White both lived "long ago and far away." However, even primary school students can investigate information about their immediate family or possibly their school. Community history as a concept may seem very abstract, but "How is second grade today different from when our parents were in school?" is a very real question about real people. From the intermediate grades up, of course, students are more likely to be able to deal with issues of local, state, or possibly even world history in a professional manner. And for secondary students, the

Historical research brings the past to life

opportunity to engage with primary sources can transform the past from a series of dry fill-in-the blanks to a story as engaging as the latest reality show.

Levy (2008) describes the transformation in a group of students who attended an alternative high school in Dubuque, Iowa, as a result of their experiences with historical research. The students in this school had not been successful in traditional high schools. In an effort to engage students with the state-standards content on World War II, their teacher introduced the topic of the Tuskegee Airmen. Even that topic held little interest until the students learned that one of the airmen had graduated from Dubuque High School. The students wrote to the airman—and others—and, as they say, the rest (really) is history! The students followed up their letters with invitations and began planning for a public forum in which the airmen would speak and a community awareness campaign in which the students spoke at community and civic organizations, did live radio interviews, and orchestrated local newspaper coverage. In addition to the public events (and with the cooperation of the English teacher), the students compiled their original research into a 230-page book that eventually sold 1,500 copies. Imagine the flexibility and problem solving required in those endeavors—and do you think any of them will ever forget what they learned about World War II?

In describing to students the tasks of historians, one effective analogy is to compare them to detectives. Like a detective, a historian looks for clues about things that have already happened, and, as with a detective, the best source for a historian is an eyewitness. Even young children are familiar enough with TV mysteries that the concept of an eyewitness usually is familiar and useful for explaining to them primary and secondary sources. Primary sources are original documents or artifacts, preferably those in which the author or creator was a direct observer of the recorded event. Secondary sources are those in which the author is reporting and analyzing information from primary documents. He or she may be one time or many times removed from the actual event.

Lesson 7.6   Children's Books: Historical Research and Language Arts (7–12)

Children's books from other regions or eras can provide students with the opportunity to view the world through another's perspective and attempt to make hypotheses about another time. Both the stories and the illustrations can provide clues to lifestyle and values. Many times, children's books can be found in local used bookstores or flea markets. One of my favorites is a reproduction of *General Lee and Santa Claus* (Bedwell & Clark, 1997), originally published in 1867. The story of children wondering if Santa still loves little rebel children gives a unique perspective on a child's view of wartime. It could spur students to additional research on children's literature of the period or on children's perspectives of other wars.

Lesson 7.7   Anonymous Women Creators: Problem Finding and Historical Research (7–12)

Share *Anonymous Was a Woman* (Bank, 1995), or, if you are very fortunate, locate the video of the same title. Discuss the forces that affected the ways women expressed their creativity in the 18th or 19th centuries. This book could inspire a number of historical research projects. Students could investigate attics or local antique shops for further examples of women's creative activities. With permission, these could be photographed for a display. Or students could interview women currently active in creative arts, framing their questions around issues raised by the film or book.

One of the key differences between historical research and typical library research is the reliance of historical research on primary sources. In a typical research report on the response of U.S. citizens to World War II, a student would go to Wikipedia, a reference book, or other secondary source, take notes, and summarize the information. A student doing historical research on the same topic would look for primary sources of information. He or she might look at magazines or newspapers of the period, listen to music of the time, and interview local citizens regarding their experiences. The student would look for similarities and variations, drawing conclusions from the data. One source for teaching students to work with primary sources is the *Exploring America* series, developed at the College of William and Mary. The series helps students explore American history by decades, through examining literature, art, and music of the period. For example, *Exploring America in the 1960s* examines the March on Washington through analyzing the "Letter from a Birmingham Jail" and Martin Luther King's famous speech, but also the music sung during the march (Sandling & Chandler, 2014). Advanced high school students can benefit from Brundage's (2013) *Going to the Sources* for a readable but professional introduction to historical method. It includes information on writing historiographic essays analyzing the ways a particular event or theme has been studied by various historians.

Most historical research is structured with a research question. Without it, research can be an unorganized, often confusing fishing expedition. The more sophisticated the student-researcher, the more fine-tuned the questioning and conclusions. Although many students might be able to draw conclusions about how women's clothing from 1860 to 1865 is different from clothing today, a more able or knowledgeable student might investigate the differences in women's clothing in the Northern and Southern states from 1860 to 1865 or the differences in women's clothing as portrayed in *Harper's Bazaar* and the Montgomery Ward catalog from 1860 to 1865. Similar investigations using the same tools of historical research could investigate trends in much more current sources, for example, questioning how the advertising or allocation of story space in *Time* magazine has changed in the past 10 years. In either case, the key is in the transformation. Students conducting historical research do not simply summarize information. They make inferences, look for patterns, and draw conclusions from data. As historical researchers, they should become aware of the difference between fact and inference and of the tentative nature of their conclusions.

Lesson 7.8   Perspectives on History 1: Using Historical Research (5–12)

The Perspectives on History series provides short collections of primary sources on a variety of periods and events selected to be accessible to young people. These are particularly valuable when multiple perspectives are available. For example, two books provide sources from the American Civil War: *Echoes of the Civil War: The Blue* (Forman, 1997a) and *Echoes of the Civil War: The Gray* (Forman, 1997b). Comparing the letters and diaries of individuals from both sides of the conflict can allow students insight into multiple points of view, as well as the universal horrors of the war.

Lesson 7.9   Perspectives on History 2: Using Historical Research (9–12)

Technology has made it possible for us to easily examine the multiple perspectives from which the same event can be reported. Have students examine news reports of the same event from several different websites—perhaps Fox News, MSNBC, and CNN along with local news channels. Compare the information found. Today, such comparisons are more important than ever, as is instruction on how to distinguish typical differences in perspective from fake news stories. There are a number of infographics online that can help students identify clues to fake news. Discuss how variations in sources may relate to differences found in historical information from other time periods.

Key to drawing reasonable conclusions in historical research is careful consideration of the motives, limitations, and biases presented in primary sources. Although primary sources are always preferable to secondary sources, it is important for students to be aware that eyewitness accounts are not necessarily accurate, complete, or even truthful. Each historical source presents a particular point of view, shaped through the lives and experiences of particular individuals. Understanding historical sources as reflections of individuals allows students to develop the flexibility in point of view that supports creative thinking. They might consider what could have caused someone to write or act in a particular way and how that perspective might differ in another individual.

Difficulties with primary sources become clear when students deal with multiple interviews. Personal accounts of the same event often differ widely. Four citizens recounting local events on VE (Victory in Europe) Day are likely to present remarkably different stories. Even student recollections of the recent past are likely to vary and can help students understand the subjectivity and variation inherent in historical sources. Such understanding and resulting habits of mind can lead students to question historical sources and raise questions that a historian would ask. Is the clothing portrayed in magazines the same as that worn by most women? (Does your closet include clothes from *Vogue* or *GQ*?) If clothing in some publications looks different from clothes in the other sources, what might be the explanation? The analysis in historical research is an outstanding opportunity to practice flexible and analytical thinking.

Access to a variety of primary sources is essential for historical research. An extraordinary variety of resources is accessible online. Other sources may be available in local libraries or museums or through interlibrary loan. In many cases, reproductions of paintings, books, magazines, or catalogs are available and more durable than the originals. You may want to consider the following:

1. *Works of art.* Look for online museum displays, reproductions, art books, or other secondary sources that may reproduce original artworks as illustrations. Much of what historians have learned about fashion, pets, architecture, household items, and even the lifestyles of particular societies has been learned through art. Consider how much of our knowledge of life in ancient Egypt has come through paintings or what could be learned by studying portraits from the 18th century.

2. *Magazines.* Many public libraries have periodicals dating to the 19th century, either in a back room or through electronic databases. Do not hesitate to ask the library media specialist for assistance. I have particularly enjoyed reading magazines written for teachers around the turn of the 20th century. It is fascinating to see how some concerns are dramatically different and others virtually unchanged.

3. *Newspapers.* Archived newspapers are even more common than other types of periodicals. Do not forget that newspapers can be used in historical research—not just research on the headline stories but also research on advertising, sports, weather, fashion, editorial cartoons, or even the history of journalism.

4. *Books and magazines.* Again, do not hesitate to ask your library media specialist for assistance in locating originals or reproductions of books from the period to be studied. For a student reading about education in the 19th century, reading about the changes in textbooks or school procedures is just not the same as reading the textbooks themselves. Museum stores, library sales, and used bookstores can also serve as sources, frequently at minimal expense. The Teaching With Documents website (www.archives.gov/education/lessons) includes material from the National Archives, ranging from the Navigation Act Broadside of 1785 to Nixon's letter of resignation. The process of working with these reproductions is virtually identical to the experience of using the actual materials—without the expense

of a trip to Washington, DC. One of my favorite sources for teaching American history to elementary and middle-level students is *Cobblestone* magazine (www.cobblestonepub. com). It includes a combination of secondary sources and primary sources selected to be accessible to young people.

5. *Music.* Song lyrics from a particular period of history can provide valuable insights into the attitudes, activities, and concerns of the time. Music stores often carry recordings of music from a particular period. I gained new insights into the attitudes and values of the 1940s by listening to an album of contemporary songs about World War II—very different from the songs about war I recalled from the 1960s and 1970s! The Lyrical Legacy area in the Library of Congress website includes songs from across American history (www.loc.gov/teachers/ lyrical). Or look for recordings of speeches and broadcasts of important moments in modern history. YouTube is full of historical footage, or the "Famous Speeches" app can bring them right to your smartphone.

6. *Interviews and surveys.* Few things students do in school can have as much long-lasting value as preserving the written and oral history of their community. Older residents can provide information and insights on local history unavailable through any other means. Other community members can recount their experiences relating to local, community, or world issues. Imagine the importance of a class project interviewing service personnel returning from Iraq or Afghanistan, factory workers affected by a local plant closing, or individuals who participated in the Women's March on Washington (or affiliated sister marches).

7. *Diaries and journals.* Either family journals or reproductions of journals available in many libraries provide information on everyday life seldom found in history texts. It is helpful to share your quest for primary sources with your school library media specialist. If the library media specialist knows the types of resources you are seeking for your class, he or she may be more likely to spend limited library funds on this type of reference material.

8. *Household items and other artifacts.* Family collections, grandparents' attics, and local museums can provide artifacts from which young historians can draw conclusions. In one area in which I taught, a local intermediate school district circulated collections of artifacts that could be examined and handled by students. Reproductions of old cookbooks can provide a fascinating glimpse into the past (see Lesson 7.11).

9. *More Online Options and Virtual Field Trips.* Many government and museum sites contain links to primary sources that can form the basis of original research for students as well as adults. For example, the National Museum of American History site includes History Explorer activities (historyexplorer.si.edu/home) and a variety of virtual exhibits. The New York Public Library has a large and ever-growing collection of online exhibits, including photographs, maps, documents, and videos (digitalcollections.nypl.org). Or perhaps you'd like to take a virtual field trip to view the ruins of Pompeii. The Google World Wonders project can take you on a 3D exploration. As new technology evolves, the world will increasingly be at our fingertips!

Thinking About the Classroom

Visit used bookstores, antique stores, or flea markets in your area. See what you can find to enhance one of your teaching units. Next, go to the Teaching with Documents website or any other major historical database and see what else you can find to add to your collection.

Locating primary source materials, for either an individual or a class project, may seem daunting, but historical research provides benefits to students that are unavailable by any other means. Aside from the obvious development of research and thinking skills it fosters, this type of investigation makes history come alive. Students who have been touched by the words and sounds and images of real people from long ago, who have considered these people's lives and points of view, and who have drawn conclusions from those lives form links with the story of history that are not forged in other ways. This power to touch the reality of history makes historical research a vital tool to consider, both to expand students' understanding of historical information and to help them ask the kinds of questions historians might ask.

Although you may find many local resources electronically, I have also found it worthwhile to search flea markets and used bookstores for items that tie to major units in the curriculum. Often for minimal expense, it is possible to locate items that can benefit students for many years. For example, a fourth-grade teacher who commonly teaches the history of the community may scout library sales or flea markets for reproductions of early maps, old postcards depicting the community, or histories of local families. Such materials could allow students to investigate questions as diverse as "How have the boundaries of our town changed since 1800?" and "What were the most common architectural styles in our community in 1920? How closely does the current restoration resemble the original buildings?" A teacher who deals with American history may want to consider old magazines, sheet music, advertising brochures, or reproductions of catalogs or news photos. Such additions might result in a class investigation into point of view in news coverage of a particular period or an individual study comparing 19th-century yellow journalism with modern tabloids. Even a primary teacher whose class studies "Our School" may want to search the district archives for old photos, records, or yearbooks that might be duplicated for class use in examining changes in school dress, studies, or personnel. In each case, students are able to experience the thrill of touching the world of the past and working as bona fide historians. They also experience history not as something one learns but as something one questions, wonders about, and investigates—certainly key activities for those who are to be creative in that field. In parallel ways, if you'd like students to explore another branch of the social studies, Sweeney and Walker's (2012) *Exploring People and Cultures* is a resource to help students learn about cultures through ethnographic research. By using field research to learn about cultures in their family and community, they come to understand how anthropologists study more distant ones—and ask good questions along the way.

Lesson 7.10   Scout Museum Shops: Sources for Historical Research (7–12)

One of my favorite sources for reproductions of historical artifacts is museum shops. A visit to the National Historic Site at Seneca Falls, New York, led me to copies of the *Report of the Woman's Rights Convention, The Lily* (August 1852), a newspaper published by Amelia Bloomer, and *The Revolution* (January 1868), a paper published by Susan B. Anthony and edited by Elizabeth Cady Stanton and Parker Pillsbury. The issue of *The Revolution* I purchased contained quotations from other newspapers' responses to the creation of the new paper. These artifacts could easily provide the beginnings of historical research examining questions such as these: How did the statements in *The Lily* differ from those in *The Revolution*? Did they reflect changes in the women's movement or differences in editors? How did other papers vary in their responses to *The Revolution*? Were these responses typical of other publicity of the time? It also might be interesting to compare these papers with current publications of the National Organization for Women or other groups lobbying for change. In what ways are their styles, strategies, and the like similar or different? Your trips to other historic sites may lead to equally valuable finds.

Students as Participants in Democracy

In addition to helping students gain important understanding from the social sciences, social studies also has the challenge of preparing students to be active participants in our democratic society. Helping students become involved citizens entails more than assisting them in understanding the branches of government but also means giving them the vision of empowered individuals affecting the community around them and the tools to achieve empowerment. Among the best ways to achieve this is to allow students to become involved in problem solving in their communities. Needless to say, this type of activity reinforces not just social studies content but also problem solving and creative thinking. The Creative Problem Solving (CPS) process (see Chapter 6) can be a particularly valuable tool in facilitating this type of activity.

Lesson 7.11   Looking at Cookbooks: Another Source for Historical Research (5–12)

Cookbooks can provide interesting sources for historical research into the lives of ordinary families. Many used bookstores contain cookbooks and various guides to homemaking from the 19th century. Other books can be found in reproduction, often in museum shops. Dover Publications, a source for many interesting reproductions, publishes *The First American Cookbook, a Facsimile of "American Cookery," 1796* (Simmons, 1984). This book, which includes many types of advice "for the improvement of the rising generation of Females in America" (p. 3), can allow students to draw conclusions about lifestyle and values as well as nutrition. Another treasure, purchased at a museum store, is a reproduction of *Directions for Cooking by Troops in Camp and Hospital* prepared for the Army of Virginia by Florence Nightingale in 1861. It includes essays on the types of food most suitable for sick or injured soldiers. Recipes like "Fresh Beef Soup for 100 Men" give a new perspective on camp life. My favorite phrase from that recipe was, "in a convenient-sized pot . . . "

Of course, like so much else, even more is available online. The Historic American Cookbooks project (digital.lib.msu.edu/projects/cookbooks) offers American cookbooks from the 18th through 20th centuries, as well as images of historic cooking implements. For older students or those who want a real adventure, Historical Cookbooks online offers cookbooks from the 13th century on, allowing explorations of both early cooking and early English language (www.angelfire.com/md3/openhearthcooking/aaCookbooks.html).

One sixth-grade class created a group called the Amesville Thinkers that set out to identify and address a community problem (Elasky, 1989). They conducted interviews with local community members in an effort to identify major problems. Whereas the most commonly cited problem, unemployment, seemed too daunting to be tackled by a group of elementary school students, the second most commonly mentioned, uncertainty about the responsibilities of elected officials, seemed more manageable. The students wrote and produced a series of public service announcements designed to educate the community on the functions of local government. The following year, the same sixth-grade teacher worked with students who chose to analyze contamination in local waterways. This group called themselves the Amesville Sixth-Grade Water Chemists.

Lesson 7.12   Historical Markers

Examine historical markers in your community or online at the Historical Marker Database (www.hmdb.org). Creating historical markers provides rich opportunities for writing succinct prose, historical research, and sometimes even flexible thinking. Consider whether your students could research and propose a potential historical site in your area, with the many associated opportunities for examining primary sources. Or, alternatively, imagine that you are creating historical markers for the sites of events being studied. As students create hypothetical markers, they have the opportunity to identify and express key ideas in a compressed format. Or perhaps you could have students create markers for the same site but from the perspective of different groups. For example, many battlefields would be differently described by the combatants on either side. What other types of sites might inspire varied perspectives?

Involving students in such projects—whether they are first-grade students planting seeds to lure butterflies to a local park or high school students making a proposal for bicycle paths to the town council—helps the young people develop both the skills and attitudes necessary for creative involvement with content. Students have the opportunity to care about the content, take risks, try strategies, make mistakes, and try again until they reach some kind of conclusion. This attitude was described by the Amesville teacher in his response to a student who said testing water made him feel "like a real scientist."

> I told him he was, because he was doing what real scientists do. The real world of scientists, writers, and teachers had invaded our room and given students reasons to begin changing the theory of content importance into the practice of meaningful content use. This didn't happen because the Amesville Sixth-Grade Water Chemists or the Amesville Thinkers were uniquely talented or gifted, or because their teacher is extraordinary, or because we handled what we did in a superior way—or even exploited it to its fullest. None of these things are true. It is because we used a process that works.
>
> (Elasky, 1989, p. 13)

Levy (2008) tells of a group of Spanish students whose engagement in Spanish content changed dramatically when they learned of an impoverished school in Guatemala where students, whose home language is Ixil, needed to learn Spanish in order to improve their opportunities for education and employment. Spanish students in the United States eagerly learned vocabulary and sentence construction in order to write stories and create learning materials for young children thousands of miles away. These examples show that community problem solving can and should involve multiple disciplines. Although community problem solving is included in this section because of the importance of involved citizenship in social studies, it is virtually impossible to address any meaningful community problem without involving language arts, math, science—and sometimes even Spanish. The complexity of the problems and the skills needed to address them is one more support for the complex, multidimensional thinking associated with creativity. If you are interested in assisting your students in community action, an outstanding resource is *The Kid's Guide to Social Action* (Lewis, 1998). In it, Lewis describes students' involvement in attacking problems from toxic waste to endangered species and provides information on numerous skills essential for social action, such as preparing a press release, taking a survey, or writing a letter to the editor. Although the examples generally involve elementary school students, the skills are appropriate for any grade level or for an adult activist. Another fine resource is the Community Problem Solving program within Future Problem Solving (www.fpspi.org). There students work on real community problems within a group competition.

Lesson 7.13 The Artifact Box Exchange Network and Other Exchanges

The Artifact Box Exchange Network (www.artifactbox.com) is a project in which students in different parts of the country create boxes giving clues about their area's geography, economy, and so on through the use of local artifacts, and then exchange the boxes with a partner class. Although the project is structured enough that it doesn't allow for generating original questions, it is a fine opportunity for students to practice drawing conclusions from artifacts across several social science areas.

If you like the idea of collaborating across the country (or the world) but the Artifact Box project doesn't fit your needs, there are many other options. You might want to visit Kathy Schrock's links for project-based learning (see the "Finding a Project section (www.schrockguide.net/authentic-learning.html) or the Virtual Architecture website (virtual-architecture.wm.edu), particularly the Telecollaboration section, to find information on dozens of options across disciplines. Some of the projects are completed; some are ongoing, but all will inspire you.

Social Studies: Creative Strengths

As a content area, social studies has numerous aspects that support especially strong ties to creativity. It provides outstanding opportunities for problem solving and data gathering, particularly in the local community. Studies of history and diverse cultures are natural vehicles for exploring multiple points of view, attempting to view events and ideas from more than one perspective. Diverse points of view may be identified in the persons or cultures studied or in the materials themselves. The Michigan Educational Extension Service (1992) described the efforts of two teachers who wanted students to examine the point of view from which their social studies text was written. After months of teaching students about the need for multiple perspectives, they found students asking questions such as "How come whenever they mention a woman it is on a gray page? And it's only a little" (p. 7) or "Why are there two pages in the book on the Boston Tea Party . . . when there's only a paragraph on the Trail of Tears? Four thousand people died on the Trail of Tears and no one died in the Boston Tea Party" (p. 4). Some of the teaching strategies that are particularly effective in helping students take on new viewpoints and explore the world from another's perspective are particularly well suited to social studies.

Finally, social studies that focuses on key concepts can provide opportunities for interdisciplinary transfer that can be both flexible and original. Concepts of interdependence, power, change, or revolution can be explored not just in history but in science, literature, or art. Helping students examine how a literary work may be powerful, how cause and effect operate in music or science, or how a painting may express the idea of revolution provides fuel for new perspectives and flexible thinking.

Think About It

1. Consider the role of point of view in the news sources you rely on most regularly. If you find that you read or watch the same sources repeatedly, for a few days, examine news sites that have varied points of view. You might even check Snopes' (or others') list of Fake News sites and examine one or more of them as well. Consider how history might be written if historians relied on only one source of information—and how that issue might be important for students.

2. Visit the ReadWriteThink website associated with the International Reading Association (readwritethink.org). Explore the lesson plans. See how many you can find that help students identify original writing topics, think flexibly, gain skills for self-expression, or create something new. Share your favorites with colleagues. Or find lessons that could be "tweaked" to insert opportunities for more divergent and flexible thinking. Sometimes a small adjustment can make a big difference.

3. Try some historical research yourself. Locate a newspaper from the day you were born. Examine the headlines. Look at the advertising, the sports section, and the classified ads. Ask any available relatives what they remember about that day. Listen to music or watch a movie that was popular then. Try to be aware of what you are learning and how you feel as the project progresses. Did history come alive for you? Discuss your feelings and think about what your experience as an authentic historian might imply for your teaching.

Try It Tomorrow

1. If you teach Shakespeare, there are a number of unusual genre variations you might consider. In *Pop Sonnets*, available as a book or on Tumblr (popsonnet.tumblr.com), Erik Didriksen transforms pop music lyrics into sonnet form, full of word play and imagery. Challenge your students to try the process. While the resulting sonnets may not be Shakespearean, the activity will help make it clear their intention is to communicate. Or how about imagining a text conversation between Romeo and Juliet or what Macbeth might tweet? Of course there are times when sticking to the original language is important, but if you want to know if students understand the dialog, creative "translations" can be helpful.

2. Experiment with other types of writing with constraints. One place to start is with six-word memoirs. You can find examples for adults and teens, as well as activities for teachers, at sixwordmemoirs.com.

3. Search for "Activity ideas from the Descriptosaurus" from the UK's National Literacy Trust. It is a treasure trove of activities for developing descriptive vocabulary for creative writing.

4. The U.S. Library of Congress is such a valuable resource that it can become a bit overwhelming. One of my favorite parts of the site is *Lyrical Legacy*, a collection of 400 years of American song and poetry. Lyrical Legacy provides tools for analyzing primary documents, including a graphic organizer for Thinking about Songs as Historical Artifacts. It also includes a listing of dozens of ideas for class activities centering on period songs and poetry. See what will fit your curriculum and budding historical researchers.

5. Have students imagine themselves as historical researchers from the future studying the artifacts in your classroom or other familiar objects. How might they interpret—or misinterpret—the things they find? Such an exercise can help students understand the tentative nature of historical documents.

Tech Tips

1. There are myriad technological options for telling stories, so these will represent just a few. Be sure to search for the latest apps—you know they are appearing every day. For example, one option for story creation is Storybird (storybird.com). The art that is available for storytelling is beautiful and varied, suitable for children and adults. The books you create can be viewed online, shared, or printed. Some of the samples are truly lovely.

   Many more options for storytelling have arrived with the advent of iPhones, iPads, and other tablets. There are lots of apps for that! One place to start is Storykit. Storykit is free, created by the International Children's Digital Library Foundation. It is simple enough for children to use to create portable stories using photos from your photo library or art created on screen with a simple drawing option. Storykit is helpful in schools that have sets of tablets because it allows for students to create stories at varied levels of complexity. Adobe Spark is a visual storytelling app that can be used to create graphics, web stories, and even animated videos. It is available online and through a variety of mobile apps (see spark.adobe.com).

   Of course there are many other options. The StoryBuddy app allows students to use the iPad's touch screen to draw then add text, page by page. With Little Bird Tales, students can create or upload artwork then record their story or presentation for each page. It is particularly helpful for students whose storytelling capacity outstrips their keyboarding skills. See their website for helpful suggestions. 30Hands allows similar options online and promises to soon integrate with Google Classroom.

2. Creaza (www.creazaeducation.com) is an integrated set of tools that allows students to create mind maps or cartoons and edit video and audio files online. The cartoonist portion of Creaza is also available as an iPad app. Like many systems, Creaza offers a free demonstration option and then a more complete option for sale. An interesting aspect of Creaza is that it is used across the globe, so demonstration videos represent students from various countries.

3. The search for primary resources can lead students to museums. Fortunately, a vast array of museum resources are available online. The Google Art Project (search for it), powered by Google, provides instant access to art museums around the world. Would you like to go to the Palace of Versailles? How about the Slate Tretyakov Gallery in Moscow or the Uffizi Gallery in Florence? A click of the mouse and you are there. Not every piece from every museum is on display, but the zoom feature allows you to get a closer view than ever would be possible in person. You can also download a selection of art from the various museums to make a personal collection. Amazing! Google Arts and Culture focuses more thematically but has many options to view art and cultural artifacts around the globe.

   Closer to my home, the Detroit Institute of Art (www.dia.org) has online resources that allow access to a number of collections online. It is fun for me to browse materials online and then visit them in person for a different view. You may have similar opportunities in a museum near you.

The Smithsonian is, of course, not a single museum but a collection of museums, from art to history to science. Collections of all kinds can be viewed online (www.si.edu/Exhibitions), and a large collection of resources for educators is available (www.si.edu/educators).

MoOM (coudal.com/moom), the Museum of Online Museums, offers portals to museums from the traditional (such as the Musée d'Orsay in Paris) to the less traditional (an exhibit of fading billboards). It is a great place to explore.

Finally, Virtual Tours (www.virtualfreesites.com/museums.museums.html) offers links to more than 300 museums, exhibitions, and tours. You can visit an ancient Roman villa, hear the sounds of various African primates, learn about Einstein, or visit scores of other sites. Not every link works, but there is enough there for much happy browsing.

8
Creativity in the Content Areas
Science, Math, and General Teaching Strategies

[A]s I see it, knowledge alone is not enough. In today's rapidly changing world, people must continually come up with creative solutions to unexpected problems. Success is based not only on what you know or how much you know, but on your ability to think and act creatively. In short, we are now living in the Creative Society. . . . New technologies play a dual role in the Creative Society. On one hand, the proliferation of new technologies is quickening the pace of change, accentuating the need of creative thinking in all aspects of people's lives. On the other hand, new technologies have the potential . . . to help people develop as creative thinkers.

(Resnick, 2007–2008, p. 18)

"If one actually set out to give as little help as possible to both aesthetics and originality in science, one could hardly devise a better plan than our educational system. . . . One rarely hears about what we do not understand in science, and least of all how to prepare for creative ideas."

(William Lipscomb, as quoted by Root-Bernstein &
Root-Bernstein, 1999, p. 13)

I once went to a bookstore in search of science books for young children. I had just one request. I wanted books that encouraged young people to engage in questioning and experimentation without telling them how the investigations would turn out. When the clerk asked if he could help, I explained my problem, showing an example of a book that made fine suggestions about planting seeds and placing the containers in different places—then on the very next page told the children exactly what they should expect to happen to each plant. "What is the point of doing the experiment," I asked, "If the book tells you the 'answer'? I want them to do experiments like real scientists." I was dumbfounded by the young man's reply. "But scientists do know the answers," he said, "They just do the experiments to show it. Even when I took college physics (evidently the ultimate in science, from his perspective), we always knew the answers before we started. Then we did the labs."

Finding and Solving Problems in Science

I've thought a lot about the clerk quoted earlier in the intervening years. Somehow, an apparently intelligent adult had come through at least 16 years of education believing that science functions like a book with an answer key. He had no sense of mystery or progress, to say nothing of conflict or controversy, in the sciences. Scientists, in his view, spent their days "proving" things they already knew. All of us who have ever taught science must think about whether the ways we teach could be part of that erroneous thinking. Of all the curriculum areas, perhaps science is the one in which the importance of finding and solving problems should be most obvious. Science, and particularly scientific investigation, is about posing hypotheses and solving problems. In the introduction to her book *Science Is Golden*, Finkelstein (2002) said, "I was struck by how much children are like scientists. They seem to have an insatiable curiosity, they love to investigate unfamiliar concepts and objects, and they analyze what they observe" (p. xiii).

Physicist David Bohm (1998) described the motivation in science as enmeshed in creativity.

> Scientists are seeking something that is much more significant to them than pleasure. One aspect of what this something might be can be indicated by noting that the search is ultimately aimed at the discovery of something *new* that had previously been *unknown*. But, of course, it is not merely the novel experience of working on something different and out of the ordinary that the scientist wants—this would indeed be little more than another kind of "kick." Rather, what he is really seeking is to learn something new that has a certain fundamental kind of significance . . . a kind of harmony that is felt to be beautiful. In this respect, the scientist is perhaps not basically different from the artist, the architect, the musical composer, etc. who all want to *create* this sort of thing in their work.
>
> (p. 2, italics original)

Unfortunately, the processes and understandings that are integral parts of real-world science have not always been translated into science teaching. Some approaches have treated the sciences as a collection of facts, rules, and definitions to be memorized. As national testing requirements grow to include science testing, the temptation to view science teaching as preparing students for multiple-choice exams is likely to increase. The *Framework for Science Education* (National Research Council, 2011) attempts to address the problem by identifying three major dimensions in science teaching: Scientific and Engineering Practices, Crosscutting Concepts, and Disciplinary Core Ideas. All three dimensions can be used in ways that are supportive of creativity. The most obvious application is in the Scientific and Engineering Practices. These include:

- Asking questions (for science) and defining problems (for engineering)
- Developing and using models
- Planning and carrying out investigations
- Analyzing and interpreting data
- Using mathematics and computational thinking
- Constructing explanations (for science) and designing solutions (for engineering)
- Engaging in argument from evidence
- Obtaining, evaluating, and communicating information

When I read that list, it sounds like science: curiosity driven, messy, and wonderful. These processes give students the opportunity to raise and address questions, as do creative scientists. The other two dimensions of the *Framework* address concepts to be addressed, both cross-disciplinary and core disciplinary concepts. These, too, can be addressed in ways that are supportive of creativity and learning for understanding.

Working Toward Conceptual Change

Teaching science concepts for understanding often requires conceptual change. Based on their experiences in the world, students come to class with prior notions of scientific phenomena. They have seen the sun come up, watched things fall to earth, and made their best sense of all manner of interactions with their environments. If those notions are inaccurate, it is necessary for students to have experiences that allow them to address their prior knowledge, question its validity, and build new concepts. Merely telling students what is true or what is our best understanding of truth at this time does not suffice. In building concepts, students should be involved in the processes of science: observing, making hypotheses, manipulating variables, and so on. All of these recommendations emphasize the sciences as explanatory in nature.

These emphases in science teaching also are supportive of the attitudes and processes of creativity. They center around student experiences and student questions, predictions, and experiences. Assisting students in building a small number of key concepts through experience instead of exposing them to myriad ideas also allows students to live the persistence, confusion, and muddiness that are essential elements of creativity in science.

Watson and Konicek (1990) set forth three key elements in assisting students with conceptual change. First, the teacher must connect new concepts to the students' everyday lives. Unless students see connections between the things they do in science class and their assumptions about the way the world operates, it is easy for them to dismiss science activities as a series of strange things that happen only in class. Second, students should be asked to make predictions. Hypothesis making creates essential ties between prior knowledge and new experiences and also practices a critical element of any scientific investigation. Third, the teacher should stress consistency. Students should be helped to see contradictions or inconsistencies in their thinking and be encouraged to address them. Science is about making sense of the world. Students should be encouraged to seek understanding that makes logical sense, not to memorize rote information. With these emphases, teachers can structure lessons so students observe phenomena that challenge their current ideas and then provide appropriate, testable alternatives.

Watson and Konicek (1990) described several days of experiments in which fourth-grade students tested their belief that sweaters generate heat. Years of experience dressing for winter weather had taught the students that heat comes from fire, from the sun—and from sweaters, hats, and coats. When the initial experiment (placing thermometers inside sweaters and hats for 15 minutes) did not provide evidence of heat production, the students designed new efforts using longer times and sealing the sweaters in enclosed spaces. Still, no heat was produced. The students were confused and probably frustrated because their predictions were not supported. Only then, when the students seemed at an impasse, did the teacher offer an alternative hypothesis that might be tested. The article ends with the students heading to recess, thermometers under their hats! This type of teaching allows students to learn both the concepts at hand and the nature of science. Recently, a friend's third-grade class spent a number of weeks investigating shadows in a similar manner. Their class blog described conclusions worthy of any scientist.

A hypothesis is a question or a theory that you think is going to be true or happen. It may be right or it may be wrong. How do scientists make or develop hypotheses? Well once we were talking and somebody said, "Look that shadow has multiple shadows!" Then someone said, "That is because even one light can make multiple shadows!" So our teacher said, "Let's test it!" When we went outside the [hypothesis] was not true. That is how scientists make a guess and find a theory in it.

Check multiple times until you are certain. Don't jump to conclusions. Voting is not a conclusion. Experimenting to find out is a more reliable conclusion.

It is essential to note that teaching for conceptual change is not limited to young children. Bransford, Brown, and Cocking (2000) cite numerous instances of misconceptions (and strategies for conceptual change) in high school and college physics students. For example, when such students are asked to describe the forces operating on a ball that has been thrown vertically, many students cite the "force of the hand." (I'll bet a few of you are now thinking, "But isn't that right?") In fact, the force of the hand is exerted only as long as the hand is touching the ball—while the ball is in the air, it is being affected by gravity and air resistance, not the hand. Often the inability to transfer science concepts to new situations can be evidence that conceptual change has not occurred. How often, for example, have you seen someone struggle to open a heavy door without moving to the edge of the door? How many of those individuals have "learned" about levers and hinges at some point in their education?

Thinking About the Classroom

Interview a student about what he or she has learned in science recently. Probe to see whether the student can apply the information to a new situation. Do you see evidence of conceptual change or misconceptions?

Teaching With Real Science

Brandwein (1962) also wrote, "The way of the scientist . . . is not to be interpreted as a calisthenics of discovery but as an art of investigation. In the long run the scientist knows a kind of success, but daily it comes from intelligent failure" (p. 8). Involving students in the successes and failures of science begins with questions. Because most class time in science classes is likely to be framed around content determined by the teacher, district, or state, one of the teacher's key responsibilities is to provide experiences that will spur students to ask questions about the content. Sometimes questions can be triggered by familiar tried-and-true demonstrations such as air pressure crushing the gas can. However, instead of explaining the phenomenon and expecting the demonstration to prove it, the teacher can use the activity in a different way. After the students watch the can deflate, the teacher might ask questions such as "What happened?" "What questions does it raise in your mind?" "Have you seen anything like this before?" "What other experiences have you had with things collapsing like this?" "Why did it happen?" "Why do you think this happened?" and "What could we do to test your ideas?"

Lesson 8.1   What Do Scientists Do?

Many online resources are available that can expose students to the day-to-day life of scientists, including all the bumps in the road. Tumble (wondery.com/wondery/shows/tumble), a podcast for students, tells stories of scientific discoveries, and museums such as the Exploratorium in San Francisco provide dispatches from scientists at the far corners of the earth (exploratorium.edu). The options for "listening in" on real science change constantly, and the best ones are in real time, allowing you to follow tweets or blogs of scientists and explorers as they go about their work. Mine the Web to find out what is happening now.

One second-grade teacher described her first attempt at adapting a standard science lesson for student investigation. The prepared lesson called for the teacher to blow soap bubbles, ask the students to observe and respond to questions, and present the necessary content. Instead, the teacher gave the bubble liquid and straws to the children. Afterward she reflected:

In no time at all everyone was blowing bubbles, big ones, little ones, stacks of bubbles and huge bubbles. Students were talking about what they did, what they saw, comparing, and analyzing. After 15–20 minutes we put the cups down and started to list questions. . . . Students listed about 40 questions. Some were very simple. "How are bubbles made?" "Why are they so messy?" Some were quite astounding. "Why do they spin? Why do they have colors? Why does your finger pop it but the straw doesn't?" . . . I was truly amazed when my students were able to answer all of the questions except one . . . I was so excited that I shared my experience with the other second-grade teachers and was met with skepticism. I guess one has to try it to believe it!

(Bingham, 1991, p. 6)

Similarly, traditional lab activities often can be revised to allow for student questioning. Many prepared labs look a great deal like recipes. Students are given a list of ingredients and materials and step-by-step directions for the procedure—like those experienced by the bookstore clerk at the beginning of the chapter. In such situations, students do not participate in the questioning or design phases of the activity. They can easily fail to grasp the purpose of such labs and their relation to the scientific process. Certainly, few scientists begin their days or their research with a set of illustrated directions! Consider whether some of your traditional science labs might be adapted to allow students to participate in the design process. The Center for Gifted Education Staff (1996) described a process of adapting labs, Uncanning the Experiment, that is appropriate for students of many ability levels. Instead of handing students the prepared lab worksheet, the authors suggested that students be engaged in a prelab class session in which they develop or are given the key question and figure out how to investigate it. The procedures are likely to be very similar to those in the prepared directions, but in this case they are the students' own, prepared purposefully.

Lesson 8.2   The Humblebee Hunter: The Nature of Science (K–3)

For an account of beginning science accessible to primary students, read Hopkinson's (2010) story of Charles Darwin's investigations of "Humblebees," ably assisted by his children. Talk about what Etty did and how it relates to the processes of science. Think about the kinds of observations your students might make of the animal life around them. With primary students, I've successfully investigated the preferred pathways of ants in the schoolyard and how those might be influenced by distributing different types of food. It was real scientific questioning and investigation at work!

The Center for Gifted Education Staff (1996) gave the example of a lab in which students are to grow seeds in pots covered with varied colors of cellophane. Uncanning this experiment requires starting with an introduction of the topic. This could include a discussion of what students know about light and plants.

Lesson 8.3   Flexible Thinking in Biology: Evolution

Even when firsthand investigations aren't possible, flexible thinking can enhance science activities. In this lesson, students choose a species of animal and list its important characteristics.

They learn about the animal's typical activities, food options, and habitat. Next, students imagine that a small population of that animal has been moved to a zoo in a different geographical location. They are to select two traits and create a genotype for each animal. Next, they hypothesize what would happen to the animal population in the new environment. Depending on the curriculum, teachers can then pose questions about genetic bottlenecks, genetic drift, or specific mutations and have students hypothesize changes in the population. If they were the zoo owner, would this animal be a good choice? (Adapted from a lesson by Krista Adair.)

Students might be given prisms and asked what they can learn about the nature of sunlight from the rainbow created by the prism and what implications this knowledge suggests for growing plants. The research question could be developed by students or posed directly by the teacher: "Do you think plants need all the colors of light, or only some of them?" Once the basic question has been established, lab groups can be challenged to develop a protocol for investigation. All lab groups need not follow identical protocols as long as their plans are reasonable and address the question. After experimentation and data collection, students can discuss information gained, questions remaining, and additional experimentation that might address remaining questions. Although not all labs can be opened to student design (particularly in chemistry, when safety considerations may limit flexibility), many can be adapted to allow students more participation in authentic scientific processes, granting them the freedom to act more like scientists than preparers of boxed macaroni and cheese.

This process of raising questions and testing hypotheses in an effort to understand observations brings students in touch with both the techniques and the habits of mind of scientists. Neither textbooks nor hands-on experiences are sufficient for either student learning or creativity. Students also must be involved in discussing, hypothesizing, defending ideas, questioning, and

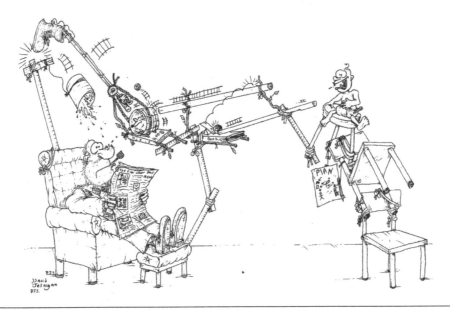

Even young children can carry out experiments

testing, both verbally and in writing. Providing students with such experiences is time consuming. However, regardless of whether our goal is to understand science concepts or to develop creativity in science, such time is essential. It is simply necessary to trade coverage for understanding.

Lesson 8.4 Uncanning Study of the Heart

A study of the heart provides several opportunities to adapt "canned" activities to support creative thinking.

1. Once students have learned to take their pulse, they can be encouraged to imagine the types of activities that might make their pulse faster or slower and then test their hypotheses.
2. When discussing circulation, students can devise a model for testing how blood flows through clear and impeded arteries. They might test the speed at which liquid can flow or how hard an artificial heart has to work. (Adapted from a lesson by Jill M. Finney.)

Thinking About the Classroom

Take a science lesson you typically plan as a demonstration or recipe lab and uncan it so that students derive the questions and plan the investigations. Note any differences you see in student involvement and understanding.

Lesson 8.5 Uncanning Biology in Kindergarten: What Gets Moldy?

Have students observe two pieces of bread, one moldy and one not. Discuss the ways scientists ask questions about things they see. Have students generate ideas about things they think might make bread get moldy faster and ways to test their hypotheses. Carry out the investigations. (Adapted from a lesson by Melinda Spicer.)

First-grade students evaluating the growth of plants in sun, shade, and darkness, sixth-grade students measuring pollution in local streams, and high school students analyzing the location of cases of an unknown disease all are asking and attempting to answer meaningful scientific questions at appropriate levels. Planning for such questioning, by both groups and individuals, is an essential part of planning science curricula. Although it is important to help students address questions within required content outcomes, there also is a place for student-generated questions. Anderson and Lee (1997) demonstrated that unless students found enough connections between science instruction and their personal agendas, even the best-planned science instruction failed. Good science requires significant student focus and effort, which are ultimately controlled only by the students. It may be that time invested in allowing students to investigate questions they care about is essential to effective science teaching as well as creativity.

Of course, students must report on their scientific endeavors, in lab reports, science fair displays, or other venues. Again, do not forget that students with special needs can be supported in these endeavors so that their scientific thinking is not lost in communication difficulties. The CAST Science Writer (sciencewriter.cast.org/welcome) is designed to help middle and secondary students write science reports. Science Writer breaks the tasks of science writing into smaller, more manageable chunks, and guides students through writing, revising, and editing. It will read sections of the report aloud so students can check their writing and even provides translations of words. Needless to say, it can be helpful for a wide range of students' needs.

It is also essential that students be supported in developing habits of mind similar to those necessary for scientists. These might include attributes such as curiosity, seeking logic and consistency, looking at a problem from multiple perspectives, and persistence in the face of confusion. We need to consider the affective components of both the content and methods of our teaching. If we want to support curiosity, we must not only respond to evidence of curiosity positively, even when it is not part of our lesson plan, but also structure activities designed to pique curiosity and model curiosity ourselves. If we want to model curiosity, persistence, and seeking, we cannot present ourselves as, nor can we be, the ones with all the answers. At least part of the time, we need to address and encourage students to address questions that truly puzzle us as well.

Lesson 8.6   Be a Naturalist

Have students select a plant from among those growing near the school. They are to observe and record the plant as carefully as they can. This should include a drawing of the plant, as well as notations on the type of environment in which it was found, the population density (how many plants per square foot), what other plants or animals were found nearby, and so on. Next, generate questions about how that plant may fit into the existing ecosystem. This is a good exercise in problem finding and observation, even if the questions are not ultimately investigated.

Problem-Based Learning

One strategy for organizing science content that supports both creativity and science processes is problem-based learning (Center for Gifted Education Staff, 1996; Coleman & Gallagher, 1997; Finkelstein, 2002; Gallagher, 2015; Lambros, 2002; Ngeow & Kong, 2001; Stepien & Gallagher, 1993). This strategy is, of course, appropriate in other disciplines as well.

In problem-based learning, students begin with an ill-structured problem. Typically, an ill-structured problem describes a real-world event for which students must formulate a solution, reaction, or explanation. As in most real problems, students often do not have most of the information needed to solve the problem at the onset, nor do they know the processes or actions necessary for solutions. They are forced to observe, seek connections, gain additional information, learn techniques, and use knowledge in particular situations, just as problems occur in the real world. Often the nature of the perceived problem may change during the course of the task. What seemed at first to be the important issues may become secondary as new information is gained. The teacher's role is to act as a model of problem solving, help students become aware of their own thinking, and allow them to take control of the problem-solving process. This role can be facilitated through the use of questions such as "What do we know?" "Do we have enough information?" "Is the information reliable?" or "What's the problem as we see it now?"

One problem-based unit developed for high-ability students in grades 4 to 6 was based on the problem of an overturned truck spilling an unknown chemical into a local creek (Center for Gifted Education Staff, 1996). Initially, students are asked to take on the role of supervisor of the State

Highway Patrol. They must decide what they know about the situation, what they need to know, and how to find out. Content emphases for the unit include the concept of systems (ecosystems and transportation systems), acid–base chemistry, and scientific processes. However, during the course of the investigation, students will, of necessity, gain and consider information on weather patterns, laboratory techniques, government responsibilities, and other content. Although this particular unit is planned for use by high-ability students over an extended time, the processes of problem-based curricula can be used at a variety of ability levels and in differing time schedules. Erskine and Krzanicki (2012) described a whole-school activity in which the staff of a primary school arranged for a large rock to be delivered to the front of the school while the students were on break. An actor friend was "found" next to the rock, portraying an injured alien. Local police came, and the newspaper sent a reporter. Because the injured alien came from a pollution-free planet where only healthy food was eaten, this led to studies in nutrition and pollution—as well as the moral dilemmas involved when simulated scientists wanted to purchase the alien.

Lesson 8.7   Uncanning the Great Gum Dilemma

Provide students with the following scenario: Your group has just been hired as gum experts for Acme Food Company because they want to produce a new chewing gum. Because the company has identified sixth graders as the target group, you must decide which type of gum to produce. Acme already makes the gum base. You are to provide information on the flavor, type of sweetener, and ratio of the flavor/sweetener to the base, as well as data to support your recommendations. The company is most interested in determining how its new product will compare with current products on the market.

It may be necessary to provide students with cues and/or modeling for them to understand that information regarding the relative amounts of sweetener and flavoring in gum can be found by weighing gum before and after chewing. This will allow them to provide data other than survey data to back up their recommendations. (Adapted from a lesson by Deborah Melde.)

Stepien and Gallagher (1993) described the use of short "posthole" problems (inquiries that delve deeply into a relatively narrow problem) when teachers want to introduce problem-based learning but do not wish to use it to structure an entire unit or course. In one example, third-year German students arrived in class one day to find a letter in German from the Nazi Ministry of Propaganda. The letter, dated 1938, addressed the students as Gallery Directors and informed them that they must review their collection and discard any work that was degenerate, because degenerate art would no longer be tolerated in Germany. Failure to comply would result in severe penalties. Similar to the students facing the truck-spilled chemical, these students started with, "What do we know?" and "What do we need to know?"—except that they did so in German. Younger students might be faced with posthole problems such as a dying patch in the teacher's vegetable garden, a kite that will not fly, or an unusual number of dead woodchucks by the side of the road. I have found the following guidelines helpful for teachers who are beginning to write posthole problems:

- Is the problem realistic, clearly tied to the real world? Problems based on demonstrations or events not naturally occurring in the world are less desirable. Students should be able to see clear connections between their efforts and real-life phenomena. If you want to focus on a problem using a prepared demonstration or activity, think about circumstances that might realistically (or close to realistically) cause the phenomenon or situation to occur.

- Is the problem situation intriguing for students of this age?
- Are both the solution and the method for the solution unknown? An ill-structured problem should not have an immediately evident solution or method of solution. Multiple methods (and usually multiple solutions) should be possible.
- Is the students' role as stakeholder intrinsic to the problem? Does it provide a logical and useful focus? Giving students a role they perceive as powerful usually is more motivating than any role asking them to be students. The role selected should logically direct students to the content on which you want to focus.
- Does the problem situation elicit the need for substantive content? Do the materials and information provided focus the students in the desired direction? Is your ill-structured problem well structured? Though "a well-structured ill-structured problem" sounds like an oxymoron, it is not. In problem-based learning, the problems are "ill structured" in that they have the messy characteristics of real-life situations, but they must be carefully planned to point students in the direction of key content.

Even with shorter posthole problems, it is important to provide scaffolding for the types of thinking required in this type of learning. It is not as simple as posing a question and then waiting for students to figure it out. Learning through problems is complex. It requires careful modeling, dividing of the task into manageable portions, and assistance in focusing on key elements of the task. Of course, problem-based learning need not be based on teacher-structured problems. Although planned problems can ensure a more structured consideration of major curriculum concepts, important learning can take place in the investigation of authentic real-world problems. The Amesville Sixth-Grade Water Chemists, described in Chapter 7, addressed this type of problem.

Sometimes technology can provide astonishing opportunities for real-world learning. Bollman, Rodgers, and Mauller (2001) described the Goldstone Apple Valley Radio Telescope (GAVRT) project, in which middle and high school students have the opportunity to collect and process telescope data as part of a larger scientific community. Similar opportunities continue to emerge online. Go to the Virtual Architecture website (virtual-architecture.wm.edu) and look under Telecollaboration or simply search for "telecollaborative projects" for one place to start.

Thinking About the Classroom

Plan a posthole experience that introduces students to problem-based learning through a short-term, ill-structured problem. Keep a journal of your experiences.

Science: Creative Strengths

Certainly, the sciences provide clear and important avenues for students to develop and pursue questions. Inquiry teaching, described later in the chapter, should be a mainstay of science instruction. Beyond the obvious ties to problem finding and problem solving, science activities can be particularly valuable in developing attitudes and values that underlie creativity. Good science demands persistence, patience, and commitment to task. It requires flexible thinking and the examination of new avenues when old ones prove fruitless. Studies of scientific discoveries can help students see the value of analogies, reframed questions, and risk taking. Experiences with puzzling situations can help develop curiosity. Perhaps most important, good science teaching shows clearly that scientific knowledge is tentative, often temporary. Science helps us understand the world and also should help us question it. Students who understand that the answers are not all in the books, that the questions change from day to day, and that the road to understanding is muddy but exciting may see the beginning of scientific creativity.

Lesson 8.8   Posthole Problems for Elementary and Secondary Students

- You own a large eagle statue that sits in front of your house. It is 10 feet tall with a wingspan of 10 feet. It weighs 1,000 pounds. One day Mr. Big arrives at your house and loves your statue. If you can deliver it to his house unbroken, he will pay you $1 million. How will you do it?

  (Kevin Learned)

- I just bought a farm although I do not know very much about farming. My farm has 600 acres. Some is in a valley, some on a hill, and some right next to my house. I would like to grow my crops without pesticides. I have come to you, experts in my county extension agency, for assistance. Can you help me figure out what crops would be best?

  (Pat Furnner)

- A recent newspaper article states that an iceberg the size of Rhode Island has sheared off the edge of Antarctica and could drift for 10 years before it melts. It rises 100 to 600 feet above the water and reaches about 1,000 feet below. It is important to predict the path of the iceberg to avoid difficulties. The National Oceanic and Atmospheric Administration has asked for your assistance in this matter. You will be hired as temporary consultants until the iceberg's path for the next 2 years has been determined.

  (John Watson)

Finding and Solving Problems in Mathematics

If you were to ask a group of people what subject they thought of first when you said the word "problems," chances are good the answer would be math. Yet if you asked the same people for the subject first associated with the word "creativity," I suspect the responses would be different. When we envision math problems, we can easily picture rows of multiplication tables and stories about Johnny giving six apples to Suzy or two trains leaving from point A and point B. Such problems, presented by the teacher, solved by a method prescribed by the teacher, and evaluated by the teacher from a prepared answer key, have little to do with creativity. They present a version of mathematics with very neat edges; every important question is in the book, and every question has one correct answer. This type of instruction eliminates the heart of mathematics. As in science, true math is muddy. Halmos (1968) stated,

> Mathematics . . . is never deductive in its creation. The mathematician at work makes vague guesses, visualizes broad generalizations, and jumps to unwarranted conclusions. He arranges and rearranges his ideas, and he becomes convinced of their truth long before he can write down a logical proof.
>
> (pp. 380–381)

Math is about raising questions as well as answering them, finding new relationships and generalizing old ones. In fact, the ability to shape and solve mathematical problems in ways that allow students to construct mathematical meaning is at the core of modern research on mathematical thinking (Kilpatrick, Martin, & Schifter, 2003; The Math Forum's Bridging Research and Practice Group, 2013).

Teaching Math for Understanding

Just like all other disciplines, math must be taught for understanding. Teaching math procedures is not enough, either for good learning or for creativity. In describing the Learning Standard, the standards overview of the National Council of Teachers of Mathematics (2000) states,

> Learning the "basics" is important; however, students who memorize facts or procedures without understanding often are not sure when or how to use what they know. In contrast, conceptual understanding enables students to deal with novel problems and settings. They can solve problems that they have not encountered before.
>
> Learning with understanding also helps students become autonomous learners. Students learn more and better when they take control of their own learning. When challenged with appropriately chosen tasks, students can become confident in their ability to tackle difficult problems, eager to figure things out on their own, flexible in exploring mathematical ideas, and willing to persevere when tasks are challenging.
>
> Students learning math should not view it as a collection of rules and procedures, but as a way of understanding and describing the world. Math should be full of "aha!" moments.

The importance of teaching mathematics for understanding is echoed in neuropsychologist Brian Butterworth's (1999; D'Arcangelo, 2001) writing on brain research regarding mathematical reasoning. He suggests that strategies for enhancing understanding include solving problems in more than one way, using a wide range of examples, and actively engaging students with numbers in different ways. Each of these suggestions entails both fluent and flexible thinking around mathematical questions.

Thinking Like an Engineer In considering the types of teaching that may allow students to raise mathematical questions, we should distinguish two types of questioning. First, we may help students explore questions in which math is used to do creative things. Students may consider how to plan a class budget, design an aluminum foil boat with maximum cargo area, build a catapult to launch a Ping-Pong ball, or calculate the total volume of air in the school. In some ways, we may consider these engineering questions because, as do engineers, students use mathematics to solve relatively practical problems. This type of math parallels the real-world problem-solving and problem-based instruction discussed in the preceding two sections. Students learn mathematics because they need it to accomplish a task. They may learn percentages to calculate acidity, volume to build boats, or geometric constructions to create a work of art. In addition to demonstrating the utility of mathematical principles, this type of problem allows for the flexibility of multiple approaches and varied solutions. It also helps students to make the problems their own, finding their own angles and following their own instincts. Of course, these problems are not found exclusively in math classes. Middle and high school engineering and technology courses (not to mention maker activities) are framed around these types of problems: designing miniature airplanes, robotic creatures, or even a better mousetrap!

Thinking Like a Mathematician The second type of question we may want to help students formulate (find) is mathematical questions. Unlike engineering questions, which are raised to accomplish a task, mathematical questions are raised to gain understanding. Here students ask the kinds of questions mathematicians ask and think the way mathematicians think. Mathematical questions are not a matter of calculation; certainly, mathematicians do not routinely contemplate the sum of 2 + 2, or even 2,837,495 + 483,882. Mathematicians—as do scientists and artists—look for patterns and try to understand them. This is what Posamentier (2003) calls "the beauty of numbers" (p. 1). Mathematicians look at the current understanding of numerical relationships and wonder, "What logically might follow next?" "Could this be true in all cases?" and "What would happen if I changed one aspect of the problem?" A mathematician friend described the process as trying to forge new paths into the body of mathematical knowledge.

Lesson 8.9   Flexible Thinking in Math: Circumference and Diameter

About a week before the lesson, have students begin bringing in spherical objects of various sizes (e.g., marbles, beach balls, oranges). Without cutting the objects, students are to use tape measures and rulers to compare the diameters and the circumferences of a variety of spheres. Teams of students work together to determine how to measure these dimensions. When it is determined that the ratio is a little more than 3 to 1, the concept of pi can be introduced. (Adapted from a lesson by Kandi Baran.)

For many of us, thinking like a mathematician presents a new challenge, particularly if we are accustomed to equating mathematics with computation. Schoenfeld (1992) described a spectrum of understanding regarding mathematics. At one end, math is seen as a body of facts, procedures, and algorithms. If one has learned the procedures, one knows math. At the other end, math is seen as the science of patterns, closely akin to the other sciences. Schoenfeld believed "a curriculum based on mastering a corpus of mathematical facts and procedures is severely impoverished—in much the same way that an English curriculum would be considered impoverished if it focused largely, if not exclusively, on issues of grammar" (p. 335).

Finding ways to help students ask and answer mathematical questions can be the basis of sound mathematical and creative thinking. Just like any other discipline being taught for creativity, math should be full of wondering, asking, and investigating questions. There is a wonderful YouTube video of Annie Fetter at an NCTM Ignite event in Indianapolis in which she raises the mathematical questions, "What do you notice?" and "What do you wonder?" (www.youtube.com/watch?v=C_DgSWEAUbQ). When students are presented with a shape or situation involving mathematics, they are first asked to observe and explore—the essence of problem finding. Then they ask questions. As Ms. Fetter describes, such questions reflect curiosity, not misunderstanding. They approach math as an interesting situation to be explored rather than a predefined problem to be solved. In fact, the talk suggests that students be presented with scenarios—mathematical stories to be explored—rather than particular problems to be solved. When students raise questions, they not only use mathematical thinking, but they present the teacher with glimpses into their current level of understanding. The student who wondered, "Do fractions only work with circles?" provided his teacher with essential instructional information. And, of course, providing a scenario rather than a story means that no one student can solve the problem quickly, leaving the rest of the students without meaningful contributions. There is always more to observe and explore. This general approach to mathematical thinking, in which students explore and ask questions about a stimulus (generally) presented by the teacher, is also called problem posing (English, 1997; Whitin, D. J., 2006; Whitin, P., 2004).

Mathematical thinking requires students to find solutions to perplexing situations

Teachers can structure the stories or graphics presented in scenarios to highlight concepts being taught—or send students in search of such questions. Imagine a scavenger hunt for examples of slopes in the environment. Students could return with drawings or photographs of the slopes, ready to calculate and then serve as the basis for new questions. Questioning can help students see that answers to a seemingly obvious question can differ. The answer to "What is the average?" will vary depending on whether you are asking for the mean, median, or mode. What about "biggest"? For example, what are the biggest cities in the world? Does that mean largest land area, largest population, or most crowded? Students can order cities by each criterion and calculate population density. Using all three categories, students can rank and justify their list of biggest cities.

You also can find sources of questions and curiosity online and in the world at large. Real World Math (www.realworldmath.org) provides lesson ideas using Google Earth to shape and solve problems from the area of oddly shaped fields to typhoon tracking and crop circles. Math in the News (www.media4math.com/MathInTheNews.asp) is exactly what it sounds like, a mathematical look at happenings in the world around us. Use the questions there, or, better yet, use the site to inspire you and your students to ask mathematical questions in your own area. Or for opening activities that practice mathematical problem finding, try the 101 Questions website (www.101qs.com) for a daily graphic to spark questioning. The Math Forum's Bridging Research and Practice Group (2013) provides models of mathematical conversations, including video examples under the Interventions link (http://mathforum.org/brap/wrap2/index.html). The more students understand math as a way to ask and answer questions, the greater the opportunities for both understanding and creativity.

As you plan your own mathematical questions, you might consider some general strategies, each beginning with something known. First, a question may ask if a specific known case might generalize to other cases. Imagine, for example, the long-ago mathematician who first recognized that the area of a particular triangle could be calculated by multiplying the length of its base by its height and dividing by two. He or she might have wondered, "Could I do this with all triangles? Does it matter if the triangle is acute or obtuse? Can I prove that this will always work?" Students could be engaged in this type of questioning in Lesson 8.9 and 8.10 in this chapter. In each case, they move from specific examples to broader opportunities for generalizations. Second, some mathematical questions attempt to tie one body of knowledge or area of mathematics to another. A mathematician might examine an interesting algebraic relationship and wonder, "What geometric shape might this describe?" Your students can experience similar processes in both mathematical and more cross-disciplinary ways. For example, Lessons 8.12 and 8.13 explore the ties between mathematical and human relationships.

Third, some mathematical questions ask the questions, "What if?" They begin with a theorem or relationship known to be true and explore what would happen if one of the assumptions were changed. For example, if the area of a triangle on a flat surface is 1/2(b × h), what would happen if the triangle were drawn on the surface of a sphere? Would the same equation still work?

Lesson 8.10   Flexible Thinking in Math: Non-Euclidean Shapes

Using string, have groups of students construct varied sizes of triangles on a beach ball. Have each group measure the angles of each triangle. Create a chart indicating the angles and sums of angles for the triangles. Have students observe patterns and make hypotheses about what is happening and why. This activity will be even better if you begin by posing the question about whether the shapes on nonflat surfaces follow the same patterns as those on flat surfaces. Students could design investigations to answer the question. If you provide a variety of balls and string, problem solving is likely to develop!

Finally, sometimes mathematicians look at a problem that has already been solved and try to solve it in a new way. Niu and Zhou (2017) describe solving problems in multiple ways as the central to creative teaching of mathematics in China. They cite the Chinese saying "one problem solved with three variations" (p. 89) as describing the characteristics of a good math teacher. Of course solving a problem in more than one way also supports students' creativity. In this type of problem, the aesthetics of math can become obvious. Mathematicians not only try to solve problems but also try to solve them beautifully. To a nonmathematician, the idea of a beautiful solution may seem curious: Either a solution works or it does not. However, some solutions may contain loose ends, unnecessary pieces, or awkward constructions, much like fixing the drooping muffler on your car using half a belt, two scraps of tin foil, several pieces of chewing gum, and three banana peels. The muffler may not drag on the ground, but it will not be beautiful, either. An expert who can weld the pieces together so that the joints barely show has also solved the problem but has done so elegantly. Soderborg (1985) argued,

> Let me explain why I feel math can be beautiful. First, mathematical statements can contain significant meaning succinctly and elegantly expressed. They can simultaneously compress the expression and generalize the meaning of significant ideas, much like well-written poems. Second, mathematical statements can produce aesthetic pleasure in the person who studies them. A well-constructed solution or proof can evoke wonder from a student aware of its fluid logic and broad implications. . . . Studying beautiful mathematics can be like listening to a symphony or studying an inspiring painting. One feels intrigue and admiration for something so well put together that produces such marvelous results.
>
> (p. 10)

To help students find and solve problems like mathematicians, we must help them see both the effectiveness and the elegance of their efforts.

When mathematicians address problems, they do not use neat, prescribed algorithms. They must have a battery of problem-solving strategies and select the methods that produce the most effective, most aesthetic solution. Deciding which strategies to use is an enormously important task and one that is eliminated in assignments in which every problem on a page demands the same kind of manipulations.

Although students in grades K–12 are not likely to generate new mathematical knowledge, they can address problems that demand mathematical thought and personal creativity. Tasks that allow students to experience the ambiguities of math may not be real-world problems, but they can be attacked in multiple ways to help students discover the relationships that constitute the field of mathematics. Mathematical tasks may help students discover patterns, series, or relationships. The teacher might demonstrate that a paper folded in half once forms two sections. Students might be challenged to figure out how many sections would be formed if the paper could be folded eight times. Some students might try folding a paper eight times; others might make a chart and see a pattern. Students who are familiar with exponents may have other insights.

Sometimes problems may help students see new systems or change previous assumptions. Our number system is based on units of 10. If that assumption is changed, many new systems can be created: base 5, base 2, and so on. Problems and activities that challenge students to think about numbers in new ways foster mathematical problem finding and problem solving. (Think about what the pattern of sections created by various folds of paper would look like in base 2 and base 8.)

Lesson 8.11   Flexible Thinking in Math: The Playscape Problem

Using the playscape as an example, develop a problem that uses one of the listed formulas, an explanation as to how to solve the problem, and a reason why someone might need the information. For example, if a student fell off the playscape bridge, the Health Department might require warning tape along the edges of the bridge. How many rolls of tape would you need to buy? Possible formulas include area of a rectangle, perimeter of a rectangle, circumference of a circle, and so forth. (Adapted from a lesson by Tamara Dodge.)

Problems that allow students to discover a new idea or find a new, possibly more elegant method of solution also foster mathematical thinking. The aforementioned paper-folding example fits this category. So do number bracelets (Burns, 1992). These are created by choosing two numbers from 0 to 9 and following this rule: Add the two numbers and record next the digit that appears in the ones place in the sum. For example, if I started with 5 and 4, I would record the number 9. Next, I would add 9 and 4 and record 3, because that was the digit in the ones place. I would continue until I got back to 5–5 4 9 3 2 5. Students are challenged to find the longest and shortest possible bracelets and to look for odd and even patterns in the bracelets. Students who look carefully for patterns may be able to find elegant solutions without recording every possible combination. Identifying and using such patterns is an "aha!" of mathematical creativity.

To add variety to your problems, you also may want to seek out activities that tie math to other disciplines, particularly the arts. Did you know the Fractal Foundation (fractalfoundation.org) has a website of activities for integrating math, art, and science through the study of fractals? The Lessons and Activities section of the National Gallery of Art (nga.gov) includes math/art activities for grades K–12. And the Student Guide Best Math Art on the Web is a treasure trove of math/art resources, organized by math content (www.studentguide.org/the-best-math-art-on-the-web). One of my favorite resources is Dr. Ron Eglash's Culturally Simulated Design Tools (csdt.rpi.edu), a collection of materials that teach principles of math and computation through varied cultures. The activities include mathematics activities based in African, African American, Native American, and Latino traditions. The site also presents activities based in contemporary youth culture, such as Cartesian and polar coordinates as they appear in graffiti or slopes and arcs as they apply to skateboarding. Think about the problem-posing activities that could inspire!

Planning Math Activities

A number of authors have presented recommendations for teaching strategies that are appropriate for both the NCTM goals for understanding and the creativity goals set forth in this book.

Burns (1992, 2007) presents examples of problem-based mathematics instruction in six strands: measurement, probability and statistics, geometry, logic, patterns and functions, and number. She puts forth four criteria for a mathematical problem:

1. There is a perplexing situation that the student understands.
2. The student is interested in finding a solution.
3. The student is unable to proceed directly toward a solution.
4. The solution requires use of mathematical ideas.

(1992, p. 17)

Students are taught to address problems using a variety of problem-solving strategies, such as looking for a pattern, constructing a table, working backward, or solving a simpler or similar problem. Burns presented strategies for using both cooperative and individual problem-solving experiences.

In cooperative experiences, the lesson starts with an introduction that includes any necessary presentation of concepts and introduction of the problem to be solved. Next, students work in cooperative groups toward solving the problem. Finally, groups share their strategies and results.

Lesson 8.12   Vertex Stories

Turn the equation of a quadratic equation in vertex form into a story. For example, $y = -2(x - 2)^2 + 3$ could represent, "Mario hit a mushroom and shrank. He ran to the right two and climbed 3 ladder rungs to save the princess."

The story describes the primary transformations of the parabola compared to $y = x^2$. When students create their own stories, they demonstrate knowledge of the vertical and horizontal translations, dilations, and reflections—and exercise their creativity. (Adapted from a lesson by Melanie Carbine.)

Discussion questions might include "How did you organize the work in your group?" "What strategies did your group use?" "Did any group use a different strategy?" "Are there patterns or relationships you can see from your solution?" and "Does this remind you of any other problems you have solved?" Problem-solving lessons may be completed in one class period or extended over several days.

Lesson 8.13   Analogies in Math: Valentine's Day Math

Use Venn diagrams to express relationships. For example, imagine the intersection of a perfect match, never rejected, and worth the trouble. The intersection is either true love or kidney donation!

Or create graphs to express the history of a relationship, such as changes in the number of Facebook posts or tweets across the history of a relationship. For example, what kind of graph would express the relationship between love and trust? (Adapted from a lesson by Melanie Carbine.)

One sample activity is designed to introduce pentominoes, geometric shapes. First, the teacher demonstrates the rule for making pentominoes and shows how to determine, by flipping or rotating, whether two pentominoes are congruent. Next, the class is presented with a problem similar to that planned for the cooperative groups: "Imagine you were trying to find all the possible arrangements of three squares. How many would there be?" The students could then try the same for four squares. Next, cooperative groups investigate possible ways to arrange five squares. They cut them out of graph paper and test for congruence. Finally, the groups come back together to compare strategies and results. Individual problem-solving opportunities are organized using a menu, or collection of problem-solving tasks. Similar to the group problem-solving experiences, menu tasks are designed to have multiple solutions and to provide students with the opportunity to develop mathematical reasoning. They also build independent thinking and working skills that are important in creative activities (see Chapter 9).

Some teachers post directions for menu tasks on a bulletin board. Others make copies that students can take to their desks when needed. Systems for recording the tasks that have been completed also may vary. A menu can be prepared for several days or longer. Menu problems are generally not hierarchical but pose problems, set up situations, and ask questions that may be addressed in any order by an individual or small group. Menus can be used from primary grades up to high school. Very young children may do menu tasks at centers, often without written directions. High school students can carry menu tasks over from one day to the next, allowing productive time to begin when the bell rings. In most classes, instructional time is likely to be divided among group problem solving, class discussions, direct instruction, and menu time. For many more examples of intriguing challenges, see Marilyn Burns's math blog. It is full of interesting problem options, easily searched by math concepts (marilynburnsmathblog.com/wordpress). You can also check the Math Solutions webpage for more Burns-inspired math activities (mathsolutions.com/free-resources).

Lesson 8.14   Flexible Thinking in Math: Lying With Statistics (9–12)

As part of a unit on statistics, have students take on the role of advertisers motivated to use statistics—accurately but deceptively—to sell their products. Students will design and conduct a sampled study (survey) about their product. They must use the data to sell their product. Students must report how they biased their sample to maximize positive results and how they used statistics selectively in order to promote their product. This activity is excellent for developing flexible thinking as well as consumer savvy. (Adapted from a lesson by Benjamin Ahronheim.)

Wiggins and McTighe (2005) present a lesson sequence for high school math that suggests a lesson sequence similar to the elementary examples given earlier. It is interesting to note that although it is a format strongly supportive of creativity, Wiggins and McTighe present it as a model for promoting deep understanding and transfer. Yet again, the procedures that are supportive of creativity also are supportive of learning.

The sequence starts with a "hook problem" (p. 39) that engages students in a puzzling situation. In the sample lesson, students are provided with finish times of 122 students in four classes competing in a 1-mile walk. Their task is to determine which class won. The next stage of the process is to discuss essential questions, in this case "What is fair? How might math be used to determine if something is fair?" Students then are given a preview of their culminating activity. In this case, students will have to decide which measure will be used to determine their math grade for the quarter—mean, median, or mode? Only then, when students have a puzzle and require the information to solve it, do traditional direct instruction and practice activities begin. This is another form of problem-based learning described earlier.

Lesson 8.15   Problem-Based Math: The Epidemic

In this activity, students are placed in the role of mathematical consultants hired by the military to deal with a biohazard. They are provided with a chart containing data on bacterial growth: day, number of bacteria per sample, number of people infected, number of deaths. Students are challenged to create equations to model the bacteria's behavior and allow the military to predict bacterial growth and risk factors. (Adapted from a lesson by Steven McGough.)

Some mathematical problems can foster flexible thinking by requiring students to look at situations from multiple points of view. Sobel and Maletsky (1999) cite a problem in which a customer buys a pair of slippers for $5, paying with a $20 bill. Unable to make change, the merchant asks the grocer next door to change the bill and sells the customer the slippers, giving $15 change. Later, the grocer discovers the $20 bill is counterfeit and demands that the merchant make good for it. The merchant does so and then must turn the counterfeit bill in to the FBI. The problem asks how much the merchant lost. It can be more easily solved by viewing the situation from a different point of view—that of the customer-counterfeiter.

Problems can be especially appealing when they spring from the environment in which students live. In materials developed for the Detroit Historical Museum, Caniglia (2003) presented a series of questions and problems to be investigated during a cemetery visit. Students use pictographs to depict the birth months of the deceased, bar graphs to compare the number of deaths by decade, box and whisker plots to analyze data regarding gender, age at death, and so forth. They use plotting to create maps to the five most interesting headstones. Such activities are challenging in their own right but also provide opportunities for students to generate and investigate their own additional questions.

Brown and Walter (1990) described activities for secondary school students that focus specifically on finding or posing mathematical problems. They suggested that, like mathematicians, students should be encouraged to ask questions about mathematical propositions. For example, they described activities derived from the equation

$$x^2 + y^2 = z^2$$

When faced with this equation, most of us (if our memories of high school math are clear enough) are likely to assume that our task is to come up with values of x, y, and z that make the equation true—for example, 3, 4, and 5. However, the equation did not actually ask us to do that. The equation did not ask anything at all; it is a statement. In fact, "What are some values for which $x^2 + y^2 = z^2$ is true?" is only one of the many possible questions one could ask about the equation. Other questions could include "Are the solutions always integers?" "What is the geometric significance of this?" "How could you find solutions without trying out every possible number?" Each of these is an example of what Brown and Walter called the first phase of problem posing—and also Annie Fetter's "What do you wonder?" question. Problem posing can be initiated by stimuli other than mathematical statements: definitions, theorems, scenarios, questions, or objects. In the first phase of problem posing, students might ask questions about a right triangle ("Why is it called right?") or about the definition of a line. In each case, the questions relate to the stimulus as it is presented.

Brown and Walter (1990) coined the phrase "What-if-Not" for the second phase of problem posing. In that case, some aspect or assumption of the stimulus is changed to create a question or problem. Remember that this is one of the key strategies used by mathematicians in developing new ideas. For example, changing assumptions for the equation $x^2 + y^2 = z^2$ might lead us to wonder, "For what values is it true that $x^2 + y^2 > z^2$?" or "What happens to the values for a triangle that is not a right triangle?" Using the What-if-Not strategy begins with listing the attributes of the stimulus to be investigated. For example, a right triangle has three sides and three angles, one of which is a right angle. It is helpful to break up the attributes so that each is listed separately and can be considered individually (do you recognize the attribute listing strategy from Chapter 6?):

1. It has three sides.
2. It has three angles.
3. One angle is a right angle.
4. The longest side is opposite the right angle.
5. $x^2 + y^2 = z^2$ (and so on).

Next comes What-if-Not. Students select some attribute to change. Suppose the shape had more than three sides. The next stage is to raise questions based on the new assumption. If the shape had more than three sides, we could ask, "Is it possible to draw such a shape so that the rest of the statements are still true?" "What would be the area of a shape like that in the figure on the board?" "Would $x^2 + y^2 = z^2 + a^2 + b^2$?" or "Would another equation better describe the relationship?" Finally, one or more of these questions could be chosen for analysis. This example illustrates the four levels of the What-if-Not strategy:

Level 1: Attribute Listing
Level 2: What-if-Not (change some attribute)
Level 3: Question Asking
Level 4: Analyzing a Problem

Another interesting strategy described by Brown and Walter (1990) is the writing of mathematical journals with students serving as authors and members of the editorial boards. Papers may include problem solutions or nonsolutions, discussions of attempted strategies, insights, and misconceptions. The journals also include abstracts of each article and letters of acceptance sent to the author—including the reflections of the editorial board on the piece, lists of interesting problem ideas, and suggested readings. The journals provide a fine outlet for the results of creative mathematical thinking. Equally important, they publish unsuccessful attempts with as much validation of the insights provided as that accorded to successful solutions. This balanced attention encourages risk taking and persistence in the face of difficulty. Students are much more likely to attempt challenging tasks when they understand that their success depends more on their thinking and learning than on their finding the correct answer to the problem.

Mathematics: Creative Strengths

Mathematics has natural ties to creativity: seeking patterns and beauty, looking in many directions, solving problems, and seeking new ideas. Unfortunately, some math instruction—always focusing on one correct way to find one correct answer—can rob from math much of its beauty and make it difficult for students to see links between creativity and mathematics. Perhaps the greatest service we could give to the development of creative thinking in math is to help students understand that math does not equal computation and that the math problems are not all in the book. Helping students to raise math questions, discover mathematical relationships, and challenge math assumptions can bring them closer to the creative thinking that brings joy to the lives of creative engineers and mathematicians.

Thinking About the Classroom

Plan a math activity that is designed to help students discover a mathematical idea or principle independently. Try to include a problem that can be solved in more than one way and see what happens.

Thinking About the Content Areas

Pondering the kinds of teaching that support creativity in the content areas, I thought of several themes. I have said that such teaching requires us to help students learn both the key concepts and the methods of the disciplines. If students are to develop new ideas, they must know the experts' ideas and how those ideas are developed. In many disciplines, problem-based instruction can provide an avenue for both strong content teaching and creative thinking. At times, real-world problems are most appropriate; at other times, teacher-structured problems are more manageable. I would hope that there also is a place for student-generated problems, questions, and ideas as the basis for instruction. I have thought recently that if I had a classroom of my own—my current teaching is actually all online—I would hang a giant sign that says, "Ask a good question." Perhaps under that I would list the questions that keep appearing whatever the discipline:

What is?
What was?
How do you know?
Why?
Why not?
What if?
What if not?

Additional Strategies for Content Teaching

This section examines lesson designs and teaching strategies that support creative thinking while presenting or using content information. Most of these strategies concern the *how* of teaching. The strategies discussed are by no means a comprehensive list, nor is the section meant to suggest that all teaching should be done in the ways described. It does provide alternatives to more direct presentation and practice strategies that may be used to increase variety, interest, and flexibility in teaching. The strategies are divided into three sections: inductive strategies, simulation and role-play, and questioning and discussion techniques.

Inductive Approaches

When an argument or process of logic is said to be inductive, it proceeds from the specific to the general. That is, individuals draw general conclusions based on particular examples. If I notice that the four small dogs in my neighborhood all bark more than the larger dogs and draw the conclusion that small dogs bark more than large dogs, that is inductive reasoning. If I read the biographies of five famous scientists and conclude that they have characteristics in common, that is also inductive. Detectives, particularly the television variety, use inductive reasoning when they draw conclusions about what happened at the crime scene from isolated bits of evidence. Whereas in direct lessons a teacher is likely to present an idea or skill and then cite specific examples of how it may be applied, in inductive lessons, the students are given the examples and challenged to figure out the concept or generalization that ties the examples together. *It is only an inductive lesson if the students engage in inductive thinking.* Inductive lessons provide opportunities for thinking independently, taking risks, and generating original ideas. Although some inductive lessons lend themselves to a relatively limited number of conclusions, others provide for multiple conclusions, strategies, or points of view.

Inductive teaching has taken many shapes, from concept attainment to inquiry-based teaching to problem-based learning (see, for example, Joyce, Weil, & Calhoun, 2009, 2014). But the underlying assumption of induction (or inquiry) in its many varieties is that because learning is a constructive task, students will learn best when they are provided with activities that allow them to discover concepts and generalizations through experience. The idea of learning as a constructive task is supported by the growing knowledge base in cognitive psychology (Bransford et al., 2000), but the processes of inquiry teaching and learning are less universally accepted and not always simple to implement.

Both a cadre of researchers and any experienced teacher can tell you that inquiry activities are not always successful (Kirschner, Sweller, & Clark, 2010; Klahr & Nigam, 2004; Mayer, 2004). Some students may explore materials without drawing the hoped-for conclusions. Other students may jump three steps down the logic path, confusing those they leave behind. Kirschner et al. (2010) argue that although cognitive psychology supports learning as a constructive process, it also explains the failures of inquiry-based teaching because of the increased cognitive demands placed on novice learners. I would argue that the "pure discovery" used to define inquiry in such critiques represents an extreme of practice seldom seen in classrooms, but still, demonstrations of limited student learning must be taken seriously.

However, lack of opportunity to explore and inquire also carries risks, what one author calls the "double-edged sword of pedagogy" (Bonawitz et al., 2011). For example, children who are directly taught about the uses of an object are less likely to explore it and discover alternatives and are more likely to imitate what they've been shown, even when it is less efficient (Bonawitz et al., 2011; Buchsbaum, Gopnik, Griffiths, & Shafto, 2011). The notion that students explore less after direct instruction is particularly problematic if explorations are likely to lead to more substantial understanding. And until students learn to draw effective conclusions on their own, they will always be at the mercy of those willing to present conclusions without evidence. And so, for now, we are left to use good judgment, careful assessment, and wise feedback in implementing inductive activities. Although they represent only one type of instruction, it is a powerful one. Recognize that all may not go smoothly the first time around, persist, and watch your students' thinking (and creativity) develop!

Taba (1967, also described in Joyce et al., 2014) identified three basic inductive thinking tasks: concept formation, interpretation of data, and application of principles. Concept formation involves identifying and enumerating data, grouping items into categories, and then developing labels. For example, students might list all the things they would buy if they were in charge of the family's budget for a month and then group the items by common attributes. Through this process, they may eventually, with some teacher guidance, develop the concepts of wants and needs.

Interpretation of data, Taba's (1967) second inductive task, entails examining data, making hypotheses about relationships, inferring causes, and building generalizations. For example, one group of students had examined magazine advertisements and developed a number of categories to describe the sales techniques the ads used. The teacher then asked them to study the ads and look for relationships between the types of products being advertised and the technique used. Students noticed that certain techniques, such as snob appeal, were more commonly used for nonessential products than for basic-needs products. They hypothesized that advertising techniques varied depending on whether the product was a want or a need. Drawing this conclusion required them to interpret data. (It is interesting to note that in this particular lesson, the conclusion reached by the students went beyond the teacher's expectations. She was anticipating that students would notice that some strategies were used more often with particular products—for example, sports figures selling athletic shoes—but she had not previously recognized a pattern around wants and needs. The teacher and students together became investigators testing this hypothesis.)

Application of principles may logically follow the interpretation of data. In this task, individuals try to predict new situations or consequences based on identified patterns. Students might predict the type of advertising most likely to be used for promoting a particular product or hypothesize as to whether their observations of print advertisements would likely hold true for television ads. The three tasks of concept formation, interpretation of data, and application of principles may be used separately or in combination in inductive lessons.

In the next sections, I discuss two basic types of inductive experiences: experiences designed to build concepts and inquiry experiences requiring the interpretation and application of data. Many of the research and problem-solving activities previously discussed also incorporate inductive thinking. Any time students draw conclusions from data, they are thinking inductively.

Experiences Designed to Build Concepts Taba's (1967) concept-formation lessons have three basic components. First, students are asked to list or enumerate data regarding a particular question or problem. In the previous example, students were asked to list all the items they would buy if they were in charge of the family budget. Next, students are asked to group items with similar characteristics. For example, they may be asked to divide into groups the items that are alike in some way. This process may be assisted by such questions as, "You said that the new TV and the new bikes go together because they both help you have fun. Would any other items on your list do that?" or "Try to divide the items into the smallest number of groups that still make sense together." The final step of a concept-formation lesson is labeling the concepts. In this lesson, the teacher hopes to develop the concepts of wants and needs.

In planning a concept-formation lesson, there are two major considerations. First, it is important to plan a question or problem that allows students to generate a list of data rich enough to include the concept you wish to develop. If I had started the lesson on wants and needs with the statement "Imagine that you had $500. Let's list all the things you might buy," it is possible that all the items listed might be wants. In that case, it would be impossible to develop the desired concepts without asking additional questions. By having students imagine they are in charge of all family purchases for an extended time, it is more likely that some students will mention food, electricity, rent, and other essentials.

The second key to a successful concept-development lesson is recognizing when students need additional direction to assist them in generating items or focusing the categories. It is always wise to try predicting in advance what types of categories may be formed initially and to think how students can be guided to the desired concepts. Sometimes very general questions or directions may be helpful. Suggesting that students generate the smallest possible number of categories is an example of a general guide. Other times, you may need to be more specific: "Let's remember that you are in charge of everything your family will buy for the month. Are there any important ideas missing from your list?" Concept-formation lessons may stand alone or be part of a sequence leading to interpretation and use of data. Additional detail on planning concept formation lessons and other Taba strategies is available in Gallagher's (2012) *Concept Development*.

A related type of lesson, the concept-attainment lesson, is also designed to help students develop new concepts. Whereas concept-formation lessons require students to determine criteria and develop categories, concept-attainment lessons require them to identify the attributes that differentiate categories already formed by someone else. They do this by analyzing examples and nonexamples of the concept to be attained (Bruner, Goodnow, & Austin, 1977). The examples and nonexamples are called exemplars.

A concept-attainment lesson begins with the teacher's presenting exemplars and categorizing them as "yes" (an example of the concept to be developed) or "no" (a nonexample). By comparing the yes and no exemplars, students begin to form ideas about the critical attributes of the concept. After a number of exemplars have been presented, students are asked to describe the characteristics or attributes held in common by the yes examples presented thus far. As additional examples are presented, students may be asked to categorize them as yes or no and to determine whether the criteria originally developed continue to hold. After additional examples are examined, students refine the criteria and develop concept labels. Next, the teacher gives the label, and students are asked to produce examples of their own. Finally, students describe their thinking and how their ideas changed as they moved through the activity. Imagine, for example, that a teacher wanted the students to attain the concept of natural resources. He or she would begin by presenting examples and nonexamples of natural resources and placing them in the correct categories. The example of the ocean would be categorized as a yes, whereas a table would be a no. As the pattern emerged, students would be challenged to determine the category of new examples, describe what the examples have in common, and generate examples and nonexamples of their own. Finally, the teacher would present the concept label—natural resources.

There are three major steps in developing a concept-attainment lesson. First, you must carefully define your concept, decide on its key attributes, and think about which attributes are critical (essential for this concept) and which are noncritical (common but not essential). For example, if the concept is mammal, critical attributes are that mammals are warm blooded, are covered with hair or fur, give birth to live young, and nurse them. Noncritical attributes are that many mammals have four legs and live on land. It is important to develop your concept-attainment lesson to clarify as many of the critical attributes of the concept as possible.

Next, you need to select your exemplars. Exemplars may be provided in the form of words, pictures, or even concrete items. You need to select examples and nonexamples that highlight critical attributes. It would be extremely difficult to provide sufficient examples to enable young students to extrapolate the characteristic of warm blooded. You could, however, provide examples that would highlight other relevant characteristics. For example, in choosing the examples and nonexamples of the concept mammals, you might anticipate that students would initially think of the concept as animals in the zoo or animals in the woods. You could help clarify these misconceptions by including a snake or an ostrich as nonexamples. If you used pictures of these animals, including their eggs, you could focus attention on important attributes. Using a whale as an example may be confusing if students do not know that whales have hair or give birth to live young. A picture of a nursing whale may be an important clue. The more straightforward the attributes of the concept, the better the match with this method. A concept-attainment lesson on acute versus obtuse angles could be very clear. An attempted lesson on liberty could be problematic, because the attributes of liberty are much more abstract and subject to interpretation.

Finally, it is important to consider the order in which you will present the examples and nonexamples. In most cases, broadly differing examples are given first, with finer and finer distinctions presented as the concept is developed. For example, you might decide to present pictures of a bear and a fish early in the lesson and save the whale photo for later fine-tuning of the concept. In determining the order of the exemplars, it is important to consider the purpose of the activity. If, as in a concept-attainment lesson, the intent is to provide students with information from which they can build a new concept, it is most appropriate to start with clear examples and save those that demand careful analysis for later in the lesson. Occasionally, activities resembling concept-attainment lessons are used to review or reintroduce concepts that have already been learned. In this case, teachers sometimes use trickier examples first and allow clues to become more and more obvious until students arrive at the concept. This activity can be a highly motivating and appropriate introduction to a lesson, but it is not a concept-attainment lesson because students are attempting to identify a concept they have already internalized.

Both concept-development and concept-attainment lessons provide opportunities for thinking logically, exercising flexibility, and drawing conclusions from data. Although the lessons generally are structured to lead students to predetermined conclusions, they still can reinforce attitudes that are important to creativity. Direct teaching of concepts sends the implicit message, "The teacher will tell me what is important or true." Concept-development and concept-attainment lessons, in contrast, imply that "I can figure this out myself."

Inquiry Lessons: Interpreting and Applying Data Experiences that require students to interpret and apply data are frequently called inquiry lessons. Inquiry lessons, naturally, require students to inquire, examine information, make hypotheses, gather data, and draw conclusions. They involve students actively in discovering a generalization that explains a puzzling event or set of data. Inquiry lessons are particularly valuable because they involve students in many processes of authentic investigation used by adults in a variety of fields.

One variety of inquiry lesson was developed by Suchman (1962). In Suchman's model, the teacher begins the activity by explaining the inquiry process and the ground rules. Students are not given any response from the teacher except "yes" or "no" during the questioning period. Next, the teacher presents a puzzling event—something that conflicts with our typical notions of reality. Then, the students ask questions to get more information and learn the conditions under which different results would occur. The students, through their questions, begin to isolate relevant variables and to form hunches about causal relationships (hypotheses). Through questions or experiments that test their hypotheses, they formulate an explanation for the puzzling event. Finally, the teacher leads the students to analyze their own thinking processes. The teacher may present a science demonstration, such as the can crushed by air pressure mentioned earlier, and challenge students to determine what happened in a method that resembles 20 Questions. Students strive to identify relevant variables and plan additional experiences that can verify their hypotheses.

More commonly, inquiry lessons involve students in drawing conclusions not about a particular puzzling event but about a set of data. The lesson described earlier in which students made and investigated hypotheses about the relationship between advertising strategies and product type could be described as an inquiry lesson. Students examined the data set (magazine ads), made hypotheses about variables (product and strategy), and tested their conclusions (looking at additional print or TV ads). The key attributes of inquiry lessons are examining data, making hypotheses, and drawing conclusions. This cycle may be repeated as many times as it seems productive.

One of my students developed an inquiry lesson based on occupations during the Revolutionary War period. Elementary students were shown photographs of artifacts of the period and asked to hypothesize what occupations must have existed in that society. The activity demanded careful observation and willingness to stand up for one's point of view. Later, during a trip to a local museum, students looked for additional information to support or refute their hypotheses. They had the opportunity to consider multiple possibilities, think independently, and support their ideas, all while learning fairly traditional social studies content. For additional detail on strategies for concept development, concept attainment, and inquiry lessons, see Joyce et al. (2014).

Simulation and Role-Play Activities

One key characteristic of creative thinking is that it is flexible, considering more than one category or point of view. Role-play and simulation activities are particularly effective strategies for developing this type of thinking because they involve looking at the world through someone else's eyes (Taylor, 1998).

Role-Play Role-play can be an effective tool for enhancing understanding of content as well as social understandings. In role-play activities, students take on a role—pretend they are a particular person—to solve a problem or act out a situation. Joyce et al. (2009) stated,

> On its simplest level, role playing is dealing with problems through action; a problem is delineated, acted out, and discussed. . . . A person puts himself or herself in the position of another person and then tries to interact with others who are also playing roles. As empathy, sympathy, anger and affection are all generated during the interaction, role playing, if done well, becomes a part of life.
>
> (p. 291)

Role-play may be done in small groups or in front of the whole class. It usually is a brief activity, often completed in less than 1 hour. Torrance (1975) has used the term "sociodrama" to describe a related process in which students solve present and future problems through a variety of dramatic techniques. The activities described as role-play in this section are most closely related to the direct presentation technique of sociodrama. For other, more complex forms of sociodrama, see Torrance (1975).

Role-play can be used to enhance content in a variety of areas. Students could role-play Emmy Noether convincing her father that she wanted to become the only woman studying math at the university, a pioneer family making the decision to stay in Missouri or travel farther west, or characters in a work of literature trying to work out a new solution to their dilemma. It also can be used to solve real-world social problems, such as a friend offering drugs, an encounter with a bully, or an argument over playground equipment. Joyce et al. (2009) stated, "The essence of role playing is the involvement of participants and observers in a real problem situation and the desire for resolution and understanding that this involvement engenders" (p. 60). Any area of content in which it is important to understand a variety of points of view can provide opportunities for role-playing.

There are four main steps in planning a role-play:

1. Decide on the general problem area to be addressed. In choosing a topic, you will want to consider your students' needs, interests, and backgrounds. In addition to selecting a problem area that is relevant and interesting, it is important for you to choose a topic about which students have sufficient prior knowledge to take on roles knowledgeably (or to provide them with such background before attempting the role play). If you are role-playing in content areas, background knowledge can make the difference between an amusing (or possibly time-wasting) skit and a powerful learning experience.
2. Once you have decided on a general problem area, define the specific situation to be portrayed. A good role-play puts the characters in a specific situation that requires action. If the topic is the causes of the Civil War, the situation might be two siblings in a Virginia family arguing over whether the sons should go to war. Students studying the Dust Bowl era could similarly debate the decision to stay or where the family should go.
3. Plan a role for the audience. It is important that students not playing particular roles have an active part in the role-playing experience. They may be listening for particularly effective arguments, deciding which of several solutions they think is best, or considering what they might do in a particular character's place.
4. Decide how you will introduce the role-play. Some role-play situations might be introduced by a story, others by a discussion of the issue or small-group sharing.

When you actually present the role-play experience, you will first conduct the introductory activities and then explain clearly and explicitly the situation to be enacted. Select students for each role and assign the observation task to the audience. Conduct the role-play one or more times. If you repeat a scenario, you can give more students the opportunity to participate as well as obtain varied points of view. For some role-plays, you may wish to discuss each version as it occurs. For others, you may prefer to delay discussion until after several versions have been portrayed. In either case, be sure to allow ample time for discussion of role-play experiences. Helping students understand why individuals made particular choices, what those individuals were thinking and feeling, and what alternative choices might be made is at the heart of role-playing activities. Some writers have used role-play to foster in-depth understanding of particular times or topics. For example, Manley and O'Neill (1997) used role-play to explore African American heritage, ranging from portrayals of the Underground Railroad to activities based on Jacob Lawrence's artwork depicting the Northern migration after World War I. Insights into decision making and alternate points of view also can be found through the use of simulations.

Simulation In role-play activities, the goal is to allow students to understand people, perspectives, and events by taking on the roles of particular individuals in specific situations. The goal of simulations is similar but more complex. Whereas role-play activities generally encompass short, tightly defined problem-solving situations, simulations allow students to experience a simplified version of reality over a more extended period. Role-play usually involves a small number of students at a time and generally is completed in a class period, whereas simulations are likely to involve many students over a period of days, weeks, or even months.

A role-play activity regarding international relations might involve a student portraying the president of Russia discussing with the president of the United States the nuclear capabilities of developing nations or terrorist groups. If several pairs of students portrayed the same situation, the activity might span approximately 45 minutes. A simulation on international relations would probably involve the entire class. Each student would have a role as a representative of a particular country. Representatives might be organized into delegations as part of a simulated United Nations. Students portraying developing nations could argue their right to nuclear protection at a meeting of the UN Security Council or other appropriate venue. Preparing for and conducting such activities could easily span several weeks.

Good simulations have a variety of roles that demand differing strengths and interests. Students address complex situations from points of view that vary with the needs and interests of their respective roles. It is important that the results of a simulation not be predetermined. Events should take place as a natural consequence of student actions. One common form of simulation is courtroom reenactments. These may range from very realistic portrayals to trials involving literary characters (Is Goldilocks guilty of breaking and entering? Who, in *Lord of the Flies* (Golding, 1999), is responsible for Piggie's death? Is Lady Macbeth guilty of murder?). The guilt or innocence of the character should be assessed by the jury based on the evidence presented. If one attorney does a better job arguing and preparing than the other, he or she is likely to win the case. Teachers may provide information on procedures or other necessary input, but they should not direct students' actions. Students should act as they believe their roles demand.

Lesson 8.16   War Room: A Simulation for High School

In this simulation, students learn about the impact of nationalism, imperialism, industrialism, militarism, and the secret web of alliances in the events leading up to World War I. Students are divided into groups representing different countries. Each group is provided with information: existing treaties, things their country knows, things the country wants, and things the country suspects but does not know. After a period of planning time, groups engage in "diplomatic activity." Groups are empowered to make alliances, dissolve alliances, plan for action in the event war breaks out, and so on. The teacher monitors treaties periodically and may choose to insert world events (preferably real) into the mix. After the simulation, students can examine the factors that influenced their decision making and how those were similar to or different from those that influenced nations at the time. (Adapted from a lesson by Darren Terry.)

Naturally, the depth and complexity of simulation that is appropriate for a group of students will vary with the age of the students and their familiarity with simulations and role-play. Primary-grade students may set up a simulated postal system that functions for several weeks or create a pioneer household that lasts only for a day. Older students may set up businesses, a banking system, or a simulated stock market. Some classes or even whole schools have created minisocieties, complete with currency, daily expenses, and employment for all students. In such minisocieties, students may spend a portion of each day earning the currency necessary to rent their desks or pay their portion of the lighting bill in classroom currency. Some may earn their hypothetical living as part of the government, others by operating banks or businesses, and still others as publishers. Minisocieties may operate for a few weeks or for most of the school year. It also is possible to simulate historical events. Students might take on roles of individuals organizing a party traveling westward or spend a day simulating life in an early schoolhouse.

Several interesting and challenging simulations are available commercially. However, not all materials labeled "simulation" actually involve students in important aspects of real life. Materials purporting to be simulations that involve students with dragons or talking space creatures probably have other goals. A number of simulations also are available online. Although computer simulations may not involve an entire class simultaneously, they allow students to experience the results of decisions that would be impossible or hazardous in real life. Computer simulations can allow students to affect their environment, travel to dangerous places, and conduct elaborate experiments that could not be managed in a school. With computers, students can build cities, manipulate gene pools, mix chemicals, or attempt to control environmental disasters without danger or enormous expense. For example, the PhET simulations, described under Tech Tips, allow physics experiments without additional materials—or danger. Students can also participate in simulations with students in other schools or countries. Interactive Communications and Simulations at the University of Michigan (ics.soe.umich.edu) links students around the globe in simulations that have included the Mideast conflicts, an environmental decisions simulation, and the creation of literary journals. The guidelines for assessing computer simulations are similar to those for other simulation materials. The simulation should present a version of reality that is simplified for students' use but is as complex and authentic as appropriate for the grade level. The results should be determined by students' participation and should be a natural consequence of students' actions and real-world forces, not primarily luck or chance.

Thinking About the Classroom

Plan a series of inductive, simulation, or role-play lessons for your class. Remember that it will probably take six or eight experiences with a new technique for you and the students to become comfortable with it. Do not give up if your first attempts are shaky.

Questioning and Strategies

In Chapter 6 we discussed helping students to become questioners. It is also important to think about the ways we use questions as part of our professional repertoire. Few skills are more important to any teacher than good questioning. Both the content strategies described in this chapter and the strategies for developing creative thinking described in Chapter 6 rely heavily on the use of questions. In particular, divergent questions, those with many possible appropriate responses, are at the heart of many activities that encourage creative thinking. After all, if the questions asked in school always have one and only one correct response, students are unlikely to believe that original ideas are valued or accepted. A complete discussion of questioning strategies is much too complex to be included here, but four key points may serve as reminders when you consider questioning strategies.

First, plan the purposes of your questioning. Many times, you may ask questions to determine whether students understand the content being discussed. However, questioning that focuses primarily on checking for understanding can lead students to believe every question is a quiz with the purpose of producing a single correct answer. In such an atmosphere, it is difficult to induce students to risk offering original ideas or opinions when they are desired. A balance of question types, including comprehension checks, questions in which students apply information, opinion questions, and "what if" questions, is more supportive of flexible student responses. If students have been taught the varied purposes of questioning, you can give them cues as to the purpose of a given activity: "I'd like to check to make sure this information is clear," "Let's talk for a minute about our own personal views on this subject," or "This time, let's really let our imaginations run wild." Such cues can help students anticipate the types of responses that are appropriate.

One purpose that can be particularly damaging to student creativity and learning is the use of questioning as a weapon. Regardless of the provocation, it is important not to use questions to bully or shame students. Although questions can appropriately be used to draw an inattentive student back into the conversation, it is important to do so in a way that maximizes the chances that the student can respond appropriately. Students who have been humiliated by pointed questioning are not likely to have a positive learning experience, nor are those who witnessed the humiliation. Such strategies are extremely detrimental to the atmosphere of acceptance and risk taking that supports creativity.

Second, consider the pacing of your questions. In a classic study, Rowe (1974) discovered that, on the average, less than a second passed between the time teachers asked a question and the time they asked another question, called on another student, or answered the question themselves. The use of wait time, a brief pause between the question and the response—typically 3 to 5 seconds— has been associated with increased student responses, more complex responses, and greater willingness to respond. If we hope to prompt diverse or original responses, it is only reasonable to give students some time to think of them. Few people do their best thinking under a barrage of rapid-fire questions.

Third, consider the distribution of your questions. Creative thinking is important for all students. Neither our society nor the global community can afford citizens who do not think flexibly and solve problems. Consequently, it is important that the questions prompting creative thinking are distributed equitably to all students. This is not as easy as it sounds. Many teachers distribute questions unequally, calling on boys more than girls, high achievers more than low achievers, majority students more than minority students, or students on one side of the room more than those on the other. Without some cues to assist you, such patterns are difficult to break. Some teachers pull students' names randomly from a collection of Popsicle sticks or index cards. Others record the names of students who respond in order to ensure more equitable distribution.

One additional advantage of random questioning—that is, asking a question and then randomly selecting a student to respond rather than choosing volunteers—is the message it sends about high expectations for all students. If teachers usually call on volunteers, students reasonably assume that if they do not volunteer, they are free of the responsibility to respond and need not necessarily concentrate on the lesson. The same message is conveyed when a teacher names the student to respond before asking the question. The question, "Bob, why do you think Castro continued to believe communism would succeed after the fall of communism in Europe?" allows everyone except Bob to breathe a sigh of relief without listening to the question. If, on the other hand, the teacher phrased the question, "Let's think for a moment, why do you think Castro continued to believe communism would succeed? . . . (wait time)" and then randomly chose a student to respond, all students would understand that they were expected to be prepared to answer.

Some teachers are concerned about calling on nonvolunteers for fear of embarrassing students who do not know the answer. Such concerns should be minimal with divergent questions, because there is no one correct response. Even so, some teachers are more comfortable allowing students a given number of pass responses per day. If a student is called on and genuinely has no response, he or she is allowed to say, "Pass," and the question goes to someone else. Limiting the number of these options per day makes it more likely that students will attend to the issue at hand and expect to think with creativity and care. Students who have difficulty focusing or are exceptionally anxious about questioning can be given cues that allow them to be prepared for a question, for example, "When I stand near your desk, you'll know I'm going to call on you next."

In addition to distributing questions equitably, make sure that you use probing and prompting responses equally for all students. Sometimes a student's initial response is unclear or incomplete. If only highly able or highly creative students are prompted for further responses, other students may come to believe they need not be concerned with questions that demand creative thought.

Thinking About the Classroom

Ask a colleague to observe your questioning technique. You might ask the observer to keep track of the number of boys and girls you question or the percentage of convergent and divergent questions you use. If the observer knows your class well, you might want him or her to note the number of high and low achievers you question. See what patterns of questioning you are using.

Fourth, remember that there is a difference between questioning and discussion. Both questioning and discussion are important classroom strategies. In questioning, most of the interaction is between the students and the teacher. The teacher asks a question, a student or students respond, and then another question is asked. In some kinds of questioning, there is a correct answer being sought. In a discussion, students talk both to the teacher and to each other. The teacher may ask a stimulus question, but the bulk of the responses and additional questions come from the students. The goal is to examine points of view or to reach consensus rather than identify a correct response. Discussion is an important classroom strategy that has particular value in communicating to students that diverse opinions and ideas are appreciated. This is an important distinction, particularly as it opens the possibility of uniqueness in student perspectives. If we want flexible thinking, we must be prepared for discussions that don't always go as planned. Beghetto (2007) found that prospective teachers reported they much preferred relevance to uniqueness in students' contributions to class discussions. While this is not surprising in inexperienced discussion leaders, it limits one of the key benefits of genuine classroom communication: exposure to new ideas.

The teacher's role in a discussion is to provide the stimulus question; paraphrase, summarize, or clarify student positions as needed; help to maintain focus; and draw the discussion to a close. True whole-class discussions are difficult to initiate and maintain. You may find that smaller discussions with partners or small groups may pave the way for larger efforts. Some teachers find that a no-hands rule helps students learn to listen to each other during discussion periods. If a teacher controls the discussion by calling on students with raised hands, a student with something to say may become more concerned with gaining the teacher's attention than following the course of the discussion. The no-hands rule simply states that no raised hands and no interruptions are allowed. Students must listen carefully to know when the speaker has completed a thought and another person may reasonably enter the discussion.

Finally, if you are interested in planning a discussion, a good discussion question is of prime importance. One good gauge for such a question is whether you, yourself, have an answer. If a question has a right answer, it may be more suited for a question-and-answer session. A good discussion question is one for which the discussion leader is truly seeking an answer, one that invites multiple perspectives. Walsh and Sattes (2015) suggest four ways teachers can plan for meaningful engagement in discussions:

- Framing questions that initiate and sustain student thinking and interactions
- Promoting the equitable participation of everyone involved in the discussion
- Scaffolding student responses to sustain and deepen thinking and understanding
- Creating a culture that supports thoughtful and respectful discourse

(p. 17)

Their book *Questioning for Classroom Discussion* is a good resource for teachers who want to think through the details of planning discussion and includes a number of protocols for adding variety and interest to students' interactions.

Content teaching provides many rich opportunities for encouraging creativity in students. The type of content we teach and the methods we use for doing so send messages to students about the types of learners and thinkers we expect them to be. Content and lessons that expect students to question as well as answer, investigate as well as comprehend, and identify problems as well as solve them allow students to learn important content while exercising their creativity—surely an unbeatable combination.

Thinking About It

1. Go to Steve Spangler Science (www.stevespanglerscience.com), Bill Nye the Science Guy (www.billnye.com), or another science activity website. Review several activities. How many include student questioning or students investigating questions? Which ones allow students to come closest to being scientists? Are there some activities you could "tweak" to allow more genuine investigations?

2. Not sure how to apply your math content to real-world problems? One source of inspiration is engineering projects designed for K–12 students. A place to start is the K–12 section of the American Society for Engineering Education website (www.asee.org/k12/index.cfm). Think about which projects might entail content that is part of your curriculum. The National Council of Teachers of Mathematics website (www.nctm.org/) also is a valuable resource.

3. To bring real-world real-time science and math content into your classroom, science blogs (which often include mathematics) can be valuable resources. You can find collections of blogs at scienceblogs.com or through the *Popular Science* or *Wired* websites.

Try It Tomorrow

In addition to the national math (www.nctm.org) and science education (www.nsta.org) sites discussed earlier, many math and science resources are available online, ranging from CSI to medieval science to the scale of the universe itself. Here, activities for Try It Tomorrow and Tech Tips blur together a bit, so read them all and see what strikes your fancy.

1. Let's start with an example for all the *CSI* fans out there. A variety of organizations have created materials for incorporating forensic investigations into science class. The materials available for free shift periodically, so you'll need to search to see what is available. Stem-Works has created a free set of materials in a 9-week course covering a wide gamut of forensics techniques. Reading the materials made me want to be in science class (stem-works.com/external/lesson_plan/175)!

   NOVA online has a whole collection of materials and lesson plans ready to download. You can find them and other similar materials with a simple search for "forensics in the classroom."

2. For an exploration that suits both math and science, explore the Scale of the Universe (htwins.net/scale2). Warning! The Scale of the Universe is addictive. You may have trouble pulling yourself away from this fascinating exploration of size, scale, and relationships. It takes a moment to load, but once it does, it presents items in order of size, from quantum foam, at 1×10^{-35} meters, to microbes, ants, giant earthworms, the Titanic, and the Tarantula Nebula, all the way to the estimated size of the observable universe at 9.3×10^{28} meters. Zoom up or down the range of sizes. Click on items to see their sizes and interesting snippets of information. Did you know that Gomez's Hamburger is a burger-shaped young star with light-reflecting dust buns? Or that if you eat a bowl of rice every day, you'll eat about 300 million grains of rice in your lifetime? Can you imagine molecules as huge? You can now.

   Even more amazing, the Scale of the Universe was created by Cary Huang, a 14-year-old ninth grader from Moraga, California, with technical help from his twin brother Michael. Inspired by a seventh-grade science teacher's video on the size of cells, Cary decided to create his own interactive version with "a wider range of sizes." That has to be some kind of understatement. What an example of students following their passion! Think about the math that could be utilized as your students create their own (likely much smaller) set of comparisons.

3. Yummy Math (www.yummymath.com) focuses on bringing real-world thinking and problem solving into the classroom. It is organized by math topic (probability, number sense, etc.) and also by subject areas, typical and not so typical. The thing I love about Yummy Math is that it doesn't just ask students to answer questions, it prompts them to create them. For example, a Veterans Day activity provides a moving chart of the number of veterans, types of service, and deaths in wars beginning with the American Revolution. The activity prompts: "Use the data above to create 3 questions to ask your class tomorrow. Your questions should help students understand the magnitude of American Veterans' service in our country."

   When students experience math in real-world contexts such as these, it not only enhances their learning, but it makes it possible for them to ask and answer original math-related questions.

Tech Tips

1. If you'd like to bring both fantasy and history to your science classes, Harry Potter's World: Renaissance Science, Magic, and Medicine (www.nlm.nih.gov/exhibition/harrypottersworld) presents an online exhibition of ideas from the wizard-world of Harry Potter and links them to Renaissance concepts in science and medicine. For example, the Herbology

section teaches that the screaming mandrakes that plagued young wizards in their herbology course were based on a Renaissance belief that mandrake roots resembled the human figure and possessed magical powers, including the fatal scream appearing in Harry Potter. The illustrations from early botanical writings look eerily Potter-esque. Aside from the literary ties, the site offers a glimpse into early science that can be a valuable part of science studies.

2. The PhET simulations (phet.colorado.edu) from the University of Colorado at Boulder present math and science content in ways that allow students to explore, experiment, and apply principles in a safe environment—nothing to spill, inadvertently combine, or explode when students follow their hunches to try new paths.

3. San Francisco's Exploratorium (www.exploratorium.edu) offers a wealth of interactive options to explore "science, art, and human perception." I particularly enjoy their explorations in the science and art of music. It makes me want to go out and create some sound!

4. And don't forget that NASA's Education section (www.nasa.gov/education) can bring both the universe and the life of a scientist to your classroom door. Click on the "For Educators" link for resources targeted to various grade levels.

9
Motivation, Creativity, and Classroom Organization

The art table in Joan's preschool was one of the most popular areas in the room. It was full of materials for a variety of projects. There was an adult nearby to supervise, and student efforts were always met with enthusiastic praise. Joan thought it strange that two of her students never went near the art table. For the first 3 months of school, neither David nor Diane touched the paints, crayons, scissors, or other available materials.

It was time for the yearly substance abuse essay contest sponsored by a local radio station, and Jim couldn't decide whether he wanted his class to be involved. He knew drug abuse was an important topic, and the contest did offer the opportunity for students to win gift certificates to local stores, but the contest never seemed to bring out the best in his students. In past years, the essays didn't seem particularly creative, and students seemed angry that no one from their class won a prize. Jim felt confused.

Mr. Monk's third-grade class was examining bean seeds. The students were to study the seeds and record their findings in their lab notebooks, including an illustration. Nancy had drawn her seed carefully and labeled each part: "baby," "blanket," "crib," and "bottle." When Mr. Monk came to her desk, he exclaimed, "Nancy, what are you doing? We don't have time for this kind of silliness in third grade—baby dolls belong in the kindergarten. I want the scientific names. Do this again, and this time use your science book."

It is not enough for students to know the content and skills that provide the grist and the mill for creativity. They also must have a secure space in which to create—a creativity-friendly classroom. A creativity-friendly classroom uses teaching strategies that are supportive of creativity, but it is more than that. It also provides an atmosphere in which it is safe to take creative risks and where exploring creative ideas and interests is a normal part of the classroom routine. This is the place in which students develop the motivation to be creative: the will, you might say, to turn the millstone. In this chapter, we will consider the type of classroom environment best suited to developing creativity and the many variables that go into creating it.

Creative Environments, Business, and the Classroom

Creativity can be found in all kinds of environments. Author Eric Weiner (2016) circled the globe, visiting places he called "historic places of genius," (p. 9), places creativity has flourished during particular eras. Weiner searched for commonalities in those places but found each largely unique, though each was characterized with diversity and some type of disorder (which should give us hope for our classrooms!) Even the most hostile environments can hold creativity within. In a visit to Prague some years ago, I saw artworks by children imprisoned in WWII concentration camps. I felt as if my heart would break with the beauty and tragedy on those pages. And certainly we've all heard stories of creative achievement against terrible odds. Yet no educator hopes for such circumstances for our students. Our goal is to consider the types of environments most likely to support and encourage young creators.

I will admit I've frequently railed against using business models to design and evaluate schools. There are so many ways schools and businesses are different that attempting to translate one to the other risks assuming children are some kind of consistent raw material that can be systematically transformed into a uniform product. And yet, when considering the types of environments in which creativity can flourish, business research has a lot to teach us. In 1998, Amabile published an article in *Harvard Business Review* titled "How to Kill Creativity." While its focus was on innovation in the business world, the problems described sound sadly relevant to schools. She describes businesses in which employees are mismatched with tasks, given little flexibility, faced with arbitrary or impossible deadlines, assigned to groups ill suited to tasks, and provided with little motivational (or sometimes material) support. Her suggestions for enhancing creativity are as applicable today as they were nearly 20 years ago.

Take, for example, her first recommendation: "Of all the things managers can do to stimulate creativity, perhaps the most efficacious is the deceptively simple task of matching people with the right assignments." Not surprisingly, assignments with too much or too little challenge afforded few options for creative insights. Sound familiar? Similarly, her recommendation that managers give choice in methods for problem solving fits a school environment. Like teachers, managers must set goals, but they can allow many ways to meet them. Without a sense of choice and autonomy, neither workers nor students are motivated to do their best.

If businesses want to succeed in today's innovation-focused economy, they need to think carefully about the work environments they create. Our needs are similar, though the available research on educational environments is sparser. Davies et al. (2013) reviewed the literature on creative learning environments and found that while there was not an abundance of research, the recommendations were not surprising: flexible use of space and time; availability of appropriate materials; working outside the classroom/school; "playful" or "games-bases" approaches with a degree of learner autonomy; respectful relationships between teachers and learners; opportunities for peer collaboration; partnerships with outside agencies; awareness of learners' needs; and non-prescriptive planning. As in the business world, students are more engaged when presented with a balance of challenge and support (Shernoff et al., 2016; Shernoff, Tonks, & Anderson, 2014). Shernoff, Tonks, and Anderson summarize:

> When students believe that what they are doing is important and has clear goals, they are more likely to interact with interest and absorb what is available in the classroom environment. When they additionally are supported to reach those goals, both emotionally (e.g., via support for autonomy and intrinsic interests and feeling understood by teachers and peers) and with timely performance feedback, they adopt attitudes characterized by excitement, fun, and interest in learning.
>
> (p. 174)

This enthusiasm, in turn, can lead to more creative responses. Creative thinking can be influenced by mood, with more positive mood leading to more creative responses (Yamada & Nagai, 2015). In one study, Chinese college students were given a divergent-thinking task, then, in an "incubation break," shown videos designed to induce a positive, negative, or neutral mood. Students in a positive mood had the highest originality scores, even higher than students who continued working without interruption (Hao, Liu, Ku, Hu, & Runco, 2015). When studying everyday creativity, Conner and Silvia (2015) tracked a large sample of young adults who rated their creativity and their emotional states over 13 days. The researchers found that positive emotions like feeling energetic, excited, and enthusiastic were most conducive to everyday creativity. Similarly, in a study subtitled "Play Some Music and Dance," Campion and Levita (2014) found that—as the title suggests—both dancing and listening to music improved mood and creativity. It makes me wonder what would happen to learning if we had periodic dance breaks in class!

Even the physical environment can affect students' creative participation—or participation at all. In one study, researchers found that simply changing the objects in a computer science classroom from those associated with male computer stereotypes (*Star Trek* posters, video games) to less stereotypical ones (nature posters, coffee maker) was enough to raise undergraduate females' interest in computer science. The male-stereotyped rooms left women feeling less interested and comfortable, even in a group of women (Cheryan, Plaut, Davies, & Steele, 2009). It is hard to be involved, take risks, or be creative when you don't feel you fit in. Recall from Chapter 1 that Mueller and colleagues found that when conditions became uncertain, individuals are less likely to generate creative ideas or even to recognize a creative solution when it is presented (2012). Stress and uncertainty appear to make creativity more difficult—just when it is likely to be needed most. Perhaps that is why Ding and colleagues found that creativity scores improved after short-term training in meditation (Ding, Tang, Tang, & Posner, 2014).

All this is consistent with Amabile's research on the environmental forces that drive creativity in organizations. Amabile and her colleagues studied the day-to-day experiences of workers in organizations focused on innovation by examining thousands of diary entries. They discovered a pattern they dubbed the Progress Principle.

> Of all the things that can boost emotions, motivation, and perceptions during a workday, the single most important is making progress in meaningful work. And the more frequently people experience that sense of progress, the more likely they are to be creatively productive in the long run. Whether they are trying to solve a major scientific mystery or simply produce a high-quality product or service, everyday progress—even a small win—can make all the difference in how they feel and perform.
>
> (Amabile & Kramer, 2011, paragraph 3)

This seems important to educators from several perspectives. If we want to be able to devise solutions to the very real problems faced in schools, we, the educators at all levels, need to unleash our own creative potential. And we are going to have a harder time doing that in uncertain environments. Amabile and Kramer continue:

> Early on, we realized that a central driver of creative, productive performance was the quality of a person's inner work life—the mix of emotions, motivations, and perceptions over the course of a workday. How happy workers feel; how motivated they are by an intrinsic interest in the work; how positively they view their organization, their management, their team, their work, and themselves—all these combine either to push them to higher levels of achievement or to drag them down.
>
> (paragraph 7)

Our "inner work lives" and those of our colleagues are major driving forces in the creativity and success of our work environments. While much of Amabile's writing is targeted at managers, we can have an important impact on our school or university environments through our own words and actions. Amabile and colleagues identified four types of triggers that can impact a workday: catalysts, nourishers, inhibitors, and toxins. As you might imagine, catalysts are actions that directly support the work. When you share materials with a new colleague or plan a new lesson with your professional learning community, you are providing catalysts to the work. Nourishers are actions that show respect or support. I still remember, 40 years later, a parent who periodically wrote notes commenting on class activities her son particularly enjoyed or a display she'd noticed in the hall. I was more enthusiastic about my job for days afterward. We can do that for each other. How often do we take time to express admiration for a colleague's work or celebrate with someone whose student showed improvement? Those small interactions really matter. They help us see the small "wins" that help us keep our creative motivation going.

Of course, those actions have their evil twins. Inhibitors are actions that actively inhibit the work, and toxins are discouraging or undermining events. Sadly, I suspect these are common enough I need not give examples. We may not be able to avoid the toxins in our environments, but we can resolve not to contribute to them. In creative work, a positive and supportive environment is much more effective than high-pressure or fear-based strategies of management. I know that many of the negative forces around us are outside our control. Fortunately, the Progress Principle tells us that small interactions and small victories can go a long way. We can be part of that progress by the ways we interact among ourselves.

We also can apply these principles with students. If we want students to be successful, particularly if we want to think creatively, solve problems, and engage in challenging tasks, they, too, must feel they are making progress in meaningful work. In Chapter 7, I talked about shaping curriculum around ideas that matter—helping the work become meaningful. But we also have to help students *see* their own progress and understand that their progress matters. We'll talk about feedback and assessments supportive of creativity later in this chapter and the next. But I also want to suggest that we may need to find ways to acknowledge progress toward goals we might not have chosen. Students who are thinking creatively may come up with ideas that take the discussion off our planned track, complete projects in ways we hadn't anticipated, or be so focused on their latest original video game or robotic prom float that they have a hard time concentrating on math or English. Of course we have to help them focus, but if, first, we take a minute to acknowledge the creative response as original and wonderful, look carefully at all the ways the unique project may have met our requirements, or listen a moment to excited stories about the latest maker-space adventure, it may change the classroom environment in important ways. Feeling successful makes everyone want to work harder. Feeling seen and valued makes students feel safe enough to try a new idea, take a risk, solve a problem. The small moments of recognition and support are not, in fact, small. They are the real stuff of human relationships that make classrooms work. They are all part of the principle behind the progress.

I know all this requires delicate balancing. In schools, time is a precious commodity. We cannot afford to waste it in activities that don't contribute to significant learning. But especially given what we now understand about the relationship between creativity and learning, we must be careful about trying to create classrooms that are "all business," especially now that we understand a stark or negative atmosphere isn't effective in business, either. There is a time for students to learn about organization, respect, and care. But this research tells us that a positive atmosphere—a place people want to be—makes a difference in their thinking. If we want to have students engage with content in multiple ways—to think creatively and flexibly—we must create spaces in which such things are possible. For example, Vass (2007) studied collaborative creative writing processes of British children ages 7 to 9. A key finding was the centrality of emotion to the creative process. She identified patterns of communication she labeled musing, acting out (playacting, not misbehaving), humor, and singing, all of which contributed to the creative endeavors. It is interesting to think how often those activities might be labeled "time wasters" as opposed to "creative stimuli." In addition to examining our classroom atmospheres, we may also want to consider how we, like the best business leaders, can communicate to students that we believe they have important contributions to make. This will help us create classrooms in which students are motivated to both learn and create.

Wagner (2012) describes a sequence of factors he believes build the intrinsic motivation for innovation—all alliteratively beginning with P: play, passion, and purpose. Playing with creative ideas is not just for children. It includes the playful exploration described as part of problem finding and more. Wagner quotes Joost Bronson of MIT, one of the United States' premier sources of innovative engineering.

> Being innovative is central to being human . . . We're curious and playful animals, until it's pounded out of us. Look at the tradition of pranks here at MIT. What did it take to put a police car on a dome that was fifteen stories high [one of the most famous MIT student pranks], with a locked trapdoor being the only access? It was an incredible engineering feat: They had to fabricate the car, get it to the base of the dome without getting caught—and then the real challenge was to get it to the top of the dome, and get yourself down without getting caught or hurting yourself. . . . Pranks reinforce the cultural ethos of creative joy.
>
> (p. 27)

While some might hope to avoid cars on the roofs of our school buildings, creating a "cultural ethos of creative joy" is part of our task, whatever level we teach. Do you hear echoes of Bloom's talent development stages here?

The second P, passion, is the center of intrinsic motivation. It drives us to explore, to learn, to conquer something difficult. Wagner identified passion for their ideas as central to the success of successful innovators. In schools, passion can often be sadly lacking. We help students find it through a careful balance of identifying the joy and excitement in the things they must learn and allowing them space to find the things they want to learn. Making room for choice and exploration in our standards-driven educational environment is not easy, but it is important.

The final P, purpose, can be thought of as a deeper and more sustainable form of passion. Purpose involves tasks that are not just interesting and exciting but have meaning. Remember David Sengeh, the young man described in Chapter 1, whose college study group developed lighting for Africa using buckets of dirt and water? Early in his high school years, David developed a sense of purpose in service, beginning with funding school supplies and malaria nets for Sierra Leone. Purpose helps us feel our struggles and creative efforts are worthwhile. Although Wagner suggests a developmental sequence from play in childhood to passion in adolescence to purpose in adulthood, I don't believe it is that clear-cut. I have known elementary school students driven by creative purpose—and I believe helping students find such purposes is one way we channel their creativity in positive directions. And so consider how your creativity-friendly classroom can build play, passion, and purpose in developmentally appropriate ways. As we do so, we build both the space and the motivation to create—making progress toward meaningful goals.

Recall from Chapter 1 that intrinsic motivation, along with more global motivation to learn, is an essential component of the Creativity in the Classroom model. We can look specifically at the motivation component of the model in Figure 9.1.

We also have seen that independence in judgment, willingness to take risks, and perseverance in self-chosen tasks are characteristics associated with creativity. We know that self-efficacy affects students' persistence—including in creative pursuits. If we are to enhance these traits in students, we must create classrooms that increase their autonomy and creative self-efficacy. If students are to be creative, they must begin to develop their own ideas, judgments, and interests instead of always pursuing paths forged by their teachers.

The remainder of this chapter considers ways to support and develop students' autonomy, self-efficacy, and intrinsic motivation in supportive environments—to create the creativity-friendly classrooms described in Chapter 6. It examines theories associated with intrinsic and extrinsic motivation, self-efficacy, classroom organization, and independent learning, each as they affect student motivation, autonomy, and creativity. It discusses how common classroom practices may undermine these goals and how such practices might be changed to support student independence, risk taking, and exploration. As you read, reflect on your own teaching practices. Look for opportunities to develop play, passion, and purpose. We'll continue the discussion in Chapter 10, examining how these factors relate to classroom assessment.

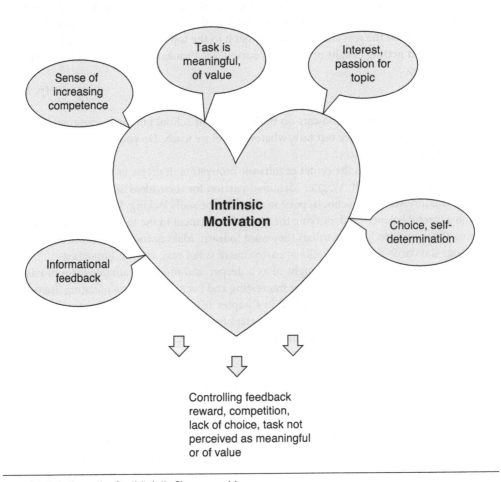

Figure 9.1 Motivation section, Creativity in the Classroom model

Psychological Safety, Intrinsic Motivation, and Flow

Psychological Safety

Rogers's (1962) concept of psychological safety, although not directly addressing the topic of motivation, expressed his understanding of the conditions necessary for an individual to develop creativity freely. Rogers, you recall from Chapter 3, believed that creativity is a natural product of healthy development but that it may be blocked by a person's need for psychological defenses. Whether an individual moves toward creativity and self-actualization can be affected by internal and external factors. In addition to the personal characteristics that enhance creative growth (such as openness to experience), Rogers believed that circumstances surrounding the individual affect his or her opportunities for creativity.

Rogers (1962) used the analogy of a farmer and a seed. Although farmers cannot force seeds to grow, they can provide the nurturing conditions that will permit the seed to develop its own potential. In the same way, teachers, therapists, and others hoping to promote human growth can establish the conditions of psychological safety that allow individuals to develop. Psychological safety is associated with three processes: acceptance of the individual, lack of external evaluation, and empathetic understanding. Think about how each of these is related to research on creative environments just described.

Acceptance of the individual as having unconditional worth is at the core of psychological safety. This type of acceptance means that whatever his or her current condition, the person is seen as having value and potential. Some individuals are fortunate enough to find this type of acceptance in a warm, loving family. In such situations, the individuals know that no matter what they do, they are loved. The love and acceptance are not tied to passing tests, winning ball games, or playing concerts; they are unconditional. Such acceptance is part of the "relatedness" that is an essential element of intrinsic motivation (Ryan & Deci, 2000).

It is impossible for any teacher to provide all the advantages of a loving home in a few hours each day. It is possible, however, to have a classroom in which students are valued just because they are there, a room in which all students, no matter what their current situation or behavior, are seen as having potential. Unconditional acceptance does not mean all student behavior is acceptable. The most loving families have rules and clear consequences when the rules are broken. However, even when the behavior is not acceptable, the child can feel accepted if he or she is treated with respect and dignity. It brings to mind a friend's young son who, when told by a school staff person that he was a "bad boy," replied, "No, I'm a good boy who sometimes makes bad choices." That young boy knew who he was—and that understanding is a gift we can give our students.

Unconditional acceptance can be manifested in many ways. Any act sending the message that students are important, valuable, and full of potential builds a foundation of psychological safety. Perhaps the most obvious type of acceptance is the teacher's willingness to examine student ideas, even when they initially appear strange or inappropriate. If Mr. Monk had asked Nancy to tell him about her illustration before he exploded, he could have determined whether her unusual labels came from a lack of understanding, inattention, or an attempt to use analogy to express the relationships among the seed parts. Nancy's use of this type of analogy could be a cue to both her understanding of content and her ability to express it in novel ways. Unfortunately, her teacher's rejection of her ideas make it less likely that Nancy will feel welcome to make similar connections in the future. Worse yet, Mr. Monk rejected not just the ideas but Nancy herself. By implying that such ideas were suitable only for a kindergarten student, he left Nancy feeling small, inadequate, and unhappy.

Most teachers would recognize Mr. Monk's behavior as unsupportive. However, other acts that undermine psychological safety may be less easily recognized. In a safe class, all students feel that they are important and that the teacher has high expectations for them. These expectations are manifested in equitable patterns of questioning, in literature that recognizes and honors the cultures represented in the class, and in classroom posters and illustrations that portray many kinds of students in positive ways. If students are to feel safe enough for exploration, risk taking, and challenge, they must feel that their teacher and the school accept students just like them. This type of classroom sends a message that says, "Of course, you are important. Of course, you'll work hard. I expect you'll make mistakes and some of your ideas will not work, but that's okay. I expect that you'll keep trying and eventually we'll all make it." If this message is sent to all students, regardless of achievement, gender, race, disability, family background, or any other factor, students have a chance to feel psychologically safe in school, whatever the rest of their lives may bring.

The second aspect of psychological safety is lack of external evaluation. Rogers (1962) believed that evaluation by external sources hinders psychological safety. It forces individuals to put up defenses and keeps them from being open to their own self-evaluation. Rogers believed that an internal locus of evaluation—the use of one's own judgment to determine the ultimate worth of a creative product—is a key to creative behavior. He made it clear that lack of evaluation does not mean lack of feedback or that outside evaluators cannot express opinions about creative efforts. Such opinions can be helpful. It does mean that the final determination about the value of a creative effort is most powerfully and safely determined by the creator.

This aspect of psychological safety poses challenges in schools. Few areas of life have more continuous outside evaluation than the classroom. Students are evaluated many times each day on numerous academic and behavioral variables. The teacher's challenge is to provide feedback and information on behaviors and ideas without leading students to believe that the only valid sources of evaluation are outside themselves. Later in this chapter, I'll discuss feedback as part of clear communication with students. Chapter 10 also discusses informational feedback and self-evaluation, essential elements in a total assessment effort.

The final aspect and pinnacle of psychological safety is empathetic understanding. Empathetic understanding goes one step beyond acceptance. It accepts not only who the person appears to be but also who he or she is inside. In empathetic understanding, we see the world from another's point of view, enter that person's private world, and still accept him or her. Empathetic understanding of all our students is a lofty goal, particularly for secondary teachers with enormous class loads, but it can allow students to feel safe and accepted in many difficult circumstances. For some students, a teacher's willingness to learn enough about them to see the world through their eyes may provide the key to both content learning and creative thinking.

Recall from the beginning of the chapter, the idea that affect matters—that creativity is most likely to occur in a positive supportive atmosphere—is at the heart of research on creativity in the business world. Traditionally, the word "businesslike" indicates an atmosphere that is far from the playfulness we associate with creativity. But for many businesses, innovation is essential to their success. Amabile, Barsade, Mueller, and Staw (2005) examined the relationship between affect (emotional environment) and creativity in seven different companies. The researchers found that positive affect is related to increased creativity; when employees have positive feelings about their work environment, they are more likely to have creative ideas. Additionally, when employees have creative ideas at work, they then feel more positive. Amabile et al. proposed an affect–creativity cycle in which positive affect leads to more freedom to have multiple ideas, which through incubation can lead to creativity, which leads to activity in the organization, which leads to more positive affect. A few years ago, Google opened an office in my hometown of Ann Arbor, Michigan. Local gossip was full of stories about the office: the free food, the lava lamps, the inflatable superheroes, and the relaxed atmosphere. Given Google's success, it is clearly doing something right, and Amabile et al.'s research would suggest that creating a positive atmosphere in which to work is one of the keys.

Thinking About the Classroom

Psychological safety requires that every child in your room feel accepted, important, and valued. Examine the images of children and adults found in your room. Consider those in textbooks, posters, calendars, and any other available materials. Think about the mixture of genders and races portrayed. Will it support psychological safety for all your students? Does it suggest you believe everyone has important things to contribute?

Intrinsic Motivation

As mentioned, some of Rogers's (1962) ideas about psychological safety—and, of course, Amabile et al.'s (2005) examination of affect and creativity—ring true in the context of research on intrinsic motivation. Intrinsic motivation comes from within, as a positive response to the task itself. It spurs a person to explore, to persist, and to achieve based on the satisfaction of the task. I note in Chapter 4 that interest, choice, relatedness, and a growing feeling of competence all contribute to an individual's intrinsic motivation regarding a particular activity. Extrinsic motivation arises from sources outside the task: evaluation, contracted for reward, external directives, and the like.

Researchers have examined factors affecting motivation in a variety of activities—some creative, others not. Several types of studies have reported the effects of external constraints on work that was originally motivated internally. Such constraints might include rewards, deadlines, and overt supervision. In a variety of circumstances, the imposition of external controls actually can decrease intrinsic motivation for the targeted task. In their classic study, Lepper, Greene, and Nisbet (1973) observed preschool students playing with magic markers. After identifying students who displayed a high level of interest in the markers, the researchers asked the students to draw some pictures with the markers. Some of the students were promised a reward if they drew the pictures; others were not. Afterward, the students who had been promised a reward demonstrated less interest in the markers than those who had drawn pictures without the promised reward. It was as if the students could conceive of no other reason to draw once they had drawn for a reward. Drawing for the sake of drawing no longer seemed worthwhile. Similar findings have been observed for varying constraints and target behaviors (Amabile, DeJong, & Lepper, 1976; Deci, 1971; Deci, Koestner, & Ryan, 2001a, 2001b; Lepper & Greene, 1975, 1978).

Taking cues from this body of research, Amabile (1987, 1989, 1996) and Collins and Amabile (1999) investigated the effects of factors affecting intrinsic motivation on creative tasks. If, as hypothesized, intrinsic motivation is an essential element of creativity, variables that decrease intrinsic motivation should also decrease the level of creativity displayed in a given task. Amabile's research has used varied types of information: retrospective reports of creative people gleaned from their writings, experimental studies of children and adults involved in creative tasks, and interviews and surveys in which individuals reflect on the factors affecting their creativity. In her studies, the creativity assessed was not a test score but the subject's response to an open-ended task or other real-world problem situation. A consensus of judges expert in the particular domain (consensual assessment) was used to evaluate the level of creativity in the responses. The experimental studies of children and adults generally involved the researchers' manipulating the circumstances under which individuals performed a creative task and assessing the responses. In one study, children were asked to tell stories from a picture book. One group was told they would be rewarded for this activity by having the opportunity to take a picture with a Polaroid camera. If they agreed to tell the story, they were allowed to take the pictures first and then complete the story task. Other children also took pictures and told stories but were simply presented with the activities as two unrelated things to do. Students who worked in the no-reward condition produced stories judged to be significantly more creative than those who told their stories for a reward (Amabile, Hennessey, & Grossman, 1986). These findings are similar to those from the Lepper et al. (1973) magic marker study, but they take the theory one step further. Whereas Lepper et al. documented the negative effects of reward on motivation toward a potentially creative activity, Amabile et al. (1986) found that the reward affected creativity itself. Numerous other studies had similar results (Amabile, 1996; Collins & Amabile, 1999; Hennessey, 2010, 2015, 2017).

Like virtually every other idea about creativity, Amabile's position on the importance of intrinsic motivation can be debated. Weisberg (1993) cited adult creators who were highly motivated by external rewards. Watson and Crick wanted the Nobel Prize for their modeling of DNA. Da Vinci, Michelangelo, Mozart, Dickens, and others frequently worked for commissions or contracts. Their creativity did not seem to be blunted by the promise of financial reward. Eisenberger and his colleagues, arguing from a behaviorist perspective, cited research in support of rewards increasing divergent thinking (Eisenberger, Armeli, & Pretz, 1998; Eisenberger & Cameron, 1996). Eisenberger and Shanock (2003) contend that the behavior leading to rewards matters—if individuals believe creativity will be rewarded, they will be more creative. If they believe more mundane responses will be rewarded, mundane responses will result. Cameron (2001) argued that negative effects of reward are very limited and that most rewards are not problematic. It is possible that the importance of internal motivation changes developmentally or varies by task or by discipline. Motivation to engage in long-term scientific enterprise seems likely to differ from motivation to complete a divergent-thinking exercise. Still, the overall relationship between creativity and intrinsic motivation seems important. A meta-analysis examining studies of intrinsic motivation and creativity conducted between 1990 and 2012 found that, overall, higher intrinsic motivation was associated with more creative products (De Jesus, Rus, Lens, & Imaginário, 2013).

As her research continued, Amabile (1993b, 1996, 2001) revised her original hypothesis. The original Intrinsic Motivation Hypothesis argued that any extrinsic motivation is detrimental to creativity. In 1996, Amabile proposed a revised Intrinsic Motivation Principle: "Intrinsic motivation is conducive to creativity; controlling extrinsic motivation is detrimental to creativity, but informational or enabling extrinsic motivation can be conducive particularly if initial levels of intrinsic motivation are high" (p. 119). That is, intrinsic motivation is supportive of creativity. Some types of extrinsic motivation are harmful to creativity; some are not. Of course, our task is to determine which is which and how best to use them in classrooms.

The key distinction between good and bad extrinsic motivation, at least in so far as it affects creativity, may be the degree to which the extrinsic factors are controlling or informational. This can make the difference between motivation that is extrinsic but goal driven (motivation to learn) and motivation that is driven entirely by factors outside the individual. Controlling extrinsic motivation is the driving force behind an activity, perhaps the only reason it is undertaken. Classrooms that operate under a constant threat of tests and grades are centering on controlling extrinsic motivation. So are those that focus students' attention primarily on prizes, stars, or accolades rather than on learning. Praise that is doled out to good students without a clear indication of what they did well can have a similar effect. Students may expend so much energy figuring out how to get the praise that they have less left for creative thinking—or learning. Global praise may be particularly damaging for students with low self-esteem. In one study, researchers found that, particularly among students with low self-esteem, what they termed "person praise," which included general statements like "You are great," can backfire in the face of failure, causing students to feel greater shame (Brummelman et al., 2014). If the student—as a person—was "great" after a success, they felt less than great after a failure. Since creativity requires risk taking and perseverance in the face of disappointment, anything that makes failure feel humiliating is a problem.

Praise that gives students information about what they did well and enhances their sense of competence is less detrimental. We know that making progress toward meaningful goals is motivating, so information about that progress can be helpful. The more broad and obvious the external motivation, the more problematic it is. A 3-foot trophy in the front of the classroom for the most creative story is likely to shift students' focus from their stories to the trophy. This is unlikely to enhance creative thinking. The prize has become the controlling factor in this situation.

Using a series of studies varying the circumstances under which subjects pursued diverse creative tasks, Amabile (1989, 1996) and Collins and Amabile (1999) identified five factors that affected creativity, particularly in children. These factors have two key attributes: (a) They have been associated with reduced student creativity and (b) they are a major part of many classroom cultures. The factors are evaluation, surveillance, reward, competition, and lack of choice. In this discussion, I examine how they may affect motivation in complex ways and how that may impact students.

I must admit that the first time I read Amabile's (1989) research, I felt discouraged. Developing creativity in classrooms is important to me, yet some of the factors she designated creativity killers are so much a part of the ebb and flow of classroom life that I began to wonder if I were working for an impossible dream. As research continued and it became evident that motivation and creativity interact in more complex ways than originally thought, I felt less discouraged—but possibly more confused! The key when considering this research is to refrain from trying to determine how to eliminate these factors from our classrooms. Few teachers will be able to eliminate all evaluation or rewards, and probably few would want to. What we can do is think carefully about the ways these factors operate in our classes and do what we can to minimize their detrimental effects on students' intrinsic motivation and creativity.

The first two factors to be considered are evaluation and surveillance. There is evidence that students whose creative efforts are evaluated express less creativity in their next efforts even if the evaluations are positive. This observation immediately brings to mind Rogers's (1962) ideas about evaluation and psychological safety. According to this theory, external evaluation forces individuals to put up defenses and makes them less open to creative ideas. Rogers's theory suggests that evaluation makes individuals less motivated to explore multiple ideas and possibilities. Regardless of the mechanism, the results are the same: Evaluation can have an inhibiting effect on creativity.

The story of Joan's preschool art table at the beginning of the chapter illustrates this effect. After reading research on intrinsic motivation, Joan decided to see what would happen if she eliminated evaluative comments on the children's artwork. She met with the preschool staff and volunteers and decided to make two changes. First, there would no longer be an adult seated at the art table. Adults would be available for assistance if needed, and they would continue to ensure that materials were used safely, but they would do so from a distance. Some studies have shown that close surveillance of individuals inhibits their creativity, possibly because it makes them feel as though they are being evaluated even if they are not. The second change was in the types of comments made to students. Rather than comments that implied evaluation such as "Good job!" or "What a nice picture," adults would limit themselves to descriptive comments such as "I see you used a lot of blue today." If they were asked directly whether they liked a picture, the adults were to turn the question around and ask the student how he or she liked it.

The results of these simple changes were remarkable. Within a week, the two students who had avoided art activities for months were both active at the art table. One student, Diane, was obviously nervous at her first attempt. She kept glancing over her shoulder to see if any adults were watching; the adults all studiously averted their eyes. When she completed her first painting, she brought it to the teacher for assessment. When it became clear her teacher was not going to pass judgment on her work, Diane heaved a sigh and returned to work. There were no further difficulties with students avoiding art activities.

Certainly, we cannot expect students to improve in their creative efforts, in visual arts or any other area, without feedback. Our goal can be to provide the type and timing of feedback that are most helpful. One consideration is the student's maturity and level of expertise. Bloom's (1985) first-level students' greatest need was to fall in love with the subjects. Second-level students needed to develop discipline and technique appropriate to the content area. Certainly, the types of feedback appropriate at these two stages differ. However, even when evaluative feedback is necessary, the type of feedback makes a difference. Just as praise can be either informational or controlling, so can other types of feedback (Amabile, 1989, 1996). Controlling, also called evaluative, feedback lets students know how the teacher assesses their progress. It answers the students' frequent question, "How did I do?" In controlling feedback, the teacher is the primary and usually the sole judge of students' success or failure. Students are told "A" or "Good work!" or "You can do better than this" or even "I'm disappointed in you." Such comments clearly let students know where they stand in the teacher's eyes and probably how they stand in relation to others in the class. They do not, however, give students any information that will help them learn much except "I'm a success" or "I'm not." This type of feedback can be called controlling because the teacher is the arbiter of good and bad, successful and not successful, valuable and not valuable.

Informational feedback assumes that students are in charge of organizing and evaluating their own learning. It provides useful information for their guidance. It addresses the questions "What did you learn?" and "Which parts of this can help you learn more?" For example, "Good work!" is controlling. It tells students that their work was good but not what made it good or how to make it better. Students are no better informed or able to learn after receiving the comment than they were before. Compare that comment to the following: "The character of Danny was really believable. His dialogue was realistic and sounded just like a real 12-year-old." "The description of the forest on page 2 became a bit wordy. Try to paint a clear picture with fewer, well-chosen words." "Good work multiplying fractions. You seem to be having some trouble with division. Read page 67 again; then see me." A note asking students to "Look at this one and compare it to example 5" or "Try this part again focusing on the number of pulleys" provokes a very different response from the response to a giant red X or an F at the top of the page. In each case, the feedback provided students with specific information about what made them successful or how they might succeed in the future. Value judgments clearly are not being made about students as individuals but about the strengths and weaknesses of various aspects of their work. Informational feedback also provides gauges against which students can assess their own work. If Alex knows that his last description was wordy, he can try next time to be more precise and economical with his writing. In a classroom atmosphere of acceptance, such comments can be considered valuable help rather than personal judgments or threats to self-esteem.

Wiggins (2012) makes a helpful distinction between feedback and advice. Advice simply tells someone what to do, for example, "You need more descriptive language here." There are three features that help clarify the difference. First, feedback reflects the learner's current effort in relationship to a particular goal, as demonstrated by the following statement: "Remember that the goal in describing the setting is to help the reader picture the place. Often, like in your ghost story, you want the reader to feel something. When you are describing walking through the woods, think about words that would help the readers see a picture—and maybe feel scared, too."

Second, informational feedback gives information as to what to do next time, even when students are successful. "Great job! A+" may make a student feel momentarily pleased, but it doesn't give any helpful information. Consider instead the information provided by the following: "You did an exceptional job locating both primary and secondary sources that related to your topic.

Your analysis of the two letters clearly tied to your main points and also made the soldiers feel very real. It is not easy to write a report that is both accurate and moving, but you did just that." In this case the student knows she did a fine job, and she also knows which aspects of her report were exceptional.

Finally, for feedback to be effective, students need to be willing and able to act on it. This means that feedback must be part of ongoing formative assessment that occurs during instruction, while students have a chance to improve their performance, rather than solely at the end, when the product is complete. It also means that the amount and type of feedback need to be carefully gauged. A paper covered with red "feedback" is no more help than a traditionally graded paper if the result is that the student feels overwhelmed and discouraged. Tackle one or two goals at a time. Particularly with struggling learners, it is better to give clear, focused feedback that helps students improve in one area rather than attempt to perfect everything simultaneously. Deciding to focus on descriptive language and capitalization doesn't mean you'll never work on quotation marks—just that you will do it another day.

Like so much about creativity, shaping our evaluation in ways that support creativity is also supportive of learning. Stiggins's concept of assessment *for* learning (as opposed to assessment *of* learning; Stiggins, Arter, Chappuis, & Chappuis, 2006) describes ways assessment can be used to facilitate students' learning, including formative assessment with clear informational feedback (see, for example, Brookhart, 2007/2008, 2012; Chappuis & Chappuis, 2007/2008; Chappuis, 2012; Fisher & Frey, 2012). This type of feedback can send two kinds of messages: "Here is what you need to do" and "I know you can do it." It supports both students' learning and their motivation for creativity. More information on formative assessment—and assessment *for* creativity—is found in Chapter 10.

As more information is gathered about the interactions of evaluation, motivation, and creativity, increased complexity emerges (Amabile, 1996; Hennessey, 2015, 2017). The prospect of evaluation may depress creativity in shy students more than in less shy students, in less-skilled students more than in more-skilled students, in students of some cultures more than others. Effects may vary with the activities that precede the creative effort. Yuan and Zhou (2008) found that the impact of evaluation differed depending on which part of the creative process was being evaluated. As the research continues to emerge, it seems sensible to work toward informational rather than controlling feedback in our classroom interactions. It seems likely that it will enhance creativity—and it is certain to be more helpful to our students in their efforts to improve.

Thinking About the Classroom

Look through a stack of papers you corrected recently, preferably those that required some creativity on the part of students. Check to see how often you used controlling versus informational feedback. Try to add informational feedback where necessary.

The second, frequently related threat to creativity is reward. In many ways this idea runs counter to our intuition, and the role of reward has been subject to considerable debate (Cameron, 2001; Deci et al., 2001a, 2001b). Students like rewards and frequently work hard to receive them. Elementary school teachers have kept sticker companies in business for many years, and secondary school students frequently have been enticed with class parties, honor rolls, and a variety of special privileges. Unfortunately, research tells us that rewards, when promised before a creative effort, can diminish both the motivation to continue similar activities later and the creativity of the activity itself. This can be called contracted-for reward—a reward that becomes the purpose of the activity. Jim, whose dilemma about the substance abuse essay contest was described at the beginning of the chapter, may well have cause for concern. Students who are writing with the possibility of a prize uppermost in their minds may not only produce less creative essays now but also may be even less inclined to write later when there is no possibility of reward.

There is a place for rewards in school. There is some evidence that individuals pursuing simple, straightforward tasks or practicing tasks already learned perform better and faster for promised rewards. I suspect I would do a much better job at housecleaning if someone were to pay me for doing it. It also is likely that students practicing math computation, handwriting, French verb conjugations, or grammar drills may benefit from some system of rewards. Rewards also may be effective for some students with learning difficulties or a history of school failure. There is even evidence to suggest that reward may be helpful in straightforward divergent-thinking tasks such as coming up with multiple uses for an object or multiple ways to use a shape (Eisenberger & Cameron, 1996). However, for complex tasks involving problem solving or creativity, rewards often can be counterproductive, and there is some evidence that the negative effect is more pronounced in children (Deci et al., 2001a). Such tasks generally should be interesting and motivating in themselves. To reward students is to imply that the tasks are dull, to suggest that without an external stimulus there is no reason students would want to think, experiment, or explore these ideas. Like seemingly all variables related to creativity, interactions can be complicated and may vary by culture and context. For example, Hennessey (2015) described cultural differences in the relationship between reward and motivation when viewing U.S. versus Saudi students.

There are times when you may want to reward an especially creative effort. If a reward is occasionally presented after the fact as a pleasant surprise rather than regularly as an expected payoff, it should not negatively affect student motivation. There is some evidence that unexpected rewards may even have a positive influence on creativity (Amabile, 1996). You also may want to devise rewards that point out the inherent value and interest of the task itself. Students who write an excellent story may be rewarded with the opportunity (not the assignment) to spend extra time in writing. Those who devise a particularly original experiment may be allowed to earn more time in the science room. Outstanding art projects may be rewarded with the opportunity to create a personal gallery or compile a special portfolio. These strategies send the message that creative activities are interesting and valuable and that participating in them is reward in itself.

Fortunately, studies have shown that just as we can use inoculations to protect children from disease, we can apply immunizing strategies to minimize the detrimental effects of reward or other extrinsic motivators (Amabile, 1993a, 1996; Hennessey, 2017). In one study, students viewed a video in which children and an adult discussed the things the children enjoyed about school. The children served as models of intrinsic motivation, explaining which subjects they enjoyed and the pleasure they obtained from learning. When they were questioned about grades, they stated that good grades were nice, but the really important thing was learning. Exposure to this modeling appeared to protect students from the negative effects of reward, perhaps by limiting its effect as a controller. Presented with a creative task, the students who had received the training did not decline in creativity when they were offered a reward, unlike the students who had not seen the videotape. In fact, students who had seen the videotape were more creative in their products when promised a reward. In this circumstance, intrinsic and extrinsic motivations seemed to work together. If we have similar conversations with students, emphasizing the interesting aspects of a task and minimizing the importance of extrinsic motivators, we may have similar results. Repeated references to tests, grades, prizes, or other external rewards, particularly with students engaged in creative tasks, are likely to have the opposite effect.

Thinking About the Classroom

In Chapter 4, you may have made a list of the strategies you used to motivate students in your classroom during the course of a week. If not, try it now. See what proportions of intrinsic and extrinsic motivations you used. Examine the types of motivation you used for different types of tasks. Are you using the same motivation strategies for both creative and mundane tasks? Do you notice any differences in the ways boys and girls respond to your motivators?

A different take on reward comes from Odyssey of the Mind's Ranatra Fusca Creativity Award. The award goes to a team whose entry demonstrates exceptional creativity, regardless of whether it is successful in solving the competition problem. The prize is named after a classification of water spider. It commemorates a vehicle built by students at Glassboro State College in a flotation device competition. The flotation devices were supposed to cross a body of water. Instead of being powered by the usual paddle wheels or sails, the Glassboro entry was designed to walk across the water like a water spider. It capsized before completing the crossing but did so spectacularly and with considerable originality (Micklus & Micklus, 1986). Prizes such as the Ranatra Fusca may give students a very different idea about rewards!

The fourth problematic factor frequently found in classrooms also is a part of Jim's essay contest dilemma: competition. However, as should be clear by now, the relationships are not straightforward. In two studies, one with children and one with adults, individuals produced less creative products in a competitive situation than in a noncompetitive situation (Amabile, 1982a, 1987). Two subsequent studies indicated that girls may be more negatively affected by competition than boys and that boys may even show higher levels of creativity in some competitive situations (Conti, Collins, & Picariello, 1995, cited in Amabile, 1996). In the world of work, there is some evidence that within-group competition is associated with lower levels of creativity, whereas between-group competition is associated with greater creativity (Amabile, 1988a, 1988b; Amabile & Gryskiewicz, 1987). Competitions in creative problem solving such as Future Problem Solving or Destination ImagiNation count on between-group competition to enhance teams' creative efforts. Competition also may be less problematic for individuals who have already developed strong intrinsic motivation. For example, the talented pianists studied by Bloom (1985) encountered many competitions in their career paths.

Finally, the last common classroom factor that can inhibit creativity is lack of choice. Collins and Amabile (1999) put it bluntly: "The best way to help people maximize their creative potential is to allow them to do something they love" (p. 305). Can you hear Amabile's Progress Principle here? Unfortunately, it is easy for students to go through years of schooling without ever having the opportunity to make meaningful choices about their learning. I have talked to many students about independent study opportunities, asking them what they would like to learn about if they could study anything they liked. On far too many occasions, such students have gazed at me as if I were from another planet. They simply could not conceive of learning anything voluntarily. Learning was something you did when it was assigned. In school, one learned what the teacher said to learn when the teacher said to learn it. Period.

Students can experience choice in school in a wide range of areas. They can have input into the class rules. They can plan games for the class parties or the destination for the yearly field trip. They can help determine the curriculum focus for particular units and pursue short- and long-term projects around individual interests. Choices don't need to be huge. Recently a young educator friend called me, excited at the success of her new middle school homework policy. She assigned five different assignments for the week, of which students were to choose three. Suddenly her homework-hating students were thoughtfully considering which of the offered options they should complete. The easiest three? The ones on topics that puzzle them? Some combination? Feeling in control of their learning made a difference in their attitude toward the assignments. And they are doing their homework! Kohn (1993) suggested that increasing student choice affects both students' attitudes and their achievement. Although much research remains to be done, the suggestion is eminently logical. If students are allowed choice in learning tasks, they may work harder and learn more than when tasks are consistently imposed from outside. Once again, a strategy that enhances students' creative thinking may increase their learning as well.

Pink (2009) describes a fascinating example of the impact of choice in the business world: Google's "20% time," in which engineers are encouraged to spend one day a week working on a project of their own choosing. According to Pink, more than half of Google's new ideas in a given year come from the 20% time, including Google News, Gmail, and Google Translate. Although most teachers don't have the flexibility to offer 20% choice time, there are structures that can support increased student choice, including classroom centers or schoolwide enrichment clusters in which students gather weekly to work on problems of mutual interest (Renzulli, Gentry, & Reis, 2014).

Older students may be more adept at individual research, but even young children can plan and pursue individual goals. One of my graduate students decided to let each of her kindergarten students pick one thing he or she would most like to investigate. They collected all the ideas, and she promised that before the school year was over, she would help each student learn more about his or her choice. Because she had two half-day kindergartens and more than 50 students, this effort took most of the school year. Projects ranged from learning how to bake a cake (they did, and the class enjoyed it) to investigating which animals run fast. Each project was photographed and recorded in a class album. Her students certainly learned much interesting content that year, but I believe the most valuable lessons were these: You may choose to learn about something you like and learn about it. Learning things you want to learn is fun! More information on choice in assessment is found in Chapter 10.

Thinking About the Classroom

In your next unit, think about how you could incorporate more choice into student activities. Plan at least one set of activities that allows students to select topics for further study.

At this point, the research regarding intrinsic motivation and creativity is complex (Hennessey, 2010, 2015, 2017). There is a considerable body of research suggesting that intrinsic motivation enhances creativity and that many sources of extrinsic motivation depress it. But it is not quite that simple. Where intrinsic motivation is well established, for example, in adult professional artists, a promised reward may not be detrimental (for which any institution commissioning an artwork can be grateful). It is possible that different types of motivation may be necessary at different stages of the creative process. Where the flexibility demanded in the initial stages of problem finding and idea generation might be best instigated by intrinsic motivation, the persistence necessary to continue a long-term creative project may benefit from the judicious use of external motivators. Certainly, many writers may get through difficult periods thinking about deadlines and promised royalties, even though those factors are not likely to be the ones supporting good problem finding.

Similarly, students engaged in a lengthy science project will be best served by a focus on interest and choice when engaged in selecting a project but may be encouraged 3 weeks into data gathering by the impending science fair. Some research suggests that the impact of intrinsic versus extrinsic motivators may vary by personality characteristic or gender, with girls more likely to be negatively affected by extrinsic motivators than boys (Amabile, 1996; Baer, 1998). "Immunization" research tells us that the conversations we have about the intrinsic and extrinsic motivators in school life influence the impact of the motivators on all students. Our daily talk about joy in learning or learning for reward has far-reaching consequences.

Grant and Berry (2011) found that in work environments, the relationship between intrinsic motivation and creativity is enhanced by prosocial motivation, or desiring to solve problems in a way that is useful to others. And research continues to examine how motivation interacts with environmental variables across cultures. As noted, Hennessey (2015) found differences in the impact of reward between U.S. and Saudi students. Hong, O'Neil, and Peng (2016) examined two different varieties of intrinsic motivation in Chinese students: motivation to do creative work and motivation to do challenging work. Not surprisingly, students who reported interest in doing creative work produced more original homework results. However, students who reported they enjoyed challenging work were less creative in their homework assignments—in fact, the more students reportedly enjoyed challenge, the less creative the homework. Maralani (2016) investigated the impact of a "creative educational environment" on both intrinsic and extrinsic motivation in female college students in Iran. In this study, a creative educational environment included freedom, supporting ideas with information, discussion, humor, risk, vitality and dynamism, contrast, and confidence. In such an environment, it was found, both intrinsic and extrinsic motivation were higher. What more could a teacher want?

The concept of motivational synergy suggests that there are times when intrinsic and extrinsic factors can come together in beneficial ways. If rewards and recognition are used in ways that confirm competence and provide information, without undermining a sense of self-determination, they may contribute to later intrinsic motivation. I observed such an incident when a friend's teenage son won special recognition for his writing at an end-of-school-year ceremony. This bright, creative young man has learning difficulties that have caused him to struggle in school. To his family's astonishment, he spent the entire summer after that award working on his writing. When questioned by a friend he replied, "Well, I'm a writer, you know." This incident illustrates the paradox of rewards and other extrinsic motivators. In many circumstances, they diminish both motivation and creative responses. Certainly, if this young man had been encouraged to write in order to enter a writing contest, he likely would have responded with characteristic reluctance and minimal creative energy. However, in this case, a wise teacher understood that public recognition of his blossoming talent—as a joyous surprise rather than a contracted-for reward—would help forge his identity as a creative writer. Finding the balance of intrinsic and extrinsic factors that best enhances your students' creativity will take similar wisdom, balance, and careful observation.

Creative Self-Efficacy

In Chapter 4, the concept of self-efficacy (Bandura, 1977, 1986) was tied to intrinsic motivation. Recall that self-efficacy referred to our level of confidence in our ability to perform a particular behavior. Self-efficacy affects which activities we attempt, how much energy we put into them, and how much we persist when things go wrong. As I have taken mosaic classes for the last few years, I have grown in self-efficacy regarding mosaic problems. If something goes wrong, I usually believe I can fix it—and I do. On the other hand, I have virtually no self-efficacy regarding my ability to hit a ball with a bat. I avoid situations in which I might be pressed into playing ball, and when I (yet again) miss the ball, I'm ever more anxious to avoid a repetition. Not surprisingly, I don't get any better at baseball.

So how did I grow in self-efficacy in my mosaic efforts? My first moments in the studio were daunting, to say the least. At that point I had virtually no confidence in my abilities, but I really wanted a mosaic mirror, so with considerable trepidation, I signed up for a community education class. My experiences there reflect Bandura's (1977) description of the sources that build self-efficacy. The most powerful experiences, not surprisingly, entail actually accomplishing the behavior, or *performance accomplishments*. In my case, when my first small mosaic was successfully completed, I was amazed, delighted, and anxious to do another one. My self-efficacy regarding mosaics had skyrocketed in that one experience. I'd also had two other important contributors to my self-efficacy. The first was *vicarious experiences*. I had watched other students in the studio make mosaics, many with no more experience than I had. Watching them surmount difficulties and succeed increased my belief that I could do the same. Watching other beginners was a much more powerful source of efficacy than watching my teacher, because her skill level was too far above my own to "count." Watching professional baseball players does nothing to increase my self-efficacy regarding ball playing. I would have to watch someone succeed whose skills are as limited as mine—a challenging task, indeed! My third source of efficacy information was what Bandura terms *verbal persuasion*. Although not as powerful as accomplishing the task myself or watching others do it, encouraging comments from my teacher (whose mantra is, "There is nothing that can't be fixed") and fellow students helped me overcome my initial lack of confidence.

All types of self-efficacy are task/discipline specific. *Creative self-efficacy* refers to a level of confidence in one's ability to accomplish creative tasks. Like other kinds of self-efficacy, the higher an individual's creative self-efficacy, the more likely that person will attempt creative endeavors and persist until he or she succeeds (see, for example, Tierney & Farmer, 2002). Creative self-efficacy will vary across disciplines or even subdisciplines. For example, my level of creative self-efficacy regarding mosaics is vastly different from my self-efficacy regarding representational drawing or metal sculpture. Within our classrooms, we will have students at all levels of creative self-efficacy across a range of subject areas. Students with high creative self-efficacy will be much more likely to attempt creative tasks, engage fully, and persist when they encounter difficulties. Students without much creative self-efficacy are more likely to resist, do a minimal job, and give up in discouragement at the first sign of difficulty. Working toward greater creative opportunities can help, sometimes in unexpected ways.

All of us have had experiences in which our classmates and colleagues have influenced the ways we think about ourselves. Sometimes being surrounded by highly successful people can be discouraging—we feel less successful by comparison. Sometimes we can be the "big fish," the best at something within our small sphere, and come to have great confidence in our abilities. This is sometimes called the Big Fish Little Pond Effect (BFLPE), when being surrounded by less-successful colleagues raises our confidence. One study investigated these phenomena regarding creative self-efficacy among Polish middle school students. What they found was the opposite, BFSPE—when students were in classes where classmates scored higher on creativity, their own creative self-efficacy was stronger (Karwowski, 2015). I suspect the dynamic might resemble my mosaic class—as I'm in an encouraging environment, surrounded by creative activities, more and more seems possible, so I keep trying.

As we consider the importance of having students engage in challenging creative tasks, creative self-efficacy becomes extremely important. Structuring these experiences so that all students experience initial success in smaller creative tasks before attempting large ones, providing models of a variety of paths to success, and pointing out positive steps forward can help students build the self-efficacy they need to persist and succeed. This can mean carefully structuring larger creative tasks into sections rather than handing over the entire task and letting students "sink or swim." For example, imagine that you were having students build a Rube Goldberg-type machine to represent a system of the human body. If you segment the project into (1) drawing a plan and explaining how it represents the system, (2) creating a materials list and experimenting with different options, (3) building the machine, and (4) presenting an explanation for how each aspect of the system has been represented, several things are accomplished. First, of course, you help students work through the project in a systematic manner rather than leaving everything until the last moment. You create multiple opportunities for formative assessment (see Chapter 10) so that if students need redirection, it occurs before the final product. You also create opportunities to build creative self-efficacy as students experience multiple small successes and watch peers do the same.

Flow

Pursuing tasks because they are fun may seem to be a frivolous objective. Yet if we think for more than a moment, we will realize that helping students learn ways to find happiness and to lead lives that are more meaningful, satisfying, or growth promoting may not just be a goal but rather *the* goal of school. Csikszentmihalyi (1990a) summarized decades of research examining happiness, focusing on the concept of optimal experience. Optimal experience is hard to describe yet easy to imagine. It encompasses those moments when one feels life is in focus, exhilarating, and satisfying. For some, it may be the moment they attain the summit of a mountain. For others, it may be understanding how the melodies of a symphony come together in a unified whole, feeling the colors on a canvas become something new, or experiencing the birth of a child. Each of these experiences adds to our richness and complexity as human beings. In a sense, it helps us create ourselves. In describing these moments, Csikszentmihalyi (1990a) wrote,

> Happiness is not something that happens. It is not the result of good fortune or random chance. It is not something that money can buy or power can command. It does not depend on outside events, but rather on how we interpret them. Happiness, in fact, is a condition that must be prepared for, cultivated, and defended privately by each person. People who learn to control inner experience will be able to determine the quality of their lives, which is as close as any of us can come to being happy.
>
> (p. 2)

Csikszentmihalyi's (1990a) research on optimal experiences began with interviews of thousands of people in all walks of life: adults in Thailand, teenagers in Tokyo, farmers in the Italian Alps, assembly-line workers in Chicago, and others. Later, his research team developed the Experience Sampling Method, which involved having subjects wear electronic pagers for a week and writing down what they were doing and how they felt when the pager signaled. From this enormous collection of data emerged the concept of flow, "the state in which people are so involved in an activity that nothing else seems to matter; the experience itself is so enjoyable that people will do it even at great cost, for the sheer sake of doing it" (Csikszentmihalyi, 1990a, p. 4).

The search for flow may be at the heart of much human discontent. For that reason alone, it seems worthy of further consideration. It certainly is related to intrinsic motivation. In fact, flow may be seen as the ultimate example of intrinsic motivation. It also seems to have ties to creativity. Many of the activities that traditionally elicit flow entail creative behavior. Artists painting, musicians practicing, and scientists absorbed in their work are classic examples of individuals in flow. In this discussion, I briefly examine the nature of flow and the conditions that allow it to occur and then consider how these variables operate in classrooms.

Csikszentmihalyi (1990a) described the researchers' surprise at the uniformity of the flow experience in widely varying cultures and activities. The subjects may have been doing very different things—sailing, meditating, painting, or working on an assembly line—but the feelings they described when the activities were at their best had remarkable similarity. Moreover, the reasons they enjoyed the activities also showed many similarities. When these key components were present, the activities caused such a deep sense of enjoyment in people that they were willing to expend enormous amounts of energy just to have the experience.

One cluster of elements found in most flow experiences was that the activities were not random but goal-directed activities that demanded some type of energy and skill (there's the Progress Principle again—progress toward meaningful goals). This type of focus is easy to see in physical activities. The mountain climber has a goal, expends considerable energy to attain it, and needs prerequisite skills. However, similar demands can be made of intellectual or psychic energy. The listener who suddenly hears the unity of a symphony is not listening casually. Such an experience demands concentration. It is enhanced by knowledge and skills. The more the listener knows about symphonic structure, the more attuned he or she is to nuances of instrumentation and performance and the more meaningful and powerful will be the experience.

One key condition of flow is the optimal match it brings between challenge and skill. Too much challenge or too little skill leads to frustration. Too little challenge leads to boredom. To maintain flow, the level of challenge must constantly be raised to match the person's increasing skills.

> In our studies, we found that every flow activity . . . had this in common: It provided a sense of discovery, a creative feeling transporting the person into a new reality. It pushed the person to higher levels of performance, and led to previously undreamed-of states of consciousness. In short, it transformed the self by making it more complex. In this growth of the self lies the key to flow activities.
>
> (Csikszentmihalyi, 1990a, p. 74)

These observations have implications for schools. If insufficient skill development precedes a challenging, potentially creative activity, it is likely to be met with frustration and resistance. It is highly unlikely that a student will be intrinsically motivated to pursue a task he or she perceives as impossible. Conversely, too little challenge also impedes motivation. A task that previously may have been motivating becomes less so as one's skills increase and the challenge diminishes. Years ago I found this to be true with my fledgling efforts at dulcimer playing and later in new challenges with my Celtic harp. Although I periodically enjoy reviewing beginning pieces, I do not want to play them for long. I enjoyed attending dulcimer classes offered by our city's community education program. They offered me a chance to learn new techniques and play harmonies I could not manage alone. However, because of the range of experience in the class, pieces that were appropriate challenges for some students were mastered in 10 minutes by others. As long as all of us worked on the same piece, we could not all be challenged. Over time, as I have attempted to teach myself to play the harp, I have different problems. Because I am alone, the level of challenge usually is appropriate, but I must work to find the strategies that are most effective for learning and practicing on my own. When I don't feel myself progressing, it is hard to stay motivated. These dilemmas seem to provide one link among motivation, autonomy, and flow. Because students will always have varied levels of skills, if we want them to develop intrinsic motivation, perhaps leading to flow, some of the activities they pursue in school must vary from student to student. For students to manage these varied challenges, they must learn to become more autonomous learners.

Flow activities have meaningful goals and some type of feedback that allows participants to know whether they are approaching the goal. Some types of feedback are obvious. The dancer

In flow, a person is so involved in an activity that nothing else seems to matter

knows when she is leaping higher, and the pianist knows when he is playing faster trills. Scientists get feedback from their research results. Other types of feedback are less obvious but still essential. The painter must be able to look at a piece and tell whether it is working, and an actor must know whether the performance reads or not. These demands seem to tie again to the need for an internal locus of evaluation, standards by which one can judge his or her own product. The demands of flow activities provide one more bit of evidence to support informational assessment and self-evaluation as keys to students' understanding the dimensions and quality of their work, not just its quantitative value.

A second cluster of elements present in most flow experiences includes concentration, loss of self-consciousness, and a diminished sense of time. People involved in activities from dance to reading to chess or rock climbing have described a level of concentration that essentially shut out the rest of the world. All of us have had occasions in which we simply could not believe time had flown by so quickly.

In considering how this variable might operate in schools, I was struck by how difficult it is to find time in schools to concentrate long on any task without interruption. It would be interesting to see how motivation and creative efforts might be affected simply by longer uninterrupted blocks of time to work. If a fifth-grade teacher usually scheduled 1 hour each for reading, math, science, and social studies every day, consider how the possible activities might change in one 2-hour block that was used for math or reading (or perhaps science and social studies) on alternate days. Or imagine social studies and reading combined in one interdisciplinary block. The block scheduling used in some middle and secondary schools can facilitate this type of involvement. Instead of scheduling individual classes and teachers, larger groups of students can be scheduled to a group of teachers for a block of time. The time and the students can be regrouped in various ways as needed. Any of these alternatives can provide increased opportunities for intense involvement in creative projects or problem solving without the interruption of the 43-minute bell.

Beyond just time, there are many variables that affect student engagement in the learning process. Speaking to Sherer (2002), Csikszentmihalyi suggested that student engagement and flow are more likely when students understand the goal of each lesson and the relevance of the material, receive clear, consistent feedback, have the opportunity to solve a problem or work together, and have the opportunity to study content of interest.

Finally, note that the constellations of factors associated with flow do not happen in passive activities. Individuals seldom find flow watching television or lying for hours in a hammock. Although enjoyment often is found in recreation, it also is found in work—and in recreation that requires work. Helping students to find this truth—that the motivation, involvement, energy, and creativity we seek from them can bring them happiness—also can bring focus and energy to our own efforts.

Thinking About the Classroom

Individuals in flow have reported a balance between the challenge of the task and their skill level. Achieving that balance for a diverse student population can be difficult. Examine your plans for the next week. How many times during the week have you planned activities that challenge each child at his or her own level? Talk about that challenge with some colleagues and share ideas.

What can we glean from all these theories that will help us organize and manage classrooms? We want to create classroom spaces of psychological safety, where students feel accepted and valued. To build intrinsic motivation, we need to help students develop an increasing sense of competence, be engaged in meaningful tasks, have experiences with choice and exploring interests, and receive informational feedback. We need to be thoughtful about our use of rewards. To move toward flow experiences, students need instruction at a level that challenges them without overwhelming them and sufficient time for engaged work. To gain creative self-efficacy, students must have successful experiences in creative tasks and see peers do the same. Whew! There is a lot to consider, but fortunately, there is also a lot of overlap. We'll consider four key principles that support both learning and creativity.

1. Students need instruction at a level that is right for them (differentiated instruction) and to see evidence of their progress.
2. Students need assessment that gives them helpful information and leads to a sense of competence.
3. Students need experiences with choice and the chance to explore their interests.
4. Students need opportunities to engage in meaningful tasks and pursue creative experiences in the classroom.

Tomlinson and Imbeau (2010) describe this as an *enabling environment*. Enabling environments are more than just orderly. They are environments in which teachers use a wide variety of strategies to help students make sense of content. Because not all learning is facilitated through direct teacher-focused instruction, teachers and students need strategies by which multiple learning activities can happen simultaneously. For the remainder of this chapter, we'll consider classroom practices that are supportive of differentiated instruction and opportunities for choice and meaningful tasks. Chapter 10 will address assessment that gives students the needed information and strategies for assessing creative projects. For more complete strategies for creating an enabling environment, see Tomlinson's (2014) *The Differentiated Classroom: Responding to the Needs of All Learners* and Tomlinson and Imbeau's (2010) *Leading and Managing a Differentiated Classroom.*

Classroom Organization, Motivation, and Autonomy: Teaching for Independence

If students are going to work at a level appropriate for them and have experiences with choice in the classroom, it goes without saying that they cannot always be doing the same thing at the same time. They must become independent learners. And their teachers must learn to organize time and materials in ways that allow students to work self-sufficiently. Neither smooth classroom organization nor students' skills of independent work happen automatically. If most of your teaching has been teacher-directed whole-group instruction, your transition to a less directive mode will be smoothest if you make it gradually. This section examines strategies for moving students toward more autonomy and choice in classroom activities. It discusses teaching students the skills of independent learning, materials and procedures that facilitate such learning, and flexible classroom grouping. These strategies work best in a classroom context in which differentiated instruction—instruction varied to meet the needs of different students—is the norm. In a classroom based on differentiated instruction, students sometimes work together, sometimes individually, and sometimes in groups, depending on the need of the moment. Students of varying skill levels can be challenged by varying activities.

Teachers' experience with independent learning strategies varies enormously, affected greatly by the time and place the teachers began their careers. As the educational pendulum has swung back and forth, individualized instruction, centers, management plans, and a host of other educational buzz words have come and gone. As with many innovations, when one aspect of a practice falls out of favor, the rest of it often follows. As a result, some teachers have had experiences with a variety of independent learning techniques. Others, whose training encompassed a different swing of the pendulum, have had none. If you have a great deal of experience teaching with a variety of grouping patterns, you may want to skim the next section. You probably will find the ideas there familiar. If you are accustomed to whole-group teaching and would like to vary the pattern occasionally but are not sure how to make the transition, read on!

Teaching Skills of Independent Learning

If students are to have opportunities to identify and pursue questions and interests and to develop creative products, all students in the class must be taught the skills of independent working. Not only is independent work a logistical necessity if students are to work at varied levels of challenge, but, as Chapter 5 explained, many creative people need time alone to pursue their creative endeavors effectively. The skills of independent learning are not just for the most able, the most creative, or the most motivated. It may be that such students ultimately have more opportunities to work independently, but if you are to interact with all your students in various groupings, at some point each student must be able to work without your direct guidance. Managing various grouping strategies also is an essential element of "flipped" classroom structures, in which students spend homework time watching core content online and then spend class time in practice or extension activities.

The first key to making the transition to independent student work is realizing that you need to *teach* students how to work independently. It is not sufficient to tell them to be independent; you must teach them how to do it. In most cases, you may start this process by planning a series of lessons on independent work time. These lessons should be planned and executed with as much care, planning, and practice as any other teaching unit. Major topics should include the following:

- Becoming independent
- Uses of independent work time (sometimes for the whole class, sometimes for a small group, and sometimes for an individual)
- Planning your time (e.g., complete assigned tasks before going on to independent projects or choice activities)
- What to do if you are stuck or do not understand a task
- How to signal the teacher for assistance or a conference (the teacher may not be available immediately, and students should know what to do in the meantime)
- Expectations about noise, conversation, and other disruptions
- Rules about materials (what may be used and how to return materials)
- Choice activities and what to do when tasks are completed

Although the specifics of the skills will vary by age, virtually all levels of students need similar types of direction. Currently, I am teaching most of my graduate courses online. Particularly in this new environment, I am finding that discussions about how to manage work independently, how to structure your time, and even how to hand in materials enhance success even among advanced students.

No set procedures are better than all others. There is no single best strategy for students to follow if they are stuck or do not understand a task. The key is that there must *be* a strategy. A friend teaching first grade had students place small balls of clay at the corners of their desks. They made signs on popsicle sticks that read, "Help me!" or "I'm stuck." In that class, students were instructed to use the following procedure if they were stuck during independent work time: (a) put up your sign; (b) go on to something you know how to do; (c) if there is nothing left that you know how to do, read your library book until Mrs. K. can help you.

Other classes have very different procedures for the same dilemma. Some students are told to ask three people before asking the teacher. Some classes are divided into teams. The teacher may not be consulted unless no one on the team can answer the question. Other classes have sign-up sheets for requesting assistance. The key in each case is that the procedure must be carefully taught. Mrs. K's first-grade students spent 20 minutes learning, modeling, and practicing using the signs before their first independent work period. The need for specific instruction, modeling, and practice, however, is not limited to young children. Even secondary students who have had limited experience with independent work benefit from careful instruction in the procedures and expectations for this work time. Once the procedures are established, independent work time can be initiated. The goal is to move students from seatwork—during which they may be quiet but for which all activities are chosen, directed, and monitored by the teacher—to a period during which many activities are planned, organized, and implemented by students.

The first time you have independent work time, do not try to introduce any new content. The important lesson is independence. Give the students an assignment (preferably one with enough challenge that some students may practice getting assistance) and two or three choices of activities. During the work time, do not try to give other instruction. You may wish to circulate and give students feedback on their independent work skills, but do not assist with content except through the procedures established for independent work time. After the independent work time, discuss the results with the class. Identify areas of difficulty and devise strategies to reduce them. Students should be aware of independence as a goal and monitor their progress toward that end.

The next stage in establishing independent work time involves having students work independently while you give your attention to individuals or small groups. This is a good opportunity to pull together groups needing practice in a particular skill or to spend time with individuals needing assessment or help with projects. Be sure you are situated so you can easily monitor the class while you are working with small groups. It is important that students know you are aware of all the activities in the room. Try not to interrupt the group to answer individual questions, but refer students to the procedures for independent work time. You may wish to circulate and answer questions between your instructional groups.

Remember that independent work skills are complex and will be built over time. Early in the year, most whole-class choice activities should be fairly simple, building in complexity as the year progresses. You may wish to progress from activities not tied directly to academic content (Sudoku or other puzzles, art activities, free reading) to activities reinforcing class content (games centering on a current unit) to activities that explore new content (interest-development centers or independent projects). Of course, some students probably will be ready for individual independent projects before the rest of the class. Providing the varied levels of challenge necessary to build intrinsic motivation in students is one purpose of independent work.

As the year progresses, you may wish to introduce other independent work skills. These might include directions for working at centers (when they may be used, how many students may use them at a time, and other rules) and instruction on planning an individual project (choosing a topic, creating a time line, making daily plans, and other steps).

Thinking About the Classroom

Think about the independent work skills your high school students will need to succeed in college or further vocational education. Consider the level of those skills currently being used in your class. Plan an assignment that will require independence, and then plan lessons about the work skills necessary to complete it successfully.

Students also may become responsible for planning and working independently for longer periods. Most students from intermediate grades and up and some younger students can learn to plan independent work responsibilities that span several days. This, too, necessitates instruction. If students have daily math assignments, a social studies assignment spanning 5 days, and an individual research project, they will need teaching, modeling, and practice in dividing the tasks into manageable chunks and deciding what to do each day. You might consider modeling several alternative plans. For example, given a 90-minute work time, Student A might decide to do one page of math each day. He might start each work period with math, work 20 minutes on social studies, and reserve the remaining time for his independent project. On Thursday, he could evaluate his progress in social studies and decide whether he needs to allot extra time to complete the project by Friday. Student B might prefer working in longer blocks of time. Perhaps, too, she has an appointment to interview the principal for her independent project on Wednesday. She might decide to try to complete three pages of math on Monday. Tuesday might be devoted entirely to her social studies project. Wednesday could be spent doing the interview and recording her notes. On Thursday, she could try to complete two pages of math and evaluate her progress in order to plan for Friday.

Either of these schedules could result in assignments completed on schedule in a style that suits a particular student. When you teach students to schedule their time, help them understand that many routes are possible as long as the goal is attained. Resist the temptation to point out the best schedule. Although some schedules are clearly inappropriate (such as "Do it all on Friday"), many are acceptable. The one that seems obviously superior to you probably suits your learning style but may not be right for every student. One fifth-grade teacher discussed planning daily work time with her students. A student with a diagnosed attention disorder found that for him, the best plan was to do five or six math problems, a little English, and some science or social studies, then a few more math problems, beginning the cycle again. In this manner, he was able to complete all his assignments successfully, something he had never been able to do when the teacher insisted that he finish one task before beginning another. Again, do not underestimate the amount of instruction necessary for many secondary students to master planning and time management. Telling them to plan ahead is not sufficient. They need direct explanations, discussions, and examples of how to manage time within and across class assignments. Time invested in these discussions is likely to pay off not just in class projects but in students' success in their continuing education, where independence is essential.

Thinking About the Classroom

Visit an elementary-grade teacher who uses centers in his or her classroom or invite such a teacher to visit your college class. Talk about getting started, rules for independent learning, and how the centers are used.

Materials and Structures for Independent Learning

Anchor Activities One of the first and most important strategies for helping students become independent is the use of anchor activities. Even when pursuing whole-class assignments, students seldom complete their work at the same time. Assuming that students who complete their work will sit quietly with nothing to do for more than a few moments is both foolish and wasteful. Time in school is precious, so we need ways to use students' time productively. Anchor activities are tasks that students should move to when they have completed a given assignment, before class begins, when they are stuck and waiting for help, or any other empty moments of the day.

High-quality anchor activities are not busy work. Anchor activities should be engaging experiences that are tied to core learning goals. Anchor activities can help students explore their interests and develop new ones by tying needed concepts and skills to attention-grabbing content. Why do yet another math worksheet when you can practice the same skills by analyzing sports statistics or conducting a survey regarding a local issue? Of course, anchor activities must also provide for a variety of levels of readiness and learning styles. They must have clear directions, allowing students to proceed without teacher guidance. Anchor activities may be ongoing or short-term activities on which students work independently (e.g., centers, "Problem of the Day," or explorations tied to current content) or long-term projects students may pursue when they have completed assigned tasks. They provide options for students to move from one learning activity to another independently, without teacher direction.

But, as indicated, start small. Begin with a few options and expand as the year progresses. Like all processes of independent learning, use of anchor activities must be taught. Remember that at the beginning, the most important thing you are teaching is how to manage time and attention. As students come to understand that learning does not come to a halt at the end of a particular assignment and that they can be responsible for their own engagement, you can present them with more complex choices.

Once you are past the beginning stages, two of the most common vehicles for implementing independent learning activities are centers and contracts. These can function as core instruction and also as anchor activities, because students can turn to ongoing activities as their work time permits. Each of these strategies has many possible variations and implementations in diverse subjects and grade levels. In this section, I describe general definitions, uses, and patterns. It will be up to you to adapt this general framework to the needs of your students.

Centers Although centers are most commonly used in elementary grades, they can be adapted for any level. Initially, I make a distinction among three kinds of centers: learning centers, interest-development centers, and exploratory centers. Physically, learning centers and interest-development centers look much the same. Each has a designated area of the classroom designed to facilitate independent work on a particular topic or discipline. Centers may be constructed in study carrels on tabletops, on a pair of desks in the corner, or on an easel, in a refrigerator box, or using virtually any structure that can store materials and provide directions. The difference between learning centers and interest-development centers is the intent. A learning center is designed to introduce and reinforce a specific part of the regular curriculum. An interest-development center is designed to spur students' curiosity and interest in areas outside the regular curriculum, often while reinforcing general skills in research, presentation, and so on. Exploratory centers are designed for more flexible use, typically in primary classrooms. In these centers are a variety of materials available for exploration but without specific directions or preplanned activities.

Because a learning center is designed to reinforce core curriculum, activities at a learning center are frequently required of students. However, the nature of a center makes it easy to provide choice within the requirements and to vary the difficulty of assignments for individual students. In constructing a center, the first decision you must make is the topic. Some centers are focused on particular skills such as reading maps or solving story problems. Some may be focused on specific materials such as geoboards or particular software. Still others are directed toward areas of content such as Native American cultures, weather, or mobiles.

Once you have determined the topic, your next step is to gather available materials. If the topic is weather, you would start by gathering books, websites, phone or tablet apps, and any other available materials on weather. Next, you would brainstorm a list of possible activities that could be pursued independently by individuals or small groups. Typically, activities focus on or branch off from key concepts and generalizations planned for the unit. Activities should include opportunities for data gathering, problem solving, individual research, and creative expression, in addition to more traditional vocabulary practice and fact-gathering exercises.

Your unit on weather might be planned around three general content clusters: basic causes of weather and weather forecasting, safety during extreme weather, and changes in weather trends. The list of possible activities could include a crossword puzzle of weather vocabulary and a worksheet on building a barometer from the science text. You might bookmark websites or find apps that allow students access to up-to-date radar and worldwide weather information to track patterns and make comparisons across regions. In addition, you might decide that students could gather and graph local temperature and pressure data for a week, research and report on climate change, design a brochure to teach young children about tornado safety, create a series of paintings of cloud types, examine state trends in temperature and precipitation over the past 10 years, and so on. Each of these activities could be carried out independently and would reinforce one of the content emphases for this unit. You would need to decide which activities might be done during class time with teacher supervision, which will be required center activities, and which will be electives. You also must decide if and how assignments will be varied to meet students' needs.

You could organize the center activities in many ways. You might decide to glue the directions for each kind of activity on a different-colored card or present them on different-colored posters. Red could be for core activities, blue for enrichment activities, and green for more challenging activities. You could give a blanket assignment, such as requiring each student to complete three red activities and at least two blue or green activities. This requirement still would allow choice within a well-defined structure. Alternatively, you could vary assignments for individual students. Some students might be required to complete only the red activities, with additional activities optional. Others who had demonstrated prior knowledge or ability in this area might be required to choose at least one green card. It also would be necessary to provide a title and some kind of backdrop for the center using a poster, bulletin board, large box, or other type of display. This part of the construction can be regarded as advertising for the center. It helps define the area encompassed by the center and serves to provoke student interest and curiosity. The same activities will be received differently if they are presented in a different setting. If your weather activities are written in pencil on white index cards and placed in a file box, they are not apt to generate a lot of excitement. The same activities on multicolored cards displayed with a collection of books and weather instruments, a colorful poster of pictures of storms, and the title "Weird Weather Wonders" may be received quite differently.

Regardless of how activities are assigned or organized, several factors can allow students to use centers more smoothly. Each activity should be accompanied by clear directions. In most cases, you should demonstrate the complex activities when a center is introduced, but do not depend on students' remembering the directions for a variety of center activities. Even young children should be given directions. For nonreaders, rebus or recorded directions not only allow students to pursue activities without teacher assistance but also accustom them to looking to the materials rather than the teacher for direction.

If some activities have correct answers, set up as many of these as possible to be self-correcting. If activities are not self-correcting or you want to see students' work, be sure to designate a location where products can be placed for your later attention. For the center to function smoothly, students must be able to pursue and complete the center activities and check their products without immediate teacher intervention. It is important to decide in advance how many students may use a learning center at one time and whether center materials must be used in place or may be taken to other parts of the room. For older students, a sign may be used to designate the number of students permitted at a given center. Younger students may retrieve colored chips or clothespins from a central location and bring them to the center. For example, green chips might be used for the weather center. When no green chips are available, students would know they must work elsewhere until someone has finished in the center and returned a green chip. The chip system works particularly well if you plan to change the activities at a center periodically. If a new center activity is particularly messy or demands a large amount of space, the number of chips can be reduced.

If the learning center activities are required, you need to consider how to keep records of completed activities. Certainly, if some activities must be checked, you can record them as you would any other student work. If graphs of the week's temperatures are required, students could deposit these in a basket, and you could evaluate them at your convenience. However, other activities might not produce a physical product (e.g., a role-playing or discussion activity) or may produce a product that is not easily saved (e.g., a completed jigsaw puzzle or a demonstration). In these cases, it may be more important for you to record the activities that have been pursued than to evaluate the end products. One possible way to organize such records is to provide students with a list of center activities. Students could check off activities as they are completed. If you are concerned about honesty in reporting, a second student's initials could also be required. Younger children can color in numbered shapes to indicate completed activities. For example, if a student completed the activity labeled "2" at the fish center, he or she would color the spot numbered 2 on a picture of a fish. Alternatively, a sign-up sheet near specific activities could be used to record students' participation.

Finally, you will need to decide when the center is to be used. Some teachers plan for students to use centers when other assignments are complete, as anchor activities. The problem with this arrangement is that some students may never complete required assignments in time to work on center activities. If center activities are considered important, other arrangements should be considered. One option is to have students rotate in and out of center time. One middle-level math teacher divided his class into three groups, which were changed for each unit, and divided the class period into two sections. At any given time, one group was working with the teacher, one was at a learning center on problem solving, and one was working at the class computers. The teacher rotated instruction among the groups, meeting with groups 2 out of every 3 days. The same type of organization is possible in an elementary school classroom during skills instruction. Similarly, a teacher could meet with a group needing a particular skill while part of the class works on seatwork and part works at the centers. The groups could rotate until all the students have worked at the centers. Still other teachers who have multiple centers schedule specific times when everyone pursues center activities.

Some teachers use centers as a key organizing feature of their curriculum. Such classrooms typically feature multiple centers that are less elaborate than the weather center described earlier, often changed on a weekly basis. One traditional way is to organize elementary classroom centers around subject areas. The result is a math center, a language arts center, an art center, a science center, and so on, with each center providing support materials for studies in these areas. Another way to use subject-focused centers is to organize all activities around a thematic unit or shared book. For example, a first-grade class reading about the three bears may do math activities adding bears, science studies on bear habitats, writing activities on adjectives describing bears, and so on. A third approach to organizing multiple centers is to create centers around multiple intelligences rather than subject areas—in this case perhaps writing about bears, creating a dance in the style of a bear's walk, measuring out the size of a father, mother, and baby bear, and so forth. In classrooms with multiple centers, the general principles of organization are similar to those of single learning centers. Students who have the chance to organize their time using multiple centers have an exceptional opportunity to develop as independent workers.

In most ways, the construction and use of interest-development centers parallel those of learning centers. They, too, start with a topic. However, the topic generally is not part of the regular curriculum. It may be selected because of student interest, as an offshoot of a unit, or as an extension of some local or national event. Next, activities are listed, but because the intent is to spur student interests rather than reinforce content, the activities are likely to be more wide ranging and less tied to specific generalizations. If I were to plan an interest-development center on photography, I could include activities on operating cameras, editing pictures, the lives and art of great photographers, the history of photography, historical research based on photographs, the use of photography in motion research, stop-action photography, the development of moving pictures, and on and on. My goal would not be to have everyone in the class understand the basic processes of photography but to have as many students as possible find some question, idea, or activity that looks interesting enough to investigate. I would want to reinforce the idea that "we sometimes choose to learn more about something because it is interesting."

Because the goal of the center is to pique interest, the activities in an interest-development center generally are optional. Some teachers require students to try at least one activity. This approach parallels a parent's insistence that children try at least one spoonful of a new vegetable—they might like it! You will need to decide whether requiring some activities will lessen or enhance your students' interest.

You also need to decide how much record keeping and assessment is necessary to meet the goals of this type of center. Some teachers prefer to keep track of the number and variety of activities explored by various students. Others feel they can gauge the general success of the center by observation and do not need more detailed records. If interest-development centers are used as an occasional source of enrichment, you probably need only minimal record keeping. If they are used as part of a concerted effort to help students identify and pursue interests, you may want to track patterns of student involvement. When you know which students are making and following through on independent learning choices at a variety of centers, you can more easily gauge whether uninvolved students lack independent learning skills and motivation or simply are not interested in a particular topic. Noting the types of activities that are most successful can give you clues to areas of student interests and needed skills.

As with learning centers, if you value the message the interest-development center sends, it is important to schedule some time for all students to explore it. Because the content of interest-development centers is not part of the required curriculum, it is tempting to view it as superfluous and appropriate only when the real work is completed. From my perspective, beginning to make choices about learning *is* part of students' real work, and it is important for all students to have that opportunity. Interest-development centers offer very appropriate activities for students who have completed other assignments or have previously mastered the day's topic for instruction. However, I hope you will not limit their use to able students or those who work quickly and successfully. The lessons of choice and independence are important for everyone. Work in interest-development centers can also be scheduled as part of a planned rotation of activities or as a specifically designated time for exploration, allowing all students to benefit from such activities.

In early grades, particularly in prekindergarten through first grade, classrooms may be organized using *exploratory centers*, or free-play areas. These areas typically are designed not to organize specific tasks but to allow students to interact with materials in ways that provide background or reinforcement for concept development. Planned well, they set the stage for many teachable moments and interaction with materials from a variety of perspectives. For example, young students studying their community might have a costume area that encourages them to role-play community workers, a block area with various vehicles, or a play store complete with goods to sell.

With careful planning and teacher interaction, exploratory areas help students develop and practice key concepts through play. Teachers observing children interacting with materials in these areas have the opportunity to help students label concepts appropriately and develop verbal skills. Many preschool teachers use interactions at the block area to help students learn concepts such as "over," "under," and "through." Conversations within exploratory centers also give teachers the opportunity to model flexible thinking. A teacher who uses a plastic kitchen bowl as a hat, a steering wheel, and a bed for a stuffed dog engages in the social interactions Vygotsky described as developing creativity through interactive play (1960; also Smolucha, 1992).

Contracts Learning contracts provide a structure for a student and teacher to agree on a series of tasks to be completed in a given time frame. Many contracts allow students to work independently through a body of required content and then carry out an individual project during times when part of the class is involved in other activities. The appropriate complexity and duration of contracts vary enormously with the students' maturity and experience with independent work. The first independent contracts completed by primary school students should entail no more than one or two work periods. Short time periods also are appropriate for many older students who have never worked outside of whole-group teacher-directed lessons before. As with other aspects of independent learning, students must develop facility with contracts gradually, starting with simple short-term forms and advancing to more complex tasks.

Most contracts entail specific assignments from the regular curriculum and optional activities that may be drawn from the curriculum or planned around student interests. Regular curriculum assignments may be specific pages to be completed or concepts that must be mastered in preparation for some type of evaluation. When basic skills are part of the agreement, many contracts can be tailored to individual students' needs through the use of preassessment. Figure 9.2 shows a contract that might be used as part of many units, particularly those emphasizing specific skills. After preassessment, the teacher can check the content an individual student needs. Other examples of contracts that are differentiated for varied students' needs can be found in Tomlinson and her colleagues' "Differentiation in Practice" books (Tomlinson & Eidson, 2003a, 2003b; Tomlinson & Strickland, 2005), Winebrenner's (2012) *Teaching Gifted Kids in Today's Classroom*, and other writings on differentiation or through an online search for "learning contracts."

Optional activities might be planned by the teacher or student. Older students more experienced in independent learning should have considerable input in planning the optional activities.

LEARNING CONTRACT

CHAPTER:____

NAME:_____

√	Page/Concept	√	Page/Concept	√	Page/Concept

ENRICHMENT OPTIONS:_____

Special Instructions

YOUR IDEA:

WORKING CONDITIONS

Teacher's signature _____
Student's signature _____

Figure 9.2 Learning contract

Source: From Winebrenner, S. (1992). *Teaching Gifted Kids in the Regular Classroom*. Minneapolis, MN: Free Spirit, p. 24. Copyright © 1992 by Free Spirit Publishing Inc. Reprinted with permission.

Open-ended activities based on student interests and those emphasizing problem finding, problem solving, and expression of creative ideas should be an important part of this section of the contract. Figure 9.3 is a simple, short-term contract. It might be used as the first independent study opportunity for both student and teacher. Although it represents a short period, it still includes clearly designated activities and opportunities for individual questioning and investigation.

Contract activities can be pursued during any independent work time: while other students are involved in skills instruction, when other assignments have been completed, or any other time designated by the teacher as appropriate for independent work. It is not necessary for all students to be working on individual contracts in any given subject. You may want to begin with a small group of students who have demonstrated independent working skills. As the year progresses, the opportunity to work on independent contracts can be expanded or rotated to other students.

Whatever structure you choose for allowing students more independence, do not assume that choice is only for the most able or successful students. Recently, one of my graduate students completed a case study examining the impact of choice on the behavior and achievement of a young man with autism. Even small choices, such as the type of writing implement and the space in which he worked, made a difference in his behavior and level of focus. And perhaps not surprisingly, he attended longer and wrote more when given open-ended topics rather than assignments that required only recall.

Thinking About the Classroom

Contracts are one way to give students diverse levels of challenge and to promote autonomy. Plan a contract for one or more students. You may want to have several of your friends try this strategy with their classes and compile the contracts into a booklet of samples to share.

I will learn about ___ *rockets*

The questions I will answer are   *What makes rockets go so fast?*

                                       How high has the highest rocket gone?

                                       How can they control a rocket that is already in space?

I will investigate by   *reading books about rockets*
                                       Talking to Mr.Connett about his model rockets

I will share what I learn by   *making a poster with a rocket diagram and Information*

If I need help I will   *sign up on Ms.Toronto's list*

I will complete my investigation by   *next Friday*

Student Signature _____

Teacher Signature _____

Figure 9.3 Independent learning contract

Helping students become autonomous, confident, and self-motivated is an important part of structuring a classroom to support and enhance creativity. Amid all the emphasis on independence, however, it is important that you not lose sight of the value to students of sharing creative activities and insights. The classroom must be an interactive community of autonomous learners, an environment Pace-Marshall (1993) called a "learning community." After all, we know much important creativity is collaborative.

Csikszentmihalyi and Sawyer (1993) described the social aspects of creativity in an interview study of eminent creative adults. Often students and adults envision creative individuals as solitary geniuses secluded in a studio or lab. In fact, Csikszentmihalyi and Sawyer found that every stage of the creative process is heavily dependent on social interaction. One scientist used the metaphor of a door.

> Science is a very gregarious business; it's essentially the difference between having this door open and having it shut. If I'm doing science I have the door open. That's kind of symbolic, but it's true. You want to be all the time talking with people. . . . It's only by interacting with other people in the building that you get anything interesting done, it's essentially a communal enterprise.
>
> (p. 9)

Although not every creative person or product requires the same amount of social interaction, students should understand that sharing thoughts, experimenting with ideas, and asking questions of peers are important parts of both individual and collaborative creativity. The interactive teaching strategies described in Chapters 6 through 8, group-learning activities, and discussions of individual creative efforts all can help to build the sense of a creative community. You also may want to structure discussions around independent work time or class think tanks to which students bring ill-structured problems, research dilemmas, or creative ideas. Achieving a balance between autonomy and community is a delicate business but an essential part of the creative process.

Classroom Environment and Routines

Classroom Space for Flexible Instruction The physical arrangement of the classroom can send messages to students about the role of independence, choice, and creativity in the class. Desks that all face the teacher make large-group instruction simpler. They also send a message to students that the source of information is found in one place. Seelig (2012) described an experience in which she inadvertently discovered the impact of furniture arrangement on creative processes. In a simulation involving creative problem solving, one group of students had tables and chairs, while the other had only chairs. This turned out to be the key variable that affected the outcome of the simulation—students who had only chairs immediately pulled together and began to collaborate. Those with tables remained anchored to their spots. Repeating the experience with other groups led to the same results. To a great degree, the thinking of these very able college students was so framed by furniture that they could not seem to get past it. And recall that the basic artifacts of a classroom influence whether students feel they belong and want to engage. The study cited previously described the way gender-associated objects made students feel more or less welcome, but the same phenomenon can occur with any other set of groups (Cheryan et al., 2009). The physical setup of the classroom influences how—and if—students will interact.

McIntosh (2010) writes about the types of spaces our students will experience, both physically and online. Think about how these spaces may operate in classrooms, because they will be the worlds for which we are preparing our students:

- *Private spaces.* These are the places we all need to stop and regroup alone, or perhaps by texting a close friend.
- *Group spaces.* Here teams may work together, preferably without furniture getting in the way!
- *Publishing spaces.* These spaces may be physical or virtual and provide a venue for sharing. Think about the options for sharing student work and thinking that did not exist just a few years ago, from online bulletin boards to slide shares, blogs, vlogs, wikis, and more.
- *Performance spaces.* In performance spaces, ideas are shared verbally or through performance. Of course, again, these may be both physical and virtual spaces, though in most cases a physical space will be required first.
- *Participation spaces.* These spaces feel a bit like the commons in an old New England town. It is a place you can be part of the ongoing community action. Whether through voting for the latest candidate on a reality show or engaging in a multiplayer simulation, these spaces engage large numbers of people at once.
- *Watching spaces.* Sometimes problem finding, problem solving, and learning require time to simply watch and listen. Those belong in schools, too.

Innovative schools, just like innovative companies, need physical spaces that literally and metaphorically move as needed. It is not by accident that companies such as Google and Pixar, with their focus on creativity, have elements of play and flexible spaces in their work spaces. Although we may not be able to bring in go-carts or zip lines, we can work to make our spaces more adaptable. If students are sometimes to work independently or in teams, these practices can be facilitated through classroom arrangements that make them convenient. If students are to pursue independent research, they should have easy access to reference books and computers or tablets. If they are to work on long-term projects, they must have safe places to store their projects and materials between work periods. If they are to develop openness to sensory experiences, they need to be exposed to a variety of materials. Isenberg and Jalongo (1993) suggested that we examine the sensory experiences of the classroom from the students' eye level. Items that are interesting from an adult perspective may be much less interesting seen from below or from an awkward angle. (Think of most crib mobiles!) If students are to create a variety of products, they need materials, models, and clear directions for product options.

Even in a small classroom, you may want to consider a variety of work areas for various purposes. Both elementary and secondary classrooms might have an area for small-group skills instruction that still allows other students space to work undisturbed. If the classroom is too small to provide this type of space while still allowing for whole-group instruction, it is possible to have two or three basic classroom arrangements. You might have one arrangement for whole-class lessons, one for team work, and another for independent work time. The basic pattern might vary from day to day. If patterns are designed to demand minimal moving of furniture, students can be taught to make the transition. You might say, "Today we'll need to be working in teams. Please turn your desks into team formation. We will begin work in 1 minute." Such transitions cause momentary chaos, but the end result allows you to conduct class activities in a room arrangement that supports the activities. Of course, whatever the arrangement, make sure that you can leave paths that allow you to circulate among groups and students to have access to materials. It can also be helpful to label areas of the room, either long- or short-term, so that you can direct a particular group to "Area 1" and be clearly understood.

Some students with an intense need for concentration benefit from personal study areas in which they can pursue individual projects. Even a cardboard box on a table can be made into a study carrel. Ongoing projects also necessitate places for storing work in progress. Milk crates or food storage containers can be used to keep young students' projects. Older students may need access to locked cabinets for the safekeeping of long-term efforts. These precautions are particularly important when incomplete projects are messy, nontraditional, or difficult to understand at first glance. One of my most haunting teaching memories is the look on the faces of a group of elementary school students who came in one morning and found their project, representing several weeks of effort, missing from the back counter. They had been planning and building artifacts for a simulated ancient civilization. A custodian had seen the pile of undistinguished art materials on a counter near a wastebasket, assumed it was junk, and thrown it away. After that experience, I have been much more systematic and careful about classroom storage.

Students must be taught to work independently

Communication and Directions If different individuals or groups of students need varied directions, do not give all directions to everyone. Asking students to spend large amounts of time listening to directions that do not apply to them wastes time and invites distracted behavior. You also may want to consider mailboxes (physical or virtual), pocket charts, or other communication vehicles that allow you to provide individual contracts, assignments, or other comments without using a large amount of time passing out paper.

Some teachers use individual pocket folders to disseminate assignments. If the folders are filled before class, the materials in each one can differ slightly. You can easily distribute the right folder to each student so students do not feel conspicuous and you do not spend time juggling piles of assignments while students are waiting.

Bulletin boards or other display areas can provide important information through assignment charts or descriptions of ongoing projects. Task cards in various areas of the room can work like mini-centers. I particularly like Tomlinson and Imbeau's (2010) notion of "hint cards" (p. 95) that provide reminders of procedures students have learned in the past but may not recall at the moment. Hint cards could include anything from how to interpret a graphed correlation to the structure of various types of poetry, allowing students to move forward independently.

It also is helpful to have a clear system for both students and teachers to indicate the need for an individual conference. You may want to consider a place where students can sign up to report progress or ask for assistance on a project. It is equally important for students to know when you want to see them. One teacher, fortunate enough to have a paraprofessional in her classroom, made a list of all her students' names. She clipped a clothespin of one color next to the names of students with whom she wanted the paraprofessional to check, with relevant folders stacked nearby. A clothespin of different color reminded her of students she wished to see herself. A similar system could certainly be used by a teacher alone.

Many other communication systems and classroom arrangements can facilitate flexibility in class activities as well as autonomy and motivation in students. A system that works well for one teacher may seem burdensome and unwieldy to another. The particular strategies themselves are not as important as the messages they send. Schools are full of unspoken curricula: values, ideas, and assumptions that shape students' lives within those walls. It is important to examine the simple things that build classroom life—the arrangement of the furniture, the possibilities for communication, the materials that surround students during their hours in school—and to make sure that the unspoken messages tell them of their importance, potential, and ability to grow and take on responsibility as independent learners.

Flexible Grouping and Organization

Classroom grouping patterns have been the subject of vigorous debate in the educational community. Negative reactions to rigid ability grouping and ineffective educational practices in lower-tracked classes resulted in calls to limit or eliminate ability grouping in schools. This trend raised concerns about the potential of heterogeneous classes to challenge high-ability students (Allan, 1991; Kulik, 1991; Slavin, 1991). Reactions to the debate have caused confusion and, in some cases, extreme positions that appear unwarranted by either research or reason. It is hard to imagine any experienced teacher who believes that all students in any class need identical experiences in all subjects. It is equally hard to believe any educator would think that high-ability students or students with disabilities should never mix in heterogeneous groups. Yet the application of grouping research sometimes seems to take this dichotomous approach: either grouping is good or bad; either we group students or we do not. Fortunately, as more schools focus on differentiated instruction, flexible groupings become a regular part of the school day.

In deciding how various groupings may impact motivation for creativity, we should consider at least four points. First, if students are to view themselves as increasingly autonomous learners and problem solvers, they must spend some of their time in school working outside teacher-directed whole-group lessons. Second, if students are to develop intrinsic motivation leading to flow, there must be a match between their skills and the level of challenge. Students have widely differing skill levels necessitating a variety of challenges. Third, we know that choice increases both motivation and quality in creative products. If students have choices, they clearly cannot always be working on identical tasks. Finally, competition can inhibit motivation and quality in creative efforts. Creating a classroom atmosphere that minimizes competition (at least for creative activities) necessitates some type of cooperation—and opportunities for creative collaboration.

Each of these factors provides support for diverse patterns of grouping in classrooms. If students are to have choice, challenge, and autonomy, they must spend at least part of the school day outside whole-group instruction, either as individuals or as small groups. If they are to learn cooperation, they must spend time in cooperative groupings. No one pattern precludes the others or meets all students' needs. Most students probably should spend parts of the school day working in larger, heterogeneous groups. They also should spend some time on individual tasks, projects, and interests and some time in small groups. The small groups may be heterogeneous or homogeneous, skills based or interest based, depending on the needs of the students and the demands of the task. At times, you may want students to work in groups based on the need for a particular skill. This type of grouping is particularly appropriate for basic skills instruction or instruction in areas that have been introduced previously but not mastered by all students. Few things will kill motivation more quickly than repeated practice in a long-mastered skill or instruction in a task that is well beyond a student's current skill level. More targeted groupings can provide an appropriate level of challenge (see Tomlinson, 2004, for additional details). However, it is essential that students who need skills support not always be relegated to skills practice while other students tackle challenging projects.

Working on complex tasks in homogeneous groups can provide advantages, particularly in differentiated classrooms in which all groups are engaged in critical and creative thinking. Particularly challenging problem-solving activities or projects demanding research in advanced resources may provide an appropriate challenge for students with demonstrated abilities or interests in a particular area, but they could be unsuitable for a whole-class task. Groups of students with more limited skills can benefit from tackling a research task that presents an appropriate challenge to them but would be less challenging to others. Managing the task alone can give them chances for problem solving and persistence that they might not have in a more heterogeneous group.

At other times, groups may be based on students' expressed interests. Sharan and Sharan's (1992) group investigation procedures suggest allowing students to generate questions they would like to investigate about a particular topic. Students then can be divided into groups according to the questions they would most like to investigate. A class studying the Renaissance may be divided into groups examining Renaissance art, music, and dance; weaponry and warfare; or other areas of interest. Some students may want to learn about culture and events in Asia or Africa during the time of the Renaissance in Western Europe. The groups may be heterogeneous in skills but homogeneous in interests. There also are tasks appropriate for groups that are heterogeneous in many dimensions.

Assigning students to groups that vary hour to hour can be challenging. One option is to create "standing groups" that last for a week or more. Standing groups don't replace groups that are based on skill level, readiness, or interest, but they are a handy way to designate groups for a particular purpose. For example, Tomlinson and Imbeau (2010) describe standing groups that could include reading partners with similar reading levels or groups of mixed skill levels that the teacher can use for checking understanding in whole-group instruction. Another option is to have several types of groups that allow students to switch as needed from pairs (perhaps strength based) to quads (mixed level) to trios (interest based or student selected). If you say, "Work with your trio . . . " the students should know what you mean.

Some of the most challenging but ultimately valuable learning can take place in heterogeneous groups. Students in such groups can learn to help one another, to get along with those who are different from themselves, and to understand the value of diversity. Unfortunately, improperly used heterogeneous groups also can cause a host of problems. Less able students can rely on more able students to carry out the tasks for them. More able students can become resentful or bored at having to explain information repeatedly to team members that they mastered easily themselves. If heterogeneous groups are to provide motivation, challenge, and interdependence for all students, cooperative tasks must be carefully planned. Fortunately, many of the factors that characterize effective tasks for heterogeneous groups also are associated with creativity.

Slavin (1990) stated that appropriate cooperative learning activities have group goals and individual accountability. The group as a whole must complete some task together, but the information to be learned or the skills to be acquired must be mastered by each individual in the group. Individual assessment ensures that no group member can slide by, assuming that others will carry the load. These certainly are important factors. However, the teacher must look carefully at the tasks and make sure that the interdependence assumed in group goals is real. Sometimes an effort toward group tasks produces group efforts that are more illusion than substance.

This type of difficulty is particularly likely in tasks that are closed. Such tasks have a single correct answer or procedure that the group is to discern. In tasks of this kind, it is likely that some students will already know the correct answer or can deduce it in very little time. Other students will not. Here there is no true interdependence. Students who do not know the answer are dependent on those who do. Those who already know the answer receive little academic benefit from their participation in the group.

Imagine a spelling team whose group goal is to have the highest possible total score on Friday's test. Jan received a score of 100% on Monday's pretest of the spelling words. Ben received a 50%. During the week, Jan and her teammates work hard to help Ben improve his score. In this case, Jan may be dependent on Ben for her team to reach a goal or receive a reward, but not to improve her spelling. Similarly, if Jan and Ben are together in a social studies group, each may be assigned to look up specific information on Sitting Bull. Jan may be a fluent reader and able to manage the research easily. Ben may work much more slowly or need help from team members to make his contribution. If the task is simple fact gathering, Jan could have carried it out more efficiently on her own. She then could have gone on to a more appropriately challenging task. In neither of these tasks did all the students really need each other. Some of the students could have completed the assignments more easily alone. Any student in the group could tell you who helped whom, who were the teachers, and who were the students. This type of dependent (rather than interdependent) relationship can undermine both the desirable level of challenge and the understanding of all individuals as important contributors that is the heart of effective group learning.

Cohen (1986) suggested guidelines for cooperative group tasks that avoid these pitfalls. The key is that cooperative tasks, particularly those for heterogeneous groups, should be tasks for which group participation is a genuine asset for everyone in the group. This emphasis reflects the way groups function in business and society. Automobile manufacturers do not typically use groups to fill out reports or gather facts. Those tasks are more efficiently done by individuals acting alone. Groups are important in design teams, in think tanks, and in many other problem-solving situations. A good group task is one that benefits from many strengths and points of view. Cohen's guidelines may be grouped in the following clusters:

1. Cooperative tasks should have more than one answer or more than one path toward a solution. No student should be able to come to the task with the solution in hand. Imagine that instead of gathering facts about Sitting Bull as a cooperative learning exercise, the class had the opportunity to learn from a movie or class discussion the basic facts surrounding Sitting Bull, General Custer, and the events at the Little Bighorn. Cooperative groups then might be charged with designing a suitable monument for the battle site at the Little Bighorn. There is no simple solution to this task. Each student's opinion could be valuable in helping the group decide on a focus and perspective for their monument.
2. Cooperative tasks should be intrinsically motivating and offer challenge to all students. They should work together to create a worthwhile product, not simply to earn team points. Intrinsically motivating tasks, such as the monument assignment, require students to make choices about interesting topics at a level of challenge suitable for their knowledge and skills. Providing reasonable challenge to all requires a variety of materials and learning options and scaffolding for those whose learning needs require it.
3. Group tasks should allow students to make different kinds of contributions by demanding a variety of abilities and skills. Jan may be able to read and analyze reference materials easily. Ben may be able to see issues from more than one point of view. Sally may be able to draw and Chris to organize materials and keep the group on the task. Each contribution is needed and valuable. Assigned roles can help ensure that each student is contributing something of substance. This means we don't assign one student as the "researcher" and one as the "materials collector." It could mean one student demonstrates solving a problem with manipulatives and another shares the equation. But both students solve the problem.
4. Cooperative tasks should involve multiple media and multisensory experiences in addition to traditional text. Complex experiences are good education under any circumstances. In a heterogeneous group, they increase the probability that each student will have the opportunity to take in information and express ideas in the form that best matches his or her learning style.

Complex, open-ended tasks such as these benefit from diverse student interests, ideas, and skills. Although some students still may prefer learning independently, as do many creative individuals, group efforts of this type are much more likely to help students see the value of diverse contributions than activities that purport to be group efforts but in fact merely demand that some students tutor others. By happy coincidence, complex open-ended tasks also are supportive of the skills and attitudes associated with creativity. Involving students in a balance of individual and group activities that can support such skills and attitudes will help them develop motivation and autonomy while learning the skills necessary for cooperation.

Thinking About the Classroom

Talk to other teachers about how they use groups in learning. Examine your own use. See what kinds of tasks are most commonly used and how they promote interdependence. Plan a group learning task that meets Cohen's (1986) criteria.

Think About It

1. Think about how you spend your time when you are not doing something required. For example, consider your week. Make a list of the things you did when there was free time—even a few minutes. Next, list the things you do during vacation or break times. Things you do by choice are likely to be things you find intrinsically motivating. Are the things that motivate you consistent with theories of intrinsic motivation? Why might that be so—or not? That could be an interesting class discussion!

2. Experiment with adding choice to a home, school, or other activity in which it might not be expected. Observe what happens, and share with a friend or colleague. How does your experience relate to research on motivation?

3. Examine how evaluation, reward, competition, and choice are operating in your home or classroom. You may find it helpful to create a table listing the variables along the top and your class/family activities underneath. Where do you see patterns that are supportive of intrinsic motivation, and where might you want to make some changes? Be sure to check the activities you give students with special needs. Are they having opportunities to develop independence?

4. When are you in flow? Consider inviting some highly creative people to speak on a panel and describe their experiences while creating. Which attributes of flow do you hear in their experiences—or find in yours?

Try It Tomorrow

1. Remember the study titled "Play Some Music and Dance" (Campion & Levita, 2014) found that both dancing and listening to music improved mood and creativity. Experiment with playing music during work times in which students are engaged in creative thinking. Have students create a classroom playlist. These can be organized in themes using keywords such as Happy, Focus, Calm, Concentration, Dance, or Silly. Streaming services like Spotify can be used for building user-friendly playlists. The class can designate appropriate times for the use of a particular list. Or perhaps you'll want to incorporate a dance break!

2. While you are considering your classroom environment, remember that the artifacts of a classroom affect how welcome and engaged students feel. Look at the images and objects in your classroom. If they could appeal to one gender or some ethnic groups more than others, work to make them more varied and inclusive.

3. What problems do you see arising when students work independently? Determine what skills or procedures would help students overcome the problems. Teach them as if they were essential content—because they are. You might want to make hint cards that provide reminders of procedures for independent working skills or directions for products students have previously learned. For example, you might have a hint card for "What to do when you are stuck" or "How to make a mind map with Popplet" (Tomlinson & Imbeau, 2010).

Tech Tips

There are many Tech Tools that can help students develop creative projects. Here are just a few.

1. As we think about tech skills for the future, coding is an undeniable priority. Scratch (scratch.mit.edu) is an amazing site, developed by the Lifelong Kindergarten Group at MIT Media Lab. (Don't you just love the notion of lifelong kindergarten excitement?) Scratch is

a programming language that allows young people to create interactive stories, animations, games, music, and art—and share their creations on the web. Scratch has many resources prepared for educators, including helpful video and print resources.

There are other sites to help students learn coding at a variety of levels. Made With Code is a Google project designed to encourage girls 8 to 22 in coding (www.madewithcode.com). It includes projects from LED-powered dresses to all manner of animations, coding parties, and female mentors. It makes me think about the impact that environment has on young women's interest in coding. This is clearly a female-friendly coding space. Would you like an app for that? Cato's Hike (ages 4+) and Hopscotch (ages 9+) teach basic coding through games. And if you are at all interested in coding and haven't yet discovered the Hour of Code website (hourofcode.com), let that be stop one. The Hour of Code is an international effort to involve students in coding, if for only one hour each year. But you don't have to worry about the date of the event to tap into the many links, tutorials, and other helps available on their website.

2. Are your students entranced by video games (and whose aren't)? Gamestar Mechanic (gamestarmechanic.com) is a program designed for students grades 4 through 9 that teaches the basic principles of game design through playing and then creating games. Well-developed materials for parents and teachers and good FAQ sections make the site accessible to adults who may not be avid game players. Gamestar Mechanic for Teachers (gamestarmechanic.com/teachers) provides both an introduction to Gamestar and materials, sample lessons, and even a teachers' manual. Like many sites, it has both free and paid options for teachers.

   An even more sophisticated option is GameSalad (gamesalad.com), a program that allows aspiring designers to create games without having to write the code that underlies them. Appropriate for anyone from game-crazed middle school students to professional designers, GameSalad has both basic (free) and professional (not free) versions that allow games to be exported to the Web, iPhones, and other devices. Although GameSalad appears too complex for most school applications, it could be just the thing for a creative gamer who needs a challenge. Stencyl (stencyl.com) offers similar free and upgraded versions specifically for iOS (phone and tablet) games.

3. Glogster (www.glogster.com) allows you or your students to create multimedia posters online. Glogster posters can include text, video, and images used in many flexible ways. You can register for Glogster as an individual for free, but educators may be more interested in Glogster.edu, a paid subscription account for educators. The Basic Teacher account is free and allows you to work with up to 50 students, with (naturally) limited functions. Still, it is a good way to experiment and see if Glogster is right for you. A number of Glogster tutorials are available via YouTube.

4. Padlet (formerly Wallwisher; padlet.com) is a free program that allows individuals or groups to create online bulletin boards. The Gallery area is full of samples to inspire you. If you wonder how this could be useful in schools, search for a Google Docs document titled "32 Interesting Ways to Use Wallwisher in the Classroom." Need I say more?

5. Prezi is an alternative presentation option for those who like to see the big picture or who just want a break from PowerPoint. Prezi is particularly helpful for anyone who likes to think holistically. It allows you to see a whole picture or jump to a detail with just a click, using text, audio, or video. To explore Prezi, start at the Prezi website (prezi.com/overview). There you can see a 1-minute introduction by the founder of Prezi and explore a few samples. The structure of the site shifts, but if you explore, you should find several short videos

that give you step-by-step directions to creating a Prezi. If you'd like a YouTube option, there are also several tutorials there.

6. Audacity (audacity.sourceforge.net) is a free open-source platform for recording and editing sounds. Students could use audacity to create podcasts, put together multimedia presentations, or record original music. Think about how different "book reports" could be with this tool. It also provides an exceptional opportunity for creative expression for students whose disabilities make writing difficult.

10
Assessment and Creativity

Barbara looked across the table at Kenneth's mother, Mrs. Greene. The conference was not going as well as Barbara had hoped. Mrs. Greene was concerned about the difficulties Kenneth was having in some areas, particularly spelling, but did not seem to see the strengths Barbara thought so important. Barbara considered Kenneth one of the most creative students she had ever taught. His comments in class frequently reflected a unique point of view, and his projects, although not always the neatest in the class, almost always included elements Barbara had never considered. Mrs. Greene was unimpressed. "Creative!" she exclaimed. "I'm not even sure I know what that means. How can you tell he's creative, anyway? In math, 100% means he did a good job. Can you be 100% creative? It looks to me as if he's pulling a fast one on you. Kenneth can be pretty tricky." Barbara didn't know what to say. How did she know Kenneth was creative? Could she prove it? Should she try?

Barbara's dilemma is not unique. Efforts to assess creativity have been as challenging as the quest to define it. The complex and elusive nature of the construct, combined with limitations in the technology of our measurements, make precise assessment of creativity a daunting task. Yet efforts to enhance creativity in children seem doomed to failure unless we can recognize creativity when it occurs. Allowing these judgments to move from the individual instincts of "I know it when I see it" to greater consistency and agreement among professionals is the goal of assessment.

There is another—and perhaps even more pressing—issue when considering assessment and creativity in the same sentence. That is, how do we manage assessment in classrooms in ways that are conducive to creativity? So much of assessment these days feels out of teachers' control. Still, there are scores of assessment opportunities each day that can support—or not support—an atmosphere in which creativity can thrive. This chapter addresses both dilemmas. First it will present the concept of assessment *for* creativity, or classroom assessment that is supportive of creativity. Next, it reviews assessment *of* creativity, efforts to assess creativity itself. It discusses why we might want to assess creativity, difficulties in assessment, creativity tests, observations, and product assessments. Finally, it describes how some schools have combined techniques in an effort to identify students with outstanding creative potential.

Creativity and Assessment *for* Learning

It is interesting when things that don't seem as if they'd go together at all come together to make something wonderful—cayenne pepper in hot chocolate or fig-flavored gelato. Assessment and creativity are like that. If I were to ask you to list the first 10 words you associate with creativity in the classroom, I'd guess that "assessment" would not be among them, unless maybe you created a list of things that made developing creativity difficult. High-stakes assessments have increased the pressure to "deliver" content in neat, test-ready bites. It is easy to think that assessment is the enemy of creativity, but it's not true. We just have to remember that assessment ≠ standardized tests. Assessment, as it goes on in classrooms day to day, is a tremendous force affecting both learning and creativity. It is a key link in the Creativity in the Classroom cycle, affecting the intrinsic motivation that is essential for both creativity and learning.

As Stiggins (2008) points out, the key decision makers in schools are not the administrators, teachers, or even the vital office professionals and custodians—the key decision makers are the students:

> The instructional decisions that contribute the most to student success are, in fact, not made by the adults. Rather, they are made by the students themselves. . . . Students decide whether the learning is worth the risk and effort required to acquire it. They decide if they believe they are smart enough to learn it.
>
> (p. 17)

To the degree that students believe they can succeed, they are willing to try. If they perceive success as beyond their reach, what sane person would continue trying? And if students stop trying, the best-designed curricula and the most-skilled teachers have little chance of success.

What determines whether students believe they are successful or not successful, capable or not capable? *Assessments.* Stiggins believes—and I've come to believe as well—that the ways we assess our students are pivotal to those students' beliefs about their academic potential and to their decisions about how to deal with school—to give up entirely, go for performance regardless of understanding, or set and achieve mastery goals that lead to genuine learning. Stiggins (2005) says,

> The driving forces must be confidence, optimism, and persistence—for all, not just for some. All students must come to believe that they can succeed at learning if they try. They must have continuous access to evidence of what they believe to be credible academic success, however small.
>
> (p. 326)

And where will they get the "credible evidence of academic success?" You guessed it, through assessments—particularly the skillful use of diagnostic and formative assessments. Assessment is used for varied purposes: diagnostic assessments to determine students' level of prior knowledge, formative assessments to evaluate students' learning "on the fly" and make instructional decisions, and summative assessments to evaluate student learning at the end of a body of content.

Stiggins has made an important distinction between assessment *of* learning—assessment focused on making judgments about what students have learned—and assessment *for* learning—assessment that supports and facilitates student learning. When we evaluate students' learning at the end of an instructional unit, our purpose is generally assessment *of* learning—we want to find out how successful we were in helping students learn. But when we think about how to assess students in ways that will support their learning and build the confidence, optimism, and persistence Stiggins describes, we are focusing on assessment *for* learning. Assessment *for* learning means using assessment at all points in the instructional cycle in ways that give students useful information and help them succeed. Clearly, assessment is an essential element in building the intrinsic motivation and confidence that are essential for learning.

Similarly, I propose considering *assessment* for *creativity* in addition to *assessment* of *creativity*. Assessment *of* creativity, of course, is assessment that attempts to measure creativity or some aspect of creativity. Although there are many difficulties in this task, contemporary researchers have been working to develop measures *of* creativity for more than 50 years. We will address assessment *of creativity* in the second half of this chapter.

But while there is plenty of discussion about the stifling impact of high-stakes testing on creativity, there has been much less conversation about how classroom assessment can be supportive of creativity. How can we have assessment *for* creativity? The first section of this chapter will address that important question. And, best of all, this is another two-for-one phenomenon. Just as teaching that supports creativity also supports learning for understanding, assessment for creativity is assessment *for* learning as well.

Assessment *for* Creativity

When I started teaching, albeit in the Dark Ages, assessment wasn't something we talked about much. Teachers taught. We occasionally gave tests. We gave grades. That was about it. Teaching and testing were typically discussed separately—when testing was discussed at all. Mostly it was considered a distasteful but necessary part of the job.

Of course, the ever-increasing emphasis on high-stakes standardized testing has been a dramatic shift since those less-stressful times. But that has not been the only important change in the ways we think about assessment. Cycles of learning and assessment are now seen as more intertwined and complex. Assessment is not seen as something that happens after instruction is completed but rather something that occurs at every stage of the process. Looking back, I realize that in my early days, we may not have talked a lot about assessment, but we did it all day long. Assessment happens before instruction, in order to make good decisions about how to begin (diagnostic assessment); during instruction, in order to adjust to student needs (formative assessment); and after important intervals of instruction are completed, in order to evaluate progress (summative assessment). One of the key assumptions of current assessment practice is: *Assessment is an essential part of instruction, not something separate from instruction. We assess in order to make instruction more effective, as well as to determine what students have learned.* When we assess for learning, we assess to support intrinsic motivation.

Perhaps because of my history, the positive links between assessment and motivation were not immediately obvious to me. Remember from Chapter 1 that my teachers' attempts to "motivate" me through threats of assessment sent me straight to the path of performance (rather than mastery) goals.

However, assessment used more wisely can be immensely supportive of learning (e.g., see Chappuis, Stiggins, Chappuis, & Arter, 2012; Stiggins, 2005, 2008). Providing an overview of all the recommendations for assessment that effectively support learning is beyond the scope of this book, but the notion leads to a relevant question. What kind of assessment is supportive of creativity? What would assessment *for* creativity look like?

Assessment *for* creativity builds bridges among creativity, learning, and intrinsic motivation. At minimum, assessment *for* creativity has three characteristics:

1. Assessment *for* creativity builds intrinsic motivation through a sense of increasing competence. This requires the wise use of diagnostic and formative assessments, as well as appropriate feedback.

2. Assessment *for* creativity builds intrinsic motivation through the use of choice and meaningful tasks.
3. Assessment *for* creativity provides opportunities to use content in new ways, through examining multiple perspectives, solving problems, and applying ideas in original situations.

It should come as no surprise by now that the assessment characteristics that are supportive of creativity are supportive of learning as well.

Building a Sense of Competence

Helping students build a growing sense of competence is not a matter of cheerleading. In most cases, students know whether they really understand what is going on. If we say they are doing well when they are not, they know it is not true—and we shake their trust. *The only way to help students develop a sense of competence is to help them actually be competent.* It sounds simplistic, but it is true. Of course this means you need good instruction focused on understanding, but it also means you need effective assessment.

Diagnostic and Formative Assessment At the risk of, again, stating the obvious, students cannot make effective progress when the instruction is not at an appropriate level. Time taken for diagnostic assessment before beginning a unit of instruction can allow you to identify students' current levels of learning and adjust accordingly. Some students may have already mastered much of the content you are about to teach. Other students may lack knowledge or skills that are essential underpinnings of your planned instruction.

Diagnostic assessments can be formal or informal, focused on individuals or more general group strengths. The best diagnostic assessments:

- Focus on the highest-priority outcomes
- Require students to apply knowledge or skills
- Are relatively brief, low-stress activities

Think "FAB": focused, applied, and brief. You do not need to give a virtual final exam before teaching the content. Such practices (except for students you have reason to believe may actually know the content) can be exercises in frustration, killing the very motivation we are trying to build. FAB tasks are more efficient, less stressful, and often more fun. For example, a teacher who asks students to create a web of information showing what they know about ancient Egypt, draw an example of an animal in the wrong habitat, solve a real-world problem using a math skill, or write a journal entry predicting what will happen next in a science demonstration is in a much better position to begin (or adapt) instruction appropriately than one who just dives in.

Similarly, formative *assessments* keep instruction "on track" for student success. Effective formative assessments

- Are based on learning goals that are clear to both the teacher and the students
- Are followed by clear informational feedback
- Allow for student self-assessment based on criteria

In other words, teacher and students are clear about the goals. The teacher uses a variety of assessment strategies during instruction to determine how students are progressing toward the goals. Both the teacher and the students are clear about the criteria for success. The teacher is able to give students informational feedback about how they are progressing (information, not simply a score), and, in time, students are able to use criteria independently to assess their own progress. The ability to assess one's own progress and to make adjustments as needed is a critical component of an increasing sense of competence. And remember, a sense of competence is tied to intrinsic motivation, and intrinsic motivation is tied to creativity.

Dozens of options for formative assessment are available, including the questioning techniques described in Chapter 8. Think about quick writes, clicker systems, exit cards, short quizzes, problem solving, graphic organizers, concept maps, journal entries, assignment drafts, or any other strategies that allow insight into students' thinking. When used to give feedback and adapt instruction to better meet students' needs (rather than just to say, "Well, you got a C on that quiz . . ."), any of these strategies can be effective as formative assessments. The key is that the assessments are intended to promote better teaching and learning rather than simply to make judgments about students.

Informational Feedback Chapter 9 described Amabile's (1996) research on the impact of informational feedback rather than controlling feedback on creativity and intrinsic motivation. Similar recommendations are made when considering the type of feedback that is appropriate for learning. Giving clear feedback is one of the most important things a teacher does, whether we are thinking about learning or creativity. Feedback gives students information about what they are doing well and not so well and guidance on how to improve. Good feedback is based on standards students understand, and it allows them to adjust accordingly.

Again, a complete review of feedback strategies is impossible here (see, for example, Brookhart, 2008; Feedback for Learning, 2012). For our purposes, one point is fundamental: Feedback is only useful when it helps students improve. This requires at least three things: (1) the criteria used to judge the work must be clear, (2) the feedback must give students information about what they did well and what needs to be improved, and (3) the process must take place in a classroom atmosphere that is supportive of constant change and improvement. Brookhart (2008) wisely says,

> Good feedback should be part of a classroom assessment environment in which students see constructive criticism as a good thing and understand that learning cannot occur without practice. If part of the classroom culture is to always "get things right," then if something needs improvement, it's "wrong." If, instead, the classroom culture values finding and using suggestions for improvement, students will be able to use feedback, plan and execute steps for improvement.
>
> (p. 2)

This same atmosphere that helps students improve their learning also allows the risk taking that is an essential element in creativity. When students understand the criteria by which their work is judged, they learn to self-assess, giving them the skills necessary for an internal locus of evaluation, another characteristic associated with creative behaviors. Creating rubrics that will facilitate self-assessment and clear feedback will be discussed in the next section.

Choice and Meaningful Tasks

Choice Choice, in many forms, is supportive of a climate of intrinsic motivation, including choice in assessment. One of the basic principles of universal design is multiple means of expression, multiple ways for students to show what they know. (Remember the CAST website?) Of course it is not feasible or wise for students to always be able to choose the means by which they will be assessed. It is important for all of us to flex into less preferred styles. But sometimes choice in assessments can provide options that better represent students' actual understanding as well as motivation that will enhance the quality of the task. Choice in assessment often entails giving students a choice of products. Will they write a paper? Create a display online? Present orally? Build a model?

Like many things in education (and life), choice in assessment brings both strengths and challenges. The strengths of choice are clear: Students are more likely to find a mode of expression that will allow them to show what they know, and they are likely to be more motivated to create a product they've chosen. However, choice in assessment also has one major challenge: *If students are to be given choices, it must be possible to demonstrate the learning target equally well across options.* For example, if students are to demonstrate their understanding of the way the religious beliefs in ancient Egypt affected the lives and culture of the people, they could reasonably do that through a traditional paper, an imaginary journal of an ancient Egyptian, or a skit presenting "a day in the life" of several Egyptians. However, building a model of a tomb or a replica of a statue does not offer the same opportunities to display complex understanding of content unless accompanied by additional information. Looking at a replica statue, I have no way of knowing how much the student understands about the statue's importance. However, if the statue is part of a "museum display" of simulated artifacts and explanatory display cards, the problem can be solved.

One key to making sure all available options are feasible is to score them all with the same content rubric. After all, the content is the thing you are trying to assess. If you also want to address attributes of the product chosen (e.g., whether actors in the skit were loud enough to be heard or the statue was well constructed), keep that as a separate "product" assessment. For example, Coil (2004) suggests using product criteria cards, listing key criteria for each possible product. A "skit" card would list the characteristics of a good skit. Using the cards allows the teacher to create a rubric that assesses the content about ancient Egypt, with a single criterion that requires that the product meet the standards on the appropriate product criteria card. Before giving students a choice of assessment options, envision how each option would look if it fully met the content criteria. If all the choices give students similar options for success, you are ready to move forward.

Meaningful Tasks One of the key attributes associated with teaching for understanding is the role of authentic performance tasks (Wiggins & McTighe, 2005) or performances of understanding (Fusaro, 2017). These reflect the authentic tasks described at the end of Chapter 1. Such assessments parallel the notion of "meaningful tasks" associated with intrinsic motivation, because they allow students to put their knowledge to use in tasks that reflect the real world. Although they can be called by a number of names, we'll refer to them as *performance assessments*.

The distinction between traditional and performance assessments is illustrated well in the procedure for obtaining a driver's license. In the traditional testing part of the assessment, potential drivers are given a paper-and-pencil test on the rules of the road. In the performance assessment, they must actually drive the car. In performance assessment, students must do something with their understanding. Those learning composition must write. Students being assessed in math or science must solve problems in those areas. In the best performance assessments, the tasks assigned mirror the ways content is used in the real world.

Imagine, for example, a high school history class in which some of the key goals came from the Language Arts Common Core:

- Integrate and evaluate multiple sources of information presented in diverse formats and media (e.g., visually, quantitatively, as well as in words) in order to address a question or solve a problem.
- Integrate information from diverse sources, both primary and secondary, into a coherent understanding of an idea or event, noting discrepancies among sources.

(National Governors Association Center for Best Practices, Council of Chief State School Officers, 2010, p. 61)

Imagine that those same students were also studying the Cold War. Students could undertake an oral history project in which they interviewed older relatives and friends about their memories of key events (launching of *Sputnik*, fall of the Berlin Wall). They could integrate material from the interviews with information gathered from print and online sources, perhaps even interviews in the online National Security Archive (www.gwu.edu/~nsarchiv/coldwar/interviews), with their own interviews to create an original product (e.g., a research report, Prezi, etc.). Criteria used to assess the project could include the degree to which students accurately integrated information from multiple print and online sources, the effectiveness with which they integrated the interviews into their historical context, and the degree of understanding of historical events evidenced in their product. For younger students, a performance assessment could entail writing a short story, creating a dialogue between historical characters, or analyzing the acidity of soil samples from the schoolyard in order to recommend plantings.

Performance assessment tasks should reflect real-world concerns and problems, using information in ways that are meaningful to students (Wiggins, 1996). Because real-world contexts rarely entail clear-cut multiple-choice alternatives to problems, performance assessments offer multiple paths to a solution.

One enormous benefit of performance assessments is that teachers no longer need to hesitate about assigning creative projects, wondering, "How will I grade this?" The techniques of performance assessment are designed to evaluate complex, open-ended tasks. And, of course, these types of tasks—solving problems, expressing ideas, and looking at information in multiple contexts and from varied perspectives—are essential for effective content mastery. Performance assessment is an ally to those promoting creativity and learning in schools, both in utilizing meaningful tasks that support intrinsic motivation and in providing technology that allows assessment of creative products.

Creating Performance Assessment Tasks Creating an authentic or performance assessment task for a particular body of content begins with the question, "What do you want the students to do?" In considering that question, imagine how the students might use the knowledge or skills being studied in a real-world context or apply them in a new way. Imagine, for example, that you are planning a unit on simple machines. You probably want students to be able to combine the machines to solve a problem. You might decide to challenge students to design a series of steps that would allow them to move a 50-pound weight from one side of the classroom to the other. The path the weight must travel is blocked by your desk, so the weight must go over your desk without touching it. Students must be able to explain why they chose the procedures and how each step minimizes the amount of work to be done. If you hope that students will move the weight in an original or unique way, that also can be part of the task. Often, creating the task can entail placing students in a real-world role, as in problem-based learning. I once had a student develop a performance task in which the class members were put in the role of an art collector who had taken delivery of a 1,000-pound statue and now must move it into place. That task required the same types of skills as my 50-pound weight task, and in a more interesting way.

When preparing a task, I like to consider the GRASPS acronym (Wiggins & McTighe, 2005). Each letter suggests something you must consider in constructing the task:

> *GR: Goal and Role.* In my example, the goal is to move the weight from one side of the room to the other. Taking the lead from my student's art collector idea, I might decide to frame the task as a demonstration for a movie producer who needs to hire a company to move heavy scenery across outdoor obstacles.

A: *Audience.* Who is the real or simulated audience for this task? Sometimes the audience is a real-world group. In this case, my audience will be the head of the imaginary movie company—perhaps played by a cooperative colleague.

S: *Situation.* For this performance assessment, the situation is that the movie company needs to hire movers and has asked students to demonstrate their ability to handle the job by moving the weight.

P: *Product.* What will students actually create? They may, of course, do a demonstration. I may decide that they should also submit a diagram of their plan, with notations as to where they are using simple machines and why they chose each one.

S: *Standards.* What are the criteria by which the performance assessment will be judged? In this case, I am most concerned with students demonstrating their ability to use simple machines to solve a problem. I'll need to think more about the details of assessment when I plan the rubric.

Once you have a general idea of the task to be accomplished, you must develop specific guidelines for the assessment. For this task, questions such as the following need to be considered: (a) Will students be required to actually arrange the machines and move the weight or merely submit the diagram? (b) Will this be an individual or group task? (c) What materials will students be permitted to use? (d) What sources of help will be allowed? and (e) What amount of time will be allotted?

After considering these questions, you can develop student directions for the task. It is important that student directions be as clear as possible. Students should be told what they are to accomplish, what resources are available to them, and how the product will be assessed. Do not be discouraged if your first attempts at designing performance tasks are unclear or confusing. As with any new skill, developing these tasks demands time and practice. If you find you have omitted essential information, explain it as well as you can and revise the task next time. A first draft of the directions for the machine assignment reads as follows:

The movies have come to town! Ms. Gonzales, head of VIMS (Very Important Movie Studio) has come to town looking to hire a team to move set pieces into place for an upcoming project. The problem is that the movie will be shot outdoors, so equipment will need to be moved over and around a number of obstacles. In order to choose which team to hire, Ms. Gonzales has issued a 50-Pound Challenge, in which teams will show how well they can use simple machines to move heavy objects. Because Ms. Gonzales has heard that you have been studying simple machines, she has invited you to try the challenge.

Your task is to move a 50-pound bag of potting soil from the door of the classroom to the plants on the windowsill. The bag must travel in a straight line. Because the path from the door to the window is blocked by my desk, your plan must include a way to get the bag over my desk without touching the desk or damaging anything on the desk. Try to design a plan that not only is effective but also uses simple machines in an original way. You will complete your plan for the 50-Pound Challenge in teams, but some work will be done individually.

1. First, teams will plan how they will combine at least three simple machines to move the bag. Each team will turn in a written plan for moving the bag, using equipment available in the science corner. Other equipment may be used with approval of your teacher.

2. After the plan is approved, your team will be assigned a time to set up your machines and move the bag.

3. Finally, team members will hand in individual diagrams illustrating the way their team moved the bag. The diagram must label each simple machine and explain why it was used and how the machine helps the bag move. The diagram should also include an explanation of how you would change the plan if you could move the bag again, and why.

Diagrams will be evaluated on two main questions:

1. Does the diagram accurately label and explain the uses of at least three simple machines?
2. Does the diagram demonstrate understanding of why the plan did or did not work?

Because VIMS values originality, Ms. Gonzales also will be looking for originality solving the problem.

Once the task has been defined, a scoring rubric must be designed. After the scoring is determined, you may find that the student directions need to be changed to make the goals of the activity clear. Creating a scoring rubric has three general stages: identifying the dimensions or variables to be assessed, determining the scale of values to be used, and setting standards or descriptors for each value. Sometimes products are scored along only one dimension. This is a holistic scoring approach. Holistic scoring might be used to rate the overall quality of a performance or product. This provides maximum flexibility for the evaluator but limited feedback to the student.

In this case, your dimensions could follow your goals. You would want to assess if the machines are labeled and explained correctly and whether the explanation demonstrates understanding of the function of the machines. If it is important to you to assess originality or some other aspect of creativity, you could either create a separate scale for that dimension of assessment or incorporate it into the three other scales. This kind of scoring, in which students receive feedback on key dimensions of the assignment, is called analytical scoring. It is particularly useful when the scoring guides are presented with the assignments, so that students can readily identify the critical attributes of a successful project.

The last step in creating a scoring rubric is the most complicated, but it is essential in creating performance assessments that are reliable and fair. You must decide what constitutes a 2 or a 9 on the 10-point scale for each dimension. It is not necessary to give a description for every possible point value. For a 10-point scale, you might create five levels: minimal achievement (1–2 points), basic achievement (3–4 points), satisfactory achievement (5–6 points), superior achievement (7–8 points), and exceptional achievement (9–10) points. You may find that three levels are simpler and more efficient. Regardless, for each level, you need to determine criteria or descriptions of a typical performance. Your completed scale might resemble that in Figure 10.1. For many assignments, you may find that three levels of assessment (unacceptable, acceptable, target) are sufficient. Descriptions of the criteria at each level allow evaluations to be consistent from product to product and keep the evaluator focused on important dimensions instead of assessing one project on its plan and the next on the quality of its artwork. Like the directions, your first rubric attempt is likely to need revision the first time you use a particular assignment. It is not unusual to identify additional criteria that need to be made explicit or areas that require clarification.

Thinking About the Classroom

Choose an open-ended task as part of your assessment for an upcoming unit. Create a scoring rubric with criteria for varying levels. If this is your first effort at performance assessment, you may wish to work with a partner or small group.

	Minimal 1–2	Basic 3–4	Satisfactory 5–6	Superior 7–8	Exceptional 9–10
Accurate Labeling and Explanation of Each Machine	Machines are not labeled correctly and/ or explanations are missing.	Fewer than three simple machines are labeled correctly or the machines' functions are not explained correctly.	At least three simple machines are labeled correctly. The explanations may be a bit unclear.	Three simple machines are accurately labeled and their functions are explained correctly.	More than three simple machines are labeled, with their functions accurately explained.
Explanation of Plan for Next Time	Plan for next time is incomplete or unclear.	Plan for next time does not demonstrate clear understanding of the how the changes will impact the system.	Plan for next time may improve the efficiency of the system, but it is not clear.	Plan for next time improves either the efficiency or originality of the plan, demonstrating understanding of how changes will affect the system.	Plan for next time improves either the efficiency or originality of the plan in more than one way, demonstrating understanding of how changes will affect the system.
Originality (5 Points Possible)	Plan is very similar to examples used in class.	Diagram demonstrates originality in either solving the problem or in revising it.	Diagram demonstrates originality in solving the problem and revising it.		

Figure 10.1 Scoring rubric for the 50-pound challenge

The techniques of performance assessment can allow flexibility for students with a variety of strengths. Hawes, Wdziekonska-Piwko, Martin, Thomas, and Nicholls (2012) describe a project created by deaf students. One student, in particular, was disheartened when he observed that his written work was not as good as that of his hearing peers. He was much more comfortable signing. So for his project (on China's one-child policy), he used images from the Internet as background and (using Green Screen) worked with two other deaf students to sign the information they wanted to communicate. With the support of a special educator, they wrote subtitles for the film. By the end, the students had created a written response, but they were able to begin their thinking using the language in which they were most comfortable. Although this project took place in a specialized school, and most teachers are unlikely to have three deaf students in a general classroom, the principle of helping students find "voice" in a manner that meets their needs and preferences still holds, whether the students literally speak a different language or are best able to convey their understanding visually. Once we are comfortable having students show their understanding in many different ways, it becomes easier to differentiate for those who need to show it differently.

Fostering Self-Assessment The techniques of performance assessment allow teachers to use complex tasks in evaluating students' understanding of content. They can also help students to understand that complex and creative tasks are not assessed at the whim of the evaluator but have qualities that add to or subtract from their value. These qualities can be learned and used to improve future efforts.

If used well, this type of assessment becomes an integral part of instruction. Because complex tasks are used to assess instruction, they become part of it. Performance assessment also can become a vehicle for informational feedback. If a product is not simply labeled A or B but is assessed along clear dimensions, the information from the evaluation can be used by students to understand the strengths and weaknesses of their products and to improve future projects. For this reason, Stiggins, Arter, Chappuis, and Chappuis (2006) include self-assessment as a critical component of assessment *for* learning. Involving students in the creation of rubrics can be a particularly powerful tool in helping students appreciate what comprises excellence and take responsibility for meeting those standards.

Understanding the criteria by which their work is evaluated brings students one step closer to effective self-evaluation. Developing the ability to assess one's own work and learning the importance of an internal locus of evaluation are important factors in creativity. It also is important that students learn to assess the creativity of their own ideas, because creative individuals must not only generate original ideas but also recognize which ideas are original (Runco, 1991b). Allowing students to correct their own spelling tests is not self-assessment. An outside source (the dictionary) is the absolute determiner of the quality of the work. Effective self-assessment requires students to measure their efforts against some scale or criterion and make judgments about how they measure up.

Beginning in primary school, students can be taught to evaluate their own products. They can assess their stories for complete sentences; a clear beginning, middle, and end; or the use of interesting descriptions. They can judge the use of color in their paintings or the precise definitions of variables in science projects. Initially, teachers should provide guide sheets or checklists to help students focus their assessments. Later, students can add their own variables or develop their own forms of assessment. The goal is to help students internalize the evaluation process, both to improve the quality of their products and to build confidence in their own judgment.

By definition, creative products are different from those that came before. Individuals who produce creative products often are faced with skepticism and doubt about the quality or validity of their efforts. Helping students to develop standards for self-assessment can help them view evaluation as a tool for improvement rather than an arbitrary or capricious judgment by either the creator or an outside evaluator. Products are not good or bad because "I say so" or "I like it" but because the product meets some standard or accomplishes some objective.

Developing self-evaluation also can help students understand that, at times, the standards or objectives by which something is evaluated may differ from standards that came before. That is how fields and domains change. Picasso's art could not be judged by the standards of his predecessors. Although some traditional ideas could be applied (e.g., the use of color or balance), Picasso changed many of the rules for evaluation. His art was not random or without standards. It simply tried to solve problems of different kinds from those that had been addressed before. Similarly, although the standards of the discipline must be taken into account, students may sometimes evaluate their products along different dimensions or focus on goals different from those of other evaluators. They should recognize that although setting new standards carries risks, such evaluations also can have value and promise. Figures 10.2, 10.3, and 10.4 are examples of forms that may help guide students in their efforts at self-assessment.

Thinking About Your Thinking

Think about how you solved today's problem. Which did you do?

____ I didn't try any of the strategies from the list.

____ I tried one strategy from the list.

     ____ The strategy helped me solve the problem successfully.

     ____ The strategy did not help me.

____ I tried more than one strategy from the list.

     ____ The strategies helped me solve the problem successfully.

     ____ The strategies did not help me.

____ I tried a strategy that was not on the list. It was _____

     ____ My strategy helped me solve the problem.

     ____ My strategy did not help me.

I used these strategies:

____ Guess and check	____ Make a table
____ Look for a pattern	____ Make a list
____ Draw a picture	____ Work backward
____ Try a simpler problem	____ Write an equation

Figure 10.2 Self-assessment, mathematical problem solving

Thinking About the Classroom

Plan a checklist or rubric that will allow students to evaluate a project according to several criteria. Discuss students' feelings about self-evaluation. If your students are already adept at using rubrics, consider developing the next rubric collaboratively.

Using Content in New Ways

Finally, assessment *for* creativity includes assessments of all types—diagnostic, formative, and summative assessments, as well as performance assessments—that require students to use the content in new ways. Of course, not every assessment will require originality. Sometimes content goals focus on analyzing content accurately and drawing appropriate conclusions. But there are other times when students' understanding of content can be deepened by using it in a new way, whether as a short brainstorming activity (What options did King George have if not to impose a tea tax?) or a significant performance assessment (Design and carry out an original investigation on factors influencing plant growth). The key is, if we want students' understanding of content to benefit from thinking about the content in multiple ways, their creativity must focus on the content itself, not just the format in which students present it.

Note that the scale reflecting originality in the 50-Pound Challenge reflects originality in the task itself rather than in presentation. There is a key difference between presenting information in an interesting (and possibly creative) manner and engaging in creative thinking regarding the information. If we want students to think creatively about content, they must be engaged in tasks that require them to *think about the ideas* in new ways, not simply rephrase ideas and then putting them in a folder with a decorated cover. Using design skills to *present* content in new ways may result in creative design, but it does not usually result in creative thinking about the content itself. Unless you are teaching design, the distinction matters. Thinking about content from multiple perspectives and using it in varied ways helps students understand it more deeply. If we only use

What Am I Learning?

This sheet will help you think about what you are learning now and what you will learn during the school year. Thinking about the things you are learning in school now, answer the following questions.

What things are you doing well?

What things are you working on and improving on?

What things are causing difficulties for you?

What do you plan to do to help with your learning?

What things are you not studying in school that would be interesting to learn?

Figure 10.3 Self-assessment, general

Student _____ Date _____			
Title _____			
I am working on:	My evaluation:		
	Not yet	Improving	Well done
Correct spelling			
Punctuation			
Capital letters			
Comments			

Figure 10.4 Self-evaluation, writing

flexible thinking for book covers and displays—or even high-tech versions of such displays—we waste the power it brings to learning. If we want to set creativity as a goal, the task itself must require creativity, not just the frame in which it is housed.

Of course, there is nothing wrong with decorated folders or graphically beautiful Prezis or Glogster posters that share basic information. Creating those things allows individuals with talents in graphics to shine and can be motivating to many students. Learning how to do technical presentations well is an important goal in and of itself. It is just not the same goal as having students use the content information (say, about simple machines) in creative ways. If I want my students to learn how to create a Voki, they can build a Voki that shares three important facts about Martin Luther King. If I want to have them build a Voki and also think more flexibly about Dr. King, I could have them build a Voki that expresses three things in the news today about which they think Dr. King would comment and what he might say. Either Voki would have to be accompanied by more detailed written explanations. Both kinds of goals can be useful—just be sure you are clear which you are aiming for.

The knowledge, skills, and attitudes associated with creativity are affected by every aspect of classroom life—from the content and method of our lessons to the arrangement of chairs and the day-to-day assessment of students' efforts. In your classroom assessments, work toward assessment for creativity. Looking at all our interactions with an eye to creativity can be a complicated business but one that may lead to schools transformed from within into places of both learning and wonder.

Assessment *of* Creativity

This section considers the second question: What types of evaluation might best support and encourage creativity in schools?

Why Assess Creativity?

The primary goal of assessing creativity in schools was expressed by Gowan (1977):

> Heretofore we have harvested creativity wild. We have used as creative only those persons who stubbornly remained so despite all efforts . . . to grind it out of them . . . If we learn to domesticate creativity—that is, to enhance rather than deny it in our culture—we can increase the number of creative persons in our midst by about fourfold.
>
> (p. 89)

The goal of assessing or identifying creativity in schools is not to generate creativity scores or to divide students into categories called "creative" and "not creative." Rather, it is to allow us to recognize creativity when it occurs and to create conditions that allow it to develop. It also can help us identify students such as Kenneth, whose exceptional creativity, as with any other special ability, should be nurtured and supported in school. Of course, valid instruments with which to assess creativity also are essential in the continuing research efforts to understand creativity and the ways it develops.

The type of assessment that is needed or appropriate varies with the purpose for which it is intended. In schools, the assessment of creativity is most likely to be used for planning instruction, for identifying students to be included in specific programs or opportunities (such as a summer arts program or school-based gifted and talented program), and occasionally for evaluating programs. If an assessment technique is to be used by a school or district to make decisions about educational opportunities for individual students, it must be the fairest and most accurate measure available. If a classroom teacher is using an assessment to plan class activities for her next unit, a more loosely constructed instrument may be acceptable. In many cases, teachers must use a combination of assessment tools to make valid judgments. The nature of creativity and the limitations of traditional forms of measurement provide challenges that can make any single form of assessment suspect.

Thinking About the Classroom

Think about the need for assessing creativity in your class or school. For what purposes might assessment be used? Compare your ideas with those of teachers in another building or district.

Difficulties Associated With Assessing Creativity

The Nature of the Beast The most obvious difficulty in trying to assess creativity is lack of consensus on what constitutes creativity in the first place. Measuring something is extremely difficult if we are not sure what it is. Varying theories and definitions of creativity will support differing types of assessment. Are we trying to assess the type of creativity that allows an Einstein to change the nature of a discipline ("big C" Creativity) or the more common creativity that might allow me to invent a new soup, play a new harp tune, or fix my leaky faucet without a washer ("little c" creativity)? A theorist interested in group creativity in an engineering firm and an individual studying history's most creative musicians or scientists may wish to measure very different things. Researchers disagree on whether general creativity can be identified and measured or whether creativity must be subject specific. Some of the variations in assessment techniques reflect these differences and represent attempts to measure variables important to various theories. The more complex the theory, the more daunting the task of assessment. If, as some theorize, creativity is discipline specific, the measurement of generic creativity will be ineffective. It is possible that each discipline will provide unique assessment opportunities. As more complex systems theories of creativity come to the forefront, attempts to measure any single factor may become less appropriate. On the other hand, if we want to measure general divergent thinking rather than a more complex constellation of creative behaviors, a simpler measurement will suffice. And, of course, to the degree that creativity varies across cultures, assessments must reflect those differences. Attempts to assess creativity also are subject to difficulties related to the nature of measurement itself.

Measurement and the Usefulness of Instruments The field of assessment is based on the assumption that the thing to be measured can be identified and quantified or judged. For these assumptions to be met, the instruments used for measurement must meet the tests of validity and reliability. At the most basic level, these two criteria mean that different observers can agree that they are measuring the thing they set out to measure and what the measurement is. For example, if I want to measure the length of the keyboard on which I am typing, I could use a ruler. If society in general has agreed on what length means and that a ruler, properly used, is an appropriate measure of length, my measurement can be considered valid. If I use a ruler, I can measure the variable I want to assess—length. To do so accurately, I must have a ruler that is consistent, or reliable. A standard ruler is reliable. If I measure my keyboard several times, I should get the same results. If someone else measures my keyboard with a standard ruler, he or she too should obtain the same measurement. If my ruler bent or stretched in hot weather, it would not be reliable. The measurements taken by that ruler would be essentially meaningless because they could differ with each attempt. I might never really know the length of my keyboard. Of course, dealing with reliability and validity in measuring abstract constructs such as creativity is more complex than determining the purpose and accuracy of a ruler.

Reliability can be generally thought of as consistency. Reliability is the foundation of quantitative measurement. Without consistency in scores, measurements cannot be valid. The most easily recognized type of reliability is stability, or test-retest reliability. Just as I would hope that two measurements of my keyboard would result in the same number of inches, test-retest reliability ensures that an individual identified as highly creative today will also be identified as highly creative next week or next month. Assuming that no major changes in creativity occur, individuals should obtain relatively consistent scores on the same instrument if they are tested more than once. Without this type of reliability, test scores are useless. We would never know whether a given score is a true reflection of the variable being measured or whether the subject might obtain a totally different score on another day. Of course, test-retest reliability assumes that the variable being measured is relatively stable. If creativity actually changes from day to day or minute to minute, test-retest reliability—and most quantitative assessment—will be impossible.

Other types of reliability also are important in measuring creativity. Equivalent-forms reliability says that scores obtained on one form of an instrument should be about the same as scores obtained on any other form. This type of reliability is particularly important in the selection of instruments to be used for program evaluation. It is very common for evaluators to use one form of an instrument as a pretest and another form as the posttest to avoid having students become familiar with the test itself. Without equivalent-forms reliability, scores on the various forms could not be compared in meaningful ways. Any differences found between pre- and posttest scores could be the result of differences in the tests rather than the effects of the program being evaluated.

A third type of reliability is interrater reliability. Interrater reliability is required for any instrument that relies on individual expertise or judgment for scoring. For it to be achieved, two raters scoring the same test or product have to produce similar scores. Interrater reliability is affected by the level of detail in the scoring guide. If scorers are merely asked to designate scores on a five-point scale, the scores are more likely to vary than if scorers are given examples and criteria for each level of the scale. This type of reliability clearly is an issue when creative products are being assessed. It would be unfair if students were judged to be creative or less creative depending more on who scored their product than on the merits of the product itself.

Perhaps the most commonly reported type of reliability is internal-consistency reliability. This type of reliability examines whether the items on a test instrument work together and seem to be measuring the same thing or whether different items are assessing different strengths. One way to test internal consistency is to correlate scores on odd-numbered items with those on even-numbered items or to compare scores on the first and second halves of the test (also called split-half reliability). If the test is intended to measure one construct, such as creativity, internal-consistency reliability should be high.

When you examine commercial instruments for assessing creativity, you should find information on reliability in the documentation accompanying the test as well as in test reviews. Reliability scores generally are expressed as correlations, with a range from .00 (no reliability) to 1.00 (perfect reliability). Be sure to examine both the score itself and the type of reliability it expresses when determining the appropriateness of a particular instrument for a given purpose.

The types of reliability may occasionally become confusing, but the issues regarding reliability are actually pretty straightforward: Either a test produces consistent results or it does not; either two judges obtain similar scores or they do not. These results can be easily and clearly expressed in numerical scores. *Validity* offers no such clean assurances. In validity, we are concerned not with the consistency of the scores but with their accuracy. Are we, in the end, measuring what we want to measure? Consistent scores are of little value if they actually are measuring the wrong thing.

Scientists of the 19th century purported to have a wonderful measurement for assessing intelligence: brain weight. The reliability scores for that measure were excellent. Given an accurate scale, brain weights were extremely consistent if weighed at different times or by different evaluators. The only problem was that brain weight does not really measure intelligence. In examining measures of creativity, we must ask the same question: If the test measures something consistently and accurately, is that something creativity?

There are five types of validity that can be considered when we make judgments about assessment instruments. Content validity asks whether the content of the test items reflects the definition or theory of creativity we accept. In its simplest form, it asks, "Do these tasks look as if they require creativity? Do they logically match creativity as we define it?" If our definition of creativity requires novel responses, the test should provide opportunities for novelty, and the scoring should reward novel responses. A multiple-choice test with specific correct responses probably would not be appropriate. If our definition also requires that responses be appropriate, the instrument should distinguish between responses that are unusual but fit the task and responses that are inappropriate.

Criterion-related validity asks whether the measure correlates with other measures of creativity. How do scores on a particular instrument relate to other standards previously identified for creativity? Criterion-related validity can be divided into two types: concurrent validity and predictive validity.

Concurrent validity examines whether a measure of creativity correlates with other current measures of creativity or assessments of creative productivity. It might ask whether individuals scoring high on a particular measure of creativity also score high on another creativity test or if their writing is rated as more creative than the writing of those who score lower. Measures used to assess concurrent validity all are given to subjects during the same general period.

Predictive validity addresses a more difficult challenge. It asks not how measures correlate with other measures today but how they may relate to activities tomorrow. Predictive validity examines whether scores on a measure of creativity predict creative performance at a later time. Are the students who score highest on a creativity test today most likely to be the creative writers, artists, or scientists of tomorrow? Developing an instrument with long-term predictive validity is a daunting task. Regardless of the power of the measure, an enormous number of factors outside the level of childhood creativity will affect whether a person is creatively productive in adulthood. School influences, values of the surrounding culture, family interactions, social unrest, personal health, and politics in the field of interest are just a few of the forces that may shape an individual's opportunities for creative activities. Some theorists have reasoned that because any creativity test can measure such a limited segment of creative behavior, and because the influences on creativity are so complex, expectations of long-term predictive validity for creativity tests are "unrealistic and inappropriate" (Treffinger, 1987, p. 109). Nevertheless, predictive validity remains an important goal of creativity assessments and can be a valid source of comparisons among measures. Researchers differ in their assessments as to whether assessments of creativity currently demonstrate useful predictive validity. A substantial discussion of the limitations of psychometrics in creativity can be found in Weisberg (2006), while a perhaps more optimistic view is available in Plucker and Makel (2010).

Both concurrent and predictive validity are affected by what Treffinger, Renzulli, and Feldhusen (1971) called "the criterion problem" (p. 105). Briefly, the criterion problem is the difficulty in identifying criteria against which to test the validity of creativity tests. If experts disagree on the nature and manifestations of creativity, how can they determine what standard to hold up as "real" creativity in order to evaluate assessments? Efforts at identifying criteria have included other standardized assessments, teacher and peer judgments, profiles of adult accomplishments, and assessment of creative products. Whereas the criterion problem is obvious in the attempt to predict future creativity, it is a factor in any determination of validity regarding creativity.

Like content validity, construct validity asks whether the tasks on an instrument match generally accepted characteristics of the construct being measured—in this case creativity. It also examines how the scores on an instrument relate to other measures of creativity. However, unlike either of the previously mentioned types of validity, construct validity also considers how the measure fits into the total pattern of theory surrounding the construct to be assessed. It is concerned not only with whether this test measures the same thing as other creativity tests but also with whether we are sure it is creativity we are measuring.

Each of these types of validity is important in our consideration of how creativity will be assessed. If educational decisions are to be based on such assessments, we must ensure that the tools being used are the most reliable and valid measures available. Unfortunately, as the following brief review of tests clearly shows, the reliability and validity of most instruments designed to assess creativity are limited. In some cases, the limitations are so severe that the instruments are inappropriate for educational decision making. In other cases, instruments, although limited, still may be the best available. Educators who are knowledgeable about the need for reliability and validity are in a better position to judge the value of assessment information and how it may be combined in a variety of ways to help make the best decisions possible with the available information. Without such knowledge, test users can be at risk of accepting scores as absolute truth—an assumption that is seldom, if ever, appropriate.

Thinking About the Classroom

Examine a standardized test manual for a test used in your district. Evaluate the types of reliability and validity information provided. Determine what types of information are given and what, if anything, is missing or unclear.

Instruments for Assessing Creativity

As you review some of the instruments that have been developed to assess creativity, you should again consider four perspectives from which the concept of creativity has been viewed: person, process, product, and press. Many assessment tools can be similarly categorized. Some instruments provide tasks that require individuals to use processes associated with creativity. They may require test takers to solve open-ended problems, pull together remote associations, or derive multiple responses for a particular question. Tasks are constructed to demand the types of thinking emphasized in the definition or theory accepted by the test constructor.

Other measures focus on the products of creativity. These assessments are less concerned with how a creative product came to be than with the quality of the product itself. Instead of presenting subjects with an artificial task, they may assess the products of wild, or at least authentic, creativity. Works of art, scientific experiments, pieces of writing, or other creative efforts can be evaluated. Although the emphasis with this type of assessment is on more real-world products, it is similar to the process-focused assessment in that the thing to be measured is the result of someone's creative effort.

Still other measures of creativity focus not on the processes or products of creativity but on the creative person. Instead of asking individuals to complete specific tasks, these measures focus on biographical or personality traits tied to creativity. Individuals may be evaluated for their willingness to take risks, internal locus of evaluation, past creative efforts, or other traits or activities commonly associated with creativity. The assumption is that individuals who have a high number of the personal characteristics found in creative individuals are likely to be creative themselves. Many times, these measures take the form of self-report surveys or observational checklists.

The fourth "P," in addition to process, person, and product, is press (Rhodes, 1961). Press refers to the external forces, or context, acting on the creative person or process. Although not as often used in schools, businesses are beginning to assess creative context in an effort to structure environments more conducive to innovation. This section reviews some of the more commonly used assessment tools in each of the four categories as well as some whose characteristics span or defy the categorization. In each case, it is important to remember what aspect of creativity is being measured and how that information fits into the complex construct of real-world creativity.

Additional information on assessment instruments can be found in Puccio and Murdock (1999) and Kaufman, Plucker, and Baer (2008). Another outstanding resource documenting reviews of assessments of creativity is the index created by the Center for Creative Learning. Information on more than 70 different assessments can be found on its website (www.creativelearning.com/index. php/free-resources/assessing-creativity-index). The website also provides essential information on test publishers and availability.

Assessing Creative Processes

The Torrance Tests of Creative Thinking Many standardized creativity tests are based on the processes of divergent thinking identified by Guilford (1967) and are most accurately described as divergent-thinking (DT) tests. The most widely researched and extensively used of these are the Torrance Tests of Creative Thinking (TTCT; Torrance, 1990, 1999, 2008). Because these tests are widely available and frequently used by both schools and researchers, the following discussion describes them in some detail.

Torrance tests are available in both figural and verbal versions, each with A and B forms. Both versions of the test ask the test taker to complete a series of open-ended tasks presented in test booklets. For example, the verbal test asks the individual to list all the questions he or she can think to ask about a given picture. Other test items require the test taker to list possible improvements for a product and unusual uses for common objects. The figural form asks the test taker to make as many different pictures as possible using a common shape (e.g., a circle) and to make and label pictures using a series of abstract forms. All subtests are timed.

The original tests were scored for fluency, flexibility, originality, and (in the figural tests) elaboration. Ball and Torrance (1980) developed a streamlined scoring technique designed to minimize scoring time and allow the scorer to assess additional dimensions of creativity, including emotional expressiveness and internal visualization. The additional dimensions are not norm referenced (i.e., they do not compare test takers with a standard degree of emotional expressiveness), but they do allow scorers to make judgments in relation to specified criteria. The flexibility score was removed in the streamlined scoring system because it overlapped so much with fluency.

The scoring procedures are described in considerable detail in the test manual, but the tests also may be sent to a scoring service. Fluency scores are simply a count of ideas listed or drawings completed. Originality scores are determined by statistical infrequency. If an item or idea was rarely expressed by the students on whom the test was normed, it is considered to be original. Each idea is listed in a table and awarded 0, 1, or 2 originality points. The test scorer matches each idea or drawing with the closest approximation in the table and judges it for creative strength.

The open-ended nature of the tasks and multiple dimensions to be evaluated make scoring Torrance tests a time-consuming endeavor. However, the detail provided in the test manual helps ensure good interrater reliability. One caution was raised by Rosenthal, DeMars, Stilwell, and Graybeal (1983), who noted that although the correlations across raters were high, there still were significant mean differences across self-trained raters. That is, although the raters ranked the tests in approximately the same order, some judges gave generally higher scores than others. This discrepancy would mean that if Torrance tests are used to compare students or groups of students, the same scorer should evaluate all students, or adjustments should be made to compensate for differences in judges. In the same way, program evaluations using Torrance tests should use the same evaluator(s) for pre- and posttest scoring. Otherwise, any differences identified may be the result of a particular scorer's rating patterns rather than true differences among students or groups. Torrance Tests have not been found susceptible to coaching, that is, students who had pretest information on how the tests are scored or brief general creativity training did not score higher than those who received no test preparation (Fairweather, Cramond, & Landis, 2015).

The predictive validity of the Torrance tests varies in different research studies. Torrance (1984) reported two longitudinal studies in which subjects' results on early versions of the TTCT were correlated with their accomplishments as adults after 12 and 20 years. Although the correlations were far from perfect (ranging from 0.43 to 0.63), they are as high as most predictive validity scores of achievement or intelligence tests. In 1999, Torrance reported similar findings after 40 years. He found that the tests were more accurate in predicting creative accomplishments for men than for women, which raises interesting questions about the factors that may have hindered women's creative achievement. Torrance and Wu (1981) found that students identified as highly creative in high school earned as many postgraduation degrees and honors as students identified as highly intelligent and surpassed the high-IQ students in adult achievement. Plucker (1999a) reanalyzed Torrance's original data with more current statistical techniques and found the DT tests were three times better than IQ scores at predicting adult creative achievement. Perhaps most impressive, in a 50-year follow-up study, researchers found that long-ago Torrance tests continue to predict personal (if not public) creativity (Runco, Millar, Acar, & Cramond, 2010). These researchers and others continue to believe that Torrance tests and DT tests in general have much to offer (Runco & Acar, 2012). Other researchers are much more critical, finding that DT tests fail to substantially predict future creative accomplishment (Baer, 1993; Kaufman et al., 2008).

In an effort to settle the question, Kim (2008) used a meta-analysis to examine DT tests and intelligence tests as predictors of creative achievement. She found that both types of test were relatively weak but significant predictors but that divergent-thinking tests were the stronger. She did not find differences between males and females, but she did find that the TTCT was a stronger predictor than any of the other DT tests examined. Interestingly, the relationship between DT test scores and creative achievement had the highest correlation at the period of 11 to 15 years. Another interesting observation comes from Silvia (2008), who noted that DT tests aren't relevant predictors for expert performance but only for novices and beginners. Of course, those are the individuals most likely to take such tests in schools.

Torrance (2003) reported that cultural differences in the expression of creativity were reflected in Torrance test scores. He noted that in the Mexican sample (from the 1960s), only males were permitted to paint pottery. In Western Samoa, males were considered the official artists of the community. In both cases, males excelled females in figural creativity. In addition, Torrance had teachers in 11 different cultural groups complete an "Ideal Child" checklist and compared those scores to their students' scores on the TTCT. The rank order was very similar—to the degree that teachers valued creativity, students scored higher. These results provide two related sets of insights. First, the degree of cultural support for creativity appears to affect degree of creativity, at least as manifested in creativity test scores. This is important information about culture. But it also demonstrates that even this most respected of creativity tests is not a culture-free demonstration of potential, and it must be interpreted with that understanding. Studies of TTCT scores across cultures continue worldwide, with varied results (Kaufman & Sternberg, 2006). In particular, originality scores are likely to be culture specific. Something that is very common in one culture could easily be unique in another (see, for example, Saeki, Fan, & Van Dusen, 2001).

In general, research on Torrance tests suggests that the conditions under which the test is taken can have a significant effect on the scores. Torrance (1988) listed 36 studies examining the results of varying testing conditions on TTCT scores. Of these, 27 studies found significant differences in scores on at least some test forms after changes in test conditions. The changes ranged from barren and enriched rooms to varying warm-up activities and differences in timing. Other differences have been related to whether the testing was preceded by an interesting or uninteresting activity (Kirkland, 1974; Kirkland, Kirkland, & Barker, 1976), whether conditions were testlike or gamelike (Hattie, 1980), and minor changes in test instructions (Lissitz & Willhoft, 1985). If students are to be compared using scores from Torrance tests, it is particularly important that testing conditions be consistent in as many details as possible. Reviews of the Torrance tests vary from the critical assessment that the tests are based on a "loosely formed" theory and best used for research and experimentation only (Chase, 1985, p. 1632) to their recommendation as "sound examples of instruments useful for research, evaluation, and general planning decisions" (Treffinger, 1985, p. 1634). Whatever their weaknesses, the TTCT remain the most widely used and researched assessments of creativity and, as such, often provide a standard against which other tools are measured. For a more complete history, reviews, and cautions, see Kim (2006) and Plucker and Makel (2010). Of course, there are other DT tests available.

Abbreviated Torrance Test for Adults Goff and Torrance (2002) developed a short form of the TTCT that can be given to adults in approximately 15 minutes. The scores obtained are similar to those in the full-length TTCT, focusing on fluency, flexibility, originality, and elaboration. Issues about the need for consistency in scoring are similar to those in the TTCT; however, the relationship between scores on the short form and those on the long form is not clear. The norming sample was quite small (175). Reviewers concur that the Abbreviated Torrance Test may have potential, but, at this point, its demonstration of reliability and validity is substantially weaker than the original TTCT. It would not currently be appropriate for high-stakes decision making (Athanasou, 2007; Bugbee, 2007).

Thinking Creatively in Action and Movement Another test developed by Torrance (1981), Thinking Creatively in Action and Movement (TCAM), examines fluency and originality as they are expressed in movement. Designed to be used with students as young as preschool age, the test asks subjects to move across the room in as many different ways as they can, to move in designated ways (e.g., like a tree in the wind), to put a paper cup into a wastebasket in as many ways as possible, and to generate possible uses for a paper cup. The tests are not timed. They are scored for fluency (number of ideas) and originality using a scoring guide similar to the TTCT guide.

Short-term test-retest reliability and interrater reliability correlations for TCAM are high. Validity evidence is less well defined. Some efforts at establishing concurrent validity have compared scores on TCAM with scores on two other measures of fluency: the Multidimensional Stimulus Fluency Measure (Godwin & Moran, cited in Callahan, 1991) and Piagetian tasks identified by researchers as divergent (Reisman, Floyd, & Torrance, 1981). In both cases, scores correlated significantly. However, Tegano, Moran, and Godwin (1986) found significant correlations between the fluency scores on TCAM and both IQ and age. This finding raises questions about whether scores on TCAM reflect creativity or intelligence and whether they might change significantly over time. Reviews have praised TCAM as an important contribution to the assessment of creativity in young children but have noted its experimental nature and the need for additional research before it can be used with confidence in educational decision making (Evans, 1986; Renzulli, 1985; Rust, 1985). Additional research appears promising, and TCAM may provide an important option for recognizing creativity in young children (Zachopoulou, Makri, & Pollatou, 2009).

Thinking Creatively With Sounds and Words Still another product of Torrance and his colleagues, *Thinking Creatively With Sounds and Words* (Torrance, Khatena, & Cunningham, 1973) uses recorded sounds to stimulate divergent thinking. The instrument actually comprises two tests: Sounds and Images; and Onomatopoeia and Images. In the Sounds and Images test, test takers are presented with four abstract sounds. After each sound, the individual jots down the mental images he or she associates with the sound. The set of four sounds is presented three times. Subjects' ideas are evaluated for originality using a scoring guide similar to those in the two tests previously described. The Onomatopoeia and Images test is similar except that instead of abstract sounds, subjects are presented with 10 onomatopoetic words such as "boom" or "fizzy." The set of words also is repeated three times and scored as in the previous test. Both tests are available in A and B forms and with instructions designed for adults or children. As does TCAM, this test presents reasonable reliability data except for some weaknesses in alternate forms but presents inadequate evidence of validity for it to be a major source in educational decision making (Houtz, 1985). Until further information on validity is available, the test may be most useful as a source of interesting creative activities in varying domains rather than a means of assessment.

Guilford and the Structure of Intellect Assessments All of the tests assessing divergent thinking are built on the work of Guilford (1967, 1973, 1977). Based on his Structure of Intellect (SOI) model, Guilford's tests emphasized divergent production and transformations. Guilford's *Creativity Tests for Children* (1973) are made up of five verbal and five nonverbal divergent production tasks. They include generating names for stories, finding letters of the alphabet hidden in complex figures, and listing alternate uses for familiar objects. His *Alternate Uses Test,* which can be used for secondary students and adults, is a single task requiring test takers to list alternate uses for six common objects and is used regularly in research with adults. The reviews of these tests have been critical. Concerns expressed by reviewers regarding the *Creativity Tests for Children* include low correlations with the Torrance tests and low reliability estimates (French, 1978; Yamamoto, 1978). The *Alternate Uses Test* was criticized for lack of interrater-reliability data, lack of correlation with other measures of divergent thinking, the influence of background experience on scores, and inadequate information in the test manual (Quellmalz, 1985). At this point, it appears that the second generation of divergent-thinking tests (notably the TTCT) have outdistanced Guilford's original measures in estimates of reliability and validity.

Meeker also adapted groups of Guilford tests in a diagnostic-prescriptive model of instruction, the *Structure of Intellect Learning Abilities Test* (SOI-LA; Meeker, 1969; Meeker, Meeker, & Roid, 1985). Students are tested on various aspects of SOI (described in Chapter 2) and provided with targeted remediation and instruction. Although not a creativity test per se, the SOI-LA does include a divergent-thinking score associated with creativity. Unfortunately, like the Guilford's tests, the SOI-LA in general and the divergent-thinking scores in particular have been seriously questioned by test reviewers. One reviewer suggested, "Maybe the SOI-LA represents an attempt to slice the intellectual pie too thinly" (Cummings, 1989). Reviewers' concerns have included limitations in reliability of both test-retest and alternate forms, with divergent-thinking scores particularly low. Certainly, limited alternate-forms reliability in divergent-thinking scores would make the use of alternate forms for pre- and posttesting inappropriate (Clarizio & Mehrens, 1985; Cummings, 1989).

The Wallach and Kogan Tests Similar to the preceding tests, the Wallach and Kogan battery also is a series of tasks requiring divergent thinking. The battery is not available from a publisher but is reproduced in its entirety in *Modes of Thinking in Young Children* (Wallach & Kogan, 1965). Although it is not commonly used in schools, the Wallach and Kogan battery is important for at least two reasons: It is used in research involving creativity, and it is conducted in a unique testing atmosphere. Wallach and Kogan (1965) believed that the formal test settings of most creativity tests are not conductive to creativity in young children, particularly if creativity requires a relaxed, playful state of mind. Consequently, their tests are designed to be given individually in an untimed, gamelike atmosphere. Their original research emphasized the relationship between tests of creativity and intelligence, a question of construct validity. In a study of 151 fifth-grade children, they found that the scores on the five subtests correlated strongly with one another but not highly with measures of intelligence. This is one piece of evidence in the debate over the relationship between creativity and intelligence.

There is one unusual aspect to the scoring of the Wallach and Kogan battery. The tests are scored for fluency (the total number of ideas listed) and uniqueness (the number of ideas given that are not given by any other member of the group tested). Although this scoring variation may help to account for cultural differences (a response that might have been unique in a norming population used to create a scoring chart might be very common in another group), it causes scores to be heavily affected by the number of individuals taking the test. If I were to take the tests in a group of 10, it is much more likely that I would generate several unique ideas than if my responses were being compared with 500 others.

Because this test battery is published as part of a research study and not as a nationally distributed standardized test, the information on reliability and validity is not as extensive nor the sample as large as might be expected for other uses. There are some data suggesting that the battery may be more reliable for students scoring higher on standardized achievement tests (Runco & Albert, 1985) and that the verbal subtests correlate with self-reports of creative activities in students identified as gifted but not in others (Runco, 1986). The relationship between Wallach and Kogan scores and general intellectual ability requires further investigation.

The Remote Associates Test The *Remote Associates Test* (RAT) was developed by Mednick (1967) as an assessment tool based on his theory of creativity. Recall from Chapter 2 that Mednick believed creativity to be the result of mental associations. The more numerous and diverse the associations an individual can make, the more opportunities he or she has for creativity. The RAT attempts to assess the number of verbal associations at an individual's disposal by providing three stimulus words and asking the test taker to generate a word that can be associated with all three. For example, the words paint, doll, and cat all can be associated with the response "house."

Some validity studies of the RAT have showed correlations between it and other assessments of creativity, whereas other studies have found no such relationships (Lynch & Kaufman, 1974; Mednick, 1962; Wallach, 1970). No validity data are available for the high school version of the test. Moreover, the validity of the RAT has been questioned on theoretical grounds. The nature of the test punishes novel or imaginative responses; an association is scored as correct only if it is the same association made by the test constructors. The test also has been criticized because studies of the processes used by individuals taking the test do not match those intended by the author (Perkins, 1981) and because scores on the RAT correlate highly with IQ scores (Ward, 1975). Another review also criticized the role of convergent production in the RAT and suggested that it "not be used for counseling or placement purposes at the present time" (Backman & Tuckman, 1978, p. 370). Finally, the RAT has been criticized for cultural bias and is difficult for nonnative English speakers. The RAT is currently out of print but is available at several websites and continues to be used in creativity research.

Measures of divergent thinking continue to expand. For example, the Unusual Box test is a nonverbal text designed to be used by children as young as 2 years old. In it, children play individually with a novel toy box and novel objects. The test shows promise, as it correlates well with other divergent-thinking measures that are appropriate for young children. This instrument is particularly interesting because it has demonstrated that children's fluency and originality scores increase with age, though this may be due to improved motor skills. Certainly it has the potential to help us learn more about the ways divergent thinking develops in young people and the variables that may affect it (Bijvoet-van den Berg & Hoicka, 2014; Hoicka, Bijvoet-van den Berg, Kerr, & Carberry, 2013).

Process Tests Yet to Come One possible adaptation in creativity testing is in the scoring procedures. To date, most tests of creative processes have examined divergent thinking, generally scored as fluency, flexibility, originality, and elaboration. However, there is considerable question as to whether these scores actually represent three different abilities. Callahan (1991) referred to fluency as a "contaminating factor" (p. 229) in the assessment of originality. Higher fluency scores accompany higher scores on originality. Similarly, higher fluency scores are associated with higher scores on flexibility. On one hand, this is logical, since the intent of fluency is to allow more flexible and original thinking, but it poses an assessment challenge. The concern about fluency as a contaminating factor has been echoed by other writers (Plucker & Renzulli, 1999; Plucker & Runco, 1998). It is possible that future research and test development may lead us to alternative scoring mechanisms for divergent-thinking tasks. The streamlined scoring procedure for the Torrance Tests of Creative Thinking (perhaps misnamed because it results in many more than four scores) is one effort in this direction.

Other researchers have investigated alternate scoring methods for divergent-thinking tasks. For example, scoring whether an idea is original is tricky. Not only does originality depend on context and experiences, but for scoring purposes, simply having more ideas can automatically generate more originality points. One proposal to solve this problem, called subjective top scoring, asks individuals to identify their most creative ideas, then scores those for originality (Benedek, Mühlmann, Jauk, & Neubauer, 2013; Silvia et al., 2008). Other researchers have investigated various combinations of objective and subjective ratings, particularly for evaluating solutions to "real-world" problems (Plucker, Qian, & Schmalensee, 2014). One group of researchers has proposed calculating a Creativity Quotient (CQ) to score DT responses, with higher scores going to pools of responses that are both fluent and flexible (Bossomaier, Harré, Knittel, & Snyder, 2009; Snyder, Mitchell, Bossomaier, & Pallier, 2004). Other researchers, building on the original CQ scale, found that an adjusted CQ score, calculated by weighting some categories based on originality, better predicted real-world creativity (Lucas, van der Wijst, Curşeu, & Looman, 2013). Although it is not wise to add or otherwise adjust current creativity test scores contrary to the instructions of the test constructors, it is possible that future research will allow us to use scores in new and more effective ways.

Still other creativity tests to come may assess process factors not yet addressed in commercial measures. Tests that attempt to measure insight, problem identification (Runco & Chand, 1994; Starko, 2000), or other process variables may one day add to our understanding of the creative process. Vessey and Mumford (2012) proposed the study of cognitive and metacognitive heuristics (strategies) in creative problem solving as a source for new assessment techniques. Sternberg (2012) describes a series of open-ended tasks based on his investment theory (e.g., story writing or cartoon captions) and suggests prompts for such tasks having potential as assessment strategies. And, of course, there is the question as to whether creative processes are similar across domains. Research such as Kaufman, Cole, and Baer's (2009) investigation of self-reported creativity lays the foundation for discipline-focused assessments. Another area of investigation is the feasibility of online assessments, particularly of divergent thinking (Hass, 2015). Clearly, there are many creative process assessments yet to come!

Assessing the Creative Person

Instruments focusing on the characteristics of the creative person include personality assessments and biographical inventories. These most often take the form of self-reports or observational checklists.

The Khatena–Torrance Creative Perception Inventory This two-part inventory includes the self-rating scales What Kind of Person Are You? (WKOPAY) and Something About Myself (SAM). It is designed to identify creative individuals ages 10 years and older (Khatena & Torrance, 1976, 1990). The WKOPAY is designed to "yield an index of the individual's disposition or motivation to function in creative ways" (Khatena, 1992, p. 134). It contains 50 forced-choice items that require the test taker to choose between items that may be socially desirable or undesirable, creative or noncreative. For example, one item might ask individuals whether they are more likely to care for others or have courage for what they believe. The scale yields five factors: acceptance of authority, self-confidence, inquisitiveness, awareness of others, and disciplined imagination.

The SAM is designed to reflect an individual's personality characteristics, thinking strategies, and creative products. Test takers review 50 statements such as "I like adding to an idea" or "I have made a new dance or song" and indicate which statements are true for them. This scale yields six factor scores: environmental sensitivity, initiative, self-strength, intellectuality, individuality, and artistry.

Reliability data for the inventory are satisfactory. Validity studies have shown moderate but significant correlations between SAM and tests of verbal originality and the Onomatopoeia and Images subtest of Thinking Creatively With Sounds and Words. Both scales correlated significantly with a measure of readiness for self-directed study (Kaltsounis, 1975; Khatena & Bellarosa, 1978). At this point, there are no data on predictive validity for either scale. Callahan (n.d.) notes, "Reliance on self-reporting relating to the behaviors that require considerable self-knowledge and reflection is a very tenuous assessment strategy" and suggests the instrument is best used for research or discussion purposes.

Group Inventory for Finding Creative Talent The *Group Inventory for Finding Creative Talent* (GIFT) is a self-report form designed to assess the creative potential of students grades 1 to 6 (Davis & Rimm, 1980). Students respond "yes" or "no" to a series of statements designed to assess the traits of independence, flexibility, curiosity, perseverance, breadth of interests, and past creative activities and hobbies (Davis, 1992). They respond to statements such as "I like to make up my own songs," "I like to take things apart to see how they work," and "I like to do things that are hard to do." The GIFT instrument yields a total score and scores for three subscales: imagination, independence, and many interests. Tests must be scored by the publisher. Although publisher scoring ensures consistency, it can cause delays and makes it impossible to examine individual responses to analyze scores.

The split-half reliability (correlating one half of the scale with the other half) for GIFT is strong, but the test-retest reliability is only moderate. Validity studies have compared GIFT scores with teacher ratings of creativity and experimenter ratings of creative stories and pictures. The relationships were low to moderate (ranging from 0.20 to 0.54) and significant. Reviewers of the GIFT have stressed the need for additional validity data and more complete information in the test manual, but they have viewed the scale as a useful tool for decision making when used in conjunction with other types of assessment (Dwinell, 1985; Wright, 1985).

Group Inventories for Finding Interests (I and II) The Group Inventories for Finding Interests (GIFFI) I and II are very similar to GIFT but are designed for junior and senior high school students, respectively (Davis & Rimm, 1982). Their strengths and weaknesses are very similar to those of GIFT. Validity studies comparing scores on GIFFI with writing samples and teacher ratings have produced an average score of 0.45. The GIFFI has been criticized for cultural bias in some of the items (e.g., "I like to attend concerts"), which may undermine its effectiveness, particularly in multicultural populations (Weeks, 1985).

Preschool and Kindergarten Interest Descriptor (PRIDE) PRIDE (Rimm, 1983) is an inventory intended to screen young children who may be identified as creatively gifted. The inventory contains 50 questions, which are completed by parents, describing their own or their child's behavior. Like GIFT and GIFFI, it must be scored by the publisher, resulting in some delay in obtaining results. PRIDE has reasonable face validity in that the characteristics on the list have been reported as characteristics of creative children. However, the norming group is too small (114), particularly for the factor analysis reported for the inventory. The technical issues, combined with the general difficulties with assessment in very young children, mean that this instrument should be used with caution until it can be more extensively tested (Galvin, n.d.).

Creative Attitude Survey The Creative Attitude Survey (Schaefer, 1971) is designed to assess subjects' attitudes associated with creativity, including confidence in one's ideas, appreciation of fantasy, theoretical and aesthetic orientation, openness to impulse expression, and use of novelty. Validity information has come through the evaluation of two training programs in which elementary school children received creativity training over a period of weeks. The students who received the creativity training had increased scores on the Creative Attitude Survey, whereas the control groups did not. Twenty months later, the differences remained. At least one reviewer has suggested that this instrument may be effective for evaluating programs designed to increase creativity in elementary school–age children (McKee, 1985).

Biographical Inventory—Creativity The Biographical Inventory—Creativity (BIC; Schaefer, 1970) is based on the assumption that the best predictor of future activity is past activity—those who have been involved in creative activities in the past are more likely to be so involved again. The inventory consists of 165 items in which the test taker is asked whether he or she has participated in a given activity. It yields four scores: creative art for girls, creative writing for girls, creative math and science for boys, and art and writing for boys. Clearly, the scales defined by gender present problems. No options for information on girls creative in math or science appear available. Research on the BIC has indicated that the instrument successfully differentiated groups of high school students who had been nominated by teachers for scientific or artistic creativity from other students matched for school, grade, and grade point average (Anastasi & Schaefer, 1969; Schaefer, 1969; Schaefer & Anastasi, 1968). It is important to recognize, however, that significantly differentiating large groups is a different task from providing reliable and valid individual scores. Additional research and development is necessary before the BIC could be recommended for educational decision making.

Behavioral Observations One common way of assessing creativity in schools is through the use of behavioral observations. Guided by a checklist or observation form, teachers identify students whose behaviors match descriptions of activities associated with creativity. One of the most commonly used tools for observation is the Creativity scale of the Scales for Rating the Behavioral Characteristics of Superior Students (Renzulli et al., 2002). This nine-item checklist describes behaviors such as imaginative thinking ability and "a non-conforming attitude, does not fear being different."

Teachers use a six-point scale to rate each student on each behavior. Both test-retest and interrater reliability data for this instrument are strong. In initial validity studies, the Creativity scale correlated significantly with verbal scores on the TTCT but not with figural scores. The authors suggest that "this finding reflects a verbal bias in the Creativity Scale items and suggests that caution should be exercised in using this scale to identify students for programs that emphasize nonverbal creativity" (p. 9). The revised scales correlate with success in gifted programs for grades 3 through 12.

Thinking About the Classroom

Use the Creativity scale of the Scales for Rating the Behavioral Characteristics of Superior Students to evaluate five randomly chosen students in your class. Do you feel the results of the scale accurately reflect the students' creative behavior in your class?

Another type of instrument, the *Kingore Observation Inventory* (KOI; Kingore, 1990), provides teachers with descriptions of target student behaviors on a large form to be kept on the teacher's desk. For several days, teachers jot a student's name next to a characteristic each time he or she demonstrates the behavior. Less commonly, teachers may plan a specific activity designed to elicit creative activity and make anecdotal records of student behaviors. The KOI is designed to identify young gifted children rather than to assess creativity. Although several of the categories of behavior may be associated with creativity (e.g., Perspective or Sense of Humor), the author has suggested that creative behaviors may be infused throughout any of the observations. No reliability or validity data are reported. The lack of reliability and validity data raises questions, and teachers wishing to assess creativity may want to use an instrument that targets key behaviors more specifically. However, the concept of observing designated behaviors over a designated period may prove fruitful as new observations are developed.

The subjective nature of most rating scales makes reliability and validity assessments difficult. In particular, school-specific homemade activities and scales are at risk of providing unreliable or invalid data. Yet observations of students' behaviors often can provide clues to strengths and abilities not accessed by written standardized tests. In addition, an observation of activities directly associated with the purpose of assessment (e.g., observations of activities in a high school industrial technology class in order to nominate students for a specialized program making creative use of technology) may provide appropriate information for particular circumstances. In no case, however, should instruments of questionable reliability and validity be the sole source of information for educational decision making.

Newer Assessments As researchers learn more about creativity and ask new questions, new instruments emerge. For example, the *Creative Achievement Questionnaire* (CAQ; Carson, Peterson, & Higgins, 2005) is like the BIC in that it asks participants to check off their accomplishments in 10 domains of creative activities, from visual arts to scientific inquiry to cooking to humor. The authors of the CAQ found that the domains tend to cluster. Studies are ongoing, but the effort to look at creative activities across disciplines has promise.

The *Runco Ideational Behavior Scale* (RIBS; Runco, Plucker, & Lim, 2000–2001) is another self-report scale. RIBS asks individuals to indicate how much they agree with statements such as, "I have many wild ideas" or "I try to exercise my mind by thinking things through." Although it does not have the research history of some of the older instruments, the RIBS has demonstrated reliability and continues to be used in research.

One of the great dilemmas in creativity theory and research is whether creativity is a global or domain-specific construct. This question can be investigated as domain-specific measures of creativity emerge. For example, the *Kaufman Domains of Creativity Scale* or K-DOCS is designed to assess domain-specific variations in everyday creativity, in a self-report format. The K-DOCS items were based on Kaufman's earlier Creativity Domain Questionnaire (CDQ, Kaufman, 2006; Kaufman et al., 2009), edited into behavioral terms. They ask the person completing the instrument to gauge their creativity in a variety of areas, as compared to their peers. The instrument provides separate scores for Self/Everyday, Scholarly, Performance, Mechanical/Science, and Artistic creativity (Kaufman, 2012; McKay, Karwowski, & Kaufman, 2016). While domain-specific creativity instruments are still in the relatively early stages (and self-reports have definite limitations), the careful development of instruments like the K-DOCS can provide statistical assistance in identifying ways creative behaviors may cluster, as well as a valid and reliable way to assess domain-specific creativity.

An interesting variation on the study of creative individuals is assessing creative self-efficacy. Recall from Chapter 9 that creative self-efficacy refers to individuals' level of confidence in their own creativity or ability to succeed at creative tasks. It is most commonly studied in the workplace, where creative problem solving is essential to financial success. Like other forms of self-efficacy (Bandura, 1977, 1986), creative self-efficacy is typically situation or discipline specific. My creative self-efficacy in the area of music or mosaics is much higher than that for painting or computer programming. Creative self-efficacy helps predict creative job performance (Choi, 2004; Tierney & Farmer, 2002).

Beghetto (2006) studied creative self-efficacy in middle and secondary school students and found that higher creative self-efficacy was associated with higher levels of motivation and academic aspirations. Students with higher creative self-efficacy also were more likely to report teachers telling them they were creative. It is interesting to consider whether creative self-efficacy is supported in the same ways as other forms of self-efficacy. Tierney and Farmer (2002) found that bosses who modeled and supported creativity were associated with higher creative self-efficacy in employees. Bandura's general self-efficacy research would suggest that self-efficacy is built through successful experiences with creativity, modeling, and verbal support. Further research (and assessment) will help us understand the impact these actions may have on the creative self-efficacy of young people.

As research on creative individuals continues, it is likely that other types of assessment instruments will emerge. As we learn more about how creative individuals solve problems, we may discover multiple variations across individuals and domains.

Instruments Assessing Creative Products

With this type of assessment, an individual is faced with a creative product and asked to make a determination: "Is this creative?" or "To what degree is this creative?" Assessments of creative products are made every day by art, literary, and theatrical critics and editors of scientific journals. Using their knowledge of the forms, standards, and history of their disciplines, these experts are able to determine where a work falls in the field at a given time. Assessments of creative products virtually always entail subjectivity, knowledge, and expertise. Packaging such assessments as standardized, easily purchased items is very difficult, but assessment of creativity must, ultimately, depend on the evaluation of its fruits.

Creative Product Assessment Matrix Few empirical studies have attempted to identify the characteristics of a creative product (Besemer & Treffinger, 1981). One effort to develop a model for

Evaluating creative products can be difficult

creative product analysis is the *Creative Product Assessment Matrix* (CPAM; Besemer & O'Quin, 1986). It suggests three dimensions for assessing creative products: novelty, resolution, and elaboration and synthesis. Novelty includes the originality of the product and its potential for generating further ideas and changes. Resolution entails how well the product serves its intended purpose, solves a problem, or fills a need. Elaboration and synthesis express stylistic attributes of the product and may include diverse complexity or simple elegance.

Student Product Assessment Form The *Student Product Assessment Form* (SPAF; Renzulli & Reis, 1997) was designed to assess students' creative products in schools. The SPAF is used to rate student products on nine factors (Figure 10.5). Although not all factors are appropriate for every kind of product, item descriptions provide clarity in the judging of each factor and contribute to the reliability of this instrument. As efforts to create a concise model for assessing creative products continue, both CPAM and SPAF may provide general guidelines for those attempting to evaluate creative products.

Instruments such as these, designed to assist in the evaluation of creative products, generally are intended to bring consistency to the endeavor. If two movie critics give widely different reviews of the same movie, the disparity may be viewed as a legitimate difference of opinion. If a particular critic consistently reviews differently from the majority of his or her colleagues, he or she will be labeled a maverick or find a new career but probably will not determine the fate of the films. If educational decisions are made on the basis of product evaluations, a maverick judge can affect children's opportunities in important ways. Therefore, although professional critics seldom sit down to review a product with a checklist in hand, such guidance may be appropriate in an educational setting.

The scoring rubrics for authentic assessment described in the first section of this chapter are a form of product assessment. Each is designed to provide a set of criteria along which complex products can be assessed. Similar patterns can be followed in the assessment of creative products, with consistent attention paid to the creativity expressed. Products to be assessed may be single items or a portfolio of creative efforts.

Portfolios In portfolio assessments, teachers and students collect samples of students' work throughout the year as a means of demonstrating student progress. In a writing portfolio, several drafts of a work may be included to illustrate thought processes, self-assessment, and developing sophistication. Similar collections of work can be made in other domains, such as science portfolios and math portfolios. These may or may not be contained in physical folders. A student whose oral history project or screenplay is best captured on video will need a different kind of portfolio.

Name(s) _____ Date _____

School District _____ Teacher _____

Grade _____ Sex _____

Product (Title and/or Brief Description)

Number of Months Student(s)Worked on Product _____

Factors	Rating*	Not Applicable
1. Early Statement of Purpose	_____	_____
2. Problem Focusing		
3. Level of Resources		
4. Diversity of Resources		
5. Appropriateness of Resources	_____	_____
6. Logic, Sequence, and Transition	_____	_____
7. Action Orientation		
8. Audience		
9. Overall Assessment		
A. Originality of the Idea		
B. Achieved Objectives Stated in Plan	_____	_____
C. Advanced Familiarity with Subject	_____	_____
D. Quality Beyond Age/Grade Level	_____	_____
E. Care, Attention to Detail, etc.	_____	_____
F. Time, Effort, Energy		
G. Original Contribution		

Comments:

Person completing this form: _____

*Rating Scales: Factors 1–8	Factors 9A–9G	
5 = To a great extent	5 = Outstanding	2 = Below /Average
3 = Somewhat	4 = Above/Average	1 = Poor
1 = To a limited extent	3 = Average	

Figure 10.5 Student project assessment form summary sheet

Source: From Renzulli, J. S., & Reis, S. M. (1991). "The Assessment of Creative Products in Programs for Gifted and Talented Students." *Gifted Child Quarterly, 35*(2), 130. Copyright © 1991 by Creative Learning Press. Reprinted with permission.

Regardless of the subject areas, portfolios provide one strategy for organizing the assessment of creative products. If, for some reason (such as participation in a particular school program), you need to identify exceptionally creative individuals in a given class or school, you may want to compile a creativity portfolio. This could document creativity in a particular discipline (e.g., if nominating students for a writing or art program) or creative activities in multiple domains. Such a portfolio might contain photographs or originals of artwork, creative writing, tapes or scores of original music, video of performances, accounts of real-life problem solving, unusual responses to class assignments, records of science projects, invention notes, or any other documentation of creative activities. These can be assessed using a scoring rubric. The rubric might include dimensions for novelty, technical quality, depth or breadth of interests, or any other factor relevant to the selection.

Thinking About the Classroom

Compile a creativity portfolio for at least one student. Include evidence of creative activities in at least three areas. Do you see patterns or large variations across domains? You may want to share the information with the student's parents.

If creativity is to be evaluated not for individual decision making but as part of general classroom assessment, a separate portfolio probably is not necessary. One possible strategy is to examine the scoring procedures currently in place for any portfolio or other performance assessment currently in use. Is there a dimension that gives credit for novelty in appropriate responses? If a writing portfolio provides numerous opportunities for teachers and students to examine proofreading and grammar skills but few chances to evaluate originality, imagery, or the use of metaphor, opportunities to evaluate and encourage creative products are being lost.

The products to be assessed may be naturally occurring—part of an individual's typical productivity—or they may be generated specifically for assessment. Both have their advantages. Products generated specifically for assessment have the advantage of consistency and often are easier to rate relative to one another. Naturally occurring products are less likely to have been produced in a constrained amount of time and may be more likely to represent an individual's best work and genuine interests. A portfolio of creative work might include one or two items created specifically for assessment purposes, some regular class assignments, and some items created outside a school setting.

Consensual Assessment Technique In some cases, particularly with advanced students, teachers may feel they do not have sufficient expertise to assess creative products. For these situations, expert judges using Amabile's (1982b, 1996) Consensual Assessment Technique (CAT) may be most effective. The Consensual Assessment Technique is one of the most well-documented and frequently used measures in current creativity research. In consensual assessment, expert judges rate creative products. If there is agreement among the judges as to the most creative products, usually at about 0.80, the judgments are considered sound. Because the judges are expert in the area being assessed, they are not provided with specific criteria for judgment but are asked to make several global assessments, such as evaluations of creativity, technical skill, and overall quality.

There is a growing body of research on the reliability of differing groups of judges in consensual assessment (Baer, Kaufman, & Gentile, 2004; Hickey, 2001; Kaufman, Gentile, & Baer, 2005; Priest, 2006) The following guidelines were offered to researchers using consensual assessment in research. They seem reasonable for others using expert judges as part of creativity assessment (Hennessey & Amabile, 1988):

1. Use experienced, knowledgeable judges. The judges need not all have the same level of expertise, but they should be knowledgeable in their domain. Of course, there are practical considerations. When judging high-level creativity—Pulitzer Prize winners, for example—we'd expect judges to have substantial expertise and experience in the field, but things can be different in schools. Judges for advanced high school science projects need much more expertise than those judging younger students. Most of you teaching elementary school will not have the option to bring in literal rocket scientists to judge rocket design projects—and even if you could, they might not be the best judges of what is exceptional for a 10-year-old. Kaufman and Baer (2013) note that quasi-experts, with some background in the area but not expert standing, may be effective judges, and also that some tasks used in creativity measures, for example, writing humorous titles under photographs, may not

have existing experts. Finding the appropriate balance between expertise and practicality is a challenge of this form of assessment. If creative products span several dimensions or domains, judges' expertise should be similarly broad. For example, if the art portfolios to be judged include sketches, paintings, advertising designs, and photographs of sculptures, a better panel would be judges whose expertise included several areas and techniques rather than those who all were landscape painters.

2. Have judges make their assessments independently. The correlations among judges become meaningless if judges have conferred. Each individual judge should bring his or her ideas of creativity to the task.

3. Make judgments of all dimensions at the same time. For example, if judges rate products on both creativity and technical expertise, it is easier to determine whether the judgments of creativity are related to or independent of technique.

4. Rate products relative to each other. It is important that judges be instructed to rate products in a student's own sphere rather than by the standards they might hold for adult colleagues. Although assessment according to adult criteria may be useful for older students, few useful purposes are served by observing that none of the elementary students' efforts meet adult standards.

5. Rate products in random order. Judges should not rate the products in the same order. Otherwise, assessment may relate more to order (e.g., specific comparisons or weariness of the judges) than to merits of particular products.

Because it is quite labor intensive, assessment by experts might be most appropriate for selecting highly creative students for advanced educational opportunities. Such processes are fairly familiar in the arts. For example, if students are to be nominated for a state-level summer art program, art students might be asked to compile a portfolio of their work. Portfolios could be judged by two or three professional artists whose combined scores could be used for decision making. Students can be taught to compile documentation of their creative efforts in other domains. They can keep records of science projects, musical compositions, writing, inventions, or historical research. Expert judges can assist in educational decision making and provide realistic feedback to older students about career opportunities.

Thinking About the Classroom

Work with colleagues to collect high-quality samples of student work in a particular domain. You may wish to focus on the work of secondary school students. Ask two or three expert judges to rate the samples separately for creativity, technical skill, and overall quality. See if your data provide support for consensual assessment as an evaluation tool.

Assessing Creative Press: Environments for Creativity

Because the organizational climate of businesses influences their creativity—which, of course, influences their success—it is not surprising that instruments for assessing creative business environments continue to be developed worldwide. Probably the most well-known effort to assess creative work environments is Amabile, Conti, Coon, Lazenby, and Herron's (1996) *KEYS: Assessing the Climate for Creativity*. KEYS is a self-report instrument that examines employees' perceptions of their work environment. It assesses four categories of variables: managerial practices, organizational motivation, resources, and outcomes. Being able to assess factors that support or depress creativity can give important guidance to leaders in business environments.

Another instrument intended to assess the creativity of organizations rather than individuals is the *Innovation Phase Assessment Instrument* (IPAI). Based on Cropley and Cropley's (2012) expansion of the Wallas model (preparation, activation, generation, illumination, verification, communication, validation), the instrument examines six dimensions of innovation (for example, process, personal motivation, and product) at each stage. It is designed to diagnose relative areas of creative strength and weakness across an organization's creative activities (Cropley, Cropley, Chiera, & Kaufman, 2013).

Ekvall's *Creative Climate Questionnaire* was translated from the original Swedish and developed over a 10-year period in a collaboration with the Center for Studies in Creativity at Buffalo State University. It identifies nine dimensions of creative climate in the workplace: Challenge/Involvement, Freedom, Trust/Openness, Idea Time, Playfulness/Humor, Conflict, Idea Support, Debate and Risk Taking (Isaksen, Lauer, & Ekvall, 1999). Bruno-Faria (2014) has developed an assessment of creative climate in the Brazilian workplace, the Indicators of Climate for Creativity (ICC). She makes the distinction between workplace creativity (generation of ideas, processes, products, and/or new services) and innovation (implementing such ideas). The scale is designed to identify Stimulants that promote expressions of creativity and Barriers that hinder it. The scale continues to be tested with various groups, but the notion of examining both the strengths and barriers in an organization would seem a promising idea. It is fascinating to think about what the parallels might be in educational environments.

Thus far there are few instruments designed to assess the creative classroom environment, but there is a beginning in Fleith's (2014) *Classroom Climate for Creativity Scale*. Based on initial testing of the scale, five factors were identified (paraphrasing the titles): teacher's support/acceptance of student ideas, student's self-perceived creativity, student's interest in learning, student's autonomy, and teacher's encouragement to think of new ideas. Pilot tests with the scale were done with third and fourth graders, with better success with the older students. Certainly the format appears most appropriate for elementary grades. Notice how the scales fit the ideas we've been reviewing about the type of environment necessary to intrinsic motivation. The scale is brief and appears easy to use. It is interesting to think about how it could be used to diagnose our teaching strengths or to assess how classroom changes are perceived by our students.

Combinations and Other Types of Assessment

It should be clear that creativity is complex enough that no single measure, no matter how valid, is enough to measure its many dimensions. While single measures may be needed for some practical purposes, understanding the nature of creativity may require a multimeasure approach. An early effort in that direction was Williams's (1980) *Creativity Assessment Packet (CAP)*. The CAP includes three tasks: the Exercise in Divergent Thinking, the Exercise in Divergent Feeling, and the Williams Scale. The Exercise in Divergent Thinking is almost identical to the picture completion subtest on the figural form of the Torrance Tests of Creative Thinking (TTCT). The Exercise in Divergent Feeling includes 50 items on which students are to rate themselves along a four-point scale for such characteristics as curiosity and imagination. The Williams Scale is a 48-item checklist to be used by a parent or teacher rating the child on creative characteristics and activities.

The combination of a divergent-thinking measure, a self-assessment of characteristics associated with creativity, and a behavioral checklist would seem, at first glance, to be a logical and possibly winning combination. Unfortunately, the CAP has been criticized severely by reviewers. Concerns have included poor norming samples and unclear and inadequate reliability and validity data. Reliabilities are characterized as "in the sixties," and "validity scores" of 0.71 and 0.76 are given without any information as to what they mean or how they were obtained (Damarin, 1985).

Two 1985 reviewers concluded that the limitations are so severe that the CAP cannot be recommended for use (Damarin, 1985; Rosen, 1985).

More recently, Agnoli, Corazza, and Runco (2016) have developed a "multifaceted test battery" for the measurement of creativity within scientific and artistic domains. The battery includes 12 different measures of convergent thinking, divergent thinking, evaluation of ideas, creative accomplishments in particular domains, intelligence, and personality measures that have been associated with creativity. Understanding the relationship of variables within the battery may be helpful moving forward in our understanding of creativity and particularly the ways it intersects with neurological processes.

An interesting assessment from Brazil assesses not creativity itself but obstacles to personal creativity (Alencar, 2014). The self-report Obstacles to Personal Creativity Inventory identifies four modalities of obstacles: Inhibition/Shyness, Lack of Time/Opportunity, Social Repression, and Lack of Motivation. In all studies conducted thus far, the most common obstacle is Lack of Time/Opportunity. It is interesting to consider whether, when reporting obstacles to personal creativity, any of us might be more likely to say we'd be more creative if we had more time or others were more encouraging rather than say we'd do more if we were less lazy and more motivated! Still, it is important to understand the barriers that block individuals from creativity, and this inventory can be a valuable beginning. It can be found in Alencar, Bruno-Faria, and Fleith's (2014) *Theory and Practice of Creativity Measurement*.

Assessing Creativity in Schools

Schools and school districts have assessed creativity in a variety of ways, depending on their needs. Working to accurately assess students' complex varieties of creativity can be demanding and often requires a balance of nuance and practicality. Treffinger, Schoonover, and Selby (2013) suggest the use of a Creative Strengths Profile to identify the various ways students demonstrate creative characteristics and strengths. It is not intended to "add up" various strengths to a creativity total but to examine students' strengths in ways that will help teachers support them. Sources of evidence could include tests, rating scales, self-reports, and observations. For me, envisioning myself completing a full Creativity Strengths Profile on a class (or five classes) full of students seems beyond what I could manage. But when creativity is assessed outside a general classroom evaluation, it is most often for the purpose of identifying students with exceptional creative potential who may benefit from particular educational opportunities. For example, if a school has a mentorship program in which community adults work with students in areas of mutual interest, all students could benefit from interaction with a concerned adult. However, it would be helpful if you could identify students who would benefit most from association with a creative cartoonist, scientist, or writer and match those students and mentors appropriately. In this case, the Creative Strengths profile or other type of creativity portfolio could be useful. The format also could be useful for thinking about a puzzling student or group of students in more complex and useful ways. If you'd like to experiment with a Creative Strengths Profile, Treffinger et al. can provide a place to start. In any such efforts, it is important to recognize that students must have the opportunity to demonstrate creative behaviors if those strengths are to be identified. Knowledgeable teachers who regularly provide students with opportunities for flexible and innovative thinking are an essential part of the process. Kerr and McKay (2013) also investigated the use of profiles in identifying creative adolescents for specialized programming. While preliminary, their profiles explore the possibility that discipline-specific creativity profiles can be used to better match students with opportunities.

Another fascinating use of creativity assessment in education is in college admissions. Sternberg (2006, 2012) reports an effort to improve predictions of college success beyond that available through the SAT through assessments of analytical, practical, and creative skills. Based on Sternberg's triarchic theory of intelligence (Sternberg, 1985a), the project indicated that use of the Sternberg Triarchic Abilities Test, in addition to the SAT, enhanced predictions of college GPA and also reduced ethnic-group differences. This success led to Tufts University adding supplemental application materials for students seeking admission in fall of 2007. Students had the opportunity to title a cartoon or write a short story on an intriguing topic. Although Tufts officials were careful to state that "We are not going to leave out high academic-achieving students and replace them with less academic-achieving, but more creative students" (Ragovin, 2006), the pilot project has the potential to transform college admissions through enhancing understanding of students' abilities. Sternberg (obviously a busy researcher!) has also collaborated in piloting a new creativity assessment designed to measure the six components of his investment model (Sternberg, 2012; Zhang & Sternberg, 2011). Although that measure is still in its early stages, it illustrates the continuing evolution of assessments of creativity to address more and more complex creativity theories.

Challenges, Lessons, and Recommendations

Whatever the process, attempts to assess creativity are full of challenges. There is no universally agreed-on theory of creativity, no criterion for identifying creativity that satisfies all critics, and no standardized test that is free from concerns about some forms of reliability and validity. Although some instruments are stronger than others, there is no sure-fire, no-fail test of creativity, no way to know for sure if an Elijah McCoy, Michelangelo, or Hypatia is waiting in your classroom. Yet we are left with the feeling that although we may not be able to quantify creativity precisely, if we look for it, we may just recognize it when we see it. Furthermore, despite the difficulties, there are lessons to be learned from research on creativity testing that may add to our understanding of both assessment and creativity in general.

Lessons From the Research Front Barron and Harrington (1981) carefully stated, "One can say that some divergent-thinking tests, administered to some samples, under some conditions and scored according to some criteria, measure factors relevant to creativity criteria beyond those measured by indices of general intelligence" (p. 448). No measure of creativity—divergent-thinking test, biographical inventory, or any other iteration—can take into account all the cognitive, affective, social, and cultural forces that ultimately shape an individual's creativity. However, even the small portion of creativity captured by tests of divergent thinking is affected by a variety of factors. These may provide clues to factors affecting the nature of creativity itself. A few of these possibilities include the following:

1. The conditions matter. Scores on tests of divergent thinking are affected both by the physical objects in the room and by the activities that precede the test. Students are more likely to generate fluent responses in a stimulus-rich than in a stimulus-poor environment (Friedman, Raymond, & Feldhusen, 1978; Mohan, 1971). They are less likely to produce creative responses if they are interrupted from an interesting activity (Elkind, Deblinger, & Adler, 1970). If these trends carry into other kinds of creativity, consideration of the physical arrangements in the classroom and of transitions from one activity to another may affect students' creative performance. It is hard to imagine how students may be intrinsically motivated to be creative if an interesting discussion is cut short because the clock says it is time for art or creative writing.

2. The directions matter. Students are more likely to give original responses if they are told that original responses are desired. Runco (1986) compared the performances of students given tests from the Wallach and Kogan battery with and without explicit directions to give

original ideas. With explicit directions, students gave fewer total ideas, but more ideas were original. Interestingly, explicit directions directing students to give original ideas increased originality scores more in students who had not been identified as gifted than in students who had been so identified. A similar phenomenon was observed by Friedman et al. (1978) and Mohan (1971). Although Mohan (1971) found that increasing the stimulation in the classroom increased scores, the increase came largely from the most creative students. Less creative students did not seem to use their environment to assist them. When Friedman et al. (1978) specifically cued students to look around them for ideas every 5 minutes, all students increased their scores. These studies suggest that if we want students to be creative, we should tell them so. If we are looking for fluency, originality, metaphor, or any other possible component of creative thinking, we are more likely to find it if students understand that we desire and value such responses. Of course, this is also useful to think about when giving assignments that are not assessments.

3. The types of stimuli matter. Scores on creativity tests are affected by the types of stimuli to which students respond. Verbal versus nonverbal and familiar versus unfamiliar stimuli may produce very different responses (Runco, 1986; Runco, Illies, & Eisenman, 2005; Sawyers, Moran, Fu, & Milgram, 1983). If exercises designed to enhance creativity are structured around familiar or mundane stimuli, they seem less likely to stimulate original responses. Even the visual design of the test can impact results. Mohr, Sell, and Lindsay (2016) found that when giving the *Alternate Uses Test* online, the size and shape of the response boxes affected the results—more space for options, more responses.

4. Some students are more affected than others by variations in the directions. Students who have been identified as gifted or highly creative may be less affected by changes in test directions than other students. Their test scores have sometimes been more reliable (perhaps suggesting they were less affected by other unintentional differences in test administration) than the scores of those not identified as gifted or highly creative. Although the relationship between creativity and intelligence remains somewhat unclear, it does appear that a variety of students may benefit from activities designed to enhance creativity, including students who may appear initially to be less able.

5. Assessments of creativity are affected by context and culture. As creativity research becomes more international, assessment issues become more complex. Because creative responses can involve nuance, word play, and judgments about relevance, using creativity measures across cultures cannot be a matter of simple translation (for example, see Yarbrough, 2016). Torrance (2003) demonstrated that students in environments in which creativity was less supported will score lower on TTCTs. Aside from the question of whether this assessment accurately represents individuals' potential for something they may have had no experience undertaking, it assumes that the same measures are appropriate across cultures. This has yet to be demonstrated. One of the themes running through the research cited in *The International Handbook of Creativity* (Kaufman & Sternberg, 2006) is that much international research has been done using Western conceptions of creativity and Western measures. New instruments continue to be developed in different parts of the world, with different goals (see, for example, Milgram & Livne, 2006; Mpofu, Myambo, Mogaji, Mashego, & Khaleefa, 2006). Mun, Mun, and Kim (2015) developed an inventory specific to assessing scientific imagination in Korean students. In Taiwan, researchers developed measures of scientific creativity and science inquiry for elementary children (Yang, Lin, Hong, & Lin, 2016), where in Latvia, scholars adapted and evaluated the *Test for Creative Thinking—Drawing Production* (first designed in Germany) as a drawing-based test of creative potential, at least initially focused on secondary students (Kālis, Roķe, & Krūmiņa, 2014). And in Brazil,

Gontijo and Fleith (2014) developed an assessment of creative thinking in mathematics for high school and undergraduate students. We have much to learn about the ways creativity may be expressed and assessed around the world, particularly in non-Western and more traditional cultures. These issues become particularly relevant in schools with diverse and international student bodies.

Recommendations With all the research, limitations, and sometimes controversy surrounding tests of divergent thinking, Runco and Acar (2012) concluded, "The word is out, DT [divergent thinking] is not synonymous with creativity but DT tests provide useful estimates of meaningful potential" (p. 73). Other estimates may be found in other assessments of creative processes, products, and personal characteristics. Although the limitations of standardized measurements of creativity can be discouraging, a few recommendations can be made.

First, match your assessment tools with the goals of your assessment. If you are working in your own classroom only for the benefit of your general instruction, consider what you know about the definition and characteristics of creativity. Then think why you are interested in assessing creativity. Perhaps you plan to try some new activities and you want to see whether they affect students' creative thinking. Because this assessment is essentially for your own benefit and will be used only for general planning, you may wish to be fairly informal. Perhaps you might plan an activity that stimulates creative thinking and score it for various types of divergent thinking. After you have conducted your activities, you could use a similar measure. Your homemade measures would not have sufficient reliability or validity for assessing individual students, but they may give you a sense of how the class is progressing.

If, however, you are responsible for planning an assessment to be used for individual identification or large-scale screening, you will need much more reliable and valid measures. Make sure that before an assessment plan is devised, there is a clear goal in mind—if not, you may rightly ask why you are assessing students in the first place! With the preliminary decisions made, you can select reliable measures that match the opportunities for which students are being selected. For some opportunities, standardized creativity tests may be appropriate. For others, subject-specific assessments may make more sense. For example, an advanced music or acting program might be better served by having auditions with expert judges instead of using the most carefully planned set of standardized assessments.

Second, no one assessment has sufficient reliability or validity to be the sole determination of individual educational opportunities. If creativity assessment is to be used for this purpose, it is important to have multiple sources of information. These could include standardized tests, performance assessments, and behavioral observations. In using multiple sources, it is best to examine each piece of data individually rather than create an artificial, summed creativity score. An individual who did not obtain a high score on a standardized creativity test but made an extraordinary creative product for which he or she earned a high score cannot be adequately described by a moderate-level score that attempts to combine the two.

Third, study all available information about the assessment tools to be used, looking particularly for information about reliability, validity, and potential bias. This review should include test reviews and research using the instruments. For example, Argulewicz and Kush (1984) found that Mexican American children scored lower than European American children on two of the three TTCT verbal scores. There were no differences between groups on the figural form of the test or on the Scales for Rating the Behavioral Characteristics of Superior Students (Renzulli, Smith, Callahan, White, & Hartman, 1976). Any school with populations for which English is not the first language would want to take this information into account when selecting test instruments. Chen et al. (2002) found consistency in the consensual assessment technique used with Chinese and European American students. This provides some support for its use in multicultural settings in which judgment of individual student products is important. Similarly, Niu and Sternberg (2002) found that American and Chinese judges were similar in their ratings of artworks.

However, Niu and Sternberg also found that the American students tended to produce artworks that were judged as more creative than the works by Chinese students. Does this mean American students are more creative than their Chinese counterparts? It brings to mind the Torrance (2003) research in which he noted cross-cultural differences in creativity scores depending on the level of support for creativity in classrooms and cultures. If Sternberg and Niu's Chinese students had fewer experiences with developing original ideas, do their artworks reflect their capacity for creativity or their current level? Only additional research will tell us. In the meantime, we must use caution when interpreting assessments for young people whose creative experiences may be limited.

Except for informal single-classroom assessments, standardized and researched scales have advantages over teacher-made instruments. Researchers with years of effort invested in the process have a difficult time producing tests or observation checklists with reasonable reliability and validity. It seems unlikely that any individual would do better in a first effort. The one exception to this rule may be assessment of creative products. As the technology for performance assessment develops, the time may come when reliable scales for assessing a variety of creative products are readily available. Until then, a consensus of expert judges or an evaluation with a clear scoring rubric designed for particular types of products may be the most reasonable path in any high-stakes assessment.

Fourth, be aware that assessments of creativity, particularly tests of divergent thinking, are affected by a variety of variables including the type of room, timing, and phrasing of the test instructions. To obtain reliable results and to be fair to all the students (as with any standardized test), you should make test administrations as uniform as possible. Perhaps more importantly, assessments are affected by the experience and support students have had with creativity—and particularly with the types of creativity required on the test. The more diverse your student population, the more flexibly you will need to think about the types of assessments that are appropriate and the preparation necessary to give them fairly.

Years ago, when I was serving as a resource teacher for gifted and talented education, a fifth-grade student who had been identified for special services came to me and announced that she believed her new friend should be identified for the same program. I asked why, and the student said that her new friend was the most creative person she knew, as evidenced by her amazing basketry. The new student in question had recently emigrated from Vietnam. As it turned out, my fifth-grade friend was absolutely right. The young woman in question was a gifted artist and creative in many other ways. Her limited experiences with English, as well as with standardized tests, did not allow her abilities to become visible in traditional testing. Her friend and peer recognized her creativity long before any of the involved adults. Because the student in question had limited English, she spent some time each day with a TESOL specialist. When the specialist substituted more creative language activities for the more typical memory activities, our new student soared!

Fifth, if the assessment of creativity is ongoing, collect a database of test information for your school. Examine how trends change over time and how scores vary among gender and racial groups in your area. Be aware that an instrument that works well elsewhere may not be right for your population. If you use performance assessment, consider using multiple raters and gathering reliability data on your rating scales. Think about saving the data and comparing them with those for other measures of creative performance in later years. This kind of effort can be invaluable in examining the validity and practicality of these measures.

Sixth, remember that teachers using observation forms or behavioral checklists need background information and instruction on the purpose and use of the forms. If a teacher is not sure what creative behaviors might look like or is not aware that they might be manifested in positive or negative ways, it will be difficult for him or her to observe professionally. If you are part of any effort to gather information on creative behavior, try to ensure that those responsible for gathering data provide the time and opportunities for all teachers to learn the necessary observation skills—and something about creativity—before proceeding with the assessment.

Observations and assessments of creative activities in class must take place in an atmosphere that makes it possible for creative behaviors to emerge. In addition to the person, process, and product aspects of creativity, the influence of the creative environment is important. If a teacher encourages flexibility, motivation, originality, and independence every day, that teacher is more likely to observe students' creative behaviors than one whose only flexible activity is planned for the day of the observation. In some schools, the assessment of creativity may be better postponed until teachers have the opportunity to learn more about creativity and how to encourage it in students. Encouraging creativity, after all, is the goal—of assessment of creativity, of teaching creative thinking, and of this book.

Blind Men, Elephants, and Farewell

When I first wrote this book, I thought repeatedly of the story about the blind men and the elephant. In the fable, several blind men surround an elephant and explore him with their hands. Each man holds a portion of the elephant's anatomy and is convinced he knows exactly what an elephant is like. The man holding the elephant's tail is certain that an elephant is very much like a snake. The one holding a leg assures him, no, an elephant is much more like a tree trunk. And so it goes, each man holding a little bit of knowledge but no one able to comprehend the whole elephant.

I concluded that studying creativity was something like that. Now, more than 20 years and five editions later, I am more convinced than ever that creativity is more than we can "grab" with any one of the scholarly tools at our disposal. We examine patterns of divergent thinking or the characteristics of creative people or strategies for generating original metaphors and believe we are learning what creativity is about. The answer, I suspect, is that creativity is all those things and more. Creativity demands some kinds of divergent thinking and problem finding, persistence and intelligence, a willingness to take risks, task motivation—and yet those things do not fully explain it. It is manifest in myriad ways in different disciplines and across the globe; whether they are all the same at the core is not yet certain. And even now, in the 21st century, creativity still contains an element of mystery and wonder—often most of all to those who engage in it.

Although all my creativity is definitely of the "little c" variety, I've done a lot of small creative things. I've written songs, made mosaics, invented research strategies, and fashioned new recipes from whatever is in the refrigerator. I've had fun telling and writing serial stories for young friends. As I invent new fantasy worlds for them to explore, there are times when I can easily identify my divergent thinking or ties to prior experience. Other times, I begin to understand the experience of authors who claim they don't know what their characters will do next until they do it—sometimes (and often the best times), the story just comes, unbidden. I suspect we have a long way to go before we can fully explain it.

Messenger (1995) quoted blues musician Robert "Pete" Williams describing his process: "All the music I play, I just hear in the air. . . . I may be walking, going along, riding along in a car, the blues just come to me. . . . I come back, I get my guitar, I play it. It's like taking photographs of your life." We understand that creativity ties to the lives, minds, and emotions of individuals and to the places and times in history they inhabit. But behind those photographs, there remains an element of mystery.

As we consider the mystery, it is essential to also consider the purpose. In Chapter 1, I introduced the question of whether creativity is necessarily good. Liu and Noppe-Brandon (2009) eloquently stated,

> Every one of us every day faces situations, whether tragic or joyous or trivial, that activate the imagination. In choosing *how* we want to activate it, we either add to or subtract from the sum total of good in the world [italics original].
>
> (p. 206)

Today that charge, to choose carefully the way we use our creativity, feels more essential than ever. The students in our classes have the capacity to add their imagination and understanding to that sum-total good in profound and wonderful ways—if only they catch a glimpse of their power to do so. The role of a teacher, helping to shape that purpose, fills me with wonder.

Human beings are amazing creatures. Even as I know something about the circulatory system, I stand in awe of the lifelong beating of a heart. In the same way, I believe we can learn about the processes and attributes of creativity and still find wonder in glimpses-of-the-elephant creativity. When we listen to Mozart or Pete Williams, when we look at Australian grave pole carvings or

Learning about creativity can be like the blind men and the elephant

Marshallese stick maps, we see the infinite variety of the human imagination at work. I believe we also can catch sight of the elephant, perhaps at least a young one, as our students find and solve problems that intrigue them, use ideas or materials in new ways, or connect concepts in patterns they have not seen before. Those paths are seldom easy. In such activities, students interact with their environment in three-dimensional ways, encountering the unfamiliar and exploring it in patterns that are at once as new and as old as human history. It is when we try to shield students from the complexities, to present neat, solvable problems and clean, clear solutions, that our view of creativity is muddied. The real world never comes in such tidy packages. True creativity involves facing challenges, looking into the unknown, and exploring ideas you do not totally understand. It is about learning to live.

The challenge I leave with you is to explore and to help your students explore as many aspects of this pachyderm creativity as you can. Knowing full well that no one piece makes the creature complete, and understanding that we do not have all the answers, join the hunt with vigor. It is the search for the unknown that brings the wonder and excitement in discovering each new inch. If new paths cause occasional stumbles, they also bring adventure and understanding. Exploring them can make for schools of joy—and curious delight.

What's Next?

1. Before diving into assessment activities, stop for a moment to consider "schools of curious delight." When are the moments when school has been delightful to you—as a student or a teacher? Do those moments include creativity? Share your ideas with a friend. Are they similar? What would *your* school of curious delight be like?

2. If you chose to accept the challenge, by now you should have made considerable progress on your creative product. Devise a scoring rubric or other assessment procedure to assess products of the type you created. Use it to assess your product. Decide how well you believe your assessment procedure worked and how you felt evaluating your product.

3. Take and score a Torrance Test of Creative Thinking (TTCT). You may want to try the new, streamlined scoring or the Abbreviated Version. Think about how the scoring process might work in a school with a large number of tests to evaluate.

Try It Tomorrow

1. For a day (or a week), keep track of all the ways you assess students—questions you ask, class activities that allow you to see their performance, homework, class assignments, projects, and so on. How many of those activities asked students to use information in new ways? Are there some you could adapt to allow choice or flexibility?

2. Experiment with informally assessing creativity through observation. Make a simple chart listing sample creative behaviors like "Showed curiosity by asking questions" or "Gave an original or unexpected answer" in different boxes. Each time a student demonstrates the behavior, note his or her name in the box. Does this exercise help you identify any creative strengths you'd previously missed?

3. Choose an assignment in which you will practice giving informational feedback. You could use an assignment from your own class or any of the many sample student essays available on the Web. Work with a colleague to see if your comments are clear and appropriate for your grade level.

Tech Tips

1. Teachers who make rubrics need not start from scratch. My favorite rubric maker is from Rubistar (rubistar.4teachers.org), whose website makes creating customized rubrics a breeze. You can start from scratch or begin with one in its collection and then adapt it to your particular students and content.

2. The phrase "There's an app for that" continues to be more true every day. Here are a few last apps for a variety of creative products.

   Pic Collage or FrameMagic can be used to create photo collages, with many opportunities for visual storytelling.

   The Green Screen app allows students to create "green screen" backgrounds for their video presentations, just as a TV weather forecaster might be broadcast in front of a virtual map or a movie actor placed in an alien landscape. Think about students presenting information on ancient Greece direct from the Acropolis!

   Shadow Puppet is a simple-to-use presentation app that can be used by students or teachers to combine pictures, video, music, text, and narration. The website has plenty of classroom stories to inspire you.

   The Sock Puppets app is used to create (you guessed it) virtual sock puppet shows by recording students' voices and linking them to digital puppets.

   A whole suite of options is available from Launch Pad Toys' new partnership with Google (launchpadtoys.com). Toontastic can be used to create and animate original cartoons; TeleStory is an augmented reality app that allows students to embed themselves in videos. It looks like there's more to come, so take a look!

   Book Creator is another option for creating online books, journals, photo books, comic books, and more.

   And finally, Skitch allows students to take a picture, write on it, decorate it, even use emoji on it. It's another way to mix media to show understanding or add knowledge.

   With all these options—and more emerging every day—why should student projects ever be repetitious? Of course it is impossible to use them all, but pick a few and experiment. You may find you enjoy them as much as your students do.

Appendix
Problem-Finding Lessons

Lesson One: People Need Problems

Materials Needed

    Two or three gadgets (vegetable peeler, pencil sharpener, etc.)

    An assortment of catalogs

    Picture of Chester Greenwood (optional, available in *Steven Caney's Invention Book* or Google Images)

Opening

Have you ever heard anyone say, "Boy, I wish I had a problem?" What kind of a problem might someone want to have? We all know that there are some kinds of problems that no one wants to have, but there are other kinds of problems that can be important—and even fun. For the next few weeks, we will be talking about why someone might look for an interesting problem and how they might do it.

Constructing Understanding

Let me start by telling you a story about a boy who found a problem and solved it. This problem started in a cold winter in Maine. A 15-year-old boy named Chester Greenwood had terrible trouble with his ears. Every time he went outside, even with his hat on, his ears were very cold. He tried wrapping a scarf around his head, but it was too uncomfortable. Finally, Chester made some loops out of wire and asked his grandmother to sew pieces of fur on one side and velvet on the other. Chester attached his fur-covered loops to a wire that went across his head. Chester Greenwood had invented the first earmuffs! In fact, Chester started an earmuff business and became a very successful inventor. [*Show a picture of Chester and his earmuffs.*]

Another option for an introductory story is the inventions of Elijah McCoy. His story provides a fine example of an African American inventor—and the source of the phrase "the real McCoy."

What problem did Chester (or Elijah) find? Do you think anyone else had ever had that problem? Why do you think no one else solved the problem the way he did? Sometimes one of the most important things that problem finders do is keep their eyes and ears open—they pay attention to the problems around them.

Another problem was solved more recently. A first-grade girl named Suzanna Goodin hated one of her chores at home. She hated feeding the cat! Now, Suzanna liked her cat, and she wanted the cat to have food. There was only one thing wrong. She hated washing the cat food spoon. Every time she fed the cat, the spoon ended up covered with squishy, smelly cat food. It was disgusting to wash. Luckily, Suzanna was a good problem finder, much like Chester Greenwood. Instead of just complaining about the smelly cat food, she thought, "aha! This is a problem I can solve." And she did. Suzanna invented an edible pet food spoon. The spoon is made of hard pet food, like a spoon-shaped dog biscuit. After you scoop the pet food out of the can, you can throw the spoon right into the bowl with the food. The cat or dog can eat it right up! For her invention, Suzanna won grand prize in that year's *Weekly Reader* invention contest.

Here is another invention. [*Hold up any convenient gadget. It may be a common object such as a vegetable peeler or pencil sharpener or something more unusual, such as electric socks.*] What kind of problem might have caused someone to invent this? Why do you think they might have decided to work on that problem? [*Repeat with two or three inventions. Select from the discussion questions that follow, as appropriate for your class. Of course, any of these inventions or stories can be exchanged for those more culturally appropriate or familiar to your students.*]

Possible Questions

What made Chester or Suzanna a good problem finder?

Why do you think that some people notice problems and some don't?

Why do you think some people complain about problems and some people try to figure out how to solve them?

What inventions can you think of that solved a problem? Why do you think someone might have chosen to work on that particular problem?

Applying Understanding

Let's see if you can find examples of someone finding a problem and inventing something to solve it. Using these catalogs, find something that you think someone invented to solve a problem. Cut out the picture of the object you choose and paste it at the top of a piece of paper. Under the picture, describe what problem this invention solves and why you think someone decided to work on it. [*This activity may be completed individually or in pairs, as appropriate for your classroom.*] An alternate activity would be to have students search websites on inventors and inventions, still looking for examples of problems and solutions.

Lesson Two: Inventors Look for Problems

Materials Needed

Assorted Oreos or other multivariety snack foods (optional)

Opening

Yesterday we talked about inventors needing to find problems. Today we are going to act like inventors and find some problems to solve. Remember the stories of Suzanna Goodin and Chester Greenwood? What did they do that made them good problem finders? Chester and Suzanna:

1. Noticed things around them.
2. Decided to solve a problem instead of complaining about it.

[*List key points on the board or chart paper. Add other ideas from the class as appropriate.*]

Constructing and Applying Understanding

Before we try to find some problems for ourselves, I need to tell you one more secret of being a good problem finder. A very famous scientist, Linus Pauling, once said that the secret of having good ideas is to have a lot of ideas. What do you think he meant by that? Finding a good problem to solve is like that. If you think of a lot of problems, you can pick an interesting problem to solve. If you think only of one problem, it might not be interesting or you might not be able to solve it. Your first idea (or problem) is practically never your best idea.

One way to find a problem to solve is to think about things that bug us. For example, it bugs me when there's only a tiny bit of ketchup left in the bottle and I can't get it out or it squirts all over me. It bugs me when people are talking on cell phones or doing other unsafe things while they are driving. [*Substitute your own things that bug you here.*] Think about things that bug you at home, at school, or any place else you go. [*It may be necessary to clarify that we are not trying to think of people who bug us but things.*] Let's brainstorm as many things that bug us as we can. [*List ideas. This may be done as a class or in small groups.*]

Sometimes, problem finders don't find things that bug them but things that can be improved or changed in some way. In this type of problem, nothing is really wrong, but something could be different or better. For example, what are some of the ways Oreo cookies have been changed to make new products? [*Possibilities include Double Stuff Oreos, miniature Oreos, giant Oreos, holiday Oreos, and reduced-fat Oreos. You may wish to bring in examples of one or more of these.*] I don't think there was anything wrong with Oreos—Oreos probably didn't bug anyone—but someone thought of ways they could be changed or improved to make something new. Let's try to add to our list of problems by thinking of things that might be changed or improved. For example, is there anything in this classroom that could be changed to make it easier or more fun to use? [*Add to list.*]

Now we have LOTS of ideas to choose from, just as Linus Pauling suggested. If you were going to choose one of these problems to solve, which one would you choose? On a piece of paper, write one problem you think would be interesting to work on and why you'd like to work on it. You may choose one of the problems from our list or think of one of your own. If you decide to solve the problem, be sure to tell the class what you invent!

Lesson Three: Authors Look for Problems

Materials Needed

Two or three children's books by the same author
Berlioz the Bear by Jan Brett (1991), if possible

Opening

We've been talking about how inventors find problems to solve or things to improve. What were some of the things good problem finders did? Yes, good problem finders:

1. Noticed things around them.
2. Thought of many possible problems.
3. Solved problems instead of complaining about them.

Today we are going to think about a very different kind of problem, one that can't be solved by an invention.

In the 1860s, Louisa May Alcott wanted to be a writer. She wrote mysteries. She wrote romantic stories. She sent her stories to magazine publishers, but no one ever wanted to buy them. In fact, one editor told her she would never be able to write anything that had popular appeal. Louisa May Alcott didn't want to find a problem she could solve with an invention. What kind of problem did Louisa need? Yes, Louisa May Alcott needed to find a problem she could solve by writing. She needed to find something she could write about that would be interesting and allow her to tell a good story. Does anyone know how Louisa solved her problem? Louisa May Alcott decided to write stories about her family, especially about her life with her three sisters. Many of you may have read some of Louisa May Alcott's stories or seen a movie of her most famous book, *Little Women*.

Just as inventors need to find problems to solve with their inventions, authors need to find their own special kinds of problems. An author looks for a problem he or she can solve with words—an interesting story to tell. One author I really enjoy is [*fill in a children's author you enjoy*]. [*The author*] writes books about [*give two or three examples*]. What do you think the author chose to write about?

Jan Brett, a children's author and illustrator, uses things around her to come up with ideas for her books. She tells the story of how she first started thinking of ideas for her story *Berlioz the Bear*. This is what she says in *Berlioz the Bear Newsnotes*.

I was listening to a Boston Symphony Orchestra concert. My husband Joe plays with BSO. While I was watching, Joe and all the double basses began to play loudly. I thought, "That is a large instrument, really huge. Something could fit right inside." Then I noticed the carved "F" holes in the front of Joe's bass. It would have to be a small something. A mouse? A caterpillar? Music does that. It leads one's thoughts to interesting places.

All this took place at an outdoor concert at Tanglewood, the Boston Symphony's summer home. Afterward the musicians were talking about their instruments. I asked Joe if his double bass changed with the weather. He looked concerned. "Jan," he said, "my bass is 100 years old. Sometimes the wood dries out and cracks. Then it makes a buzz." "A loud buzz," I asked, "that people can hear?"

At that moment I knew what kind of creature might live in a double bass, and my story had begun.

(p. 1)

[*You may want to share a few pictures from* Berlioz the Bear *or ask if anyone knows what kind of animal Jan Brett wrote about. In the book, there is a bee inside the string bass. Alternatively, go to your favorite author's website and see if you find similar information about another story.*]

Does anyone here have a favorite author or an author whose stories they especially like? How do you think that author decides what he or she is going to write about?

Applying Understanding

Today we are going to try to imagine why some of our favorite authors decided to write about the things they did. Maybe they wrote about their favorite places. Maybe they wrote about something they really had done, or maybe they wrote about something based on a favorite animal or object or dream. Pick a book you have enjoyed. Pretend you are the author. Write a paragraph explaining why you wrote the book and what first gave you the idea.

Lesson Four: Looking for Interesting Objects

Materials Needed

A bag of miscellaneous small objects

Opening

Today I want to tell you about another author who could not think of anything to write. The author's name was E. L. Doctorow, a famous author of adult books. He already had one best-selling novel, *The Book of Daniel*. But now he was stuck. He couldn't think of anything to write. Have you ever felt that way? Have you ever had journal time or a writing assignment and were not able to think of anything to write about? Well, that is exactly how E. L. Doctorow felt. Fortunately, E. L. Doctorow was a good problem finder. So, what do you think he did? He did many of the same things the inventors did when they were being good problem finders. He tried to think of many possible problems to solve and choose one of them to work on. Every day he sat down to write and tried to write something, even if he didn't think it was a very good idea. E. L. Doctorow knew that if he kept thinking of ideas, eventually he'd think of a good one. Where do you think he got his ideas? Where did the inventors get their ideas? Yes, they noticed things around them. E. L. Doctorow noticed things around him and tried to find ideas for his writing.

One day he couldn't think of anything to write about, so he sat staring at a spot on the wall in front of him. He just kept thinking of more and more ideas. First, he just thought about the spot. Then he thought about the wall the spot was on. Thinking about the wall made him think about the house. Thinking about the house made him think about how old the house was. Thinking about how old the house was made him think about who might have lived there long ago and who might have been their neighbors. Thinking about that gave him an idea for a story about people who lived back when his house was first built. Eventually, after a lot of work and a lot more thinking, that idea grew into his next famous book, *Ragtime*.

Other authors sometimes get ideas from objects around them, too. Lawrence Yep, a Chinese American author, once got ideas for two mystery books by looking at some old coins. He thought the coins were interesting, so he thought about them until he had many good story ideas. If you are stuck and can't think of anything to write about, one thing you can do is try what E. L. Doctorow did. Pick something near you or something interesting and just let your mind wander. See if it leads to any interesting story ideas. Let's try a few. Sometimes asking questions about the object can help us. We'll choose an object from this bag to help us. [*Pull an item from the bag.*]

1. What is interesting about this object?
2. What interesting place might this object have been?
3. What interesting place might this object go?
4. Does this object remind you of anything interesting?
5. What story ideas does this object give you?

[*With the children, model the problem finding-process. It is not necessary to come up with a full-blown story, just the general story idea. For example, a wooden box might be interesting because of the designs on the lid or because we wonder what is inside. It might have been in someone's attic or on a bookshelf in a fancy house. Maybe someone will hide it under a bed, using it to hide a secret note from a friend. This could lead to ideas for a story about a mysterious box in the attic, an artist who paints magic boxes, or a friend with a secret she is afraid to share.*]

Looking for Interesting Objects

Name _____ Date _____

What object did you choose?

What is interesting about this object?

What interesting places might this object have been?

What interesting places might this object go?

What does this object remind you of?

What story ideas does this object give you?

Put your best story idea here.

Figure A.1 Finding a story in an interesting object

Applying Understanding

Now it is your turn. Pick an object from the bag or choose another object in the classroom. On your worksheet (Figure A.1), answer the questions listed. Try to come up with the most interesting story idea you can. Remember, you probably will have to think of many different ideas before you choose the idea you think is the most interesting. [*Do not assign students to write the story at this time. They may, of course, if they choose to do so.*]

Tonight, look around you for an object that you think might be interesting to think about. It must be something small enough to carry to school. Bring the object to school tomorrow. [*At a convenient time, repeat the worksheet with the objects chosen by the students. This time, assign students to choose their favorite idea and actually write about it.*]

Lesson Five: Looking for Interesting Characters

Materials Needed

Two or three photographs of faces from magazines or Internet images

Opening

[*Hold up first photograph.*] What do you think this person might be thinking? Where do you think the person might be? What might the person be doing? What kind of story about this person might be most interesting to tell? [*Make sure students generate several alternatives. Briefly repeat with a second photograph. Use a third if you think it is necessary.*]

By now you can tell that good problem finders, whether they are inventors or authors, really have to keep their eyes and ears open. They notice the things around them, think of many possible problems or possible ideas, and then work on them. The last time, we talked about finding writing possibilities by looking for interesting objects. Today, we will talk about another way that problem-finding authors get their ideas—looking around for interesting characters.

Constructing Understanding

If you are going to be a problem-finding author, you will need to notice not just the objects around you but the characters as well. Take out a piece of paper. On it, make a list of all the people you have seen today. You do not have to list every single name. Sometimes you might list a whole group of people at once like, "students in my class" or "people on the bus" or "my family." See how many people you can remember. Did you see a bus driver? A police officer? Someone driving a car?

Sometimes authors get ideas for characters by looking at the people around them. They might write about people they know, as when Louisa May Alcott wrote *Little Women* about her sisters. Laura Ingalls Wilder wrote about her family, too, in her Little House books. At other times, authors write about characters because someone they know is interesting and helps them think of interesting ideas. For example, remember how Jan Brett got the idea for *Berlioz the Bear* at a concert? She got the idea for her version of *Goldilocks and the Three Bears* a different way. Jan Brett met a girl named Miriam who was very, very curious. Miriam was very adventurous and spunky, and she made Jan think that she'd like to write about a little girl who was adventurous and spunky like Miriam. That is where her ideas for Goldilocks got started. When he wrote *Where the Wild Things Are*, Maurice Sendak started out to write a book about wild horses. When he found he wasn't very good at drawing horses, he drew wild things instead—designed to look like his relatives!

Look at your list. Think about the people you have seen today. Is there anyone on your list who has an especially interesting personality? Who do you think might be interesting to read about in a story? Pick two or three characters from your list who you think are the most interesting. Put a check mark by them.

Of course, characters are not always people. Jan Brett's ideas for her book *The First Dog* started when she tried to guess what her dog was thinking. Did you see any interesting animals today? Are there any animals in school that might make interesting characters? Add them to your list.

Applying Understanding

Look at your list. Choose one character from your list. Use the worksheet (Figure A.2) to help you think how that character might help you think of a story idea—a problem you can solve by writing a story. [*Again, do not require students to write the story at this time. They may, of course, if they wish.*]

Tonight, look carefully at the people and animals around you. Try to find a character that might bring you interesting story ideas. Remember to think of many possibilities—your first idea is practically never your best idea. [*At a convenient time, have students repeat the worksheet with their chosen character. This time they should write at least a paragraph about their character.*]

Looking for Interesting Character

Name _____ Date _____

What character did you choose?

Why did you think that character was interesting?

List at least six words that describe your character.

List at least three places this character could go.

List at least three problems the character could have.

What story ideas does this character give you?

List your best story idea here.

Figure A.2 Finding a story in an interesting character

Lesson Six: Scientists Look for Problems

Materials Needed

Soap bubbles and wand
Hershey's Hugs or other candy with a hidden center, enough for each student to have one. If candy is not appropriate for your class, filled pretzels or an unfamiliar fruit can also be used as long as the objects can be cut with a plastic knife.
Plastic knives
Paper towels

Opening

So far, we have talked about how inventors and authors both need to look for problems they can work on. Inventors look for problems they can solve through inventions. Authors look for interesting ideas or stories they can try to write. Today we will talk about another type of person who needs to find problems to investigate. Who do you think that might be? [*Discuss student responses and acknowledge the many types of people who need to find things to investigate. Tell students that although many types of people need to find problems, today they'll be talking about scientists.*]

Constructing Understanding

Today I'd like to tell you about a scientist who made a very important discovery that saved many lives. Listen carefully and decide how you think this scientist is like the other problem finders we have talked about.

Alexander Fleming was working in the laboratory. He was doing an experiment for which he had to grow bacteria. One day in his lab, he noticed something that probably did not make him very happy. Some of his petri dishes, in which he was growing the bacteria he needed, had mold growing on them. The mold had killed the bacteria, so his experiment was ruined. What do you think most people would have done with those moldy dishes? I suspect many scientists would have thrown them away. Luckily, Alexander Fleming did not do that. He wanted to know why the bacteria had died. Was there something about that mold that killed them? Now he had a new problem to investigate. The things Alexander Fleming learned from his moldy petri dishes led to the development of penicillin, an antibiotic that has saved many, many lives.

How do you think Alexander Fleming was like the other problem finders we've talked about? [*Make sure the discussion includes the ideas that he noticed things around him. He did not just complain about things he did not understand; he tried to understand them; and he thought of more than one problem he could investigate.*]

Scientists who are problem finders do many things, but three of them are especially important. Problem-finding scientists

1. Observe (notice) things around them.
2. Ask questions for which they don't have answers.
3. Try to find answers to their questions.

Today we are going to act like problem-finding scientists by practicing asking some of the kinds of questions scientists might ask. Alexander Fleming asked at least three questions. He asked, "*What* happened in these petri dishes? *What* is growing here?" "*Why* did the bacteria die?" and "*How* did the mold kill the bacteria?" "What," "why," and "how" are three important words that many scientists (and other problem finders) use when they are asking questions. What, why, and how questions help us think about what we observe and why things happen the way they do.

Let's imagine we are scientists who have gone to the park one sunny afternoon. As we are sitting on a bench, we notice a child blowing soap bubbles. I'll pretend I'm the child and blow a few bubbles. [*Blow bubbles.*] You be scientists. What are some of the problems or questions we might think about if we saw these bubbles? Remember, scientists ask questions for which they do not have answers. Think about questions that begin with what, why, and how. [*Students should generate questions such as "What are the colors on the sides of the bubbles?" "Why do some bubbles end up bigger than others?" or "How do bubbles stick together?" If students ask obvious questions such as, "What are those?" or "What color is the bubble wand?" remind them that scientists ask questions for which they do not already have answers.*]

Those are interesting problems to think about. What other things might scientists notice in a park that might lead to interesting questions? [*Spend a few minutes brainstorming other things that might be observed and how they might lead to questions or problems to be investigated.*]

Applying Understanding

Now, imagine that a scientist looked on the ground and saw one of these. [*Hold up a Hershey's Hug or other similar candy.*] Think about all the what, why, and how questions you could ask about this. I am going to give you each an object just like this one. Please examine it carefully. If you wish, you may use a plastic knife to help you. Be sure to put a piece of paper towel on your desk to protect it. As you observe your item, imagine that you are a scientist. Write down as many scientific questions about this object as you can. Try to use the words *what*, *how*, and *why*. The more carefully you observe, the more questions you will be able to ask. Circle the question you think is most interesting. [*After the activity is complete, let the students eat the candy!*]

Lesson Seven: Making Comparisons

Materials Needed

Scotch tape and masking tape

Opening

The last time, we talked about how scientific problem finders observe the things around them and ask questions. We talked about questions that started with three special words. What were the words we used? Yes, we thought of lots of questions that started with *what*, *why*, and *how*. Today I'd like to tell you a story about two groups of scientists who asked a different kind of question. Listen carefully and see if you can figure out how their questions were alike.

Both groups of scientists I will tell you about were elementary school children—in fact they were only 6 or 7 years old—but they found interesting problems to work on. The first group of students had a fish tank. What are some of the things the students might have wondered about the fish or the fish tank? [*Briefly brainstorm possible questions or problems. If you have an aquarium in your classroom, you may want to point it out.*]

Those are interesting problems to think about. In this class, the students became curious watching the bubbler that blew oxygen into the fish tank. They knew that fish in streams and ponds did not have bubblers to bring them oxygen. Most fish depend on plants to produce the oxygen they need. This made the students wonder if their fish would be healthier in a tank with a bubbler or in a tank with plants. They designed an experiment to find out. [*If your students are curious, you may explain that the class set up two fish tanks, one with a bubbler and one with plants. At set times of the day, they counted how many times the fish swam across the tank in 5 minutes, assuming that healthy fish are more active. The fish in the tank with plants were more active.*]

The second group of student scientists found a very different kind of problem. The weather was nice, and many students had been playing jump rope on the playground. The problem-finding students observed the jumping and wondered whether older or younger students could jump rope longer. They thought that younger students, with more energy, might be able to jump longer than older students. They conducted an investigation into their problem and studied whether first- or fifth-grade students could jump rope longer. [*In this study, fifth-grade students did, much to the disappointment of the first-grade investigators!*]

Think about the questions these two groups of students wondered about—the problems that they found to study. The first group wondered, "Will fish be healthier in a tank with a bubbler (and no plants) or one with plants (and no bubbler)?" The second group wondered, "Who can jump longer, first graders or fifth graders?" How are these questions alike? [*In your discussion, help students determine that, although there are several possible similarities, one important one is that both questions are comparisons.*] Yes, both of these questions compare one thing with another. They ask which is healthier or better or longer. Comparisons are another type of question scientists ask. They might compare things and think about whether one thing is stronger, heavier, faster, or more efficient than another. They might wonder which antibiotic works best for a particular infection, which formula will create the bounciest ball, or which type of paper towel is most absorbent.

Applying Understanding

Look around the classroom. Imagine that you are a scientist looking for comparison problems to study. Think about what ideas you may discover just by looking at things around you. For example, looking at this tape might make me wonder if it is very sticky. I could write the comparison question, "Which is stickier, Scotch tape or masking tape?" When you have finished your list, circle the question you think would be the most interesting to investigate if you were a scientist and had a big laboratory. Put a star next to the question you think would be the most interesting to investigate in a school like ours. [*Do not require students to investigate the questions at this time. They may, if they choose to do so.*]

Lesson Eight: Wondering What Would Happen

Opening

Have you ever done a real experiment? What did you do? Today we are going to talk about the kinds of problems that lead scientists to do experiments. I'm going to tell you about one more young problem finder who found a question that led to an interesting experiment and an unexpected difficulty.

This problem finder, named Alex, was studying plants in school. He had learned about things plants need. Can you guess some of the things Alex learned? Yes, Alex studied about how most plants need sun, water, and soil to grow properly. One day when Alex was thinking about plants growing, it made him think about the things he needed to grow. He didn't need soil to grow, but he did drink water. Thinking about how he drank water and the plants took in water gave Alex an idea. He knew that drinking milk helped him grow and develop strong teeth and bones. He wondered if he poured milk on plants instead of water whether the plants would grow stronger, too. Alex's question was a very important type of question that scientists ask. We have already talked about what questions, why questions, how questions, and comparison questions. Alex's question was a different type. He asked a "what if" question. What if questions lead to problems in which we investigate what would happen if we did something different from the things we usually do. In this case, Alex's question asked, "What if we put milk on the plants instead of water; what would happen?"

Alex was so interested in his problem that he did an experiment to find out. He used a group of bean plants. Half of the bean plants were watered every day, just as usual. Half of the bean plants received milk instead of water. After 2 weeks, Alex did not notice any difference in the beans, but he did notice something he had not expected—something he had not predicted before the experiment. See if you can imagine what it might have been. Imagine Alex pouring milk on the plants every day. Imagine those milky plants sitting in the warm sun on the window sill. After a few weeks, can you guess what happened? [*If no one guesses, tell the students that the soured milk began to smell horrible. It smelled so bad that no one wanted to go near the windowsill, and they had to throw the plants away!*]

This story is a little silly, but it helps us think about three important things. First, it helps us think about what if questions and the interesting problems they can help us find. When George Washington Carver was a child, he asked what if questions about plants, too. He was always trying to find ways to help make sick plants healthy again. He grew up to be an important botanist. Perhaps Alex will, too. Second, it helps us remember that, because problem finders look for questions to which they do not already have the answers, problem finders sometimes run into unexpected results. When we find interesting questions or problems we never know exactly what will happen when we investigate them. That is what makes problem finding so exciting. But it also leads to the third important idea. If you find an interesting scientific problem, especially a what if question, you should always share your problem with an adult before you investigate it. Some investigations can be dangerous. All of us can think of lots of interesting problems that might be interesting to investigate. If we decide really to investigate them, it is important to tell an adult our plans before we conduct any experiments. Alex's unexpected results did not hurt anyone, but good scientists are careful scientists.

Applying Understanding

There are lots of ways to think of interesting what if problems. Sometimes, like Alex, we think of things we do and wonder what would happen if we did it differently. At home, listening to music while I cook, I might wonder whether students would do a better job on their homework with music playing or with no music playing. (Some sixth-grade students actually investigated that problem.) Sometimes we might look at something and wonder what would happen if we changed it in some way. For example, I might look at my flashlight and wonder if a flashlight with four batteries would shine brighter than one with two batteries. Or I might wonder if a colored filter on the flashlight made it easier or harder to see in the dark.

Today I'd like you to practice asking what if questions by thinking about how Bob and Cristina (Figure A.3) spent the morning. Pretend you are Bob or Cristina thinking about all the things you are doing and seeing. List as many what if questions as you can. Try to wonder about many interesting things. When you are finished, put a star by the problem that makes you the most curious.

Wondering What Should Happen

Name _____ Date _____

Bob and Cristina's Morning

This morning Bob woke up to the sound of the alarm clock ringing at 7:30. Cristina woke up at 7:15, when her dog, George, jumped on her bed. Cristina and Bob both dressed warmly because it was a cold morning. They put on jeans, shirts, and sweaters. After they were dressed, Cristina and Bob ate breakfast and fed their pets. Cristina ate eggs and tortillas with milk. She fed her dog, George, dry dog food and water. Bob ate cold pizza and milk. He fed his cat, Alex, a can of cat food.

After breakfast, Cristina and Bob left for school. Cristina put on her backpack and got on her bike. She rode next door to her friend Chris's house. Cristina and Chris rode their bikes to school together. They noticed that the snow had melted on the sidewalk and on the roads but not on the grass. The snow on the grass was still deep and was starting to look dirty and gray.

Bob walked to the corner to wait for the bus. His friend Sam waited there, too. Bob and Sam got cold waiting for the bus to come. Bob wished he had a warmer hat. His Tigers cap did not keep his head very warm. When the bus came, Bob and Sam hurried to the back seat. They liked the way the back seat bumped when they rode over the railroad tracks.

When Bob, Cristina, and their friends arrived at school, they walked down the hall to their classroom. Their feet sounded loud on the tile floor. They could hear children laughing and could smell something good baking in the cafeteria. In the classroom, they could see that their teacher had a big box on her desk. Maybe it was the pet snake she had talked about yesterday. Bob and Cristina hoped so! They went to their desks, took out pens and pencils, and got ready for the day.

Think about all the questions Bob and Cristina might ask about things they observed this morning. List all the questions or problems they might find. Use the back of this paper for more space. Put a star next to the question that makes you the most curious.

Figure A.3 Bob and Cristina's morning

Lesson Nine: Trapping Your Ideas

Materials Needed

Pictures from Leonardo da Vinci's journals, available several places online; see Google Images

Small notebook or pad of paper for each student

Opening

We have talked a lot about different problem finders and some of the things they do. Today we will talk about something that all problem finders have to do, no matter what kinds of problems they are searching to find. Have you ever had a really good idea and then forgot what it was before you had a chance to do it? You might have thought, "Oh, no. I had an idea and now I can't remember what it was." Do you think that ever happens to the problem finders we have been talking about: to inventors or writers or scientists? It can, if they are not careful. That is why good problem finders have to be very careful to trap their ideas before they get away. What kind of trap do you think you might use to trap an idea? A mousetrap? Probably not. Many problem finders trap their ideas in a special problem-finding notebook.

Constructing Understanding

Just as there are many kinds of problems to find, there are many kinds of things to write in a problem-finding notebook. Inventors might keep an inventor's log. In their inventor's log, they write down all the interesting problems they notice or ideas they get for inventions. They write down the ideas even if they don't plan to use them right away. Someday they may want to come back to an idea, and if the idea is trapped in a notebook, they will always be able to find it.

A very great problem finder named Leonardo da Vinci lived around the time of Columbus. He kept problem-finding notebooks that people still study today. Leonardo da Vinci recorded notes and drawings for many different kinds of problems. He made sketches for paintings he might paint someday and inventions he might want to build. He trapped ideas for different kinds of buildings. Leonardo da Vinci must have been a careful observer of the world around him. He certainly thought of many different problem ideas! [*Show pages from da Vinci's notebooks.*]

Writers also trap ideas. They might write down interesting ideas for characters, interesting places to write about, or titles they'd like to use some day. What other kinds of ideas might an author want to record? How about a scientist? What kinds of things might a scientist write in a notebook? Can you think of other kinds of ideas a different kind of problem finder might want to record? (For example, an artist might record interesting ideas for works of art, or a dancer might make notes about a new movement.)

Applying Understanding

Today you will be creating your own problem-finding notebooks. You may use a purchased notebook or pieces of paper stapled together. The important thing about a problem-finding notebook is not how elegant it looks but how much you use it. Keep your problem-finding notebook with you so you can jot down ideas for different kinds of problems. You may want to divide your notebook into sections for different kinds of problems or leave it all together. It is up to you. Tonight, see if you can record at least three interesting problems in your problem-finding notebook. [*Have students create their notebooks. Decorations may be as plain or elaborate as students choose. Effective problem-finding notebooks will easily fit in pockets or packs so that they are easy to transport.*]

Lesson Ten: Wondering and Wondering

Opening

If I say something is a habit, what do I mean? What are some examples of habits you have? Have you ever heard the phrase "habits of mind?" What do you think habits of mind might be? Yes, habits of mind are ways of thinking that someone does over and over. Your habits of mind determine how you notice things and how you think about the world. Today I'd like to tell you about a few more problem finders. Think about them and about the other problem finders we've discussed and decide what kinds of habits of mind you think a good problem finder should have.

Constructing Understanding

The first problem finder I'd like to tell you about was named Charles W. Turner. Charles W. Turner was a very curious person. When he was young, he always wondered how ants could find their way home. He spent many hours on the ground observing ants, bees, and other insects. When he grew up, Charles became a naturalist, a person who studies nature. He discovered many things, including the finding that insects can hear and bees can see colors.

The second problem finder was named Vera Rubin. When Vera was growing up, she liked to look at the sky. Sometimes she would stay up all night looking at the stars and wondering what she saw. After she grew up and got married, she still wondered about the stars. Finally, she decided she should study to become an astronomer. Vera Rubin studied galaxies far from our solar system. In fact, in 1979, she discovered the largest galaxy ever seen. It is 10 times larger than our Milky Way galaxy.

Langston Hughes found problems to solve with his writing. He loved the people and the sights and sounds of his neighborhood in Harlem. He found many ideas for poems there. Some of his most famous poems are about the things he saw and people he met in Harlem.

Edgar Degas found problems to solve with art. Degas was an artist who lived more than 100 years ago. He painted many things, but his most famous paintings and sculptures are of ballet dancers. Degas did not just paint the dancers while they were on stage dancing. He observed behind stage and in practice rooms, watching the dancers work. He watched carefully to find the most interesting moments. Those moments gave him ideas and problems to express with his art. Even when he grew older and his eyesight was failing, Degas continued to use his art to portray dancers through sculpture.

Think about Charles W. Turner and Vera Rubin, Langston Hughes and Edgar Degas. What kinds of habits of mind do you think they might have had? What about the other problem finders we've talked about; what kinds of habits of mind do you think they might have had? Do you think different kinds of problem finders have different types of habits of mind, or do you think inventors, writers, and scientists have some similar habits of mind?

Applying Understanding

[*With the class, use the preceding discussion questions to help generate a list of "Rules for Problem Finding" or "What Makes a Good Problem Finder?" The rules should include such habits as observe things around you and think about what you see; think about things for a long time; think about many different ideas; don't give up; and think about any other ideas reasonably derived from this or previous lessons. Have students copy the list in the front of their problem-finding notebooks. Encourage students to continue to think like problem finders as they find interesting problems at home and at school.*]

References

Abraham, A., Thybusch, K., Pieritz, K., & Hermann, C. (2014). Gender difference in creative thinking: Behavioral and fMRI findings. *Brain Imaging and Behavior, 8*, 39–51. DOI: 10.1007/s11682-013-9241-4

Abraham, A., & Windmann, S. (2008). Selective information processing advantages in creative cognition as a function of schizotypy. *Creativity Research Journal, 20*, 1–6.

Abuhamdeh, S., & Csikszentmihalyi, M. (2004). The artistic personality: A systems perspective. In R. J. Sternberg, E. L. Grigorenko, & J. L. Singer (Eds.), *Creativity: From potential to realization* (pp. 31–42). Washington, DC: American Psychological Association.

Aghababyan, A. R., Grigoryan, V. G., Stepanyan, A. Y., Arutyunyan, N. D., & Stepanyan, L. S. (2007). EEG reactions during creative activity. *Human Physiology, 33*(2), 252–253.

Agnoli, S., Corazza, G. E., & Runco, M. (2016). Estimating creativity with a multiple-measurement approach within scientific and artistic domains. *Creativity Research Journal, 28*(2), 171–176. DOI: 10.1080/10400419.2016.1162475

Albert, R. S. (1990). Identity, experiences, and career choice among the exceptionally gifted and eminent. In M. A. Runco & R. S. Albert (Eds.), *Theories of creativity* (pp. 13–34). Newbury Park, CA: Sage.

Albert, R. S. (1993, May). *The contribution of early family history to the achievement of eminence.* Paper presented at the Henry B. and Jocelyn Wallace National Research Symposium on Talent Development, Iowa City, IA.

Alencar, E. M. L. S. (2014). Obstacles to personal creativity inventory. In E. M. L. S. Alencar, M. F. Bruno-Faria, & D. S. Fleith (Eds.), *Theory and practice of creativity measurement* (pp. 21–35). Waco, TX: Prufrock Press.

Alencar, E. M. L. S., Bruno-Faria, M. F., & Fleith D. S. (Eds.). (2014). *Theory and practice of creativity measurement.* Waco, TX: Prufrock Press.

Alfonso-Benlliure, V., Meléndez, J. C., & García-Ballesteros, M. (2013). Evaluation of a creativity intervention program for preschoolers. *Thinking Skills and Creativity, 10*, 112–120.

Aljughaiman, A., & Mowrer-Reynolds, E. (2005). Teachers' perceptions of creativity and creative students. *Journal of Creative Behavior, 39*, 17–34.

Allan, S. D. (1991). Ability grouping research reviews: What do they say about grouping and the gifted? *Educational Leadership, 48*, 60–65.

Amabile, T. M. (1982a). Children's artistic creativity: Detrimental effects of competition in a field setting. *Personality and Social Psychology Bulletin, 8*, 573–578.

Amabile, T. M. (1982b). Social psychology of creativity: A consensual assessment technique. *Journal of Personal and Social Psychology, 43*, 997–1013.

Amabile, T. M. (1987). The motivation to be creative. In S. G. Isakesen (Ed.), *Frontiers of creativity research* (pp. 223–254). Buffalo, NY: Bearly.

Amabile, T. M. (1988a). A model of creativity and innovation in organizations. *Research in Organizational Behavior, 10*, 123–167.

Amabile, T. M. (1988b). A model of creativity and innovation in organization. In B. M. Shaw & L. L. Cummings (Eds.), *Research in organizational behavior* (Vol. 10, pp. 123–167). Greenwich, CT: JAI Press.

Amabile, T. M. (1989). *Growing up creative.* New York: Crown.

Amabile, T. M. (1993a, May). *Future issues.* Panel discussion at the Henry B. and Jocelyn Wallace National Research Symposium on Talent Development, Iowa City, IA.

Amabile, T. M. (1993b, May). *Person and environment in talent development: The case of creativity.* Paper presented at the Henry B. and Jocelyn Wallace National Research Symposium on Talent Development, Iowa City, IA.

Amabile, T. M. (1996). *Creativity in context: Update to the social psychology of creativity.* Boulder, CO: Westview.

Amabile, T. M. (1998, September/October). How to kill creativity. *Harvard Business Review.* Retrieved from https://hbr.org/1998/09/how-to-kill-creativity

Amabile, T. M. (2001). Beyond talent: John Irving and the passionate craft of creativity. *American Psychologist, 56*(4), 333–336.

Amabile, T. M., Barsade, S. G., Mueller, J. S., & Staw, B. M. (2005). Affect and creativity at work. *Administrative Science Quarterly, 50*, 367–403.

Amabile, T. M., Conti, R., Coon, H., Lazenby, J., & Herron, M. (1996). Assessing the work environment for creativity. *Academy of Management Journal, 19*, 1154–1184.

Amabile, T. M., DeJong, W., & Lepper, M. (1976). Effects of external imposed deadlines on subsequent intrinsic motivation. *Journal of Personality and Social Psychology, 34*, 92–98.

Amabile, T. M., & Gryskiewicz, S. S. (1987). *Creativity in the R&D laboratory.* Technical report No. 30. Greensboro, NC: Center for Creative Leadership.

Amabile, T. M., Hennessey, B. A., & Grossman, B. S. (1986). Social influences on creativity: Effects of contracted-for reward. *Journal of Personality and Social Psychology, 50*, 14–23.

Amabile, T. M., & Kramer, S. J. (2011, May). The power of small wins. *Harvard Business Review.* Retrieved from https://hbr.org/2011/05/the-power-of-small-wins

Ambrose, D., & Sternberg, R. J. (Eds.). (2012). *How dogmatic beliefs harm creativity and higher-level thinking.* New York: Routledge.

Ames, C. (1992). Classrooms: Goals, structures, and student motivation. *Journal of Educational Psychology, 84*(3), 261–271.

Ames, C., & Archer, J. (1988). Achievement goals in the classroom: Students' learning strategies and motivation processes. *Journal of Educational Psychology, 80*(3), 260–267.

Anastasi, A., & Schaefer, C. E. (1969). Biographical correlates of artistic and literary creativity in adolescent girls. *Journal of Applied Psychology, 53*, 267–273.

Anderson, C. W., & Lee, O. (1997). Will students take advantage of opportunities for meaningful science learning? *Phi Delta Kappan, 78*, 720–724.

Anderson, N., Potočnik, K., & Zhou, J. (2014). Innovation and creativity in organizations: A state-of-the-science review, prospective commentary, and guiding framework. *Journal of Management, 40*(5), 1297–1333. DOI: 10.1177/0149206314527128

Apol, L. (2002). What do we do if we don't do Haiku? Seven suggestions for writers and teachers. *English Journal, 91*(3), 89–97.

Argulewicz, E. N., & Kush, J. C. (1984). Concurrent validity of the SRBCSS Creativity Scale for Anglo-American and Mexican-American gifted students. *Educational and Psychological Measurement, 4*, 81–89.

Ariely, D. (2012). *The (honest) truth about dishonesty.* New York: HarperCollins.

Arlin, P. K. (1975). A cognitive process model of problem finding. *Educational Horizons, 54*(1), 99–106.

Arlin, P. K. (1990). Wisdom: The art of problem finding. In R. J. Sternberg (Ed.), *Wisdom: Its nature, origins, and development* (pp. 230–243). New York: Cambridge University Press.

Armstrong, D. (2012). The contributions of creative cognition and schizotypal symptoms to creative achievement. *Creativity Research Journal, 24*(2–3), 177–190.

Armstrong, T. (2016). *The power of the adolescent brain: Strategies for teaching middle and high school students.* Alexandria, VA: Association for Supervision and Curriculum Development.

Armstrong-Ellis, C. F. (2015). *I love you more than moldy ham.* New York: Harry N. Abrams.

Ashby, F. G., Isen, A. M., & Turken, A. U. (1999). A neuropsychological theory of positive affect and its influence on cognition. *Psychological Review, 106*, 529–550.

Athanasou, J. A. (2007). Test review of abbreviated Torrance test for adults. In K. F. Geisinger, R. A. Spies, J. F. Carlson, & B. S. Plake (Eds.), *The seventeenth mental measurements yearbook.* Retrieved from http://marketplace.unl.edu/buros/

Auger, E. E. (2005). *The way of Inuit art: Aesthetics and history in and beyond the arctic.* Jefferson, NC: McFarland & Co.

Baas, M., De Dreu, C. K. W., & Nijstad, B. A. (2008). A meta-analysis of 25 years of mood-creativity research: Hedonic tone, activation, or regulatory focus? *Psychological Bulletin, 134*(6), 799–806.

Backman, M. E., & Tuckman, B. W. (1978). Review of remote associates form: High school form. In O. Buros (Ed.), *The eighth mental measurements yearbook* (Vol. 1, p. 370). Highland Park, NJ: Gryphon Press.

Baer, J. (1993). *Creativity and divergent thinking.* Hillsdale, NJ: Erlbaum.

Baer, J. (1993–1994). Why you shouldn't trust creativity tests. *Educational Leadership, 51*(4), 80–83.

Baer, J. (1998). Gender differences in the effects of extrinsic motivation on creativity. *Journal of Creative Behavior, 32*, 18–37.

Baer, J. (2010). Is creativity domain specific? In J. C. Kaufman & R. J. Sternberg (Eds.), *The Cambridge handbook of creativity* (pp. 321–341). New York: Cambridge University Press.

Baer, J., & Kaufman, J. C. (2005). Bridging generality and specificity: The amusement park model of creativity. *Roeper Review, 27*(3), 158–163.

Baer, J., & Kaufman, J. C. (2008). Gender differences in creativity. *Journal of Creative Behavior, 42*(2), 75–105.

Baer, J., Kaufman, J. C., & Gentile, C. A. (2004). Extension of consensual assessment technique to nonparallel creative products. *Creativity Research Journal, 16*, 113–117.

Baird, B., Smallwood, J., Mrazek, M. D., Kam., J. Y. W., Franklin, M. S., & Schooler, J. W. (2012). Inspired by distraction: Mind wandering facilitates creative incubation. *Psychological Science, 23*(10), 1117–1122. DOI: 10.1177/0956797612446024

Baird, B., Smallwood, J., & Schooler, J. W. (2011). Back to the future: Autobiographical planning and the functionality of mind-wandering. *Consciousness and Cognition, 20*, 1604–1611.

Ball, O. E., & Torrance, E. P. (1980). Effectiveness of new materials developed for training the streamlined scoring of the TTCT, figural A and B forms. *Journal of Creative Behavior, 14*, 199–203.

Bandura, A. (1977). Self-efficacy: Toward a unifying theory of behavioral change. *Psychological Review, 84*, 191–215.

Bandura, A. (1986). *Social foundations of thought and actions: A social-cognitive view.* Englewood Cliffs, NJ: Prentice Hall.

Bank, M. (1995). *Anonymous was a woman.* New York: St. Martin's Griffin.

Barker, J. E., Semenov, A. D., Mechaelson, L., Provan, L. S., Snyder, H. R., & Munakata, Y. (2014). Less-structured time in children's daily lives predicts self-directed executive functioning. *Frontiers in Psychology, 5*, 1–16. DOI: 10.3389/fpsyg.2014.00593

Barron, F. (1955). The disposition towards originality. *Journal of Abnormal and Social Psychology, 51*, 478–485.

Barron, F. (1969). *Creative person and creative process.* New York: Holt, Rinehart & Winston.

Barron, F., & Harrington, D. M. (1981). Creativity, intelligence, and personality. *Annual Review of Psychology, 32*, 439–476.

Basadur, M., Runco, M. A., & Vega, L. A. (2000). Understanding how creative thinking skills, attitudes and behaviors work together: A causal process model. *Journal of Creative Behavior, 34*(2), 77–100.

Bateson, P., & Martine, P. (2013). *Play, playfulness, creativity, and innovation.* Cambridge, UK: Cambridge University Press.

Batey, M., & Furnham, A. (2006). Creativity, intelligence, and personality: A critical review of the scattered literature. *Genetic, Social, and General Psychology Monographs, 132*(4), 355–429.

Baum, S. M., & Owen, S. V. (2004). *To be gifted and learning disabled.* Mansfield Center, CT: Creative Learning Press.

Beach, J. K. (2003). *Names for snow.* New York: Hyperion Books for Children.

Beaty, R. E., Benedek, M., Kaufman, S. B., & Silvia, P. J. (2015). Default and executive network coupling supports creative idea production. *Scientific Reports, 5*(10964), 1–14. DOI: 10.1038/srep10964

Beaty, R. E., Benedek, M., Wilkins, R. W., Jauk, E., Fink, A., Silvia, P. J., Hidges, D. A., Koschutnig, K., & Neubauer, A. C. (2014). Creativity and the default network: A functional connectivity analysis of the creative brain at rest. *Neuropsychologia, 64*, 92–98.

Beaty, R. E., & Silvia, P. J. (2012). Why do ideas get more creative across time? An executive interpretation of the serial order effect in divergent thinking tasks. *Psychology of Aesthetics, Creativity, and the Arts, 6*(4), 309–319.

Bechtereva, N. P., Korotkov, A. D., Pakhomov, S. V., Roudas, M. S., Starchenko, M. G., & Medvedev, S. V. (2004). PET study of brain maintenance of verbal creative activity. *International Journal of Psychophysiology, 53*, 11–20.

Bedwell, R., & Clark, L. (1997). *General Lee and Santa Claus.* Nashville, TN: Spiridon Press.

Beghetto, R. A. (2006). Creative self-efficacy: Correlates in middle and secondary students. *Creativity Research Journal, 18*(4), 447–457.

Beghetto, R. A. (2007). Does creativity have a place in classroom discussions: Prospective teachers' response preferences. *Thinking Skills and Creativity, 2*, 1–9.

Beghetto, R. A. (2008). Prospective teachers' beliefs about imaginative thinking in K–12 schooling. *Thinking Skills and Creativity, 3*, 134–142.

Beghetto, R. A., & Kaufman, J. C. (2017). Ever-broadening conception of creativity in the classroom. In R. A. Beghetto & J. C. Kaufman (Eds.), *Nurturing creativity in the classroom* (2nd ed., pp. 67–85). New York: Cambridge University Press.

Belenky, M. F., Clinchy, B. M., Goldberger, N. R., & Tarule, J. M. (1997). *Women's ways of knowing: The development of self, voice, and mind* (19th anniversary ed.). New York: Basic Books.

Benedek, M., Borovnjak, B., Neubauer, A. C., & Kruse-Weber, S. (2014). Creativity and personality in classical, jazz, and folk musicians. *Personality and Individual Differences, 63*, 117–121.

Benedek, M., Jauk, E., Sommer, M., Arendasy, M., & Neubauer, A. C. (2014). Intelligence, creativity, and cognitive control: The common and differential involvement of executive functions in intelligence and creativity. *Intelligence, 46*, 73–83.

Benedek, M., Mühlmann, C., Jauk, E., & Neubauer, A. C. (2013). Assessment of divergent thinking by means of the subjective top-scoring method: Effects of the number of top ideas and time-on-task on reliability and validity. *Psychology of Creativity, Aesthetics, and the Arts, 7*(4), 341–349. DOI: 10.1037/a0033644

Bengtsson, S. L., Csikszentmihalyi, M., & Ullén, F. (2007). Cortical regions involved in the generation of musical structures during improvisation of pianists. *Journal of Cognitive Neuroscience, 19*(5), 830–842.

Berger, W. (2016). *A more beautiful question: The power of inquiry to spark breakthrough ideas.* New York: Bloomsbury.

Berlin, L. (2008, September 28). We'll fill this space, but first a nap. *New York Times.* Retrieved from www.nytimes.com/2008/09/28/technology/28proto.html

Berliner, D. (2012). Narrowing curriculum, assessments, and conceptions of what it means to be smart: Creaticide by design. In D. Ambrose & R. J. Sternberg (Eds.), *How dogmatic beliefs harm creativity and higher-level thinking* (pp. 79–93). New York: Routledge.

Berlyne, D. E. (1960). *Conflict, arousal and curiosity.* New York: McGraw Hill.

Besemer, S. P., & O'Quin, K. (1986). Creative product analysis: Testing a model by developing a judging instrument. In S. G. Isaksen (Ed.), *Frontiers of creativity research: Beyond the basics* (pp. 341–357). Buffalo, NY: Bearly.

Besemer, S. P., & Treffinger, D. J. (1981). Analysis of creative products: Review and synthesis. *Journal of Creative Behavior, 43*, 997–1013.

Bijvoet-van den Berg, S., & Hoicka, E. (2014). Individual differences and age-related changes in divergent thinking in toddlers and preschoolers. *Developmental Psychology, 50*(6), 1629–1639.

Bingham, C. (1991). *Journal of creative activities.* Unpublished manuscript, Ypsilanti, MI.

Bloom, B. (Ed.). (1985). *Developing talent in young people.* New York: Ballantine.

Boden, M. A. (1980). *Jean Piaget.* New York: Penguin.

Boden, M. A. (1991). *The creative mind: Myths and mechanisms.* New York: Basic Books.

Boden, M. A. (1992). Understanding creativity. *Journal of Creative Behavior, 26*, 213–217.

Boden, M. A. (Ed.). (1994). *Dimensions of creativity*. New York: Cambridge University Press.

Boden, M. A. (1999). Computer models of creativity. In R. J. Sternberg (Ed.), *Handbook of creativity* (pp. 351–372). New York: Cambridge University Press.

Boden, M. A. (2004). *The creative mind: Myths and mechanisms* (2nd ed.). London: Routledge.

Boden, M. A. (2015, October 20). Artificial creativity: Why computers aren't close to being ready to supplant human artists. *MIT Technology Review*. Retrieved from www.technologyreview.com/s/542281/artificial-creativity/

Bohm, D. (1998). *On creativity*. New York: Routledge.

Bollman, K. A., Rodgers, M. H., & Mauller, R. L. (2001). Jupiter Quest: A path to scientific discovery. *Phi Delta Kappan, 82*(9), 683–686.

Bonawitz, E., Shafto, P., Gweon, H., Goodman, N. D., Spelke, E., & Schulz, L. (2011). The double-edged sword of pedagogy: Instruction limits spontaneous exploration and discover. *Cognition, 120*(3), 322–330. DOI: 10.1016/j.cognition.2010.10.001

Bornstein, M. H., Hahn, C., & Suwalsky, J. T. D. (2013). Physically developed and exploratory young infants contribute to their own long-term academic achievement. *Psychological Science, 24*(10), 1906–1917.

Boss, S. (2012). *Bringing innovation to school: Empowering students to thrive in a changing world*. Bloomington, IN: Solution Tree Press.

Bossomaier, T., Harré, M., Knittel, A., & Snyder, A. (2009). A semantic network approach to the creativity quotient [CQ]. *Creativity Research Journal, 21*, 64–71.

Bowden, E. M., & Jung-Beeman, M. (2003). Aha! Insight experience correlates with solution activation in the right hemisphere. *Psychonomic Bulletin & Review, 10*(3), 730–737.

Boykin, A. W. (1994). Harvesting talent and culture: African American children and educational reform. In R. Rossi (Ed.), *Schools and students at risk* (pp. 116–138). New York: Teachers College Press.

Boykin, A. W., & Bailey, C. T. (2000). *The role of cultural factors in school relevant cognitive functioning: Synthesis of findings on cultural contexts, cultural orientations, and individual differences*. Report No. 42. Washington, DC: Office of Educational Research and Improvement.

Boykin, A. W., & Cunningham, R. T. (2001). The effects of movement expressiveness in story content and learning context on the analogical reasoning performance of African American children. *Journal of Negro Education, 70*(1–2), 72–83.

Bradbury, R. (1996). *Zen and the art of writing: Essays on creativity*. Santa Barbara, CA: Joshua Odell Editions.

Brandt, R. (Ed.). (1993). Authentic learning [Theme issue]. *Educational Leadership, 50*(7), 3–82.

Brandwein, P. F. (1962). *Elements in a strategy for teaching science in the elementary school*. New York: Harcourt Brace.

Bransford, J. D., Brown, A. L., & Cocking, R. R. (Eds.). (2000). *How people learn: Brain, mind, experience and school* (expanded ed.). Washington, DC: National Academies Press.

Bransford, J. D., Brown, A. L., Cocking, R. R., Donovan, M. S., & Pellegrino, J. W. (Eds.). (2000). *How people learn: Brain, mind, experience, and school*. Washington, DC: National Academies Press.

Bransford, J. D., Sherwood, R., Vye, N., & Rieser, J. (1986). Teaching thinking and problem solving. *American Psychologist, 41*, 1078–1089.

Brett, J. (1991). *Berlioz the bear*. New York: G.P. Putnam's Sons.

Bronson, P., & Merryman, A. (2010, July 10). The creativity crisis. *Newsweek Magazine*. Retrieved from www.thedailybeast.com/newsweek/2010/07/10/the-creativity-crisis.html

Brookhart, S. M. (2007/2008). Feedback that fits. *Educational Leadership, 65*(4), 54–59.

Brookhart, S. M. (2008). *How to give effective feedback to your students*. Alexandria, VA: Association for Supervision and Curriculum Development.

Brookhart, S. M. (2012). Preventing feedback fizzle. *Educational Leadership, 70*, 25–29.

Brophy, J. (2010). *Motivating students to learn* (3rd ed.). New York: Routledge.

Brown, J. S., Collins, A., & Duguid, P. (1989). Situated cognition and the culture of learning. *Educational Researcher, 18*(1), 32–42.

Brown, S. (2009). *Play*. New York: Avery.

Brown, S. I., & Walter, M. I. (1990). *The art of problem posing* (2nd ed.). Hillsdale, NJ: Erlbaum.

Brummelman, E., Thomæs, S., Overbeek, G., Castro, B. O. de, Hout, M. van den, & Bushman, B. J. (2014). On feeding those hungry for praise: Person praise backfires in children with low self-esteem. *Journal of Experimental Psychology, 143*(1), 9–14. DOI: 10.1037/a0031917

Brundage, A. (2013). *Going to the sources: A guide to historical reading and writing* (5th ed.). Malden, MA: John Wiley & Sons.

Bruner, J., Goodnow, J., & Austin, G. (1977). *A study of thinking*. New York: Wiley.

Bruno-Faria, M. F. (2014). Indicator of the climate for creativity in the workplace. In E. M. L. S. Alencar, M. F. Bruno-Faria, & D. S. Fleith (Eds.), *Theory and practice of creativity measurement* (pp. 85–102). Waco, TX: Prufrock Press.

Buchsbaum, D., Gopnik, A., Griffiths, T. L., & Shafto, P. (2011). Children's imitation of causal action sequences is influenced by statistical and pedagogical evidence. *Cognition, 120*(3), 331–340. DOI: 10:1016/j.cognition.2010.12.001

Buckner, R. L. (2012). The serendipitous discovery of the brain's default network. *NeuroImage, 62*, 1137–1145.

Buckner, R. L., Andrews-Hanna, J. R., & Schacter, D. L. (2008). The brain's default network: Anatomy, function, and relevance to disease. *Annuals of the New York Academy of Science, 1124*, 1–38. DOI: 10.1196/annals.1440.011

Bugbee, A. C. (2007). Test review of abbreviated Torrance test for adults. In K. F. Geisinger, R. A. Spies, J. F. Carlson, & B. S. Plake (Eds.), *The seventeenth mental measurements yearbook*. Retrieved from http://marketplace.unl.edu/buros/.

Burns, D. E. (1990). The effects of group training activities on students' initiation of creative investigations. *Gifted Child Quarterly, 34*, 31–36.

Burns, M. (1992). *About teaching mathematics*. White Plains, NY: Math Solutions Publications.

Burns, M. (2007). *Teaching mathematics: A K–8 resource* (3rd ed.). White Plains, NY: Math Solutions.

Butterworth, B. (1999). *The mathematical brain*. London: MacMillan.

Cabra, J. F., Talbot, R. J., & Joniak, A. J. (2005). Exploratory study of creative climate: A case from selected Columbian companies and its implication on organizational development. *Cuadernos de Administración, 18*(29), 53–86. Retrieved from www.scielo.unal.edu.co/scielo.php?script=sci_arttext&pid=S0120-35922005000100004&lng=pt&nrm=

Cajete, G. (2000). *Native science: Natural laws of interdependence*. Santa Fe, NM: Clear Light Publishers.

Callahan, C. M. (1991). The assessment of creativity. In N. Colangelo & G. A. Davis (Eds.), *Handbook of gifted education* (pp. 219–235). Boston: Allyn & Bacon.

Callahan, C. M. (2005). [Test review of *The Khatena—Torrance creative perception inventory*]. In R. A. Spies & B. S. Plake (Eds.), *The sixteenth mental measurements yearbook*. Retrieved from http://marketplace.unl.edu/buros/.

Cameron, J. (2001). Negative effects of reward on intrinsic motivation—a limited phenomenon: Comment on Deci, Koestner, and Ryan. *Review of Educational Research, 71*(1), 29–42.

Campbell, J. (1996). *The eastern way: Creativity in oriental mythology*. Joseph Campbell audio collection, Vol. 3, Tape 5. San Anselmo, CA: Joseph Campbell Foundation.

Campion, M., & Levita, L. (2014). Enhancing positive affect and divergent thinking abilities: Play some music and dance. *The Journal of Positive Psychology, 9*(2), 137–145. DOI: http://dx.doi.org/10.1080/17439760.2013.848376

Caney, S. (1985). *Steven Caney's invention book*. New York: Workman.

Caniglia, J. (2003). *Math and the great fire of 1805*. Detroit, MI: Detroit Historical Museum.

Carlsson, I., Wendt, P. E., & Risberg, J. (2000). On the neurobiology of creativity: Differences in frontal activity between high and low creative subjects. *Neuropsychologia, 38*, 873–885.

Carpenter, E., Varley, F., & Flaherty, F. (1968). *Eskimo*. Toronto: University of Toronto Press.

Carson, D. K., & Runco, M. A. (1999). Creative problem solving and problem finding in young adults: Interconnections with stress, hassles, and coping abilities. *Journal of Creative Behavior, 33*(3), 167–190.

Carson, S. H., Peterson, J. B., & Higgins, D. M. (2003). Decreased latent inhibition is associated with increased creative achievement in high-functioning individuals. *Journal of Personality and Social Psychology, 85*(3), 499–506.

Carson, S. H., Peterson, J. B., & Higgins, D. M. (2005). Reliability, validity, and factor structure of the creative achievement questionnaire. *Creativity Research Journal, 17*, 37–50.

Cautilli, J. (2004). Toward a behavioral theory of creativity. *The Behavioral Analyst Today, 5*(1), 126–140.

Center for Gifted Education Staff. (1996). *Acid, acid everywhere: A unit designed for grades 4–6*. New York: Kendall/Hunt.

Chan, S., & Yuen, M. (2014). Creativity beliefs, creative personality and creativity-fostering practices of gifted education teachers and regular class teachers in Hong Kong. *Thinking Skills and Creativity, 14*, 109–118.

Chappuis, J. (2012). How am I doing? *Educational Leadership, 70*, 36–40.

Chappuis, J., Stiggins, R., Chappuis, S., & Arter, J. (2012). *Classroom assessment for student learning: Doing it right using it well* (2nd ed.). New York: Pearson.

Chappuis, S., & Chappuis, J. (2007/2008). The best value in formative assessment. *Educational Leadership, 65*(4), 14–18.

Chase, C. I. (1985). Review of Torrance tests of creative thinking. In J. Mitchell, Jr. (Ed.), *The ninth mental measurements yearbook* (Vol. 2, pp. 1630–1632). Lincoln, NE: Buros Institute of Mental Measurement.

Chen, C., Dong, Q., Greenberger, E., Himsel, A. J., Kasof, J., & Xue, G. (2002). Creativity in drawings of geometric shapes: A cross-cultural examination with the consensual assessment technique. *Journal of Cross-Cultural Psychology, 33*(2), 171–187.

Cheng, V. M. Y. (2010a). Infusing creativity into Eastern classrooms: Evaluations from student perspectives. *Thinking Skills and Creativity, 6*, 67–87.

Cheng, V. M. Y. (2010b). Tensions and dilemmas of teacher in creativity reform in a Chinese context. *Thinking Skills and Creativity, 5*, 120–137.

Cheryan, S., Plaut, V. C., Davies, P. G., & Steele, C. M. (2009). Ambient belonging: How stereotypical cues impact gender participation in computer science. *Journal of Personality and Social Psychology, 97*, 1045–1060.

Cho, S. H., Nijenhuis, J. T., Vianen, A. E. M. van, Kim, H. B., & Lee, K. H. (2010). The relationship between diverse components of intelligence and creativity. *Journal of Creative Behavior, 44*(2), 125–137.

Choi, J. N. (2004). Individual and contextual predictors of creative performance: The mediating role of psychological processes. *Creativity Research Journal, 16*(2–3), 187–199.

Clarizio, H. F., & Mehrens, W. A. (1985). Psychometric limitations of Guilford's Structure of the Intellect Model for identification and programming for the gifted. *Gifted Child Quarterly, 29*, 113–120.

Cohen, E. G. (1986). *Designing group work*. New York: Teachers College Press.

Coil, C. (2004). *Standards-based activities and assessments for the differentiated classroom*. Marion, IL: Pieces of Learning.

Coleman, L., & Gallagher, S. A. (Eds.). (1997). [Theme issue]. *Journal for the Education of the Gifted, 20*(4).

Collins, M. A., & Amabile, T. M. (1999). Motivation and creativity. In R. J. Sternberg (Ed.), *Handbook of creativity* (pp. 297–312). New York: Cambridge University Press.

Colzato, L. S., Ozturk, A., & Hommel, B. (2012). Meditate to create: The impact of focused-attention and open-monitoring training on convergent and divergent thinking. *Frontiers in Psychology, 3*(116). DOI: 10.3389/fpsyg.2012.00116

Conklin, H. (2014). Toward more joyful learning: Integrating play into frameworks of middle grade teaching. *American Educational Research Journal, 51*(6), 1227–1255. DOI: 10.3102/0002831214549451

Conner, T. S., DeYoung, C. G., & Silvia, P. J. (2016). Everyday creative activity as a path to flourishing. *Journal of Positive Psychology*. Published online: 17 Nov 2016. DOI: 10.1080/17439760.2016.1257049

Conner, T. S., & Silvia, P. J. (2015). Creative days: A daily diary study of emotion, personality, and everyday creativity. *Psychology of Aesthetics, Creativity, and the Arts, 9*(4), 463–470.

Conti, R., Collins, M. A., & Picariello, M. (1995). Differential effects of competition on the artistic creativity of girls and boys. Unpublished manuscript, Brandeis University, Waltham, MA.

Cramond, B. (1994). Attention deficit-hyperactivity disorder and creativity: What is the connection? *Journal of Creative Behavior, 28*(3), 193–209.

Cramond, B., Martin, C. E., & Shaw, E. L. (1990). Generalizability of creative problem solving procedures to real life problems. *Journal for the Education of the Gifted, 13*, 141–155.

Crawford, R. P. (1954). *The techniques of creative thinking.* New York: Hawthorn Books.

Cropley, D. H., & Cropley, A. J. (2012). A psychological taxonomy of organizational innovation: Resolving the paradoxes. *Creativity Research Journal, 24*(1), 29–40.

Cropley, D. H., Cropley, A. J., Chiera, B. A., & Kaufman, J. C. (2013). Diagnosing organizational innovation: Measuring the capacity for innovation. *Creativity Research Journal, 25*(4), 388–396. DOI: 10.1080/10400419.2013.843330

Csikszentmihalyi, M. (1988). Society, culture, and person: A systems view of creativity. In R. J. Sternberg (Ed.), *The nature of creativity* (pp. 325–339). New York: Cambridge University Press.

Csikszentmihalyi, M. (1990a). *Flow: The psychology of optimal experience.* New York: Harper & Row.

Csikszentmihalyi, M. (1990b). The domain of creativity. In M. A. Runco & R. S. Albert (Eds.), *Theories of creativity* (pp. 190–212). Newbury Park, CA: Sage.

Csikszentmihalyi, M. (1994). The domain of creativity. In D. H. Feldman, M. Csikszentmihalyi, & H. Gardner (Eds.), *Changing the world: A framework for the study of creativity* (pp. 135–158). Westport, CT: Praeger.

Csikszentmihalyi, M. (1996). *Creativity: Flow and the psychology of discovery and invention.* New York: HarperCollins.

Csikszentmihalyi, M. (1999). Implications of a systems perspective for the study of creativity. In R. J. Sternberg (Ed.), *Handbook of creativity* (pp. 313–335). New York: Cambridge University Press.

Csikszentmihalyi, M., & Sawyer, K. (1993, May). *Creative insight: The social dimension of a solitary moment.* Paper presented at the Henry B. and Jocelyn Wallace National Research Symposium on Talent Development, Iowa City, IA.

Cummings, J. A. (1989). [Test review of the Structure of Intellect Learning Abilities Test]. In J. C. Conoley & J. J. Kramer (Eds.), *The tenth mental measurements yearbook.* Retrieved from http://marketplace.unl.edu/buros/

Cummings, J. A. (2007). Review of structure of the intellect learning abilities test In K. F. Geisinger, R. A. Spies, J. F. Carlson, & B. S. Plake (Eds.), *The seventeenth mental measurements yearbook.* Retrieved from http://marketplace.unl.edu/buros/

Dacey, J. S. (1989). *Fundamentals of creative thinking.* Lexington, MA: Lexington Books.

Dahl, R. (1961). *James and the giant peach.* New York: Puffin Books.

Damarin, F. (1985). Review of creativity assessment packet. In J. Mitchell, Jr. (Ed.), *The ninth mental measurements yearbook* (Vol. 1, pp. 410–411). Lincoln: University of Nebraska Press.

Damian, R. I., & Robins, R. W. (2012). Aristotle's virtue or Dante's deadliest sin? The influence of authentic and hubristic pride on creative achievement. *Learning and Individual Differences.* Retrieved June 12, 2012, from www.sciencedirect.com/science/article/pii/S1041608012000817

Damian, R. I., & Simonton, D. K. (2015). Psychopathology, adversity, and creativity: Diversifying experiences and the development of eminent African Americans. *Journal of Personality and Social Psychology, 108*(4), 623–636.

D'Arcangelo, M. (2001). Wired for mathematics: A conversation with Brian Butterworth. *Educational Leadership, 59*(3), 14–19.

Darwin, C. (1859). *On the origin of species.* London: John Murray.

Davies, D., Jindal-Snape, D., Collier, C., Digby, R., Hay, P., & Howe, Al. (2013). Creative learning environments in education—a systematic literature review. *Thinking Skills and Creativity, 8*, 80–91.

Davis, A. (2009). Understanding the relationship between mood and creativity. *Organizational Behavior and Human Decision Processes, 108*, 25–38.

Davis, G. A. (1992). *Creativity is forever* (3rd ed.). Dubuque, IA: Kendall/Hunt.

Davis, G. A. (1998). *Creativity is forever* (4th ed.). Dubuque, IA: Kendall/Hunt.

Davis, G. A., & Rimm, S. (1980). *Group inventory for finding talent.* Watertown, WI: Educational Assessment Service.

Davis, G. A., & Rimm, S. (1982). Group inventory for finding interests (GIFFI) I and II: Instruments for identifying creative potential in the junior and senior high school. *Journal of Creative Behavior, 16*, 50–57.

de Bono, E. (1970). *Lateral thinking.* New York: Harper & Row.

de Bono, E. (1986). *CoRT thinking: Teacher's notes* (2nd ed., Vols. 1–6). New York: Pergamon.

de Bono, E. (1991a). *Six thinking hats for schools: Adult educators' resource book.* Logan, IA: Perfection Learning.

de Bono, E. (1991b). *Six thinking hats for schools: 3–5 resource book.* Logan, IA: Perfection Learning.

de Bono, E. (1992). *Serious creativity.* New York: HarperCollins.

de Bono, E. (1999). *The new six thinking hats.* New York: Little, Brown & Company.

Deci, E. L. (1971). Effects of externally mediated rewards on intrinsic motivation. *Journal of Personality and Social Psychology, 28*, 105–115.

Deci, E. L., Koestner, R., & Ryan, R. M. (2001a). Extrinsic rewards and intrinsic motivation in education: Reconsidered once again. *Review of Educational Research, 71*(1), 1–27.

Deci, E. L., Koestner, R., & Ryan, R. M. (2001b). The pervasive negative effects of rewards on intrinsic motivation: Response to Cameron (2001). *Review of Educational Research, 71*(1), 43–51.

de Giere, C. (2008). *Defying gravity: The creative career of Stephen Schwartz from Godspell to Wicked.* New York: Applause.

De Jesus, S. N., Rus, C. L., Lens, W., & Imaginário, S. (2013). Intrinsic motivation and creativity related to product: A meta-analysis of the studies published between 1990–2010. *Creativity Research Journal, 25*(1), 80–84. DOI: 10.1080/10400419.2013.752235

Delcourt, M. A. B. (1993). Creative productivity among secondary school students: Combining energy, interest, and imagination. *Gifted Child Quarterly, 37*, 23–31.

Dewey, J. (1920). *How we think*. Boston: Heath.

Dewey, J. (1938). *Experience and education*. New York: Macmillan.

Dillon, J. T. (1982). Problem finding and solving. *Journal of Creative Behavior, 16*, 97–111.

Dillon, J. T. (1988). *Questioning and teaching*. New York: Teachers College Press.

Ding, X., Tang, Y., Tang, R., & Posner, M. (2014). Improving creativity performance by short-term meditation. *Behavioral and Brain Functions, 10*(9), 1–8. Retrieved from www.behavioralandbrainfunctions.com/content/10/1/9

DiPucchio, K. (2008). *Sipping spiders through a straw*. New York: Scholastic.

Doctorow, E. L. (1971). *The book of Daniel*. New York: Random House.

Doctorow, E. L. (1975). *Ragtime*. New York: Random House.

Doron, E. (2016). Short term intervention model for enhancing divergent thinking among school aged children. *Creativity Research Journal, 28*(3), 372–378.

Dougherty, D. (2014). The maker mindset. In M. Honey & D. E. Kanter (Eds.), *Design make play: Growing the next generation of innovators* (pp. 7–11). New York: Routledge.

Drapeau, P. (2014). *Sparking student creativity*. Alexandria, VA: Association for Supervision and Curriculum Development.

Duggleby, J. (1994). *Artist in overalls: The life of Grant Wood*. San Francisco: Chronicle Books.

Dwinell, P. L. (1985). Review of group inventory for finding interests. In J. Mitchell, Jr. (Ed.), *The ninth mental measurements yearbook* (Vol. 1, pp. 362–363). Lincoln: University of Nebraska Press.

Eberle, R. F. (1977). *SCAMPER*. Buffalo, NY: DOK.

Eberle, R. F. (1996). *SCAMPER* [Reissue]. Waco, TX: Prufrock Press.

Ehlert, L. (1989). *Color zoo*. New York: J. B. Lippincott Pub.

Eisenberger, R., Armeli, S., & Pretz, J. (1998). Can the promise of reward increase creativity? *Journal of Personality and Social Psychology, 74*, 704–714.

Eisenberger, R., & Cameron, J. (1996). Detrimental effects of reward: Reality of myth? *American Psychologist, 51*, 1153–1166.

Eisenberger, R., & Rhoades, L. (2001). Incremental effects of rewards on creativity. *Journal of Personality and Social Psychology, 81*, 728–741.

Eisenberger, R., & Shanock, L. (2003). Rewards, intrinsic motivation and creativity: A case study of conceptual and methodological isolation. *Creativity Research Journal, 15*(2–3), 121–130.

Ekvall, G., & Ryhammar, L. (1999). The creative climate: Its determinants and effects at a Swedish university. *Creativity Research Journal, 12*, 303–310.

Elasky, B. (1989). Becoming. *Democracy and Education* (Occasional Paper No. 3), 6–13.

Elkind, D., Deblinger, J., & Adler, D. (1970). Motivation and creativity: The context of effect. *American Educational Research Journal, 7*, 351–357.

Ellamil, M., Dobson, C., Beeman, M., & Christoff, K. (2012). Evaluative and generative modes of thought during the creative process. *NeuroImage, 59*, 1783–1794.

Ellenbogen, J. M., Hu, P. T., Payne, J. D., Titone, D., & Walker, M. P. (2007). Human relational memory requires time and sleep. *Proceedings of the National Academy of Science, 104*(18), 7723–7728.

Elliott, E. S., & Dweck, C. S. (1988). Goals: An approach to motivation and achievement. *Journal of Personality and Social Psychology, 54*, 5–12.

Engel, S. (2011). Children's need to know: Curiosity in schools. *Harvard Educational Review, 81*(4), 625–645.

Engel, S. (2015). *The hungry mind: The origins of curiosity in childhood*. Cambridge, MA: Harvard University Press.

Engel, S., & Randall, K. (2009). How teachers respond to children's inquiry. *American Educational Research Journal, 46*(1), 183–202.

English, L. D. (1997). Promoting a problem-posing classroom. *Teaching Children Mathematics, 4*(3), 172–179.

Eric Carle Museum of Picture Book Art. (2007). *Artist to artist*. New York: Philomel Books.

Erlbach, A. (1999). *The kids' invention book*. Minneapolis: Lerner Publications.

Erskine, I., & Krzanicki, C. (2012). The vernacular and the global: Fulbridge Primary School. Peterborough. In N. Owen (Ed.), *Placing students in the heart of creative learning* (pp. 14–29). London: Routledge.

Evans, E. D. (1986). Review of thinking creatively in action and movement. In D. Keyser & R. Sweetland (Eds.), *Test critiques* (Vol. 5, pp. 505–512). Kansas City, MO: Testing Corporation of America.

Fabricant, M., Svitak, S., & Kenschaft, P. C. (1990). Why women succeed in mathematics. *Mathematics Teacher, 83*, 150–154.

Fairweather, E. C., Cramond, B., & Landis, R. N. (2015). Are creativity tests susceptible to coaching? *Asia Pacific Education Review, 16*, 177–182. DOI: 10.1007/s12564-015-9365-x

Feedback for learning [Theme issue]. (2012). *Educational Leadership, 70*(1).

Fehr, K. K., & Russ, S. W. (2016). Pretend play and creativity in preschool-age children: Associations and brief intervention. *Psychology of Aesthetics, Creativity and the Arts, 10*(3), 296–308.

Feist, G. J. (1999). The influence of personality on artistic and scientific creativity. In R. J. Sternberg (Ed.), *Handbook of creativity* (pp. 273–296). New York: Cambridge University Press.

Feist, G. J. (2010). The function of personality in creativity: The nature and nurture of the creative personality. In J. C. Kaufman & R. J. Sternberg (Eds.), *The Cambridge handbook of creativity* (pp. 113–130). New York: Cambridge University Press.

Feldman, D. H. (1994). Child prodigies: A distinctive form of giftedness. *Gifted Child Quarterly, 37*, 188–193.

Feldman, D. H. (1999). The development of creativity. In R. J. Sternberg (Ed.), *Handbook of creativity* (pp. 169–186). New York: Cambridge University Press.

Feldman, D. H. (2003). The creation of multiple intelligences theory: A study in high-level thinking. In R. K. Sawyer, V. John-Steiner, S. Moran, R. J. Sternberg, D. H. Feldman, H. Gardner, J. Nakamura, & J. Csikszentmihalyi, *Creativity and development* (pp. 139–185). New York: Oxford University Press.

Feldman, D. H., Csikszentmihalyi, M., & Gardner, H. (1994). *Changing the world: A framework for the study of creativity.* Westport, CT: Praeger.

Feynman, R. (1997). The dignified professor. In F. Barron, A. Montuori, & A. Barron (Eds.), *Creators on creating* (pp. 63–67). New York: Putnam.

Fine, E. C. (2003, Summer). Stepping. *American Legacy, 9*(2), 19–22.

Fine, S. M. (2014). "A slow revolution": Toward a theory of playfulness in high school classrooms. *Harvard Educational Review, 84*(1), 1–23.

Finke, R. A. (1990). *Creative imagery: Discoveries and inventions in visualization.* Hillsdale, NJ: Erlbaum.

Finkelstein, A. (2002). *Science is golden: A problem-solving approach to doing science with children.* East Lansing: Michigan State University Press.

Fisher, D., & Frey, N. (2012). Making time for feedback. *Educational Leadership, 70*(1), 42–47.

Fleck, J. S., & Weisberg, R. W. (2013). Insight versus analysis: Evidence for diverse methods in problem solving. *Journal of Cognitive Psychology, 25,* 436–463.

Fleith, D. S. (2014). Assessment of the climate for creativity in the classroom. In E. M. L. S. Alencar, M. F. Bruno-Faria, & D. S. Fleith (Eds.), *Theory and practice of creativity measurement* (pp. 37–49). Waco, TX: Prufrock Press.

Fleming, T. (2006). *Everybody's revolution.* New York: Scholastic.

Forman, S. M. (Ed.). (1997a). *Echoes of the Civil War: The blue.* Carlisle, MA: Discovery Enterprises.

Forman, S. M. (Ed.). (1997b). *Echoes of the Civil War: The gray.* Carlisle, MA: Discovery Enterprises.

Forthmann, B., Gerwig, A., Holling, H., Çelik, P., Storme, M., & Lubart, T. (2016). The be-creative effect in divergent thinking: The interplay of instruction and object frequency. *Intelligence, 57,* 25–32.

Forthmann, B., Wilken, A., Doebler, P., & Holling, H. (2016, September). Strategy induction enhances creativity in figural divergent thinking. *Journal of Creative Behavior,* available online in advance of publication. DOI: 10.1002/jocb.159

French, J. W. (1978). Review of creativity tests for children. In O. C. Buros (Ed.), *The eighth mental measurements yearbook* (Vol. 1, pp. 363–365). Highland Park, NJ: Gryphon Press.

Friedman, F., Raymond, B. A., & Feldhusen, J. F. (1978). The effects of environmental scanning on creativity. *Gifted Child Quarterly, 22,* 248–251.

Fusaro, M. (2017). What is teaching for understanding? *Usable Knowledge.* Retrieved January 3, 2017, from www.gse.harvard.edu/news/uk/08/05/what-teaching-understanding.

Gallagher, S. A. (2012). *Concept development.* Unionville, NY: Royal Fireworks Press.

Gallagher, S. A. (2015). The role of problem-based learning in developing creative expertise. *Asia Pacific Education Review, 16,* 225–235. DOI: 10.1007/s12564-015-9367-8

Galvin, G. A. (1989). [Test review of the preschool and kindergarten interest descriptor]. In J. C. Conoley & J. J. Kramer (Eds.), *The tenth mental measurements yearbook.* Retrieved from http://marketplace.unl.edu/buros/.

Gardner, H. (1982). *Art, mind, and brain.* New York: Basic Books.

Gardner, H. (1983). *Frames of mind: The theory of multiple intelligences.* New York: Basic Books.

Gardner, H. (1993a). *Creating minds.* New York: Basic Books.

Gardner, H. (1993b, May). *From youthful talent to creative achievement.* Paper presented at the Henry B. and Jocelyn Wallace National Research Symposium on Talent Development, Iowa City, IA.

Gardner, H. (1994). The creators' patterns. In D. H. Feldman, M. Csikszentmihalyi, & H. Gardner (Eds.), *Changing the world: A framework for the study of creativity* (pp. 69–84). Westport, CT: Praeger.

Garland, D. (1993). *The lotus seed.* New York: Harcourt Brace Jovanovich.

Garner, B. K. (2007). *Getting to "Got it!"* Alexandria, VA: Association of Supervision and Curriculum Development.

Getzels, J. W. (1964). Creative thinking, problem solving and instruction. In E. Hilgard (Ed.), *Sixty-third National Society for the Study of Education yearbook: Part 1, Theories of learning and instruction* (pp. 240–267). Chicago: University of Chicago Press.

Getzels, J. W. (1982). The problem of the problem. In R. Hogath (Ed.), *New directions for methodology of social and behavioral science: Question framing and response consistency* (pp. 37–49). San Francisco: Jossey-Bass.

Getzels, J. W. (1987). Problem finding and creative achievement. *Gifted Students Institute Quarterly, 12*(4), B1–B4.

Getzels, J. W., & Csikszentmihalyi, M. (1976). *The creative vision: A longitudinal study of problem finding in art.* New York: Wiley.

Ghiselin, B. (1985). *The creative process.* Berkeley, CA: University of California Press.

Gilhooly, K. J., Georgiou, G. J., & Devery, U. (2013). Incubation and creativity: Do something different. *Thinking and Reasoning, 19*(2), 137–149.

Gilhooly, K. J., Georgiou, G. J., Sirota, M., & Paphiti-Galeano, A. (2015). Incubation and suppression processes in creative problem solving. *Thinking and Reasoning, 21*(1), 130–146.

Gilligan, C., Lyons, N., & Hammer, T. (Eds.). (1990). *Making connections.* Cambridge, MA: Harvard University Press.

Glăveanu, V. (2009). Paradigms in the study of creativity: Introducing the perspective of cultural psychology. *New Ideas in Psychology, 28,* 79–83. DOI: 10.1016/j.newideapsych.2009.07.007

Glăveanu, V. (2010). Principles for a cultural psychology of creativity. *Culture and Psychology, 16*(2), 147–163.

Goff, K., & Torrance, E. P. (2002). *Abbreviated Torrance test for adults.* Bensenville, IL: Scholastic Testing Service.

Golden, J. (2001). *Reading in the dark: Using film as a tool in the English classroom.* Urbana, IL: NCTE.

Golding, W. (1999). *Lord of the flies*. New York: Penguin.

Goldman, S., & Kabayadondo, Z. (Eds.). (2017). *Taking design thinking to school*. New York: Routledge.

Golman, R., & Loewenstein, G. (2015, April 16). Curiosity, information gaps, and the utility of knowledge. Retrieved from http://ssrn.com/abstract=2149362 or http://dx.doi.org/10.2139/ssrn.2149362

Gontijo, C. H., & Fleith, D. S. (2014). Assessment of creativity in mathematics. In E. M. L. S. Alencar, M. F. Bruno-Faria, & D. S. Fleith (Eds.), *Theory and practice of creativity measurement* (pp. 65–84). Waco, TX: Prufrock Press.

Gordon, W. J. J. (1981). *The new art of the possible: The basic course in synectics*. Cambridge, MA: Porpoise Books.

Gordon, W. J. J., & Poze, T. (1972). *Teaching is listening*. Cambridge, MA: SES Associates.

Gordon, W. J. J., & Poze, T. (1975). *Strange and familiar*. Cambridge, MA: SES Associates.

Gordon, W. J. J., & Poze, T. (1979). *The metaphorical way of learning and knowing*. Cambridge, MA: SES Associates.

Gordon, W. J. J., & Poze, T. (1981). *The new art of the possible*. Cambridge, MA: SES Associates.

Gordon, W. J. J., & Poze, T. (1984). *Presenter's manual for the SES seminar for teachers*. Cambridge, MA: SES Associates.

Goswami, U. (2006). Neuroscience and education: From research to practice? *Nature Reviews Neuroscience, 7*, 406–413. DOI: 10.1038/nrn1907

Gotlieb, R., Jahner, E., Immordino-Yang, M. H., & Kaufman, S. B. (2017). How social-emotional imagination facilitates deep learning and creativity in the classroom. In R. A. Beghetto & J. C. Kaufman (Eds.), *Nurturing creativity in the classroom* (2nd ed., pp. 308–336). New York: Cambridge.

Gowan, J. C. (1977). Some new thoughts on the development of creativity. *Journal of Creative Behavior, 11*, 77–90.

Grandits, J. (2004). *Technically, it's not my fault*. New York: Clarion Books.

Grant, A. M., & Berry, J. W. (2011). The necessity of others is the mother of invention: Prosocial motivations, perspective taking, and creativity. *Academy of Management Journal, 54*(1), 73–96.

Grant, H., & Dweck, C. S. (2003). Clarifying achievement goals and their impact. *Journal of Personality and Social Psychology, 85*, 541–553.

Gray, P. (2011). The decline of play and the rise of psychopathology in children and adolescents. *American Journal of Play, 3*(4), 443–463.

Gray, P. (2013). Play as preparation for learning and life: An interview with Peter Gray. *American Journal of Play, 5*, 271–292.

Grazer, B., & Fishman, C. (2015). *A curious mind: The secret to a bigger life*. New York: Simon & Schuster.

Greenfield, P., Maynard, A., & Childs, C. (2003). *Historical change, cultural learning, and cognitive representation in Zinacantec Maya children*. Washington, DC: American Psychological Association.

Gregory, G., & Kaufeldt, M. (2015). *The motivated brain: Improving student attention, engagement, and perseverance*. Alexandria, VA: Association for Supervision and Curriculum Development.

Gruber, H. E. (1981). *Darwin on man: A psychological study of scientific creativity* (2nd ed.). Chicago: University of Chicago Press.

Gruber, H. E., & Davis, S. N. (1988). Inching our way up Mount Olympus: The evolving-systems approach to creative thinking. In R. J. Sternberg (Ed.), *The nature of creativity* (pp. 243–270). New York: Cambridge University Press.

Gruber, H. E., & Wallace, D. B. (1999). The case study method and evolving systems approach for understanding unique creative people at work. In R. J. Sternberg (Ed.), *Handbook of creativity* (pp. 93–115). New York: Cambridge University Press.

Gruber, H. E., & Wallace, D. B. (2001). Creative work: The case of Charles Darwin. *American Psychologist, 56*(4), 346–349.

Gudipati, M., & Sethi, K. B. (2017). Adapting the user-centered design framework for K–12 education: The Riverside School case study. In S. Goldman & Z. Kabayadondo (Eds.), *Taking design thinking to school* (pp. 94–101). New York: Routledge.

Guilford, J. P. (1959). Three faces of intellect. *American Psychologist, 14*, 469–479.

Guilford, J. P. (1967). *The nature of human intelligence*. New York: McGraw-Hill.

Guilford, J. P. (1973). *Creativity tests for children*. Orange, CA: Sheridan Psychological Services.

Guilford, J. P. (1977). *Way beyond the IQ*. Buffalo, NY: Creative Education Foundation.

Guilford, J. P. (1986). *Creative talents: Their nature, use, and development*. Buffalo, NY: Bearly.

Guilford, J. P. (1988). Some changes in the Structure-of-Intellect model. *Educational and Psychological Measurement, 48*, 1–6.

Günçer, B., & Oral, G. (1993). Relationship between creativity and nonconformity to school discipline as perceived by the teacher of Turkish elementary school children, by controlling for their grade and sex. *Journal of Instructional Psychology, 20*, 208–214.

Gute, G., Gute, D. S., Nakamura, J., & Csikszentmihalyi, M. (2008). The early lives of highly creative persons: The influence of the complex family. *Creativity Research Journal, 20*, 343–357.

Hall, M. (2011). *Perfect square*. New York: Greenwillow Books.

Halmos, P. R. (1968). Mathematics as creative art. *American Scientist, 4*, 380–381.

Han, K., & Marvin, C. (2002). Multiple creativities? Investigating domain specificity of creativity in young children. *Gifted Child Quarterly, 46*(2), 98–109.

Hanaford, P. A. (1882b). *Daughters of America or women of the century*. Augusta, ME: True.

Hao, N., Liu, M., Ku, Y., Hu, Y., & Runco, M. A. (2015). Verbal divergent thinking facilitated by a pleasurable incubation interval. *Psychology of Aesthetics, Creativity, and the Arts, 9*(3), 286–295. DOI: http://dx.doi.org/10.1037/a0038851

Harmon, D. (2002). They won't teach me: The voices of gifted African American inner-city students. *Roeper Review, 24*(2), 68–75.

Hass, R. W. (2015). Feasibility of online divergent thinking assessment. *Computers in Human Behavior, 48*, 85–93.

Hattie, J. (1980). Should creativity tests be administered under testlike conditions? An empirical study of three alternative conditions. *Journal of Educational Psychology*, 72, 87–98.

Haught-Tromp, C. (2017). The *Green Eggs and Ham* hypothesis: How constraints facilitate creativity. *Psychology of Aesthetics, Creativity, and the Arts*, 11(1), 10–17. DOI: http://dx.doi.org/10.1037/aca0000061

Hawes, S., Wdziekonska-Piwko, D., Martin, K., Thomas, J., & Nicholls, J. (2012). Engaging deaf students through ICT. In E. Sellman (Ed.), *Creative learning for inclusion: Creative approaches to meet special needs in the classroom* (pp. 68–79). New York: Routledge.

Healey, D. (2014). Attention-deficit-hyperactivity disorder and creativity: Ever the twain shall meet? In J. C. Kaufman (Ed.), *Creativity and mental illness* (pp. 236–249). Cambridge: Cambridge University Press.

Heinig, R. B. (1992). *Creative drama for the classroom teacher* (4th ed.). Upper Saddle River, NJ: Prentice-Hall.

Helson, R. (1983). Creative mathematicians. In R. Albert (Ed.), *Genius and eminence: The social psychology of creativity and exceptional achievement* (pp. 211–230). London: Pergamon.

Hennessey, B. A. (2010). The creativity-motivation connection. In J. C. Kaufman & R. J. Sternberg (Eds.), *The Cambridge handbook of creativity* (pp. 342–365). New York: Cambridge University Press.

Hennessey, B. A. (2015). Creative behavior, motivation, environment and culture: The building of a systems model. *Journal of Creative Behavior*, 49(3), 194–210.

Hennessey, B. A. (2017). Intrinsic motivation and creativity in the classroom: Have we come full circle? In R. A. Beghetto & J. C. Kaufman (Eds.), *Nurturing creativity in the classroom* (2nd ed., pp. 227–264). New York: Cambridge University Press.

Hennessey, B. A., & Amabile, T. M. (1988). The conditions of creativity. In R. J. Sternberg (Ed.), *The nature of creativity* (pp. 11–38). New York: Cambridge University Press.

Hickey, M. (2001). An application of Amabile's consensual assessment technique for rating the creativity of children's musical compositions. *Journal of Research in Music Education*, 49(3), 234–244.

Hill, W. E. (1977). *Learning: A survey of psychological interpretations* (3rd ed.). New York: Harper & Row.

Hoffman, J., & Russ, S. (2016). Fostering pretend play skills and creativity in elementary school girls: A group play intervention. *Psychology of Aesthetics, Creativity, and the Arts*, 10(1), 114–125.

Hoffman, J., & Russ, S. (2012). Pretend play, creativity, and emotional regulation. *Psychology of Aesthetics, Creativity, and the Arts*, 6(2), 175–184.

Hofstede, G. (2001). *Culture's consequences: Comparing values, behaviors, institutions, and organizations across cultures*. Thousand Oaks, CA: Sage.

Hoicka, E., Bijvoet-van den Berg, S., Kerr, T., & Carberry, M. (2013). The Unusual Box Test: A non-verbal, non-representational divergent thinking test for toddlers. *Creativity and (Early) Cognitive Development: Papers from the 2013 AAAI Spring Symposium*, 32–37. Retrieved from www.aaai.org/ocs/index.php/SSS/SSS13/paper/viewFile/5801/5932

Hollingsworth, S., & Gallego, M. A. (Eds.). (2007). Special issue on no child left behind. *American Educational Research Journal*, 44(3), 454–629.

Holt, D. G., & Willard-Holt, C. (2000). Let's get real: Students solving authentic corporate problems. *Phi Delta Kappan*, 82(3), 243–246.

Hon, A. H. Y., & Leung, A. S. M. (2011). Employee creativity and motivation in the Chinese culture: The moderating role of organizational culture. *Cornell Hospitality Quarterly*, 52(2), 125–134.

Hong, E., O'Neil, H. F., & Peng, Y. (2016). Effects of explicit instructions, metacognition, and motivation on creative performance. *Creativity Research Journal*, 28(1), 33–45. DOI: 10.1080/10400419.2016.1125252

Hong, H., & Lin-Siegler, X. (2012). How learning about scientists' struggles influences students' interest and learning in physics. *Journal of Educational Psychology*, 104(2), 469–484.

hooks, b. (1995). *Art on my mind: Visual politics*. New York: The New Press.

Hoover, S. M. (1994). Scientific problem-finding in gifted fifth grade students. *Roeper Review*, 16, 156–159.

Hopkinson, D. (2010). *The humblebee hunter*. New York: Hyperion Books.

Houtz, J. C. (1985). Review of thinking creatively with sounds and words. In D. Keyser & R. Sweetland (Eds.), *Test critiques* (Vol. 4, pp. 666–672). Kansas City, MO: Test Corporation of America.

Howard-Jones, P. A., Blakemore, S., Samuel, E. A., Summers, I. R., & Claxton, G. (2005). Semantic divergence and creative story generation: An fMRI investigation. *Cognitive Brain Research*, 25, 240–250.

Howard-Jones, P. A., Samuel, E. A., Summers, I. R., & Claxton, G. (2005). Semantic divergence and creative story generation: An fMRI investigation. *Cognitive Brain Research*, 25, 240–250.

Hucko, B. (1996). *A rainbow at night: The world in words and pictures by Navajo children*. San Francisco: Chronicle Books.

Hughes, L. (1951). Dream deferred. In *The panther and the lash: Poems of our times* (p. 14). New York: Knopf.

Hughes, L. (Ed.). (1968). *Poems from black Africa*. Bloomington: Indiana University Press.

Hunter, J. P., & Csikszentmihalyi, M. (2003). The positive psychology of interested adolescents. *Journal of Youth and Adolescence*, 32(1), 27–35.

Immordino-Yang, M. H. (2016). *Emotions, learning, and the brain: Exploring the educational implications of affective neuroscience*. New York: W. W. Norton & Co.

Innamorato, G. (1998). Creativity in the development of scientific giftedness: Educational implications. *Roeper Review*, 21, 54–59.

Isaksen, S. G., Dorval, K. B., & Treffinger, D. J. (2000). *Creative approaches to problem solving* (2nd ed.). Dubuque, IA: Kendall/Hunt.

Isaksen, S. G., Lauer, K. J., & Ekvall, G. (1999). Situational outlook questionnaire: A measure of the climate for creativity and change. *Psychological Reports*, 85, 665–674.

Isaksen, S. G., & Treffinger, D. J. (1985). *Creative problem solving: The basic course*. New York: Bearly.

Isenberg, J. P., & Jalongo, M. R. (1993). *Creative expression and play in the early childhood curriculum.* New York: Merrill.

Jagiellowicz, J., Xu, X., Aron, A., Aron, E., Cao, G. et al. (2011). The trait of sensory processing sensitivity an neural responses to changes in visual sciences. *Social Cognitive and Affective Neuroscience, 6*(1), 38–47.

Jauk, E., Benedek, M., Dunst, B., & Neubauer, A. C. (2013). The relationship between intelligence and creativity: New support for the threshold hypothesis by means of empirical breakpoint detection. *Intelligence, 41,* 212–221.

Jepma, M., Verdonschot, R. G., Steenbergen, H. van, Rombouts, S. A. R. B., & Nieuwenhuis, S. (2012). Neural mechanisms underlying the induction and relief of perceptual curiosity. *Frontiers in Behavioral Neuroscience, 6*(5), 1–9. DOI: 10.3389/fnbeh.2012.00005

Jirout, J., & Klar, D. (2012). Children's scientific curiosity: In search of an operational definition of an elusive concept. *Developmental Review, 32,* 125–160.

Johnson, C. (1997). Lost in the woods. In F. Barron, A. Montuori, & A. Barron (Eds.), *Creators on creating* (pp. 59–62). New York: Putnam.

Johnson, L. G., & Hatch, J. A. (1990). A descriptive study of the creative and social behavior of four highly original young children. *Journal of Creative Behavior, 24,* 205–224.

Johnson, S. (2010). *Where good ideas come from.* New York: Penguin Books.

John-Steiner, V. (2000). *Creative collaboration.* New York: Oxford University Press.

Joosse, B. M. (1991). *Mama, do you love me?* San Francisco: Chronicle Books.

Joyce, B., Weil, M., & Calhoun, E. (2009). *Models of teaching* (8th ed.). Boston: Allyn & Bacon.

Joyce, B., Weil, M., & Calhoun, E. (2014). *Models of teaching* (9th ed.). New York: Pearson.

Jung, C. G. (1972). *The spirit in man, art, and literature.* Princeton, NJ: Princeton University Press.

Jung, R. E., Gasparovic, C., Chavex, R. S., Flores, R. A., Smith, S. M., Caprihan, A., & Yeo, R. A. (2009). Biochemical support for the "threshold" theory of creativity: A magnetic resonance spectroscopy study. *Journal of Neuroscience, 29*(16), 5319–5325.

Jung-Beeman, M., Bowden, E. M., Haberman, J., Frymiare, J. L., Arambel-Liu, S., et al. (2004). Neural activity when people solve verbal problems with insight. *PLoS Biology, 2*(4), e97. DOI: 10.1371/journal.pbio.0020097

Kagan,J.(1972). Motives and development. *Journal of Personality and Social Psychology, 22,* 51–66.

Kālis, E., Roķe, L., & Krūmiņa, I. (2014). Investigation of psychometric properties of the Test for Creative Thinking—Drawing Production: Evidence from study in Latvia. *Journal of Creative Behavior, 50*(1), 47–63. DOI: 10.1002/jocb.68

Kaltsounis, B. (1975). Further validity on something about myself. *Perceptual and Motor Skills, 40,* 94.

Kang, M. J., Hsu, M., Krajbich, I., Loewenstein, G., McClure, S., Wang, J., & Camerer, C. (2009). The wick in the candle of learning: Epistemic curiosity activates reward circuitry and enhances memory. *Psychological Science, 20*(8), 963–973.

Karwowski, M. (2015). Peer effect on students' creative self-concept. *Journal of Creative Behavior, 49*(3), 211–225. DOI: 10.1002/jocb.102

Kashdan, T. B., Afram, A., Brown, K. W., Birnbeck, M., & Drvoshanov, M. (2011). Curiosity enhances the role of mindfulness in reducing defensive responses to existential threat. *Personality and Individual Differences, 50,* 1227–1232.

Kashdan, T. B., DeWall, C. N., Pond, R. S., Silvia, P. J., Lambert, N. M., Fincham, F. D., Savostyanova, A. A., & Keller, P. S. (2013). Curiosity protects against interpersonal aggression: Cross-sectional, daily progress, and behavioral evidence. *Journal of Personality, 81*(1), 87–102. DOI: 10.1111/j.1467-6494.2012.00783.x

Kashdan, T. B., McKnight, P. E., Fincham, F. D., & Rose, P. (2011). When curiosity breeds intimacy: Taking advantage of intimacy opportunities and transforming boring conversations. *Journal of Personality, 79,* 1067–1099.

Kashdan, T. B., Rose, P., & Finchma, F. D. (2004). Curiosity and exploration: Facilitating positive subject experiences and personal growth opportunities. *Journal of Personality Assessment, 82,* 291–305.

Kashdan, T. B., Sherman, R. A., Yarbro, J., & Funder, D. C. (2013). How are curious people viewed and how do they behave in social situations? From the perspectives of self, friends, parents, and unacquainted observers. *Journal of Personality, 81*(2), 142–154. DOI: 10.1111/j.1467-6494.2012.00796.x

Kashdan, T. B., & Yuen, M. (2007). Whether highly curious students thrive academically depends on perceptions about the school learning environment: A study of Hong Kong adolescents. *Motivation and Emotion, 31,* 260–270.

Kaufman, J. C. (2001). The Sylvia Plath effect: Mental illness in eminent creative writers. *The Journal of Creative Behavior, 35*(1), 37–50.

Kaufman, J. C. (2005). The door that leads into madness: Eastern European poets and mental illness. *Creativity Research Journal, 17*(1), 99–103.

Kaufman, J. C. (2006). Self-reported differences in creativity by ethnicity and gender. *Applied Cognitive Psychology, 20,* 1065–1082. DOI: 10.1002/acp.1255

Kaufman, J. C. (2012). Counting the muses: Development of the Kaufman Domains of Creativity Scale (K-DOCS). *Psychology of Aesthetics, Creativity and the Arts, 6*(4), 298–308.

Kaufman, J. C. (Ed.). (2014). *Creativity and mental illness.* Cambridge: Cambridge University Press.

Kaufman, J. C., & Baer, J. (2013). Beyond new and appropriate: Who decides what is creative? *Creativity Research Journal, 24*(1), 83–91. DOI: 10.1080/10400419.2012.649237

Kaufman, J. C., & Beghetto, R. A. (2009). Behind big and little: The Four C Model of creativity. *Review of General Psychology, 13,* 1–12.

Kaufman, J. C., Cole, J. C., & Baer, J. (Eds.). (2005). *Creativity across domains: Faces of the muse.* Mahwah, NJ: Lawrence Erlbaum.

Kaufman, J. C., Cole, J. C., & Baer, J. (2009). The construct of creativity: Structural model for self-reported creativity ratings. *Journal of Creative Behavior, 43*(2), 119–132. DOI: 10.1002/j.2162-6057.2009.tb01310.x

Kaufman, J. C., Gentile, C. A., & Baer, J. (2005). Do gifted student writers and creative writing experts rate creativity the same way? *Gifted Child Quarterly, 49,* 260–265.

Kaufman, J. C., Plucker, J. A., & Baer, J. (2008). *Essentials of creativity assessment*. New York: Wiley.

Kaufman, J. C., & Sternberg, R. J. (Eds.). (2006). *The international handbook of creativity*. New York: Cambridge University Press.

Kaufman, J. C., & Sternberg, R. J. (2010). *The Cambridge handbook of creativity*. New York: Cambridge University Press.

Kaufman, S. B. (2009). Faith in intuition is associated with decreased latent inhibition in a sample of high-achieving adolescent. *Psychology of Aesthetics, Creativity, and the Arts, 3*(1), 28–34.

Kaufman, S. B. (2013). *Ungifted: Intelligence redefined*. New York: Basic Books.

Kaufman, S. B., & Gregoire, C. (2015). *Wired to create*. New York: Perigee.

Kaufman, S. B., Quilty, L. C., Grazioplene, R. G., Hirsh, J. B., Gray, J. R., Peterson, J. B., & DeYoung, C. G. (2016). Openness to experience and intellect differentially predict creative achievement in the arts and sciences. *Journal of Personality, 84*(2), 248–258.

Keating, D. P. (1983). The creative potential of mathematically gifted boys. In R. Albert (Ed.), *Genius and eminence: The social psychology of creativity and exceptional achievement* (pp. 128–137). London: Pergamon.

Keats, E. J. (1962). *The snowy day*. New York: Scholastic.

Kelley, T. (2001). *The art of innovation: Lessons in creativity from IDEO, America's leading design firm*. New York: Doubleday.

Kemmelmeier, M., & Walton, A. P. (2016). Creativity in men and women: Threat, other-interest, and self-assessment. *Creativity Research Journal, 28*(1), 78–88. DOI: 10.1080/10400419.2016.1125266

Kerr, B., & McKay, R. (2013). Searching for tomorrow's innovators: Profiling creative adolescents. *Creativity Research Journal, 25*(1), 21–32. DOI: 10.1080/10400419.2013.752180

Kestly, T. A. (2014). *The interpersonal neurobiology of play*. New York: W. W. Norton & Co.

Khaleefa, O. H., Erdos, G., & Ashria, I. H. (1997). Traditional education and creativity in an Afro-Arab Islamic culture: The case of Sudan. *Journal of Creative Behavior, 31*(3), 201–211.

Khatena, J. (1992). *Gifted: Challenge and response for education*. Itasca, IL: Peacock.

Khatena, J., & Bellarosa, A. (1978). Further validity evidence of something about myself. *Perceptual and Motor Skills, 47*, 906.

Khatena, J., & Torrance, E. P. (1976). *Manual for Khatena-Torrance creative perceptions inventory*. Chicago: Stoelting.

Khatena, J., & Torrance, E. P. (1990). *Manual for Khatena-Torrance creative perception inventory for children, adolescents, and adults*. Bensenville, IL: Scholastic Testing Service.

Kilpatrick, J., Martin, W. G., & Schifter, D. (Eds.). (2003). *What research says about the NCTM Standards*. Reston, VA: National Council of Teachers of Mathematics.

Kim, K. H. (2005). Learning from each other: Creativity in East Asian and American Education. *Creativity Research Journal, 17*, 337–347.

Kim, K. H. (2006). Can we trust creativity tests? A review of the Torrance Tests of Creative Thinking (TTCT). *Creativity Research Journal, 18*(1), 3–14.

Kim, K. H. (2007). Exploring the interactions between Asian culture (Confucianism) and creativity. *Journal of Creative Behavior, 41*(1), 28–53.

Kim, K. H. (2008). Meta-analyses of the relationship of creative achievement to both IQ and divergent thinking test scores. *Journal of Creative Behavior, 42*, 106–130.

Kim, K. H. (2016). *The creativity challenge: How we can recapture American innovation*. New York: Prometheus Books.

Kim, K. H., Cramond, B., & VanTassel-Baska, J. (2010). The relationship between creativity and intelligence. In J. C. Kaufman & R. J. Sternberg (Eds.), *The Cambridge handbook of creativity* (pp. 395–412). New York: Cambridge University Press.

Kim, K. H., & Hull, M. F. (2012). Creative personality and anticreative environment for high school dropouts. *Creativity Research Journal, 24*(2–3), 169–176.

Kingore, B. (1990). *Kingore observation inventory*. Des Moines, IA: Leadership Publishing.

Kinney, D., Richards, R., Lowing, P. A., LeBlanc, D., Zimbalist, M. E., & Harlan, P. (2000–2001). Creativity in offspring of schizophrenic and control parents: An adoption study. *Creativity Research Journal, 13*, 17–25.

Kirkland, J. (1974). On boosting divergent thinking scores. *California Journal of Educational Research, 25*, 69–72.

Kirkland, J., Kirkland, A., & Barker, W. (1976). Sex difference in boosting divergent thinking score by the context effect. *Psychological Reports, 38*, 430.

Kirschner, P. A., Sweller, J., & Clark, R. E. (2010). Why minimal guidance during instruction does not work: An analysis of the failure of constructivist, discovery, problem-based, experiential, and inquiry-based teaching. *Educational Psychologist, 41*(2), 75–86. DOI: 10.1207/s15326985ep4102_1

Klahr, D., & Nigam, M. (2004). The equivalence of learning paths in early science instruction: Effects of direct instruction and discovery learning. *Psychological Science, 15*, 661–667.

Kleibeuker, S. W., Koolschijn, P. C. M. P., Jolles, D. D., De Dreu, C. K. W., & Crone, E. A. (2013). The neural coping of creative idea generation across adolescence and early adulthood. *Frontiers of Human Neuroscience, 7*, 905. DOI: 10.3389/fnhum.2013.00905

Kohn, A. (1993). Choices for children: Why and how to let students decide. *Phi Delta Kappan, 75*(1), 8–20.

Kounios, J., & Beeman, M. (2015). *The eureka factor: Aha moments, creative insight, and the brain*. New York: Random House.

Kounios, J., Fleck, J. I., Green, D. L., Payne, L., Stevenson, J. L., Bowden, E. M., & Jung-Beeman, M. (2008). The origins of insight in resting-state brain activity. *Neuropsychologia, 46*, 281–291.

Kounios, J., Frymiare, J. L., Bowden, E. M., Fleck, J. I., Subramaniam, K., Parrish, T. B., & Jung-Beeman, M. (2002). The prepared mind: Neural activity prior to problem presentation predicts subsequent solution by sudden insight. *Psychological Science, 17*, 882–890.

Koustaal, W., & Binks, J. T. (2015). *Innovating minds.* New York: Oxford University Press.

Kris, E. (1976). On preconscious mental processes. In A. Rothenberg & C. R. Hausman (Eds.), *The creativity question* (pp. 135–143). Durham, NC: Duke University Press. Reprinted from *Psychoanalytic explorations in art* (pp. 303, 310–318). New York: International Universities Press.

Kubie, L. S. (1958). *Neurotic distortion of the creative process.* Lawrence: University of Kansas Press.

Kühn, S., Ritter, S., Müller, B. C., van Baaren, R. B., Brass, M., & Dijksterhuis, A. (2014). The importance of the default mode network in creativity—a structural MRI study. *The Journal of Creative Behavior, 48*(2), 152–163.

Kulik, J. (1991). Findings on grouping are often distorted. *Educational Leadership, 48,* 67.

Kushner, T. (1997). Is it a fiction that playwrights create alone? In F. Barron, A. Montuori, & B. Barron (Eds.), *Creators on creating* (pp. 145–149). New York: Putnam Books.

Kyaga, S., Landén, M., Boman, M., Hultman, C., Långström, N., & Lichtenstein, P. (2013). Mental illness, suicide and creativity: 40-year prospective total population study. *Journal of Psychiatric Research, 47,* 83–90.

Kyaga, S., Lichtenstein, P., Boman, M., Hultman, C., Långström, N., & Landén, M. (2011). Creativity and mental disorder: Family study of 300,000 people with severe mental disorder. *The British Journal of Psychiatry, 199,* 373–379. DOI: 10.1192/bjp.bp.110.085316

Lambros, A. (2002). *Problem-based learning in K–8 classrooms: A guide to implementation.* Thousand Oaks, CA: Corwin Press.

Lan, L., & Kaufman, J. C. (2013). American and Chinese similarities and differences in defining and valuing creative products. *Journal of Creative Behavior, 46,* 285–306.

Landgraf, S., Ilinykh, A., Haller, C. S., Shemelina, O., Cropley, D. H., Von Treskow, I., Razumnikova, O. M., Kutscher, T., & van der Meer, E. (2015). Culture makes the difference: The "creativity-schizotypy" association varies between Germans and Russians. *The International Journal of Creativity and Problem Solving, 25,* 35–60.

Langer, E. J. (2000). Mindful learning. *Current Directions in Psychological Science, 9*(6), 220–223.

Langer, E. J. (2005). *On becoming an artist: Reinventing yourself through mindful creativity.* New York: Ballantine Books.

Larsen, M. (2016). *How to put your parents to bed.* New York: Harper Collins.

Lee, C. S., & Therriault, D. J. (2013). The cognitive underpinnings of creative thought: A latent variable analysis exploring the roles of intelligence and working memory in three creative processes. *Intelligence, 41,* 306–320.

Lee, C. S., Therriault, D. J., & Linderholm, T. (2012). On the cognitive benefits of cultural experience: Exploring the relationship between studying abroad and creative thinking. *Applied Cognitive Psychology, 26,* 768–778. Published online July, 19, 2012, in Wiley Online Library (wileyonlinelibrary.com) DOI: 10.1002/acp.2857

Lee, J., & Cho, Y. (2007). Factors affecting problem-finding depending on degree of structure of problem situation. *Journal of Educational Research, 10,* 113–124.

Leno, J. (1992, September 30). [Interview with D. Hoffman]. In H. Kushinick (Ed.), *Tonight Show.* New York: NBC.

Lepore, S. J., & Smyth, J. M. (2002). *The writing cure: How expressive writing promotes health and well-being.* Washington, DC: American Psychological Association.

Lepper, M., & Greene, D. (1975). Turning play into work: Effects of adult surveillance and extrinsic rewards on children's intrinsic motivation. *Journal of Personality and Social Psychology, 31,* 479–486.

Lepper, M., & Greene, D. (1978). *The hidden costs of reward.* Hillsdale, NJ: Erlbaum.

Lepper, M., Greene, D., & Nisbet, R. (1973). Undermining children's intrinsic interest with extrinsic rewards: A test of the "overjustification" hypothesis. *Journal of Personality and Social Psychology, 28,* 129–137.

Leung, A. K., & Chiu, C. (2010). Multicultural experience, idea receptiveness, and creativity. *Journal of Cross-Cultural Psychology, 41*(5–6), 723–741.

Leung, A. K., Maddux, W. W., Galinsky, A. D., & Chiu, C. (2008). Multicultural experience enhances creativity. *American Psychologist, 63*(3), 169–181.

Levy, S. (2008). The power of audience. *Educational Leadership, 66*(3), 75–79.

Lewis, B. A. (1998). *The kid's guide to social action.* Minneapolis, MN: Free Spirit Press.

Lewis, C., & Lovatt, P. J. (2013). Breaking away from set patterns of thinking: Improvisation and divergent thinking. *Thinking Skills and Creativity, 9,* 46–58.

Liep, J. (2001). *Locating cultural creativity.* Sterling, VA: Pluto Press.

Lillard, A. S., Lerner, M. D., Hopkins, E. J., Dore, R. A., Smith, E. D., & Palmquest, C. M. (2013). The impact of pretend play on children's development. *Psychological Bulletin, 139,* 1–34. DOI: 10.1037/a0029321

Limb, C. J., & Braun, A. R. (2008). Neural substrates of spontaneous musical performance: An fMRI study of jazz improvisation. *PLoS One, 3*(2), e1679. DOI: 10.1371/journal.pone.0001679

Lindsay, J., & Davis, V. A. (2012). *Flattening classrooms, engaging minds: Move to global collaboration one step at a time.* New York: Pearson.

Lissitz, R. W., & Willhoft, J. L. (1985). A methodological study of the Torrance tests of creativity. *Journal of Educational Measurement, 22,* 1–11.

Litman, J. A. (2005). Curiosity and the pleasures of learning: Wanting and liking new information. *Cognition and Emotion, 19*(6), 793–814.

Liu, E., & Noppe-Brandon, S. (2009). *Imagination first.* San Francisco: Jossey-Bass.

Londner, L. (1991). Connection-making processes during creative task activity. *Journal of Creative Behavior, 25,* 20–26.

Loewenstein, G. (1994). The psychology of curiosity: Review and reinterpretation. *Psychological Bulletin, 116*(1), 75–98.

Lubart, T. I. (1990). Creativity and cross-cultural variation. *International Journal of Psychology, 25,* 39–59.

Lubart, T. I. (1999). Creativity across cultures. In R. J. Sternberg (Ed.), *Handbook of creativity* (pp. 339–350). New York: Cambridge University Press.

Lubart, T. I. (2010). Cross-cultural perspectives on creativity. In J. C. Kaufman & R. J. Sternberg (Eds.), *The Cambridge handbook of creativity* (pp. 265–278). New York: Cambridge University Press.

Lubart, T. I., & Guignard, J. H. (2004). The generality-specificity of creativity: A multi-variant approach. In R. J. Sternberg, E. I. Grigorenko, & J. L. Singer (Eds.), *Creativity: From potential to realization* (pp. 43–56). Washington, DC: American Psychological Association.

Lucas, G. J. M., van der Wijst, A.m, Curşeu, P. L., & Looman, W. M. (2013). An evaluation of alternate ways of computing the creativity quotient of a design school sample. *Creativity Research Journal, 25*(3), 348–355. DOI: 10.1080/10400419.2013.813811

Ludwig, A. M. (1992). Culture and creativity. *American Journal of Psychotherapy, 46*, 454–469.

Ludwig, A. M. (1995). *The price of greatness.* New York: Guilford Press.

Lynch, M. D., & Kaufman, M. (1974). Creativeness: Its meaning and measurement. *Journal of Reading Behavior, 4*, 375–394.

Lyons, M. E. (1997). *Stitching stars: The story quilts of Harriet Powers.* New York: Aladdin Paperbacks.

McCaslin, N. (1999). *Creative drama in the classroom and beyond* (7th ed.). White Plains, NY: Longman.

McIntosh, E. (2010, December 14). Learning spaces. Virtual spaces. Physical spaces. *Ewan McIntosh's edu.blogs.com.* Retrieved from http://edu.blogs.com/edublogs/2010/12/learning-spaces-virtual-spaces-physical-spaces.html

McKay, A. S., Karwowski, M., & Kaufman, J. C. (2016, August 25). Measuring the muses: Validating the Kaufman Creativity Scale (K-DOCS). *Psychology of Creativity, Aesthetics, and the Arts.* Advance online publication. DOI: http://dx.doi.org/10.1037/aca0000074

McKee, M. G. (1985). Review of creativity attitude survey. In D. Keyser & R. Sweetland (Eds.), *Test critiques* (Vol. 3, pp. 206–208). Kansas City, MO: Test Corporation of America.

MacKinnon, D. W. (1978). *In search of human effectiveness.* Buffalo, NY: Creative Education Foundation.

McTighe, J., & Wiggins, G. (2013). *Essential questions: Opening doors to student understanding.* Alexandria, VA: Association for Supervision and Curriculum Development.

Maddux, W. W., Adam, H., & Galinsky, A. D. (2010). When in Rome . . . learn why the Romans do what they do: How multicultural learning experiences facilitate creativity. *Personality and Social Psychology Bulletin, 36*(6), 731–741.

Maddux, W. W., & Galinsky, A. D. (2009). Cultural borders and mental barriers: The relationship between living abroad and creativity. *Journal of Personality and Social Psychology, 29*(5), 1047–1061.

Magnuson, C. D., & Barnett, L. A. (2013). The playful advantage: How playfulness enhances coping with stress. *Leisure Sciences, 35*, 129–144.

Manley, A., & O'Neill, C. (1997). *Dreamseekers: Creative approaches to the African American heritage.* Portsmouth, NH: Heinemann.

Manning, M. J. (2003). *The aunts go marching.* Honesdale, PA: Boyds Mills Press.

Mansilla, V. B., & Gardner, H. (2008). Disciplining the mind. *Educational Leadership, 65*(5), 14–19.

Maralani, F. M. (2016). The mediation role of intrinsic and extrinsic motivation in the relationship between creative educational environment and metacognitive self-regulation. *Journal of Education and Learning, 5*(3), 272–277. DOI: 10.5539/jel.v5n3p272

Martín-Brufau, R., & Corbalán, J. (2016). Creativity and psychopathology: Sex matters. *Creativity Research Journal, 28*, 222–228. DOI: 10.1080/10400419.2016.1165531

Martinez, S. L., & Stager, G. (2013). *Invent to learn: Making, tinkering, and engineering the classroom.* Torrance, CA: Constructing Modern Knowledge Press.

Maslow, A. H. (1954). *Motivation and personality.* New York: Harper & Row.

Maslow, A. H. (1968). *Toward a psychology of being* (2nd ed.). Princeton, NJ: Van Nostrand.

The Math Forum's Bridging Research and Practice Group. (2013). Encouraging mathematical thinking: Discourse around a rich problem. Retrieved from http://mathforum.org/brap/wrap2/index.html

Mayer, R. E. (2004). Should there be a three-strikes rule against pure discovery learning? The case for guided methods of instruction. *American Psychologist, 59*, 14–19. DOI: 10.1037/0003-066X.59.1.14

Mednick, S. A. (1962). The associative basis of the creative process. *Psychological Review, 69*, 220–232.

Mednick, S. A. (1967). *Remote associates test.* Boston: Houghton Mifflin.

Meeker, M. N. (1969). *The structure of intellect: Its use and interpretation.* Columbus, OH: Merrill.

Meeker, M. N., Meeker, R., & Roid, G. (1985). *Structure-of-intellect learning abilities test (SOI-LA).* Los Angeles: Western Psychological Services.

Meier, D. (2009). Democracy at risk. *Educational Leadership, 66*(8), 45–49.

Menon, V., & Uddin, L. Q. (2010). Saliency, switching, attention and control: A network model of insula function. *Brain Structure and Function, 214*, 655–667.

Messenger, B. (1995). Lecture 4: Blues. In *Elements of jazz: From cakewalks to fusion* [CD]. Chantilly, VA: The Teaching Company.

Michigan Educational Extension Service. (1992, Winter/Spring). *Changing minds: A bulletin of the Michigan Educational Extension Service.* East Lansing, MI: Author.

Michigan Future Problem Solving Program. (n.d.). *The Michigan future problem solving program.* Ann Arbor, MI: Author.

Micklus, C. S., & Micklus, C. (1986). *OM program handbook.* Glassboro, NJ: Odyssey of the Mind.

Milgram, R. M., & Livne, N. L. (2006). Research on creativity in Israel. In J. C. Kaufman & R. J. Sternberg (Eds.), *The international handbook of creativity* (pp. 307–336). New York: Cambridge University Press.

Miller, A. (1990). *The untouched key: Tracing childhood trauma in creativity and destructiveness.* New York: Doubleday.

Miron-Spektor, E., Paletz, S. B. F., & Lin, C. (2015). To create without losing face: The effects of face cultural logic and social-image affirmation on creativity. *Journal of Organizational Behavior, 36*, 919–943.

Mohan, M. (1971). *Interaction of physical environment with creativity and intelligence.* Unpublished doctoral dissertation, University of Alberta, Edmonton, Canada.

Mohr, A. H., Sell, A., & Lindsay, T. (2016). Thinking inside the box: Visual design of the response box affects creative divergent thinking online. *Social Science Computer Review, 34*(3), 347–359. DOI: 10.1177/0894439315588736

Moore, M. (1985). The relationship between the originality of essays and variables in the problem-discovery process: A study of creative and noncreative middle school students. *Research in the Teaching of English, 19,* 84–95.

Moore, S. G., & Bulbulian, K. N. (1976). The effects of contrasting styles of adult-child interaction on children's curiosity. *Developmental Psychology, 12*(2), 171–172.

Morimoto, J. (1988). *Inch boy.* New York: Penguin Putnam.

Morrison, T. (1987). *Beloved.* New York: Penguin.

Morrisseau, N. (1997). *Norval Morrisseau: Travels to the house of invention.* Toronto, ON: Key Porter Books.

Mostafa, M. M., & El-Masry, A. (2008). Perceived barriers to organizational creativity: A cross-cultural study of British and Egyptian future marketing mangers. *Cross Cultural Management, 15*(1), 81–93.

Mottweiler, C. M., & Taylor, M. (2014). Elaborated role play and creativity in preschool age children. *Psychology of Aesthetics, Creativity, and the Arts, 8*(3), 277–286.

Mouchiroud, C., & Lubart, T. (2006). Past, present, and future perspectives on creativity in France and French-speaking Switzerland. In J. C. Kaufman & R. J. Sternberg (Eds.), *The international handbook of creativity* (pp. 96–123). New York: Cambridge University Press.

Moyers, B. (1990). *A world of ideas II.* New York: Doubleday.

Mpofu, E., Myambo, K., Mogaji, A. A., Mashego, T., & Khaleefa, O. H. (2006). African perspectives on creativity. In J. C. Kaufman & R. J. Sternberg (Eds.), *The international handbook of creativity* (pp. 456–489). New York: Cambridge University Press.

Mueller, J. S., Melwani, S., & Goncalo, J. A. (2012). The bias against creativity: Why people desire but reject creative ideas. *Psychological Science, 23*(1), 13–17. DOI: 10.1177/0956797611421018

Mullen, B., Johnson, C., & Salas, E. (1991). Productivity loss and brainstorming groups: A meta-analytic integration. *Basic and Applied Social Psychology, 12,* 3–23.

Mun, J., Mun, K., & Kim, S.-W. (2015). Exploration of Korean students' scientific imagination using the Scientific Imagination Inventory. *International Journal of Science Education, 37*(13), 2091–2112. DOI: http://dx.doi.org/10.1080/09500693.2015.1067380

Nakamura, J., & Csikszentmihalyi, M. (2001). Catalytic creativity: The case of Linus Pauling. *American Psychologist, 56*(4), 337–341.

National Council for Social Studies. (n.d.). Retrieved April 9, 2009, from www.ncss.org

National Council for the Social Studies. (2013). *The college, career, and civic life (C3) framework for social studies state standards: Guidance for enhancing the rigor of K–12 civics, economics, geography, and history.* Silver Spring, MD: Author.

National Council for Teachers of English. (2016a, November, 3). Position statement: Professional knowledge for the teaching of writing. Retrieved from www.ncte.org/positions/statements/teaching-writing

National Council for Teachers of English. (2016b, November 3). Strategy guide: Implementing the writing process. Retrieved from www.readwritethink.org/professional-development/strategy-guides/implementing-writing-process-30386.html

National Council of Teachers of Mathematics. (2000). Principles and standards for school mathematics. Retrieved April 16, 2009, from http://standards.nctm.org/document/chapter2/learn.htm

National Governors Association Center for Best Practices, Council of Chief State School Officers. (2010). *Common core state standards.* Washington, DC: Author.

National Research Council (NRC). (2011). *A framework for K–12 science education: Practices, crosscutting concepts, and core ideas.* Washington, DC: National Academies Press.

Neihart, M. (1998). Creativity, the arts, and madness. *Roeper Review, 21,* 47–50.

Newmann, F. K., & Wehlage, G. G. (1993). Five standards of authentic instruction. *Educational Leadership, 50,* 8–12.

Ng, A. K. (2004). *Liberating the creative spirit in Asian students.* Singapore: Prentice Hall.

Ngeow, K., & Kong, Y. (2001). Learning to learn: Preparing teachers and students for problem-based learning. *ERIC Digest.* ED457524.

Nitengale, F. (1861). *Directions for cooking by troops in camp and hospital.* Reproduction. Laramie, WY: Sue's Frou Frou Publications.

Niu, W., & Kaufman, J. C. (2005). Creativity in troubled times: Factors associated with recognitions of Chinese literary creativity in the 20th century. *Journal of Creative Behavior, 39*(1), 57–67.

Niu, W., & Kaufman, J. C. (2013). Creativity of Chinese and American cultures: A synthetic analysis. *Journal of Creative Behavior, 47*(1), 77–87.

Niu, W., & Sternberg, R. J. (2002). Contemporary studies on the concept of creativity: The east and the west. *Journal of Creative Behavior, 36,* 269–288.

Niu, W., & Zhou, Z. (2017). Creativity in mathematics teaching: A Chinese perspective (An update). In R. A. Beghetto & J. C. Kaufman (Eds.), *Nurturing creativity in the classroom* (2nd ed., pp. 86–107). New York: Cambridge.

Nottage, L. (2005). Out of east Africa. *American Theater, 22*(5), 26–27, 66–68.

Nusbaum, E. C., & Silvia, P. J. (2011). Are intelligence and creativity really so different? Fluid intelligence, executive processes, and strategy use in divergent thinking. *Intelligence, 39,* 36–45.

Nusbaum, E. C., Silvia, P. J., & Beaty, R. E. (2014). Ready, set, create: What instructing people to "Be creative" reveals about the meaning and mechanisms of divergent thinking. *Psychology of Aesthetics, Creativity, and the Arts, 8*(4), 423–432.

Oppezzo, M., & Schwartz, D. L. (2014). Give your ideas some legs: The positive effect of walking and creative thinking. *Journal of Experimental Psychology, 40*(4), 1142–1152.

Osborn, A. F. (1953). *Applied imagination.* New York: Scribner's.

Osborn, A. F. (1963). *Applied imagination* (3rd ed.). New York: Scribner's.

Ostroff, W. L. (2016). *Cultivating curiosity in K–12 classrooms*. Alexandria, VA: Association for Supervision and Curriculum Development.

Ozkal, N. (2014). Relationship between teachers' creativity-fostering behaviors and their self-efficacy beliefs. *Educational Research and Reviews, 9*(18), 724–733. DOI: 10.5897/ERR2014.1816

Pace-Marshall, S. (1993, May). *Our gifted children: Are they asking too much?* Keynote address presented at the meeting of the Michigan Alliance for Gifted Education, Dearborn, MI.

Palatini, M. (1999). *Ding dong, ding dong.* New York: Hyperion Books.

Paletz, S. B., & Peng, K. (2008). Implicit theories of creativity across cultural domains: Novelty and appropriateness in two product domains. *Journal of Cross-Cultural Psychology, 39*, 286–302. DOI: 10.1177/0022022108315112

Panksepp, J. (2008). Play, ADHD, and the construction of the social brain: Should the first class each day be recess? *American Journal of Play, 1*(1), 55–79.

Park, G., Lubinski, D., & Benbow, C. P. (2007). Contrasting intellectual patterns predict creativity in the arts and sciences: Tracking intellectually precocious youth over 25 years. *Psychological Science, 18*(11), 948–952.

Parker, W. C. (1991). *Renewing the social studies curriculum.* Alexandria, VA: Association for Supervision and Curriculum Development.

Parnes, S. J. (1963). Education and creativity. *Teachers College Record, 64*, 331–339.

Parnes, S. J. (1981). *Magic of your mind.* Buffalo, NY: Bearly.

Paulus, P. B., & Nijstad, B. A. (Eds.). (2003). *Group creativity: Innovation through collaboration.* New York: Oxford University Press.

Pennebaker, J. W. (1995). *Emotion, disclosure, and health.* Washington, DC: American Psychological Association.

Perkins, D. N. (1981). *The mind's best work.* Cambridge, MA: Harvard University Press.

Perkins, D. N. (1988). The possibility of invention. In R. J. Sternberg (Ed.), *The nature of creativity* (pp. 362–385). New York: Cambridge University Press.

Perkins, D. N. (1994). Creativity: Beyond the Darwinian paradigm. In M. A. Boden (Ed.), *Dimensions of creativity* (pp. 119–142). Cambridge, MA: MIT Press.

Perkins, D. N. (2001). *The eureka effect: The art and logic of breakthrough thinking.* New York: W. W. Norton & Co.

Perry, S. K. (1999). *Writing in flow.* Cincinnati, OH: Writers Digest Books.

Piaget, J. (1969). *The psychology of intelligence.* New York: Littlefield, Adams.

Piechowski, M. M., & Cunningham, K. (1985). Patterns of overexcitability in a group of artists. *Journal of Creative Behavior, 19*, 153–174.

Piirto, J. (2004). *Understanding creativity.* Scottsdale, AZ: Great Potential Press.

Pink, D. (2009). *Drive: The surprising truth about what motivates us.* New York: Riverhead Books.

Plucker, J. A. (1998). Beware of simple conclusions: The case for content generality of creativity. *Creativity Research Journal, 11*, 179–182.

Plucker, J. A. (1999a). Is the proof in the pudding? Reanalyses of Torrance's (1958—present) longitudinal study data. *Creativity Research Journal, 12*, 103–114.

Plucker, J. A. (1999b). Reanalysis of student responses to creativity checklists: Evidence of content generality. *Journal of Creative Behavior, 33*(2), 126–137.

Plucker, J. A., & Esping, A. (2015). Intelligence and creativity: A complex but important relationship. *Asia Pacific Education Review, 16*, 153–159. DOI: 10.1007/s12564-015-9374-9

Plucker, J. A., & Makel, M. C. (2010). Assessment of creativity. In J. C. Kaufman & R. J. Sternberg (Eds.), *The Cambridge handbook of creativity* (pp. 48–73). New York: Cambridge University Press.

Plucker, J. A., Qian, M., & Schmalensee, S. L. (2014). Is what you see what you really get? Comparison of scoring techniques in the assessment of real world divergent thinking. *Creativity Research Journal, 26*(2), 135–143.

Plucker, J. A., & Renzulli, J. S. (1999). Psychometric approaches to creativity. In R. S. Sternberg (Ed.), *Handbook of creativity* (pp. 35–61). New York: Cambridge University Press.

Plucker, J. A., & Runco, M. A. (1998). The death of creativity measurement has been greatly exaggerated: Current issues, recent advances, and future directions in creativity assessment. *Roeper Review, 21*, 36–39.

Porath, M., & Arlin, P. (1992, February). *Developmental approaches to artistic giftedness.* Paper presented at the Esther Katz Rosen Symposium on the Psychological Development of Gifted Children, Lawrence, KS.

Posamentier, A. S. (2003). *Math wonders to inspire teachers and students.* Alexandria, VA: Association of Supervision and Curriculum Development.

Preckel, F., Holling, H., & Wiese, M. (2006). Relationship of intelligence and creativity in gifted and not gifted students: An investigation of threshold theory. *Personality and Individual Differences, 40*, 159–170.

Preiser, S. (2006). Creativity research in German-speaking countries. In J. C. Kaufman & R. J. Sternberg (Eds.), *The international handbook of creativity* (pp. 167–201). New York: Cambridge University Press.

Priest, T. (2006). The reliability of three groups of judges' assessments of creativity under three conditions. *Bulletin of the Council for Research in Music Education, 167*, 47–60.

Prince, G. (1968). The operational mechanism of synectics. *Journal of Creative Behavior, 2*, 1–13.

Puccio, G. J., & Cabra, J. F. (2010). Organizational creativity. In J. C. Kaufman & R. J. Sternberg (Eds.), *The Cambridge handbook of creativity* (pp. 145–173). New York: Cambridge University Press.

Puccio, G. J., & Murdock, M. C. (1999). *Creativity assessment: Readings and resources.* Buffalo, NY: Creativity Education Foundation.

Puccio, G. J., Murdock, M. C., & Mance, M. (2007). *Creative leadership: Skills that drive change*. Thousand Oaks, CA: Sage.

Quellmalz, E. S. (1985). Review of alternate uses. In J. Mitchell, Jr. (Ed.), *The ninth mental measurements yearbook* (Vol. 1, p. 73). Lincoln: University of Nebraska Press.

Ragovin, H. (2006, May). Amplified application will provide additional cues about prospective students. *Tufts Journal*. Retrieved January 29, 2009, from http://tuftsjournal.tufts.edu/archive/2006/may/features/index.shtml

Raine, A., Reynolds, C., Venables, P. H., & Mednick, S. A. (2002). Stimulation seeking and intelligence: A prospective longitudinal study. *Journal of Personality and Social Psychology, 82*(4), 663–674.

Ramos, S. J., & Puccio, G. J. (2014). Cross-cultural studies of implicit theories of creativity: A comparative analysis between the United States and the main ethnic groups in Singapore. *Creativity Research Journal, 26*(2), 223–228.

Rao, C. R. A. (2005). Myth and the creative process: A view of creativity in the light of three Indian myths. *Creativity Research Journal, 17*, 221–240.

Ratey, J. J. (2001). *A user's guide to the brain*. New York: Vintage Books.

Reis, S. M. (1987). We can't change what we don't recognize: Understanding the special needs of gifted females. *Gifted Child Quarterly, 31*, 83–89.

Reis, S. M. (1998). *Work left undone*. Mansfield Center, CT: Creative Learning Press.

Reis, S. M. (2002). Toward a theory of creativity in diverse creative women. *Creativity Research Journal, 14*(3–4), 305–316.

Reisman, F. K., Floyd, B., & Torrance, E. P. (1981). Performance on Torrance's thinking creatively in action and movement as a predictor of cognitive development of young children. *Creative Child and Adult Quarterly, 6*, 205–210.

Reiter-Palmon, R., & Arreola, N. J. (2015). Does generating multiple ideas lead to increased creativity? A comparison of generating one idea vs many. *Creativity Research Journal, 27*(4), 369–374.

Renzulli, J. S. (1977). *The enrichment triad model*. Mansfield Center, CT: Creative Learning Press.

Renzulli, J. S. (1978). What makes giftedness? Re-examining a definition. *Phi Delta Kappan, 60*, 180–184.

Renzulli, J. S. (1985). Review of thinking creatively in action and movement. In J. Mitchell, Jr. (Ed.), *The ninth mental measurements yearbook* (Vol. 2, pp. 1619–1621). Lincoln: University of Nebraska Press.

Renzulli, J. S. (2012). Reexamining the role of gifted education and talent development for the 21st century: A four-part theoretical approach. *Gifted Child Quarterly, 6*(3), 150–159.

Renzulli, J. S., Gentry, M., & Reis, S. (2014). *Enrichment clusters: A practical plan for real-world, student-driven learning* (2nd ed.). Waco, TX: Prufrock Press.

Renzulli, J. S., & Reis, S. M. (1997). *The schoolwide enrichment model: A how-to guide for educational excellence* (2nd ed.). Mansfield Center, CT: Creative Learning Press.

Renzulli, J. S., Smith, L. H., Callahan, C., White, A., & Hartman, R. (1976). *Scales for rating the behavioral characteristics of superior students*. Mansfield Center, CT: Creative Learning Press.

Renzulli, J. W., Smith, L. H., White, A. J., Callahan, C. M., Hartman, R. K., & Westburg, K. (2002). *Scales for rating the behavioral characteristics of superior students* (rev. ed.). Mansfield Center, CT: Creative Learning Press.

Resnick, M. (2007–2008, December/January). Sowing seeds for a more creative society. *Learning and Leading with Technology, 35*, 18–22.

Reynolds, P. (2003). *The dot*. Somerville, MA: Candlewick Press.

Reynolds, P. (2004). *Ish*. Somerville, MA: Candlewick Press.

Rhodes, J. (1961). An analysis of creativity. *Phi Delta Kappan, 42*(7), 305–310.

Richards, R. (2007). Everyday creativity: Our hidden potential. In R. Richards (Ed.), *Everyday creativity and new views of human nature* (pp. 25–53). Washington, DC: American Psychological Association.

Rietzschel, E. F., Nijstad, B. A., & Stroebe, W. (2014). Effects of problem scope and creativity instruction on idea generation and selection. *Creativity Research Journal, 26*(2), 185–191.

Rimm, S. (1983). *PRIDE: Preschool and kindergarten interest descriptor*. Watertown, WI: Educational Assessment Service.

Ringgold, F. (1991). *Tar beach*. New York: Crown.

Ritter, S. M., Damian, R. I., Simonton, D. K., Baaren, R. B. van, Strick, M., Derks, J., & Dijksterhuis, A. (2012). Diversifying experiences enhance cognitive flexibility. *Journal of Experimental Social Psychology, 48*, 961–964.

Robinson, K. (2001). *Out of our minds: Learning to be creative*. Chichester, West Sussex, UK: Wiley.

Robinson, K. (2005). *How creativity, education and the arts shape a modern economy: Arts and minds*. Denver, CO: Education Commission of the States.

Robinson, K. (2015). *Creative schools: The grassroots revolution that's transforming education*. New York: Viking.

Rodrigue, A. L., & Perkins, D. R. (2012). Divergent thinking abilities across the schizophrenic spectrum and other psychological correlates. *Creativity Research Journal, 24*(2–3), 163–168.

Roe, A. (1952). *The making of a scientist*. New York: Dodd Mead.

Rogers, C. R. (1961). Toward a theory of creativity. In C. Rogers (Ed.), *On becoming a person: A therapist's view of psychotherapy* (pp. 347–362). Boston: Houghton Mifflin.

Rogers, C. R. (1962). Toward a theory of creativity. In S. J. Parnes & H. F. Harding (Eds.), *A source book for creative thinking* (pp. 63–72). New York: Scribner's.

Rohmer, H. (Ed.). (1999). *Our ancestors*. San Francisco: Children's Book Press.

Root-Bernstein, R. (2015). Arts and crafts as adjuncts to STEM education to foster creativity in gifted and talented students. *Asia Pacific Education Review, 16*, 203–212. DOI: 10.1007/s12564-015-9362-0

Root-Bernstein, R., Allen, L., Beach, L., Bhadula, R., . . . Weinlander, S. (2008). Arts foster scientific success: Avocations of Nobel, National Academy, Royal Society and Sigma Xi members. *Journal of Psychology of Science and Technology, 1*(2), 51–63. DOI: 10.1891/1939–7054 1.2.51

Root-Bernstein, R., & Root-Bernstein, M. (1999). *Sparks of genius: The 13 thinking tools of the world's most creative people*. New York: Houghton Mifflin.

Root-Bernstein, R., & Root-Bernstein, M. (2004). Artistic scientists and scientific artists: The link between polymathy and creativity. In R. J. Sternberg, E. L. Grigorenko, & J. L. Singer (Eds.), *Creativity: From potential to reality* (pp. 127–151). Washington, DC: American Psychological Association.

Rosen, C. L. (1985). Review of creativity assessment packet. In J. Mitchell, Jr. (Ed.), *The ninth mental measurements yearbook* (Vol. 1, pp. 411–412). Lincoln: University of Nebraska Press.

Rosenthal, A., DeMars, S. T., Stilwell, W., & Graybeal, S. (1983). Comparison on interrater reliability on the Torrance tests of creative thinking for gifted and nongifted children. *Psychology in the Schools, 20,* 35–40.

Rostan, S. M. (1992, February). *The relationship among problem finding, problem solving, cognitive controls, professional productivity and domain of professional training in adult males.* Paper presented at the Esther Katz Rosen Symposium on the Psychological Development of Gifted Children, Lawrence, KS.

Rothenberg, A. (1990). *Creativity and madness.* Baltimore: Johns Hopkins University Press.

Rothenberg, A., & Hausman, C. R. (1976). *The creativity question.* Durham, NC: Duke University Press.

Rothstein, D., & Santana, W. D. (2011). *Make just one change: Teach students to ask their own questions.* Cambridge, MA: Harvard Education Press.

Roukes, N. (1982). *Art synectics.* Worcester, MA: Davis Publications.

Rowe, M. (1974). Wait time and rewards as instructional variables: Their influence on language, logic, and fate control. *Journal of Research in Science Teaching, 11,* 81–94.

Ruas, C. (1984). *Conversations with American writers.* New York: McGraw-Hill.

Rubenson, D. L., & Runco, M. A. (1995). The psychoeconomic view of creative work in groups and organizations. *Creativity and Innovation Management, 4,* 232–241.

Rudowicz, E., & Yue, X. (2000). Concepts of creativity: Similarities and differences among Mainland, Hong Kong, and Taiwanese children. *Journal of Creativity Behavior, 43*(3), 175–192.

Rueda, M. R., Checa, P., & Cómbita, L. M. (2012). Enhanced efficiency of the executive attention network after training in preschool children: Immediate changes and effects after two months. *Neuroscience & Education, 2*(Supplement 1), S192–S2014.

Runco, M. A. (1986). Divergent thinking and creative performance in gifted and nongifted children. *Educational and Psychological Measurement, 46,* 375–384.

Runco, M. A. (1991a). *Divergent thinking.* Norwood, NJ: Ablex.

Runco, M. A. (1991b). The evaluative, valuative, and divergent thinking of children. *Journal of Creative Behavior, 25,* 311–319.

Runco, M. A. (2010a). Divergent thinking, creativity and ideation. In J. C. Kaufman & R. J. Sternberg (Eds.), *The Cambridge handbook of creativity* (pp. 413–446). New York: Cambridge University Press.

Runco, M. A. (2010b). Education based on a parsimonious theory of creativity. In R. A. Beghetto & J. C. Kaufman (Eds.), *Nurturing creativity in the classroom* (pp. 235–251). New York: Cambridge University Press.

Runco, M. A. (2014). *Creativity* (2nd ed.). Waltham, MA: Elsevier.

Runco, M. A., & Acar, S. (2012). Divergent thinking as an indicator of creative potential. *Creativity Research Journal, 24*(1), 66–75.

Runco, M. A., & Albert, R. S. (1985). The reliability and validity of ideational originality in the divergent thinking of academically gifted and nongifted children. *Educational and Psychological Measurement, 45,* 483–501.

Runco, M. A., & Chand, I. (1994). Problem finding, evaluative thinking, and creativity. In M. A. Runco (Ed.), *Problem finding, problem solving, and creativity* (pp. 40–76). Norwood, NJ: Hampton.

Runco, M. A., Illies, J. J., & Eisenman, R. (2005). Creativity, originality, and appropriateness: What do explicit instructions tell us about their relationships? *Journal of Creative Behavior, 39,* 137–148.

Runco, M. A., & Jaeger, G. J. (2012). The standard definition of creativity. *Creativity Research Journal, 24*(1), 92–96.

Runco, M. A., Johnson, J., & Gaynor, J. R. (1999). The judgmental bases of creativity and implications for the study of gifted youth. In A. S. Fishkin, B. Cramond, & P. Olszewski-Kubilius (Eds.), *Investigating creativity in youth: Research and methods* (pp. 115–143). Cresskill, NY: Hampton Press.

Runco, M. A., Millar, G., Acar, S., & Cramond, B. (2010). Torrance tests of creative thinking as predictors of personal and public achievement: A fifty-year follow-up. *Creativity Research Journal, 22,* 361–368.

Runco, M. A., Plucker, J. A., & Lim, W. (2000–2001). Development and psychometric integrity of a measure of ideational behavior. *Creativity Research Journal, 13,* 393–400.

Runco, M. A., & Sakamoto, S. O. (1999). Experimental studies of creativity. In R. J. Sternberg (Ed.), *Handbook of creativity* (pp. 62–92). New York: Cambridge University Press.

Russ, S. W. (2014). *Pretend play in childhood: Foundation of adult creativity.* Washington, DC: American Psychological Association.

Russ, S. W., & Fiorelli, J. A. (2010). Developmental approaches to creativity. In J. C. Kaufman & R. J. Sternberg (Eds.), *The Cambridge handbook of creativity* (pp. 233–249). New York: Cambridge University Press.

Rust, J. O. (1985). Review of thinking creatively in action and movement. In J. Mitchell, Jr. (Ed.), *The ninth mental measurements yearbook* (Vol. 2, p. 1621). Lincoln: University of Nebraska Press.

Ryan, R. M., & Deci, E. L. (2000). Intrinsic and extrinsic motivations: Classic definitions and new directions. *Contemporary Educational Psychology, 25,* 54–67. DOI: 10.1006/ceps.1999.1020. Retrieved from www.idealibrary.com

Sacher, J. (2012). *The amazing story generator.* San Francisco: Chronicle Books.

Sadker, D. (2002). An educator's primer on the gender war. *Phi Delta Kappan, 84*(3), 235–240, 244.

Sadker, D., & Sadker, M. (1986). Sexism in the classroom: From grade school to graduate school. *Phi Delta Kappan, 67,* 512–515.

Sadker, D., & Sadker, M. (1995). *Failing at fairness: How American schools cheat girls.* New York: Simon & Schuster.

Saeki, N., Fan, X., & Van Dusen, L. V. (2001). A comparative study of creative thinking of American and Japanese college students. *Journal of Creative Behavior, 35*(1), 24–38.

Sandling, M., & Chandler, K. L. (2014). *Exploring America in the 1960s.* Waco, TX: Prufrock Press.

San Souci, R. D. (2000). *Cinderella skeleton.* New York: Voyager Books.

Sawyer, R. K. (2006). *Explaining creativity: The science of human innovation.* New York: Oxford University Press.

Sawyer, R. K. (2007). *Group genius: The creative power of collaboration.* New York: Basic Books.

Sawyer, R. K. (2011). The cognitive neuroscience of creativity: A critical review. *Creativity Research Journal, 23*(2), 137–154. DOI: http://dx.doi.org/10.1080/10400419.2011.571191

Sawyer, R. K. (2012). *Explaining creativity: The science of human innovation.* New York: Oxford University Press.

Sawyer, R. K., & DeZutter, S. (2009). Distributed creativity: How collective creations emerge from collaboration. *Psychology of Aesthetics, Creativity, and the Arts, 3*(2), 81–92. DOI: 10.1037/a0013282

Sawyers, J. K., Moran, J. D., Fu, V. R., & Milgram, R. M. (1983). Familiar versus unfamiliar stimulus items in measurement of original thinking in young children. *Perceptual and Motor Skills, 57*, 51–55.

Sayre, A. P. (2011). *If you're hoppy.* New York: HarperCollins.

Scalin, J. (2011). *Unstuck.* Minneapolis, MN: Voyager Press.

Schack, G. D., & Starko, A. J. (1998). *Research comes alive.* Mansfield Center, CT: Creative Learning Press.

Schaefer, C. E. (1969). The prediction of achievement from a biographical inventory. *Educational and Psychological Measurement, 29*, 431–437.

Schaefer, C. E. (1970). *Biographical inventory creativity.* San Diego, CA: Educational and Industrial Testing Service.

Schaefer, C. E. (1971). *Creative attitude survey.* Jacksonville, IL: Psychologists and Educators, Inc.

Schaefer, C. E., & Anastasi, A. (1968). A biographical inventory for identifying creativity in adolescent boys. *Journal of Applied Psychology, 52*, 42–48.

Schanzer, R. (2004). *George vs. George.* Washington, DC: National Geographic.

Schiefele, U. (1999). Top interest, text representation, and quality of experience. *Contemporary Educational Psychology, 21*, 3–18.

Schiefele, U. (2001). The role of interest in motivation and learning. In J. M. Cholis & S. Messick (Eds.), *Intelligence and personality: Bridging the gap in theory and measurement* (pp. 163–194). Mahwah, NJ: Lawrence Erlbaum.

Schlichter, C. (1986). Talents unlimited: Applying the multiple talents approach in mainstream and gifted programs. In J. S. Renzulli (Ed.), *Systems and models for developing programs for the gifted and talented* (pp. 352–389). Mansfield Center, CT: Creative Learning Press.

Schlichter, C., Palmer, W. R., & Palmer, R. (1993). *Thinking smart: A primer of the Talents Unlimited model.* Mansfield Center, CT: Creative Learning Press.

Schoenfeld, A. H. (1992). Learning to think mathematically: Problem solving, metacognition, and sense making in mathematics. In D. Grouws (Ed.), *Handbook of research on mathematics teaching and learning* (pp. 334–370). Reston, VA: National Council of Teachers of Mathematics.

Science Olympiad. (1990). *Student manual division B.* Rochester, MI: Author.

Scieszka, J. (1989). *The true story of the three little pigs.* New York: Viking Kestral.

Seelig, T. (2012). *InGenius: A crash course on creativity.* New York: HarperCollins.

Seo, H., Lee, E. A., & Kim, K. H. (2005). Korean science teachers' understanding of creativity in gifted education. *Journal of Secondary Gifted Education, 16*, 98–105.

Seuss, Dr. (1954). *Horton hears a who.* New York: Random House.

Shamay-Tsoory, S. G., Adler, N., Aharon-Peretz, J., Perry, D., & Mayseless, N. (2011). The origins of originality: The neural bases of creative thinking and originality. *Neuropsychologia, 49*, 178–185.

Sharan, Y., & Sharan, S. (1992). *Expanding cooperative learning through group investigation.* New York: Teachers College Press.

Sherer, M. (2002). Do students care about learning? A conversation with Mihaly Csikszentmihalyi. *Educational Leadership, 60*(1), 12–17.

Shernoff, D. J., Kelly, S., Tonks, S. M., Anderson, B., Cavanagh, R. F., Sinha, S., & Abdi, B. (2016). Student engagement as a function of environmental complexity in high school classrooms. *Learning and Instruction, 43*, 52–60.

Shernoff, D. J., Tonks, S. M., & Anderson, B. (2014). The impact of the learning environment on student engagement in high school classrooms. In D. J. Shernoff & J. Bempechat (Eds.), *Engaging youth in schools: Evidence-based models to guide future innovations* (pp. 166–177). New York: NSSE Yearbook, National Society for the Study of Education, Volume 113, Issue 1, by Teachers College, Columbia University.

Silverman, I. W. (2016). In defense of the play-creativity hypothesis. *Creativity Research Journal, 28*(2), 136–143.

Silvia, P. J. (2006). *Exploring the psychology of interest.* New York: Oxford University Press.

Silvia, P. J. (2008). Creativity and intelligence revisited: A lent variable analysis of Wallach and Kogan (1965). *Creativity Research Journal, 20*(1), 34–39.

Silvia, P. J., & Beaty, R. E. (2012). Making creative metaphors: The importance of fluid intelligence for creative thought. *Intelligence, 40*, 343–351.

Silvia, P. J., Beaty, R. E., Nusbaum, E. C., Eddington, K. M., Levin-Aspenson, H., & Kwapil, T. R. (2014). Everyday creativity in daily life: An experience sampling study of "little c" creativity. *Psychology of Aesthetics, Creativity, and the Arts, 8*(2), 183–188.

Silvia, P. J., & Kashdan, T. B. (2009). Interesting things and curious people: Exploration and engagement as transient states and enduring strengths. *Social and Personality Psychology Compass, 3/5*(2009), 785–797. DOI: 10.1111/j.1751-9004.2009.00210.x

Silvia, P. J., & Kaufman, J. C. (2010). Creativity and mental illness. In J. C. Kaufman & R. J. Sternberg (Eds.), *The Cambridge handbook of creativity* (pp. 381–394). New York: Cambridge University Press.

Silvia, P. J., Winterstein, B. P., Willse, J. T., Barona, C. M., Cram, J. T., Hess, K. I., . . . Richard, C. A. (2008). Assessing creativity with divergent thinking tasks: Exploring the reliability and validity of new subjective scoring methods. *Psychology of Aesthetics, Creativity, and the Arts, 2*, 68–85. DOI: 10.1037/1931-3896.2.2.68

Simmons, A. (1984). *The first American cookbook: A facsimile of "American Cookery," 1796.* New York: Dover.

Simonton, D. K. (1986). Biographical typicality, eminence, and achievement style. *Journal of Creative Behavior, 20*, 14–22.

Simonton, D. K. (1988). Creativity, leadership, and chance. In R. J. Sternberg (Ed.), *The nature of creativity* (pp. 386–426). New York: Cambridge University Press.

Simonton, D. K. (1999). *Origins of genius: Darwinian perspectives on creativity.* New York. Oxford University Press.

Simonton, D. K. (2004). *Creativity in science.* New York: Cambridge University Press.

Simonton, D. K. (2009). Varieties of [scientific] creativity: A hierarchical model of disposition, development, and achievement. *Perspectives on Psychological Science, 4*, 441–452.

Simonton, D. K. (2010). Creativity in highly eminent individuals. In J. C. Kaufman & R. J. Sternberg (Eds.), *The Cambridge handbook of creativity* (pp. 174–188). New York: Cambridge University Press.

Singer, M. (2010). *Mirror mirror: A book of reversible poetry.* New York: Dutton Children's Books.

Sio, U. N., & Ormerod, T. C. (2009). Does incubation enhance problem solving: A meta-analytic review. *Psychological Bulletin, 135*(1), 94–120.

Skinner, B. F. (1972). *Cumulative record: A selection of papers* (3rd ed.). Englewood Cliffs, NJ: Prentice-Hall.

Slavin, R. (1990). *Cooperative learning: Theory, research, and practice.* Englewood Cliffs, NJ: Prentice-Hall.

Slavin, R. (1991). Are cooperative learning and "untracking" harmful to the gifted? *Educational Leadership, 48*, 68–69.

Sligh, A. C., Conners, F. A., & Roskos-Ewoldsen, B. (2005). Relation of creativity to fluid and crystallized intelligence. *Journal of Creative Behavior, 39*(2), 123–136.

Sloan, G. D. (1991). *The child as critic* (3rd ed.). New York: Teachers College Press.

Smolucha, F. (1992). A reconstruction of Vygotsky's theory of creativity. *Creativity Research Journal, 5*, 49–68.

Snyder, A., Mitchell, J., Bossomaier, T., & Pallier, G. (2004). The creativity quotient: An objective scoring of ideational fluency. *Creativity Research Journal, 16*, 415–420.

Sobel, M. A., & Maletsky, E. M. (1999). *Teaching mathematics.* Boston: Allyn & Bacon.

Soderborg, N. (1985). Å{%&*(=)-Å}. *Insight, 2*(1), 9–10, 13.

Sofaer, J. (2015). *Clay in the age of bronze: Essays in the archaeology of prehistoric creativity.* New York: Cambridge University Press.

Sosniak, L. A. (1985). Phases of learning. In B. Bloom (Ed.), *Developing talent in young people* (pp. 409–438). New York: Ballantine.

Sowden, P. T., Clements, L., Redlich, C., & Lewis, C. (2015). Improvisation facilitates divergent thinking and creativity: Realizing a benefit of primary school arts education. *Psychology of Aesthetics, Creativity, and the Arts, 9*(2), 128–138.

Sowden, P. T., Pringle, A., & Gabora, L. (2015). The shifting sands of creative thinking: Connections to dual process theory. *Thinking and Reasoning, 21*, 40–60. DOI: http://dx.doi.org/10.1080/13546783.2014.885464

Spielberg, S. (1985, July 15). The autobiography of Peter Pan. *Time, 126*(2), 62–63.

Starko, A. J. (1989). Problem finding in creative writing: An exploratory study. *Journal for the Education of the Gifted, 12*, 172–186.

Starko, A. J. (1993, May). *Problem finding in elementary students: Two explorations.* Paper presented at the Henry B. and Jocelyn Wallace National Research Symposium on Talent Development, Iowa City, IA.

Starko, A. J. (1995, May). *Problem finding in elementary students: Continuing explorations.* Paper presented at the Henry B. and Jocelyn Wallace National Research Symposium on Talent Development, Iowa City, IA.

Starko, A. J. (1999). Problem finding: A key to creative productivity. In A. S. Fishkin, B. Cramond, & P. Olszewski-Kubilius (Eds.), *Investigating creativity in youth* (pp. 75–96). Cresskill, NJ: Hampton.

Starko, A. J. (2000). Finding the problem finders: Problem finding and the development of talent. In B. Shore & R. Freedman (Eds.), *Talents unfolding: Cognition and development* (pp. 233–249). Washington, DC: APA Books.

Starko, A. J., & Schack, G. D. (1992). *Looking for data in all the right places.* Mansfield Center, CT: Creative Learning Press.

Stein, M. I. (1953). Creativity and culture. *Journal of Psychology, 36*, 31–322.

Steiner, J. (1998). *Look alikes.* New York: Little, Brown & Company.

Stepien, W., & Gallagher, S. (1993). Problem-based learning: As authentic as it gets. *Educational Leadership, 50*, 25–28.

Sternberg, R. J. (1985b). Critical thinking, Part 1: Are we making critical mistakes? *Phi Delta Kappan, 67*(3), 194–198.

Sternberg, R. J. (Ed.). (1988a). *The nature of creativity.* New York: Cambridge University Press.

Sternberg, R. J. (1988b). A three-facet model of creativity. In R. J. Sternberg (Ed.), *The nature of creativity* (pp. 125–147). New York: Cambridge University Press.

Sternberg, R. J. (Ed.). (1999). *Handbook of creativity.* New York: Cambridge University Press.

Sternberg, R. J. (2000b). Identifying and developing creative giftedness. *Roeper Review, 23*(2), 60–64.

Sternberg, R. J. (2001). What is the common thread of creativity? Its dialectical relation to intelligence and wisdom. *American Psychologist, 56*(4), 360–362.

Sternberg, R. J. (2003). The development of creativity as a decision-making process. In R. J. Sternberg (Ed.), *Creativity and development* (pp. 91–138). New York: Oxford University Press.

Sternberg, R. J. (2004). *International handbook of intelligence.* New York: Cambridge University Press.

Sternberg, R. J. (2006). The Rainbow Project: Enhancing the SAT through assessments of analytical, practical and creative skills. *Intelligence, 34*, 321–350.

Sternberg, R. J. (2012). The assessment of creativity: An investment-based approach. *Creativity Research Journal, 24*(1), 3–12.

Sternberg, R. J. (2015). A model of institutional creative change for assessing universities as learning organizations. *Creativity Research Journal, 27*(3), 254–261.

Sternberg, R. J., & Kaufman, S. B. (2011). *Cambridge handbook of intelligence.* New York: Cambridge University Press.

Sternberg, R. J., & Lubart, T. I. (1991). An investment theory of creativity and its development. *Human Development, 34,* 1–34.

Sternberg, R. J., & Lubart, T. I. (1993). Creative giftedness: A multivariate investment approach. *Gifted Child Quarterly, 37,* 7–15.

Sternberg, R. J., & O'Hara, L. A. (1999). Creativity and intelligence. In R. J. Sternberg (Ed.), *Handbook of creativity* (pp. 251–272). New York: Cambridge University Press.

Stickgold, R., & Walker, M. (2004). To sleep, perchance to gain creative insight? *Trends in Cognitive Science, 5,* 191–192.

Stiggins, R. (2005). From formative assessment to assessment for learning: A path to success in standards-based schools. *Phi Delta Kappan, 87*(4), 324–328.

Stiggins, R. (2008). *An introduction to student-involved assessment for learning* (5th ed.). Upper Saddle River, NJ: Pearson.

Stiggins, R., Arter, J., Chappuis, J., & Chappuis, S. (2006). *Classroom assessment for student learning: Doing it right.* Portland, OR: Educational Testing Service.

Stravinsky, I. (1997). Poetics of music. In F. Barron, A. Montuori, & A. Barron (Eds.), *Creators on creating* (pp. 189–194). New York: Putnam.

Subotnik, R., & Arnold, K. (1995). Passing through the gates: Career establishment of talented women scientists. *Roeper Review, 13*(3), 55–61.

Subramanian, K., Kounios, J., Parrish, T. B., & Jung-Beeman, M. (2009). A brain mechanism for facilitation of insight by positive affect. *Journal of Cognitive Neuroscience, 21*(3), 415–432.

Suchman, J. R. (1962). *The elementary school training program in scientific inquiry* (Report to the U.S. Office of Education). Urbana: University of Illinois.

Swan, G. E., & Carmelli, D. (1996). Curiosity and mortality in aging adults: A 5-year follow-up of the Western Collaborative Group study. *Psychology and Aging, 11,* 449–453.

Sweeney, M. E., & Walker, B. (2012). *Exploring people and cultures: Help kids learn about culture through challenging research activities.* Waco, TX: Prufrock Press.

Szekely, G. (1988). *Encouraging creativity in art lessons.* New York: Teachers College Press.

Taba, H. (1967). *Teacher's handbook for elementary school social studies.* Reading, MA: Addison-Wesley.

Tadmor, C. T., Galinsky, A. D., & Maddux, W. W. (2012). Getting the most out of living abroad: Biculturalism and integrative complexity as key drivers of creative and professional success. *Journal of Personality and Social Psychology, 10*(3), 520–542. DOI: 10.1037/a0029360

Tadmor, C. T., Satterstrom, P., Jang, S., & Polzer, J. T. (2012). Beyond individual creativity: The superadditive benefits of multicultural experience for collective creativity in culturally diverse teams. *Journal of Cross-Cultural Psychology, 43*(3), 384–392. DOI: 10.1177/0022022111435259

Takeuchi, H., Taki, Y., Hashizume, H., Sassa, Y., Nagase, T., Nouchi, R., & Kawashima, R. (2011). Failing to deactivate: The association between brain activity during a working memory task and creativity. *NeuroImage, 55,* 681–687.

Tamannaeifar, M. R., & Motaghedifard, M. (2014). Subjective well-being and its sub-scales among students: The study of the role of creativity and self-efficacy. *Thinking Skills and Creativity, 12,* 37–42.

Tan, T., Zou, H., Chen, C., & Luo, J. (2015). Mind wandering and the incubation effect in insight problem solving. *Creativity Research Journal, 27*(4), 375–382. DOI: 10.1080/10400419.2015.1088290

Tang, M., Werner, C., Cao, G., Tumasjan, A., Shen, J., Chi, J., & Spörrle, M. (2015). Creative expression and its evaluation on work-related verbal tasks: A comparison of Chinese and German samples. *Journal of Creative Behavior,* online. DOI: 10.1002/jocb.134

Tanggaard, L. (2015). The creative pathways of everyday life. *Journal of Creative Behavior, 49*(3), 181–193.

Tardif, T. Z., & Sternberg, R. J. (1988). What do we know about creativity? In R. J. Sternberg (Ed.), *The nature of creativity* (pp. 429–440). New York: Cambridge University Press.

Taylor, P. (1998). *Redcoats and patriots: Reflective practice in drama and social studies.* Portsmouth, NH: Heinemann.

Tegano, D. W., Moran, J. D., & Godwin, L. J. (1986). Cross-validation of two creativity tests designed for preschool children. *Early Childhood Research Quarterly, 1,* 387–396.

Tierney, P., & Farmer, S. M. (2002). Creative self-efficacy: Its potential antecedents and relationship to creative performance. *The Academy of Management Journal, 45*(6), 1137–1148.

Tischler, L. (2009, February 1). IDEO's David Kelley on "design thinking." *Fast Company.* Retrieved from www.fastcodesign.com/1139331/ideos-david-kelley-design-thinking

Tomlinson, C. A. (2004). *How to differentiate instruction in mixed-ability classrooms* (2nd ed.). Alexandria, VA: Association for Supervision and Curriculum Development.

Tomlinson, C. A. (2014). *The differentiated classroom: Responding to the needs of all learners* (2nd ed.). Alexandria, VA: Association for Supervision and Curriculum Development.

Tomlinson, C. A., & Eidson, C. C. (2003a). *Differentiation in practice: A guide for differentiating curriculum grades K–5.* Alexandria, VA: Association for Supervision and Curriculum Development.

Tomlinson, C. A., & Eidson, C. C. (2003b). *Differentiation in practice: A guide for differentiating curriculum grades 5–9.* Alexandria, VA: Association for Supervision and Curriculum Development.

Tomlinson, C. A., & Imbeau, M. B. (2010). *Leading and managing a differentiated classroom.* Alexandria, VA: Association for Supervision and Curriculum Development.

Tomlinson, C. A., & Strickland, C. A. (2005). *Differentiation in practice: A guide for differentiating curriculum grades 9–12.* Alexandria, VA: Association for Supervision and Curriculum Development.

Torrance, E. P. (1975). Sociodrama as a creative problem-solving approach to studying the future. *Journal of Creative Behavior, 9,* 182–195.

Torrance, E. P. (1981). *Thinking creatively in action and movement*. Bensenville, IL: Scholastic Testing Service.

Torrance, E. P. (1983). The importance of falling in love with something. *Creative Child and Adult Quarterly, 8*(2), 72–78.

Torrance, E. P. (1984). Some products of 25 years of creativity research. *Educational Perspectives, 22*(3), 3–8.

Torrance, E. P. (1988). The nature of creativity as manifest in its testing. In R. J. Sternberg (Ed.), *The nature of creativity* (pp. 43–75). New York: Cambridge University Press.

Torrance, E. P. (1990). *Torrance tests of creative thinking*. Bensenville, IL: Scholastic Testing Service.

Torrance, E. P. (1999). Forty years of watching creative ability and creative achievement. *Celebrate Creativity: Newsletter of the Creativity Division of the National Association for Gifted Children, 10*(1), 3–5.

Torrance, E. P. (2003). Reflection on emerging insights on the educational psychology of creativity. In J. Houtz (Ed.), *The educational psychology of creativity* (pp. 273–286). Cresskill, NJ: Hampton Press.

Torrance, E. P. (2004). Creative achievements of sociometric starts in a 30-year study. *Journal of Secondary Gifted Education, 16*(1), 5–13.

Torrance, E. P. (2008). *The Torrance tests of creative thinking: Norms-technical manual*. Bensenville, IL: Scholastic Testing Service.

Torrance, E. P., Khatena, J., & Cunningham, B. F. (1973). *Thinking creatively with sounds and words*. Bensenville, IL: Scholastic Testing Service.

Torrance, E. P., & Torrance, J. P. (1978). The 1977–1978 Future Problem-Solving Program: Interscholastic competition and curriculum project. *Journal of Creative Behavior, 12*, 87–89.

Torrance, E. P., & Wu, T. H. (1981). A comparative longitudinal study of the adult creative achievement of elementary school children identified as highly intelligent and as highly creative. *Creative Children and Adult Quarterly, 6*, 71–76.

Treffinger, D. J. (1985). Review of Torrance Tests of Creative Thinking. In J. Mitchell, Jr. (Ed.), *The ninth mental measurements yearbook* (Vol. 2, pp. 1632–1634). Lincoln, NE: Buros Institute of Mental Measurement.

Treffinger, D. J. (1987). Research on creativity assessment. In S. G. Isaksen (Ed.), *Frontiers of creativity research: Beyond the basics* (pp. 103–119). Buffalo, NY: Bearly.

Treffinger, D. J. (1995). Creative problem solving: Overview and educational implications. *Educational Psychology review, 7*, 301–312.

Treffinger, D. J., & Isaksen, S. G. (1992). *Creative problem solving: An introduction*. Sarasota, FL: Center for Creative Learning.

Treffinger, D. J., & Isaksen, S. G. (2005). Creative problem solving: The history, development, and implications for gifted education and talent development. *Gifted Child Quarterly, 49*, 342–353.

Treffinger, D. J., Isaksen, S. G., & Dorval, K. B. (1994). Creative problem solving: An overview. In M. A. Runco (Ed.), *Problem finding, problem solving, and creativity* (pp. 223–236). Norwood, NJ: Ablex.

Treffinger, D. J., Isaksen, S. G., & Dorval, K. B. (2000). *Creative problem solving: An introduction* (3rd ed.). Waco, TX: Prufrock Press.

Treffinger, D. J., Isaksen, S. G., & Dorval, K. B. (2003). *Creative problem solving (CPS Version 6.1 TM): A contemporary framework for managing change*. Retrieved from Center for Creative Learning, Inc. (www.creativelearning.com).

Treffinger, D. J., Renzulli, J. S., & Feldhusen, J. F. (1971). Problems in the assessment of creative thinking. *Journal of Creative Behavior, 5*, 104–112.

Treffinger, D. J., Schoonover, P. F., & Selby, E. C. (2013). *Educating for creativity and innovation*. Waco, TX: Prufrock Press.

Treffinger, D. J., Young, G., Selby, E., & Shepardson, C. (2002). *Assessing creativity: A guide for educators*. Storrs, CT: The National Research Center on the Gifted and Talented.

Vallerand, R. J., Salvy, S., Mageau, G. A., Elliot, A. J., Denis, P. L., Grouzset, F. M. E., & Banchard, C. (2007). On the role of passion in performance. *Journal of Personality, 75*(3), 505–534.

van de Kamp, M , Admiraal, W., van Drie, J., & Rijlaarsdam, G. (2015). Enhancing divergent thinking in visual arts education: Effect of explicit instruction of meta-cognition. *British Journal of Educational Psychology, 85* (1), 47–58.

Vaske, H. (2002). *Why are they creative?* Maplewood, NY: fivedegreesbelowzero Press.

Vass, E. (2007). Exploring processes of collaborative creativity: The role of emotions in children's joint creative writing. *Thinking Skills and Creativity, 2*, 107–117.

Vernon, P. E. (Ed.). (1975). *Creativity*. Baltimore: Penguin.

Vessey, W. B., & Mumford, M. D. (2012). Heuristics as a basis for assessing creative potential: Measures, methods, and contingencies. *Creativity Research Journal, 24*(1), 41–54.

Viki, G. T., & Williams, M. L. J. (2013). The role of identity integration in enhancing creativity among mixed race individuals. *Journal of Creative Behavior, 48*(3), 198–208.

von Stumm, S., Hell, B., & Chamorro-Premuzic, T. (2011). The hungry mind: Intellectual curiosity is the third pillar of academic performance. *Perspectives on Psychological Science, 6*(6), 574–588. DOI: 10.1177/1745691611421204

Vygotsky, L. S. (1967). Imagination and its development in childhood. In L. S. Vygotsky (Ed.), *The development of higher mental functions* (pp. 327–362). Moscow: Izdatel'stvo Academii Pedagogicheskikh Nauk RSFSR. (Originally a lecture presented in 1930.)

Waber, B. (1972). *Ira sleeps over*. New York: Scholastic.

Wagner, T. (2008). Rigor redefined. *Educational Leadership, 66*(2), 20–24.

Wagner, T. (2012). *Creating innovators: The making of young people who will change the world*. New York: Scribner.

Wakefield, J. F. (1985). Towards creativity: Problem finding in a divergent thinking exercise. *Child Study Journal, 15*, 265–270.

Wakefield, J. F. (1992, February). *Creativity tests and artistic talent*. Paper presented at the Esther Katz Rosen Symposium on the Psychological Development of Gifted Children, Lawrence, KS.

Walberg, H. J. (1988). Creativity and talent as learning. In R. J. Sternberg (Ed.), *The nature of creativity* (pp. 340–361). New York: Cambridge University Press.

Wallace, C. E., & Russ, S. W. (2016). Pretend play, divergent thinking, and math achievement in girls: A longitudinal study. *Psychology of Aesthetics, Creativity, and the Arts, 9*(3), 296–305.

Wallace, D. B., & Gruber, H. E. (1989). *Creative people at work*. New York: Oxford University Press.

Wallach, M. A. (1970). Creativity. In P. Mussen (Ed.), *Carmichael's manual of child psychology* (3rd ed., Vol. 2, pp. 1211–1272). New York: Wiley.

Wallach, M. A., & Kogan, N. (1965). *Modes of thinking in young children*. New York: Holt.

Wallas, G. (1926). *The art of thought*. New York: Harcourt Brace.

Walsh, J. A., & Sattes, B. D. (2015). *Questioning for classroom discussion*. Alexandria, VA: Association for Supervision and Curriculum Development.

Ward, T. B. (2001). Creative cognition, conceptual combination, and the creative writing of Stephen R. Donaldson. *American Psychologist, 56*(4), 350–354.

Ward, T. B., & Kolomyts, Y. (2010). Cognition and creativity. In J. C. Kaufman & R. J. Sternberg (Eds.), *The Cambridge handbook of creativity* (pp. 93–112). New York: Cambridge University Press.

Ward, T. B., Patterson, M. J., & Sifonis, C. (2004). The role of specificity and abstraction in creative idea generation. *Creativity Research Journal, 16*, 1–9.

Ward, T. B., Smith, S. M., & Finke, R. A. (1999). Creative cognition. In R. J. Sternberg (Ed.), *Handbook of creativity* (pp. 189–212). New York: Cambridge University Press.

Ward, W. C. (1975). Convergent and divergent measurement of creativity in children. *Educational and Psychological Measurement, 35*, 87–95.

Wasserspring, L. (2000). *Oaxacan ceramics*. San Francisco: Chronicle Books.

Watson, B., & Konicek, R. (1990). Teaching for conceptual change: Confronting children's experience. *Phi Delta Kappan, 71*, 680–685.

Watson, J. W., & Schwartz, S. N. (2000). The development of individual styles in children's drawings. *New Directions for Child and Adolescent Development, 90*, 49–63.

Webb, A. N., & Rule, A. C. (2014). Effects of teacher lesson introduction on second grader's creativity in a science/literacy integrated unit on health and nutrition. *Early Childhood Education Journal, 42*, 351–360. DOI: 10.1007/s10643-013-0615-4

Webb, J. T., Amend, E. R., Webb, N. E., Goerss, J., Beljan, P., & Olenchak, F. R. (2005). *Misdiagnosis and dual diagnosis of gifted children and adults*. Scottsdale, AZ: Great Potential Press.

Wechsler, S. M. (2000). Talent development in Brazil: As viewed by adult writers and poets. *Roeper Review, 22*, 86–88.

Weeks, M. (1985). Review of group inventory for finding interests. In J. Mitchell, Jr. (Ed.), *The ninth mental measurements yearbook* (Vol. 1, pp. 362–363). Lincoln: University of Nebraska Press.

Wei, D., Yang, J., Li, W., Wang, K., Zhang, Q., & Jiang, Q. (2014). Increased resting functional connectivity of the medial prefrontal cortex in creativity by means of cognitive stimulation. *Cortex, 51*, 92–102.

Weiner, E. (2016). *Geography of genius*. New York: Simon & Schuster.

Weiner, R. P. (2000). *Creativity and beyond: Cultures, values and change*. Albany: State University of New York Press.

Weinstein, E. C., Clark, Z., DiBartolomeo, D. J., & Davis, K. (2014). A decline in creativity? It depends on the domain. *Creativity Research Journal, 26*(2), 174–184.

Weisberg, D. S., Hirsh-Pasek, K., & Golinkoff, R. M. (2013). Guided play: Where curricular goals meet a playful pedagogy. *Mind, Brain and Education, 7*(2), 104–112.

Weisberg, D. S., Zosh, J. M., Hirsh-Pasek, K., & Golinkoff, R. M. (2013). Play, language development and the role of adult support. *American Journal of Play, 6*(1), 39–54.

Weisberg, R. W. (1986). *Creativity: Genius and other myths*. New York: Freeman.

Weisberg, R. W. (1988). Problem solving and creativity. In R. J. Sternberg (Ed.), *The nature of creativity* (pp. 148–176). New York: Cambridge University Press.

Weisberg, R. W. (1993). *Creativity: Beyond the myth of genius*. New York: Freeman.

Weisberg, R. W. (1999). Creativity and knowledge: A challenge to theories. In R. J. Sternberg (Ed.), *Handbook of creativity* (pp. 226–250). New York: Cambridge University Press.

Weisberg, R. W. (2006). *Creativity: Understanding innovation in problem solving, science, invention, and the arts*. Hoboken, NJ: Wiley.

Weisberg, R. W. (2010). The study of creativity: From genius to cognitive science. *International Journal of Cultural Policy, 16*(3), 235–253.

Weisberg, R. W. (2013). On the "demystification" of insight: A critique of neuroimaging studies of insight. *Creativity Research Journal, 25*(1), 1–14. DOI: 10.1080/10400419.2013.752178

Weisberg, R. W. (2015). Toward an integrated theory of insight in problem solving. *Thinking & Reasoning, 2*(1), 5–39. DOI: 10.1080/13546783.2014.886625

Welter, M. M., Jaarsveld, S., van Leeuwen, C., & Lachmann, T. (2016). Intelligence and creativity: Over the threshold together? *Creativity Research Journal, 28*(2), 212–218. DOI: 10.1080/10400419.2016.1162564

Wentzel, K. R., & Brophy, J. E. (2014). *Motivating students to learn* (4th ed.). New York: Routledge.

Westby, E. L., & Dawson, V. L. (1995). Creativity: Asset or burden in the classroom? *Creativity Research Journal, 8*, 1–10.

Whitebread, D. (2012). *The importance of play*. Brussels, Belgium: Written for Toy Industries of Europe (TIE).

Whitin, D. J. (2006). Problem in the elementary classroom. *Teaching Children Mathematics, 13*(1), 14–18.

Whitin, P. (2004). Promoting problem-posing explorations. *Teaching Children Mathematics, 11*(4), 180–086.

Wiggins, G. (1996). Designing authentic assessments. *Educational Leadership, 153*(5), 18–25.

Wiggins, G. (2012). 7 keys to effective feedback. *Educational Leadership, 70*(1), 11–16.

Wiggins, G., & McTighe. (2005). *Understanding by design* (2nd ed.). Upper Saddle River, NJ: Pearson.

Wilcox, A. (2013). *Descriptosaurus.* New York: Routledge.

Williams, F. E. (1980). *Creativity assessment packet.* East Aurora, NY: DOK.

Winebrenner, S. (1992). *Teaching gifted kids in the regular classroom.* Minneapolis, MN: Free Spirit Press.

Winebrenner, S. (2012). *Teaching gifted chidren in today's classroom: Strategies and techniques every teacher can use* (3rd ed.). Minneapolis: Free Spirit Press.

Wolk, S. (2008). Joy in school. *Educational Leadership, 66*(1), 8–14.

Wolters, C. A. (2004). Advancing achievement goal theory: Using goal structure and goal orientations to predict students' motivation, cognition, and achievement. *Journal of Educational Psychology, 96*, 236–250.

Woo, S. E., Chernyshenko, O. S., Longley, A., Zhang, Z.-X., Chiu, C.-Y., & Stark, S. E. (2014). Openness to experience: Its lower level structure, measurement, and cross-cultural equivalence. *Journal of Personality Assessment, 96*(1), 29–45. DOI: 10.1080/00223891.2013.806328

Worsley, D., & Mayer, B. (1989). *The art of science writing.* New York: Teacher and Writers Collaborative.

Wright, D. (1985). Review of group inventory for finding interests. In J. Mitchell, Jr. (Ed.), *The ninth mental measurements yearbook* (Vol. 1, p. 363). Lincoln: University of Nebraska Press.

X, M. (1965). *Autobiography of Malcolm X.* New York: Grove Press.

Xu Bing. (2001). *Words without meaning, meaning without words: The art of Xu Bing.* Washington, DC: Smithsonian Institute.

Yamada, Y., & Nagai, M. (2015). Positive mood enhances divergent but not convergent thinking. *Japanese Psychological Research, 57*(4), 281–287. DOI: 10.1080/10400419.2016.1162571

Yamamoto, K. (1978). Review of creativity tests for children. In O. C. Buros (Ed.), *The eighth mental measurements yearbook* (Vol. 1, pp. 365–367). Highland Park, NJ: Gryphon Press.

Yang, K.-K. , Lin, S.-F. , Hong, Z.-R., & Lin, H.-S. (2016). Exploring the assessment of an relationship between elementary students' scientific creativity and science inquiry. *Creativity Research Journal, 28*(1), 16–23. DOI: 10.1080/10400419.2016.1125270

Yarbrough, N. (2016). Assessment of creative thinking across cultures using the Torrance Tests of Creative Thinking (TTCT): Translation and validity issues. *Creativity Research Journal, 28*(2), 154–164.

Yi, X., Plucker, J. A., & Guo, J. (2015). Modeling influences on divergent thinking and artistic creativity. *Thinking Skills and Creativity, 16*, 62–68.

Yoruk, S., & Runco, M. A. (2014). The neuroscience of divergent thinking. *Activitas Nervosa Superior, 56*(1–2), 1–16.

Yuan, F., & Zhou, J. (2008). Differential effects of expected external evaluation on different parts of the creative idea production process and on final product creativity. *Creativity Research Journal, 20*, 391–403.

Yue, Z. D., & Rudowicz, E. (2002). Perception of the most creative Chinese by undergraduates in Beijing, Guangzhou, Hong Kong, and Taipei. *Journal of Creative Behavior, 36*(2), 88–105.

Zabelina, D. L., & Robinson, M. D. (2010). Child's play: Facilitating the originality of creative output by a priming manipulation. *Psychology of Aesthetics, Creativity, and the Arts, 4*, 57–65.

Zachopoulou, E., Makri, A., & Pollatou, E. (2009). Evaluation of children's creativity: Psychometric properties of Torrance's "Thinking Creatively in Action and Movement" test. *Early Child Development and Care, 179*(3), 317–328.

Zenasni, F., Besançon, M., & Lubart, T. (2008). Creativity and tolerance for ambiguity: An empirical study. *Journal of Creative Behavior, 42*(1), 61–73.

Zhang, L., & Sternberg, R. J. (2011). Revisiting the investment theory of creativity. *Creativity Research Journal, 23*(3), 229–238.

Zhao, Y. (2012). *World class learners: Educating creative and entrepreneurial students.* Thousand Oaks, CA: Corwin.

Zmigrod, S., Colzato, L. S., & Hommel, B. (2015). Stimulating creativity: Modulation of convergent and divergent thinking by transcranial direct current stimulation. *Creativity Research Journal, 27*(4), 353–360.

Author Index

Abraham, A. 66, 117
Abuhamdeh, S. 103
Acar, S. 340, 357
Adam, H. 120
Adler, D. 355
Adler, N. 68
Admiraal, W. 157
Afram, A. 130
Aghababyan, A. R. 66
Agnoli, S. 354
Aharon-Peretz, J. 68
Albert, R. S. 119, 343
Alencar, E. M. L. S. 354
Alfonso-Benlliure, V. 157
Aljughaiman, A. 23
Allan, S. D. 314
Amabile, T. M. 9, 72, 84–9, 93, 280–1, 286–93, 295, 325, 351–2
Ambrose, D. 6
Ames, C. 9
Anastasi, A. 346
Anderson, B. 280
Anderson, C. W. 251
Anderson, N. 94
Andrews-Hanna, J. R. 67
Apol, L. 225
Archer, J. 9
Arendasy, M. 102
Argulewicz, E. N. 357
Ariely, D. 22, 116
Arlin, P. K. 40
Armeli, K. S. 55, 288
Armstrong, D. 117
Armstrong, T. 8
Armstrong-Ellis, C. F. 223
Arnold, K. 126
Arter, J. 291, 323, 331
Arutyunyan, N. D. 66

Ashby, F. G. 72
Ashria, I. H. 47
Athanasou, J. 341
Auger, E. E. 76, 78
Austin, G. 268

Baas, M. 72
Backman, M. E. 343
Baer, J. 17, 80, 89, 124–5, 156, 295, 339–40, 344, 351
Bailey, C. T. 47
Baird, B. 32, 67, 71
Ball, O. E. 339
Bandura, A. 87, 295–6, 348
Bank, M. 234
Barker, W. 128, 341
Barnett, L. A. 128
Barron, F. 12, 101, 355
Barsade, S. G. 72, 286
Basadur, M. 156
Bateson, P. 128–9
Batey, M. 101
Baum, S. M. 135
Beach, J. K. 184
Beaty, R. E. 68, 102
Bechtereva, N. P. 66
Bedwell, R. 234
Beeman, M. 12, 63, 66, 68–9, 72
Beghetto, R. A. 17, 22, 275, 348
Belenky, M. F. 126
Bellarosa, A. 345
Benbow, C.P. 102, 134
Benedek, M. 68, 101–2, 104, 344
Bengtsson, S. L. 66
Berger, W. 155
Berlin, L. 32
Berliner, D. 22
Berlyne, D. E. 130
Berry, J. W. 295

401

Subject Index